'Thunderingly good; a classic, heavyweig   substance at last on soccer's flimsy bookshelf' Frank Keating, *Punch*

'A first-class book that every statistician should save for' Association of Football Statisticians

'Of all the books I have read on football, none has given me more pleasure than *Soccer at War*' Stan Cullis, Wolves and England

'Another must for every collector' *Football Monthly*

'While it will be compulsive reading for nostalgia buffs, those too young to remember gasmasks and ration books should still find the work a rewarding experience' David Lacey, *Guardian*

'A valuable social history as well as an invaluable work of soccer reference' Patrick Collins, *Mail on Sunday*

'A special present for dads and grandads and a must for the libraries of every amateur and professional football club' *Aberdeen Evening Express*

'The definitive record of football amidst the blackouts and skirmishes engineered by Adolf Hitler' John Richardson, *Newcastle Journal*

'An absolute must for anyone with an interest in football history or for that matter war history' Cliff Butler, *Manchester United Review*

'Any football fan who lived through that historic period will surely derive great pleasure from this nostalgic story' Donald Saunders, *Daily Telegraph*

'A buff's buff book' Simon Barnes, *The Times*

'Indispensable for supporters, historians, journalists; compiled with painstaking patience' *France Football*

'A fascinating study of Association Football while Adolf Hitler was trying to conquer all' *North London News*

'An authoritative and fascinating study of what happened to the game when war broke out in 1939' *The Chronicle*

'The best football book I've ever read' Tom Watt, BBC Radio London

SOCCER *at* WAR

1939 - 45

Recent books by Jack Rollin

Sky Sports Football Yearbook (with Glenda Rollin)
Playfair Football Annual (with Glenda Rollin)
The Essential History of England (with Andrew Mourant)
Rothmans Book of Football Records

SOCCER
at WAR
1939 - 45

JACK ROLLIN

headline

This edition first published in 2005
by HEADLINE BOOK PUBLISHING

1

A CIP catalogue record for this title is available from the British Library

ISBN 0 7553 1431 X

Typeset by Wearset Ltd, Boldon, Tyne and Wear

Printed and bound in Great Britain by
Mackays of Chatham PLC, Chatham, Kent

Headline's policy is to use papers that are natural, renewable and recyclable products and
made from wood grown in sustainable forests. The logging and manufacturing processes
are expected to conform to the environmental regulations of the country of origin.

HEADLINE BOOK PUBLISHING
A division of Hodder Headline
338 Euston Road
London NW1 3BH

www.headline.co.uk
www.hodderheadline.com

DEDICATION

To my grandson Harry

ACKNOWLEDGEMENTS

The author would like to express his appreciation to the late Don Aldridge for his research into a mountain of queries raised in the original work.

Other acknowledgements: Geoff Allman, Anne Alvarez, Mike Braham, Dave Batters, Harry Berry, Mike Blackstone, Jack L. Bloomfield, Arthur Bower, Bob Brunskell, Cliff Butler, Colin Cameron, Garry Chalk, Scott Cheshire, Tim Clapham, Roy Cope, Bob Crampsey, Datasport, Mike Davage, Gareth Davies, Roger Desouches, David Downs, Dave Drage, Reg Drury, Garth Dykes, Keith Farnsworth, Peter Fay, Grenville Firth, Michael Firth, Raymond Gaspard, Maurice Golesworthy, Frank Grand, Dave Harrison, John W. Harrison, Jack Hellier, Malcolm Henderson, Paul Hetherington, Peter Hewitt, Tony Higgins, Brian Hobbs, Ron Hockings, Bryan Horsnell, Keith Howard, Alan Jenkins, Leslie James, Karl-Heinz Jens, Paul Joannou, A. Kelleher, John Kirkby, Fred Lee, G. Lewis, Richard Lindsay, Billy Lucas, Gordon Macey, John Maddocks, Max Marquis, Brian Marshall, Wade Martin, Tony Matthews, Keith Mellor, Jack Mills, Gerald Mortimer, John Moynihan, John Musgrove, Ian Nannestad, Jimmy Nicholson, John Northcutt, Fred Ollier, Derek Orme, Bob Perkins, Christine Phillips, Steve Phillips, Paul Plowman, G. M. Readyhough, Ian Rennie, Mick Renshaw, Ian Rigby, Dennis Samuels, Rev. Nigel Sands MA, Stan Searl, Richard Shepherd, Bill Simmons, Gordon Smailes, Dave Smith, Les Smith, Lionel E. Smith, H. Ellis Tomlinson, John Treleven, Roger J. Triggs, Dennis Turner, Jack Turton, Frank Tweddle, Martin Tyler, Keith Warsop, Roger Wash, Reg Weller, Richard Wells, Richard West, Eric White, Sandra Whiteside, Dick Williamson, Ian Willars, Harold Wolfe, Andrew Wood, Sid Woodhead, Ray Spiller and the Association of Football Statisticians, the Football League, the Football Association and secretaries of Football League clubs past and present; also 'A History of Professional Association Football in England during the Second World War'— by John Ross Schleppi BSc MA;

and Glenda Rollin.

The author would also like to thank John English for his meticulous proof-reading; John Anderson, Simon Dunnington and the team at Wearset for their contribution to the production of this book; and finally Lorraine Jerram and David Wilson of Headline Book Publishing for their enthusiasm and support.

CONTENTS

INTRODUCTION

ACCORDING TO THE late J. B. Priestley, that precise observer of society, the British people were at their best during the Second World War and have never been quite as good since. The same was arguably true of Association Football, which not only survived hostilities but became a morale-stimulating, therapeutic pastime and even increased its popularity as a spectator sport. Its story has never been properly told in detail but that historical void is now filled.

Official attendances at Football League games in pre-war days had never been recorded except for the 1937–38 season which celebrated the competition's half-centenary. They aggregated 28,132,933. A survey by Mass Observation in 1940, the first year of the war, found that 65 per cent of pre-war Saturday followers were not attending for a variety of wartime reasons. By the 1945–46 transitional season, however, crowds were streaming through the turnstiles in increasing numbers. The post-war boom, which reached a record aggregate of 41,271,414 spectators in 1948–49, was fashioned in the dark days of war-torn, fortress Britain.

Despite alarming difficulties in fielding full teams, instances of sides taking the field without a full complement were rare; there were always volunteers. Goals were plentiful and added to the uncertainties and excitement of Soccer at War.

In pure footballing terms, many hundreds of players lost seven seasons out of their official careers. For many this was their only exposure to the first-class game. Some merely appeared in the aborted pre-war matches.

Naturally, in such traumatic times the game did not always fall easily on the ear. Reg Smith serving in one of HM ships told me of the understandably uncomfortable reaction on board in the wake of the Dunkirk evacuation, listening to a radio broadcast of the first War Cup Final while fishing bodies out of the English Channel. But just as life went on, so did soccer.

There were other harrowing stories. Teenager Leo Goldstein had been herded along with the rest of his Jewish family to a concentration camp awaiting their fate and inevitable death march to the gas chamber. But a Nazi guard asked the group in which the youngster was assembled if anyone had knowledge of the rules of football. Though Leo did not have a clue about the game and had showed no previous interest in it, he thought this might provide at least a ray of hope amid the gloom. It did. In fact, being summoned to referee a match between two German teams saved his life, though, alas, not the other members of the Goldstein family.

After the war Leo emigrated to the United States and, since he owed his life to officiating at a football match, he took up refereeing seriously to become one of the best-known officials in New York.

Such was his progress that he attained FIFA status and was one of the linesmen appointed for the 1962 World Cup finals in Chile. He ran the line in the infamous 'Battle of Santiago' when the host nation met Italy, refereed by Ken Aston.

OVERTURE TO THE INEVITABLE

W HEN PRIME MINISTER Arthur Neville Chamberlain returned from Munich on 30 September 1938 to give that frail, futile flutter for appeasement in our time, it signalled just one more complete season of normal football before the advent of that strangely still September Sunday nearly a year ahead. Prospects for a continuation if war came seemed as slight as any lasting expectation that there would be peace.

Already in June the Department of Air Raid Precautions (ARP) under the Home Office had discussed plans for closing entertainments both inside and outside if hostilities started. A re-opening after one week was not ruled out but would depend on the intensity of air attacks and be at the discretion of the police. Since sport as a whole, let alone Association Football, would scarcely be a priority consideration for the Home Office it made any provision under such circumstances pure speculation.

In September the Consultative Committee of the Football Association had decided that 'in the event of war a meeting be convened comprising the officials of the FA and the Management Committee of the Football League for the purpose of deciding the course of action to be taken with regard to the game'. This was no more than an acknowledgement of the inevitable, but not knowing the prospective enemy's intentions left the summer months of 1939 as much in the dark as the gathering gloom over the future.

During the 1938–39 season, many professional footballers had joined the Territorial Army or other national service organisations to spend their leisure preparing for the worst. They were encouraged so to do by a Football Association circular in April 1939 which hoped that the game would display a patriotic example to the youth of the country. While many opted for the Terriers and Militia, others chose different uniforms. Brentford players, for example, joined the War Reserve Police and attended classes conducted by police officers at Griffin Park.

However, Liverpool had been the first to join the Territorials as a club. Their entry included manager George Kay and assistant secretary Jack Rouse, but not all clubs shared this collective desire to volunteer. Manchester United's directors totally dismissed the idea, recording that 'it is a matter for the individual to decide'. Bolton Wanderers and West Ham United were indeed the only two others to enlist virtually as a unit.

On Easter Monday the entire Bolton Wanderers first team led by captain Harry Goslin enlisted in the 53rd Field Artillery Regiment of the Bolton Artillery. It had been pointed out to all players that there would be no guarantee of a posting near their homes.

With the call-up of more reservists, the Football League Management Committee meeting minutes in July recorded that

> there is no onus on clubs to pay players called up for military service during their period of military training. If, however, arrangements can be made with the military authorities for the players' services on match days, then liability would arise during such week or weeks as the players are available for the club.

As ever, the clubs were acutely aware that paying absentee footballers was not a sound business principle. Understandably, since the conscription was for six months, they wanted the period for footballers to be restricted to the summer and reduced to four months.

The Annual General Meetings of the Association and League in the summer of 1939 made virtually no reference to war apart from the FA's International Selection Committee meeting in June 1939, which deferred arrangement of a match with France in Paris scheduled for May 1940.

If the civilian game had been rendered impotent in controlling its own destiny, the Army FA was at least conceiving some plans for itself. At its AGM the Army Cup rules were amended to allow soldiers to play for professional clubs provided permission was obtained, but also to exclude professionals from playing in the Army Cup.

However, there had been a number of purely domestic decisions taken. The bottom two clubs in each of the Southern and Northern sections of the Third Divisions were re-elected. In the South, Bristol Rovers received 45 votes, Walsall 36, Gillingham 15, while Chelmsford City and Colchester United with one each were not elected. Hartlepools United with 38 and Accrington Stanley 29 were re-elected in the North while Shrewsbury Town 22, South Liverpool 5 and Scunthorpe and Lindsey United with 4 were unsuccessful along with Burton Town and Wigan Athletic who failed to muster a vote between them.

The watering of pitches was officially sanctioned and regulated as permissible except in the months of November to February inclusive. Also, by a majority of 24 to 20, it was agreed for the first time that all players must be numbered in Football League matches. Derby County's proposal that promotion and relegation should be increased to four up and four down was defeated by 28 votes to 21.

There were a number of changes in the game's hierarchy, ironically foreshadowing the loss of personnel through other causes. As the *Athletic News Annual 1939–40* put it, 'during 1938–39 time took heavy toll of football's leaders'. William Pickford, President of the Football Association and Chairman of the Council with 50 years' service on the FA Council, died on 5 November 1938 aged 77. Charles E. Sutcliffe, Jubilee President of the League who had served nearly 40 years on the Management Committee, died on 11 January 1939 aged 74. The League was celebrating its Jubilee, the FA their 75th anniversary. W. C. 'Willie' Cuff of Everton was elected President of the Football League, the Rt. Hon. The Earl of Athlone, KG, President and Mark C. Frowde, Weymouth, the Chairman of the FA.

Charlie Buchan in the *News Chronicle Football Annual* editorial of the same year referred to 'an eventful season that proceeded merrily despite alarms of war and crises in world affairs'. Their four Players of the Year were: England internationals Stanley Matthews (Stoke City), Willie Hall (Tottenham Hotspur), Joe Mercer (Everton) and Billy Morris (Wolverhampton Wanderers). Yet there had been some anxiety when England undertook a tour of Europe in May playing Italy, Yugoslavia and Romania, drawing 2-2, losing 2-1 and winning 2-0 in that order. It seemed at one stage that the Foreign Office would prevent the trip taking place. Wales lost to France 2-1 in Paris during the same month. The previous October the FA had commemorated their anniversary with England beating a Rest of Europe selection 3-0 at Highbury, the opposition including five Italians and two Germans.

Players reported back to their clubs for training in an atmosphere of unreality, but with typical British bravado they either ignored the situation or treated the portents of doom light-heartedly. Ronnie Burgess was a young Tottenham winghalf at the time and spoke of the tentative opening to the season: 'Each time we took the field we wondered if it would be our last game together . . .' Newspaper headlines were predicting 'Football to go if war comes?'. On 21 August 1939 the FA waived Rule 33 which stated that 'no player serving in His Majesty's Forces could be registered as a professional footballer'.

In late summer, the cinema release of *The Arsenal Stadium Mystery* had one clip of film showing a newspaper placard outside Highbury which read 'WE WARN HITLERS BRITISH FRIENDS'.

When the official opening of the 1939–40 League season arrived on 26 August it was witnessed by more than 600,000 spectators, figures down on normal levels for a full programme of 44 games played in traditionally good weather. After the usual midweek games, Friday 1 September saw the start of the evacuation of children from London, but it was announced that the fixtures for the following day would go ahead as planned.

That Saturday saw the invasion of Poland, but a bulletin from the Home Office stated that the situation did not warrant cancelling matches. Arsenal's game with Sunderland kicked off at 5 p.m, Fulham's an hour later. Both clubs

had decided to delay their start because of the evacuation scheme and its atten-
dant operation of one-way traffic on certain adjacent roads up to late afternoon.

Attendances shrunk to 380,000. People had other duties and everyone's mind
was elsewhere. Arsenal's Ted Drake scored four times in the 5-1 win over Sunderland, aided by some fine scheming from Bryn Jones, at £14,000 the world's
most expensive player. Newport County arrived 40 minutes late for their game
against Nottingham Forest, and Tottenham Hotspur only just turned up at West
Bromwich Albion in time for the kick-off, but won 4-3, though Cecil Shaw
missed a penalty which would have levelled the scores. At Blackpool a bottle was
thrown on the pitch near Alec Scott the Wolves goalkeeper. The referee
instructed two policemen to patrol the area.

Many amateur games were cancelled with players called up and others unable
to travel because of ARP and other duties. In what was to be an oft-repeated
gesture, Liverpool only managed a full side thanks to the generosity of some of
their Territorial friends, eight of whom volunteered for sentry duty in place of
Kemp, Ramsden, Busby, Bush, McInnes, Fagan, Balmer and Done. Stationed
'somewhere in the north', these players had snatched a few hours' sleep on the
floor of a railway station waiting-room before turning out for four hours' sentry
duty at 5 a.m. It caused little adverse effect as they beat Chelsea with a goal from
Cyril Done on his debut and despite having Jim Harley sent off mid-way
through the second half. His case was never heard.

Though Newcastle United beat Swansea Town 8-3, the top scorers that day
were Bournemouth who beat Northampton Town 10-0 at Dean Court. The
weather on the south coast, nearest to the unhappy continent of Europe, was in
keeping with the occasion. There was an air of depression, and thunder rumbled
for a while before heavy rain fell half-an-hour prior to the kick-off. One of the
linesmen appointed for the game was G. T. Chivers of Chippenham. He had not
arrived. An announcement appealing for a local referee produced no response
from the 1,500 estimated attendance. The reporter on the local evening paper was
asked to deputise, but declined. He suggested approaching Cliff Hayward, son of
the Bournemouth chairman and once a local referee. Hayward accepted and the
kick-off was delayed by ten minutes. Subsequently, a telephone message was
received from the Football League which said that Chivers would not officiate
and no substitute had been appointed.

Bournemouth scored first in six minutes but Northampton were not out of it.
They hit an upright and the Bournemouth goalkeeper was forced to make several
brilliant saves. With Bournemouth leading 3-0 after 22 minutes the rain stopped
and the sun came out. The sixth goal broke the net and struck a spectator standing behind the goal in the face. In that day's *Bournemouth Evening Echo Sports Final*
there were numerous references to the impending situation. Ken Bird, the
Bournemouth goalkeeper, was serving in the Militia and consequently he was
absent from the team group photograph which was reproduced.

It was reported that Stoke City had 13 of their professional staff on military duty, Aldershot had seven players who came within the scope of the Military Training Act, and Southampton's two Spanish refugee footballers, Barinaga and Perez, had been evacuated to Salisbury and were unavailable for the 'A' team.

Northampton's luckless goalkeeper was John Clifford, a Londoner who had been discovered in junior football and signed for the club by Warney Cresswell from Crystal Palace in January 1939. He had made his debut in March at Bournemouth and kept a clean sheet in three of the last eight games, conceding only one goal in four others. He was to be involved in another unusual game later on.

Only two clubs had taken maximum points from their three games: Blackpool in Division One and Accrington Stanley in Division Three (North). Top scorers were Hugh Billington (Luton Town) and Ernie Waldron (Crystal Palace) with five goals each.

Statistics apart, as Spurs' Ronnie Burgess recalled, there were weightier issues pressing the mind.

> We talked about the uncertainty of the future, of course, but the general opinion was that war would not come. But it did. On the Sunday morning (3 September) we all reported at White Hart Lane, for we were due to play Southampton on the Monday, but no preparation was necessary. War had been declared.

The immediate effect was a ban on the assembly of crowds until further notice. Yet, on 5 September Football League President W. C. Cuff announced that clubs should retain their players under contract to stand by, as a result of the Government's order to close places of entertainment. Fred Howarth, the League Secretary, referred to the fact that the loss of fixtures in this hold-up had meant a hopeless dislocation of the programme, but at an emergency meeting of the Management Committee at Crewe the next day the following points effectively ended the League competition.

1. The advice to the clubs to keep players standing by was cancelled and clubs were liable to pay players up to 6 September.
2. Signing-on bonuses and removal expenses were to be cleared immediately.
3. Season ticket refunds could not yet be given but must be made uniform.
4. Those matches already played in the League were to be counted as cup-ties and if the regular schedule resumed later the return matches would be played on similar terms.
5. Injured players were to follow end-of-season procedures when making claims.
6. Proposed Inter-League games with Scotland and Ireland were cancelled.
7. Any alternative schemes for competition when soccer resumed were deferred.

Transfers were one of the first casualties of war. Harold Cothliff, a Torquay United wing-half was about to be transferred to Chelsea in a £6,000 deal on the eve of hostilities breaking out.

In Scotland the Scottish FA meeting in Glasgow suspended all contracts between players and clubs, pre-empting the obvious move south of the border which came two days later when 15 representatives of the Association and League met at FA headquarters at 22 Lancaster Gate to act on the decision taken twelve months before. Thus, the first meeting of the War Emergency Committee took place.

By far the most important decision taken was that in accordance with the Government's proclamation and under Rule 27 of the Association, all football except for that of the Forces, under 'the jurisdiction of the Association would be suspended until official notice to the contrary was given'. All players' service contracts were suspended. They were, like many thousands of others, out of a job. Those in the Militia or Terriers had either been called to the colours or were soon so to be, but conscription for others would take longer.

Clubs still retained not only the players' registrations but with it the feudal hold they had over their servants, which was ingrained in the system of the professional game. The players were far removed from being free agents, yet without some call by clubs upon their own players there would have been no subsequent organisation. Ultimately it was as much the determination of the clubs as the desire of the players themselves to participate for whatever reasons which kept the game alive.

At the same meeting the FA Secretary, Stanley Rous, reported that he had already discussed with the General Officer Commanding Home Forces the possibility of utilising the Association's facilities in respect of their panel of coaches, trainers and masseurs, and the proposals had seemed to have been favourably accepted. Several clubs offered the Armed Services the use of their grounds and amenities for recreational purposes and their gestures were passed on to the War Office. The FA made its first donation, £1,000, to be spent on footballs and other equipment for the Army. A decent ball could cost as little as £1 and a waterproof one just a few shillings more.

This new cooperation between the game and the services, which was to become the basis of wartime football, was put into immediate effect with a hastily arranged game between Queens Park Rangers and the Army at Shepherd's Bush on the following afternoon. It was the only match staged on a Football League club's ground that day and was played behind closed doors.

Rous had also said that approval for friendlies in the areas specified as safe could be obtained from local police but at such short notice would be chiefly 'recreational entertainment for the young people'. The QPR players, ground staff and office staff had all enlisted in the Metropolitan Police but they managed to field a side with those players not on duty. This was soon to become a familiar pattern.

Under a blazingly cloudless sky, Rangers shot the Army to pieces with such military precision that they scored five times in each half to once by the soldiers and won 10-2. Perhaps it was as much to prevent sporting embarrassment as to maintain military secrecy that the names of the Army team were not disclosed.

Regional football was already being considered and on 11 September the Players' Union announced that, if the FA did introduce it and the clubs charged for admission, they would be prepared to allow their players to play for nothing provided the money was given to charity. The Football League Management Committee subsequently said that no payment could be made to players as yet, since the FA had cancelled players' contracts, but they would be insured against accidents under the Work Compensation Act.

Thus, the total black-out of civilian football had lasted only a few days. Indeed, it was announced on 14 September that friendly matches could be arranged even in areas banned by the Home Office under the Defence Regulations, provided there was local police approval. Several other games had already been played the day before, including Cardiff City v Arsenal (3-4) at Ninian Park and Leicester City against an Army XI (7-2) at Filbert Street.

In neutral and reception areas, existing pre-war fixtures could be played provided they were designated as friendly and not as games in a competition. After consultation with the Home Office the FA announced on 21 September that it would lend its full support to the organisation of both friendly and competitive matches confined to local and district groups on Saturdays and public holidays, as long as there was no interference with the National Service and the general war effort. However, in the interests of public safety the number of spectators would be limited to 8,000 or half the capacity of the ground, whichever the less, in evacuation areas or as fixed by the local police. Large crowds travelling to and from grounds would have to be avoided. For grounds in other areas with a capacity of 60,000 the Chief Constable had discretion to allow crowds of 15,000 provided they were all-ticket matches with tickets purchased in advance.

These arrangements were revised, with London clubs being allowed gates of 15,000 from tickets purchased on the day of the game through the turnstiles. Brentford, in commendably attempting to comply with the original ground limit, printed 8,000 programmes to be distributed free to spectators and when supplies ran out the gates were closed.

The London Combination, which had organised a first team tournament in the First World War, said it had a scheme to organise a similar regional competition. On 16 September some 31 first-class friendlies were played on amateur lines, attracting more than 120,000 spectators. Results included Southend United beating Norwich City 6-2 and Peterborough United (Midland League) winning 4-3 against Nottingham Forest. Liverpool won 5-0 at Chester.

Commenting on the changing face of soccer, the *Yorkshire Post* acknowledged that while the wartime game 'would lack the keenness and excitement of League competition, there was the opportunity for spectacular exhibitions with skilful manoeuvre and finesse to be exploited, enabling players to display whatever ball craft they possessed'. Alas, their verdict on the Halifax Town 3 Leeds United 2 game: 'that usually associated with the village green'. Receipts were about £120.

The following day the Scottish League held a two-hour conference and decided that the competition would be resumed on 23 September. Wages in Division One would be £2 a week, £1 in Division Two. Any clubs making a profit in the season would pay their players back pay to the extent of £1 per week for Division One and ten shillings (50p) for Division Two. However, and presumably after some further fiscal findings the plan was suspended just a few days later!

On 20 September E. Holland Hughes, Secretary of the Pools Promoters' Association, said that public demand and the desire of members to give employment to as many as possible had resulted in them deciding to reintroduce football pools from 7 October. Irish League fixtures would be used together with whatever English and Scottish games were available. In the event they restarted at a later date.

Two days later it was agreed that professionals in England would receive no more than 30 shillings (£1.50) for each match, paid to eleven men and one reserve. There would be no championships, trophies or bonuses paid to players, but the League had circulated clubs and upon their response would determine how the game could be organised on a regional basis. Registered players could be permitted to assist other clubs within a reasonable distance of their residence or work by consent of their own clubs. Minimum admission price had been fixed at one shilling (5p) but clubs could charge less to servicemen, women and boys. Two per cent of net receipts would go to the League, partly for insurance purposes.

Further friendlies were played on 23 September with non-league clubs previewing the advent of hastily assembled teams and the resultant shock scores. Tottenham were beaten 4-2 at Chelmsford City and Crystal Palace by five clear goals at Guildford City. Bill Edrich scored for Chelmsford playing against his own club. Elsewhere Plymouth Argyle beat Bristol City 7-1, Coventry City won 6-0 at Shrewsbury Town and there was a 6-1 win for Brighton & Hove Albion over Millwall, watched by 8,000 and 6-4 for Leicester against Birmingham.

A further easing of the situation came on 25 September when the 50-mile travelling limit was lifted, provided clubs could make the return journey on the day of the game. London clubs announced they would start their regional competition on the last Saturday in October, but James Fay, Secretary of the Players' Union, was unhappy about the size of the proposed payment for players which he described as 'not adequate' and a further meeting was arranged.

League Secretary Howarth forecast that there would be seven sections of regional football with no more than 18 teams in each because there were at most

34 more playing days left in the season. One of the first clubs to close down had been Sunderland, who said they would take no part in any regional competition.

Despite the restriction on the numbers of spectators, only two grounds reached the limit of 8,000 on 30 September, Elm Park and Upton Park. Arsenal were the attractive visitors at Reading where they won 3-1 while West Ham United beat Millwall 2-1 in their London derby. Spurs lost 4-2 again, this time at Chelsea in front of 6,338. West Bromwich Albion took six goals off Stoke City without reply and Forest won similarly at Lincoln City. Stoke were without Stanley Matthews who had previously stated that he would be unable to leave work in time for the kick-off. The all-Mancunian affair at Old Trafford was attended by only 7,000, City beating United 3-2. Leeds' 3-1 win at Derby had been well received by the modest assembly of 2,500. Despite the hard ground caused by the too close cutting of the grass – a feat accomplished by the Derby players themselves – Leeds displayed some 'pretty footwork'.

The *Yorkshire Post* voiced its opinion that 'the wartime game would be played at a slower pace, because of a lack of training and an absence of tension caused by the fact that there would be no points awarded or bonuses paid'. But it also hoped 'that it would afford the chance for players to show greater accuracy and introduce experimental movements'.

At a meeting at Crewe on 2 October plans were finalised for the Football League's regional competition to commence on 21 October. Teams would be split into eight geographical groups regardless of their pre-war status. Of the 88 clubs in the League only six had declined to take part: Aston Villa, Sunderland, Derby County, Exeter City, Ipswich Town and Gateshead. Arsenal and Birmingham said they would be unable to play home games on their own grounds. Arsenal had already made arrangements to share White Hart Lane with Tottenham. At their meeting the Scottish League announced it would also operate on a regional basis.

Twenty-one clubs had wanted to play in the London area. The problem was solved by moving Luton Town in the Midland Section and splitting the remainder into two Groups, South A and South B. It was agreed that points would be awarded on the usual basis, two for a win, one for a draw and League tables would be compiled. With about 33 playing days remaining, the fixture list seemed adequate.

The Players' Union reported that it would accept whatever minimum payment the Football League decided to give the players but for an experimental period only, acknowledging that regional competition would benefit the game more than the meaningless scratch affairs which were now taking place and which were not proving an attraction. They also wanted to explore the possibility of pooling the gate money, with any surplus being paid to the players as a bonus as well as the interest from the Jubilee Fund. With many players experiencing financial hardship, the Union made numerous grants to their members.

The Football Association were also quick to respond to the Lord Mayor of London's Red Cross Appeal with a first donation of 500 guineas (£525) and shortly afterwards the Red Cross and St John's formed a sports sub-committee to raise money from sporting events. The FA and League accepted invitations to be represented on it.

However, the growing discontent among London clubs which was to manifest itself seriously at a later date now emerged. The eleven teams in the capital were reported to be furious about the way in which they had been 'carved up' in the regionalisation. They made it clear that with the addition of four clubs outside the area they could have a competition of 28 games run by the London Combination under the auspices of the London Football Association. They pointed out that clubs in a five-mile radius had been split up in a totally unrealistic way, four of them being asked to play games on the coast and the other seven in another competition.

The League denied that there was any breakaway threat and surprisingly a further meeting of the eleven accepted the groupings provided they could be guaranteed their fixtures on consecutive playing days. It was something of a compromise solution as it would enable them to run a separate competition in the second part of the season organised by the London Combination with sixteen clubs split into two groups, but taking into account pre-war divisional distinctions. One group would be composed of Arsenal, Brentford, Charlton, Chelsea, Fulham, Millwall, Tottenham and West Ham, the other of Aldershot, Brighton, Clapton Orient, Crystal Palace, QPR, Reading, Southend and Watford.

Meanwhile, everyone made the most of whatever fixtures could be arranged. On 7 October the Bristol clubs City and Rovers shared ten goals, Arsenal won 3-0 at Chelsea and Millwall beat Brentford 8-4, while Billington hit four for Luton in a 5-2 win over Fulham. Tyne-Tees rivalry was recaptured in somewhat lukewarm form when Newcastle and Middlesbrough met for the first time in six years. There was a 8,000 crowd and United won 3-2. Everton were 4-1 winners at Liverpool in the Merseyside derby and it was reported that there was 'some difference of opinion between spectators'.

The provisional list of regional fixtures was now out and would be finalised by the following week after clubs had sent in their objections. Meanwhile the friendlies continued, drawing little more than apathy from the spectators. One interesting aspect was the continued likelihood of surprising and unexpected results, partly affected by the amount of time players had been able to give to voluntary training since they were no longer under the day-to-day control of their clubs.

A few days later West Ham decided to pay all their players 30 shillings (£1.50) a week whether or not they played. About 24 of their players were in the Army and the club considered they should not suffer financially for their patriotism. Shortly afterwards the Management Committee of the League passed the following resolution: 'Permission is granted to any club to implement any promise made to players on joining HM Forces up to and including 8 September when all players' service agreements were suspended.' But this would mean a maximum payment of 30 shillings (£1.50) a week, with no extra for playing.

West Bromwich generously decided to pay their players an extra week's wages. Barrow, with 14 available, agreed to split the money for the dozen permitted between all of them.

Leeds had not played at home since the series of friendlies had been introduced, but they prepared for their first one with Grimsby. Motor cars would not be allowed in the club car park or in streets around the ground, but could be left in other car parks in the vicinity.

At Sheffield the problem was infinitely worse. There had been no football at all in the city following the outbreak of war and, while both United and Wednesday were happy about the 8,000 crowd restriction, they were not in agreement with the local police authority's insistence on advance booking which the clubs had rejected as impractical. United's game with Leicester had to be switched to their opponent's ground.

On 14 October in another crowded programme of matches Blackpool beat Manchester United 6-4 in a match broadcast by the BBC and picked up by a French radio station which relayed it to British troops based there. Jim Shankley scored five in Orient's 6-1 win over Finchley, Arsenal won 7-0 at Swindon Town and West Ham, doubtless inspired by their club's recent benevolence, waded into Charlton 9-2. Carlisle United shared eight goals with Clyde.

Then, the first of what was to become a firm and frequently used facet of the friendly soccer scene – the representative game – arrived on 18 October at Aldershot three days before the regional competition's debut. An FA XI with eight internationals played a combined team known locally as 'Camp and Town' which had five players from Aldershot FC and six capped Army players from other clubs. The only goal of the game was credited to the FA's Lester Finch, one of two amateurs in their side.

Len Goulden was a late replacement for Cliff Britton who was unfit; again a sign of what was to become a familiar story of late, late changes in wartime. The Royal Artillery Band's selection ranged from 'Colonel Bogey' and 'South of the Border' to 'Blaze Away' and, inevitably, 'We're Going to Hang Out the Washing on the Siegfried Line'. Gate receipts and a collection on the ground among the 10,000 spectators realised £364. At the time, Aldershot's record League attendance was 15,611.

The size of the crowd was interesting for two reasons. First, that a town which was the home of the British Army could not be described as a safe or neutral area. Second, that the instant appeal of seeing first-class players in a match for a worthy cause attracted so many spectators. Then there was the 8,000 limit which had been waived.

Thus, the initial hurdles were overcome and within 48 days of war being declared some form of competitive football had been restarted; but there was no question of the League competition resuming. Disruption of civilian life had been less than anticipated but transport difficulties alone would prevent nation-wide travelling. Yet, there was a willingness to restore the game to a level that would interest the people and prove an important boost to morale.

PLAYERS FACED UNCERTAIN FUTURE

O UT-OF-WORK FOOTBALLERS WERE faced with few options: enlistment in one of the three Armed Forces or national service organisations, taking on essential war work or waiting for their call-up. Outside of these alternatives any kind of temporary employment was preferable to no income at all. Those players who had previously signed on either in the Territorials, the Militia or as War Reserve policemen reported almost immediately. Their foreseeable future was sorted.

But Manchester City and Northern Ireland international inside-forward Peter Doherty was one of those in a dilemma. He applied to Leyland Motors and then Vickers Armstrong without success. A friend offered him a job in Greenock, but City insisted that he stayed in the area! One of the club's directors found him a job as chauffeur to a local businessman, but Doherty gave it up after a few days.

He helped out in the building firm run by Bert Sproston's brother as a paint-ordering clerk and eventually found work at an ordnance factory on the outskirts of Warrington, continuing to play for City. Early in 1940 he volunteered for the RAF rather than hang around waiting for his call-up in the services and went on a PT course at Uxbridge with other players like Ted Drake and Alf Kirchen both of Arsenal, Charlton's Sam Bartram plus Sam Barkas and Jackie Bray from his own club. In Sproston's case, as a former apprentice plumber he found himself in the tank corps!

Ronnie Burgess and his Tottenham colleagues had various ideas. 'Some of them decided to join up straight away. Others said they would go home and think things over, while 11 of us reported on the Monday morning at the local police station to be sworn in as War Reserve policemen,' he recalled. So Messrs Burgess, Willie Hall, Albert Page, Arthur Hitchins, 'Taffy' Spelman, Len Howe, Fred Cox, Percy Hooper, Vic Buckingham, Bert Gilroy and Harry Tompkin were thus enrolled.

It was not long before the authorities ruled that no one below the age of 23 was eligible for the police because of the demands of the three branches of the Armed Forces. Burgess returned to South Wales, awaiting his call-up papers and worked in a local foundry, travelling each weekend to play for Spurs. Then in

February 1940 he volunteered for the RAF and completed his basic training at Padgate, near Warrington. After not making much progress on an RAF police course, he applied for a PT job, which he was duly given two years later!

Frank Swift was another who favoured the Bobbies' Blue. 'When the war broke out, I became a special constable in Manchester, but on my very first day of traffic point duty, I got everything so muddled that, on the advice of a colleague, I walked away, leaving the traffic to sort itself out! I felt at that moment how many full-backs must have felt when playing against Stanley Matthews,' he added.

Some others like Len Shackleton had had to look around for jobs before the war even started. In company with his Arsenal groundstaff colleague Harry Ward, Shackleton had been axed by Manager George Allison in the spring of 1939. The two rejected players decided to go along to the London Paper Mills at Dartford where it was said that footballers could be found jobs provided they turned out for the firm's team. Shackleton remained there for a time even after the war began, returning to Bradford in April 1940 where he played the odd game for Park Avenue as an amateur. At this time he was employed by GEC on aircraft wireless, which was considered as a skilled occupation.

He tried to volunteer for the RAF but, because of his reserved civilian employment, was turned down as were his subsequent applications to enlist in the Fleet Air Arm and then the Army. In 1945 his firm moved back to Coventry and rather than pull up his roots, Shackleton decided to stay in the area. Since the war was over he saw little point in being called up in the services, so he was forced into his only remaining alternative and became a Bevin Boy in the coal mines.

Raich Carter's first reaction was to join the Auxiliary Fire Service with whom he served for two years. He explained: 'I could join immediately, start the same day and once again there would be money if only £3 a week coming in to pay for the rent and some food. And so I enlisted right away.' In fact he became so interested in the service that he seriously thought about making a career of it and turning his back on football, but his physical well-being suffered with the arduous shifts worked in the service and for the first time he found himself hurt by the unfair taunts that many firemen received from using the Fire Service to escape the Armed Forces. He applied for permission to join the RAF and started basic training at Blackpool in October 1941.

The two groups of sportsmen, mostly footballers, accepted into the Physical Training course at Aldershot included Joe Mercer, Don Welsh (both in Group One) and Cliff Britton, Billy Cook, Wilf Copping, Arthur Cunliffe, Bert Sproston and Eric Stephenson. Only two others were turned down by the Medical Board. There was a similar scheme put into operation by the RAF where commissions were granted to, among others, Walter Winterbottom and Tom Whittaker, both given the rank of Pilot Officer. Thus their operation began on 28 December 1939.

In the first six months of the war 154 men from the Association's list of nominations had been accepted by the Services for courses and of these 109 were in the Army and 45 in the RAF. Direct recruitment of civilians to the Army PT staff ceased at the end of February 1940, but the Association was asked to recommend serving men to be considered for any subsequent vacancies which occurred. In November 1939 every one of the players and trainers selected for enlistment in the Army passed out successfully and qualified for the rank of Sergeant-Instructor on the PT staff. The negligible proportion of footballers who were fortunate enough to become PTIs was far outweighed by those who were drafted into many other units at the sharp end of the war.

Of the clubs who had joined the Territorials en masse, Bolton Wanderers gave exemplary service. In May 1939, 15 professionals from the club had enlisted in the 'terriers' and when war came they were called up at once and with the exception of two, Sydney Jones and Charlie Hanks, who were too young to go overseas, they all went to France with the Bolton Artillery before they had even completed training.

They were involved in the Dunkirk evacuation and ten of them later went to the Middle East and later served in the Italian campaign where the skipper, Lieutenant Harry Goslin, was killed and others received minor wounds. When time permitted they played together virtually as a team in such foreign fields as Cairo, Baghdad and Italy. The 13 were: Stan Hanson, Danny Winter, George Catterall, Jimmy Thompson, Harry Goslin, Jack Hurst, Ernie Forrest, Jack Ithell, Albert Geldard, Tommy Sinclair, Jack Roberts, Don Howe and Ray Westwood.

Winter was in hospital when his colleagues went out East, while Geldard and Ithell were transferred to other units before the Artillery went overseas a second time. According to Tommy Lawton, Geldard who once scored 22 goals in a schoolboy game was 'the fastest thing on two legs over ten yards – he could catch pigeons'. Geldard had been the game's youngest debutant at 15 years 158 days, playing for Bradford Park Avenue against Millwall on 16 September 1929. A TA member at the time, of course when war was declared he rushed to his local centre only to be told to go home!

Of the 35 players on the staff in 1939, 32 went into uniform. The other three went into the coal mines and munitions. The club's other fatality was Walter Sidebottom, drowned when his ship was torpedoed in the Channel. Additionally, Harry Hubbick was in the mobile police, George Hunt and Jack Atkinson acting as ARP wardens.

Liverpool, who had a similar record for pre-war enlistment found themselves with several of their players being promoted even before a shot was fired. Twenty were called up immediately. Among those who had volunteered for the 9th King's Liverpool Battalion of the Territorials, Arthur Riley and Dick Kemp were made sergeants, Tom Cooper, Willie Fagan, Bernard Ramsden and Tommy Bush promoted to lance corporals. Fagan became a trench mortar expert. Cooper later lost his life in a motor-cycle accident. Phil Taylor and Jackie Balmer were learning to drive tanks.

Even those fortunate enough to be selected for Army touring sides found they were sometimes close to the fighting. 'Often we played matches only a few miles behind the front lines with the noise of gunfire sometimes tending to drown the sound of the referee's whistle,' recalled Matt Busby.

Like Busby, Mercer was another of the early intake of PT instructors from the FA's scheme and enlisting with the APTC on the promise that the rank of Sergeant-Instructor would be bestowed immediately. He was in the first batch of men sent to Reading where they soon discovered that the stripes would not be automatic. Then they perpetrated a most unsoldierly act. 'When we were told we were not going to become sergeants right away we mutinied,' said Mercer. 'We refused to obey orders!'

A solution was found after an urgent message to Stanley Rous at the FA who was responsible for the operation with the Army. The intake became temporary sergeants and as such given a rough time of it by the proper NCOs in the mess! 'I suppose I was at my peak during the war years,' Mercer added. 'I could call on stamina and never feel tired. You get tired when you are young and when you are old. There are five or six years in between when you don't. The Army made me fitter than I had ever been before.'

On the periphery of the professional scene short-term employment varied widely. One of the busiest of civilian employees at the time of the first air raids was Leicester winger Charlie Adam. He became a member of the Building Trade's Flying Squad, who were rushed to blitzed towns for essential repair work.

Some of those who were able to find employment in reserved occupations remained in them throughout hostilities. Albert Stubbins was a draughtsman in a Sunderland shipyard and as such rather more available on a regular basis to turn out for Newcastle United. Leslie Compton was another early police recruit. In fact he was what might be termed the imperfect 'flatfoot'. But a chiropodist corrected his problem and he was later taken into the Army.

Other players had assorted occupations in the early days of the war. Luton coach George Martin opted for the night shift at a nearby car factory so that he could put in a training stint at the ground at 10 a.m. in the morning. Berry Nieuwenhuys of Liverpool worked as a driller on Merseyside, his trade from his South African days. He worked nights to get in a daytime game of golf! Footballer-cricketer John Arnold of Fulham and Fred Sargent the Spurs outside-left both packed cigarettes and tobacco for the troops. Maurice Dunkley the Northampton and Manchester City outside-right worked in an Army boot factory. Cyril Block the Charlton forward became an accounts clerk in the RASC. Then the Bournemouth trio of 'Shorty' Wilson, Jack Kirkham and 'Blondie' Paton worked on farms before joining the Army, while Ken Bird their goalkeeper was in the Army Ordnance Corps tinkering with electrical faults on tanks. Wilson's speciality was hedge-trimming. Sam Bartram the Charlton goal-keeper was an RAF Sergeant-Instructor. Stockport's John Bowles picked his father's plums for a while!

Birmingham defender Ted Duckhouse helped to build ARP shelters, Hugh Billington of Luton 'Hatters' fame was appropriately making hats for service-women, while his former colleague Bill Fellowes, then with Exeter, looked after his three shops in Tavistock. Two Wolves players had differing jobs: Cyril Sidlow went to a Mills bomb factory, while Dennis Westcott was fixed up at the local gas works. Halifax's full-back Harold Jackson became an Air Ministry inspector for an engineering firm. Jack Ormandy, Southend winger, found himself detailed to guard an aerodrome while in the police. Spurs centre-forward John Morrison, used to having goalscoring ammunition supplied to him, became a munitions lorry driver.

Reg Mountford of Huddersfield, who always had a yearning to be a school-teacher, did help out as a sports master at a prep school and became an ARP Control Officer, Another Huddersfield player, Ken Willingham, capped 12 times at wing-half for England, became a fitter and turner in a munitions works, but Bury's Archie Livingstone found the spice of life. A slater by trade, he had two different jobs at an aircraft factory, one at a stone quarry, another at a paper mill and then one as a clerk at a food control office, all in the first season of the war. Two Newcastle players, Jim Denmark and Jimmy Woodburn, found diverse occupations. Denmark, of Scottish-Canadian descent, had been a hosiery worker and was handed an ARP hose, while Woodburn worked as an electrician in the mines. Tom Olsen of Bury went back to his grocer's shop in Swansea. One of his colleagues, George Davies, became an expert on naval guns in a shell factory.

A couple from Sheffield Wednesday eventually found themselves attached to the medicos. Full-back Ted Catlin became a medical officer's orderly, Allen Driver batman to the medical officer. Manchester United goalkeeper found work as a sanitary inspector.

Alex Robinson, the Burnley half-back, was stationed at Bury in the AFS and guested for Bury. He quit when he realised that firemen were not allowed to move out of the area at any time, but his superior officer made him re-sign and gave him each Saturday off duty with permission to play outside Bury as well. Alec Hall, the Grimsby half-back and skipper, was another in the AFS, while Everton full-back George Jackson was working inside shipyard boilers. Stoke's Arthur Tutin was with several City players employed digging trenches. It dra-matically improved his arm strength for throw-ins.

Idris Hopkins of Brentford became a steeplejack then worked a foot-operated metal trimming machine in an aircraft factory, while Dickie Dorsett, the Wolves forward, made bomb racks. Everton centre-half Charlie Gee became a demoli-tion worker with the ARP, working a shift from 8 p.m. to 8 a.m., although he was an expert joiner by trade. Brentford's Bob Thomas found himself as a naval stoker after working as a shell loader before his call-up. Three Bury players were postmen: Reg Halton, Jack McGowan and Bobby Hulbert. Later McGowan and Halton joined the same regiment.

Orient's Bob Shankly fitted fuses to naval shells, while his colleague Charlie Fletcher, an ex-lorry driver, became a foreman in a munitions factory. Reading centre-forward Magnus Tony MacPhee fitted ear pieces to respirators, his club mate Bob Dougall was fixed up in a jam factory, while Chelsea's Jack Smith and Vic Woodley went from being special constables to RAF PT instructors. Villa defender George Cummings, an iron moulder by trade, was employed in an air-craft factory.

Leicester goalkeeper Sandy drove a taxi; his colleague Johnny King worked on a farm and used to cycle to matches. The Everton centre-half Tom Jones worked in an aircraft factory. So keen was he that he took up aircraft modelling before enlisting in the RAF. The Goodison Park club took on 15-year-old Harry Cooke, grandson of first-team trainer Harry Cooke, to work in the office. Southampton outside-right Bill Bevis, a keen yachtsman and sea angler, appropriately joined the Navy. Chesterfield goalkeeper Ray Middleton went into the mines but insured his hands for £2,000.

Many players put on weight in the forces, but not all. Davy Cochrane, Leeds right-winger, returned to Ireland, but the club did not want him to play in Irish football. 'During his lay-off', said manager Bill Hampson, 'he lost no less than a stone in weight. He was only nine stone at the best of times.'

Charlton's John Oakes became a special traffic policeman, Charlie Hillam an accomplished tenor singer and pianist and this Southend United goalkeeper was also in the police. Chesterfield's Tommy Lyon went back to Scotland, worked in the ambulance service and became a demolition worker, while Gordon Bremner, who combined office work with playing at Arsenal, joined the RASC as a clerk.

Bob Pryde of Blackburn Rovers, a fine violinist off the field, broke his nose in his first match guesting for Aldershot but carried on in traditional Army spirit, revealing another string to his bow. Billy Wrigglesworth was employed building secret aircraft. He kept his footballing ability more in the open, hitting a hat-trick in 11 minutes and scoring twice more in the game against Port Vale on 23 November 1939 as Manchester United won 8-1.

Alfie Anderson, former Bolton winger, who was playing for Third Lanark, returned to Lancashire and was fixed up with a job at a Bolton firm as an uphol-sterer, his former trade. He played for Rochdale but they had to insure him for £1,000. Sergeant Pilot Reg Trim, a Nottingham Forest full-back, was once a tele-graph boy before he swapped his cycle for a message of more national impor-tance. He had had over 80 hours' solo flying experience before he enlisted. Tottenham's Freddie Cox became an RAF fighter pilot, then switched to Trans-port Command, clocking 2,000 hours in the Far East.

If players and officials wondered whether the desire to carry on was worth-while they should not have been in any doubt, for within a month of the out-break of war one police chief was quoted in the *Topical Times*:

> Football is the best teetotal agency we can produce for the worker and others left behind at home. If there is no football each week our cells will be full because the young men of today will have nowhere to go and will fall into mischief. The collection of people at churches is not barred and the collection of football crowds, should not be hindered. Let us have them in their customary winter quarters, not on the streets or in the pubs.

However, perhaps the biggest curse of the war for players was that the black-out made it impossible to play cards in the coach on away trips!

Players used a variety of ingenious methods to arrive at matches; lifts from milk and coal lorries, on the backs of motor cycles, generally hitch-hiking to save expenses. Charlton goalkeeper Sam Bartram thumbed his way to play for York at Hartlepools in a snowstorm. A fire engine on a call picked him up! It was a haz-ardous journey on the icy roads and he arrived late to find the game had started with a replacement in goal. He watched York lose.

Delays on road and rail made team travel just as uncertain. Huddersfield took nine hours to reach London for a War Cup game in May 1940. On another occa-sion Millwall arrived at Norwich an hour late. It was agreed that a shortened game of 35 minutes each way would be played, but it had to be abandoned in the second half.

As far as servicemen were concerned, officers travelled first class, all other ranks third class, but players were only insured if they travelled with the rest of their team and not alone. Young players still had to be groomed and granted opportunities to reveal whatever natural talent they might possess. Leon Leuty had been promised a private trial by Notts County manager Frank Womack. It was a Sunday morning and only a few days earlier a bomb had dropped on one end of the Meadow Lane ground. A few groundstaff recruits filled in the crater with loose earth. It was a makeshift attempt which ended disastrously for Leuty, who fell into the hole after ten minutes and damaged the cartilage in his left leg. He was signed but could not play for a year!

In fact his first taste of football came while playing for Derby as a guest against Mansfield in a 10-0 win. After that he even played for Notts against Derby when they won 3-1 at the Baseball Ground in a North Cup tie in 1942, marking Dave McCulloch so well that Derby persuaded him to turn professional.

Variety was common. Charlie Wayman was a miner who left the pits to become an asbestos roofer. He then served three years in the Royal Navy as an Able Seaman before volunteering for the mines again following two years abroad. As a youngster at inside-left he had scored 65 goals for Chiltern Boys. But a trial for Newcastle was successful. He had a dozen games for the reserves and made his senior debut against Huddersfield in a 3-0 win and was immediately signed by manager Stan Seymour.

Bradford defender Jimmy Stephen was first in the RAF, switched to the pits but, when the Coal Board became unhappy about the time off he was having for football, they sent him back to the service!

Doug Flack, a 19-year-old goalkeeper, emerged in the 1939–40 season. Discovered by Arsenal's Bernard Joy as a pupil at his school, he was given a start by Fulham and also turned out for West Ham. Roy Bentley was not quite 16 and a bit when he scored two goals for Bristol City in their 6-0 win over Aldershot on 26 October 1940, and Arthur Rowley joined Manchester United at 14 and made his debut for them two days after his 15th birthday at outside-right. His brother Jack was on the other flank. Arthur also guested for Wolves and while playing for Blakenhall St Luke's signed for West Bromwich as a professional in April 1944 after asking United to cancel his registration. By this time he had moved to centre-forward but while guesting for Brighton against Crystal Palace he was used at left-back. He later served in Germany and Palestine.

Joe Walton was 14 when war broke out. He was born and raised in Manchester. When most of his friends at school were evacuated to Preston, he stayed at home because he was allowed to look after his invalided mother. He was able to develop as a footballer and with the aid of his schoolmistress, who was keen on soccer, he found his way on to United's list of amateurs when he was 16.

Ted Passmore was just one of many footballers who experienced a classic chequered career. Born Moorsley, Durham on 28 April 1922 he was spotted by Middlesbrough playing with Crook Colliery Welfare at 14. He had trials at Ayresome Park and also at Leeds, who both advised him to return to the pits, but in 1939 he joined Portsmouth from Horden Colliery and enlisted in the Army on the outbreak of war. While serving in the Middle East he played in the same team as Wilf Mannion and, when released, joined up with Swansea, scoring goals from centre-forward in the League West. He signed forms for them against the wall of a cinema.

Middlesbrough's Mannion found himself on a 13-hour trip from the northeast to Aldershot. He joined the 7th Battalion of the Green Howards and was sent to Bridlington for basic training back in the north-east in January 1940. Sent to France he was one of the lucky escapees from Dunkirk along with 700 other soldiers who were taken back by a supply ship SS *Neptune*, though there had been rumours in Middlesbrough that he had perished.

Millwall winger Reg Smith was one of the first to realise that the absence of regular training had affected his performance. Against Tottenham he confessed that he had missed four easy goal chances, hitting the ball way over the bar. 'It's the easiest thing in the world to get underneath the ball – I'm finding that out,' he said. 'I've been unable to get in any training and consequently I've been feeling a little out of touch.'

One of the first on-field casualties was Tom King, the Luton full-back, who badly tore ligaments in the first friendly after war was declared. He missed the rest of the season. Reg Smith himself suffered a war work injury in a crane accident at Shrewsbury in November 1941. He was in hospital for a month and also missed the remainder of the season.

Eddie Carr had been an Arsenal starlet pre-war. He had the misfortune to smash his knee so badly in a game against Charlton that he was told he would never play again. He returned to Durham and played in local football. But for the opportunities that the war presented he would probably not have tried to play at professional level again, but he recovered his confidence and fitness, scoring 29 goals for Newcastle in 1944–45, 18 for Huddersfield the following season and then joined Newport.

Jack Smith, the Chelsea full-back who guested for West Bromwich, slipped on a Wolverhampton kerbstone in the war and a bus ran over his foot. His thick-soled shoe minimised the injury but the accident ended his playing career. Wolves had been Smith's former club and the bus driver turned out to be a Wolves fan.

Len Tyler was invalided out of the Rifle Brigade and then started what appeared to be a promising film career in the close season when not playing football for Millwall. He understudied Tommy Trinder and acted with Robert Donat and Harry Randle.

One of the most consistent of wartime players was Spurs' former Bradford Park Avenue full-back Ralph Ward. He was transferred to Crewe Alexandra in August 1945, having been commissioned in the Home Guard with the rank of lieutenant. An all-round sportsman, he was a fine boxer, once acting as sparring partner to Reggie Meen, heavyweight champion of Great Britain.

Alf Miller – inevitably Dusty – was another whose prowess in the noble art of self-defence was exploited. In India he twice deputised for Al Robinson of Leeds in exhibition bouts against Freddie Mills. At 16, Miller had been on the same bill as Jack Hood. As a wing-half with Southampton, Plymouth and Portsmouth, he guested for Aldershot along with his brother-in-law Bob Royston, an Argyle colleague.

Other club officials were equally concerned with patriotism. George Hicks was a member of Orient's office staff. He joined the Army in 1939, served with Wingate's Chindits in South-East Asia and was demobbed with the rank of captain in 1945. Walter Griffiths had joined Wolves in 1935, combining amateur football with work in the Molineux offices. He turned professional a year later and served in the Royal Navy during hostilities. Of the younger fraternity, Les Olive joined the Manchester United office staff in 1942 at 14 and signed on in the RAF in 1945.

Arthur Rowe was coaching in Hungary from May 1939 until just before the war and 12 British coaches escaped on the last boat to leave Holland. One of them was Sam Wadsworth, coach to DWS Amsterdam. 'I lost everything I had when the Germans kicked me out of Holland,' he said. 'I was one of the last Englishmen to leave Amsterdam in May 1940. I left Jerry my football boots, but remembered at the last minute to bring my international caps.'

Pre-war injuries to players presented increased agonies. Gilbert Wassell, a former Blackpool, Millwall and Tranmere full-back who broke his leg a year beforehand, was living in London near The Den when war came. He had had 22 operations on his leg and was told his career was finished. His leg was in plaster for a further year. Wassell was receiving just 30 shillings (£1.50) a week from the League, out of which his rent was £1.

3 FUN OF THE FARE?

THE PUBLIC'S INITIAL response to the substitute regional competition ranged from the apathetic to the patchy. In many instances, attendances were only marginally better than those for the friendly fixtures which had barely kept the financial ball rolling and, although clubs had greatly reduced expenses, their income was scarcely enough to stay ahead of running costs. Five per cent of all net gate receipts were paid to the League, chiefly for the insurance of players, the rest being equally divided between the two competing clubs.

It took four weeks for a five-figure attendance to be recorded, and that came when Arsenal visited Norwich, drew a crowd of 12,000 and the game ended 1-1. Most League games were scheduled for the Midland and South-West Divisions where the eight clubs in both sections were to meet each other four times for a total of 28 games per club. Other sections played 20 or 22 matches.

However, for the potential spectator the Football Association's liberal spreading of representative games around the country allowed that rare wartime luxury – choice. Such matches with an almost guaranteed ingredient of international-class players provided an attraction that club games could not offer.

The first such large-scale affair set the standard to follow. Played on Everton's Goodison Park ground between a Football League XI and an all-British team, it was considered as a 'great success' and full value for the restricted attendance of 15,000 spectators who paid £1,244 when all receipts from programme sales, etc. were counted, the proceeds going to the Red Cross. Twenty international players were on view and the game ended in a 3-3 draw.

This was followed by the first wartime international fixture, although the 'England' team was selected solely from London clubs and the Welsh themselves had six players from clubs in the London area. Later, like all wartime internationals, it was given an unofficial England label and the crowd of 28,000 at Ninian Park was the highest attendance since crowd limits had been imposed. A sum of £1,627 was raised for the Red Cross.

Already the Lord Mayor's Appeal had benefited from FA representative games by £3,784. In addition, soccer's governing body had donated 500 guineas (£525); the FA had also paid all expenses for these matches which it was estimated had cost them a further £1,000. By March, the Red Cross had received £9,138 from the game.

Two first-class representative games were even fixed for the same day. On 2 December an FA XI met Doncaster Rovers on Rovers' Belle Vue ground while an England team were taking on Scotland at St James' Park, Newcastle. Receipts from the 15,000 crowd there yielded £1,200. Interest aroused in the Doncaster match was such that 2,000 tickets were sold within a couple of days of the announcement of the fixture and the gate was 9,000. Rovers led 2-0 until ten minutes from the end when the FA equalised.

Towards the end of November many clubs were supporting the Players' Union in their plea to increase pay to their members and institute a bonus scheme. The proposal made by the Union to the League was that £2 should be paid for appearance money with ten shillings (50p) for a win and five shillings (25p) for a draw. The Union pointed out in a letter that the players were giving of their best and though attendances had not reached expectations they felt that the extra increment would be a further incentive and help the players to meet their increased liabilities. The Union had already dispensed £400 in grants to players. These requests were turned down: the increase in wages because attendances had not increased appreciably and the bonus on a matter of principle.

Even so, there was something of a return to normality with the first transfer of the war when Wolves paid a 'substantial' fee for Bob King, Northampton Town's outside-right on 22 November.

The League and FA had been strict about players guesting indiscriminately for teams outside the jurisdiction of the competition, in Ireland and Scotland, for example, and when King's Park approached Preston North End for permission to use their wing-half Bill Shankly, the Deepdale club made a condition that their Scottish international be insured for £2,000.

To make up a sufficiently viable fixture list there were numerous friendlies and in November 1939 the belligerent London clubs arranged their own second half of the season programme. Clubs were to be split into First and Second Division teams in one group, South C, and another of Third Division teams under South D. They were unable to complete their South A and South B fixtures before tackling this new competition, but with one exception all outstanding fixtures were fitted in, often using midweek dates.

The winter was a severe one which did nothing to facilitate venturing out to watch the game. Fog caused postponements on 23 December but newspapers and radio were forbidden from giving weather reports. On 3 February 1940 only one Regional League match was played. The contestants did their best to make up for the decimated programme, Plymouth Argyle beating Bristol City 10-3 before 836 spectators. Rationing had started the previous month. On 27 January only seven of 59 games were played in weather which was the coldest recorded since 1894 and which caused hundreds of deaths.

On 1 March the clubs asked for an extension of the season to allow for a War Cup, which was agreed three days later and also to permit the payment bonuses of £1 for a win and ten shillings (50p) for a draw in this competition. A Preston director echoed many thoughts when he said clubs needed their own Red Cross Fund! The Football Association extended the season to 8 June, and on 11 March the Football League launched their War Cup scheme following Scotland's lead in playing ties home and away after the preliminary round. A trophy and medals would be awarded to the finalists, rescinding earlier decisions in this connection.

The preliminary round of the cup began on 13 April with the draw made on a fairly strict regional basis involving 38 Third Division clubs. There were six replays and these were completed in the following midweek. Attendance restrictions were also relaxed on 18 April for the start of the first round proper. Provided police permission was granted, 50 per cent of the ground capacity could be taken up. It had a heartening effect on attendances, the 64 first round games attracting half a million spectators.

Guest players were banned in the cup except in an emergency but this shortsighted attempt to impose peacetime rules produced its problems. Many players refused to return to their own clubs for the competition. In one instance five players appealed to the Management Committee to be allowed to stay with the club near their service depot. In others, war workers stated that their present employers had refused to allow them to travel.

The first round was decided over two legs with the First and Second Division clubs joining in except for Tranmere Rovers, who did not compete. Sunderland did, however. The respective winners of the two sections of the Third Division in 1938–39, Newport County (South) and Barnsley (North), were given byes, but with the absence of Exeter and Ipswich from competitive football it was necessary to allow two other clubs, Crystal Palace and Chester, similar treatment, although like Sunderland, Gateshead did enter the cup.

Again the draw was regionalised but without any reference to pre-war divisions and the first leg took place the following Saturday with the return games one week later. The second round was also on a home-and-away basis and this was completed in successive weekends. On 18 May the third round reverted to one-match, sudden-death ties with one replay needed, and the rest of the competition was played on a similar straight knock-out system.

Tickets for the terraces at the Wembley final were one shilling (5p) and two shillings (10p). Other tickets ranged from three shillings (15p) to ten shillings and sixpence (52p). The match kicked off in the evening at 6 p.m. to allow war workers to attend. The Hammers' semi-final with Fulham the previous week had started at 6.40 p.m.

The entire competition of 137 games including replays and final had been condensed into nine weeks. The final itself was attended by 42,399 from a capacity restriction of 50,000. It was the week of the retreat from Dunkirk. Both West

Ham, the winners with a Sam Small goal, and runners-up Blackburn Rovers managed to field teams composed entirely of their own players. A. V. Alexander, the first Lord of the Admiralty, presented the cup and medals. Among the crowd were some Dunkirk survivors admitted free of charge.

Thus, the first wartime season ended and coincided with England's darkest hour. It was as if night had closed in with no certainty of a dawn to follow it. Even before the War Cup final there had been talk of football closing down for the duration of the war, but the miracle of evacuation from Europe's beaches helped to revive a stunned populace to the realisation of how close they had been to a catastrophe. The subsequent Dunkirk spirit flourished as a reflection of it once everyone's senses were restored, yet for the game the outlook seemed bleak. England was enveloped by her enemies. Invasion seemed imminent. It never happened. But the Battle of Britain did.

The AGM of the Football League was held on 29 July. It was decided to carry on with whatever number of clubs were prepared so to do. They would be divided into two groups, North and South. There would be no professionalism, trophies or medals. Clubs would be allowed to choose their own opponents, but each First and Second Division club must play at least two Third Division teams. Matches would have to be localised and sanctioned by local Regional Commissioners. It was hoped clubs would play at least 20 matches each.

For the first time there would be no points awarded for either wins or drawn games. Instead, the League tables would be compiled purely on goal average, so that any equality of games played would not be detrimental to competing clubs. No attempt would be made to replay abandoned games – the scores would stand. Fixtures would be compiled only up to the end of the year when the position for the second half of the season would be reviewed. There was some cross-matching of the two divisions between clubs geographically close to the split. These were called 'Inter-League' games and counted in the relevant teams' respective section. The tables only made sense if you added them together!

These rather revolutionary plans were adopted by 26–13, although the clubs decided to veto the Management Committee's no-pay plan and agreed to pay the players 30 shillings (£1.50) a week as in 1939–40 with no bonuses. Referees would receive ten shillings and sixpence (52p) and local linesmen five shillings (25p) each plus travelling expenses.

In many respects the 1940–41 season proved one of the most arduous of any in the war period. Winston Churchill was the new Prime Minister. Gone were the half pretences of the so-called 'Phoney War', the Battle of Britain was to become a reality.

Only 68 clubs restarted the competition and, although two more came in, Charlton Athletic closed down at the end of the year, Hull City in the middle of April. There were numerous, and some lengthy, hold-ups of matches because of air raid alerts and scores stood as full-time results in the unfinished games.

On 19 September the FA relaxed their ban on Sunday football to provide recreation for war workers and permission was given for works teams to play games on that day. Manchester City had even wanted League games to be played on Sundays.

Early in November the FA refused permission to clubs to adopt the 'spotter' system on League club grounds during air raid alerts which would have prevented the automatic suspension of play when the sirens sounded. Later on it became accepted practice. However, the Football League did agree to allow referees wearing spectacles to officiate at Regional League matches; a decision depriving patrons of one of their most frequently laboured wisecracks.

The Russians might have invaded Finland but there was minor sporting revolution here, too. Discontent among the London clique was never far below the surface, and on 16 December the League Management Committee discussed protests from southern clubs who had been left out of the London Cup. They submitted alternative proposals for two sections, one to include the out-of-London sides. Six days later the London clubs rejected the new scheme and decided to start their own cup tournament. Then, on 11 January, Portsmouth, Bournemouth, Brighton, Watford, Southend and Southampton started their own Regional South competition and were later joined by Luton and Norwich. Thus, the cracks which had been observed as early as the start of regionalisation the season before were beginning to widen.

On 5 April the FA announced an extension of the season to 7 June. There were two major cup competitions, the national one and London's own additional tournament. In the national tournament teams were split into northern and southern groups right up to the semi-finals. In the northern group the last six clubs in the Regional League table on 25 January joined with Blackpool and Bolton Wanderers, who had not competed in the first half of the season, in a preliminary round decided over two legs. A similar scheme for the southern group failed to materialise because of withdrawals. Birmingham were allowed in the cup, taking Coventry's place.

The competition continued on a home-and-away basis and Wembley was again chosen as the venue for the final, which Preston and Arsenal drew 1-1 before an all-ticket crowd of 60,000. The 40,000 terrace tickets were sold in 24 hours. Ewood Park, Blackburn was chosen as the replay venue and the game was played three weeks later, Preston winning 2-1 – the delay was to accommodate service matches. Players received savings certificates instead of medals.

London's cup had a dozen entries split into two groups of six, playing home and away on a League basis, the top two in each section qualifying for the semi-final. Reading beat Brentford 3-2 at Stamford Bridge in a final watched by a mere 9,000. Having thus distanced themselves further from the rest of the League by organising another competition of their own, the London clubs took their rebellious measures to even greater lengths in 1941–42 by breaking away completely. The simmering dissatisfaction had finally boiled over into outright revolt.

The Football League had to rearrange its fixtures with the loss of the 11 London clubs plus, first, Aldershot and Reading then later Brighton, Watford and, finally, Portsmouth, who all joined up with the rebels. Crewe Alexandra also found themselves embroiled in the argument after they protested about being included in the Southern Section of the proposed League Championship. Thus, this section was left with 13 clubs scattered as far apart as from Swansea to Norwich and Southampton to Northampton. Charlton, Sunderland and Wolves returned to Regional League competition but Birmingham opted out to play in the Birmingham and District League along with Aston Villa.

Shortages of almost every commodity were beginning to bite into the game. The Board of Trade refused a plea to allow clubs to purchase kit without clothing coupons, though they were free to beg or borrow them from generous supporters.

The War Cup took on a different complexion. North and South sections combined for the ten games in the qualifying competition. Each club played five others home and away, their opponents selected by the League. The leading 32 teams at the end of this qualifying period then entered the competition proper. However, all games played in the cup were included in the League tables for the second half of the season.

On the League Championship which was completed by 25 December 1941, northern teams met nine opponents home and away for an 18-match schedule. In the southern section, on the other hand, because of unplayed games the table was calculated on the average of points which would have been gained had teams played the maximum of 18 matches. Thus Leicester won by 0.1 from West Bromwich.

Transport was another continuing headache. Petrol supplies were scarce and could not be given priority rating for sport, but the teams struggled on to fulfil fixtures. The Government took over the offices of the Football League in Winckley Square, Preston so they moved to 102 Fishergate. Weather conditions worsened in late January and early February but the League tried to obviate wasted journeys by arranging postponements 24 hours in advance wherever possible.

The loss of Singapore also hit the supply of football bladders.

The Japanese had bluffed the Allies into surrender, despite being outnumbered 3-1 and short of ammunition. Rubber controls limited manufacture to a quarter of its pre-war production and with leather supplies also restricted, it meant footballs being used for more than one game. Newsprint became scarce and petrol for pleasure was banned. A Doncaster supporter en route to a game was stopped by the police and upon his destination being discovered was charged and later fined in court.

The backlog of fixtures caused the League to order cup games to take precedence over League fixtures which under the designation of a Second Championship in the remaining half of the season were little more than games to fill the calendar. In March the season was extended to 30 May.

Interest in the cup was again greater compared with League matches, though the overall average attendance only went up from about 3,000 to 4,000 in the opening games. But eight ties in April produced a total of 110,000 with 35,000 recorded at Goodison Park, Everton.

Admission charges rose again, this time by 3d (over 1p) to 1s.4d (7p) because of further increases in Entertainments Tax, though it was later reduced to 1s.3d (6p). It was even mooted that a reduction to 7d (3p) would encourage more people to attend and be below the price to qualify for the tax, but football clubs, understandably not noted for acquiescing at price reductions, decided against the idea.

By April the differences between the Football League and the London area rebels was settled at last and at the same time Crewe were welcomed back into the fold. The London Cup semi-final at Stamford Bridge between Brentford and Arsenal drew a crowd of 40,000. The War Cup final first leg ended in a 2-2 draw with 35,000 attending it at Roker Park, Sunderland. In the return match at Wolverhampton, Wanderers won 4-1.

These crowds were eclipsed on the last day of the season with 72,000 at the London War Cup final at Wembley to see Brentford beat Portsmouth 2-0. It was as if the London area clubs had made some kind of point about their lone stand. The number of available footballs also decreased as a result of this match because, on the final whistle, the ball disappeared into the crowd and was apparently carried away by some excited airmen, presumably for a billet room trophy.

This was not quite the end of the official season, because the winners of the two cups met each other in a match arranged in aid of the King George's Fund for Sailors to cement the newly restored friendship with the former London 'revolutionaries'.

The changing face of the war was noted in the Football League's AGM in June 1942, which for the first time actually mentioned the setting-up of a committee to discuss post-war arrangements. Reorganisation continued and the structure for 1942–43 was for the League to be split into two main sections, North and South, as before but with the addition of a smaller Western group which included the admission of three non-League teams, Aberaman Athletic, Bath City and Lovell's Athletic. This was to allow the surviving League teams in the area to have some local competition. The size of the Northern group again necessitated teams playing a restricted number of games within smaller geographical areas but with all matches counting in the overall table.

Norwich withdrew to play only friendlies because of the distances required to travel for competitive fixtures. Bournemouth also called a halt. But Aston Villa,

Birmingham, Derby County and Notts County rejoined. Preston North End had to concentrate on a junior team in the local District League after ground problems. Admission charges had risen again but only in the League South where they increased by 3d (1p) to 1s.6d (7p). In the League North referees and linesmen were now being appointed by the League rather than the clubs.

The opening schedule of matches was watched by 150,000 with 15,000 welcoming Aston Villa back to competitive senior football for the first time in the war. Villa had upped many of their prices to 1s.6d (7p) and fell foul of the League, but they were charging less than the minimum rate of 10d (4p) to servicemen. Eventually they came into line as only the League South had been granted permission for an increase.

Another sign of the times was that Arsenal were unable to obtain elliptical goalposts because the firm manufacturing them had gone out of business. However, the game was taking a more optimistic look to the future although the war continued to fluctuate for the Allies. Further discussions were held by the League about post-war problems and a Victory Cup was purchased at the cost of £36.

A number of other trophies were bought, though pointedly none for the League South! Was this a gentle dig at the London area for the events of the previous year or were the increased admission prices considered sufficient aid?

The return of evacueees and the proliferation of troops in the London area gave clubs the potential for greater spectator catchment. In December 1942 the Army Sport Control Board agreed to pay professionals serving in the forces a match fee in sanctioned games against civilian professional teams.

Christmas Day now marked the end of the League Championship and first half of the programme. A total of 261,000 spectators were present at games with 35,000 watching the Sheffield derby between United and Wednesday. Meanwhile, the League South carried on into February. Cup games on Boxing Day were even better attended, an aggregate of 323,000 watching them. Restrictions on midweek matches meant that abandoned games could not be replayed and scores had to stand.

Another pointer reflecting the improved outlook, if not the reality, on the war front was that the FA decided to reprint 5,000 copies of the referees' chart, some no doubt for bespectacled officials. In the New Year's Honours List, Stanley Rous received the OBE, a fitting reward for his industry, diplomacy and enthusiasm in the war period. The League also mentioned for the first time in January 1943 that a transitional season would have to be implemented after the end of the war before the normal peacetime formula could be resumed. There was still to be no trophy for the League South. Instead, savings certificates would be given to the cup competitors.

Not only the League but some member clubs were also thinking about the future. Birmingham wanted clubs to be limited to spending £10,000 on transfer fees per year as well as the moving of the League's offices to a more accessible city.

The League's 1938 Jubilee book, *Story of the Football League* was still available at 10s.6d (52p) and a sales campaign was launched through club programmes which by now were shrinking in size and heavy with small print. Again cup crowds were up. Sixteen North Cup games in March attracted 200,000 and the four quarter-final games the following month drew more than 100,000. Receipts doubled over the previous season.

A further complication to the already difficult-to-follow Second League Championship came when the League announced that, as cup games also counted in it, the score after 90 minutes would be considered as the result. Extra-time goals would merely determine the winners of the tie!

Even the Inter-Allied Services Cup final at Stamford Bridge in which the Army and the RAF drew 2-2 was watched by 31,000. The United States Army had entered a side in it and were crushed 11-0 by the British Army. There was something at last which could be added to one opinion of the Americans as 'over-dressed, over-paid, over-sexed and over-here' – 'over-done!'

Blackpool became winners of the North Cup, beating Sheffield Wednesday 4-3 on aggregate while down south Arsenal had an emphatic 7-1 win over Charlton. In the Cup-winners meeting Blackpool defeated Arsenal 4-2. Arsenal were still able to field all their own players. The gates were closed with 55,195 present. A token trophy was presented along with war certificates to the players.

In the *Athletic News Annual 1943–44* it was said: 'While it must be regretted that neither Norwich City, nor Bournemouth & Boscombe can be found accommodation by the southern clubs in their 1943–44 League and Cup competitions, the Annual General Meeting of the League satisfied itself that the exclusion of the clubs was inevitable and was not due to selfish motives.' Carlisle's plea to come back was also turned down for similar geographical reasons.

A survey in 1943 undertaken by the FA at the request of the Government found organised football was being carried on in 39 of the counties with 6,570 clubs active. There was an agreed rise in players' remuneration to £2 but limited to 14 players per club. It was also proposed that the transitional season following the war would have to be followed by a post-war period during which there would be a competition for the Victory Cup.

Clubs who were still chasing debts on transfer fees from pre-war transactions were told to deal with the matter themselves and not involve the Management Committee. Bournemouth and Norwich were granted a full share of the cup pool as a gesture towards their financial circumstances, after being left out of the South's competition.

The FA also held a full-scale meeting in June 1943 which discussed a wide range of topics for the post-war period. On the eve of the season the Chairman of Chester surprisingly hoped that after the war at least Third Division football would be composed of amateurs and part-time professionals, as he did not believe 'that after the war the country would be able to afford to let all her fittest and best citizens go into what was after all a blind-alley occupation'.

Over 200,000 saw the start of the 1943–44 season. Although the Government steadfastly refused any relaxtion of the Entertainments Tax, the Board of Trade agreed to release 40,000 clothing coupons among the professional clubs of the four home countries. Meanwhile, the Players' Union pressed for the abolition of the maximum wage or a substantial increase in it and a superannuation scheme.

The Christmas period again reflected increased crowds. Some 320,000 attended on Christmas Day and 440,000 for the opening cup games and League South fixtures on Boxing Day. More than 40,000 saw Tottenham beat West Ham in January. Later in the month the Merseyside derby at Goodison Park drew 43,000 who saw Liverpool beat Everton.

Air raids became more intense in the south than for four years but despite this an international at Wembley between England and Scotland produced a sell-out crowd of 80,000, producing £18,000 for charity: the largest single contribution from a sports event in Britain. In one incendiary raid the FA offices were hit. Rous and his wife helped to extinguish the flames.

Another running sore was the complaint by many clubs of the increasing demands of the services on their players. It was a double-edged sword, because the League was continually swiping at clubs over their abuse of using guests.

In April the rekindling of interest in the game with the tide of war turning to flow for the Allies and the promising Second Front invasion of Europe expected in the summer contrived to boost attendances further. The League South Cup final at Wembley saw Charlton beat Chelsea 3-1 with 85,000 present.

So many people had applied for tickets to Aston Villa's North Cup semi-final with Sheffield United on the same day that it took weeks to return the money to disappointed applicants. Some 45,000 had attended. The following week the Scotland v England game at Hampden Park was watched by 133,000, the highest wartime gate.

Villa's following was rewarded when they defeated Blackpool 5-4 on aggregate in the North Cup. The Villa Park gate was 54,824. As a fine gesture Villa later donated the trophy to the Red Cross to auction off for charity. However, as plans for the invasion heightened, the AGM of the Football League was postponed indefinitely.

The formula which appeared to present fewest pitfalls was again adopted for the 1944–45 season. Now the advance into Europe from D-day was continuing to lengthen expectations of a shortening of the war, despite pilotless V1 'doodle bugs' and V2 rocket raids. London and the south-east was especially vulnerable to these attacks and the spotter system was again adopted at grounds.

Preston and Hull came back, but applications from Barrow, Carlisle, Bournemouth and Norwich were rejected, the former pair because of the distances involved in accommodating fixtures for them, the latter two ostensibly for the same reasons but really because of the continued opposition by the London area clubs. Later Accrington and Port Vale were also re-admitted.

The dispatch of military personnel into Europe in the wake of the Second Front brought renewed problems for clubs who had enjoyed the use of either their own players or guests stationed within a reasonable distance of their grounds. It also meant the cessation of the Inter-Allied Cup for the same reason, although there were still a large number of representative games to watch. Wembley's first international of the season attracted 90,000 for England v Scotland. The amateur game also witnessed its biggest resurgence since the start of the war and an FA County Youth Cup for Under-18s was successfully launched.

Transport problems prior to the build-up of men and materials before D-day had led to the AGMs of both the FA and League being postponed until October when there were some unexpected setbacks on the European war front with the German breakthrough in the Ardennes. It was agreed that if and when a transitional season could be started the number of guest players would be restricted to six per club and then gradually reduced.

However, the post-war committee of the FA reported the establishment of eight sub-committees to deal with a variety of topics for the time when hostilities would be at an end. In December the Third Division clubs turned down a suggestion for the formation of a Fourth Division from the existing North and South sections of the Third Division and instead confirmed as their prior concern an increase in the number of clubs promoted to Division Two from two to four.

The New Year produced crowds of over 300,000. Fred Howarth, the League secretary reported that attendances were 40 per cent up on the previous year. Nevertheless, inclement weather at the end of the month caused postponements and led to calls in the now almost annual plea for an extension to the season which was later granted by three weeks to 26 May.

In March the 16 opening games in the League North Cup were witnessed by 290,000 including 40,000 at Goodison Park for Liverpool's 1-0 win over Everton. The following month the League South Cup final at Wembley attracted 90,000 and brought receipts of £29,000 of which £13,300 was swallowed up by Entertainments Tax. In the final Chelsea beat Millwall 2-0 and of the 22 players on view, only 10 were playing for their own clubs!

Interest continued at a lively pace in the north, with the aggregate attendances for the North Cup quarter-finals reaching 142,000. By May an end of hostilities in Europe was at last in view and the FA announced the approval of friendlies to mark the celebrations on VE Day.

On 26 May over 57,000 saw Bolton clinch the League North Cup final on a 3-2 aggregate over Manchester United, and on the same afternoon the first international since the war against a foreign side took place at Wembley between

England and France. The following week the season was wound up a week later than originally anticipated but within four days of the anniversary of D-day. Bolton beat Chelsea 2-1 in the meeting of North and South Cup winners. The Greyhound Racing Association provided Stamford Bridge free of charge, each club paying its own expenses, with Chelsea footing the match expenses. A few minutes from the end some spectators swarmed over the dog track. One or two encroached on to the pitch and kept the ball after a fight. The incident had been sparked by a penalty kick.

The Japanese war was also drawing to what was to prove a doomsday-like Atom Bomb finale, when the plans for the transitional season of 1945–46 were approved. While the Management Committee were keen to revert to as near pre-war conditions as possible, the clubs vetoed the idea because of the shortage of players and persistent problems associated with travel and accommodation.

First and Second Division clubs were combined and split into North and South, the River Trent used as a dividing line, leaving the Third Division with its own pre-war regions, but these Associate Members decided against this idea and the two sections were further sub-divided into smaller geographical groups, making four area sections in all. Just to illustrate the complexity of their labels, one was called Third Division South (North Region)!

One casualty was the League War Cup which had proved popular and a source of much needed revenue for the clubs. However, the FA agreed to reinstate the FA Cup and at the request of the League teams it was decided to follow the War Cup principle of home-and-away legs from the first round proper for extra revenue purposes. Otherwise the competition was one along pre-war lines.

Players were still receiving £4 a match and, as Ivan Sharpe reported in the *Athletic News Annual 1945–46*, 'this is not a living wage for a demobilised player of Football League status, but, at this writing demobilisation is a much-used word rather than a fact as far as first class footballers are concerned'.

For League games, guest players were limited to a maximum of six per team and from 3 November that was further reduced to three. Tottenham wanted guests in the early FA Cup rounds but in the light of experience of the abuse of the system in the War Cup's last season it was unlikely to be tolerated by the FA. The old cup was a tremendous attraction after an absence of seven years and the matches over two legs helped to swell the coffers. In the final Derby beat Charlton 4-1, watched by 98,000 spectators who paid £45,000. The tragedy at Bolton overshadowed the entire tournament.

Charlton came close to a 'double' but fell short of both aims. In the League South they could have won the championship on the last day but were held to a draw. Six different clubs won the fragmented and regionalised Third Division including separate North and South cup competitions.

In a general review of the season by Charles Buchan in the *News Chronicle Annual 1946–47* he said that it 'provided a lot of excitement and bright entertainment for huge crowds, which in several cases reached record proportions'. On the international front a Victory International tournament for the four home countries was organised on the lines of the pre-war British International Championship. Belgium and Switzerland visited both England and Scotland, while England fulfilled its fixture in Paris, shelved on the eve of war. The circle was finally complete.

4 DESPITE THE BOMB DAMAGE

MANY FOOTBALL LEAGUE grounds suffered damage through enemy action. Others had either parts or the whole of their premises requisitioned by the military and defence authorities. Some clubs were forced into a quick evacuation from their headquarters on the outbreak of war. A few decided not to continue for the duration or while their individual problems persisted. Some found alternative accommodation.

One of the earliest casualties in terms of a club losing its amenities was Arsenal, whose Highbury ground became a First Aid Post and Air Raid Patrol Centre. Later an RAF barrage balloon was flown from the practice pitch by the adjacent college. The dressing-rooms were utilised as a casualty clearing station with the windows boarded over and a blast wall was built inside the main entrance to the famous marble hall. The wardens' reporting post was in the main stand.

Neighbours Tottenham speedily came to Arsenal's rescue and the two clubs shared White Hart Lane for the duration of the war and the transitional season following it. Meanwhile Highbury itself suffered some damage. A 1,000lb bomb fell on the training pitch, five incendiaries destroyed the North Bank roof, which collapsed like a pack of cards and the set of goalposts was burnt to the ground. The college behind the Clock End was destroyed by fire in the latter stages of the war.

White Hart Lane was undamaged although there were sections of the ground used for other purposes. The top of the East Stand became a mortuary for blitz victims, while another area was taken over for the manufacture and production of gas masks.

This spirit of close cooperation between neighbouring clubs enabled others to carry on with almost normal service being resumed in rival camps and was as well illustrated as anywhere by the plight of Manchester United. On 5 September 1939 part of Old Trafford was taken over by the military. The club's Cliff Ground training area at Lower Broughton was commandeered by the RAF Balloon Squadron. Old Trafford first sustained some damage on 22 December 1940. Then in March 1941 one bomb destroyed the main stand, another the terracing and cover. The pitch was also badly scorched.

Manchester City offered Maine Road, and United were still sharing with their neighbours after the war ended. In the spring of 1944 when the army released the Cliff Ground, City and United reserves shared it. By August 1945 the War Damage Commission had granted Manchester United £4,800 to clear debris at Old Trafford and £17,748 to rebuild the stands.

Of the clubs who decided to participate in regional leagues in the first season of wartime football, Birmingham had to look elsewhere simply because the local Chief Constable closed St Andrews. He was worried that there was the risk of a serious loss of life from air raids if crowds gathered to watch football there. The club made strenuous efforts to have the ban lifted and sought higher authority. After several unsuccessful attempts Birmingham City Council finally passed a resolution on 12 March 1940 asking the Chief Constable to reconsider. With only eight dissentients they recommended a reappraisal of the situation in order to supply recreation on Saturdays for the thousands of industrious munitions workers and others in the city.

The matter was raised in Parliament by local MPs and, although the Home Secretary refused to overrule the decision, when it became known that Birmingham's was the only ground in the country to be shut completely, the ban was lifted. The first home game was against Walsall on 23 March with 12,000 present.

In defence of the Chief Constable's stance it should be stressed that he might have had a point. St Andrews was hit on 18 different occasions! Dressing-rooms and other buildings were damaged. While being forced to seek alternative venues, Birmingham played home games at Coventry's training ground at Leamington and later at Villa Park. The mid-November bombing of Coventry caused that club to cancel the rest of the fixtures for the season.

Yet Birmingham suffered disastrously from a most bizarre error which was self-inflicted. In January 1942 when the main stand was destroyed by fire it was doing duty as an auxiliary fire station. One day one of the firemen tried to put a brazier out with what he imagined to be a bucket of water which turned out to be petrol. All the playing kit was lost, but fortunately the current minute book and other records were at the Secretary's home.

Greyhounds caused problems for both Bristol Rovers and Newport County. Rovers had had a pre-war debt of £16,000 and the following year the club chairman Fred Ashmead sold Eastville stadium for £12,000, against the agreement of the rest of the board, to the local greyhound company. Because Bristol greyhounds ran on Saturday afternoons there could be no football, so during 1939–40 Rovers had to play home games at either Bristol City's Ashton Gate or at Kingswood. They opted out of football until 1945–46 by which time two members of the greyhound company had purchased a controlling interest in the club.

Ashton Gate did not escape. The No. 1 stand was destroyed on successive nights, half by an unexploded bomb one night and the other by one that exploded the next evening in February 1941.

Newport were hounded by similar problems. They were also affected by the switch from evening to afternoon greyhound racing under the auspices of the Cardiff Arms Park Greyhound Racing Company. County moved to Rexville, the ground of Lovell's Athletic. Their own Somerton Park ground was commandeered by the Civil Defence and for a while the club used the Rodney Parade Rugby Ground but then they, too, gave up the struggle, although later in the war Lovell's themselves were able to keep the flag flying at a similar height in Newport.

However, by far the most seriously affected of the West Country clubs was Plymouth. Their Home Park ground was pockmarked with craters, the grandstand devastated in February 1941 by high explosives and fire set off by incendiaries. Furniture stored for safety under the stand by families in the vicinity after heavy raids on the naval base acted as tinder to the flames. Argyle played in only the first and last seasons of the wartime competition, although they appeared in some competitive games during the latter stages of the 1944–45 season. When they did return, they were forced to use old trams as offices, Army huts for dressing-rooms and railway sleepers for footing on the terraces.

Exeter City, who did not take part again until the transitional season, turned their ground over to the military. The United States Army used the pitch for training and the stand for catering purposes.

Swindon Town's County Ground became a POW camp with huts built on it. Southend United were evicted by the Army and though they moved to Chelmsford eventually they, too, had to admit defeat. In July 1940 they approached West Ham for the use of Upton Park on a sharing basis, but the Hammers said it would interfere with the plans for developing a junior side. Southend itself was a restricted area.

West Ham themselves lost their records in the blitz. The West Stand had to be evacuated along with what remained of the club administration. They set up offices in Green Street House, the oft-referred-to Boleyn Castle. The South Bank was also badly damaged and in one season the Hammers played only away games in the first half of the campaign.

Across the Thames on the Isle of Dogs, Millwall's ground at The Den was also in the wars with damage to a stand and part of the terracing. On the last day of the 1942–43 season, one hour after the match, the Main Stand seating 2,000 was burnt to the ground. In the autumn Millwall moved their games to The Valley, Charlton's ground, whose reserves went to war-torn New Cross. Millwall received permission from the authorities to erect a temporary stand but, although they had hoped it would have been completed by November 1943, it was not ready until March 1944.

When Millwall returned home, the directors had to be accommodated on a couple of wooden benches by the track and the press were similarly placed behind one of the goals. Charlton's North Stand was hit, although pre-war rumours here had given the impression that the ground would be closed completely. It was local gossip at the time that The Valley would be taken over as an ARP and Decontamination Centre. In the event, part of the ground was used for ARP purposes.

Blackpool's Bloomfield Road was partially used for storage and by the RAF as a training centre while the Army moved in at Deepdale, the home of Preston North End in May 1941. Prisoners of war were held there for a while and the military gave the club £250 a year in compensation. Then, in March 1943 they donated the princely sum of £5 per annum for use of the car park.

Preston missed two whole seasons and also played some games four miles away at Leyland Motors. They came back in March 1944. Bolton's Burnden Park playing area was used other than on match days by the Education Authorities and the stands by the Ministry of Supply. In fact, the stands were full of food at the time of the ground's tragedy in 1946.

On Merseyside close proximity to Liverpool docks caused damage to Everton's Goodison Park, while at Tranmere Rovers the car park was used as a post for sending up smoke screens to confuse German aircraft seeking out shipping in the nearby Birkenhead dock area. Rovers also had tank traps in an adjacent road and lost the cover of a stand in a raid.

Stoke City's Butler Street Stand was used as an Army Camp, Stockport County shared their Edgeley Park ground with Broughton Park RFC and Aston Villa could claim to be unique in that ground improvements being carried out when war started were allowed to be completed in February 1940. While their Holte End banking was receiving this attention, the Trinity Road Stand was refitted as an air raid shelter and the home team's dressing-room occupied by a rifle company of the 9th Battalion of the Royal Warwickshire Regiment.

Leicester applied to the FA for a loan to repair air raid damage but were referred to the local authority, and New Brighton, who pulled out of regional football after the first three seasons, found their ground requisitioned by Wallasey Corporation and were one of only two League clubs who did not return to the game when the transitional season of 1945–46 opened. Hull City were the other absentees after Anlaby Road was rendered uninhabitable, the Tigers being left to forage around their old haunts at the Rugby Club in 1944–45.

The siting of the other Humberside club, Grimsby Town, at Blundell Park in Cleethorpes was considered too vulnerable to enemy action to risk large crowds, and Scunthorpe United's Old Show Ground often acted as their home as well as staging games for several other League clubs. At York, a bomb fell at Bootham Crescent on the Shipton Street End, while Derby's Osmaston Stand was damaged.

Both Nottingham clubs were inconvenienced in different ways. Forest's City Ground suffered £75 worth of damage to the pitch in May 1941 but across the Trent at Meadow Lane Notts County had the northern wing of their main stand destroyed by bombs and the playing area was so badly cratered that the club had to pull out of the regional competition in 1941–42 for one season. On the open terrace there was even a machine gun emplacement, but Norwich went one better. The nearness of the Boulton Paul aircraft factory made Carrow Road a danger area. Norwich had two gun emplacements built in their car park overlooking the Wensum and manned by the Home Guard.

Down in Suffolk, Captain Cobbold, the chairman of Ipswich Town, had closed his ground immediately on the declaration of war so that 'every man might do his duty'. Some £13,000 worth of damage was done to Portman Road by enemy action. The ground housed a Naval Unit.

Sunderland, who followed Ipswich's early decision to pull out by announcing they would take no part in regional competition, entered the War Cup in the latter part of 1939–40 and eventually returned to full participation. But bombs fell on the Roker Park pitch and just outside the ground in March 1943 killing a policeman. Two months later more bombs destroyed the car park and the club-house.

Two other League grounds affected by raids were those of Sheffield United and Southampton. Ten bombs hit United's Bramall Lane in December 1940, demolishing half the John Street Stand, the roof of the terracing and badly cratering the pitch. United's ground was also used for storage purposes. The club transferred games elsewhere for a time.

The close proximity of The Dell in Southampton to the docks left it exposed to attack. In November 1940 a bomb struck the pitch at the Milton Road End causing one of the underground water culverts to break and flood the pitch under a couple of feet of water. On 8 April 1941 fire broke out in the West Stand but was dealt with before dark. The Saints used the Pirelli General Works Sports Ground in Eastleigh and later played a few games at Portsmouth's Fratton Park before being able to return home.

Even housing the club offices away from the ground was no answer for Reading. Their administration, then situated in the town centre, was also wrecked by a bomb while Elm Park itself escaped.

Chelsea suffered air raid damage and were allowed to erect a temporary stand following application to the local authority and it was opened in September 1943. Other disruption at Stamford Bridge occurred after the war in November 1945 when 74,496 people paid through the turnstiles to watch the touring Moscow Dynamos, but gates and fences were flattened as between 90,000 and 100,000 packed into the ground spilling on to the greyhound track and touchlines in a repeat of Wembley's inaugural 1923 Cup Final scenes. Some spectators who had climbed the roof of the main stand fell and were injured.

Wembley Stadium received an oil bomb on the pitch which made a mess but caused little damage, but in August 1944 a flying bomb exploded in the grounds outside, 50 yards from the greyhound kennels. Several animals escaped, none were injured and the last of those AWOL was rounded up a week later! At various times in the war the Empire Stadium was used as a temporary accommodation for refugees from Europe and servicemen released early to help rebuild bombed sites.

5 GUESS WHO'S PLAYING TODAY!

WITHOUT GUEST PLAYERS the wartime game would have collapsed as an organised entity. By the apparent restriction of its local catchment area, the system worked in favour of visiting teams turning up short of a full complement. They could legitimately accept anyone in the vicinity!

Unfortunately, like many sound ideas, once at the mercy of human frailty and greed it became abused. While its initial implementation was as a last resort when clubs were short of players, it became the custom for some to seek a guest at the expense of their own registered and available members.

The higher the status of the club in question the more likely it was that they were able to attract 'star' guests. It might have been questionable ethics but it was good box office. It caused bad feeling and even led to some players asking for a transfer. Events reached the height of absurdity in the 1945 South Cup final. Chelsea had eight guests while a ninth was a comparatively recent signing from Airdrieonians. Millwall fielded four strangers. One critic called it the 'lease-lend' final. With a nice touch of irony the 12th man was the same for both sides and, needless to add, Willie Hurrell, a Scot, was neither a member of the Stamford Bridge staff nor just released from The Den of Lions.

Both teams were subsequently censured for playing ineligible players without the consent of the League Management Committee, though undoubtedly the publicity attached to a game of such importance was the reason for the outcry since it was by no means an uncommon occurrence. In their defence, several of the guests had been assisting these clubs for some time.

Naturally there were many more instances of teams being unable to afford the luxury of picking and choosing whom they wanted to play in their teams. They were often lucky to field a side at all. The occasions when teams arrived short of players and had to rely on the home team to supply them with replacements, or answer urgent appeals for volunteers to fill in the numbers, were numerous.

Despite all these problems teams rarely had to take the field short of a full complement. Frequently players would arrive late, but a team would start without a man or even two, provided they knew the missing men were on their way. Substitutes were not allowed in club games at least, although there was one occasion involving Preston when a player who appeared in the first half was replaced by a late-arriving colleague for the second 45 minutes!

The Football League did its best to control what was virtually uncontrollable, officially noting in 1941–42 that Nottingham Forest had used guest players on 75 occasions and that Northampton had fielded them 95 times out of 99 in Cup qualifying games alone, using two of their own registered players. Clubs with players selected for representative games often had no alternative. Northampton and Aldershot were among the clubs who turned out complete elevens of guests. Yet Villa used just three.

The League also had to accept what was termed 'a multitude of explanations by clubs appearing before their registrations were completed'. Yet, as the war went on and problems mounted, the fact that the game was continuing on organised lines was regarded as the overriding consideration. A system later introduced of notifying the League by telegram of players being signed was an almost instant way of obtaining clearance, at least for those players registered with another League side.

Many clubs were caught by 'impostors' posing as experienced replacements, their fake credentials being explained as either reserves of Scottish clubs, colts from other League clubs or amateurs from leading non-league teams, and so on, when in fact they had little or no ability except amazing audacity. Some clubs were understandably so embarrassed at being duped they did not send in the name of the player concerned. Others' real names were never disclosed. However, some charlatans had done their homework well enough.

A young man called to see Chelsea manager Billy Birrell purporting to be a certain Motherwell player whose name appeared on that Scottish club's strength. Birrell asked him to turn up the following day in case of an emergency arising, which it did.

'It was ludicrous,' reflected Birrell. 'I walked into the dressing-room a few minutes before kick-off and the sight of the newcomer with his shirt outside his shorts told me that he had never had a stud on his sole.

'But there was no one else and we couldn't turn out ten men. His first kick out in the middle confirmed my fears and the good-humoured crowd were not slow to spot it. At half-time I told the lads to keep him out of the game and all seemed to be going well when someone forgot himself and put the ball out to our new-found friend. And to the lone, penetrating cry of "Come on, Enoch" from the back of the crowd, he missed it completely.'

Leeds United heard that Chelsea's much sought-after winger Alf Hanson was billeted at Harrogate and the wheels were set in motion to have a taxi collect him for the match with York on 21 November 1942. Despite arriving ten minutes after the start, he took his place on the vacant right wing. A portly figure, not what was expected in appearance – they had the wrong man. The newcomer was an Irishman called Stanley Anson.

There were genuine instances of course. Alexander Cross was a qualified doctor and serving officer in the RAMC. An inside-forward or wing-half with Queen's Park and a Scottish amateur international he was posted to a new unit and sought out his Welfare Officer in a bid for Saturday leave.

Slightly built and wearing spectacles, off the field he never quite looked the part and there was some disbelief when he repeated his CV to his superior. A non-committal reply was forthcoming and it was left like that. But a couple of weeks later Cross renewed his request, quickly adding that he had had an invitation to play for Arsenal! Thus on 15 December 1945, Dr A. Cross turned out for the Gunners in a 2-2 draw with Nottingham Forest at White Hart Lane.

In these trying times, printing players' names on a football programme literally put it in the fiction category. On 14 September 1940 the Tottenham programme produced ten changes, the centre-forward being a 16-year-old local lad. On that Battle of Britain day of countless air raid interruptions, the match was halted after a quarter of an hour and restarted after 75 minutes. Spurs eventually won 3-2 before a crowd of 1,622. George Ludford scored a couple of their goals against Chelsea.

Where clubs knew at the time of going to press that one or two positions were doubtful, they would use the cryptic 'A. G. Player' (a guest player), 'A. N. Other' or even 'Newman'; but the prize for the most original of these designations must have gone to Fulham who produced 'S. O. Else'. Could it have been a promising amateur from a nearby team? In fact it was simply 'Someone else'. Ironically it turned out to be Ludford and he bagged another couple of goals! Portsmouth also announced an Else, but it transpired it was their usual leader, Jock Anderson.

Even so, there were many occasions when the opposite was the case and progammes able to be printed on the morning of the match often had few if any changes in them.

Clubs, of course, began by insisting that their players were insured by other teams with whom they were to guest, but again this led to problems. While clubs might agree, the player himself might have other ideas. In 1940–41, York wanted Andy Cowie of Aberdeen to assist them at full-back. Aberdeen agreed for £5,000 insurance. York lost interest.

In 1943 in an attempt to prevent players in England playing for Scottish clubs while on holiday north of the border, only those resident in service camps would be eligible in future. Tommy Lawton had spent his honeymoon playing in Scotland! In 1943 he hit eight goals in four more Morton games.

With an internationally accepted reputation, it was obvious that Peter Doherty would be eagerly sought after. The usual practice was for the player to inform his club whether he was likely to be around on a particular Saturday. 'I wired Mr Wilfred Wild (the manager of Manchester City) to say I had an unexpected short leave and would be available on the Saturday, requesting him to send instructions to my Blackpool home.

'When I arrived there, I found a letter from the manager informing me that the team had been selected and that Albert Malam had been chosen as inside-left.

'I could understand this of course, as Malam was available every week and I was not. What annoyed me was the fact that after a long, overnight journey made with the specific intention of playing, no assistance was given to me in the matter of expenses. It was a thoughtless omission and one that remained in my mind for a long time.'

It should be said here that Malam was at the time a registered Doncaster Rovers player. It was the start of many problems for Doherty with City, which were ultimately to result in his leaving the club. On another occasion he had agreed to play for Walsall but was informed by City that he would have to play for West Bromwich, because the insurance of players of Doherty's calibre were high and smaller clubs could not always afford the premiums.

Another time he was due to play at Crewe in a cup-tie but was forced to hitch-hike there. He picked up a lorry the driver of which thought that if players arrived late they could take over from whoever had started the game. Doherty's progress might have been slowed by this misguided notion for he arrived as the team was coming on the field without him.

Doherty was approached to guest for Port Vale but City disagreed, saying instead that he could turn out for Manchester United if he wished. After Shamrock Rovers showed interest in him, City agreed to transfer Doherty and on his demobilisation from the RAF he joined Derby County for whom he had frequently guested. This was after being posted to No. 3 Medical Rehabilitation Unit, Loughborough, where he was engaged in restoring injured airmen to health by remedial exercises. While there, he was involved in a nasty accident when knocked down by a motor vehicle in camp, but he rapidly recovered.

Apart from the vexed question of availability on a Saturday and whatever legitimate complaints players had over their treatment, clubs had their own headaches multiplied by up to eleven times that number each week. Players were usually sensitive to taking the place of fellow professionals who might otherwise have been available for selection. Diplomatically, the clubs would often not inform a newcomer that he was being included at the expense of a colleague. Arsenal's Dave Nelson was one who had to play in various positions or would be omitted at the last minute.

Doherty went to Blackpool to watch Liverpool and on calling in at the dressing-room to chat to one or two friends he was asked to turn out for Liverpool. It was only afterwards that he discovered George Ainsley, the Leeds United forward, had been left out of the team on his account. There were repercussions.

Liverpool were censured, since the RAF had given permission for Ainsley to obtain leave. The RAF said that they would release no more players for Liverpool, but the club apologised to them and the League. This was not uncommon and even the star names found themselves on the receiving end of such unpleasant situations. As Bernard Joy recollected at Arsenal, Ted Drake was talking in the car park at White Hart Lane before a game, then dashed into the dressing-room in order to strip only to find his shirt had been given to Bobby Flavell, the Scottish inside-forward from Airdrieonians.

The named players were not the only ones who drew clubs like magnets. George Murphy, the Bradford City forward, reckoned he played for eight different clubs in one spell of nine weeks. Doherty himself admitted to turning out for six in just over a week and Jock Dodds's posting to the London area brought him offers from practically every team in the metropolis. Dodds decided to assist West Ham, but when he found out that George Foreman was being overlooked in his favour after returning from a spell helping Tottenham, Dodds was upset and went to Fulham.

However, the record over a short period of time probably went to Arsenal's Welsh international inside-left Leslie Jones who guested for Fulham on Monday 3 June 1940, West Ham on the Wednesday and for Southampton the following day – three clubs in four days.

Goalkeepers, being specialists, were at a premium. The Charlton goalkeeper Sam Bartram played in three successive Wembley cup finals, two of them admittedly for his own Charlton, but in the middle of the trio he guested for Millwall in 1945.

There was certainly evidence that the game attracted its share of mercenaries, not only soldiers of fortune, but sailors and airmen plus those in the Civil Defence. Their bounty was modest enough; increment in fees and expenses but still selling their services to the highest bidder. Clubs knew where and how to contact them. Bill Shankly said: 'People found me. They came looking for the players who had reached international standing. It was easy to be found out, even in big camps where there were maybe thousands of men. Well, it soon got around. I played for many teams and had a game every Saturday.'

The money was not the only incentive. Getting a regular game was something not all servicemen were privileged to be given. Many would risk 'jankers' to turn out even when there was no weekend pass for them. Shankly himself appeared at right-half for Norwich as 'Newman' in a friendly in January 1943 against an Army XI. He scored twice in an 8-4 win watched spookily by 484 people!

Wherever possible clubs protected players who chanced getting caught for being AWOL, often only releasing their names a week or so after the match in which they played. Crystal Palace listed 'Marksman' in their side for a couple of weeks in the 1941–42 season. It transpired that it was Jack Blackman. That same season Watford included 'Newman' in their attack against Brighton on 21 February, his real identity being withheld for 'security reasons'. Subsequently he was discovered to have been the Grimsby forward Fred Kurz, stationed at Woolwich Arsenal. However, when Watford signed 'A. Newman' in October 1944 that turned out to be the real name of the Amersham left-winger! But even the official history of Spurs still lists their No. 7 against Aldershot on 26 April 1941 as A Newman . . .

Moreover, team changes were not always noted and reporters, often not sports minded because of the skeleton staffs at newspapers at the time, frequently accepted what the programme printed without checking on possible changes. One journal even reproduced the teams from a match with the players clearly listed from Nos 1 to 11 on one side and 11 to 1 on the other, simply because they had appeared this way in the programme.

Frequently team changes were chalked up on a blackboard and paraded around the ground. It was not always possible for spectators positioned some distance away from the touchline to make note of the necessary alterations.

The ace soccer reporters who were still around were often in on the concealment of players who should have been guarding some important installation instead of 'punting a pill' about and the truth was the exact composition of some teams has never been accurately recorded and may never be so.

Naturally clubs had to send in names of their team after a match, but the Football League largely had to accept whatever was presented to them. There were no resources to do anything else. Of course the uncertainties led to openings for aspiring would-be professionals. It was possible that youngsters might be called upon in an emergency and turning up with your football boots was often a smart move.

On 22 November 1941 the clarion call of stardom rang out for a soldier who went to Ewood Park to watch Blackburn Rovers play Burnley. Sergeant-Major William Bryson volunteered to fill a gap in Rovers' side and had the distinction of scoring their winning goal in a 3-2 win. Blackburn were in trouble in another match against Manchester United and only completed an eleven with the inclusion of an enthusiastic youngster called Hallam, who 'missed kicks, was knocked flat, derided with laughter, then cheered for his doggedness'. On 16 January 1943 the player subsequently listed by the League as Millington, 'a last minute player', scored one of Southport's two goals at Tranmere but finished on the losing side in a 3-2 defeat.

Arsenal were at Charlton on one occasion with goalkeeper George Swindin unavailable at the eleventh hour. The management heard that Spurs goalkeeper Percy Hooper was in the ground and an announcement was made for him to report to the dressing-room. Unfortunately, the Hooper who presented himself was Mark Hooper, the Rotherham and former Sheffield Wednesday winger!

On another occasion goalkeeping problems caused Arsenal to cancel their game at Brighton. Due to go there on 9 November 1940, not one of their four goalkeepers was available, two other outfield men were away on duty, four more playing in an RAF representative game and two were injured. The previous month Brighton, at home to Chelsea, had six professionals and made the number up with five amateurs. Only 50 people turned up to watch, but the game was abandoned after five minutes because of an air raid alert with the score 0-0.

London clubs operated a system of pooling resources and the same excellent service of cooperation existed in other areas just to prove that clubs were not continually squabbling over players. In November 1940 West Ham went to Brentford and played with nine men for 20 minutes, expecting the other two to arrive. Only a tenth turned up, so Brentford loaned them another player to complete the side. The Hammers thanked them and promptly won 2-0. In January West Ham played one short throughout the first half at Millwall knowing that a replacement was almost certain to arrive at the interval.

However, the guest system ran into a few bottlenecks. Stoke gave permission for four of their players to appear for Nottingham Forest, only for Forest to ask for the same quartet to assist them against Stoke a few weeks later! The request was refused.

Jackie Chew, a Blackburn Rovers amateur, served in the RAF. He played for Leeds at Burnley as a guest, then for Burnley at Leeds where he was asked to change sides! He never played for Leeds again but subsequently joined Burnley.

When Arsenal met Southampton in 1940, one of the West Ham directors was present and persuaded eight of the team to assist his club against Charlton on the eve of the first War Cup final! The cup final of the following year saw Andy Beattie at full-back for Preston against Arsenal. Only seven days before he had appeared for Arsenal in the London Cup against Millwall. Beattie was paid the maximum of £650 for his benefit by Preston on 10 July 1942.

Some players had little difficulty in shining for whatever team they assisted. For example Jack Rowley hit all eight goals for Wolves in their 8-1 win over Derby on 21 November 1942. However, some others did not always receive the recognition due to them. Aldershot's two goals by 'Jones' at Bristol Rovers in a 5-4 win on 10 September 1945 proved to be a brace by the away-play scoring specialist Bill Hullett.

Stoke goalkeeper Norman Wilkinson guested for Luton at Tottenham on 12 February 1944 and Rowley hit seven past him. The following Saturday the two were on opposing sides in an FA v Army match.

Tommy Lawton on his honeymoon also scored for Morton against Hamilton in a 3-3 Scottish Southern League draw on 18 January 1941. But Partick Thistle's centre-forward in a 5-2 win over Dumbarton on 10 August 1940 had been recorded as 'A. N. Other 2 goals . . .'

Lawton also played twice on Christmas Day 1940: for Everton at Liverpool in the morning in a 3-1 defeat and again the same afternoon scoring both goals for Tranmere in a friendly at Crewe in a 2-2 draw. In fact, there were a number of such double-headers on that day, the morning kick-offs being the matches counting in the tables, so Lawton was not alone in this respect. Easter Monday saw a similar pattern of double-headers.

Len Shackleton was another on a second shift. He had just become a professional. 'By way of celebration, I played immediately for Bradford against Leeds

United on Christmas morning at Elland Road, had a cup of tea in Leeds and at the invitation of Bradford City, Park Avenue's rivals, travelled to Huddersfield as a City guest player in the afternoon,' he recalled. It was something of a day for Shackleton, for though Park Avenue lost 2-1 he actually headed a goal in a 4-3 win for City, a rare feat for him.

Some clubs lost track of their staff. Huddersfield had signed goalkeeper Archie Hughes in 1939 from Newry Town. He made no senior appearances before the war. Arsenal's George Allison asked the club for permission to use him for the Gunners, only to be told: 'We don't know him!' Actually a former Welsh youth cap who had also played for Colwyn Bay, Hughes had once had a month with Manchester United pre-war but suffered an attack of nerves against Manchester City in a Central League game. Later he kept goal for Spurs as a guest in 1944–45 and was then transferred to them for £1,500.

Playing with unfamiliar teams produced humorous moments. When Arsenal goalkeeper Swindin joined the Bradford Police in 1939 he guested for Leeds against Grimsby. He called for a dropping ball but United centre-half Tom Holley jumped to head it, only to find himself flattened by his goalkeeper. The pointed manner in which Holley avoided Swindin for the rest of the game greatly amused the crowd. In December 1939 when Holley joined the Army, his place in the United side went to ex-schoolboy international Leslie Thompson, 20.

Soliciting players was a hazardous business. Swindon's senior professional and trainer Harry Cousins was searching the local railway station for a sailor who was due to play for them at Millwall in 1945–46. After a lengthy and fruitless foray he returned muttering: 'I'm not doing any more looking. Molesting sailors is not my job, I'll get locked up.'

The missing matelot was waiting for them at The Den.

6 INTERNATIONAL STATUS GROWS

INTERNATIONAL GAMES GRADUALLY regained their pre-war prestige during these seven seasons, despite unfairly carrying the mark of unofficial matches. Many were first-class in execution, regardless of their second-rate status and truncated list of varied fixtures.

Of the four home countries, England played 36 times including half-a-dozen Victory Internationals in the 1945–46 transitional season. Of these they won 22, drew six and lost eight. Scotland were met 16 times, Wales on 15 occasions. One game was played against Ireland in September 1945 as part of the unofficial Home International Championship that season. France appeared at Wembley in May 1945 and a return game in Paris was played the following year. Belgium visited Wembley in January 1946, while Switzerland appeared at Stamford Bridge later the same year.

In spite of England's domination for most of the war, particularly between February 1943 and September 1945 when at their peak they had a run of 15 games unbeaten (12 wins and three draws), Scotland won all three 1945–46 Victory games and England scored just one goal in this championship, beating only Ireland. Overall England scored 98 goals and conceded 49, a ratio of exactly two to one, but in their virtually irresistible period they scored 60, an average of four goals per game.

Scotland and Wales did not meet each other until 1945–46, though it was the Welsh who provided England with more difficult opposition than the Scots on many occasions. In fact, of England's eight defeats, Wales were responsible for four of them, the Scots three and France one.

Wales also managed to win at Wembley on their first appearance at the Empire Stadium and, despite having fewer players from whom to choose a team, displayed characteristic Welsh fervour. Nevertheless, Scottish pride was restored in some measure during the transitional season to at least allow all three countries a degree of satisfaction for wartime activity.

England called upon 78 different players, one complete team for each season. Yet, including the substitution in the opening game, England used 31 different players in the three opening internationals when teams were chosen as little more than strong representative sides, awarded an England tag without much thought being given to any form of (even unofficial) international recognition. Scotland used 79 players themselves including a replacement.

The number of changes effected by Scotland can be gauged from the fact that only one player managed to achieve double figures in appearances and he was Tommy Walker of Hearts. The Scots played 20 times, all but four of their fixtures against England.

Don Dearson was the chief Welsh stalwart, missing only two of their 17 matches and appearing in both wing-half positions, inside-right, outside-left, right-back and centre-forward. Wales had to use an Englishman as substitute on one occasion while England were forced to play a Scotsman in a full game.

Matthews, with 29 matches, made the most wartime appearances. Mercer played in 27 and Lawton 23, while Cullis with 20 matches would have added to his total but for a broken leg. Lawton with 24 goals was the highest scorer. Carter was something of a lucky mascot for England, being on the losing side only once in 17 games and that was in the last of them in France. He also scored 18 goals and missed two penalties, neither failure proving costly.

In 1939 there were three internationals within four weeks between 11 November and 2 December, the first two involving England and Wales, the third between England and Scotland. At Ninian Park, Cardiff, some kind of history was recorded as no fewer than 17 players taking part were drawn from London clubs. Also England used a substitute for the first time when Joe Bacuzzi, the Fulham right-back, was injured. He was replaced by Jim Lewis, the Walthamstow Avenue amateur.

Both goals in the game had a tinge of fortune about them; Wales scored after a ball from Bryn Jones struck the referee and rebounded for Pat Glover to score, while England's reply came when Tommy Jones turned a shot from Len Goulden past his own goalkeeper. Roy John was keeping goal for Wales that day, his last appearance for his country. On the following Saturday at the Racecourse Ground, Wrexham, the same two countries met again, John's place went to Cyril Sidlow the Wolves goalkeeper. The opposition had a more representative England appearance with 11 changes, while the Welsh kept six from the previous week's side. Glover was unable to make the long journey from Plymouth.

There had been a useful crowd of 17,000 at Wrexham and two weeks later a limit of 15,000 for the first wartime renewal of the age-old skirmish between the English and the Scots at Newcastle. For once the Scots outnumbered the English on the field. Sam Barkas and Eric Brook were involved in a car crash at Dishforth and England had to recruit two Newcastle players, Joe Richardson and Tommy Pearson, a Scot, to make up a team.

The unavailability of Cullis at centre-half meant a first game in such company for Bernard Harper the Barnsley player, untried at such a level but who did well against the lively Scottish leader Jock Dodds. England won 2-1 and another

Newcastle player, Harry Clifton, had the distinction of scoring one of the goals when he threw himself full length to head in a Matthews centre. Carter, often credited with this goal, failed from a spot kick in the 86th minute.

There were many unique features in these wartime replacements for full internationals. When Wales made their first ever appearance at Wembley on 13 April 1940, the crowd was 40,000 and the Welsh won with a long-range shot from Bryn Jones which spun out of Bartram's hands and into the net. Willie Hall had a missed a penalty for England. Another interesting note was the predominance of London club players on view, each team having six. Outstanding for Wales was debutant centre-half Bob Davies from Nottingham Forest.

By the time England journeyed to Hampden Park for a return with the Scots on 11 May 1940, the war situation was so fraught with dire possibilities that it seemed the game might not take place at all. Indeed such rumours swept Glasgow and resulted in 6,000 ticket holders failing to appear; but there were still 75,000 in the ground. German radio propaganda even forecast that their Luftwaffe would lead a raid on the ground in the second half. The RAF themselves had refused leave to Sam Bartram, who had been selected in goal. In his place Vic Woodley was asked to catch the sleeper from London, but England officials had to wait anxiously for the train to steam into Glasgow to make sure not only that he was present but also that Cullis, Mercer, Sproston and Welsh had been given Army leave. Injury robbed Willie Thornton of his first appearance in Scotland's colours, though his selection by one letter post had been followed by his Army call-up papers in the next. The game took place without interruption and finished as a 1-1 draw. Film of the not too inspiring game was distributed to troops to show how life was continuing virtually as normal at home.

There were no more internationals until 8 February 1941 when Newcastle was once more chosen as the venue for England v Scotland. This the Scots won with a late own goal when the unfortunate Bacuzzi misplaced a back header to give them a 3-2 win. The 25,000 crowd was again an improvement on the earlier St James' Park encounter.

England's next game was a personal triumph for Welsh against Wales. Mightily flowed the Don that day, 16 April, with all four of his side's goals in a 4-1 victory at Nottingham. Seventeen days later England went up to Hampden and won 3-1, Welsh again claiming a couple of goals, while on 7 June at Ninian Park, England just edged the Welshmen out 3-2. In this game Lester Finch, the Barnet amateur, was given a game on England's left wing.

The Scots paid an early visit to Wembley on 4 October 1941. Relaxations in attendance limits resulted in a 60,000 gate. Welsh and Jimmy Hagan, who had provided the goals in the previous match, again scored in a 2-0 win.

Towards the end of the month, on 25 October, England beat Wales 2-1 at St Andrews, Birmingham, an odd if intriguing choice of venue since the club itself was not in regional competition at the time, though the interest was sufficient to draw a 25,000 crowd. Dearson missed a penalty for Wales.

On 17 January 1942 the snow lay thick and uneven at Wembley. A game seemed unlikely, but it was decided that a layer of the white covering would not be hazardous and with the lines painted blue it proved no problem. This game's charity was Mrs Churchill's Aid to Russia. The Prime Minister's wife herself attended, was presented to the teams and then announced before the kick-off that her husband had returned that morning from signing the Atlantic Charter. England won 3-0 with two goals from Lawton and another from Hagan.

At Hampden on 18 April 1942 the most competitive game between the old rivals during the whole of the war period was well contested. Both centre-forwards scored hat-tricks, Dodds for the Scots, Lawton for England but the former was on the winning side. The fact that eight of the Scottish team were playing regularly in English football was an important factor in their success. And even a Hagan goal in 50 seconds did not ruffle their purpose. Bill Shankly scored the winning goal. He hit a speculative lob towards the England goal. Goalkeeper George Marks came out, hesitated and allowed the ball to bounce over his head into the net.

The responsibility for players getting to these games was a heavy one. The FA's instructions laid down: 'Players will make their own travelling arrangements to arrive in Glasgow by ten o'clock on Friday evening. Members of the party are advised to obtain a meal before leaving and to provide themselves with any refreshments for the journey.'

Though 75,000 had been expected and the Chief Constable of Glasgow had said that would be the limit, 91,000 turned up and were allowed in. Then on 9 May England lost by the only goal to Wales in Cardiff. A last minute exchange of jerseys by the two Welsh inside-forwards Frank Squires and Billy Lucas led the majority of the crowd into thinking that the winning goal for Wales had been scored by the former when it had been Lucas.

By now the England team was drawn almost exclusively from soldiers and airmen, but the Scots still had a number of their own players engaged in essential war work along the industrial Clyde. The game at Wembley on 10 October 1942 ended in a goalless draw. It was only the second occasion in the history of England v Scotland that this had happened. The first official meeting had been in 1872.

Two weeks later England played Wales at Molineux and lost again, this time to a Welsh team which included Horace Cumner on the left wing. He scored both goals in their 2-1 win. Only a few weeks before he had been recovering in hospital from severe burns to his hands and face after a hydrogen container had exploded while on naval service. It seemed at one stage to have ended all hope of a career in football being resumed.

However, there was revenge for England at Wembley on 27 February 1943 when they beat Wales 5-3 despite a memorable performance from George

Lowrie, who hit all the Welsh goals. Dennis Westcott leading the England attack also had a hat-trick.

At Hampden Park on 17 April 1943 the authorities had been expecting the 75,000 restriction to be observed. Again, 105,000 turned up. They stormed the gates and there were 64 injured. The Scottish team, short of jerseys, was kitted out by Tommy Walker from his collection of 17! England won an unpleasant game by four clear goals. Near the end Stan Cullis suffered a nasty injury when a Scottish forward grabbed at his shorts while the players were lining up for a free-kick. A mêlée developed, but was brought to order and the offender, Dougie Wallace, was never subsequently selected for Scotland. Cullis said of the incident: 'He came very near to depriving me of the facility of creating two children at a later stage!'

Lowrie and Westcott were again the respective marksmen when Wales and England drew 1-1 at Cardiff on 8 May and, though Lowrie hit two on their next encounter at Wembley on 25 September, other events in the match overshadowed his effort.

England's 12th man that day was Stan Mortensen. He was sitting on the touchline bench in his RAF uniform when the Welsh left-half Ivor Powell was taken off with a collar-bone injury. It was agreed that as Wales had no spare man, Mortensen could substitute for Powell. So anxious was the adopted Welshman to get on the pitch that he began to peel his best blues off before being persuaded to change in the dressing-room. Wales, who were 4-1 down at one stage, pulled back to 4-3 before eventually losing 8-3.

Before the game Wales left-back Billy Hughes had stated his intention of not allowing Matthews a kick. England decided on a different ploy to counter this threat. They deliberately starved Matthews of the ball. Again as Cullis recalled: 'In the absence of any England team manager, I, as captain, usually made a few brief remarks to the players regarding the tactics we should employ and I arranged with the full cooperation of Stan Matthews that we would concentrate any attacks from the left side.

'I think we won the match fairly easily, but the vituperative abuse I heaped on myself from the soccer journalists was my reward!' he added.

Lawton was restored to the attack in the next game against the Scots at Maine Road on 16 October. Again England scored eight, this time without reply and gave an irresistible display of power and precision which won unqualified critical acclaim from participants and onlookers. When Scotland's team was announced, Bill Shankly said that he was relieved he had not been selected! His place went to Adam Little, Rangers right-half, who sat for a degree in medicine then travelled through the night to play.

Former England player and FA member, Charles Wreford Brown, the Oxford University student of the previous century who had been generally considered responsible for the adoption of the word 'soccer', said of it: 'This England team which has won such a magnificent victory showed perhaps the greatest combination and team work in the whole history of international football. I myself have never seen anything like it before.'

Lawton managed a hat-trick in ten minutes and his haul of four included one acrobatically achieved while sitting on the ground with his back to the goal. The players tried to present Matthews with a goal but though Lawton teed one up for him, the maestro miscued straight to Lawton who promptly popped the ball into the net. But Matthews did get on the scoresheet. Taking the ball through from the half-way line he went through the entire defence and even dribbled round goalkeeper Joe Crozier. All this and a Carter missed penalty soon after the interval! Interest in this game was such that a capacity 60,000 had also seen a number of forged tickets being produced by 'spivs' bent on making a few quid.

There was more trouble for the Scots at Wembley on 19 February 1944. The FA wanted them to be numbered for the first time. After much deliberation, the Chairman of the Scottish FA said: 'Numbers are all right for horses and greyhounds but not for humans.' But it was England who won at a canter 6-2. On 22 April the Scots tried desperately to stem the flood tide of failure against the 'auld enemy'; too physically at times, because this was a rough-and-tumble affair before a massive 130,000 Hampden gate. England squeezed through 3-2.

Down at Cardiff the following month on 6 May, England's relentless flow continued, though Wales were only beaten by two clear goals and had the handicap of debutant Walley Barnes hobbling injured on the wing in the second half.

On 16 September 1944 England began the new season's international programme with another game against the Welsh. This time Anfield was the venue. A rearranged Welsh side did well to hold England to a 2-2 draw, coming close to victory in a game in which they matched their opponents in every respect.

While the Welsh often fared better, the Scots were in for more punishment at Wembley on 14 October. The crowd was 90,000. Shankly was chosen for Scotland, but had an injury and after a fitness test at Stamford Bridge on the morning of the game was declared unfit. The night before the Scots could have recalled Matt Busby to the squad but they did not. Their only alternative now was Sergeant Bob Thyne, a Darlington centre-half on convalescent leave. Blown up when a shell hit the trench in which he was sheltering on D-day plus six, he had been suffering from shock and shrapnel wounds. Anyway, he was pitchforked into the side at right-half, wearing Shankly's shorts.

Even so, the Scots scored in the fourth minute and clung to that lead until the 56th minute when Lawton took command with a hat-trick as England finally emerged as 6-2 winners again. The breakthrough might have come earlier had the balding veteran George Cummings not held Matthews as well as he did.

On 3 February 1945 England renewed the struggle with the Scots at Villa Park when 66,000 turned up in the bomb-scarred ground where the stand seats, which had been hidden in Birmingham shelters since early in the war, were dusted off and restored to their rightful place. By now many of the stalwarts of England's success were abroad with the Armed Forces and there were new faces appearing, notably Neil Franklin, the Stoke centre-half. Though the Scots did better in this match, they were still losers by the odd goal in five. Yet the debt they owed to goalkeeper Petty Officer Bobby Brown, the Queen's Park amateur, was immeasurable.

Alas, their biggest humiliation in front of their own supporters was to come on 14 April. Tommy Bogan was making his debut for Scotland. He played only 40 seconds before crashing into Frank Swift. The England goalkeeper cradled the diminutive Hibs player in his arms and carried him to the touchline amid an unjustified storm of booing. Leslie Johnstone took Bogan's place and scored before half-time. With England 3-1 up the Scots were awarded a penalty. Busby refused to take it but as fast as he tossed the ball to a colleague it came back. The Scottish skipper knew only too well the number of penalty kicks he had practised with Swift at Manchester City in pre-war days. But he placed the ball, tried a couple of feints, thought of a double bluff, then hit the way he would have if guessing Swift would settle for the obvious. He was wrong and England eventually won 6-1.

Another curiosity was that Scotland had two John Harris's in their team – the Wolves centre-half and the Queen's Park amateur centre-forward. Before the game there was a minute's silence for President Roosevelt, who had died the day before. As the echoes of the 'Last Post' then sounded across a distinctly dampened Hampden, a lone bomber flew overhead and dipped its wings in salute.

It was tougher again for England on 5 May at rain-soaked Ninian Park, but once more they came through 3-2, Carter scoring a hat-trick. George Edwards's goal for Wales knocked a leek hanging in the net into a watching fan's hand. The war was nearly over and when France came to Wembley three weeks later they became the first foreign side to avoid defeat on English soil. They deserved their share of the spoils, even though several of the England team had been engaged on hectic tours in the days leading up to the game. The French were a colourful crew and several of them had unique wartime experiences of their own.

Sergeant Julien Darui, the goalkeeper, had been captured at Dunkirk but remained a prisoner for just three weeks before escaping to Lille and somehow managing to play with distinction for them in French League and cup games in the unoccupied zone of the country. Right-back Maurice Dupuis had become a policeman at Versailles when France surrendered and joined the Underground. In the days before the liberation of Paris he became a crack rooftop sniper. His partner Jean Swiatek, one of two Polish-born players in the team, had escaped from the Germans after spending six months in a forced labour camp. Both wing-halves were airmen: Sergeant Lucien Jasseron, who served in Algiers, Tunisia and Italy and Jean Samuel who was only 20.

In the transitional season Northern Ireland was rewarded with its first semi-official visit since pre-war days. Mortensen scored the only goal of the game which attracted 45,061 to Windsor Park on 15 September. But it would have been a different result had the Irish, inspired by Peter Doherty, taken their chances. Northern-based players of the England squad travelling to Stranraer en route to Belfast had been asleep when their double-headed train was involved in a mishap at Kendal. The pilot engine left the rails but Messrs Swift, Mercer, Soo, Franklin, Watson and Carter slept through, unaware of the incident.

The following month records were broken at West Bromwich when England lost 1-0 to Wales on 20 October. The crowd was 54,611 and receipts a massive £8,573.8s. Then on 10 November Scotland and Wales met for the first time since more peaceful occasions. The Scots won 2-0 at Hampden before a 97,000 gate. Then it was Scotland's turn to visit Belfast and they had plenty of support in the 53,000 crowd on 2 February 1946. Twice behind, they won 3-2.

Then at last there was some consolation for Scotland after suffering so many wartime hammerings at the hands of the English. On 13 April they had to wait until the 89th minute before Jimmy Delaney scored the only goal, but it was worth it. The Scots' other hero was Frank Brennan, a last-minute deputy for George Young at centre-half and he celebrated his 22nd birthday in style.

Ireland gained some recompense for their labours when they beat Wales at Cardiff on 4 May, Doherty again inspiring them while wearing a pair of lacrosse boots on the hard ground.

The programme of Victory Internationals also included visits from Belgium and Switzerland, who played both England and Scotland. England beat the Belgians 2-0 and the Swiss 4-1 at Wembley and Stamford Bridge respectively, while the Scots drew 2-2 with Belgium and beat Switzerland 3-1. Belgium's visit on 19 January to Wembley had several interesting features. The game started in brilliant sunshine but during half-time fog closed in. The two linesmen had luminous flags which had been used to signal aircraft landing and taking off on an airstrip in Burma. Before the kick-off the FA team wore sky-blue track suits and had three footballs, a trick picked up from the Moscow Dynamo tour. France entertained England in Paris and won 2-1 in May 1946 with Darui their goalkeeping hero chaired from the field.

In addition to the supply of international fixtures, the proliferation of other representative matches sometimes caused exasperation to the clubs, brought excitement to the spectators and invariably provided excess remuneration to the various charities to whose benefit they were directed. Many were simply exhibition games of immense appeal. Teams with either an England, Scotland, Wales or even Ireland label also played games against the Army and the RAF as well as the Civil Defence Services.

The clubs did not complain about the staging of such games for worthy causes but rather that the difficulties of fielding teams for League matches were made much more severe by the continual tapping of their sources of personnel by the Armed Forces and other national service bodies.

These representative games were on two distinct levels: the national scale and localised affairs. They both produced similar problems for clubs; they were not always played in midweek, though the more important games had to be held on Saturday for fear of interrupting essential war work.

One of the earliest games staged was on 4 November 1939 when a Football League XI met an All-British team at Goodison Park. On 25 November an FA XI played an Army XI at Reading and won 4-1. Then Boxing Day saw another Football League XI v All-British XI at Molineux attended by 18,000 and again oddly enough resulting in the same 3-3 scoreline which had resulted from the first match between these two selections.

After an FA XI had beaten Chelmsford 5-0 on 6 January 1940, an England XI beat the Army 4-3 at Selhurst Park in front of 10,000. Then there was a renewal of the old Amateurs v Professionals encounter, though this was a local affair with the players drawn from London teams. The pros won 4-2, the match again held at Crystal Palace before 5,515 spectators on 10 February. The following day the Army started a three-match tour of France specifically designed to entertain the Allied troops of the BEF. The party included two players, Harry Goslin and Eric Stephenson, who would not survive the war and another, Reg Allen, who was to spend many years as a POW.

The first was played in Paris before 35,000 and ended in a 1-1 draw. Four days later the two sides met again before 13,000 in Lille with the Army side winning by the only goal. The French fielded different teams in both games. The final match was in Rheims on 18 February and the Army won 2-1 in front of 15,000.

In the opening encounter the Army goal had been scored by Maurice Edelston, the only amateur in the side and a Reading player who had played for Great Britain in the 1936 Olympics. He was the soccer lecturer on the Army Physical Training Corps course at Aldershot and was one of a party of 18 players detailed for the trip.

Nine of the French team in Paris had been serving on the Maginot Line only three days before the game. They included Rudi Hiden, the Austrian goalkeeper much sought after by Arsenal in the 1930s. Despite an injury to Emile Veinante, the French had much the better of the exchanges and only Reg Allen in goal plus a booted goal-line clearance by Mercer when the goalkeeper was beaten saved the Army from defeat.

Both Football League and FA XIs deliberately spread their matches around the country and this regionalisation of representative games was well received. At Bradford on 2 March 1940 the League and All-British teams played their third high scoring draw. This time it was 4-4 with 14,575 present. A week later the Army beat the Football League XI 5-2 at Anfield in front of 14,205. Another Army team composed entirely of players with Scottish clubs met a Scottish XI and drew 2-2 on 16 March. Unbelievably the fourth League v All-British game was also drawn 1-1 at Blackpool before 24,000. The size of the attendance for these games usually outstripped League attendances on the same grounds.

Representative FA XIs also played games that season against Oxford University, Surrey County, Kent County, a Yorkshire XI, the RAF, the Metropolitan Police, Sussex County and the Herts FA as in peacetime. Barely a week passed without some kind of charity game being put on. In January 1941 another League v All-British game produced the first definite win for one side, the League winning 5-3 at Sheffield.

Belgian, Dutch, Norwegian and Czech Army sides also started playing representative games in 1940–41 and on 15 March 1941 the Army beat an Allied Armies selection 8-2 at Stamford Bridge, watched by 10,794. The visitors included players from Holland, Norway, Czechoslovakia, Poland, Belgium and France, recruited from servicemen from those countries now stationed in Britain.

The Police had enough professionals in their ranks to play their own representative team as did the Civil Defence, who by definition could also include policemen in their team. In an Allied Services game on 17 April 1941 at Millwall between them and the Free French Forces, the Civil Defence scored a 17-3 win, with Leslie Compton leading the attack and scoring eight goals. Naturally the foreign teams had only a handful of footballers available.

Two days later there was a more balanced feast of scoring in the now accepted League v All-British team events at Anfield. Only 12,000 were present, but the League won 9-7, Lawton scoring a hat-trick for the winners despite being marked by his England opposite number, Cullis. That same day in Aberdeen a Scottish XI was playing an Army team again drawn from players stationed north of the border, the Scots winning 2-1. Early in 1941–42, the Army paid a visit to Belfast, playing three games in the space of five days, beating Ireland 4-1, the Army in Ulster 6-1 and the Irish League 5-0.

On 11 October Belgium and Holland met in a friendly at Wembley, watched by 7,000, the game ending in a 5-4 win for the Belgians. Both teams were composed of servicemen, of course. That same day the first Football League v Scottish League game of the war was played at Blackpool before 20,000, the FL winning 3-2.

Area Service Command matches also featured Anti-Aircraft (AA), London, Eastern, South-East, Northern, Western, Scottish area, the South of England etc., adding to the fixture pile-up but for worthy charitable causes. The Free French Air Force, the London National Fire Service not to mention the Combined Services were also involved. The Police were even able to stage their own Professionals v Amateurs game and the Canadian Army had a side in action.

At the start of 1942–43 the Army went back to Belfast for another whirlwind tour, losing 3-2 to the Irish FA XI, beating the Army in Ulster 5-3 and the Irish

League 3-2. When France beat Holland 5-4 at Dulwich on 20 February 1943, Farago scored all five for the winners. On 13 March the Metropolitan Police beat the United States Army 3-0. Two weeks later the Army beat the Americans by 11 clear goals at Southampton, Johnny Shafto of Liverpool scoring six goals.

The calibre of some of the Army and RAF personnel was of the highest. At Stamford Bridge on 26 April 1943 the game ended 2-2 before 30,812 with 21 internationals playing. These matches produced considerable rivalry between the respective branches of the services and were as eagerly contested as internationals, with pride at stake. At the beginning of 1943–44 the Army made their customary visit to Ulster, this time playing Ireland and losing 4-2 and then beating the Irish League 5-1.

Aston Villa even made the long trip to Tynecastle to play an Edinburgh Select on 5 August 1944 and won 4-3. Two weeks later a large 40,000 were at Blackpool for the RAF against Western Command, which finished 2-2. For local interest five Blackpool players as well as three guests who were regularly assisting the seaside club were in action.

In September it was a Combined Services team which kept open the link across the Irish Sea, beating Ireland 8-4 and the Irish League 4-0. In the former match, the attendance of 49,875 produced receipts of £4,457. By then it was more difficult to find representative material as the war was moving into Europe and with it more servicemen. In the first game Peter Doherty had hit four goals for Ireland and Carter four for the Services.

That same month the FA assembled a Services XI to play in Paris, shortly after the liberation of the French capital. The air lanes were crowded corridors in those Second Front days. While crossing the Channel in an RAF Dakota, the party was nearly involved in an accident. As the aircraft came out of the clouds over the French coast it missed a homeward bound transport by less than 20 feet!

The match was played at the Parc des Princes which had been used as a concentration camp by the Germans during the occupation and still retained its six-foot wire fence round the perimeter of the pitch. Frank Swift, who kept goal for the Combined Services team in the game, recalled 'more than half of the 35,000 crowd had come to the match by cycle, including large numbers of fashionably dressed girls nearly all of them wearing silk stockings.' Clearly the liberating Yanks had wasted little time.

With Carter scoring a hat-trick, the Services won easily by five clear goals and then flew to Brussels to play Belgium and beat them 3-0 on the Daring club's pitch, which had been used by the Nazis as a tank training ground only months earlier.

Even the Army internationals played between Scotland and England raised almost as much fervour as the one designated as the substitute 'real thing'. On 28 October 1944 there were 41,558 at Hampden to see England beat the Scots 2-1 at service level. In January a Scottish Services team played two games in Belgium, beating the national team 3-2 in Brussels but losing 6-4 to a Flanders selection in Bruges.

When the Army met the RAF on 10 March 1945 at St James' Park, Newcastle, 51,000 were on hand for a goalless draw. A week later in a Western Command v London District game at Stoke, Don Welsh scored all five goals for the former including three in the first 15 minutes.

Two weeks later the FA sent a strong representative side to Belgium for a couple of games on successive days against the national team, winning 8-1 in Bruges with Lawton scoring four and 3-2 in Brussels with the Everton leader claiming all three. Within two weeks the FA were back again in Liège. By this time most Dakotas had been commandeered for a paratroop drop over the Rhine and so a smaller party was split into several Ansons, one of which contained Bert Sproston, the two Smiths Les and George, plus George Hardwick. The aircraft was about to land when it discovered a Liberator broken down on the runway and the pilot had to take evasive action over the control tower. The games were drawn 1-1 and 0-0 with Bob King, remembered as the first transferred player of the war, scoring the FA XI's only goal.

Then the Army tours broadened their own horizons as the war began to foreshorten on many fronts. The orders for a trip to Italy included the following instructions:

'All players will report to the Great Western Railway Hotel, Paddington, London W in time for dinner early on Saturday evening 5 May. This is of the greatest importance as very little notice of airlift is given in advance. Separate instructions will be given to anyone playing for England or Wales at Cardiff on this date.

'Will Officers Commanding please furnish this office by return with regimental number, next of kin and address, religion and vaccination and typhus inoculation up-to-date of players under their command.

'Uniform will be worn by all ranks and AB 64 will be carried. If necessary, arrangements will be made for a temporary issue in Italy of khaki drill. Baggage is limited to 55lbs per man and provision should be made for an adequate supply of towels, soap, razor blades, tooth paste etc. Players will also supply their own football boots.

'The tour will begin on 6 May and will end on 2 June with the proviso that any players selected to play for England at Wembley on 26 May will be flown back on 23 or 24 May in time to take part in this match.'

The Italian trip comprised games on 9 May in Naples against No. 3 Army District (a selection of units between Bari and Gibraltar) which was won 6-0; 12 May against an Army in Italy team beaten 10-2 in Rome; 15 May in Ancona bringing a 7-1 win over a District Services XI; 17 May against the Naples Area team, champions of the Central Mediterranean Forces in Rimini, resulting in a 2-0 success and finally 20 May versus the Fifth Army XI (which included a few

Brazilians) and also won 10-0 in Florence. All transport was by bumpy Army truck.

The players who made this exhaustive tour were: Goalkeepers: Swift, Sidlow; Full-backs: Bacuzzi, Sproston, Winter; Halves: Britton, George Smith, Busby, Mercer; Forwards: Elliott, Martin, Edelston, Lawton, Rowley, Watson, Hunt, Welsh (unable to make the trip and replaced by Macaulay) and Mullen. All had either been capped before the war or made wartime international appearances for the home countries. On the players return Mercer and Lawton were included in England's game with France at Wembley on 26 May, while four others from an RAF contingent had just returned from a gruelling seven games in an eight-day tour of Scotland.

7 RISING STANDARD OF PLAY

ARGUMENTS HAVE REVERBERATED about the quality of performance at the top level in what were unusual circumstances, but sound reasoning has echoed its praises. Selection of players was frequently restricted to the availability of servicemen, since the large proportion of international players came from military sources. It did not inhibit enterprise.

Players of this standard were probably physically fitter than they had been as peacetime professionals and, while the rigours of service training were not necessarily conducive to improving football skills, the heavy programme of games at service and civilian level for the privileged few meant the players were certainly match fit as well. However, with the calendar of fixtures crammed with other representative matches involving full international players and the majority of the England, Scotland and Wales personnel appearing with or against each other on a far more regular basis than in peacetime, there were more opportunities at a higher level.

Playing more representative games than in pre-war days smoothed away many of the rough edges of their skills to a finer finish than would have resulted from half-a-dozen international games per season plus a couple of Inter-League games, which was the average prior to 1939.

The national state of emergency in the country was such that it was not a practical proposition to have a committee attempting to select an international team. Thus this was left in the extremely capable hands of Stanley Rous, the FA Secretary. He was in touch with service chiefs and knew the likelihood of the various choices being made available. Given the headache of the last-minute failure of someone to turn up, which was a constant agony, this simple sole selection managed to achieve a reasonable amount of success.

As Rous explained: 'Picking the team was no problem. There were many fine players in the game and I had my own ideas who should play. And if I had doubts, then the captain and the senior and more experienced professionals were there to be asked.

'The hardest part was not picking them but getting their release from their Army units. This was managed more often than not by the generosity of the people involved,' he added. 'Major Sloan, Welfare Officer of the Army Sports

Council, Frank Adams and Jimmy Jewell of the RAF . . . these were the people who knew how to go about it.

'But we relied a lot, too, on the help of people I never met and whose names no one will ever know . . . the soldiers and sergeants who agreed to switch duties, or do an extra guard or something, so that these players could get away to play. It may all sound a bit casual. In fact it worked well. This was an absorbing time in football,' Rous concluded.

This one-man, one-vote for an international team in England was unique. There had been moves to introduce it in pre-war days, but the concept of an international team manager had always been discouraged. It was said that the one occasion this was alleged to have happened was in Rome in the early 1930s when Arsenal's Herbert Chapman had been given the job, though it was strongly denied afterwards.

The man detailed to look after England as trainer in wartime days was Bill Voisey, 'Banger' to his friends, a stalwart for his country on many fields including those in far-off lands and in the First World War itself. Enlisting in the Royal Field Artillery, he served in France and Belgium, was promoted to sergeant and awarded the DSM, MM and Belgian Croix de Guerre for gallantry._

Another developing factor as far as the England team was concerned was that, as the years passed, the nucleus of selection came down to virtually one half of the team recruited from the Army and the remainder from the RAF. This meant two halves being integrated, which was a vastly superior situation than expecting up to eleven separate units to knit together effectively. No peacetime country could have had such advantage.

Scotland was not so fortunate. Again they had the problem of Anglo-Scots and this was made more difficult since their leading contenders were not only spread about in the Armed Forces but had others still working in essential industry. Those who were involved in this civilian war work were unlucky compared with their service compatriots because they did not have the time for training or keeping fit, which at least was the case for most soldiers and airmen or at least those able to be involved with physical training. This was probably why Wales, with fewer players from whom to choose their team, came out slightly better in their encounters with England than the Scots.

England performances reached a peak in the match with Scotland at Maine Road, Manchester. Understandably several of the players taking part considered it was out of the ordinary. Lawton referred to it as 'one of the most cohesive displays of team work in the history of international football'.

Cullis said: 'This was the finest football I had ever seen.' Mercer added: 'The greatest game I can remember.' For Swift the ultimate accolade: 'The finest team I ever played in.'

Frank Butler in the *Daily Express* thought the match ceased to be a contest after half an hour, 'but I doubt if an English crowd will enjoy a football exhibition as much again'. Ivan Sharpe, a respected observer, writer on the game and former amateur international, encapsulated the impression given by this performance when he said: 'The 1943 team that defeated Scotland 8-0 was perhaps England's best since 1907. For this there was a reason. Services football brought them into action more frequently than is possible in normal times. They developed understanding.'

Wales probably reached some kind of peak themselves when they played England at Anfield in September 1944, their merited 2-2 draw coming from a strong performance from their half-back line of Dearson, Hughes and Burgess. Again it was not hard to analyse the strength of this particular department of the team. Dearson was already so versatile that no position appeared to offer him anxiety; Hughes, too, was adaptable either at full-back or in the centre-half role, while Burgess was an attacking wing-half often used as an inside-forward. A contemporary report said of it: 'A first-rate half-back line accomplished for the Principality what England's Britton-Cullis-Mercer line achieved last season.'

That particular England trio was interesting when you consider that both wing-halves had figured in the successful Everton team which won the League Championship in 1938–39, the last completed peacetime season. Or rather, it was not quite as it seemed, because it was Mercer who was switched to right-half in that team, displacing Britton who in fact made only one League appearance in the season.

Neither was Britton a first choice at the start of 1939–40. Actually, it was at Aldershot that he gained a new lease of life in senior football. At the time of the opening of the war, Britton was 30. Thus, he entered an Indian summer of a career in which he certainly contributed towards thrusting sunlight on to many England performances.

Mercer, bowed of leg but strong in the tackle and with a consuming passion for the game, was the complete foil to Britton's naturally adventurous spirit. Mercer was 25 when war broke out, Cullis at centre-half not yet 24. Cullis dominated opposing centre-forwards but was just as keen to reveal his distributive qualities when in possession. Behind this line were full-backs Laurie Scott, quick in the tackle as well as off the mark, and George Hardwick as smooth in skill as he was sleek of hair.

Lawton and Hagan developed their striking partnership again while playing for Aldershot and the Army. Hagan was an inside-forward for the aficionado. Lawton mentioned one game for Aldershot in which they beat Luton 9-1 and that 'Hagan's brilliance and unobtrusive and unselfish cooperation helped me to score six of the nine goals ... I don't think Jimmy has played a better club game ... all six were made in a different way.'

The Matthews–Carter wing was at times almost untouchable. They were regulars in the RAF side and of course on England duty as well. At outside-left Denis Compton, who admitted being fitter in the war than at any other time in his career, certainly enjoyed these years as a footballer. In goal was Frank Swift, that larger-than-life character whose huge frame never prevented him getting down to the most difficult of ground shots.

Peter Doherty captained Ireland in three wartime matches, one of which on 11 September 1943 was against a strong Army team which included eight England internationals and one each from Scotland and Wales. Ireland won 4-2. In his words: 'The Irish forward line consisting of Cochrane (Leeds), Stevenson (Everton), McAlinden (Portsmouth), Doherty (Manchester City) and Bonnar (Belfast Celtic), was the finest line in which I have ever played for Ireland.'

The composition of this front line was interesting since it contained no recognised centre-forward, McAlinden being essentially a provider rather than a scorer himself. But the ability of the five to combine was obvious and Cochrane stole the individual honours with a rousing hat-trick while his partner Stevenson scored the other Irish goal.

Scotland's best-of-the-war display prior to the transitional season was arguably in their 5-4 win over England in April 1942. The *Daily Herald* reported: 'England's sequence of conquests was broken in a match which must live with the greatest in international memory.

'Pride of the crowd became Billy Liddell, the Liverpool boy. After equalising Lawton's opening goal, he could do no wrong.'

He scored three and although England were without the injured Cullis, George Mason of Coventry taking his place, nothing could have detracted from Scotland's revitalised if isolated performance.

Universally there was every incentive to express individual ability, from the encouragement of older players who continually passed experience gained over the years to the younger members. They had no fear of being dropped. Unrestricted, they developed their own styles which by frequent exposure became akin to the repertoire of a jazz musician whose impromptu solo performances are easily accommodated because of the knowledge of the main theme and overall accomplishment of his fellow artists.

From the pinnacle of these international summits there were other strong candidates for outstanding reference. The second of the wartime cup finals between Preston and Arsenal was high on the list. Many critics considered it as Wembley's finest. Preston were easily the most accomplished team in the country during that 1940–41 season.

Stanley Matthews considered that the best team in which he played was the Blackpool side which won the League North Cup beating Sheffield Wednesday over two legs in May 1943. They also went on to win the North v South cup against luckless Arsenal. One of the Blackpool players in that side was George Farrow, described by Matthews as 'one of the greatest footballers who never played for England'. Blackpool had one run of 35 unbeaten home games.

In 1943 at the AGM of the Football League, successful moves by Tottenham and Arsenal to have the match fees for players raised to £2 a game came after glowing tributes to the high standard of play. According to Arsenal's manager George Allison, wartime football was 'better in quality than pre-war League football'. Arsenal had cause to be brightly reflective about their own players as they had not only won the League South competition by five clear points, scoring a massive 102 goals, but had trounced Charlton 7-1 in the South Cup final.

Even allowing for this purple parochial precis, there was sufficient evidence to suggest that the half-way point in the war game had produced a high in performance, well endorsed by Blackpool's subsequent success in emerging as the all-conquering side in the country after winning the cup-winners' meeting against Arsenal.

One of the outstanding efforts by a Scottish club undoubtedly came from Hibernian on that epic occasion when they routed Rangers 8-1 at Easter Road on 27 September 1941. Rangers were virtually untouchable in the war years and, allowing for some problems caused in this particular match, it was one in which the foundations were laid for Hibs to emerge as a force themselves. They scored four times in each half. Rangers had Alex Venters sent off after scoring from the penalty spot and Willie Woodburn was injured. The Hibs team was: Crozier; Shaw, Hall; Hardisty, Baxter, Keen; Smith, Finnigan, Milne, Combe and Caskie. Bobby Combe scored four, Arthur Milne and Gordon Smith a couple each. When Milne missed an easy chance later in the game, Rangers goalkeeper Jerry Dawson shouted to him: 'Have you stopped trying now, Arthur?'

Naturally there were many League matches of uneven balance and poor quality. Considerable discrepancies in standards came when teams were short of recognised League players and had to fill in with whatever material was at their disposal. Teams simply had to recruit whoever they could on the spot to make up an eleven. Inevitably these games resulted in high scores and could only be classed as of less than average standard though the goal ratio often made up for any lack of a contest. These were the exception rather than the rule and whatever the composition of sides there was little evidence that games were played in anything less than a determined manner. Indeed the examples of rough play were no more nor less than in peacetime. Certainly, the notion that wartime football consisted of scratch teams thumping the ball from one end of the pitch to the other without much skill and watched by small handfuls of largely uninterested spectators was a totally erroneous one.

The more successful sides were those who were able to make as few personnel changes as possible. Clubs who were forced to alter their team from week to week could not hope to establish any rhythm as would have been the case in pre-war times.

If it was the uncertainty which originally made the relatively simple game of Association Football so popular, then the multiple hazards of its wartime substitute merely heightened that attraction. No one could be quite sure of what was going to happen until it did!

Normally the pooling of players from three divisions would have resulted in a lowering of standards as in the natural levelling process, but there were several factors which prevented this dilution of talent. For Third Division clubs the influx of guest players from higher divisions often improved their performances at a time when individualism was paramount. For First and Second Division teams their leading players were frequently called upon for representative matches which not only kept up their own domestic standard but enhanced it with regular exposure with and against other top-class players.

The speed of the wartime game was also considered to be about a yard faster than its pre-war counterpart, though it was slow to slip into gear in the opening seasons. Again, in the game where one side had players who were able to keep fit, usually those in the Armed Forces, they had the advantage over those who were engaged in civilian work, often in shifts.

An interesting insight into the standard came from Aldershot full-back Hedley Sheppard. He described the period thus: 'They were the easiest games I have ever played in. Cliff Britton was in front of me, every player knew what to do and the ball did the work!'

Aldershot's wartime goalscoring success, Harry Brooks, assisted several other clubs as a guest player while in the RAF. He turned out for Chester, Norwich, Cardiff, Bristol City, Aberaman Athletic and Manchester City on one occasion scoring their goal in a 1-1 draw at Bolton. Signed from Doncaster Rovers in 1939 he had made only spasmodic appearances for the Yorkshire club before joining Aldershot in the close season. He had even started his Aldershot career leading the reserves attack in the Southern League, but wartime opportunities revealed his true ability.

However, the proliferation of professionals in service teams might have resulted in a high standard of play when even the most modest unit could field its share of League players, but it had its problems for others less well known. Doug Lishman was an amateur with Paget Rangers, a midland club, at the time of his enlistment. 'I was kept out of unit teams by professional players with established reputations and in consequence, scarcely touched a ball during the war years.' Apart from half a dozen games in India in 1942 and four months in Germany at the end of the war, he was confined to a spectator's role, although it did not dampen his enthusiasm. 'On one occasion I travelled three hundred miles across Germany in the back of an Army truck to watch the Combined Services team play Wolves at Hanover,' he added.

In fact, this universal spectator appeal was another indication that there was sufficient attraction in the game to provide more than mere recreational escapism. Attendances gradually rose after the first two seasons as the war changed from defence to attack, mirroring not only the increasing optimism on the war situation but also satisfaction with what was being offered on the field of play.

8 YOUTH HAS ITS FLING

OPPORTUNITIES FOR YOUNG players were substantial given the abnormal conditions under which the game needed to be staffed. With senior players invariably unavailable because of National Service or war work, vacancies were numerous, although the usual channels of grooming youngsters through reserve and junior ranks no longer existed.

The first club to benefit from a youth policy to any marked degree was Preston North End, who owed success in 1940–41 to their exceptional pre-war structure. By 1938 the club was already running two teams in local junior circles, when their chairman James Taylor decided upon a scheme to fill the gap between school leavers and junior clubs by forming a Juvenile Division of the Preston and District League open to 14–16 year olds. Preston bore the entire cost of the operation, including the equipment for all the teams and even entered two further sides of their own which bore the insignia of Preston North End C and D.

In the Junior Division for those aged 16–18, North End gave £5 to each club to help equip themselves properly and in this league Preston also entered its A and B teams. Preston's enterprise was rewarded with their teams taking the two top positions in each division. Half a dozen of the colts were taken onto the groundstaff. They received expert coaching from members of the club and were given a pint of milk each morning!

North End started 1939–40 with seven teams, one in the First Division of the Football League, the reserves in the Central League, a side in the Mid-Week League and four in the District League as previously described. Will Scott was head of Deepdale training and on some days there were more than 100 players being trained in groups with eight of the club's senior players voluntarily assisting in evening coaching.

When the war started, Preston Chairman Jim Taylor gave season ticket holders free tea, cakes and biscuits, match programmes and car parking. Players like Jim Milne, Jack Fairbrother and Willie Hamilton joined the police. Hamilton had 40 arrests to his credit on one occasion but all of them were sheep. He found them wandering along a country lane far away from their field of play!

The club produced a 17-year-old goalkeeper in Ken Groves to take over from Harold Holdcroft and Fairbrother, who was assisting Blackburn where he was stationed. Even in 1939–40 Preston were still operating on a near normal level. Scott had to prepare kit for seven teams each week and had to repair and stud nearly 100 pairs of boots! George Mutch the Preston forward knocked in different nails and became a class-1 riveter, building aeroplanes.

Bobby Beattie reckoned the first impact wartime football made was that it was 'easier for the inside-forward. The centre-half is no longer purely defensive. With no serious issues at stake defences are trying to play more attractive football and that's helping us fellows a lot!' Beattie helped out with training as Archie Rawlings and Hugh Rose were on war work.

Those footballers who had no trade on which to fall back were hardest hit. Beattie added: 'I tried for many jobs, but when I was asked what experience I had, my chances were nil. I went straight into football from school and had never learned any trade.'

Immediately war broke out there was a halt called to the coaching scheme, but in 1940–41 Preston still managed to run two sides in local football and of those pre-war youngsters, several made it to the first team that season. Preston had eight players among their professionals who were only two years out of the North End Juniors. In an official history of the club it was said: 'Though wartime football was but the country cousin of the real thing, North End won both the North Regional League and the League War Cup, an ersatz emulation of the Invincibles.'

One of those who shone was Tom Finney, a plumber's apprentice. When training he used to wear a football boot on his right foot and a soft shoe on the left, his stronger foot. He signed part-time forms for Preston at 10s (50p) a week in January 1940. He made his debut at Anfield against a Liverpool team which included Don Welsh of Charlton and Stan Cullis of Wolves at centre-half. Finney scored but Liverpool won 2-1. Yet, it was only a momentary disappointment as the club that had produced the original League and Cup double in 1888–89 achieved a substitute version, losing only four competitive matches all season. Finney was the only ever-present in the team.

Of the 26 players who were called up for duty, all but two of them were registered North End players, Hugh O'Donnell from nearby Blackpool who appeared in ten games and James McPhie a Scot who made a solitary appearance. O'Donnell was even a former Preston player who had played in their successful 1938 FA Cup-winning team.

Including the final replay, North End played 12 matches, winning nine and drawing the other three cup games. They scored 42 goals against 11 conceded. These included a 20-2 aggregate win over Tranmere in the first leg of which O'Donnell scored four times in the 12-1 win, though his feat that day was overshadowed by his colleague Andy McLaren, who hit five goals.

McLaren was aged just 19 and a former Scottish schoolboy international who had joined Preston from Larkhall Thistle as a 16-year-old in 1938. On the last day of the 1940–41 season he surpassed even his five goal performance by scoring all six for Preston in a 6-1 win over Liverpool on 7 June. According to Finney this double hat-trick, which included four in the first half, was unique because 'any one of them was good enough to win a match'.

Even so, North End's top scorer was Scottish international centre-forward Jim Dougal, with 32 League and Cup goals. Dougal had scored Scotland's goal against England in the last pre-war international, which his side had lost 2-1. On 28 September Dougal scored four for Preston in their 6-2 win against Burnley, including three goals in three minutes to equal the fastest hat-trick up to that time.

In the final against Arsenal, Preston fielded Gallimore, Shankly, Smith and Bobby Beattie from their 1938 side and the game began in a fairly sensational manner. After only three minutes play, Arsenal were awarded a penalty for hands, following a goalmouth scramble. Leslie Compton, chosen to lead the Arsenal attack, hit the foot of the post with a ferocious drive which bounced the ball back almost to the half-way line.

After their escape, Preston snapped back quickly, Finney rounding Hapgood to square the ball knee high to McLaren who hooked it on the volley past Marks in the Arsenal goal. Then the other Compton, brother Denis, made up for his elder's miss by equalising in a breakaway to force a replay. For this, Arsenal had one change, Ted Drake in at No.9 and it was the Gunners who pressed, only to be kept out by the goalkeeping of Jack Fairbrother and the defensive covering of Andy Beattie.

It was Beattie who set up the first goal again after three minutes but this time in the second half. Preston attacked down the left before transferring across to Finney on the opposite flank. He found Dougal with a square pass, a flick on to Bobby Beattie and the ball was in Arsenal's net. Frank Gallimore put through his own goal following a corner to level the scores, but within six seconds of the restart, Beattie scored again. A touch, a dart and a shot and Preston became worthy winners of a memorable match.

For this second leg, North End had made two changes. Andy Beattie moved from left-half to left-back displacing the injured Bill Scott, while Cliff Mansley came in to fill the vacancy. Scott had played in ten cup games and was a locally born product of the A team which had discovered Finney. Mansley also played in ten cup games and was just 20. Outside-left in six earlier cup matches had been Billy Jessop before he reached his 19th birthday, while others who figured in that side included Richard Finch at right-half and Tom Hough at inside-forward, another local discovery and barely 19 himself.

The *Athletic News Annual 1941–42* said of Finney that he 'reminds people of Stanley Matthews by reason of his variety of moves skill due in a measure to ability to use both feet as the result of being an inside-left before shining at outside-right'.

Chasing youth had not been sensational news for the pre-war game. That last pre-war Cup final which the odds-on favourites, Wolves, had lost, had been a blow to the midland club's manager Major Frank Buckley, whose reputation for discovering young players, blooding them and often transferring for handsome profit was unsurpassed. Stan Cullis captained the reserves at 18, the first team at 19, but in March 1939 Buckley had raised eyebrows even further by selecting two 16-year-old wingers, Alan Steen and Jimmy Mullen, to make their debut against Manchester United. Like most groundstaff boys, they were sent home at the onset of war, but several were recalled, found jobs in local factories and given a chance to shine in regional football.

Mullen turned professional in January 1940, celebrating his 17th birthday on 6 January with a 3-0 win at Coventry. Left-half that day was Dennis Thornhill, 16. On 16 March the Wolves team which defeated Birmingham 3-1 had an average age of 19 years, seven months. In addition to Mullen, there were two 16-year-olds, Billy Wright on the left wing and Terry Springthorpe at right-back.

Wolves did not operate in regional football in 1940–41, but Wright and Mullen were allowed to guest for Leicester. Wright actually turned professional for Wolves at 17 while assisting City. That season Mullen scored 15 goals, Wright 12. Steen did not have such a happy time of it. Serving in the RAF he was reported missing on a bomber raid in Germany in October 1943. Later it was discovered that he had been captured after parachuting to safety and became a POW.

Wright, axed by the club in July 1939 then reprieved, joined the King's Shropshire Light Infantry in August 1942 and became a PT instructor. Later he volunteered for the job of coaching Dutch soldiers at the Princess Irene Camp at Wolverhampton. He had recovered from a broken ankle sustained in May.

By a strange twist of fate it was at Leicester of all grounds that Wolves put on their youngest ever display of cubs, fielding a team on 27 September 1941 which had an average age of 17. The veteran was Derek Ashton at 19. They lost 2-0. For the corresponding match day a year later on 26 September 1942 they created a record with the youngest player to make his debut in senior football. He was Cameron Campbell Buchanan, a Scottish lad aged 14 years, 57 days. He made his bow against West Bromwich on the right wing in a 2-0 win.

Buchanan, who came from a Lanarkshire mining village called Chapel Hall, became the subject of an FA inquiry. They did not object to Wolves playing a lad of 14, but considered it wrong to take one of such tender years so far from his home! On 15 April 1944 at Chester, he succeeded in scoring twice in a 3-1 win.

Mullen, who made several representative appearances for the Army, was chosen to play for England against Wales at Molineux on 24 October 1942 and again against the same opposition at Anfield on 16 September 1944. Wright followed him into the team on 13 April 1946 against Scotland.

Buckley was continually looking for talent and his scouting system still functioned efficiently enough for him to learn of the ability of a 15-year-old called Tom Burden, a London evacuee. He arranged for the lad to have a trial in 1940, but when Burden arrived from Somerset it was snowing hard and the game had to be cancelled. Buckley realised the problems of trying to get back for another shot so he decided to try the lad at taking penalty kicks and signed him literally on the spot as an amateur!

Wolves played 36 games in 1941–42 and were rewarded in the North Cup when they beat Sunderland in the final on a 6-3 aggregate. They used 54 players that season, only 15 of whom were guests. Guest appearances accounted for only 53 of a possible 396 and Hull City's right-back and ex-Wolf John Dowen alone made 21 of these. Wing-half Billy Crook had one game before his 16th birthday. He had been with Boulton Paul, the aircraft manufacturers.

On the opening day of the season Buckley fielded two 16-year-olds, seven aged 17 and two aged 18, of whom only Mullen had any pre-war experience. At the end of the season when Wolves drew 1-1 with Brentford in the meeting of the cup winners at Stamford Bridge, Mullen was their scorer. Wolves finished with ten men. It was a blazing hot day in June. Right-half Eric Robinson collapsed just before half-time and again 15 minutes from the end apparently with concussion. Weather reports were forbidden so it was three years before the story that he was suffering from sunstroke could be revealed. Robinson tragically lost his life on military service when he was drowned on exercises.

Ashton, 18, was at centre-half, Ernie Stevenson, 18, at inside-left. Thornhill and Stevenson had both played against Sunderland in the first leg. On another occasion, Wolves skipper was Laurie Kelly at 17. Then on 24 March 1945 Wolves won 2-1 at Aston Villa, the penalty which beat them scored by 20-year-old Jimmy Alderton his first ever spot-kick.

Newcastle United, who canvassed widely for youngsters, gave Jackie Milburn a chance in two trial matches after spotting him with Ashington ATC. He scored two in the first of these and six in the second all in the second half and was signed in August 1943.

The snag about young players was that there was little opportunity for them to be nurtured in the usual fashion because organised junior football was either restricted or logistically impossible to operate. However, amateur registrations with League clubs had become farcical by 1944. Once signed, they had to be cancelled before a player could join another team. After that annual renewals cut the numbers.

The London clubs managed to run a junior competition for Under-19s called the London Junior Combination, but clubs like Arsenal and Tottenham, who were sharing White Hart Lane, were unable either to compete or provide any facilities. However, as the war years progressed the League managed to recruit a few more numbers.

Tranmere also introduced a number of teenagers. Harold Bell made his debut at the age of 16 and a half and later joined the Navy. On 14 November 1942 they had a 16-year-old goalkeeper, Robert Yeardsley, and four others under 18. The team won 5-3 at Everton after being 3-1 down at half-time. Then, at Maine Road they gave Stanley Wright his debut at 15, leading the attack against Manchester United.

Team shortages invariably provided unexpected opportunities. Brighton called upon one of their juniors, Reg Bowles, to fill the left-back role against Millwall on 29 November 1941. He was 15 years, 258 days old. Bury also blooded a full-back, George Griffiths, at 16 years, 296 days and he became a regular choice.

In 1939–40 Queens Park Rangerettes, as their juniors were known, discovered a promising youngster during one of their games. After the match the club approached him regarding his travelling expenses. 'I walked here, guv'nor,' he said. 'But the fare home is tuppence.' Clasping this modest recompense the youth went happily on his way . . .

9 LEAGUE EXPELS SIXTEEN CLUBS

IN THE SUMMER of 1941 the Football League sensationally expelled 14 clubs for refusing to play in an official competition. They included eight full members: Arsenal, Chelsea, Charlton, Brentford, Fulham, Millwall, Tottenham and West Ham plus Aldershot, Clapton Orient, Crystal Palace, Queens Park Rangers, Reading, Crewe Alexandra all associate members.

The event made little impact outside the immediate environs of the game though astonishingly more than John Logie Baird's successful experiments with 3-D and colour television which he displayed at a press conference in Sydenham Hill shortly afterwards.

The rebel clubs considered as unacceptable, fixtures which called upon some of them to travel to coastal areas like Southend, Southampton, Bournemouth and Swansea as well as Luton and Norwich. Crewe were not involved in this dispute but had objected to being asked to play in the Southern Region for reasons of geographical logic, although they were prepared to compete in the North. Watford and Brighton later enlisted with the rebels as did Portsmouth, making 16 London area clubs and the 17th at Crewe.

The League Management Committee had reacted to the initial withdrawal thus:

> Whereas at a duly convened meeting of the members of the League held in Nottingham on 9 June 1941, it was unanimously agreed and resolved that a League Championship competition in two sections North and South, with fixtures made by the League, be instituted and whereas in compliance with that resolution the Management Committee of the League have compiled and issued to the members fixtures made by them, having due regard to the circumstances and the just claims of all members and whereas the members set out below have intimated their intention to retire from this competition ...
>
> The Management Committee have given due consideration to such decision and consider if necessary to direct the attention of those members to the Articles of Association of the Football League and in particular to

Articles 8 and 15(c) thereof. The Management Committee have therefore resolved that such withdrawal shall not be accepted and call upon the clubs proposing to take part in football to fulfil the obligations voluntarily entered into and unless the clubs concerned shall on or before 2 August 1941 notify the Secretary of the their compliance with the decision, the Management Committee will have no alternative but to put into operation the Articles of Association above referred to, the effect of which is that the non-complying clubs would cease to be members of the Football League.

The Committee also pointed out that Article 15(c) read as follows:

Any affiliated club which shall retire from a division of the Competition organised by the League in accordance with the Regulations for the time being of the League without passing into another Division of the said competition and any affiliated club which shall be expelled from the said competition in accordance with the said regulations shall cease unless the Management Committee shall otherwise determine, to be entitled to hold any share or to appoint a representative to hold any share on its behalf and any person who shall be a representative of such affiliated club shall on its own retirement or expulsion as aforesaid be deemed to have ceased to be a representative within the meaning of Article 8.

Legal jargon for being thrown out!

On 5 August after a Management Committee meeting at Preston, the League Secretary announced that the shares of the full members had been cancelled. It was only then that the League took a step back from the brink. League Secretary Howarth pointed out that it was wrong to say the London group had been expelled. The clubs had put themselves out.

The London clubs appealed against the expulsion, though the League agreed to allow them to proceed with their own competition without prejudice to their case. The implications might have been far-reaching since the League could have taken over the registrations of the players attached to these clubs and prevented them from playing (although in practice this would have been difficult to enforce and merely have brought the question of the legality of the retain and transfer system into the limelight). The sixteen London area clubs were unanimous that they would act in unison and face whatever consequences arose when the war ended. Their attitude was that all or none of them would be taken back.

It should be remembered that the London clubs had formed their own cup competition the previous season and were not sanctioned for so doing. In that they might have had some kind of legal point of their own to make. However, the plight of the provincial clubs like Aldershot was summed up by their manager

Bill McCracken. 'When the London clubs decided to break away it scattered our programme. We had no alternative but to go in with them, because otherwise it might mean closing down for the duration.'

No attempt was made by the League to stop players with the London area clubs guesting for League teams or vice versa. Arsenal's manager George Allison was the spokesman for the rebels. He had been elected Chairman of the clubs in the South in the early days of the war. The London Combination under the London FA organised administration and appointed referees. The London clubs reckoned that, since the League was not properly constituted during the war period, they had virtually no authority to impose peacetime legislation on any clubs. They might well have had a legal point and the League could have been fully aware of the situation.

Also, the government was anxious that excess travel should be avoided, which seemed to be in line with the London case, but the Football League said that clubs would each average only 484 miles under their scheme, against the 427 or so of the London group. Luton and Southampton had both tried to gain admittance to the London League without success. General opinion swung in favour of a compromise but the London area, led by Arsenal, stuck to their guns. Peace meetings in mid-August failed to reach a settlement and the Football Association decided to sanction the London League.

In October the Appeals Committee met Allison, but the meeting was inconclusive as was one in January. The rift was finally healed in April when the London teams agreed to send letters of regret, withdraw appeals and each pay a £10 fine to be reinstated. Crewe were also welcomed back at the same time.

While this off-the-field wrangling had been taking place, the League itself managed to complete a not unsuccessful season. More than 1.2 million spectators watched the matches. Perhaps it was appropriate that, as the prime movers behind the action, Arsenal should win the League. More people watched them away than at White Hart Lane: on average 11,800 to 8,440. Since their 'home' was at Tottenham's ground, they could claim to have been the first League side to win a title without once playing on their own ground.

Even so they made an inauspicious start to the programme, losing 4-1 at Brentford before 12,000, the day's biggest crowd. The other seven games failed to produce another 5-figure gate but the aggregate for the League as a whole that weekend amounted to 41,640, an average of more than 5,000, a figure which was sustained throughout the season.

A week later Reg Lewis hit five goals for Arsenal in a 7-2 win over Crystal Palace, including two in four minutes, but the opening day's highest score had been credited to Reading, 8-3 winners at Clapton Orient. They also registered the first of the rebel goals through Jack Bradley in the first minute. Altogether, 45 goals were scored. The start at Charlton, who went on to beat Chelsea 2-1, was put back to six o'clock to allow war workers to attend.

Brentford established a 1-point lead after three weeks but Arsenal's pre-war pulling power was pre-eminent. They went to the top on 4 October after beating Chelsea 3-0 and stayed there. The same day Watford secured their first point in a 2-2 draw at home to Orient.

Arsenal went into a 3-point lead on 18 October but the following week suffered a surprise 3-1 defeat at Watford against the bottom club. Yet, there were mitigating circumstances as they took the field 15 minutes late with only eight players; but during the pre-match kick-in, the missing trio arrived and they had a full complement, though it clearly upset their rhythm.

On the same afternoon during Portsmouth's 2-1 win over Brentford, the visitors protested at Pompey's second goal, claiming the ball had gone through a hole in the roof of the net. Referee Robbins allowed the goal but on continued Brentford protests he ordered both teams off the field. Yet, as they were leaving, a touchline conference resulted in a quick resumption of play.

On 1 November the Charlton team bus hit a telegraph pole on the way to Brighton. Most of the players were badly shaken but they still won 5-3. The same day Harold Cothliff scored inside ten seconds in Reading's 3-2 win over West Ham. The Hammers also lost 5-0 at home to Crystal Palace on 22 November, but because of a road accident had had to play pivot Jim Barrett in goal. Arsenal's next reverse was by 3-1 at White Hart Lane, again to Brentford who completed the double over the Gunners on 13 December.

Christmas Day attendances were the highest of the London League programme so far with two 5-figure gates: 10,578 for Arsenal's 2-0 win over Fulham and 10,500 for the 2-2 draw between West Ham and Charlton. Aggregate crowds were 69,269. On Boxing Day, Arsenal completed the double over Spurs, winning 2-1 before 16,777. They had won 4-0 watched by 17,446 in September. On 3 January Arsenal also hit Portsmouth 6-1, Lewis scoring three in less than 15 minutes in the second half. (Only two days earlier he had turned out for the RAF against the Army at Ayr. The airmen were a man short, so the soldiers' 12th man Lewis 'guested'.) This was another impressive home and away success, as at Fratton Park they had won 5-1.

The London League's first double figures score was also logged on 3 January when Crystal Palace beat Brighton 10-1. Palace were now four points behind Arsenal the leaders and the two teams still had a game against each other in hand, but Palace's challenge faded after a 4-0 defeat on 17 January at Orient. The following week Arsenal themselves lost by three clear goals at West Ham on a day of fixture disruptions, but the 20,000 at Upton Park was the highest attendance in the League and the Hammers had closed the gap to four points though Arsenal had played one less game.

On 31 January, Arsenal hit 11 against luckless bottom-placed Watford, wreaking terrible revenge for their earlier reverse. Lewis again hit five goals. Jock Davie of Brighton was similarly rampant against Chelsea in an 8-2 win despite missing the kick-off. He scored two in the first half, three after the interval.

West Ham lost 2-1 on the following Saturday at Queens Park Rangers and Palace had caught up with them, leaving both teams six points behind Arsenal. On 7 February Arsenal suffered a further defeat, going down to a Tommy Lawton goal at Aldershot before a crowd of nearly 9,000. Aldershot fielded only one of their own players, George Raynor. On the same day a mere 900 watched Charlton beat Brentford 8-2. This cut Arsenal's lead to four points, though there were by now an irregular number of games completed and Portsmouth running into top form were the nearest challengers. The Gunners handed Millwall a 10-0 hiding a week later with Lewis helping himself to his third set of five goals that season.

The following week Arsenal had a 5-point advantage and were almost certain of the championship. On 28 February Pompey trounced a depleted Orient side 16-1 at Fratton Park, hitting ten goals in the second half. Orient were struggling for a goalkeeper in this match and a soldier named Hedges, serving in the RAOC, answered the call, duly donned the jersey and apparently was not to blame for the score, with the naval team's firing, notably from chief marksman Andy Black, who scored eight times, rivalling that of the Arsenal artillery.

Nonetheless, though Pompey had played up, Drake was in his hammock not a million miles away, having scored the all-important goal for Arsenal at Queens Park Rangers to ensure their title of London League champions.

Arsenal's mystique manifested itself marvellously in south London. At Charlton the car park was filled to capacity with military vehicles and civilian cars while young autograph hunters clustered around the players' entrance. Then, at The Den so many turned up to see them, that the kick-off was delayed 15 minutes while an SOS was sent out to the New Cross greyhound stadium for extra gatemen. Eight reported for duty.

The last official London League games were due on 14 March, though only Portsmouth and Chelsea had actually completed their fixtures by then. The London League Cup then took over, split into four groups. Again Arsenal's visit to West Ham produced a sizeable crowd of 19,000 on 28 March. On Easter Monday overall attendances rose noticeably. They produced four 5-figure gates at White Hart Lane where the Hammers gained 4-1 revenge over Arsenal before 18,405; at Portsmouth where the sailors beat Crystal Palace 2-1 in front of 12,000; at Stamford Bridge with 10,986 for Chelsea's 2-2 draw with Fulham and 10,000 at Millwall for the similar division of spoils and goals against Brentford. The eight games attracted 71,000.

Twelve thousand spectators were attracted by Arsenal to Brighton the following week and, despite that reverse against the Hammers, the champions won their section on goal average from the east Londoners as did Portsmouth over Fulham. Brentford and Charlton had more to spare in winning their groups.

The semi-final at Stamford Bridge on 25 April between Charlton and Portsmouth was watched by 19,036. Black scored the only goal. On the same day, some missing League games were completed and Aldershot, who had had a miserable time in the Cup, recorded their seventh successive unbeaten League game in winning 5-1 at Watford. The other semi-final was completed the following week, but ended in a goalless draw between Arsenal and Brentford, again at Stamford Bridge. Here the attendance was a massive 41,164 with receipts of £2,651. Arsenal completed their League programme with a 3-3 draw at Crystal Palace.

On the next Saturday the cup replay at White Hart Lane was attended by 40,000 with receipts of £2,700 and, despite Arsenal's 'home' advantage, Brentford who had been the first to lower their colours in the London League did so again this time 2-1 to reach the final. A plea by the players for extra money was refused. The maximum match fee was 30 shillings (£1.50).

Arsenal captain Hapgood reckoned 'Brentford were always a bogey in wartime games'. Despite enjoying most of the play, Arsenal went 2-1 behind five minutes from time when Doug Hunt scored. From the kick-off Lewis ran through the Brentford defence and was brought down. But the resultant penalty from Cliff Bastin was saved by Johnny Jackson, the Chelsea goalkeeper guesting for Brentford.

The London League was wound up on 23 May when Fulham beat Palace 4-3 and Brentford won the Cup final beating Portsmouth 2-0 at Wembley before 72,000. Jimmy Guthrie missed a penalty for Pompey just before half-time. Admission to the enclosure was 3s (15p), numbered and reserved seats were 6s (30p), 10s.6d (52p), 15s (75p) and 21s (£1.05), all inclusive of Entertainments Tax. A week later Brentford drew 1-1 with Wolves in the meeting of the cup winners.

While average crowds in the cup had produced an average of 6,270, the semis and final boosted the figure to an even healthier 9,100. Brentford's own elliptical goalposts were transported to Wembley for the final. Receipts were £15,000. The finalists received £2,500 and all clubs were given £250 each from the final pool. No medals were awarded, but a bonus of five war savings certificates was given for winners and three for the runners-up. The competition had been a success. In this third wartime season it had been the first tournament in which as many as sixteen teams had played each other home and away.

The London League had insured 12 players for each club under better terms than those operated by the Football League. A sum of £500 would be paid on death or total disablement; £2 a week for 52 weeks for partial disablement.

The average number of goals scored was 4.75 but the games in which double figures were produced invariably came through depletion rather than a poor overall standard of play. Indeed the disparity of the Third Division sides mixed in with First and Second Division teams passed generally unnoticed, though the lower division teams were often grateful for the experience of better-class guest players. Arsenal called upon 31 players, only six of them guests. In contrast Watford used 83, just 11 of them their own players.

Moreover, the compromise settlement was achieved without the London area clubs noticeably changing their intention or attitude towards those outside the fringe of their interest and in fact they influenced events in the League until the end of the war period.

10 THE ARMY GAME

Aldershot

Aldershot was the home of the British Army. The football club was a modest and relatively new addition having completed only its seventh season in the Third Division in 1938–39. This had been their most successful term in the competition, yet they had finished only tenth after being one of the pacesetters early on. Alas, financial embarrassment was a boardroom fixture and had necessitated the transfer of left-back George Williams to Millwall for £2,000. The defence was never the same again and, when in early December Harry Egan, the previous season's leading scorer, joined Cardiff for £1,500, the attack suffered similarly.

The Aldershot players, like many others, began the war filling sandbags. Three of the new signings, Robert Bigg and Albert Dawes from Crystal Palace and Ron 'Ginger' Palmer from Millwall, were called into the Metropolitan Police Reserve. Some of the other players returned home. A few found local work. Nineteen were still in the district to be called upon if some form of football returned. Then there was the post-dated cheque for Dawes which had to be cancelled!

Nonetheless, deep in the heartland home of the Army there was no lack of talent available. Aldershot's manager Bill McCracken was smartly off the mark without a 'one-pause-two', once the all-clear was given to start playing again and off he went with his infectious Irish brogue. Stationed in the vicinity they all qualified as legitimate guest player material, he recalled. 'Now, I always reckoned I was a reasonable mixer and I got myself a pass into the barracks. So as soon as these chaps came down, I collared them straight away.

'And I must say this about the offices down there. There were one or two good chiefs. I remember one of them was Michael Green, the cricketer. When I went down to the camp I'd see the officer and he'd say "morning, Mac". And I'd give him a big salute back, "morning, sir".

'"Who do you want for Saturday?" he'd say. "Well, sir," I'd reply, "it might be a bit difficult for you because the chara's leaving at so and so, you see."

'"You just tell me who're the players you want," he'd say and he would work it for me,' added McCracken.

After the collection of friendlies indulged in by most clubs until the regional competition started, Aldershot played their first serious game of the war at

Brighton and, despite including Billy Cook and Cliff Britton of Everton, Wilf Copping and Eric Stephenson from Leeds plus Hull's Arthur Cunliffe, all internationals from the Army PT School, the lack of understanding was most marked and, after missing three open goals in the first ten minutes, Aldershot were well beaten 4-0. In fact, they did not have a win until their sixth game, at home to Brentford in November and on a day when the APTS were playing an FA XI and had taken all available internationals in the area.

In the club programme there was ample confirmation of the jocular attitude to the 'phoney war' period. Spectators were warned that if they left their gas masks behind at the ground they would not be able to collect them until Monday morning. They were also asked to admire the dandelions growing on the pitch . . .

Aldershot did nothing to inspire confidence in their South B fixtures and when the South D section started they fared little better. The team was constantly being swapped around and players drifted in and out. Postponements due to bad weather meant many midweek games which presented further headaches of team selection.

On one Wednesday afternoon in March, however, Chelsea visited the Recreation Ground and guesting for Aldershot for the first time were Frank Swift and Tommy Lawton. After just three minutes play, Jimmy Hagan was brought down and Lawton scored from the penalty with a shot which went in off the goalkeeper's legs. Aldershot won 5-1 and at Southampton a week later Lawton scored twice again but missed a spot kick, his fiercely hit effort knocking the goalkeeper into the back of the net with the ball spiralling over the bar!

Lawton had put on nine pounds during his PT course and considered it harder than anything else he had done. A regular on the wing was England winger Arthur Cunliffe, another Sergeant Instructor, who as an accomplished violinist was invariably 'volunteered' for concerts.

In the League Cup, Shots almost managed to comply with the League's instructions and with the help of Reg 'Nobby' Clarke, the pre-war skipper who had been guesting for Torquay, they scraped up nine of their own players on duty when losing 2-0 to Bristol Rovers. Towards the end of April they beat Brighton 4-1 with Harry Brooks revealing his potential by scoring all four goals. In another game at Brighton trainer Jack Middleton had to play in goal and two juniors completed the side. The season wound up at Bournemouth on 8 June 1940 where they lost 2-1 and the gate receipts were two guineas (£2.10).

Including the Jubilee Fund game with Reading, the three abortive Division Three (South) matches and wartime Regional League games, Aldershot had completed 49 fixtures, winning just 13. Seventy-three different players were called upon, including 26 of their own players.

In 1940–41 a junior side was raised and played at home on alternate Saturdays. Average crowds settled down to 3,000. Away games were still a nightmare. At Bristol City in October they had to recruit two Army lads who had been playing in the juniors and were beaten 6-0. On 9 November Chelsea, the only London side to then play at Aldershot, were beaten 5-3 with Denis Compton scoring three times. But even a gate of 2,500 was better than many London teams were getting. The game at Swansea on 16 November had to be cancelled because Aldershot could not raise a side for the long journey and a week later Bournemouth arrived at Aldershot two short and had to be loaned Shots' George Raynor and Luton's Charlie Clark.

As the charabanc was about to leave for Brighton on 30 November, word arrived that Aldershot's regular guest goalkeeper Charlie Briggs from Halifax Town had been injured in an air raid. Centre-half Tom Cross, home on leave, was commandeered and Middleton for the third time played in goal. On the coach trip to the coast an enemy aircraft ominously circled overhead for several miles! On 7 December Norwich set out for Aldershot at 8 a.m. and arrived at 2 p.m. Aldershot won 5-4 but a week later a weakened side were thrashed 10-1 at Norwich, the club's worst reverse in wartime football. Fortunately, there was some good news that day: Aldershot, along with Reading, were elected by secret ballot to the newly formed London Combination which was to run its own cup competition for London area clubs.

After seven matches in their London Cup group, Aldershot were top with nine points and in with a chance of going into the semi-final as one of the first two. But they managed only one other point. Lawton was back to assist and in a match with QPR on 10 May he scored one of his finest goals, pivoting on a centre with his left foot and crashing in a right-footed shot from 35 yards. The following week he played in an incredible Hampshire Cup semi-final at Portsmouth. Aldershot led 4-1 at one time with Dawes scoring a hat-trick but were beaten 10-5 in extra time having been all square at five each after 90 minutes!

Two weeks later in a League game at Aldershot the teams met again. This time Aldershot were four up at half-time and 9-2 against virtually the same Pompey side. Aldershot had Stan Cullis making his debut at centre-half. Lawton scored a treble in this game and another in the last match of the season at Watford. Bizarrely, the match originally counting in the South Regional League was subsequently omitted on the request of the teams!

In the following 1941–42 season, the London area clubs broke away on their own and Aldershot went with them. In pre-war standing it meant five opponents from the First Division, four from the Second and the rest from the Third. Aldershot's well-publicised trial match in aid of the Lord Mayor of London's Distress Fund was ruined by rain. Only 200 braved the elements, despite the fact that some £50,000 worth of talent was on view in the Reds v Black and Whites game.

Aldershot started their London League programme impressively, winning 6-2 at Fulham and a crowd of 5,300 saw Tottenham beaten 3-2 in the first home game. Watford crashed 8-1 at the Recreation Ground with Lawton scoring three and at White Hart Lane against Arsenal, Raynor gave Leslie Compton the runaround in a game broadcast by the BBC.

After 13 games Aldershot were well placed, with seven wins and three draws and unbeaten at home, but December proved a poor month. Three defeats were sustained and the important home record was lost. But in February Arsenal were beaten by a single goal before almost 9,000 spectators.

Aldershot finished fourth in the table, a creditable position considering the unavailability of their international guests on numerous occasions. The 13 Aldershot players who appeared in 1941–42 made 106 appearances between them. Just ten pre-war or wartime internationals turned out that season, making only 72 out of a possible 396 League and Cup appearances. Only Britton with 23 games and Hagan and Lawton with 16 each even reached double figures and Aldershot's most used players among the 72 featured were their own men Hedley Sheppard with 25 and Raynor with 31.

Lawton mentioned that 'chopping and changing week after week when men were unable to get leave upset our side!' It was a reasonably good-natured and happy mixture at the club. McCracken was constantly at the risk of having his leg pulled by his 'stars', but he gave as good as he received.

'They were a great set of lads', added Mac. 'I said to them once – you're all kidding. You're not the set of internationals you think you are. You're not bringing the crowds in. Let's have something a bit more spectacular just to get them going.

'Or other days I'd say – this is a bad team you're playing today. I suggest you keep the ball up in the air and don't let them have a kick at it.'

Most of the verbal battering McCracken took inevitably came from the phoney expenses that Mercer and company pretended were due to them. 'Sometimes when they came in for their money, I used to say – what money? You told me you'd play for nothing. Just joking. That really used to upset them,' added McCracken.

However, when truly riled, the Irish in him would really blow its lid off and he would come on with 'Ah! bejabers! – You and Hagan and Lawton and Swifty and Britton – Dick Turpin was a gentleman compared with you lot!'

Of course, there was usually someone on the make, somewhere along the line but McCracken was not the type to be blackmailed about filling places in his team. 'Mind you a sergeant once asked to be put on the pay list to make sure the players were free!' he said. 'But I wouldn't have it. And I always kept a few boys standing by in case someone couldn't get away to play, but usually they could.'

Aldershot's programme took full credit for the club after England had beaten Scotland 3-0 at Wembley in January 1942. Lawton scored twice and Hagan once. As the notes later remarked: 'Jimmy Hagan came to prominence and earned international honours through his play with us.' There was some evidence that this was true, especially as during the period from 1939 to 1944 he played twice as many times in Aldershot's colours as he did for his own club Sheffield United. At various times the Shots had the assistance of half a dozen guests from other League clubs who were stationed locally in the Military Police.

Aldershot made another impressive start to the 1942–43 season. After 12 games they were lying second with ten wins and only two defeats. With Lawton partnering Dave McCulloch in a new spearhead, they piled up 42 goals in this period. On 31 October against Millwall they fielded six internationals: Britton, Cullis, Hagan, Lawton, McCulloch and Cunliffe.

Then on 21 November, Arsenal reappeared at the Rec. The crowd of 11,000 was the second largest seen at Aldershot. Lawton described the match as 'perhaps the most exciting game in which I played during wartime . . . with 35 minutes to go we led 3-0. It was money for old rope as they say in the Navy. We lost 7-4. Arsenal scored six times in a row to pull off a really gallant victory . . . I still don't know where we went wrong that day!'

The reverse did them momentary harm. They lost the next two games before hitting Luton for nine goals, six of them coming from Lawton and all laid on by Hagan, whose close control, marksmanship, vision and unorthodox approach were unmatched.

Nevertheless, Aldershot dropped to sixth and in January at home to Tottenham were reminded of the vagaries of the times. Torquay's goalkeeper Phil Joslin was due to guest for them but failed to appear as kick-off time drew near. Although there were any number of outfield players spare, there was no alternative goalkeeper. An appeal was made to the crowd for an experienced custodian and up came a youngster who said he had been a Yorkshire club trialist. He was given the jersey but after a few minutes it was obvious he was not what was required and at half-time having let in two he was swapped for 'Ginger' Palmer and went on the wing. Aldershot lost 3-0. His name was Broome. In another era he might have been a sweeper . . .

Lawton was posted away in February but the team showed that it was capable of winning without him and other star names by going to White Hart Lane and beating Arsenal by the only goal of the game, sweet revenge for their humiliation at the Rec. and without an international in the side!

At the start of the 1943–44 season, Aldershot fielded the contemporary England half-back line of Britton, Cullis and Mercer in the opening game at Southampton which ended in a 2-2 draw. During the season these three made ten appearances together as a middle line. Aldershot remained unbeaten until their sixth match. When they played Arsenal again on 23 November they were leading 3-2 when fog halted play 23 minutes into the second half. Mercer missed the whole game suffering the after-effects of an inoculation and Cullis the first five minutes after arriving late. That would have been Aldershot's first home win, but they had to wait a further seven days for this, then celebrated with a handsome 10-1 win over Southampton. Lawton, back again, had six of the goals. The team was: Briggs (Halifax); Horton, Royston (Plymouth), Britton (Everton), Cullis (Wolves), Halton (Bury), Bell, Hagan (Sheffield U), Lawton (Everton), McCulloch (Derby), Cunliffe (Hull).

'Arbiter' (F. W. Carruthers) of the *Daily Mail* remarked: 'Lawton was the best centre-forward in England for 20 years.' Ernie Bell, a pre-war Aldershot player at outside-right, was making his reappearance having been repatriated from a German prison camp a few weeks earlier.

There were more fluctuations of form, but in February the best crowd of the season, 9,124, saw Spurs beaten 2-1 and in the return at White Hart Lane the following month, Briggs gave a brilliant display in a 2-0 defeat watched by 39,226. The rearranged game with Arsenal attracted 7,600 but the Gunners provided all the shots and won by three clear goals. At Millwall Brooks, who had had an injured leg for two months, came back and scored twice in a 3-2 win. A friendly with Fulham was watched by 6,000, two-thirds of them in khaki. Brooks struck all three in the 3-3 draw. Eighty-three players were used in the season. Royston, Fred Marsden of Bournemouth, Britton and Hagan making the most appearances.

Hagan, Cullis and Britton had been posted overseas by the start of the 1944–45 season but Mercer, who was thought likely to retain the England captaincy, was also appointed Aldershot skipper. In a letter to the club, Cullis pointed out that on one occasion the previous season the England and Scottish team captains were available to play for Aldershot and Matt Busby had stood down. He never did play for Aldershot.

Brooks, who had clocked even time for the 100 yards in the summer, was switched to the right wing, partnering George Antonio, the Stoke inside-forward, in the opening game which Aldershot won 6-3 against Millwall, Antonio scoring five. In October in a match against Brighton, the game had been 30 minutes under way, when with the Aldershot goalkeeper holding the ball, Jimmy Horton and Ted Crawford, the visitors' forward, squared up to each other and were both sent off. It was the first time in Aldershot's history that a player had been sent off in a first-team game.

Horton had made the transition from Third Division to the higher status enjoyed by Aldershot in wartime football as successfully as anyone. He had guested for several other clubs including Blackpool when stationed there in the RAF and deserved to be remembered for his overall performances rather than this unfortunate milestone.

Heavy defeats followed and, though in November Aldershot had led Arsenal 2-0 after 55 minutes, they still lost 3-2. Reg Halton, the versatile Bury player, was now captain and the 'Aldershot Commandos' had all departed. Then, in January the first away win of the season came, thanks largely to Jack Rowley of Manchester United guesting in a 3-1 win; home from France on a course and scoring a goal. He was the 49th pre-war or wartime international to assist the club during the period.

The South Cup was a disaster. All six games were lost and 19 goals conceded. Twenty-nine players appeared in half-a-dozen games! Youngsters from the Colts were often given a chance and there was no other win until 21 April. Ninety-six different players appeared in the season: Horton, Royston and Brooks being the most frequently used.

In 1945–46 two factors stood out: Brooks's marksmanship and the FA Cup run which saw Aldershot overcome neighbours Reading in a thrilling tie, Newport (Isle of Wight) and Plymouth Argyle before losing out to Brighton. The reserves reappeared in the Combination staffed chiefly with young soldiers, but the seniors had only spasmodic success. Cunliffe was the only survivor from the club's palmy days of earlier wartime fare and the defence took some hurtful hammerings. At Bournemouth they introduced Ron Reynolds, a 17-year-old in goal. He let in seven, but kept his place and noticeably impressed. Crowds averaged 4,000. Trying to find at least five non-guest players each week was a problem and Raynor, who was now assistant trainer, had to fill in during an emergency at Brighton.

Against Reading in the opening FA Cup game, Horton, Sheppard, Hold, Ray, Bell and Brooks of the pre-war Aldershot were on duty. The second leg at the Rec. was a feast of attacking football. Ten goals were scored and an eyewitness recorded an incredible 37 shots by Aldershot and 24 by Reading. Aldershot won 7-3 and 8-6 on aggregate. They had lost the Elm Park leg 3-1 and were trailing 2-1 at home in the return!

Between rounds, however, Aldershot played Northampton at home in a friendly and lost 7-2! Also in the second half of the season they went ten games without a win. Reading revenged themselves for the club slaughter twice beating them, 7-2 and 5-1, and in the last game at home to Brighton Brooks took his senior haul for the season to 36 but Oscar Hold was sent off. The season almost concluded on a novel note. The reserves had two fixtures to fulfil on the same day; the first team was split with the home side beating Crystal Palace 5-0, the team at Luton winning 1-0 with inevitably perhaps, Brooks the scorer.

THE NAVY'S HERE

Portsmouth

UNLIKE ALDERSHOT, WHO were practically spoilt for choice, Portsmouth had a mere sprinkling of internationals at their disposal, the Navy having far fewer footballing talents in their intake compared with the other two services. However, there appeared to be less shortage of work in the vicinity, with essential services backing up the war effort and opportunities which did not exist elsewhere available in the Portsmouth area. Financially the players, who were paid fortnightly, were a week out of pocket when war came.

In the last full peacetime season the club had finished sixth from the bottom of the First Division, escaping the clutches of relegation after their surprise but fully merited FA Cup final win in which Guthrie dropped back as an extra defensive cover and McAlinden replaced him in midfield in a 4-2-4 formation ahead of its time.

In this, the psychological battle was supposed to have been won beforehand in the dressing-room when the autographs of the Wolves players were handed back, revealing distinctly shaky handwriting. This was eagerly seized upon by Pompey's manager Jack Tinn, a walking superstition in himself. Tinn's ritual was to have a pair of lucky spats adjusted before each cup game by the same player, Freddie Worrall, not averse himself to the mysticism surrounding the game's performing rites.

Although Fratton Park was situated in a city which had a major port, munitions works and railway yard close by, it suffered no bomb damage. Apart from minor storage by engineers neither was there any handicap to accommodation. The club was virtually organised by three people: Secretary-Manager Tinn, a groundsman and the tea lady whose duties were vast and ranged from fire-watching to polishing the FA Cup on match days.

Portsmouth had summer problems of an entirely different nature to concern them after a car accident in which Jimmy Guthrie was severely injured during an ARP blackout practice in July 1939. There were even fears for his life at one point. He missed the season's start, was turned down by the Navy, but recovered his fitness and worked in a factory.

Tinn soon found another occupation when the war finally arrived. He was packing footballs for the troops and organising a 20,000 sixpences fund to equip them with gear. Two others on the staff who found themselves packing up their troubles were trainer Jimmy Stewart, boxing up limbs for a naval surgeon and Jock Anderson, Portsmouth's centre-forward in the cup final, packaging naval stores in the dockyards. Centre-half Reg Flewin started to build Army huts and full-back Phil Rookes joined the RNVR. His full-back partner Bill Rochford was employed fixing metal caps on aircraft propellers.

There was a fairly high proportion of Portsmouth regulars still in the area and this applied to a relatively stable degree all through the war years. The club also reached a remarkable consistency in the number of players they used in wartime regional football. Apart from the 1941–42 London League campaign their inclusive seasons from 1939–40 to 1945–46 saw them call on 43, 42, 37, 40, 44 and 39 players respectively.

Significantly, perhaps, in 1941–42 they came as close to honours as in any season in this period. Of the 29 players turning out there were 14 guest players alone and apart from Andy Black of Hearts, who appeared in 30 games and scored a phenomenal 46 League and Cup goals, six of the FA Cup-winning team, Walker, Morgan, Rochford, Guthrie, Barlow and Parker, were fairly regular. Between them they missed only 15 League and Cup outings. In addition Guy Wharton made 11 appearances and Worrall one.

When the War Cup started, Worrall said: 'I'm glad to be cup-fighting again.' It was to be a short-lived delight, because West Bromwich Albion knocked Portsmouth out in the first round 5-4 on aggregate, though Worrall was one of the scorers in the 3-2 win at Fratton Park on 27 April 1940 watched by 19,000 – far and away the biggest gate of the season for Pompey. In addition to eight of their Cup-winning team, they had to use two guests, George Summerbee from Preston and Jimmy Mason of Third Lanark.

Nevertheless, the result was in keeping with Portsmouth's indifferent form. Attendances improved from an average of 3,006 in the first half of the campaign to 4,789, but results were exactly the opposite. In fact Pompey were bottom of the South C section. Yet 1940–41 was even worse. Average gates slumped to 2,073 although they did win three more games than they lost in the South Regional League.

At the start of the next season they introduced Peter Moores, a Royal Marine, into the Hampshire Cup game with Southampton. He scored four goals in an 8-1 win, but did not quite live up to his dramatic beginning in the next two seasons. However, others showed more promise. Fleet of foot if not by trade – he was a joiner – was outside-right Peter Harris, discovered working in a local aircraft factory. Born with the shadow of Fratton Park on his cradle, Harris was given his first chance in the senior side at Watford on 21 October 1944 when two months short of his 19th birthday. He had been recommended by Harold Crawshaw, an ex-Pompey player with whom he worked at Airspeed Ltd. He was then playing at inside-left.

Left-half Jimmy Dickinson came in during a friendly against Reading on May Day 1943. He had been recommended to the club by Eddie Lever, another former player and Dickinson's schoolteacher. He had also played in a trial game for the juniors which had been held on a Sunday. A week after his 18th birthday he turned professional on 8 January 1944, shortly before the game against Aldershot, and a few weeks later captained the ATC against a Scottish team at Shawfield Park. His side won 2-0.

Shortly afterwards he joined the Navy. At school he had wanted to be a boxer but had been spotted by Frank Taylor, the Wolves full-back who played against him for an Army team against Alton, Dickinson's club. His naval service took him to India, Ceylon, Singapore and Malta over the next three and a half years.

Jack Froggatt made a scoring debut on the left flank at Southampton on 15 September 1945 having been signed on his return from RAF service in Italy, despite fierce competition for his signature from Manchester United. He had been a schoolboy international brought up in the Hillsborough area of Sheffield as a left-half. His cousin was Wednesday's inside-forward Redfern Froggatt. His father sent signing-on forms to Italy for him and after playing centre-half in the reserves the previous week, Jack was signed a week later.

Dickinson and Jimmy Scoular, a sailor from HMS *Dolphin*, were totally contrasting wing-halves, respectively bringing grace and granite to the Pompey middle line. Scoular was introduced at Charlton on 15 December 1945, having had the distinction of playing in the FA Cup for Gosport Borough and then for Portsmouth in the same season. Scoular's father Alec had been a centre-forward with Alloa, Stenhousemuir, Leith, King's Park, St Bernard's, Broxburn and Armadale, so he had the right pedigree.

Len Phillips, a Londoner, served and learned his football in the Royal Marines, becoming an amateur with Portsmouth in 1944 and making his debut against Wolves on 9 February 1946 at inside-right. Pompey's lone wartime international was the polished pivot Reg Flewin, signed from Isle of Wight club Ryde Sports at 17 in 1937. He joined the Marines later in the war. He had taken over from Tommy Rowe, who with Jimmy McAlinden had been the only members of the successful 1939 Cup-winning side not to play in the regional leagues. However, Rowe made a friendly appearance and played in the public trial at the start of the 1945–46 season. Worrall had been capped twice in pre-war days and McAlinden for Northern Ireland.

Portsmouth's most frequently called-upon guest player was George Summerbee, then on Preston's books and like his brother Gordon, a former Aldershot player. George was the only Pompey player sent off during the war period, at Chelsea on 12 September 1942 in a 2-1 defeat.

Aldershot and Portsmouth had a few interesting tussles in the period themselves including the London League game on 13 September which had to be abandoned 13 minutes from the end when a goalpost broke. The score stayed officially at 2-2.

Harry Walker was absent merely on a score of occasions and one of his missing matches was on 2 December 1939 against Southampton when he was best man at a wedding. In addition to finishing runners-up to Arsenal in the London League, Portsmouth reached the London War Cup final but again had to take second place to Brentford. Led by Guthrie, the players staged a pre-Wembley revolt in the dressing-room, demanding the week's money docked in September 1939. The directors gave in eight minutes before the kick-off.

A missed penalty proved costly a few minutes before half-time with Brentford leading by a single goal. For rebel leader Guthrie it was ironic. He miskicked the spot kick straight at the Bees goalkeeper and the second Brentford goal went in off his head. Portsmouth had six of their 1939 Cup team on duty.

On their way to the Cup final at Wembley in 1942 they had a couple of curious results. At home to Fulham they had a comfortable 9-1 win, with Barlow and Steve Griffiths collecting hat-tricks. Two weeks later they fielded the same side at Fulham and were beaten by the odd goal in three! This was their only Cup defeat and of the sixteen players they used there was only one guest, Les Laney from Southampton, who played at home to Chelsea. In the return with the Stamford Bridge club, the game ended in a goalless draw and Portsmouth did not have one shot at goal in the game. Walker, Rochford, Guthrie, Flewin, Griffiths and Barlow were ever-present during the tournament.

Attendances had improved noticeably, to average 5,000. In 1942–43 they rose further to an average of 7,078 for League games when Pompey finished fourth after losing only one of their last eight matches. It was up to 8,455 in 1943–44. Again in 1944–45 they reached 11,203 and, despite a disappointing season in 1945–46, averaged 19,855. That season all but McAlinden and Rowe of the Wembley wonders appeared, though Rowe and Summerbee turned out in the public trial, they were their last games for the first team.

Players who made 200 or more League and Cup appearances in the seven war seasons were Walker, Morgan, Parker, Guthrie, Flewin and Rochford. In addition Bert Barlow, who had been signed in 1938–39 from Wolves and helped to defeat his old colleagues, was the most consistent marksman with 98 goals in 192 games. On 25 January 1941 he scored six in a 10-2 win over Bournemouth including a hat-trick in just over three minutes.

In 1945–46 Portsmouth managed a trip to Germany in one of the many games arranged to entertain the occupying troops. They were beaten 3-1 by a Combined Services team in the Hindenburg Stadium, Hanover.

Portsmouth's metaphorical grip on the FA Cup had been the longest in its history and included a night of near disaster when the cup's hiding place in a Portsmouth bank was bombed. There were fears for its safety until it was discovered that Tinn had taken it home and had sat nursing it in a cupboard beneath the stairs during the air raid. On another occasion the cup was loaned for exhibition at Havant Park in aid of the local Red Cross. During the parade it was dropped but was undamaged and afterwards placed in the custody of the Havant police, who locked it up in the cells overnight.

Unfortunately, it proved easier to prise away from Portsmouth on the field of play. Birmingham were able to beat them with an own goal by Flewin. Walker, Morgan, Guthrie, Worrall, Anderson and Barlow played in the away leg and Parker took Harris' place in the second game, from Portsmouth's original Cup-winning side.

There were other momentous events. Rowe had been reported missing from a mission but turned up later. Then in December 1943 he was awarded the DFC. In March 1944 when he had reached the rank of Squadron Leader he was captured after being shot down. By May 1945 he was back home.

Seven-a-side games were held during factory dinner breaks in the middle of the war to raise money for London Bomb Children and the club also had a similar game against Southampton for Mrs Churchill's Aid to Russia fund.

In 1944–45 there had been an amazing sequence of games from 25 November to 6 January 1945 during which there was only one win in eight matches. That came on Boxing Day against Crystal Palace and resulted in a 9-1 win with Ted Drake guesting from Arsenal scoring four goals and Fred Evans, discovered originally with Havant Rovers, netting three. In the other seven matches Portsmouth scored only two goals.

By 1945 Wharton was guesting for Darlington and skippering their side. Goalkeeper Ernie Butler spent three years at sea as a Royal Navy PT instructor, then guested for his former club Bath City before a posting to the north-west found him assisting Tranmere Rovers.

Tinn celebrated 25 years as a manager in March 1944, 17 of them at Portsmouth. Field Marshal Montgomery became Pompey's President. It was not a strange choice, since the roots of the club were more firmly military than naval and D-day was planned and executed from Portsmouth.

12 MORE OF THE FEW

Blackpool

IF NEITHER ALDERSHOT nor Portsmouth had had their grounds commandeered by either the civilian or military authorities, Blackpool were not so fortunate. Bloomfield Road became an RAF training centre and as late in the war as 29 April 1944 their official programme for the War Cup final with Aston Villa bore the inscription 'Ground has been loaned by kind permission of Air Commodore J. H. Simpson.'

Nevertheless, the club was more than grateful to the RAF for the availability of guest players. They became arguably the best wartime team in the north of England as the proliferation of camps in the vicinity made a variety of choice possible, and if Preston proudly unveiled their youthful local wares in the early war seasons, nearby Blackpool assumed the mantle with an older generation at their disposal.

Appropriately, perhaps, Blackpool began in 1939–40 by losing the Jubilee Match 1-0 to Preston; but they won all three of their First Division games to head the table on the eve of war, after winning by the only goal at Huddersfield and following it with two wins at home against Brentford and Wolves. In that last pre-war game, Jock Dodds leading the Blackpool attack gave Wolves centre-half Stan Cullis a rare chasing, scoring both goals. George Farrow missed a penalty, his shot being saved by Alec Scott the Wolves goalkeeper. Dodds's winning goal came from a long throw by Bob Finan.

However, Blackpool players were immediately concerned with finding employment for themselves. Some were taken on by the GPO, others went to an ordnance factory at Risley near Warrington. The services claimed others, of course.

After a series of friendlies against Everton (2-1), Blackburn (1-1), Bolton (2-0) and Queen of the South (2-1), Blackpool completed their successful run with a 6-4 win over Manchester United the week before the first Regional League game. Finan scored a hat-trick in this one.

However, there were some team-selection problems once the competitive games began. The Post Office did not always cooperate in releasing players, so this gave an opportunity for others to be tried out. In this way Jimmy Ashworth proved a useful deputy centre-forward for Dodds, of whom much had been expected pre-war. Signed from Sheffield United on 10 March for £10,000, Dodds was the forceful, thrusting centre-forward the club needed. He did not let the club down, despite the changed circumstances presented by the substitute wartime competition.

He scored more than twice the goals achieved by any other Blackpool player throughout the war, despite his absence when unavailable for selection on many days of representative and international match duty in addition to being posted away from the area with the RAF. If any one player was responsible for Blackpool outscoring all other English teams in these seven seasons it was Dodds. He was in his prime when the war started, celebrating his 24th birthday four days after the declaration. Naturally without the excellent service from the rest of the team, his task would have been more difficult.

From the start of the regional matches, Blackpool were unbeaten in the first four of them and after losing 3-1 at Bolton on 2 December they were undefeated until June 1940. They lost 3-1 at Carlisle a week before the last game. On the last day of the season Blackpool lost 4-2 at Oldham. Dodds scored both Seasiders' goals, his second being his 50th in competitive and friendly games that season. Any kind of win would have been enough for Blackpool as Bury had finished their programme and were two points ahead. Blackpool eventually finished third as Preston surprisingly had a better goal average. Dodds's best haul was seven goals in an 11-2 win over Oldham.

Even as early as this first campaign the signs that Blackpool were to become a force were recorded by Dai Astley, who had spent some part of the season down south guesting for Charlton and Orient. 'Somehow there is a lack of enthusiasm in the south', he recalled. 'At Blackpool some of our matches have been fought in a cup-tie spirit. Needless to say I've found that type of game far more enjoyable', Astley added.

Then, Blackpool were nearly lost to the game completely the following season. It seemed unlikely any part of the ground would be released for football, but in October 1940 the club announced that it was the intention to restart in the New Year at Bloomfield Road. Meanwhile, friendlies would be played at the Greyhound Stadium in St Annes Road.

They returned somewhat earlier on 21 December 1940, when a crowd of 7,000 turned up to see them beat an Army XI 4-2. Having not appeared previously in any competitive games, they had to go into the preliminary round of the War Cup, where they swamped Stockport 12-3 on aggregate. Dodds helped himself to eight goals in the 9-2 second leg win. Manchester City knocked them out in the next round, achieving a 4-1 win at Bloomfield Road, Blackpool's only home reverse. This proved too great a deficit for Blackpool, though they did win the second leg 1-0 at Maine Road.

However, in half a season Blackpool were already gearing themselves for the better prospects of 1941–42, which was to prove a vintage season for them. In 40

League and Cup games they hauled in shoals of goals, 183 in all. They were League North champions in the first half of the season and finished runners-up in the Second Championship. There were only 16 different players on the score sheet and three own goals. Dodds own catch was 65, just over a third of the total. In successive weeks at the end of February and the beginning of March they beat Tranmere 15-3 and then Burnley 13-0.

Blackpool certainly made one Preston player pay, he who had kept a clean sheet against them in the pre-war Jubilee match – Harold Holdcroft, guesting for Burnley that season. Blackpool put 28 goals past him in three matches: 13 December 1941, 9-0 at home; 7 March 1942, 13-0 at home; and 21 March, 6-0 away. Dodds scored seven of them.

His overall total was all the more remarkable as he missed ten games with RAF representative calls and leading Scotland's attack against England at Hampden Park in April when he scored three in their 5-4 win.

Two other players contributed substantially to the total: Ronnie Dix of Spurs with 32 and Birmingham's Charlie Wilson-Jones with 31. In the North Championship, Blackpool managed 75 in 18 games while they stepped up even this impressive rate in the second half of the term with 108 in 22 games. Dodds highest individual effort was seven in the 15-3 win over Tranmere after Blackpool had led 1-0 at the interval. In this match he scored a hat-trick in less than three minutes, a record. He also hit two fives, a four and six hat-tricks.

Yet, there had been nothing startling about Blackpool's opening on 30 August – a 3-1 defeat inflicted by Preston at Deepdale. Dodds inevitably scored and a week later the balance was redressed with Preston losing by two clear goals at Bloomfield Road.

Blackpool remained unbeaten until losing 2-1 at Blackburn on 25 October. During this run at Southport on 20 September, Stanley Matthews scored direct from a corner kick in the second minute. Blackpool dropped only one more point in a 2-2 draw at Burnley and were virtually assured of the title before they completed their League North fixtures with a Christmas Day game at home to Rochdale, cushioned by their superior goal average.

Lincoln City and Preston were in a position to catch Blackpool on points but it would have taken a fantastic scoring achievement to prevent Blackpool from taking the title. Yet it was something of a festive anti-climax when Blackpool lost 1-0 to Rochdale while Lincoln were beating Mansfield 6-0 and Preston were losing 2-1 at home to Blackburn. Of course Lincoln did not play Blackpool as all fixtures were localised.

Blackpool might well have added to their honours that season but for withdrawing from the League War Cup when due to meet Manchester City at Maine Road over Easter. Because of a ban placed on the movement of servicemen at this time, their RAF personnel could not be transported and Blackpool declined to fill their places and withdrew from the competition. According to their secretary:

'the game would have been a farce'. Blackpool were censured but nothing else happened to them. City had refused to switch the leg to Blackpool. Bloomfield Road patrons had to make do with a game between two RAF teams, refereed by Arthur Ellis.

Blackpool retained their League North title in 1942–43, scoring more goals in this particular competition than the term before and, though they were less impressive in the Second Championship, achieved a double with their League North Cup success which drew many admiring comments. They were able to crown even this by winning the clash between the winners of the two regional cups, at Arsenal's expense. L. N. Bailey, football correspondent of *The Star* reckoned they played 'the finest wartime football'.

The pace of their performance in the opening League games was such that they rattled up 11 straight wins, lost only once and dropped just three points. Of the 93 goals they scored in these 18 games, Dodds had 29, although in one game at least he was overshadowed by Dix who helped himself to five, one more than Dodds managed in an 11-1 win. Dix had been an early convert to goalscoring; at 15 years, 180 days old and a week after his debut, he scored for Bristol Rovers against Norwich on 3 March 1928 to become the League's youngest scorer.

In the League North Cup final Blackpool began badly in the first leg, being held at home by Sheffield Wednesday. In fact only an equaliser two minutes from the end by Eddie Burbanks, guesting from Sunderland, saved them. He was one of six guests in the side. But they had scored first through Finan, who headed in a Matthews centre. Wednesday drew level from the penalty spot after a handball incident. Jackie Robinson put Wednesday in front and Dodds appeared to have squared the scores again only for the referee to disallow it for offside.

A week later at Hillsborough, it was an entirely different story even though Blackpool were without the services of Matthews, playing for England at Cardiff that afternoon. Dodds skippering Blackpool was the first to score. After being felled by Walter Millership, the Seasiders leader took the free kick himself ten yards outside the area, beating the Wednesday goalkeeper with the spin of the ball on the greasy surface.

The long-striding Tom Gardner from Burnley was a useful deputy for Matthews and topped his memorable performance by scoring Blackpool's winning goal. However, a week later in the prestige match with Arsenal, Matthews was brought back in his familiar No. 7 shirt for an encounter which began sensationally. Reg Lewis and Denis Compton blasted the Gunners into a 2-0 lead with just six minutes of play gone, but Blackpool slowly took control and goals by Dix, Burbanks, Dodds and Finan saw them through safely for a memorable 4-2 victory.

In 1943–44 Blackpool completed a trio of successive championships but had to settle for runners-up spot in the Cup final. This time the defence took its due share of the honours as the forwards recorded what was for them a modest total of 56 goals in the 18 games, while the rearguard conceded just 20. Yet, this figure was one more than they let in when they won the League in 1941–42.

Previously, goalscoring had achieved almost everything for Blackpool, but it was different in 1943–44. They won the northern title on goal average from Manchester United, both teams scoring the same number, though United conceded 30. A crowd of 25,000 saw Blackpool clinch it, beating Southport 5-0. Certainly the system which operated in the north encouraged goalscoring. Not every team played every other team – as hitherto explained – which meant there were more teams in contention often until the last day of the championship.

In the Cup Blackpool made heavy weather of their first semi-final at home to Manchester City and allowed Peter Doherty to equalise late on and then almost score the winner. Blackpool were without the injured Stan Mortensen, but soon had the crowd on its toes with a goal straight from the kick-off in under 30 seconds, Dodds sending Dix through perfectly. His shot hit Frank Swift but Dodds was on hand to tuck in the rebound.

A week later Blackpool were more decisive throughout, although it was again Doherty who gave City a first-half lead before goals from Finan and a late choice Fred Tapping put them into the final against Aston Villa. They proved a tougher proposition and were the far superior side in the Bloomfield Road leg. Only Matthews appeared to be able to make headway, but George Cummings policed him well. Two minutes after the interval Billy Goffin deservedly shot Villa ahead and they seemed comfortable with it. But they reckoned without Dodds. With just nine minutes remaining, fine work by Newcastle's Tommy Pearson gave Blackpool's leader the chance to equalise and, hardly had the crowd's cheers of relief died away, when he scored the winner with a typical individual effort.

Nevertheless, Blackpool knew they were up against it in the return at Villa Park and their worst fears were realised as early as the first minute when Bob Iversen passed to Frank Broome whose goal in 40 seconds looked suspiciously offside. From the restart Blackpool replied through Dodds, also in an apparent offside position. His shot was parried by Alan Wakeman only for Dix to score in-off Cummings. They were level only until the tenth minute when George Edwards appeared to handle before scoring!

There had been two goals in 75 seconds and a couple more before a quarter of an hour had elapsed because Pearson brought the game level at 2-2. Villa, however, were not to be shaken out of their resolve and seven minutes before the interval Eric Houghton's shot was only partially saved by Savage and Iverson gave them the lead. It was Houghton who laid on number four for Broome.

In 1944–45 the departure of Dodds and others had a marked effect on the club's fortunes, which fluctuated alarmingly. He was posted away and first assisted West Ham, then Fulham. Mortensen turned out for Arsenal and also Bath City. Not more than three matches in a row were played without defeat and in the North Championship they finished 21st out of 54. Blackpool qualified for the Cup cut by one point and beat Wrexham in the first round proper. But Bolton were 4-1 winners at Bloomfield Road, a personal triumph for Nat Lofthouse who scored all four goals.

Though Blackpool recovered their composure to win 2-1 at Burnden Park, the demise had set in during the first game in which their domination for half an hour resulted in opportunities squandered by Hugh O'Donnell and Micky Fenton. Then injury to Mortensen disjointed their attempts.

Mortensen was still top scorer that season with 14 goals. Farrow the wing-half was the next most reliable marksman with 13 including four in one game, an 8-1 win over Preston. Perhaps significantly, Blackpool's best win in the season was 10-2 against Southport with Mortensen scoring four and the returned Dodds two.

The transitional season was only marginally better in that ninth place was achieved in the League North and Middlesbrough defeated them in a fourth round replay of the FA Cup. Earlier in the season Blackpool had again been assisted by Fenton the 'Boro leader.

Mortensen was top scorer with 38 League and Cup goals, his best total for the club and twice as many as his nearest rival, Dodds, but the team ended the term in undistinguished fashion, winning only three of their last nine games. The average home crowd was 15,000. In April 1946 the club announced that, due to wear and tear from RAF use, the main stand seating 3,500 would be closed for the rest of the season. Repairs would take place to enable it to be in full operation by the beginning of the next term. Thus, the influence and presence of the boys in blue remained at Bloomfield Road almost to the end.

GROUNDS FOR COMPLAINT 1

Manchester United

I N THE SUMMER of 1939 Manchester United were preparing for their second
term back in the First Division after a season which could scarcely be described
as more than adequate, having finished in 14th place. Only one player had made
as many as 39 appearances that season – centre-half George Vose – but their
strength was to come from latent talent in the youth of the team. The Manchester United Junior Athletic Club (MUJAC) was the pride of the parent club.

United's reserves had won the Central League for the first time in 18 years,
the A side with an average age of 17 had carried off the Manchester League title,
and the MUJACs had won their division of the Chorlton League. For good
measure the Manchester Senior Cup had also reappeared in the trophy room.
Moreover the club had stated that its far-reaching ambition was to assemble three
teams of first-team status.

There were two notable additions to the staff that summer, the Barnsley
forward Beau Asquith and Ben Carpenter from Burton Town. Also back on a
month's trial was Walter Winterbottom, having recovered from an ankle injury
sustained the previous season and anxious to be given a further chance to prove
himself as a centre-half. He was a lecturer on PT at Carnegie College, Leeds.
Youngsters like wing-half Johnny Anderson were waiting for their first crack at
senior soccer. He had come from Brindle Heath Boys Club and been signed as
an amateur at 16. There were five players in the Militia: Jack Rowley, Stan
Pearson, Carpenter, Reg Gibson and Harry Worrall, but all were available for the
start of the season.

In the public trial match Jack Smith, a centre-forward signed from Newcastle
United a couple of years previously for £6,500, impressed with a hat-trick. Billy
McKay had been appointed first team captain while Bill Porter was made skipper
of the Central League side. In the Jubilee Game with Manchester City, honours
were even in a 1-1 draw and there was satisfaction from the opening First Division
game in which Grimsby were beaten 4-0, but then came a draw with Chelsea and
defeat at Charlton on the eve of the declaration of war. Two days afterwards, part
of Manchester United's Old Trafford ground was requisitioned as a military
depot and they lost their training facilities at Lower Broughton for similar reasons.

Like many other clubs they found their staff despatched to the four corners of the islands. Goalkeeper Tommy Breen went to Northern Ireland and assisted Belfast Celtic. He had touched the ball for the first time as a United player after being signed from the same Irish club. Sixty seconds on his debut at Leeds in 1936 he was picking the ball out of the back of the net. Anyway, he was back with his former club.

Centre-forward Rowley guested for Shrewsbury Town and later Wolves, his original club. But United had guest players, too. Two of the earliest to render assistance were Len Butt from Blackburn and Bolton's Tommy Woodward. Pearson was one of the first United players to enlist in the Forces. He was stationed in Ireland for a time and later went to India where he played for Denis Compton's touring side late in the war.

Two weeks after hostilities were declared, United played their first friendly, ending in a 2-2 draw with Bolton. The initial Regional League game was at home to rivals Manchester City who won 4-0 at Old Trafford before a modest crowd of 7,000. City completed a kind of League and Cup double at United's headquarters when they won there by the only goal of a wartime cup game on 20 April 1940. Including a friendly played on 30 September which they had won 3-2, it was in fact a City treble. There were some freak results. On 2 May United beat New Brighton 6-0 at Old Trafford. Two weeks later the scores were exactly reversed in the return fixture.

However, United managed to turn the tables on their Maine Road neighbours, who had also scored a League success against them on the ground, when a week later in the Cup they won by two clear goals, only for Blackburn to knock them out in the next round.

That previously mentioned defeat by New Brighton was the second of four successive defeats in the last weeks of the term which cost United the championship of the Western Division, won by Stoke two points ahead of them. In their last game against Everton on 1 June an Alec Stevenson hat-trick turned United over in the last five minutes

While attendances in the League had been averaging just a few thousand, the Cup produced 21,874 for City's visit and 12,551 for the Blackburn tie. The club's deficit on the season amounted to £6596. All but seven of the club's 40 players were in the forces, these others on essential war work: Breedon, Roughton, Warner, McKay, Carey, Smith and Bryant.

Heavy raids on Manchester on 22 December 1940 caused the club to switch its game with Blackburn to Stockport on 28 December. Rovers had to recruit four spectators to complete their team. United found the surroundings to their liking as witness their 9-0 victory with Smith scoring five goals. Less than three months later, severe damage to the Old Trafford ground on 11 and 12 March caused a more permanent transfer of headquarters to Maine Road.

Walter Crickmer, the club's secretary, carried on single-handed in charge of United's administration. He joined the Old Trafford special constabulary and had a narrow escape from death that night in 1941. In the blitz on Manchester the nearby police station was hit by a bomb and he was buried under the debris for several hours, while several of his colleagues were killed. Crickmer suffered arm and leg injuries and severe shock, but was soon back working for the club.

United's last game at Old Trafford was on 8 March 1941 and 3,000 saw United win 7-3 with both Rowley and Carey scoring hat-tricks. Blackpool were the first team to play United at their foster home and beat them 3-2 on 5 April. On Easter Monday United showed scant regard for their neighbours' hospitality by beating City 7-1, Rowley claiming four goals, Pearson two and Smith the other one.

On 17 May came United's first wartime honour, albeit a modest one. They won the Lancashire Cup after a hard fought single goal win against Burnley. Johnny Carey was the scorer, but John Breedon save them by stopping a Bob Brocklebank penalty.

Placed eighth in the North Regional League the average gate was even lower than in 1939–40. At the start of the 1941–42 season, United beat New Brighton 13-1, fielding a full-strength side. Rowley with seven goals was their top scorer, Smith (three), Bryant (two) and Mitten completing the rout. On 29 November at Liverpool, United gave a second outing to Rowley's 15-year-old brother Arthur on the left wing in a 2-2 draw in which the elder Rowley scored both goals.

There was no success in the Cup, in which Wolves beat them in extra time after Carey had a goal disallowed for offside, but consolation came two weeks later when they not only beat rivals City 3-1 but clinched the Second Championship of the League North on goal average over Blackpool. It had been Blackpool who had won the first competition on goal average, with United themselves in fourth place three points behind them.

The 1941–42 campaign was probably the best of the club's wartime seasons. Of the competitive games against Manchester City, who also became their hosts during the period, United won nine, drew four and lost 14. Not until late in the war was it possible to run the old-style reserve side, although this did not prevent the club searching diligently for talent. By 1941 they had 64 players registered. A year later it went up to 76 and after remaining at that figure for 1943 it increased to a peak of 82 by 1944, naturally not all of them professionals.

Newcomers included Henry Cockburn, who came to the club through illness. Blackpool had already noted his ability playing for the amateur club Goslings and as an Accrington Stanley guest. They arranged a trial for him. Alas, Cockburn contracted influenza and had to cry off, which was where United stepped in to sign him in August 1944.

Goalkeeper Jack Crompton signed as a professional the same year, having originally started his career as an inside-forward. Not that United were unused to players in a variety of positions. John Aston signed in January 1940 from Clayton as an inside-forward or wing-half, and later switched to full-back. Carey, the

Irish international, had arrived in 1937 from St James Gate at the reasonable cost of £200. He could also play inside-forward, but eventually appeared for the club in nine different positions before settling down at full-back himself.

Charlie Mitten made his debut on 11 November 1939. He served in the Azores with the RAF and once scored all 13 goals for unit side against a local team. War service also took Johnny Morris, who had made his debut on 30 August 1941, across the Rhine in a tank while he was serving with the Royal Armoured Corps. Johnny Hanlon was wounded serving with the Durham Light Infantry and spent three years as a POW. He had joined United in pre-war times from St Wilfred's, Hulme.

Hanlon went out East in 1942 and in the fighting on Crete was captured and spent the rest of the war first in an Italian camp and when they changed sides, was transferred to Stalag IVB in Germany. He had turned professional in November 1935 at 17 and in two and a half years with the third team scored 133 goals. He also managed 9 in five Central League outings and in 1938–39 scored 12 in twenty-seven appearances in the First Division.

Carpenter was killed on active service. Redwood, invalided out of the forces, contracted TB in the Army and died in October 1943. Gladwin was so badly wounded that he was unable to play again. Allenby Chilton was also wounded, but less seriously.

Centre-half Chilton was another who served in the DLI and was involved in the D-day Normandy landings. He was also wounded at Caen. At the start of the 1939–40 season he had taken Vose's place in the Jubilee Match and also in the last pre-war League match at Charlton. Ironically, he was to guest for the south London club in the war.

Rowley was an outside-left until converted into a centre-forward of prolific scoring ability. He spent six years in the South Staffs Regiment, was landed at D-day but by Christmas was back from France on a course and assisting any number of clubs within reach.

On 19 May 1945 United's path was again crossed by Bolton in the final of the League North Cup. En route, United had had a few scares. The qualifying competition had seen them lose both games to Manchester City, but in the final game of the series they were struggling for the win which would qualify them for the knock-out rounds. On 17 March, having lost by the only goal at The Shay, they played the return with Halifax and a contemporary report paraphrased their performance as one lacking in confidence, guileless and shirking responsbiliity! There was no score and three minutes remained. Then somehow they clicked. John Roach, a full-back playing on the left wing, crossed the ball and Cliff Chadwick the Middlesbrough player headed in. Roach hit a speculative effort which the Halifax goalkeeper totally misjudged. From then on United strode confidently on beating Burnley, Stoke, Doncaster and Chesterfield with only the latter holding them to a draw in one leg of the semi-final.

However, Bolton won by the only goal at Burnden Park and held United 2-2 at Maine Road before 57,395, the highest crowd to watch them in the season. United fielded four guests in that team: Crompton; Walton, Roughton, Warner, Whalley, R. White (Spurs amateur), Bryant, Astbury (Chester), Sloan (Tranmere), Glidden (Tranmere) and Wrigglesworth. They showed two changes from the first leg. Bellis and Smith had been unable to play and both Sloan and Warner were injured during the game. Chadwick and Chilton did not play in the second leg and several positional changes also had to be made. Chadwick trained paratroopers and dropped saboteurs over enemy-occupied Europe!

Though Bolton's equaliser only came inside the last minute, they had been the more balanced side in a match fought with pace and spirit. Wrigglesworth had put United ahead after 21 minutes but Wanderers had drawn level within two minutes of the interval after a four-man move which ended with Malcolm Barrass scoring. Bryant regained the lead for United six minutes into the second half and they held it until Barrass's last-minute header.

When Matt Busby took up his position as manager of United on 22 October 1945, the offices were still temporarily located at the Cornbrook Cold Stores, the premises of Chairman James Gibson. There were no training facilities and the dressing-rooms were as derelict as the ground, from whose terraces had grown a large tree. The club's overdraft was £15,000 and they were still fostered out at Manchester City for home games.

For Busby's first game as manager against Bolton, he was able to field a team composed entirely of United's own players: Crompton; Walton, Roach, Warner, Whalley, Cockburn, Worrall, Carey, Smith, Rowley and Wrigglesworth. They had won only one League game, had seven points and were 16th. Carey was home on a short leave to make his first appearance for a couple of years, soon to return to duties in Italy.

United won 21 and went on to a run of eight games without defeat. Improvement was not immediate, but solid, and at the end of the season the changing face of the side was such that it was being fielded thus: Crompton; Hamlett, Chilton, Aston, Whalley, Cockburn, Delaney, Pearson, Rowley, Buckle and Wrigglesworth. The only guest among them, oddly enough again a Bolton player, Lol Hamlett.

Attendances increased appreciably. For the derby with City 61,144 saw City win 'away' and 50,440 at 'home'. This Maine Road hoodoo apart, United had climbed to fourth place. Average crowds were 30,000 in the League games.

These were changing times at United as elsewhere. George Roughton became manager of Exeter City, Bill Bryant was transferred to Bradford City and Jimmy Delaney arrived from Celtic for £4,000. In 1940 Delaney had been thought to have brittle bones and, as no insurance company would cover him, he could not play for Scotland. But despite several fractures he did!

Guest players still had to be called upon but when the club was invited to play a BAOR side in Germany on 20 March 1946, there were none in the team: Tapken; Whalley, Walton, Carey, Chilton, Cockburn, Delaney, Smith, Hanlon, Pearson and Wrigglesworth. There was a crowd of 25,000 British servicemen. The Germans were forbidden to attend, but some locals climbed nearby trees to snatch a view. United lost 2-1.

Proving that the support of servicemen was not restricted to merely viewing in 1945, both Manchester United and City had received sets of jerseys subscribed for and sent by a party of soldiers serving in India.

14 GROUNDS FOR COMPLAINT 2

Birmingham

BIRMINGHAM HAD TO suffer the indignity of being the only Football League club who wanted to play at the beginning of the war, but were prevented from so doing because Chief Constable, C. H. H Moriarty, albeit with sound reasoning, refused permission for them to use their own ground.

In the first season of the war they were forced to forage elsewhere while the debate about their plight continued. Four 'home' games were played on opponents' grounds and five at Leamington. Those were indeed dark days for the Blues, illustrated by a return journey from a trip to Luton when their coach crashed through a road island in the blackout; fortunately no one was injured.

On another occasion the entire coach party was almost put under arrest by the police after an unintentional breach of wartime regulations not disclosed at the time save for the cryptic comment that 'the position was only saved by a record quick changing act by one of the jokers of our party'.

Even so, Birmingham were the first club to pay a wartime benefit to a professional, their long-serving goalkeeper Harry Hibbs. Signed in May 1924, he retired in May 1940 and had played 25 times for England in the 1930s. They were a compact, happy outfit. Bill Camkin was honorary manager, trainer George Blackburn, a former Villa and England international half-back, looked after the teams.

The ban on their headquarters was finally lifted on 12 March 1940. Apart from the police chief's concern, eight of the Council held the same opinion. They were in a minority, however, since hundreds of Birmingham supporters were toiling on long shifts in munitions factories and were missing their weekly soccer ration. On 23 March 13,241 watched the Blues against Walsall. In May a six-a-side tournament was held there. Nevertheless, the Chief Constable's worry became a reality the following season when enemy action restricted them to 16 League games. There were 20 direct hits sustained on the ground during the war.

After a match at Walsall on Christmas Day which was lost 6-3, there were two cup-ties both at Leicester in February and another at Luton won 5-2 on 1 March 1941. Individual highlight of this contracted season was provided by the five goals Cyril Trigg scored in a 6-2 win over Stoke on 16 November and three in a 3-3 draw at Notts County in their next game; indeed a trigger-happy attacker, he scored 20 of the 38 League goals.

On 18 May 1940 they surprised Arsenal 2-1 in the War Cup at White Hart Lane and, though Trigg scored first, they lost 4-2 against West Ham in the quarter-final.

More serious damage to St Andrews and buildings in 1941–42 convinced the club of the wisdom of indulging in friendlies only. At the start of the season, Birmingham had decided not to compete in the Regional League. They arranged a fairly attractive fixture list including visits from an RAF XI and a Czech team. They beat the boys in blue 3-1 and their wartime Czech mates 3-2. On 13 September they even defeated Wolves 4-0 and again the following week at Molineux 4-2, but the Army stopped them on 4 October, 4-2. A week later Birmingham defeated Northampton 4-1.

That same month the FA offered them the England v Wales match, rather surprisingly in view of the prevailing circumstances, but the gesture was much appreciated. A crowd limit of 23,000 was imposed, but the club received more than 60,000 written applications and these had to be returned by overworked voluntary helpers. Birmingham's effort was officially recognised by the FA who termed the match a 'complete success from every point of view'.

Then, on 21 January 1942 all the players' kit was lost in the accidentally tragic fire which gutted the stand. A report on the destruction said that 'not so much as a lead pencil was saved from the wreckage'. Birmingham's season almost came to an abrupt halt then and there, one in which a full international match had been staged on the ground for the first time in the club's history.

Fortunately, the current minute book and club's typewriter were at the home of the secretary Sam Richards. Fixtures continued. A friendly at West Bromwich was lost 4-1 with both sides awarded two penalties.

In 1942–43 the club played at Villa Park by kind permission of their neighbours but had to borrow kit. However in 1943–44 they were back at St Andrews, though the players had to use the facilities of an adjacent factory as a changing room. There was no shelter for the spectators from the elements, but playing prospects had improved by then, despite the handicaps which seemed to be a constant shadow over their efforts. In the Second Championship in 1943–44, Birmingham finished a creditable fourth and were unbeaten in their home games, dropping just two points in ten matches.

The club's official handbook later referred to that season as the turning point in the club's wartime travails.

> It seemed as though our adversities had sponsored a real desire to be of help and perhaps it is not too much to say that it was this particular period which saw the birth of our new-found spirit and in some part supplied the foundation of the successes which the team has since achieved.

Birmingham reached the last eight in the cup, losing by the odd goal to Manchester City on aggregate over two games which were both titanic struggles.

In 1944–45 the ground was made to look slightly more presentable, though the scars of war remained deeply etched for all to see. Debris had lain around for years. When it was removed, workmen found an apple tree growing from a core thrown away by a pre-war spectator.

In the Cup there was another single-goal defeat, this time at the hands of neighbours Wolves, the second of which on 14 April was literally a marathon which lasted two hours and 33 minutes, the winning goal being scored at 5.45 p.m. But the main event that season was the addition of the word 'City' in November 1944.

Birmingham held middle-of-the-table positions in both competitions that season, but the following term all their troubles seemed to have been worthwhile when they crowned their wartime achievements in the same breathtaking manner as they had endured their problems. On 1 June 1945 the club appointed Harry Storer, a talker and a tactician as manager after many years' service in a similar position at Coventry. His defensive-minded inclinations on the field were in contrast to his open-handed attitude to players off it.

Arthur Turner was skipper. A product of the Potteries, he had played as a schoolboy for Stafford County at right-back and after playing for several local sides joined Stoke as an amateur. He turned professional in 1930–31 and had been captain for three seasons when Birmingham signed him in February 1939. In 1945–46 he missed only two League games, only Dennis Jennings with 41 outings making more and Harry Bodle the same number as himself. Turner was to retire at the end of the season.

As the complete record of Birmingham City recorded: 'The transitional season of 1945–46 produced some brilliant performances from the Blues.' Yet, the club made a dreadful start, losing home and away against West Ham. They were unbeaten in the next eight, which included home wins in successive weeks of 5-0 and 8-0 against Swansea and Tottenham respectively. Another run of eight games without losing put them in fine fettle for the start of the FA Cup, making a welcome return to the calendar, but before the semi-final they lost in consecutive weeks at home by a single goal against Arsenal and then against Plymouth.

Then, on 27 April a crucial home defeat by Wolves, again by the only goal, appeared to have been costly, but they drew 0-0 at Charlton two days later. League leaders Aston Villa had completed their programme three days before Birmingham's last game at Luton on 4 May. Despite a lead of two points, Villa had an inferior goal average. Not so Charlton, who were level with Birmingham City and had home advantage over Wolves. At half-time both championship contenders were one goal up but, while Charlton could only draw, Birmingham won 3-0 at Luton, which finally ended memories of that night crash in 1939–40.

The day Charlton probably lost their chance had come much earlier in the season when, before a crowd of 56,615, City were leading Charlton 1-0 when the visitors were awarded a last-minute penalty. Sam Bartram ran the whole length of the field to take the kick, which hit the bar. He had to turn and scamper all the way back; but, having taken three points from each of their nearest rivals, perhaps Birmingham deserved the crown.

The *Birmingham Evening Despatch* said of them:

> The best tribute that can be paid to Birmingham City FC is that 12 players were mainly responsible for taking the club through to this much envied football distinction . . . A grandstand finish to an exciting football race as has ever taken place found City on top, worthy of the championship because of their consistency.

Much of this consistency had come from the home programme despite the odd goal reverses previously mentioned. From 3 September to 23 February, they accumulated 14 successive home wins.

Birmingham also reached the semi-final of the FA Cup. An aggregate of 143,420 spectators watched the original tie at Sheffield and the replay at Maine Road. The total receipts of £28,205 were a record for an FA Cup semi-final. Their first victims had been the pre-war holders, Portsmouth.

However in that semi-final replay there had been no score. Gil Merrick the goalkeeper said: 'We were drawing with only half a minute to go to the end of ordinary time when Harry Bodle our inside-forward, was sent clear about 20 yards from the Derby goal. Woodley the Derby goalkeeper stayed on his line to everyone's amazement. It was surely a gift. Bodle took the ball to within eight yards of the goal but hit the ball so near to Woodley that he was able to beat the ball away.' Alas Birmingham lost four goals in extra time.

Merrick had played in the Solihull Town trial game in August 1939. He had been long sought by Birmingham, who in earlier days did not run a junior team, but when a vacancy occurred they quickly snapped him up with a £5 signing-on fee. An apprentice sheet metal worker by trade, he received £2 from his job and £3.10s (£3.50) from football. He made his debut for Birmingham in their 'A' side against Wolves in the Birmingham Combination. Leading the Wolves attack was Billy Wright, who scored twice as Wolves won 3-1. Merrick was dropped from the team, but then came the war.

He did not play any serious football for a year and was then loaned to Sutton Town, had a couple of games for a Birmingham reserve side which was occasionally assembled, and guested for one or two other League sides including West Bromwich.

Merrick was a key figure in City's successful League team which included the ubiquitous Dearson, while top scorer was Charlie Wilson-Jones, who contrived

20 League goals in only 27 games, but had an able deputy in Dave Massart who contributed nine in 11 outings himself. Massart had been signed pre-war, but service in the Middle East caused him to wait four years ten months for his debut, scoring at Nottingham in the Cup during the previous season.

Jones said that he scored two hat-tricks, one on Christmas Day in a 6-2 win over Leicester City and another in a 3-2 win at Plymouth on All Fools' Day, but the opening goal against Leicester was subsequently claimed by Ambrose Mulraney, Charlie claiming a touch to the shot! In fact the other treble-shooter was Mulraney himself in the FA Cup against Watford on 26 January in a 5-0 win. The average attendance in League games was a healthy 26,000.

Oddly enough the silver trophy which Harry Morris, Chairman of Birmingham, presented on behalf of the directors of the club to HMS *Birmingham* in 1938 remained in the mess room undisturbed during the cruiser's several actions at sea. It clearly fared better than St Andrews on dry land.

Birmingham's war service was such that 40 professionals of the club served in HM Forces, 24 in the Army, 15 in the RAF and one in the Royal Navy. Tom Farrage (Army), Ray Harris (RAF) and Bill Taylor (Army) were killed in action.

GROUNDS FOR COMPLAINT 3

Charlton Athletic

DOWN IN THE VALLEY at Charlton they had other worries. Rumours had been rife that, if war came, the ground would immediately be taken over as an ARP and Decontamination Centre. But the club were optimistic and even bought an extra car park.

Charlton had three players touring South Africa with an England team: John Oakes, Sam Bartram and 'Sailor' Brown. They returned to take part in the season's opening game in which Charlton lost 4-0 at Stoke. Don Welsh appeared to have been badly injured that day and likely to be out for three months. This seemed to be of more concern to local opinion than any continental conflict.

Players who were either Territorials or who had joined the local volunteer organisations had to report at once. Part of the ground was used by the ARP and the Government ban on all football in the area was relaxed the following week. Friendly matches were arranged for the end of September and the beginning of October. On most Saturdays two teams were fielded.

Charlton waived all rents for players who lived in club houses and helped them to find jobs wherever possible. Albert Brown, who earned his 'sailor' nickname from his rolling gait, joined the RAF! By the beginning of October the regional competition plan for London clubs was announced. The first resulted in a high-scoring defeat at White Hart Lane where Arsenal won 8-4.

In an area of high evacuation, crowds were meagre. The last game of 1939 against Arsenal, a foggy affair, was watched by only 2,000 people. Even January 1940 games in better weather had crowds of under 3,000. By February, Charlton's average gate was only 1,600. Teams of varying strength, the uncertainties of the moment and defeat by pre-war Third Division sides produced an apathy which hung like a mist over The Valley. The competition was reorganised but the players and crowds seemed uninterested.

Putting aside contemporary calamities, the club wisely looked ahead. Manager Jimmy Seed advertised a training scheme for 16- to 19-year-olds. Fifty boys were selected for training under the guidance of trainer Jimmy Trotter and a series of trial matches took place. From the most promising of these a junior team was formed and played friendlies towards the end of the 1939–40 season. After this the juniors continued to function under the name of Charlton Rovers.

Support for the seniors slumped even further. From a fixture against Fulham in late 1939–40, the two clubs shared the £14.18s.8d (under £15) receipts between them. Only 855 showed up to watch Portsmouth, the reigning Cup holders. Receipts were £35. But if finances flopped, fortunes fluctuated fluidly on the field.

On 7 April Charlton won 4-1 at Chelsea in a sensational finish which produced three penalty kicks in the last five minutes. Charlie Revell was brought down in the area and scored from the spot himself for Charlton. Then Joe Payne hit a penalty for Chelsea and with the last kick of the match, Revell added another for a foul on Harold Hobbis.

On 7 September 1940, the first game of the season, the siren sounded with one minute left for play. Millwall were leading 4-2. The raid was heavy, shrapnel fell on the ground. Whisky from the boardroom was used to fortify fainting women. When the all-clear sounded, the teams returned to play the remaining 60 seconds, but many of the 2,000 spectators could not be persuaded to return that season!

Frequent air raid warnings soon caused crowds to dwindle to a few hundreds. The Home Office order that play must stop whenever an alert was sounded was no inducement to attend, because of the refusal to implement the spotter system and its early warning of imminent danger. Play was often suspended for periods up to an hour, and on one occasion when the second half had just started, there was an 'alert' and the game had to stop for over an hour. When the 'all-clear' sounded, the referee discovered that half the players were in the bath and the rest preparing to go back to their jobs. The score stood. By November gates were down to an average of under 300. Takings in two weeks totalled £27. The club was losing £60 a week and was preparing to close after 28 December. They lost 3-1 at Portsmouth that day.

Average crowds amounted to 400, many being servicemen and children admitted half price. Average takings were £12. On 7 December they used a spotter for the first time in a 5-0 win over Arsenal and play continued during an air raid alert. The gate was 1,000. Seed said: 'The public don't want football, the Directors don't want football, the players don't want football so why go on?'

The Manager's notes afterwards reiterated the situation: 'Last match of the season. Club closes down for duration of War or until conditions make it advisable to restart.'

The ground suffered four high explosives on the terraces, two on the pitch including one on a penalty spot and a direct hit on the ambulance hut. When they packed up, the locally based players like Hobbins and Green played as guests for West Ham, Jobling for Orient and Robinson and Revell for Fulham. However, it was Seed, who had served in the Durham Light Infantry in the First World War and had been badly gassed in France, who kept Charlton Rovers going. Daylight bombing virtually ceased by the start of the following season and the populace had adapted themselves to a routine of sleeping in shelters at night and following normal activities by day. So The Valley resumed operations.

A gate of 7,000 turned up for the first London League game of 1941–42. In contrast to their experiences in the first wartime season, the London League Cup semi-final against Portsmouth was watched by 20,000, admittedly at neutral Stamford Bridge. Hobbis skippered Charlton from outside-left and in addition to the disappointment of defeat he returned home to find his house had been burgled and he had lost his 15 soccer medals.

Attendances continued at a reasonable level but there were complaints about the 1s.6d (7p) admission charge, thought to be too high for the standard of football being played. It was costing £60 a week to run the club even on reduced overheads.

Charlton's Cup form was infinitely better than its League performances. In 1942–43 they again reached the semi-final, beat Reading 2-1 at neutral White Hart Lane before 19,000 and prepared for a first visit to Wembley to meet Arsenal, then sharing Spurs' ground. A crowd of nearly 75,000 saw Arsenal win 7-1 and Charlton's share of the gate was £2,919, some consolation at least.

On 2 October 1943 Charlton suffered their only case of being hoodwinked. Chelsea were the visitors and Fred Scott who had been expecting to appear for the home team was unavailable. With no alternative, a certain J. Rogers deputised and subsequently proved his CV to be a complete fabrication. Manager Seed apologised in his next programme notes. Chelsea won 1-0.

Charlton beat Spurs 3-0 at Stamford Bridge in the semi-final the following year before 35,000, and 85,000 turned up at Wembley for the final against Chelsea. Charlton had nine of their own players on duty plus Allenby Chilton of Manchester United and Leith Athletic's Chris Duffy. Charlton won 3-1 in a freak weather cloudburst and were presented with the cup by General Eisenhower who was reported to have commented on the game: 'I started cheering for the Blues but when I saw the Reds winning, I had to go on cheering for the Reds!'

The club presented the match ball to Jobling, the longest-serving player in the side, who had actually come out of retirement to play in the match. The gate share for each team was £3,718. Charlton played Aston Villa, the winners of the North Cup, at Stamford Bridge in a brilliant display of football according to the critics, which ended 1-1, a late equaliser by Revell saving Charlton's run of 11 games without defeat. He literally revelled in goalscoring in 1944–45. On 11 November his three goals at Arsenal took his total to 12 in three games.

The Gliks[tens who ran Charlton had become involved in dealing with Government contracts by virtue of their position as timber merchants, which left manager Seed almost solely in charge. He started a physical training scheme for the public at The Valley and himself served in the Observer Corps. Club physician Dr Montgomery became a medical officer in the Home Guard and reached the rank of Major.

Jimmy Trotter helped in the PT scheme, went on training duties for Charlton Athletic and Charlton Rovers, did ambulance work and was eventually himself commissioned in the Home Guard. Alex Hird was in the local ambulance unit before being called into the Pioneer Corps, despite qualifications as a trained masseur – a decision which served to underline service thinking on most subjects . . .

Duffy was signed for £330 and there were eight or nine graduates from Charlton Rovers including Arthur Turner, an amateur who scored 34 goals in all matches during 1945–46. Turner had served as a Coastal Command air gunner and almost lost his life when his aircraft crashed into the Bay of Biscay. The only survivor, he floated around for hours before being rescued. Prior to this he had made his debut against Arsenal on 27 November 1943, scoring twice. A month after the Cup final in 1946 he asked to be released. This was refused so he joined non-league Colchester United.

Another player who found himself with flying problems was goalkeeper Jim Sanders, a product of the juniors. An RAF gunner, too, he completed three flight tours taking part in nearly 200 operational sorties. On his third tour he was severely wounded in an engagement with an enemy fighter. He was invalided out of the service and his career seemed at an end, but he did play again and was transferred to West Bromwich on 14 November 1945.

One of the earliest Charlton guests was Dai Astley, who had cost Blackpool £10,000. He arrived in London in November 1939 to stay with his brother-in-law Bert Turner, the Charlton Athletic and fellow Welsh international. Blackpool's manager Joe Smith had given Astley permission to play for whom he chose. Jimmy Mason, a Scot serving in the Middlesex Regiment, was a Third Lanark player. He assisted Charlton, though his club insisted he was heavily insured. But for a Britisher through and through, Duffy was the man. He had previously assisted Charlton while stationed at Maidstone. Born in Scotland, he married an Irish girl, joined the Welsh Regiment and was playing for an English club. Oddly enough Duffy's initial outing for Charlton had not impressed Seed.

Charlton players, like others, often used to pool their clothing coupons in order to buy new kit. They also had the interest of the club at heart in other ways. Charlie Sargeant had just come off a night shift at Woolwich Arsenal when he discovered on the Saturday morning that Charlton wanted him to make his debut against Arsenal, which he did quite cheerfully, making his bow along with 'Tubby' Warboys at right-half. Then Freddie Ford, just back on convalescence and minus a finger after being wounded crossing the Rhine, had his first game for three seasons on 4 April 1945 when he played against Brighton.

The supporters also felt concerned about their players. Welsh, who had been in the Navy pre-war before signing for Torquay, became a CSMI in the Army. Later in the war he was in charge of troop transports and earlier had been appointed PTI and coach to the Canadian Army. In 1941–42 his various service commitments caused supporters to be worried that he was playing too much football, since he looked somewhat jaded. In 1945–46 he scored 26 senior goals, one behind Arthur Turner's tally.

There had been no Happy New Year 1940 for Welsh. On leave from his regiment he travelled by road to play at Southend. The car skidded and was completely wrecked though neither he nor his wife were injured. He still wanted to play but Seed persuaded him otherwise.

Charlton came within a whisker of a League and FA Cup double; as close to it as half-time in their last match in the former competition and at the end of normal time in the latter. In the Cup final it was one view that a last-minute tactical talk cost Charlton any chance they had of beating Derby. It was decided that the two Berts, Turner and Johnson, would shadow Doherty and Carter wherever they went. It was a partially successful strategy before extra time but they were unable to supply their own inside-forwards with the ball and were eventually overrun.

That season's Cup competition over two-legged ties provided the only example of a team being beaten in an earlier round yet still reaching the final. Taking a 3-1 lead over Fulham in the first leg, Charlton lost 2-1 at Craven Cottage, but went through on a 4-3 aggregate.

The disappointing end to the season should not, however, have detracted from what was a complete vindication of the club's wholehearted resolve to foster local talent in the most difficult of circumstances. Five days after the Wembley final the Charlton board decided to award Trotter a £100 bonus and increased his salary by £2 a week. Seed received the gift of a motor car and had his money improved to £2,000 a year.

16 PARTICIPATION WAS EVERYTHING

For the other Football League clubs just managing to fulfil fixtures represented success. If more games were won than lost, this was a bonus in itself. To record more victories than anyone else was ample reward in the circumstances.

The north-east and Merseyside were the black areas if one looked upon tangible reward as a witness to their efforts. Blackpool was the most successful team in terms of honours and arguably one which played the most attractive football. Preston might well have developed, but they lost the use of their ground temporarily and had to withdraw from the Regional League for a time.

In the south, the density of clubs in the London area and style of competition afforded more opportunities for honours. Arsenal dominated the early seasons while their north London neighbours and wartime hosts Tottenham Hotspur assumed control in the latter stages.

The successful clubs in the midlands area were hit by missing out some seasons completely. But Aston Villa and Birmingham were able to record significant progress; Villa at the expense of the classical Blackpool side in the War Cup and Birmingham City, as they became, in the League South transitional season. Wolves' youth policy was interrupted in 1940–41 but they had their moments.

Interestingly enough, while Blackpool had at least half of their best team composed of guests, Preston was virtually a home-grown team; Arsenal and Spurs achieved a mixture of success with a blend of the two ingredients.

Team building was arbitrary and impossible for all but the few fortunate clubs. Availability of players depended on the strength of local industry or close proximity to service camps. The transitional season was too short a period in which to provide for peacetime conditions, although it was remarkable how the clubs who were able to persist in encouraging youth managed to make some impact, as did a few who missed several seasons.

Teams playing away from home on 2 September 1939 experienced unhappy journeys. Stoke were at Middlesbrough on this eve of war. The team drove back by motor coach in a storm and a blackout. Only side lights were permissible.

Home was reached at four o'clock on Sunday morning. War was declared at 11 a.m.

Stoke City were left with only three professionals: Brigham, Little and Sale. Twenty-two Territorial Army players were immediately called up but became available later on. Stanley Matthews' first job was as an inspector in a munitions factory making shells.

In 1939–40 Stoke topped the Western Section. Their manager said that within three years the club would have a team drawn from within a seven-mile radius of the club, Frank Bowyer and 16-year-old Frank Mountford included. The same year they signed Mountford as a professional. He had hit 60 in 25 games for the juniors. In 1940–41 John McCue from the B team was one of seven from this grade to play against Leicester.

Crowds were poor. One home gate of 3,441 was recorded against West Bromwich and only 800 watched them at Cardiff in December 1940. Mountford scored 29 goals. In 1941–42 Stoke finished fifth. John Sellars turned professional in October 1941 as the club did their best to look after the interests of local talent. They must have succeeded, because in 1942–43 their retained list of 48 professionals included all but four locally born.

Even so, Frank Soo was unhappy about being asked to move to inside-forward. He had played at wing-half for England with two other Stoke players, Stanley Matthews and Neil Franklin. Eventually he was transferred to Leicester for £5,000 in September 1945. He had been the first player of Chinese extraction to appear in the Football League.

While Stoke were able to maintain the momentum of regular competition, Port Vale were forced to pull out after the 1939–40 season. Club President Major W. M. Huntbach died and his debentures had to be called in leaving the club in a parlous state. The ground had to be sold to the council for £13,000, though later they leased it back. A junior team kept the club nominally in existence until a restart was made in 1944–45. The re-emergence produced a healthy crowd of 8,768 for a 3-0 win over Birmingham. George Hannah, one-time England schoolboy cap, became a regular policeman and reverted to amateur status with Vale.

The midlands area suffered more than most as far as first-class teams missing seasons. While Birmingham were blacked out because of their initial ground ban, Aston Villa held a meeting on 26 September 1939 to decide whether to carry on. They had 16 players in the Police and War Reserve. One friendly had been played at Leicester where Villa had lost 3-0 ten days earlier.

Villa's Trinity Road stand became an air raid shelter and storage, the home dressing-room being utilised by the 9th Royal Warwickshire Regiment's rifle company. Several Villa players helped Birmingham against Wolves in the 1-0 defeat on 14 October and again 3-2 at Stoke. They did not play as a team themselves again until 13 April 1940 when they went to St Andrews for Harry Hibbs's benefit game watched by a maximum crowd of 15,000. Hibbs's 16-year service was marked with a silver salver and a cheque for £650. In May, Villa won a six-a-side competition on the same ground with Alan Wakeman, Ernie 'Mush' Callaghan, Alex Massie, George Lunn, Stan Batty and Billy Goffin.

The first wartime game at Villa Park took place on 13 September 1941 against RAF Hednesford in the Birmingham & District League. That same season the club created a record, beating more boys in blue from RAF Lichfield 19-2 on 21 March 1942. Broome, Parkes and Goffin had four goals each, Kerr, Houghton and Cummings two each plus one from Iverson. That year Villa won the League, its Challenge Cup, the Keys Cup and Worcester Infirmary Cup.

It was their second season in it, using Solihull Town's ground at Shirley. In 1942–43 they returned to Regional competition and even made a profit of £5,837. By 1944 they had started a junior team. Their loyal fans showed their appreciation: when the League North Cup was won and the trophy auctioned for the Red Cross, the winner John Wright gave it back to the club!

Villa came within a whisker of snatching the League South in 1945–46 from their Birmingham neighbours, the outcome being settled after an exciting finale with goal average of 0.3.

Westwards into the Black Country, West Bromwich Albion were not affected by the Birmingham ban but they had their struggles and three times in 1940–41 played before home crowds of under 1,000. They had 80 members of the club serving in the Forces at one time. In 1942–43 they had to use 54 different players. They were badly affected by casualties. Three reserve players were killed in action, Cliff Wright, George Dale and George Foulkes lost a leg each and Bill Harris, Dick Pike and Tommy Griffiths received injuries. However, they did manage to keep the successful pre-war junior team going in the Birmingham JOC League.

Wolves suffered a loss of £4,000 by their inactivity in 1940–41 and were rewarded by winning the League Cup the following season. Three times they had to enlist the assistance of a spectator at home games in 1943–44. On another occasion, Tom Smalley of Northampton Town, and an ex-Wolves defender, went to watch his former club at Molineux and was pressed into service for them again.

Walsall were ever-present themselves. They mined a few gems like winger Johnny Hancocks, inside-left Dennis Wilshaw and goalkeeper Bert Williams, transferred to Wolves for a then record fee for a goalkeeper of £3,500 on 15 September 1945. Wilshaw actually developed while loaned to the Fellows Park club from Wolves.

Coventry courageously missed only one full season through bomb damage, the result of heavy bombing on the night of 14 November 1940. A return was possible in August 1942. Their only pre-season capture had been Welshman George Lowrie. He was able to prove just how wrong Swansea and Preston had been at letting him slip through their hands and was a reliable scorer at centre-forward, guesting for several clubs as well as leading his country's attack.

Another player who suffered from lack of regular training was their centre-half George Mason. He even lost his place in the Coventry side. 'He gained exactly a stone in three months,' said manager Storer, 'and he is finding this a tremendous handicap.'

Mason's loss was Tom Crawley's gain and he played in various positions including centre-half. The granite-like Mason, an ex-warehouseman in a brass foundry, worked as a checker of spare parts in an aircraft factory and, for all his problems, did get an England international call.

Arsenal and Tottenham not only shared Spurs' pitch, but took the metropolis's major honours. The Gunners were especially badly hit in that they lost six senior players and a trainer killed in action, and three others suffered injuries while playing which resulted in their premature retirement.

Honours on the field were even. Of the 20 League and Cup clashes, Arsenal and Spurs won seven each and drew the remaining six. Arsenal won the South A section in which Tottenham were second from bottom. Spurs then won the South C while Arsenal were third. The Gunners were champions of their League in 1941–42 and again the following season before handing the title over to Spurs in the next two campaigns. Arsenal had more success in knock-out competitions, winning the 1943 South Cup with the availability of many of their pre-war staff.

In 1942–43 Arsenal's 37 games were watched by 670,000, then a wartime record. That season Spurs, with an excellent defence, were runners-up, but their most successful campaign was 1944–45, when they lost only one League game and failed to score only three times. On a dozen occasions they kept a clean sheet – a rarity in the prevailing free-scoring conditions. This performance was all the more remarkable as they also had a complete eleven guesting for other teams up and down the country.

Both north London teams rendered fine service to the colours. In 194243 Spurs had 48 players in the forces at home, in the Far East, Canada, USA and Ireland. Another was reported missing. Six others were on war work. Twenty Arsenal players joined the Territorials in the summer of 1939. In three years 32 of their staff were in the Army, 18 in the RAF, one in the Royal Navy and another in the Marines.

By early 1940 six Arsenal players – Ted Drake, Jack Crayston, Norman Sidey, Alf Kirchen, Laurie Scott and George Marks – were in preliminary training with the RAF as instructors, but they all had to do their stint of square-bashing before taking special PT courses, not to mention their share of chores and fatigue duty. 'I'd never seen so many dirty plates in my life', said Drake. 'And I had to wash them up!' His initial wartime job had been as a factory night watchman.

Subsequently, the posting of many of their service personnel marked a change in fortunes with the reliance of guests. Ironically, injuries to both Kirchen and

Crayston occurred at West Ham. Kirchen, who tore ligaments in his knee, was discharged from the RAF as a result, but Crayston carried on in the service. Drake was injured at Reading and played only a few more games after slipping a disc.

Norman Bowden, who turned professional in 1943, was an RAF pilot who survived a serious crash, while another less serious playing injury but costly to his career at international level was sustained by goalkeeper Marks. He had made his Arsenal debut in April 1939 and had forced his way into the reckoning as England's No. 1 in the war when he sustained a head injury playing at Wembley against Wales in 1943 which caused the temporary development of a blind spot in his vision.

For a Third Division (South) club, Crystal Palace did well to finish top of South D in 1939–40 and follow it up with the South Regional title the following season. They were one of the clubs who benefited in the area from the comparative nearness of the Royal Artillery depot at Woolwich which was mostly full of first-class players in the early years. Palace also ran a reserve side in to give four registered players a game but found it costly at times. After one game their share of the gate was a bill of £5! One guest stationed nearby for a time was centre-forward Fred Kurz of Grimsby, who was the leading marksman for them in the transitional season.

West Ham were conscious of the duty they felt to give their available players an equal chance of a game. Whenever possible they would rotate the pool each week, regardless of any attempt to keep a settled side. This exceptional demonstration of the correct attitude was at least rewarded when they won the first of the wartime cups, beating Blackburn with a goal from Sam Small who used to travel from Birmingham each week. The Hammers were runners-up in both sections of the mini-leagues that term and showed the most consistent form of any club, finishing 2nd, 3rd, 6th, 2nd, 2nd and 7th in the remaining seasons. Centre-forward George Foreman was a useful goalscorer and assisted Spurs as well, accumulating more than 200 wartime goals in seven seasons.

Full-back Arthur Banner suffered cartilage trouble while playing in the Army. West Ham arranged for his operation. Charlie Paynter acted as trainer and care-taker for the Hammers, even to the extent of keeping an eye on things at Upton Park by sleeping on the premises!

Queens Park Rangers, to whom had fallen the honour of the first wartime friendly, were winners of the South B section and came second in South D. However, it was not until 1945–46 that they neared further success as runners-up in the Third Division (South) Cup. Mindful of the need to retain the interest of youth, the club was among the earliest to promote a junior team. However, they had reached the semi-final of the War Cup in 1942–43 before losing to Arsenal the eventual winners 4-1 at Stamford Bridge in front of a crowd of 54,008.

Life for Clapton Orient on the other side of the capital was never easy. On the receiving end of a 15-goal barrage from Arsenal in a London Cup tie, the luckless goalkeeper MacIlroy was described as having had no previous League experience; it was to prove a short one. Worse was to follow. They pluckily ploughed on, struggling for players and spectators, rarely away from the bottom two places apart from the first season and 1942–43, their most successful campaign, when they finished 11th in the South Regional League, averaging almost a point a game. Alas, the following season the first win came in the 20th match, having taken only two previous points from drawn affairs. Trainer Billy Wright was appointed manager in November 1939 and occasionally had to deputise in goal.

Millwall's most successful season was, paradoxically, nearly their worst. Reaching the final of the South Cup in 1944–45 was outstanding, but only goal average kept them off bottom place in the League. They owed that Wembley place to Arsenal missing two penalties and an open goal against them. Chelsea beat them 2-0 at Wembley. Far-sightedly, the Lions organised free training to all at the start of 1941–42 and received over 200 responses including several Czechs and Poles. Tragically, after bomb damage to the ground a discarded cigarette end probably caused the destruction of the main stand in 1943. Home games were accommodated at Selhurst Park, The Valley and Upton Park at various times.

The Lions also finished as champions of the what was the last London Combination for reserve teams in 1945–46. Because of the difficulty in fitting in fixtures and availability of players, not all clubs finished their programme, but it was a valiant effort all round, since the restriction on guests similarly applied.

Luton were one of those clubs in limbo land around the fringe of the London area and as such forced to an existence in the midlands set-up. By 1942–43 they had at least returned to the South Regional League but finished bottom and again the following season. In 1939–40 Hugh Billington, the Second Division's top scorer the previous season with 28 goals, had accounted for almost half of their goals including a five, a four and two hat-tricks. His total that season was 42 from 24 League games alone.

Fulham and Chelsea were, oddly enough, among clubs in the city with the poorest media coverage, at local newspaper level at least, though the London evening journals gave whatever space they could to all London clubs. Fulham reached the semi-final of the first War Cup just losing out 4-3 to West Ham in a thriller at Stamford Bridge. Attendances at games with Chelsea varied, but often topped the 5-figure mark. Chelsea's cup successes were later in the period and they reached successive finals, losing 3-1 to Charlton in 1944 and beating Millwall 2-0 the following year. In 1944–45, Chelsea's fourth place was the highest either of these west London neighbours managed.

Ronnie Rooke was a consistent marksman for Fulham until posted to Italy, while the Blues' ace scorer, Joe 'ten-goal' Payne, recovered from injury and illness set-backs to become the scourge of defences late on. In November 1941

Payne was seriously ill with pneumonia. On a come-back in December 1942 he broke his ankle, but by 1944–45 he was back in full flow, finding the net in 12 successive matches and totalling 27 goals in this sequence. His ten goals had come for Luton against Bristol Rovers on 13 April 1936 in a 12-0 win. Previously a wing-half, it was his first senior game at centre-forward.

At Stamford Bridge between 1943 and 1945 the middle line of Bobby Russell, John Harris and Dicky Foss had many admirers and was rarely bettered at club level. Russell was signed from Airdrie for £3,500 in 1944–45 after guesting and Harris was added later as expensive captures like Len Goulden and Tommy Lawton were taken on the payroll.

Brentford reached the final of the London Cup in 1941, losing to Reading but topped this performance by winning the London War Cup the following year, beating Portsmouth 2-0 at Wembley and upholding the south's name in a 1-1 draw in the Cup-Winners' game with Wolves. Their best season in the League South was 1944–45 when they finished third.

Watford were tenth in 1944–45 but otherwise often found difficulty in fielding the same team two games in a row. They introduced a number of promising youngsters including Reg Williams, an amateur wing-half who later joined the Fleet Air Arm, and Bedford Jezzard, a schoolboy. Jezzard made his debut for Watford as a 17-year-old on the left wing. His partner was Maurice Edelston and at inside-right was Stan Mortensen. In 1945–46 they were forced to play an FA Cup tie against Nottingham Forest which had to be abandoned after 143 minutes, and 24 hours later were required to fulfil a League fixture! Only one of the players turned out in both games ...

Slightly overshadowed by their 'foster' team from United, Manchester City's claim to fame was modest enough; they scored more goals in 1940–41 than any other team in Regional League games. Of their 104 haul, Jimmy Currier bagged 47 and in their biggest away win, 9-1 at Stockport, Alec Herd scored four and Currier three. City were also third in the Second Championship in 1942–43 when they also topped the Cup-qualifying competition. In 1943–44 they reached the League North Cup semi-final with Herd regularly travelling to games through Friday nights. Benefits were awarded to six players in 1944.

Four games early in 1939–40 gave Stockport County an indication of the topsy-turvy nature of the times. In consecutive weeks they beat Tranmere 5-0 at home, drew 6-6 at Manchester City – after being 5-2 down in 69 minutes, lost 7-4 at home to Manchester United and then also lost 8-1 at Chester ... Duggie Reid's potential power as a forward eventually attracted Portsmouth's attention. In the first three games of that sequence top scorers were Reid (four), Fred Howe of Grimsby (four) and Reid (three).

Neither Oldham Athletic nor Rochdale were able to reveal much in the way of honours. Oldham's best seasons were probably the first two. In 1939–40 Ron Ferrier scored 19 goals and went one better the next term when the Latics won one more match than they lost and scored one more than they conceded. Picked up pre-war from Manchester United where he had once scored seven in a reserve match, Ferrier was a stylish and effective spearhead.

Rochdale made a breathless start to the 1943–44 season losing 6-1 away, then 6-2 at home to Blackpool, but in the next match defeated Southport 6-1 with Jack Harker contributing five and the same player had all four goals in a 4-4 draw at Southport the following week. After that Rochdale won all their home games in the opening championship. However, in 1941–42 they had twice managed to lower the colours of all-conquering Blackpool. In 1944–45 Jimmy Constantine emerged as a formidable marksman. He had learned his football in the Grenadier Guards and in 1944 was found playing for Ashton National. Centre-half Ernie Robson was even forced to play in goal on one occasion.

As runners-up in the first War Cup, Blackburn Rovers had the misfortune to lose two of their final team, one killed in action, the other in an accident. Frank Chivers died in a pit tragedy in April 1942, Earlier he had operated a first aid station. Albert Clarke was killed on active service in 1944. Percy Dickie passed the PT instructor's course but was failed because of a slight physical ailment. He successfully passed after a minor operation. Rovers had Bob Pryde, Jack Burton, David Davidson and trainers Len Evans and Ted Harper on the same course along with Jock Wightman. In 1941–42 they were placed seventh in the North League, only three points behind the champions, but in the transitional season had slipped to second from bottom.

Bolton's achievement in winning the League North Cup in 1944–45 was naturally forgotten following the Burnden Park disaster the following season. They succeeded in building a new team, having had one join up en masse at the start of the war, and youngsters like Nat Lofthouse, Malcolm Barrass and Willie Moir began to make an impression.

The same Castle Hill School which had turned Lawton out so well was the homing ground for Lofthouse. He chose the Monday morning after the declaration of war as the day he went to start life as a groundstaff boy at Burnden Park! He was 14 but was given his debut only a year later. By his 16th birthday he had already played 20 times and scored some 30 goals in three seasons. In 1944–45 he had 30 alone and in November of the following term started his stint as a Bevin Boy down the pits. Wally Sidebottom, who was discovered by Walter Rowley in the Leeds area playing park football, had proved an able wartime replacement for Ray Westwood until his unfortunate demise.

Consistent marksmanship from George Davies was also the chief source of success for Bury over the period as a whole, though the club's main honour came in 1939–40 when they finished two points clear at the top of the North West Division. Bury swept into the Lancashire Cup semi-final with a grand hat-trick from Davies. Despite cartilage trouble which flared up so much that he had to be heavily strapped up when he played, he had reckoned that 'the cleverer type of soccer in wartime had helped to bring my confidence back'. Trainer David Robbie had to be pitchforked into action at the age of 41 years, 290 days on one occasion. The club even made a profit of £1,752.

Burnley's nearest approach to highlights came in 1940–41 when they finished as runners-up to Manchester United in the Lancashire Cup, losing by the only goal. They had previously had a titanic struggle with Everton, losing 3-2 at home before forcing an extra-time win at Goodison Park.

Len Martindale, Burnley's utility player, left his apprenticeship as a fitter to become a professional. He was 19 when war came and changed to a different firm but renewed his old job. Gordon Bentley had a chance in goal for the Turf Moor club when Ted Adams was injured. Still an amateur, he saved two penalties in his first game and was signed on as a professional.

No club suffered a more marked change of fortune after war started than Accrington Stanley, who had won all three pre-war Football League games in the Third Division (North), then had to wait until March 1940 before they won a regional one. But in 1945–46 they finished top of their section once more, benefiting from a fairly settled side.

Barrow and Carlisle, those geographical outcasts in the far north-west, operated in only the first and transitional seasons themselves. Barrow had a reasonable run in the FA Cup, beating Netherfield before accounting for Carlisle 4-2 at home and 4-3 away. Kevin Clarke achieved hat-tricks in these games and had Barrow's two in the 6-2 defeat at Manchester City in the following round. For the second leg, during which honours were shared 2-2, the gate was 7,377.

Carlisle returned to action and had the services of Ivor Broadis, an RAF navigator and commissioned officer stationed at Crosby Field with a Dakota Squadron. He had been a Spurs amateur and Millwall discovery in earlier seasons. Ipswich's Jack Connor rattled in an average of a goal a game for United in 1945–46.

Şheffield United won the League North title in the same season. Better off than many for players, they did have to use trainer Reg Wright, 39, as emergency right-back on one occasion at Doncaster in 1940. Another United trainer, Dougie Livingstone, took extensive courses with the Red Cross and St John's Ambulance Brigade and won proficiency badges with both.

Rivals Wednesday were runners-up in the League North Cup in 1942–43. Of 20 League and Cup encounters between the two teams, Sheffield Wednesday had the advantage over the Blades with seven wins to five with eight drawn. Wednesday's best win in the period came on 13 February 1943 at Hillsborough in the North Cup qualifying competition when they won 8-2. In Wednesday's 1943 cup run, Hugh Swift had to be switched from the left-wing to left-back because of injury to another player and did so well against Stanley Matthews that he stayed there.

Consolation, too, for Owls supporters in 1945–46 when the first team finished fifth and the reserves won the Central League championship for the first time in 17 years. In the course of the campaign the second team achieved 63 points and were unbeaten from 1 September 1945 to 16 February 1946, a run of 25 matches of which 20 were won and 5 drawn. They scored 83 goals and conceded 22.

Four United players reached double figures in goalscoring in the same season – Albert Nightingale, Walter Rickett, George Jones and Colin Collindridge. The master touch was provided by inside-forward Jimmy Hagan. Yet, United's opening fixture on 25 August 1945 heralded anything but the sound of ultimate triumph, since they lost 6-0 at Newcastle, while Wednesday, with nine players discovered in the war years, were beating Sunderland 6-3.

United recovered quickly to beat Newcastle 3-0 a week later while Wednesday lost by the only goal at Roker Park. On 8 September United were further embarrassed when in the local derby Wednesday won 3-1 at Bramall Lane, their third goal four minutes from the end from Charlie Tomlinson being considered as the most spectacular in 50 years of rivalry between the two sides. Having outwitted both Fred Furniss and George Tootill, by an attempted hook shot then a header, he volleyed the loose ball into the net.

However, with general enthusiasm and spirited forward play United went on to lose only one game after a 5-2 reverse at Preston on 8 December – that an incredible 7-2 home defeat to Middlesbrough – until the Easter programme which yielded home and away defeats against Manchester City. But United had five points to spare at the conclusion.

Wednesday's 1943 Cup final defeat by Blackpool was disappointing, especially after a plucky performance at Bloomfield Road in the first leg despite Jackie Robinson carrying an ankle injury and Ted Catlin off the field for a quarter-of-an hour after coming off second best with a clash with Jock Dodds. He could only hobble about on the left wing when he returned. A Hillsborough wartime record crowd of 47,657 watched the second leg, paying £5,165, and crowds of 35,000 were not uncommon at this juncture.

Robinson, Wednesday's inside-right, scored 91 goals during wartime and the transitional season. In 1942–43 he achieved the hat-trick six times and scored 35 goals. He had made his Wednesday debut in April 1935. One of Wednesday's discoveries was Redfern Froggatt. In November 1936 Jack Froggatt had been left-half and his cousin Redfern inside-right in the Hillsborough Schools team. Redfern joined Wednesday from Sheffield YMCA in 1942.

Rotherham deservedly achieved a modest double of League and Cup in the Third Division (North) in 1945–46 with a team chiefly composed of miners playing the game on a part-time basis. Centre-forward Wally Ardron was an exception; he was an engine driver. Most of the side came from a radius of ten miles. Among eight regulars, all pitmen, were George Warnes in goal; the half-backs Jack Edwards, Horace Williams and Danny Williams; inside-right Jack Shaw and right-back Jack Selkirk.

Alf England was given his chance by Barnsley after the several Scots on their books had gone back home. He had been a local discovery but was snapped up by Wolves, who failed to keep him and allowed Barnsley to step in. He made his debut at 16 against Huddersfield. Most of the Barnsley players were also working down the mines, including Cliff Binns, Bernard Harper, Rob Shotton, John Logan and George Bullock. Their traditional association with the pits was much in evidence in the war years. One of those first Bevin Boys was centre-half Harper, signed in 1932 and given an unexpected chance of wearing England national colours in the war. He was also responsible for something of a freak, wind-assisted goal from ten yards inside his own half in a 2-1 win over Sheffield United.

Barnsley also found George Robledo at Huddersfield, a Chilean-born forward whose mother refused to allow him to join Wolves in 1940. At the tender age of 13 he had registered 57 goals in a season. He joined Barnsley and made his mark at 17 against Sheffield Wednesday in 1943-44, crowning his debut with a stunning goal in a 3-1 win.

Interest in the FA Cup in 1945-46 was such that local collieries put up the following notice: 'In order that the management may have knowledge of the number intending to be absent on Wednesday afternoon, will those whose relatives are to be buried on that day please apply by Tuesday for permission to attend.' A crowd of 27,000 turned up, Barnsley won the third round tie 3-0 and 5-4 on aggregate against Newcastle.

In 1943-44 Doncaster Rovers were fourth in the League North but just a point below the winners. Their goalscoring discovery was Clarrie Jordan, while leading marksman was the Birmingham guest player Harold Bodle. Rovers used outside help sparingly and had a fine junior policy. They also recruited from the mining industry. Jordan was one such and in the marathon cup game with Stockport in 1945-46 which was abandoned in poor light after 203 minutes, he had come off a double shift to play in the game!

Syd Bycroft the centre-back joined the regular Police service and was available enough to complete 150 appearances during the seven seasons.

Grimsby Town achieved their best run when they reached the War Cup semi-final in 1941-42, drawing goalless at Sunderland but losing the return game 3-2, their scorers being guests Peter Doherty and Albert Nightingale. Neighbours Hull City were disrupted by the war after the first two seasons. They returned in 1944-45 but lost their ground at Anlaby Road through the blitz and had to cry off until fresh accommodation could be found. Their young goalkeeper Billy Bly was working in a Newcastle shipyard early on. In 1940 Hull arranged for him to move to a local ship repairers before he was called up in February 1941.

Huddersfield ran away with the North-Eastern section in the first war season finishing 10 points clear of their rivals, but they had to wait until 1944–45 before their next success when they achieved the League North Championship losing only once 2-1 at home to Darlington. Billy Price proved an excellent spearhead with 21 of their 50 goals in this 18-match programme and was well supported by ex-Altofts inside-forward Jimmy Glazzard, who was in Bolton Wanderers reserves before joining Huddersfield in 1943. While with the Burnden Park club, he had lodged with Sidebottom. Another wartime find was outside-left Vic Metcalfe, an Air Force amateur who turned professional in 1945 after his demobilisation.

Price had been a pre-war signing from Wrockwardine Wood Juniors from the Wellington area in 1937. He scored on his debut against Derby in April 1938; his wartime exploits included twice hitting the 40-goal mark in a season.

As might have been expected, in normal times Park Avenue were the more successful of the two Bradford teams thanks to their status as a Second Division club. They finished higher in almost every season without causing any appreciable waves of their own. In derby matches they were to savage their City neighbours, Park Avenue's best win being 10-0 at Valley Parade on 19 December 1942. Len Shackleton enjoyed his best scoring season in 1944–45 with some 40 goals for the club including five in a 6-1 win over Hull on 23 December 1944. Another player who took five off City was Eddie Carr guesting for Park Avenue and the same player hit six for Newcastle in an 11-0 success over Bradford City on 18 November 1944.

Considerable interest was engendered in the North Cup in 1943–44 when Park Avenue reached the third round against Blackpool. On 1 April 1944 the teams drew 2-2 at Bloomfield Road with Arthur Farrell scoring one of Bradford's goals. Farrell, who had been signed in 1940 and was working in munitions, turned out in the second leg a week later just two hours after getting married. Despite a record crowd of 32,810 it was not a happy outcome as Blackpool won 2-1. In 1943–44 City's principal marksman was Joe Harvey who scored 17 goals including two in the opening game against Newcastle, for whom Jackie Milburn was making a scoring debut.

York City reached the semi-final of the North Cup in 1942–43 losing 3-0 away to Sheffield Wednesday but drawing 1-1 at home in front of a gate of 16,350. George Lee scored their goal from the penalty spot, his 100th for the club – signed at midnight, 30 seconds into his 17th birthday in 1936. Ironically it was Wednesday who ended their FA Cup run in 1945–46 with emphatic 5-1 and 6-1 wins.

Leeds United made little headway during the period and finished last in the League North in 1945–46. Their best season was 1940–41 but then overall they won only four more competitive games than they lost. Gerard Henry, who was leading scorer for the club, managed to score in ten consecutive games in 1943–44. He had started his career with the quaintly named Outwood

Stormcocks, joined Leeds before he was 16 and turned professional a year later. The turnover of players after the first season was enormous, making any claim to consistency on the field impossible. The club's England international inside-forward, Major Eric Stephenson, was killed in Burma on 8 September 1944.

Once the football pools restarted, Halifax Town became the punters' delight in 1940–41 as the Shay Ground inhabitants drew 13 of their games and finished in a respectable seventh place. Bill Allsop was a rock in defence during the period while Jimmy Moncrieff, a Sowerby Bridge Grammar School boy, was introduced in 1940–41 before going up to Oxford University.

As might have been expected from the Jubilee Match in which Liverpool beat Everton 2-1, the Anfield club enjoyed rather the better of the wartime exchanges against their rivals from Goodison Park, winning twice as many League and Cup games as their Merseyside rivals. Neither team managed to record any of the major honours, though Liverpool were runners-up in the 1939–40 Western section and again in the League North in 1942–43, the year they also won the Second Championship. That same season Liverpool won the Liverpool Senior Cup but failed against Everton in the Lancs competition. Liverpool were third in both opening and closing championships in 1943–44 and third again in the Second Championship race of the following season.

One of the players who had impressed in Liverpool's pre-1939–40 season trials was Bob Paisley, a wing-half recruited from Bishop Auckland. When the abortive League programme began, the last pre-war goal was scored by Cyril Done who became Liverpool's highest scorer in the regional matches. Twice he topped 40 goals in a season and might well have added handsomely to his final figure had he not had the misfortune to break his leg on 9 September 1944. As for Paisley, he spent most of the war overseas in the Army. Winger Billy Liddell was described by manager George Kay in March 1940 as 'the best thing that has come out of Scotland in the past ten years'. He was 18 at the time and training to be a chartered accountant. At the start of the war Liverpool already had 20 players in the Territorials.

Everton, League Champions when hostilities began, recorded their three best attendances against Liverpool, the first two of them setting up wartime club records. The first was on 11 April 1942 when Liverpool lost 2-0 at home to the Toffeemen in front of 33,445 and the second on 29 January 1944 when the Reds returned the compliment, winning 3-2 at Goodison Park with an attendance of 45,820. The third impressive gathering was 60,926 at Goodison during 1945–46, the match ending appropriately enough in a 2-2 draw.

George 'Stonewall' Jackson, the Everton right-back, also assisted Liverpool. Moreover he kept goal for both teams in emergencies including for the Reds against the Blues on one occasion! Liverpool won 3-1.

Everton were involved in two matches in which double figures were recorded and they amply illustrated that these irregular, one-sided affairs often had a revealing story of their own. On 7 March 1942 Everton crashed 11-1 at Wolves. They lost Walter Owen, injured after five minutes. He reappeared in the second half with a plaster over his left eye and was virtually a passenger. When Everton were 2-0 down, they lost centre-half Tommy Jones, who went to hospital and did not return. Mercer went to centre-half from inside-right. As Manchester United's game had been postponed, Wolves had the assistance of Jack Rowley, who scored five goals himself and made another three, after volunteering to play when Reg Kirkham failed to appear. Leading the Everton attack that day was Tommy Lawton, who played well without support. Despite guesting elsewhere on frequent occasions, Lawton managed over 150 League goals for Everton and, with 23 in internationals and at least 66 in representative games, he amassed an incredible haul.

During the initial war season, Everton managed not to have recourse to guest players, though understandably it was not possible in the prevailing circumstances to stick to this policy in later years. The club was also on the winning side of a big score on 27 February 1943 when they defeated Southport 10-2; but the visitors' goalkeeper was handicapped with a shoulder injury mid-way through the second half.

In 1945–46 Everton had eight of their pre-war championship side, but were playing inconsistently according to contemporary records. The exceptions were Wally Boyes on the wing and Wally Fielding at inside-forward who had 'a delicate, intellectual approach, the man who silenced the get-rid-of-it brigade'.

New Brighton's scoring quartet of 'Pongo' Waring, Alf Hanson, Albert Malam and Arthur Frost achieved the unusual feat of scoring all but 12 of their 110 goals in 1940–41. Waring was on Accrington's transfer list, having signed for Southern League club Bath City in July 1939. Frost had been transferred to Newcastle from New Brighton and Malam was a Doncaster player.

· With scarcely any of their own players available, it was becoming increasing difficult for the club to carry on. Then bomb damage to the ground and the Council's subsequent requisitioning of the premises caused a shut-down at the end of 1941–42.

In 1943–44 Wrexham lost only one cup qualifying match and were well placed in the Second Championship table. Their only reverse was in the first game against Liverpool on Boxing Day when losing 4-0. They did win the return 4-2 and also had a double success over Everton winning 3-2 at Goodison Park and 2-1 at the Racecourse Ground. However, in the first round proper they lost 4-1 at home to Manchester United, drew 2-2 away and were eliminated. At various times they had the assistance of some notable guests including Cyril Sidlow, Willie Watson, Neil Franklin, Tommy Jones, Johnny Hancocks and Jesse Pye.

Chester had to wait until the transitional term themselves before coming close to honours. They were runners-up in the Third Division (North) Cup, losing 5-4 on aggregate to Rotherham. Included in the team was Frank Marsh at right-half, who had been a forward until Peter Doherty spotted him in an RAF game and advised him to move back. Tommy Astbury, a wartime discovery, was much sought after and won Welsh international recognition. Harold Howarth their former captain was the first player in their history to be awarded a benefit in 1939–40. The brothers Hollis, Ken and Harry, emerged too, and made guest appearances elsewhere.

The 1942–43 season was a reasonable one for Southport. They were placed eighth in the League North and Jack Rothwell scored 24 goals for them plus another ten for Bath. On 26 September 1942 both Rothwell and Jack Deverall the Reading player had hat-tricks in Southport's 10-0 win over Crewe. In 1943–44 Southport had the distinction of beating Everton in the final of the Liverpool County Cup. After being held at home 1-1 they won with a goal from Preston's Jim Dougal at Goodison.

Crewe Alexandra, after winning only two games in the North Regional League in 1940–41, found themselves embroiled in the argument which led to the London clubs being expelled from the League the following season. There was no improvement in their playing fortunes until 1944–45 when Jack Boothway, signed from Manchester City, enhanced his reputation with 29 League and Cup goals and 38 the next term.

Nottingham Forest were not alone in having to cannibalise other teams in their area for players. Their chief suppliers were Aston Villa, Birmingham, Coventry and Derby, all of whom missed deployment at some stage or another and had players available. Forest also managed to run a Colts side in the Notts Amateur League, the only local competition at this level able to function. A Minor League with 14- and 15-year-olds nurtured youthful promise and according to the club's Centenary Yearbook 'played dazzling football, achieved cricket scores, were delightful to watch and long remembered'.

Centre-half Bob Davies had cartilage trouble three seasons before the war, then a nasal operation followed by a bout of pneumonia necessitating a long lay-off. He was then taken into hospital for the removal of his tonsils, but he recovered sufficiently to be awarded Welsh international recognition in 1939–40.

Notts County, across the River Trent, missed one season through enemy action but like Derby managed to run a reserve side, and local derbies with Forest were as keenly fought as ever. Notts' players were widely scattered and their turnover of guests was bewildering at times. In 1943–44 a staggering 129 different players appeared. Two inside-forward discoveries of their own were Jack Marsh and Jackie Sewell, both in 1942.

Northampton Town finished top of the 1941–42 Cup-qualifying competition with the best average of points. They were also third in the League placings. Two-thirds of the players used that season were guests, George Lowrie from Coventry and Liverpool's Willie Fagan sharing the scoring honours, the Birmingham utility player Don Dearson, another valuable addition.

In 1943–44 Mansfield completed nine home games with only 19 goals scored in them. The Stags' tally was 13, the opposition just six, rare indeed for the era. Oddly enough in the last completed pre-war campaign, Mansfield had failed to score in half their League games. Yet in 1940–41 Charlie Rickards scored 14 goals in eight consecutive outings.

Chesterfield were top of the East Midlands Division in 1939–40, unbeaten at Saltergate, winning all ten. In 1944–45 they accounted for Halifax after extra time in the Cup, then Barnsley before a memorable encounter with Liverpool. After drawing 0-0 at Anfield they won the second leg with a goal from Albert Collins in front of 27,000 on 28 April 1945. In the semi-final they put up a stout fight against Manchester United, drawing 1-1 at Maine Road and only losing the return by a single goal with the crowd swollen to 32,000.

Lincoln were creditable runners-up to Blackpool on goal average in the League North Championship in 1941–42, unbeaten at home and losing only two away. Though they started the Cup qualifying games with a 9-3 win over Don-caster, Bert Knott scoring five, they failed to qualify. The Imps had another distinction: twice one of their players hit seven goals, Cyril Lello at home, Bill Hullett of Manchester United away.

Derby County sharpened the edge of their FA Cup sword in the Midlands Cup in 1944–45 with two substantial victories over Aston Villa, 3-0 at Villa Park thanks to a Raich Carter hat-trick, and 6-0 at the Baseball Ground, a game in which Peter Doherty's five goals overshadowed all else.

Leicester's youth policy was well conceived. When Don Revie joined them in 1944 from their Middlesbrough Swifts nursery, the club's most experienced player Sep Smith gave him sound advice:

1.   When in possession, get into position.
2.   Never beat a man by dribbling if you can beat him more easily with a pass.
3.   It's not the man on the ball but the man running into position to take the pass who constitutes the danger.
4.   The aim is to have a man spare in a passing move, then soccer becomes easy.

In the widespread South Regional League in 1941–42, they pipped West Bromwich for top spot on 0.10 of average points! The previous season they had several inactive Wolves players as guests including Billy Wright and Jimmy Mullen.

Reading won the London Cup final in 1940–41 in impressive fashion. They were unbeaten in their ten qualifying matches, finishing immediately above Spurs, West Ham and Arsenal. In the final they accounted for Brentford by the odd goal in five. Magnus 'Tony' MacPhee was top scorer while Maurice Edelston, who had a spell with Brentford pre-war, provided the service from inside-forward. Edelston, whose father was Reading's secretary, was an outstanding amateur. He played for Corinthians, Queen's Park, captained London University and was honoured in wartime at full level. He had been in the British Olympic team in 1936.

The club had centre-half Bill Ratcliffe wounded and captured in Italy and Frank Ibbotson killed in action in Normandy. In August 1944 Wilf Chitty was injured in a flying bomb raid near his London home.

Bournemouth's trials and tribulations seemed to have been well worthwhile enduring when they became winners of the South Cup in 1945–46. The only goal of the final at Stamford Bridge against Walsall went to Jack McDonald, originally discovered as a junior in the Rotherham area. He had started his League career with Wolves against Chelsea on 1 April 1939 before being transferred to Bournemouth a month later. He guested for Chelsea in his RAF days and scored their first goal in the 1945 South Cup final, also at Stamford Bridge.

The other south coast teams, Southampton and Brighton, had mixed fortunes; Southampton were especially harsh on Luton, twice reaching double figures against them. The first time was 11-0 on 16 January 1943 when Alf Whittingham, the Bradford City guest, scored eight, out of 31 in the season for the Saints. The next occasion was on 3 March 1945 in the League South Cup when they won 12-3. Whittingham had four of these as did Alf Ramsey, a former Dagenham grocer's assistant serving in the Duke of Cornwall's Light Infantry, who had been on Pompey's books as an amateur in 1942–43 before going to The Dell the next season. Another marksman that day was Ted Bates.

Brighton frequently struggled for a full complement. Occasionally they had useful guests. In *Soccer Calling* one of their directors Alec E. Whitcher ruefully recalled: 'We received a rude awakening when we lost them in a batch, for the Liverpool FC contingent left us overnight, when the seven players were appearing regularly in our team.' On another day their side was completed by the son of the Watford President! Trainer Sam Cowan was also drafted in during an emergency at the age of 44 years, 156 days.

Even so, they were not without their success and Watford themselves featured in it. In 1940–41 incomplete fixtures and some teams entering at a late hour, Watford disputed Brighton's right to be champions. Accordingly, a challenge match was arranged and Brighton won emphatically 4-1 with the aid of five of the Liverpool irregulars.

Brighton also had two Polish players, Felix Bojar, an international left-back and an airman, Bishek Szajina-Stankowski, whose first appearance at the Goldstone had been playing for an RAF team as 'A. Pole' for fear of recriminations against his family by the Germans.

In the west country travelling problems were not conducive to participation. Exeter City took no part until the transitional season, while Bristol Rovers, Newport County, Plymouth Argyle, Swindon Town and Torquay United functioned only in the first and last campaigns, though Argyle did enter a cup competition late in 1944–45 and a Rovers side even appeared in a Gloucester Cup game with rivals City one Christmas. Swindon took on ten of the successful 1945–46 Wiltshire Youth side upon return.

Thus, with Bristol City, Cardiff City and Swansea Town isolated and finding opponents unable to have players off duty long enough to make lengthy journeys there and back to them, by 1940–41 the crisis point was reached. Swansea were particularly badly hit by opponents cancelling games. A fully regionalised League West from 1942–43 gave them regular competition if on rather a monotonous scale, their fixtures being augmented by the three non-league teams co-opted: Aberaman Athletic, Bath City and Lovell's Athletic.

Swansea managed to win the League West Cup in 1942–43, but Cardiff could only manage runners-up place in both League and Cup the following season, a fate which befell Bristol City in the 1944–45 campaign, though Cardiff pipped them for the championship on goal average. Bristol City discovered Roy Bentley, a local schoolboy, who had been with Rovers as a youngster. During the war the club was run by manager Bob Hewison and chairman George Jenkins, a local publican.

Cardiff, whose major goalscoring discovery was Billy Rees, also groomed a number of other useful forwards including Roy Clarke towards the latter stages of the seven seasons. But a broken leg in 1942 ended Trevor Morris's career. Swansea provided the top scorer in the 1945–46 League South in Trevor Ford.

Lovell's and Bath did best of the new recruits, Lovell's taking the first two League titles, Bath the last two cups, while Aberaman did at least slightly better than Swansea in League matches. However, the installation of an anti-aircraft site at the Vetch Field forced Swansea to share the local St Helen's rugby ground for a spell until 1944–45.

Up in the north-east Darlington, who had missed three whole seasons earlier on, provided the leading scorer in the Third Division in 1945–46 in Harry Clarke, who helped the club to run Rotherham close for the North Championship. He hit 48 of their 114 League and Cup goals that season, scoring in nine consecutive games and recording five, a four and two hat-tricks. Ironically his five goals came in a 6-1 win over Rotherham on 13 October as Darlington completed a double over United. More interestingly, Clarke, who had started his career with Goole, had been signed from Rotherham!

Gateshead returned after opting out of the first two campaigns. In 1941–42 they unearthed Cecil McCormack as a goalscorer and later he was joined by the veteran Newcastle striker Billy Cairns. These two were particularly effective in 1945–46, Cairns hitting four in successive games against Lincoln in a season in which he scored 40 including five against Rotherham. The previous season Gateshead had beaten Huddersfield in extra time with a goal by Harry Dryden which put them into the Tyne, Tees and Wear Cup final, where they lost 6-3 to Sunderland at Newcastle.

Newcastle United, with Albert Stubbins a feared sharp-shooter, nurtured youth to a considerable extent but failed to capture any honours. They did reach the semi-final of the Cup in 1940–41 and were the only team to prevent Preston from scoring in their run, although it was a goalless draw and they lost the tie overall. Not one of the 23 North Regional League games was drawn.

Interest remained at a high level in the FA Cup in 1945–46. The first leg of their game with Barnsley was watched by the day's biggest crowd, 60,384. Stubbins also turned out for Sunderland as a guest in the latter stages of their cup run in 1941–42 after Newcastle had been knocked out. Sunderland notched up 103 goals that season with Cliff Whitelum, who served in the Royal Artillery, leading their sharpshooters, closely followed by Raich Carter and well supported by Johnny Spuhler. Wolves in the event proved too strong for them in the final, which exposed Sunderland's often poor form in front of their own Roker Park crowd. Sunderland also missed a season and a half during the period.

Spuhler later joined Middlesbrough, where the war years saw the transition from George Camsell to Micky Fenton as chief spearhead in attack. George Stobbart was another useful scorer for the Ayresome Park team, which nonetheless functioned only fitfully as a force. In this they mirrored the abortive pre-war trio of games from which 'Boro had taken just one point.

Hartlepools United remained in the Regional League for the first season, then missed the next three before a return. In such circumstances they did well to win just a few more games than they lost during that 1943–44 return. Even the transitional season saw them having to scratch around for players, with more than 60 being called upon.

Norwich City finally had to admit that their East Anglian base was too far removed from sufficient opposition, but they buckled down to an impressive calendar of friendly fixtures and were well supported for their efforts. They were top scorers in the North Region in 1945–46 in finishing second. Suffolk neighbours Ipswich Town only returned that same season and discovered Tom Parker, a sailor stationed at nearby HMS *Ganges*, as a potential goalscoring inside-forward whose few goals included a hat-trick in the FA Cup against Wisbech.

Although Southend United's ground, used as an Officers' Training School, was returned to them in 1944, the team did not play for another year. However, numerous representative games were played at the Greyhound Stadium as well as matches involving local units. In one, Gunner Alex James stationed at nearby Shoebury Barracks appeared. James had retired at Arsenal in 1937 and became a Pools director. The FA refused to allow him back as a manager or as a wartime guest for Northampton. In the summer of 1939 he had taken a coaching job in Poland, returning a few weeks before the German invasion.

17 WITH SNOW ON THEIR BOOTS

IT WAS SAID that a last-minute stowaway boarded the Aeroflot charter carrying the Moscow Dynamo football team to London in November 1945; one used to soloing but not at such a distance and known as *Lepidoptera*. It was of course a moth.

This hardy insect had survived the early onslaught of the Russian winter and was probably seeking a warmer clime. Alas, Croydon in November was grey, cheerless and barely rating a much higher temperature. But it was probably the first passenger to disembark and vanished.

The unknown Soviet players were to do a similar disappearing act after a brief but enlightening visit and they, too, revealed similar surprising skill, fitness and stamina given the ravages of war. They were inquisitive visitors shrouded in an air of mystery, darkly suspicious of their recent allies; the first Soviet footballers to set foot in the country.

Officially it was said they had either served in the Armed Forces or been engaged on essential factory work towards the war effort. Yet, they became the chief talking point in the transitional season between the war and normal service.

Although the eastern front had moved dramatically well into Germany in the early months of 1945 and the Soviet Union had restarted its domestic championship for the first time since 1940 in the spring with Moscow Dynamo champions, it remained a puzzle.

Moscow Dynamo had presented the FA with plenty of problems and a set of conditions which they insisted were imperative to their willingness to play. The points they made were:

- They were a club side and wished to play matches against clubs, and they could not play more than one match in seven days.
- They wished to play on the day which was normally a football day in England.
- They hoped that one of their opponents would be Arsenal.
- They were unable to number their players.
- They wanted the referee who had accompanied them to officiate in one or more matches.

- They would take all their meals at the Soviet Embassy.
- They wished substitutes to be permitted (this was agreed, provided that substitutes replaced injured players).
- They wished to practise before the match on the grounds of the clubs against which they were playing.
- They aimed to give a good exhibition of football and they did not wish much social entertainment to be arranged for them.
- They asked that ample tickets should be made available on payment, for the Russian Colony (600) for the matches in London
- They wished to have an assurance that the English game would not be changed from the names submitted to them before the match unless they were first consulted.
- They wished to be given opportunities to see their opponents in action in their normal League matches.
- They were agreeable to the financial terms suggested for each of their matches, namely that, after Entertainments Tax and the usual ground expenses had been deducted, the balance should be divided on a 50–50 basis (cup-tie terms) between the competing clubs. It was also agreed that the share due to the Dynamo FC should, in the first place, be sent to the Football Association, from which the administrative and other expenses incurred on their behalf should be paid.

The Soviet team was billeted in an Army barracks. Unimpressed at first glance they sought the more homely comforts of their embassy, but were offered the Park Lane Hotel, owned by Arsenal chairman Bracewell Smith. They were due to watch Arsenal at Fulham and trained at the White City prior to their opening match at Chelsea. The impact they made they made before that fixture was dramatic, having captured the public's imagination to the extent that tens of thousands swarmed to west London on a Wednesday afternoon.

Queues began forming as early as 8 a.m. Mounted police were on duty. In addition to the grown-ups, many schoolchildren also bunked off classes. By kick-off time the ground had not only bulged at the seams but had split open in one or two places. Spectators climbed on neighbouring roofs for a better view and Chelsea's main stand appeared to have half as many on top of it as were seated underneath. More than one spectator unexpectedly came down to earth or concrete and suffered injury.

Fifteen minutes before the start the Dynamo side came out to practise, and when the teams emerged side by side each Russian carried a bouquet of flowers. They were all blue with a large, white elaborate letter D on the left breast of their jerseys and a white hem around the bottom of their shorts, which surprisingly were longer than those of their English opponents. Chelsea wore red!

Once under way, the game soon showed that the Dynamo players were well fed, physically fit, scientifically trained and well coached. The game ended in a 3-3 draw. Most onlookers seemed more than intrigued with what they had seen.

The FA received 34 requests for fixtures with the Russians from clubs in Britain and one or two organisations abroad. Rumours spread that the squad had led a spartan existence, training for weeks in mountain regions. Otherwise how could a country so war ravaged produce a team displaying such a high standard of football?

Moscow Dynamo's origins were wrapped up in the days of the Czar before the turn of the century. Two Englishmen, the Charnock brothers, Clement and Harry, owners of a mill, founded the Morozovtsi club in 1887. They even advertised in *The Times* for 'engineers, mechanics and clerks capable of playing football well'. This factory team wore the owners' favourite Blackburn Rovers colours, blue and white, and not even the changing political shades in Russia altered that, even when Moscow Dynamo were adopted by the Electrical Trades Union in 1923.

Although this was their first visit to Britain, they had made a tour of France and Czechoslovakia in the late 1930s prior to the outbreak of war. Their present captain and centre-half, Mikhail Semichastny, had been in that team. After their next game, a 10-1 win against an understrength Cardiff City at Ninian Park watched by 40,000, their already rising reputation soared. If there was some colour clash confusion – Dynamo were in all blue again, Cardiff sporting their usual blue shirts with white sleeves – it obviously upset just one team. City reserve goalkeeper Kevin McLoughlin bore the brunt of the Russian attack and another player when questioned about the performance said: 'To play well you have to have the ball and I hardly had a kick throughout the match!'

Speculation grew that perhaps this was not a club side but the national team which had trained secretly far away from the war zones. After the 1940 season there had been no official championship in the country. But one or two facts of note had emerged so that the jigsaw could be pieced together.

Certainly the majority of Dynamo players under the direction of coach Mikhail Yakushkin were their own, but they did have at least two guests in the side – Nikolai Dementieve from Moscow Spartak and Vsevolod Bobrov, who had been with Dynamo Leningrad from 1939 to 1941.

Further information came in a letter sent early in 1943 by Alexander Divochkin, captain of the Central Red Army House (CSKA) team and Hero of the Soviet Union to Eddie Hapgood the Arsenal captain. After graphically describing his own courageous front line actions under fire which earned him his country's honour as an artilleryman, Divochkin revealed some soccer facts. In 1942 Dynamo Leningrad had undertaken a tour throughout the country which included playing three games in Omsk. The same year Moscow Spartak won a League competition in the capital without suffering the loss of one point. Divochkin also pointed out, however, that the Leningrad players had helped train reserves for the front line, so clearly their time was not entirely devoted to football. In 1942 the FA received cables from the Soviet FA outlining their activities. This would seem to have been odd considering the priorities facing the country at the time.

In the spring of 1945 Moscow Torpedo had visited Sofia to play several matches when the political climate changed in Bulgaria, but a year earlier Dynamo Tbilisi had gone to Iran for two fixtures in Teheran, followed in 1945 with three games in Bucharest to celebrate the communist regime's emergence in Romania. Neither was Yugoslavia ignored. CSKA had two matches in Belgrade, one each in Zagreb and Split.

Of the 1945 Dynamo side, the centre-forward Konstantin Beskov had joined the club in 1941 from Metallourg. Alexei Khomich, soon to be nicknamed 'Tiger' by the British fans, a supple, squat but spectacular, shaven-headed goal-keeper, had first come to prominence in the Russian Army team which had won the Shah's Cup in Iran in 1943. Clearly, the game had been safely nurtured in some parts of this vast nation.

Dynamo's next game was against Arsenal, which presented manager George Allison with a giant-sized headache. Clearly, he had no wish to become further football fodder for a formidable foe. Unfortunately, it was a fact that of the 46 professionals on the Arsenal club's books, all but two were in the fighting services and as the programme for the match pointed out, only two servicemen had been demobbed, and one of these, Leslie Jones, was injured. Others were serving in various parts of the world. Denis Compton and George Curtis were in India, Bryn Jones, Alf Fields and a few more were in Italy, George Male in Palestine, Leslie Compton, Reg Lewis and George Swindin in Germany plus George Marks in Northern Ireland. Drake, Kirchen and Crayston had suffered injuries which had ended their careers. Many were stationed away from London. Moreover it was a Wednesday; weekend leave was days away. On top of this, Arsenal were not playing too well in the domestic competition and clearly needed strengthening for a match of this importance.

Nonetheless, Allison did manage to field five of his own players including Bernard Joy, flown home from Germany where he was serving in the RAF. Leslie Compton and Lewis had been required for a BAOR representative game there. Hapgood, in Brussels at the time, failed to arrive because he was fog-bound there. Strictly speaking, since the deadline for a maximum of six guests had passed earlier in the month and been reduced to three, Arsenal were even contravening Football League rules!

Allison's ace was to select Stanley Matthews and, with Stan Mortensen also an Arsenal guest that season, the side appeared to be more respectable, though the composition of it infuriated the Russians, who claimed it was an England team despite the presence of two Welshmen, Horace Cumner and goalkeeper Wyn Griffiths of Cardiff City.

However, all this appeared academic. There seemed little chance of the match even taking place, since fog had descended on the capital. This was the game in which the Russians used their own referee and after their customary 15-minute, seven-a-side practice match, the game began. Dynamo were soon in front, their speed and change of direction catching Arsenal out. Unfortunately, Griffiths was kicked in the head in the process and staggered about until half-time when he had to be replaced. Arsenal led 3-2.

A call went round the ground for another goalkeeper and Queens Park Rangers' Harry Brown arrived in the dressing-room just before Sam Bartram of Charlton. During this lengthy interval of 15 minutes, the Russians jettisoned the tea provided for them and drank vodka instead! Whether this helped their vision is not clear because the weather had closed in even more, reducing visibility to only 30 yards. Nikolai Latyshev the referee had already adopted his own method of controlling the game, patrolling close to one touchline, while his two English linesmen operated on the other.

Tempers frayed in the fog farce. Spectators saw glimpses, the players little more. Semichastny at one stage climbed on Ronnie Rooke's back only to be shaken off with a black eye for his attempted leap-frog, while Rooke proceeded to score what should have been the equaliser at 4-4. But the referee awarded a free-kick against Rooke. Latyshev tried to send Arsenal's George Drury off but his attempt was ignored. Then came a Russian substitution. Trofimov was replaced but remained on the field for several minutes. The Russians had 12 men. With Dynamo still leading, Allison asked the First Secretary of the Soviet embassy to approach the referee about abandoning the game, but this was refused; and thus it ended. Receipts from the 54,620 crowd were £10,500.

Yet again, however, through the mist there had been more than the myth of the Dynamo's play to be suitably impressed. Joy the Arsenal centre-half said of them: 'The ball was not held but pushed first time, not to a man, but into a space between two opponents. One, two and sometimes three men closed in at top speed after the ball and when it was accepted, the rest of the team moved quickly to adjust their positions.'

Oddly enough, Johnny Harris, who had occupied the centre-half position when Chelsea had originally played them, had been impressed only with what they did without the ball. 'They weren't as good footballers – at least I didn't think they were – in general play, as our fellows, but they had us beaten in the art of moving into the open space.'

Their style was such that they had a fluidity about them which had everyone up when they attacked, all back on defence, though they were noticeably much happier going forward. At the banquet after the Arsenal match it was noted that the only Russian player to take part in the subsequent dancing was Trofimov, who revealed amazing powers of recovery, showing no sign of the limp which had developed at White Hart Lane.

The biggest crowd to watch the Russians was at Ibrox, where 90,000 saw the 2-2 draw with Rangers. The Russians took exception to George Young, who had been off injured and who, they suspected, was not eligible. They also objected to Jimmy Caskie, labelling him an Everton player. Anyway, once it started, Dynamos went two up, Khomich saved one penalty hit straight at him by Willie Waddell, but was beaten from the spot by another hotly disputed award after the English referee changed his mind when a Scottish linesman flagged. George Young scored. Jimmy Smith had earlier reduced the arrears. Dynamos had 12 on the field for a time here, too!

At the end of the match the Dynamos physician said: 'Rangers are the fittest athletes we have ever played against.' Their trainer added: 'Rangers are easily the best footballers we have met in Britain. We have no complaint.'

A total of 271,000 spectators had watched the four games involving the Russians. The FA were preparing for a fifth to be played at Villa Park against a representative team. They selected as follows: Swift; Scott, Hardwick, Soo, Franklin, Mercer, Matthews, Carter or Pye, Lawton, Shackleton and Leslie Smith. It was virtually an England eleven. Aston Villa printed 70,000 tickets in anticipation of another bonanza at the box office. Then came the bombshell. The news was picked up in England from a Moscow radio station that Dynamo had been called home.

The Russians apparently knew nothing of this and had expected to play the FA XI at Villa Park on the following Wednesday. But off they went; not straight back home as it happened, because they stopped off in Sweden to beat Norrköping 5-0, underlining perhaps the politics which had quickly removed them from western deviousness.

18 TRAGEDY AT BOLTON

THERE WERE SOME poignant stories of what was then the worst disaster in the history of British football at Bolton on 9 March 1946. None was more heartrending than of the wife who packed her husband's lunch so that he could finish work early and get to the cup-tie in time for the kick-off. It was his and others' last meal.

Part of the Home Office report read: 'The disaster was unique. There was no collapse of a structure, it was the first example in the history of football following, of serious casualties inflicted by a crowd upon itself.'

Spectators were slow to assemble that day considering the importance of the occasion: a sixth-round second-leg FA Cup-tie against Stoke City for whom Stanley Matthews was playing. Bolton were 2-0 up on the first leg. It was not before one o'clock that the railway embankment at the northern end of Burnden Park began to fill, but soon after half past two it was full, with people still filing in and thousands waiting outside to gain admittance. There was a delay in closing the turnstiles and even this did not deter those keen enough to climb over the obstacles to entry.

In the north-west corner of the embankment as the Home Office report put it:

> A boy on the fence, just inside the entrance, finds the press too great for him and his father wanted to take him out. The only way out the father can find is by picking the padlock which locks the exit gate at the side of the 'shelter' containing the two turnstiles. Between 2.45 and 2.50 p.m. he and his boy get out and the wide open door invites, and gets, a rush of people from the crowd outside the turnstile.

At five minutes to three the teams came on to the field while police and officials tried to cope with a situation which was already out of hand and rapidly worsening. The sheer weight of numbers pressing forward forced two barriers to collapse, piling spectators on top of each other, three or even four deep and others trodden underfoot.

There was a prompt kick-off at three o'clock with police, ambulance and doctors from the crowd attending the casualties. The majority of the huge crowd were unaware of the tragedy. On discovering fatalities, referee George Dutton of Warwick was informed and at twelve minutes past he took the players off into the dressing-room.

Thirty-three spectators had died. Five hundred were treated at First Aid posts and 24 of these were taken to hospital. All the casualties occurred in the space of ten square yards near a corner flag.

At 3.20 p.m. the Chief Constable urged a resumption of play to avoid panic, since all but a few spectators outside the immediate area of the disaster were oblivious of it. The closed stand which was used as a Ministry of Food store was opened for a thousand spectators, while another thousand were spread around the running track to ring the touchlines, which had to be redrawn with sawdust, shrinking the pitch slightly. The game restarted at 3.25 p.m. with no interval and ended goalless at five o'clock. A total of 65,000 people paid for admission while almost another 20,000 either attempted or succeeded in gaining access to the ground.

During the hold-up a goods train was stopped at a signal near the ground. A score of people clambered on to the coal tender of the locomotive to obtain a view of the game. The signal arm fell and the train moved off with its recently acquired complement of passengers.

The full impact of that horrendous afternoon was to dawn the following day and was aptly summed up by Matthews himself. 'The shock next morning was even worse. I sat down to breakfast, but when I picked up a Sunday newspaper and read the tragic facts, I pushed the food before me aside and went to my room. I felt sick.'

The inquest verdict was one of accidental death. Recommendations from the inquiry included an examination of grounds for safety standards and mechanical calculation of turnstile entries. Alterations to the railway embankment cost £5,500. The Mayor of Bolton's Disaster Fund realised £40,000.

By an odd irony the *Bolton Evening News* had commented on exactly the same day 17 years earlier that 'one means of entrance to the huge railway embankment is tragically inadequate'.

19 THE CUP THAT CHEERS

T HE RETURN OF the FA Cup was a sign that getting back to something approaching normality was not far off. True, there was a new look to the competition as two legs of each tie were to be played on alternate Saturdays for the first two rounds proper, then on the Saturday plus the following midweek for the third to the fifth rounds inclusive. For the sixth round it reverted to alternate Saturdays, but the semi-finals were single knock-out games.

The FA had wisely decided that every club should have the opportunity of a home game in order to distribute as fairly as possible much-needed finance after the war years, even though many clubs had turned deficits into the black through cutting down on players wages, if nothing else. But it was a gesture much appreciated.

If the aggregate score was level, there were to be ten minutes each way extra time. If still undecided, the match would be determined by the first subsequent goal scored. Only if daylight failed was a third match to be played.

The 1939–40 competition had managed to complete its extra preliminary round, minus one replay, before the close-down. This was of course scrapped, as there were understandably fewer entries six years on with clubs still sorting themselves out. The extra preliminary round had shrunk from 32 to 4 ties. The two-legged tag did not apply until the competition proper. Strangely enough, Third Division Chester were exempt to the third round. The FA explained it was because of finishing in the top half of the table in 1944–45 but, in reality, they had been nearer the bottom!

Guest players were not permitted, or at least this was the intention. There was a spate of instances contravening the ruling, either through ignorance or by design. The usual manner in which the culprits were discovered was when the opposition, having lost a tie, managed to winkle out the identity of an ineligible player or some other misdemeanour. Not that bigger clubs were against guests. Spurs for one wanted them. With players still scattered around at home and abroad serving in the forces, it was often a headache finding eleven legitimate players. Jock Davie, the Brighton centre-forward had been assisting Chesterfield, but was stationed in Newcastle. He arrived in Brighton at 1 a.m. one morning and had to spend the night in a police cell!

Perhaps the FA directive on guests had not reached Wales, because in the first qualifying round there were three cases of clubs being thrown out. Bangor City beat Rhyl 4-1, Aberaman & Aberdare, now a combined team, disposed of Llanelli 6-1 and Ebbw Vale defeated Cardiff Corinthians 3-1. However, there was ample evidence that any protest had to be made within a certain period and there was some laxness on the FA's part in dealing with queries arising. Anyway, the losing Welsh trio were reinstated for the second qualifying round. However, Barry Town's 10-0 win over Clevedon Town went unnoticed apart from the scoreline, despite the presence of a certain Charlton Athletic player and Welsh international, Bert Turner.

The *Clevedon Mercury* reported: 'Barry included several well-known League players such as Ross of Sheffield Wednesday, McCarthy of Liverpool, Ferguson and Turner of Charlton and Clayton the old Wolves captain.' *The Wiltshire Times* and *Trowbridge Advertiser* confirmed Turner's appearance at right-half.

However, according to the *Barry Herald*, Ferguson was a Raith Rovers player. This newspaper listed the team as: Harris; Snowden, Bellfield, Turner, Jones, Ross, Martin, McCarthy, Masters, Clayton and Ferguson. For the second qualifying round it added: 'Clayton did not play by mutual arrangement, because of FA ruling he would not play against Lovell's.'

Turner's last match for Barry was against Llanelli on 20 October – a 7-1 FA Cup win – as he had been posted to another service station prior to demob. Clearly, there had been no attempt to disguise his appearances for the Welsh club. He did not play for Charlton again until 10 November. Barry missed Turner against Lovell's; they lost 5-1.

In the third qualifying round Newport (Isle of Wight) protested under the rule which required players to be registered 14 days before a tie. Thus, their 1-0 defeat by Cowes Sports in the local derby attended by 2,500 was overturned. There were problems elsewhere. Bedford Avenue defeated Letchworth Town 1-0. Letchworth protested unsuccessfully, although they did have their fee refunded.

From the pages of the *Leiston Observer* on 27 October: 'Leiston go into the next round of the FA Cup against Chelmsford City at Chelmsford on 3 November due to the FA upholding their protest against the inclusion of unregistered naval players in the Lowestoft side.'

In mitigation, the *Lowestoft Journal* reported: 'After considerable difficulty the side was made up of seven players from HMS Martello and four from local clubs.' Somewhat surprisingly Lowestoft Town had drawn the game 2-2.

On 19 October the *Nuneaton Observer* reported:

It was announced yesterday that Nuneaton Borough FC officials had received a letter from the FA stating that Worcester City had protested against Bolan who was a member of the side that defeated them 1-0 in the last round of the FA Cup.

The letter pointed out that the protest had not been handed in within the prescribed period and therefore was not valid, but asked for the club's observations on the matter.

Though the club requested a ruling re-availability of club players in the FA Cup, nothing appeared to be forthcoming until the *Nuneaton Observer* again sprang into print on 2 November as follows: 'Nuneaton Borough have been ruled out of the FA Cup and fined ten guineas [£10.50] for playing guest players against Bourneville Athletic.'

The match had ended in an 8-1 win for Nuneaton. The newspaper went on to explain that as the club had not received the requested ruling they fielded their strongest team.

There was a protest of some kind brought by Coalville Town against Kettering Town after their 2-1 fourth qualifying round defeat. Nothing came of it and the remainder of the competition was mercifully free of such squabbles. Oddly enough, Jimmy Scoular playing for Gosport Borough in an earlier qualifying round was well known even though he subsequently played for the then Cup holders Portsmouth without any problems.

Already, the growth in attendances had been evident as the wartime seasons went on and prospects of ultimate victory increased. The return of the Cup enforced this to an amazing degree.

These home and away matches heightened interest and new attendance records were established along with increased receipts. Though the Burnden Park tragedy cast a grim shadow over the tournament as a whole, the official attendance there of 65,419 yielded a sum of just over £6,600, much of which was lost in ground improvements effected in the wake of the disaster.

Previously, on 9 February other records had been established. Sunderland's game with Birmingham City was watched by 44,820 and brought in some £4,631; the Preston v Charlton match on the same day was attended by 39,303 with receipts of £3,730. Four days later Bradford and Barnsley met with 29,341 crowded into Park Avenue and the takings were £2,886, while Middlesbrough against Bolton attracted 49,329 who paid £5,672. On 2 February Aston Villa's meeting with Derby had been played before a massive 76,588 at Villa Park which provided receipts of £8,651. A new Rotherham gate record had been set up on 31 January when United played Barnsley in front of 19,563 who paid £1,715.

There was equally impressive support for both semi-finals. At Maine Road the Birmingham v Derby replay had 80,483 in attendance with £13,202 taken. At Villa Park it was 70,819 for the Charlton v Bolton affair. Receipts here of £18,011 were a record for any game outside London or Glasgow.

Increased prices of admission for the final at Wembley were responsible for a steep rise in receipts compared with pre-war days. The gross amount was £43,378 but after Entertainments Tax deductions of £19,840 the net receipts of £23,538 were lower by £725 than the best pre-war figure!

With two bites at each tie, there was ample opportunity for teams to stage recoveries without losing the essential ingredient of the Cup's uncertainty which had made the competition traditionally famous. In fact the early giant-killers in the competition proved to be the reprieved Newport (Isle of Wight), Shrewsbury Town and Lovell's Athletic. Surprisingly, Newport accounted for Clapton Orient 3-2 on aggregate while Shrewsbury established a commanding 5-goal lead over Walsall from their first leg which saw them safely through despite losing the return 4-1.

Lovell's experience in the Football League West rubbed off well on them because they had a 4-1 win at home against Bournemouth and only lost the second game 3-2, after being pulled back to 4-4 overall after 31 minutes. Lovell's, managed by Ray McDonald, a former Newport County Welsh amateur international, had several of their wartime players on parade. The attraction of the Dynamos at Cardiff kept the gate down to under 4,000.

Mansfield needed extra time to take care of Gainsborough Trinity, while both Chorley against Accrington and Yorkshire Amateurs over Lincoln had first leg success but lost out on aggregate. Yet, for retrieving a lost situation, few bettered Aldershot's performance against local rivals Reading. At Elm Park, The Shots were beaten 3-1 and at half-time in the return at home they were losing 2-1 which left them 5-2 down on aggregate. Aldershot twice levelled the score before they managed to rifle through the Reading defence to win 7-3 for an 8-6 aggregate win. Harry Brooks scored five times for them and also forced a defender to put through his own goal.

Brooks hit another five in his next Cup match against Newport in a 7-0 win, the first player in the history of the Cup to hit as many in successive games. Aldershot followed up with a 5-0 win away. This 12-0 aggregate was the highest margin of success in the competition.

There were the usual mishaps en route. The Slough coach broke down on Mitcham Common, the team arrived 40 minutes late and eight minutes from time bad light stopped play with Bromley leading 2-1. They tried again the following Thursday. This time fog nearly caused another abandonment with Bromley 6-1 ahead, but after consultation with both linesmen, the referee allowed a finish. Bromley's takings were a club record £450. They eventually succumbed to Watford with two 40-year-olds, Clark and Mallett, in the team. Walthamstow Avenue put up a spirited show against Brighton and also collected club record receipts of £640, from a 5-figure gate.

In the return leg on the south coast Jim Lewis skippered Avenue. He had been only 23 when he appeared in an FA Cup tie for the club on the same Goldstone Ground against Southwick on 15 December 1930.

Lovell's renewed acquaintance with their old League West sparring partners from Bath City in the second round, Lovell's winning 7-3 on aggregate, but as the only non-league survivors, their aspirations ended against Wolves. In the first leg they led 2-0 at half-time and had missed a penalty. It proved costly. Wolves won 4-2 towards a massive 12-3 aggregate in round three.

There was no shortage of goals. The highest aggregate came in the third round where Leeds and Middlesbrough drew 4-4 at Elland Road with Boro winning the return 7-2. Yet Portsmouth, the holders, quietly went out to Birmingham via an own goal by Reg Flewin. Queens Park Rangers and Crystal Palace could only manage one goal between them and their games included a replay. The draw for the round had also been made in four regions to cut down on travelling.

Arsenal suffered their worst defeat in the competition, losing 6-0 at West Ham and they retrieved little more than their honour in the second leg, winning by a single goal. At Upton Park some 3,000 gained admission after the gates had been shut by clambering over bomb damaged walls and fences. The Hammers chairman W. Cearns pleaded with them to send entrance money so it could be donated to the East Ham Memorial Hospital.

Another remarkable result occurred in the fourth round when Manchester City had a comfortable 3-1 win at Bradford only to find themselves humiliated in front of their own supporters at Maine Road a few days later. Bradford beat them 8-2 with Jackie Gibbons scoring four goals to win 9-5 on aggregate. Top scorers in this round were Aston Villa, who beat Millwall 9-1 at Villa Park and 4-2 at The Den.

In the fifth round it was appropriate that the eventual finalists Derby and Charlton each scored 6-0 wins in the home legs of their respective matches against Brighton and Preston. Derby also won 4-1 at Brighton while Charlton drew 1-1 at Preston.

Charlton again scored six goals this time in the sixth round against Brentford, recording a 6-3 win at home and 3-1 at Griffin Park. Birmingham also managed half a dozen against Bradford after a 2-2 draw and then forced a semi-final replay with Derby, drawing 1-1 at Hillsborough before losing by four clear goals at Maine Road, but only after extra time.

Clearly, Derby's ability to press home advantage in extra time was to prove of benefit to them in the final itself. Only a week before they had lost to Charlton 2-1 at The Valley in a League game, but had then omitted their two pricey signings, Raich Carter and Peter Doherty. With this formidable pair of inside-forwards restored to the team they eventually overcame Charlton, though it was not until after normal time. Derby had gone through the ritual of having a gypsy curse removed from them and it seemed to have worked when Bert Turner had the misfortune to put through his own goal to give them the lead.

Within 30 seconds, however, Turner had the opportunity to equalise and did so from a free-kick which struck Doherty's left leg and was deflected in. Thus, Turner became the first finalist to score for both teams, having made his season's debut, of course, for another . . .

For Charlton it was not their first defeat in the Cup that season. They had lost 2-1 at Fulham in the third round to become the first club to reach the final having already been beaten at an earlier stage.

Derby took their goal tally in the competition to 37, of which Carter had notched 12 and Doherty 10, but the pair were not the leading scorers in the 1945–46 tournament. Brooks's two individual efforts of five each for Aldershot helped to take his total to 13.

The Carter–Doherty partnership was the inspiration for Derby's success. Doherty had been transferred from Manchester City just before he was demobbed from the RAF in 1945. His transfer fee was £7,000. Carter's signing was for £500 less but at rather more of a hectic pace and was a close call to beat the deadline for third-round eligibility.

Carter and Jack Catterall, the Derby secretary, travelled from Derby to York by train. Telephoning the Baseball Ground to check whether the move was still on, they tried for a train to Sunderland but were held up by the first peacetime Christmas rush, missed their connection and hurriedly had to hire a taxi, arriving with just an hour to spare.

They made a tiring return journey all the way by taxi and, not surprisingly, Carter was not at his best the following day when he made his debut for a Derby side beaten 1-0 at Birmingham in League South.

The combination of Carter and Doherty was natural and instinctive. The two blended perfectly and, having already played together as guests for Derby, knew each other's play at first hand. Derby had started their impressive run by winning the Northern League and Midland Cup in 1944–45. Carter's strengths were his vision as a schemer and powerful shot; Doherty was tireless in defence and attack using his speed to turn one into the other, but always dwelling delightfully on the ball.

The Rams were by no means a two-man team. Even injuries to stalwarts like Sammy Crooks, Jack Parr and Frank Boulton in the Cup run had not affected their performances. In goal there was the veteran Vic Woodley, given a new lease of life when signed from Bath City. In front of him were the two Jacks, skipper Nicholas 'Old Faithful' and Howe, recently back from war service in India.

The middle line of Jimmy Bullions, Leon Leuty and Walter Urban Musson known as 'Chick', was as varied in construction as it was successful in action: the industrious Bullions a miner, Leuty a cool, commanding pivot and the stodgy-looking but skilful, strong and stamina-stacked Musson.

Fledgling Reg Harrison, deputising on the right wing, body-swerve specialist Dally Duncan on the opposite flank, plus Jackie Stamps, another miner, leading the line and scoring two typically opportunist goals, were all equally important parts of the whole functioning team.

Brentford players receive gas mask instruction from Police Inspector Clark as war clouds gather in April 1939. Left to right: Jack Holliday, Bobby Allen, Ted Gaskell, Sam Briddon, George Poyser, Charlie Longdon and Billy Scott.

A pre-war innovation was the numbering of shirts. Suitably designated, Chelsea players take the field for the public trial game at Stamford Bridge in August 1939.

Bolton Wanderers, one of the first teams to enlist *en masse*, in step for this 1939 parade. Left to right: Jack Ithell, Danny Winter, Jack Roberts, George Catterall, Don Howe and Harry Goslin.

The first Wartime Cup final: West Ham United triumph over Blackburn Rovers 1-0 during the week of evacuation from Dunkirk. Sam Small scored the only goal. Archie Macaulay holds the cup with pride surrounded by his delighted West Ham colleagues. Left to right: Corporal Norman Corbett, Ted Fenton, Charlie Bicknell and George Foreman.

Arsenal players spent part of the 1939 summer filming the *Arsenal Stadium Mystery*. Action for it was taken from the Arsenal v Brentford match; the Oxford University team was used for close-up shots. The group here includes George Male, Alf Fields, Jack Crayston, Eddie Hapgood, Alf Kirchen and George Swindin.

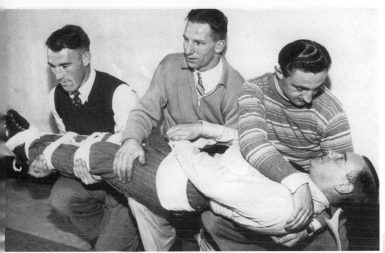

Preston North End players Emlyn Williams, Andy Beattie and Lloyd Iceton practise first aid at their local ARP centre in November 1939.

D.C. Thomson

Sunderland's Raich Carter joined the Auxiliary Fire Service and even contemplated making a career of it rather than continue to play football. But he changed his mind and later enlisted in the RAF.

Topical Times, January 20, 1940.

They're Army P.T. Instructors Now—By MAC

TOM HOLLEY
LEEDS UNITED C.HALF
Fine Athlete
wanted to be a
Policeman or a
Teacher one time.
Among other
accomplishments
is a LINGUIST

BERT SPROSTON
MANCHESTER
CITY & ENGLAND
BACK

Att'd.
TANK
CORPS.

AT PRESENT
HELPING THE
ARMY TO
"MASTER
GERMAN"!

was an
apprentice
PLUMBER

HE
MAKES
'EM
"JUMP"
TO IT!

Six footer
—moustache
—& one of
football's

arresting
personalities!

RIGHT MAN TO GET
TANKS IN CONDITION

ANDREW BEATTIE PRESTON N.E.
& SCOTLAND BACK—once
an Aberdeen Quarryman

JOE MERCER
EVERTON & ENGLAND
WING HALF

Fine all rounder
—TOP GRADE
SWIMMER

His classes
have got to
FEEL AT
HOME IN
THE
WATER!

like
Andy,
his boys
will KEEP COOL
& BE AS
TOUGH AS
GRANITE

MAC
'40

The *Topical Times* kept a light-hearted note of the activities of footballers in uniform during 1939–40 through the artistry of 'Mac'.

The second Wartime Cup final and the Preston defence is under attack from the Arsenal front line, though it was the Lancashire team which eventually won after a replay.

Old Trafford was just one of a number of football grounds damaged by bombs during the Second World War. In fact it was out of commission until well after hostilities ceased.

Manchester Evening News

On RAF guard duty: Ted Drake of Arsenal (left) and Charlton goalkeeper Sam Bartram, before they both became PT instructors.

Cliff Bastin – once known as 'Boy Bastin' – sporting his ARP helmet as he and others found war work in the early days of the conflict.

Birmingham's patience at being shunned for early wartime participation was rewarded with an England v Wales international in October 1941. England back row left to right: Harry Goslin, Joe Bacuzzi, George Marks, Denis Compton, Stan Cullis. Front: Stanley Matthews, Jimmy Hagan, Eddie Hapgood, Don Welsh, Joe Mercer, Maurice Edelston.

Wales often provided England with strong opposition in the war years. They were narrowly beaten 2-1 at St Andrews. Back row left to right: George Green, Billy Hughes, George Poland, Tommy Jones, Horace Cumner, Kendrick (trainer). Front: Idris Hopkins, Doug Witcomb, Bert Turner, Don Dearson, Leslie Jones, Billy James.

Informally happy group of Arsenal players after their 1943 League South Cup final win over Charlton Athletic. Left to right: Laurie Scott, George Marks, George Male, Bernard Joy, Ted Drake, Alf Kirchen, Denis Compton.

The beginning of hostilities in the Second World War meant footballers had to look around for employment before being conscripted for the services. Tommy Lawton signs on the dole.

'Wizard of the Dribble' Stanley Matthews turns autograph hunter and manages to persuade Field Marshal Bernard Montgomery to sign on the dotted line.

In February 1941 exiles from Holland and Belgium met in an international at Walthamstow, east London, the teams composed mainly of servicemen. Prince Bernhard in army uniform holds a watching brief and two favours.

In 1914 after the Germans overran Luxembourg they invaded Belgium and so precipitated the start of the First World War. The formation of the First Footballers Battalion was a much appreciated gesture from the sport – a tradition carried on through the Territorial Army before the outbreak of war in 1939.

20 THE GOAL RUSH

WHATEVER ARGUMENTS ARE raised about the substitute regional competitions, there was no denying that goalscoring reached hitherto unmatched proportions. The freedom of any fear of relegation and the realisation that entertainment was paramount produced the right attitude on the field. Take this, together with the uncertain nature of teams and their composition, and the natural outcome was a surfeit of scoring: an integral part of the overall spectacle.

Inevitably, individuals were provided with the opportunity to enhance their reputations as marksmen. No one did better in this respect than Jock Dodds of Blackpool, who scored more club goals than any other player in the seven seasons. His haul was 253, 227 of them for Blackpool.

Born in Grangemouth, Stirlingshire on 7 September 1915 he went to live in Durham when he was only 12. He learned his football there and it was only in a bid to emphasise his Scottish background that he called himself 'Jock' since he had been christened Ephraim.

At the age of 15 he was taken onto the ground staff at Huddersfield Town, turning professional with them at the age of 17 in 1932. He spent two unsuccessful years there before being given a free transfer to Sheffield United. Although on the losing side in the 1936 FA Cup final, he was the youngest player on the field at 20 and near the end of the game he had hit the foot of an upright.

He was transformed at Bramall Lane. In five seasons he was United's top scorer in each League term with 19, 35, 23, 21 and 27 goals respectively. He asked for a transfer and in March 1939 he was sold to Blackpool for £10,000.

Dodds developed into a bustling leader, difficult to knock off the ball when in full flow but capable of considerable skill. He was rarely dominated in the air and as an extravert character endeared himself to crowds. He did receive one FA warning for 'over robust' play. His most prolific wartime season was 1941–42 when he notched 77 goals in all games including a record run in which he registered in each of 17 consecutive games. In seven successive matches between March–April 1940 he had also notched up 18 goals.

One player who did manage to score more goals overall was Tommy Lawton. He achieved 252 League and Cup goals plus another 92 in international and representative games. Albert Stubbins of Newcastle, employed locally and almost consistently available, reached 230 goals for his club alone in the period. His overall total included 15 goals in five consecutive games in 1941: 4, 3, 3, 3, 2. Five times he scored five goals in a match.

International and representative honours did not come his way to the same degree as Dodds or Lawton, but he was a forceful centre-forward on the ground and with his head as well as possessing clever footwork plus the ability to hold his forward line together. Stubbins was 20 when the war started. As a youngster he had spent some time in the USA but returned and was signed by Newcastle in 1937. He made his debut for United in 1938–39 and scored four times in 23 League games.

Understandably, Newcastle boss Stan Seymour came down in favour of Stubbins over Lawton. He said: 'The only advantage Lawton might have over Stubbins is with his heading, Stubbins is cleverer on the ball.'

Lawton had shot to fame at 16, baby-faced, at Burnley. He scored a hat-trick in his first game after turning professional at 17, and in December 1936 Everton paid £6,500 for his signature. In the last pre-war campaign he had been the First Division's leading scorer with 35 League goals and had scored four of his team's five when war was declared.

His heading ability was masterful; he had the knack of being able to rise above opponents, seeming to hover momentarily and then stretch his neck muscles further to obtain extra height and force. He was just as lethal on the deck with either foot, placing his shots with precision and power. He also possessed an inborn sense of unselfishness and would defer acceptance of a half-chance if a colleague was better positioned and available to take a pass.

His greatest asset on the ground was, however, his ability to gain control and hit the ball in the same movement, which gave him the edge over defenders in tight situations. On 27 January 1945 he scored his 400th goal at the Gwladys Street end of Goodison Park. The *Athletic News Annual 1945–46* said that Lawton 'has physique with speed, thrust with eagerness to dash between the backs, ability to hold together the forward line and to seize scoring chances with head and foot'.

Lawton was useful at athletics. He was pressed into service in the Aldershot District Military Athletic Championships while stationed there and won the 100 yards and the long jump – all this, bearing in mind that he was flat-footed and needed arch supports in his football boots.

Others had their own special qualities. Ted Drake's directness had a wholehearted honesty about it and, though he was the toughest of the leaders in many respects, he was scrupulously fair in his shoulder to shoulder encounters. His marksmanship was unerring: witness on 14 December 1935 when he scored seven goals for Arsenal at Aston Villa with eight shots. His first six efforts produced goals.

Ronnie Rooke, the Fulham centre-forward, was a solid, immovable leader who could hit the ball hard with scarcely any backlift to his shots and like Dodds could swerve the ball wickedly at times.

Jack Rowley was feared because of the unexpectedness of his shooting, chiefly with his left foot. His finishing prowess came to fruition in 1941–42 when he and Arsenal's Reg Lewis were vying for the goalscoring honours. Rowley scored 11 in the first two matches, made it 15 in three while Lewis had reached ten. As a result the Manchester United forward was selected to play for the Football League against the Scottish League on 11 October 1941.

Despite the claims of these players and others of established scoring reputations elsewhere, it was a fact that the highest individual performances achieved home and away were contributed by others.

Leslie Compton, a reserve full-back in pre-war times at Arsenal, was converted to centre-forward in an emergency early in the war and responded with several outstanding performances. He was the only player with a League club in the war period to reach double figures, a feat he achieved on 8 February 1941 when he scored ten goals in Arsenal's 15-2 win over Clapton Orient at White Hart Lane. Six were headed in. Compton's switch also brought praise from Charlton's manager Jimmy Seed on another occasion: 'He must have had something like 30 shots at goal against us and every one of them was bang between the sticks.'

Away from home, the best performance came from Bill Hullett who notched seven of Lincoln's goals in their 8-1 win at Mansfield on 11 April 1942. Hullett was a Manchester United player who had graduated at Old Trafford from New Brighton and Plymouth Argyle. Given that Arsenal were playing away throughout the war, Leslie Compton would claim to have topped this effort.

Tommy Sale of Stoke City was another who blossomed. He was in his second spell with the club and had been a professional for over a decade. He had gone to Blackburn in 1935–36 after seven years' service, returning in March 1938. In 1941–42 he scored 55 League and Cup goals for Stoke including a record 12 hat-tricks. One of these was a 'double' treble against Walsall on 3 January 1942 in the Cup during an 8-0 win and another feat was five goals in a 9-0 win over Tranmere on 22 November 1941. In 1943–44 Sale hit 30 goals and Freddie Steele 20. The following season Sale's tally was 33 and his overall career total topped 300.

When Southampton met Chelsea on 29 December 1945, the visitors included a useful sprinkling of names including Lawton and Payne, but they were overshadowed by the sensational display given by Saints' centre-forward Doug McGibbon who opened the scoring with a goal timed at four and three-fifths seconds. McGibbon went on to rattle up six goals in the 7-0 victory.

Lawton had also been overlooked as the ace sharp-shooter on 17 February 1945 when he was guesting for Millwall at Brighton and was on the losing side as the locals won 6-2. Cyril Hodges guesting from Arsenal scored four times for

Albion. Two West Bromwich players Billy Elliott and Harry 'Popeye' Jones scored in 11 successive games. Jones did so in 1939–40, Elliott in 1941–42. Albion were twice breathlessly involved in 1941. On 29 March they defeated Walsall 4-1. Three goals two from Albion came in 90 seconds of the first half. Then, on 22 November they scored eight goals inside 32 minutes of the second half after leading 2-0 at half-time. They won 10-1 with Billy Richardson getting six.

Walsall also had their moments. On 9 November 1940 in their 11-1 victory over Notts County, Ted Vinall scored four including a hat-trick of penalties in the second half. On 11 October 1941 they scored two out of three first half penalties and beat Nottingham Forest 8-2.

Other penalty curiosities included York's Arthur Jepson, their Port Vale guest, saving two spot kicks in the closing stages to enable his team to win 4-3 away at Bradford City in a War Cup first-round game on 22 February 1941. That same day Len Butt of Blackburn scored a hat-trick of penalties in a 5-1 win at Oldham.

On 1 February 1941 Leicester beat Nottingham Forest 6-2 and scored three goals in three minutes including two penalties by Bert Howe. Harold Barton of Sheffield United also had a trio of spot kicks for Rotherham on 8 November 1944, but they still lost 6-5 at Barnsley.

Spurs' amateur centre-forward Jack Gibbons was particularly harsh on Clapton Orient. He scored a hat-trick in each of four consecutive games against them: 21 December 1940 (9-0), 28 December (7-0), 5 January 1941 (3-0) and 11 January (9-0). The first two games were in the League, the last couple in the London Cup.

Jimmy Currier, leading the Manchester City attack, scored five in each of two games in successive weeks against Rochdale. On 4 January 1942 he did so in a 9-1 win and on 11 January when City won 6-1 at Rochdale.

When Mansfield beat West Bromwich 6-2 in a second round War Cup game on 8 March 1941, Charlie Rickards scored a hat-trick in three and a half minutes. Only a week earlier probably the fastest-ever threesome had occurred when Peters did so in only two minutes for Cambridge University in a friendly against Kettering.

West Bromwich were also involved in another high-scoring affair against Cardiff on 30 August 1941 when in their 6-3 win they hit five goals in the first 11 minutes. Beriah Moore opening the scoring for Cardiff in the third minute, Billy Elliott equalised three minutes later. Albion added three more in the space of three minutes. In the four-all draw between Bury and Bolton on the same day, three goals were scored in the first three minutes. The opener went to Bolton and then Bury replied with two.

In a Cup game in 1941–42 West Bromwich were five goals down to Stoke before recovering to reduce the arrears to 5-3. In the return Albion won 6-1 for an aggregate score of 9-6.

In Aldershot's 7-4 win over Millwall on 31 October 1942 there were three individual hat-tricks: Dave McCulloch and Lawton for Aldershot, Wilf Heathcote for the Lions. On 14 November West Ham were beating Millwall 6-1 at half-time but just held on to win 7-5.

Yet, one of the highest scoring games was watched by a mere handful of people. When Huddersfield whacked 11 past Rochdale on 22 March 1941, only 356 people were scattered around the ground.

Luton suffered three successive heavy defeats in 1943, losing 11-3 at home to Millwall on 2 January, 8-0 at Brighton a week later and 11-0 at Southampton seven days after that. Later in the same year Liverpool won consecutive games 9-0, beating Chester on 13 November and Southport the next week.

Top scorer in the 1945–46 season among the First and Second Division clubs was Trevor Ford of Swansea. He had joined the club as a 17-year-old left-back, but while in the Army was converted to centre-forward where he put on height and weight to become a real handful of a bustling leader for defences to combat.

That between-the-wars-living-goalscoring-legend Dixie Dean, famous for 379 goals in 437 League games alone, had joined Sligo Rovers in the League of Ireland in January 1939 when still only 32, though slowed by a series of injuries. He was largely lost to the game in the war years. His tally for Sligo had been 11 in 11 matches. They had finished runners-up in both League and Cup, but on the outbreak of war he returned to Merseyside, taking a job in a slaughterhouse before being called up for the Army in 1940.

He joined the King's (Liverpool) Regiment and later transferred to the Royal Tank Regiment where he became a corporal mechanical instructor. Dean rarely played, but during his basic training at Formby he was asked to pick a team to play against the PT instructors and his scratch team of 'unknowns' won 8-3. He also scored eight as a guest for Cambridge Town in a 15-1 drubbing of an RAF XI, including six in 39 minutes. Most of his other games were in unit football, but on 13 September 1941 he scored three in a 5-2 win for an Army team against Southampton at Warminster. However, he did turn out for York against Gateshead two months later on 22 November and scored a goal in a 4-3 defeat. The ex-Everton striker made no other appearances for them.

Individual goal contributions accumulated towards huge totals for clubs. On 5 December 1942 a new record of goals on a single day of League matches in England was established when the 39 regional fixtures produced 225 goals for an average of 5.77 goals per game. Only seven teams failed to score at all, but Chelsea could only draw goalless with Brighton. Blackpool's 8-3 win over Oldham was the highest aggregate.

Massive scores produced fast rates, too. On 9 March 1940 West Ham were leading Fulham by a George Foreman goal just before the interval. Afterwards the Hammers hit four in five minutes mid-way through the half, the F force of Foreman, Foxall (two) and Fenton being the marksmen. Fulham themselves were on the happy end of some snappy scoring later in the season. On 25 May in a War Cup game against Everton they were two goals ahead in 60 seconds. Horace Woodward scored in six seconds after a pass by Rooke and just three touches of the ball. Then Rooke himself added a second as Woodward returned the compliment.

There were other unusual scoring feats. Ron Greenwood, who had joined Bradford Park Avenue in December 1945, was dropped into the reserves against Grantham. He was centre-half when Grantham won 9-6 and the winning side's centre-forward Jack Macartney scored eight times.

Certain clubs seemed to spark off scoring sprees when paired against each other. In the FA Cup third round in 1945–46, Middlesbrough drew 4-4 at Leeds then won 7-2 at home. Micky Fenton scored three and then five goals in the League match three days later in a 7-2 win at Sheffield United.

In the fourth round first leg, Blackpool beat 'Boro 3-2 and the return, watched by 46,566 who paid record receipts, saw the teams level on aggregate at 5-5 after 90 minutes. Ten minutes extra time each way plus another 40 minutes failed to produce a further score. A third game at Leeds attracted 30,000 who paid, plus another 10,000 who broke in! The deadlock was finally broken when after 51 minutes more of extra time, Johnny Spuhler was brought down and George Hardwick scored from the penalty spot. The fifth round was almost an anti-climax; Bolton beat Middlesbrough 1-0, while the second leg finished 1-1.

In 1942–43 Leeds and Newcastle met each other six times. A total of 47 goals resulted from their encounters. Newcastle scored 28 of them. Each side won twice away and once at home. The Newcastle scores were: 3-5, 9-0, 4-5; Leeds: 1-7, 7-2, 1-3. In the last match of this particular series at St James' Park, Newcastle were leading 4-0 with 20 minutes left. Then Leeds scored five!

Without communications and supply in the form of service from half-backs and other forwards, the scoring opportunities would not have presented themselves. Naturally, sub-standard defending was another major factor. But outside-right Stanley Matthews was at times almost unplayable. His own style had changed by the time of the war's arrival. He admitted himself that he had become 'fascinated with dribbling'. While he might have been in raptures about this, his opponents were totally frustrated. A quotation in *Picture Post*, Britain's best-selling magazine, encapsulated his qualities when it referred to him 'as a football equation without an answer'. The *Athletic News Annual 1945–46* said: 'Unequalled as artist or crowd magnet. Matthews of Stoke City realised to the full during the war, his tremendous skill at outside-right.'

Obviously, goalkeepers bore the brunt of these barrages and had a harrowing time of it, but the best of them emerged through the bombardments. Again it was the *Athletic News Annual 1945–46* which said of Frank Swift: 'His height, reach, cool judgement and kicking and throwing combine to create a truly wonderful defender.' Thus, there were those who acted not merely as a last line of defence but as a first line of attack.

21 THE SPIRIT OF THE GAME

IF DODDS, STUBBINS, Lawton, Payne, Sale and their ilk of goal plunderers were the substance of the game, Stan Mortensen typified its spirit. He survived a parachute jump that went badly wrong, a horrific aeroplane crash and took the risk of permanently damaging his leg after a football injury in a bid to start playing again.

Nothing appeared serious enough to prevent him from turning out and, while 1939 was a pretty appalling year for almost everything, it did mark his return to a Football League club when fortune seemed to have passed him by. He had turned professional with Blackpool at the age of 17, having joined them in April 1937, a month short of his 16th birthday. He had starred as a 'schoolboy' for South Shields.

In fact, he first came to Blackpool's attention in December 1936 when a South Shields newspaper advertised for players under 16 to play other ex-schoolboys. Leeds accepted the challenge and beat them 4-3. Two of the Shields goals were scored by Mortensen and two of the Leeds foursome came from Len Shackleton, an England schoolboy international.

Blackpool tried Mortensen in a number of positions – centre-forward, inside-forward and wing-half – and he was often only in their third and fourth teams. Mortensen himself reckoned that manager Joe Smith merely suffered him because he was a good worker and kept the dressing-room clean and the boots shining!

He went to play for Ashington before the war and settled down at centre-forward after Blackpool released him, but he returned to Bloomfield Road when the war started to play at inside-forward and wing-half again. However, the new Mortensen soon emerged. He was quicker off the mark, dashing, brave and a fine finisher.

His versatility was not confined to football. Before he enlisted, he had five jobs at various times: in a biscuit factory, garage, butcher's shop, wood yard and as a shipyard joiner. Later, he even toured with Ralph Reader's Gang Show. In February 1941 he joined the RAF. Though he failed to get a game with Bristol City, he did manage one or two for Bath. This was after he had a frightening experience when he was almost strangled by the rip cord of his parachute during a training exercise on 13 February 1943.

Posted to Lossiemouth, he assisted Aberdeen. Then, while on aircrew training as a wireless-operator-air-gunner on his last 900-mile flight before being assigned to a squadron, the Wellington bomber in which he was flying crashed into a forest near Lossiemouth. The pilot and bomb aimer were killed, the navigator lost a leg. Mortensen literally missed death by a hair's breadth, surviving with a dozen stitches in his head. Three weeks later he was playing football again.

Convalescing at Newport, he took the Saturday off to watch the League West Cup final between Lovell's and Swansea. The visitors arrived one player short. Morty volunteered to play outside-right and helped Swansea to a 4-2 win.

Having made his international debut for the 'wrong' country, Wales against his own England, he also managed to play for a third. While still on sick leave he went to watch an Aberdeen Scottish Select XI play the Army, again offered his services and scored all four goals in a 5-4 defeat. All this and a Norwegian grand-father . . .

During a cup game against Rochdale in March 1944 he suffered a knee injury early on. As a result, Blackpool, who had beaten the same side 8-0 the previous week, lost 2-1. Three specialists agreed that a cartilage operation was necessary, but as it was not essential for a serviceman, no surgery was allowed immediately and for four months he could not play. He was excused marching, drill and PT duties, but during the summer he strengthened the knee by keeping wicket for Blackpool Services cricket team.

A fourth specialist in Newcastle added his confirmation that the injury was indeed cartilage trouble, but persuaded Mortensen to take a chance and when the opportunity next arose he should attempt to kick the ball as hard as he could with his injured leg. Walking down Blackpool promenade, 'Morty' noticed some lads kicking a ball about on the sands. As it had had more than one sea soaking it was more like a medicine ball, so when it came in his direction he swung his leg at it, connected and although the impact was dreadfully painful, he experienced no further problems!

Mortensen had the midas touch for goals. While guesting for Watford he scored the only goal, but the match was abandoned because of fog. It would have been their first win of the season. He scored goals for other clubs including Hud-dersfield, Aberdeen and Arsenal. In London for a medical examination, he had agreed to continue guesting for Bath. He informed them that he was on his way, while at the ground loudspeaker announcements were made to the crowd that he was making progress on the road. He arrived 25 minutes late and proceeded to score with his first kick.

It was at Blackpool that he first linked up with Matthews. His partnership with him began with Matthews telling him 'just play your normal game. We'll sort things out.' Mortensen eventually forced his way into the side and by the

1945–46 season had overtaken the prolific scoring Dodds as the club's top marksman.

George Hardwick, whose pre-war introduction to League football had been unnerving in as much as he put through his own goal with his first touch of the ball for Middlesbrough, was another who served in the RAF and was almost lost to the game. During an air attack on the aerodrome where he was serving he was seriously wounded. There were fears he would not make a complete recovery. But he did.

Then there was Doug Wright, capped for England at left-half against Norway on 9 November 1938 on his own St James' Park ground and helping in a 4-0 victory. He landed in Normandy soon after D-day and also received serious wounds. Not only was he told once that he would never play again but a second opinion confirmed it! They were wrong and he also made a successful comeback.

Wright had joined the Tyneside Scottish, The Black Watch, along with colleagues Willie Scott and Dave Hamilton. Scott was one of the 30,000 who did not get away from Dunkirk. Hamilton was luckier. The retreat from Dunkirk appeared to have ended the aspirations of amateur wing-half Roy White, who had played many times for Spurs. He was a sergeant in the BEF, and the boat on which he was returning to England was torpedoed. White was in the water for several hours before being picked up. It was then discovered he had lost his sight, though he recovered it after two months. He subsequently rose to the rank of major, took part in the invasion of Europe and was also to resume his career in the game. Jackie Stamps, one of Derby's 1946 FA Cup finalists, fought at Dunkirk and was wounded. In 1942 he had been told prematurely he would never play again.

On the day of the last competitive match in the 1945–46 transitional season, Walsall played Bournemouth in the final of the Third Division (South) Cup. Immediately opposing each other were Reg Foulkes the Walsall centre-half and Jack Kirkham leading the Bournemouth attack. Foulkes had been a ground-staff boy with Birmingham before the war. He won schoolboy international honours for England and turned professional after his 17th birthday. On the eve of the war he played for the A team against Wolves, marking a 15-year-old Billy Wright.

Foulkes joined the RAF, qualified as a pilot but was so badly injured in a crash that he was told he would have to forget a career in the game. To add to his problems, he was given a free transfer by Birmingham City in 1945. At that point Walsall signed him and he helped them reach the final. His opponent, Kirkham, was a former Wolves centre-forward who had set out on the same trail undertaken by other Molineux graduates who had moved to Dean Court.

After scoring three goals in five games for Wolves he came to Bournemouth to hit another 14 in 24 matches for the Cherries to finish as their leading scorer in 1938–39. After guesting for Queens Park Rangers early in the war, he went abroad with his Army unit as a private. He was taken prisoner by the Germans in Tunisia. Three times he escaped from Italian prison camps over a period of 18 months. He finally linked up with French and Italian partisans in the mountains and spent three months there before making his way into Switzerland and then being repatriated.

In November 1944 he had returned to England and led the Wolves attack against Birmingham. It was the same Kirkham who had played in Bournemouth's 10-goal spree over Northampton on 2 September 1939 . . .

22 THE KING OF SPORTS

SOCCER'S STATURE INCREASED perceptibly during the war period for a complex set of reasons, not all of them obvious. While it was easy to see that, as the number 1 spectator sport, it had a groundswell of morale boosting appeal for the war workers, servicemen and young people of the country, enjoying the favours of the higher echelons of society required an explanation. It truly became the King of Sports.

There were sound enough arguments for gazing benevolently upon the professional game, though the amateurs were largely left to their own ingenuity to remain in existence. Employment may of necessity have been reduced to a minimal part-time capacity and administrative staffs decimated, to leave only the over-aged or unfit, and players may have been handed match fee rewards alone – nevertheless, it all added up to an industry operating efficiently despite a greatly reduced scale and providing much-needed revenue for government and, more important, for a myriad of charities.

For a while there had to be enough income to make it a viable proposition for clubs – the rake-off for the swingeing Entertainments Tax, and generous donation to war charities derived from the mass of representative games, provided the game with a special status symbol. In return, although there were no special concessions, there were some gestures of appreciation which were so rare that the charge of privileged treatment could not be fairly levelled. One move came in October 1940 when the Ministry of Food authorised permits for clubs to provide refreshments.

Perhaps it was from the patronage of the 'Establishment' that soccer was given its seal of approval. Scarcely any top-level representative game went by without the attendance of at least one named dignitary. Eddie Hapgood, who was England's captain in the early war years, said: 'The Royal Box was nearly always crowded when we played a charity international at Wembley.'

As early as April 1940 when England played Wales at the Empire Stadium, the celebrities included royalty in the presence of Princess Alice and Princess Helene Victoria. By then the game had clearly demonstrated its ability to help fund worthy causes like the Red Cross and St John Ambulance Fund.

Yet, something of a record was set up in October 1941 when Wembley staged an international against Scotland. Prime Minister Winston Churchill was introduced to the players and he was accompanied by seven Cabinet members: Messrs Herbert Morrison, Ernest Bevin, A. V. Alexander, Clement Attlee, Lord Woolton, Sir James Grigg and Lord Leathers. For a Royal touch, there was the King of the Hellenes. Peacetime could not have achieved the same line-up!

The corresponding fixture in January 1942 was handsomely to benefit Mrs Churchill's Aid to Russia Fund. The Prime Minister's wife was present, along with King Peter of Yugoslavia, a strange political juxtaposition in other circumstances in view of the beneficiaries. But it was one frequently repeated.

The visit of Wales a year later, again for the Aid to Russia charity, coincided with Hapgood's 43rd international appearance. He had then made more appearances for his country than any other player, regardless whether it was peace or wartime. He could not have expected a more regal occasion. King George VI and the Queen, King Haakon of Norway and members of the Soviet Embassy were present. The King congratulated Hapgood on his achievement and consented to autograph a photograph to commemorate the day.

Naturally it had been the policy of the Crown and Government to be seen actively participating in events of everyday life alongside the very people with whom the wartime struggles were being conducted. As a public relations exercise it worked admirably.

The upper crust not only supported the international matches, but could be seen at other games, rendering more than a crumb of comfort. When the British Army met the Allied Armies at Stamford Bridge in March 1941, Captain David Margesson, the War Minister, was presented to the teams. For the FA XI v Civil Defence at Brentford, the Minister for Home Security, Herbert Morrison, was in attendance. King Haakon even appeared for the Inter-Allied Services Cup final in April 1943. In February 1944 the England v Scotland game at Wembley was watched by King George, Princess Elizabeth and Field-Marshal Montgomery.

Cup finals were also well graced by VIPs. In April 1944 in the lead-up to D-day, hundreds of American servicemen were among the spectators for the Charlton v Chelsea final, along with guest-of-honour General Eisenhower. The Right Hon. A. V. Alexander, First Lord of the Admiralty, was himself a frequent spectator and said to be a Chelsea supporter. For Chelsea's 1945 Cup final, the King, Queen and Princess Elizabeth were present. Deputy Prime Minister Attlee was often seen at matches standing in for Churchill, who was also trying to plot the winning of the war!

Much of the credit for this high-society acceptance was thanks to the efforts of the Football Association and the League's Management Committee, who coordinated their operations from the moment they were given the green light by the Government to restore the game on an organised basis. Cooperation with the services and liaison with the police authorities from the early wartime days was also well received in official quarters. As early as December 1939 the Ministry of Home Security announced that the limit for crowds could be overcome if tickets were sold ahead of the match and the FA dealt with the local police rather than leaving it to the clubs themselves.

Clubs had also earned credit from the outset of hostilities. In some instances grounds had been put at the disposal of the military and equipment freely donated to the war effort. In some respects clubs gave so generously in gear that when they found themselves needing to replace worn-out items they were unable so to do. This certainly resulted in the Board of Trade's eventual granting of their clothing coupon donation. But again there was no favouritism. The FA had given £1,000 for footballs and equipment to the Army and in January 1940 some 456 footballs and 424 pairs of boots had been switched from the domestic game to the services.

Even before the war, the example set by soccer's two governing bodies calling for enlistment in the Territorials and other national service organisations had been duly noted and fostered a climate of goodwill.

On 22 June 1940 the FA launched its Fitness for Service campaign on football grounds in conjunction with the Central Council for Recreative Training. Within two months the number of grounds cooperating in the scheme approached 200. After three months more than 40,000 young men had participated in it.

Not surprisingly, there was barely a voice raised in Parliament against soccer, though there was some condemnation and criticism in the early stages of the war when MPs complained at the excessive absorption of footballers and other athletes into the Physical Training Corps. But these were swiftly dealt with in the press by Colonel T. H. Wand-Turley, Inspector of Physical Training.

'By their experience gained from sport, these instructors know the best PT methods to adopt,' he said. 'Irreparable damage can be done to recruits if the training is too severe. In the last war there were many cases of heart trouble caused by instructors who did not know their business,' concluded the Colonel.

There were just a few other matters raised over the war period, including one from a Labour MP in Easter 1940 who questioned the case of a tube manufacturer in Oldbury who was apparently employing between 12 and 18 West Bromwich Albion players on munitions. The club responded in their programme notes, but by the end of the season nothing more was heard about the matter.

Other sports, however, were savaged. In February 1942 Sir Stafford Cripps hit out at the 'business or pleasure as usual' attitude in many sports, chiefly those in which gambling was the prerequisite for interest. Soccer was never mentioned in the criticism of people wasting petrol and taking their minds off the war effort. Only in the respect of football pools was there any redress, and even here no legislation was put through to affect the alternative system which enabled the working class to indulge itself in the relatively harmless escapism of filling in a weekly coupon for a few pence. All this despite the fact that at the time both the FA and League were definitely anti-pools, since there was no copyright on their fixtures at that stage and therefore no revenue generated.

Neither was there much public outcry against the continuation of the professional game, although footballers occasionally had to bear the brunt of jibes of either being cushioned by moving into reserved occupations or found comfortable, safe billets in the armed forces, which in the vast majority of cases was far from reality.

FA Secretary Stanley Rous was personally responsible for the liaison work with the Home Office, and once again his availability to negotiate for a resumption of the game when all entertainments had closed down was another important factor in soccer's recovery. A less individual approach might have resulted in problems with which to deal in the wake of hostilities being declared.

The FA's decision to provide the armed services with a ready-made list of coaches who could speedily be trained as Physical Training instructors was another idea much appreciated. Again Rous, in contacting the General Officer Commanding Home Forces and its subsequent link with the War Office, made for likely cooperation.

Officials in the FA and League had the ear of many influential people in Government circles and were able to cut through the red tape that might otherwise have delayed or even prevented positive measures being taken on behalf of the game. Not that the propaganda value of soccer was lost on the authorities. It was soon arranged for radio commentaries to be resumed on Forces and Home Service stations of the BBC, subject to the agreement of the two competing clubs.

With just one or two hitches, the reorganisation of the League into regions met with official approval and, since it was generally confined to localised and approved areas, there were few problems. Even when places like Brighton became a restricted area, permits were issued for the football team and their opponents to come and go.

In the last days of the European war in April 1945 there was the hint of a possible London v Moscow game at Wembley for the Aid to Russia Fund. At the time Mrs Churchill was in the Soviet capital and actually acted as an unofficial ambassador for the FA. From this came the eventual arrival of the Moscow Dynamo team later in the year.

Numerous Footballer's Day collections were made for a variety of charities including POW Funds, and this was another indication to the public at large that the image being created by football and footballers and the people who were continuing to support it was worthwhile. In 1945 the FA's accounts showed a loss on the year, but they still had assets at their disposal and as a gesture they decided to forgo their interest on £32,400 War Stock investment.

23 WITH THE SCOTS

T HE SCOTTISH GAME, which had carried on with one division of its normal
League programme during the First World War, made a tentative attempt to
repeat the venture once the all-clear was sounded to resume organised activities.
Nothing came of this plan or the notion of paying substantially more money to
the players than those in England, but if the ambitions had been pitched rather
too high, no time was lost in organising two regional competitions. There were a
number of non-starters among the ranks and one or two names destined to dis-
appear from the scene completely.

Two Regional Leagues were formed, one in the East, the other in the West,
each comprising 16 clubs. Six of the pre-war Second Division teams did not take
part – Brechin City plus oddly enough the last five in the 1938–39 table: Mon-
trose, Forfar Athletic, Leith Athletic, East Stirling and Edinburgh City.

However, the severity of the winter caused endless problems. Some grounds
were closed for months and financial difficulties grew. Cowdenbeath shut down
in February 1940 and by May eight of the 38 pre-war teams had ceased to function. To help them, a 5 per cent levy was imposed on receipts from all League
matches. One of the clubs to close for the duration that summer was King's Park,
the Stirling club. The following year a bomb destroyed the grandstand and later
the ground was sold.

In the spring of 1940 ideas had been again entertained about restarting the
First and Second Divisions because of the minimal war activity at home, but the
sudden collapse of the Allied Front on the continent dramatically changed this
thinking.

The Scottish League suspended its competitions but gave permission for local
leagues to be formed. Thus, in the summer a Southern League was fashioned
with 16 clubs. At the same time an attempt to form a North Eastern League was
made, but it had to be postponed for a year, chiefly through the reluctance of
Dundee and St Johnstone to enter. In addition there was a Southern League Cup
and a Summer Cup, while competitions like the Glasgow Cup and Glasgow
Charity Cup also ran uninterrupted and a Second XI Cup was similarly maintained.

The Scottish Cup itself was abandoned just as it had been in the First World War, but the development of the Southern League Cup on somewhat revolutionary lines was well received and even copied by the Football League for its own wartime competition to replace the FA Cup. Other experiments were imaginative and kept interest alive. Immediate post-war suggestions included a British League and the scrapping of promotion and relegation. The *Athletic News Annual 1941–42* commented: 'We saw some of the best football that has been played in recent years.'

Rangers won at least three trophies each season of wartime football, many of their pre-war squad remaining available locally. They did suffer from the occasional bout of Achilles heel trouble, notably inflicted by Hibernian. The Ibrox club won the first Regional League, beating Falkirk 2-1 in a play-off between the winners of the Western and Eastern Sections and the Southern League for the next six seasons! A contemporary observation put it that they were 'for periods almost in a class by themselves'.

Naturally, in spite of this dominance, they had the kind of team selection and availability problems experienced by all clubs. On 29 November 1941 they arrived at Aberdeen a man short. The vacancy was filled by Cameron, a one-time Rangers trialist who, though he had later played for St Johnstone, had not kicked a ball for two years. Wing-half Scot Symon had to play in goal in a game against Clyde, but Rangers won 8-2; and despite the comparative abundance of players Willie Thornton, for instance, was serving abroad and did not play at all for two years.

Like Falkirk and Hearts, Rangers also fielded a reserve team in the North-Eastern League and its League Cup equivalent, the Mitchell Cup, winning the first of these competitions. However, not unexpectedly Aberdeen proved the giants of the northern region. Ironically, it was William Mitchell, chairman of Aberdeen, who put up the trophy.

The gaps in the calendar caused by the shrivelled League programme prompted the League Management Committee to devise an additional competition. William MacAndrew, Secretary of the Scottish League, came up with the idea and Rangers made something of a monopoly of it, winning four of these five Southern League Cup tournaments.

A start was made on the regional programme on 21 October 1939. Rangers led all the way apart from a short period in April when they had played two fewer games than leaders Queen of the South, though they soon caught up and finished eight points clear of the Dumfries club.

Falkirk themselves had won the Eastern Section by five points from Hearts, who were the only club to achieve a 3-figure total of goals after Cowdenbeath's record was deleted. Perhaps the play-off reflected what might have happened under normal circumstances, since when the pre-war League programme had had to be abandoned after five games, Rangers were leading Falkirk in the First

Division by a point. In the championship decider Alex Venters and Adam Little gave Rangers their brace of goals while Charlie Napier replied for Falkirk.

An Emergency Cup competition was started quite late in the season, the first round being towards the end of February played over two legs. Attendances were moderate at this stage, the only 5-figure gate being that at Paisley where St Mirren beat Queen of the South 6-0 with Alec Linwood claiming four of their goals. Thereafter, the tournament reverted to a knock-out system with Rangers winning the final at Hampden Park by the only goal against Dundee United, scored by Jimmy Smith before a crowd of 71,000.

In the semi-final, United had met Airdrie. After a goalless draw, the pre-match build-up to the replay was sensationally spiced up when Airdrie drafted in no less a personality than Stanley Matthews. The neutrals went over to Dundee United's side! And a moral 3-1 victory pitched them into the final. Because of their geographical position, United had to bow out for a season, but a United Juniors side played on until the seniors returned.

Dunfermline Athletic had part of their ground taken over by the RASC but the £50 rent was most welcome. Later a Polish army unit moved in and even the pavilion was occupied by the military at one time. The Pars did have the assistance of some notable guests including local boy Billy Liddell from Liverpool. In one game his accurate crosses made five goals for Jackie Hunter, guesting from Morton.

Kilmarnock's ground was commandeered by the Army as a fuel dump in 1940 and that brought an end to football at Rugby Park until 1945, though a reserve team played at Hurlford in 1944–45. German POWs helped to get the ground in order for the transitional season.

Partick Thistle operated throughout and were fortunate to have Bill Shankly stationed for a while at Bishopbriggs in the RAF. He made 69 guest appearances, scoring 12 goals. The Jags won the Summer Cup in 1945 beating Hibs 2-0, courtesy of another guest right-winger, Johnny Johnson from Stockport. Willie Newall and Willie Sharp proved two reliable goalscoring discoveries.

For the 1940–41 season there was a curtailment of the number of clubs entering. The two from Dundee, Aberdeen, St Johnstone, Arbroath and the Fife quartet did not take part. Sixteen competed in the Scottish Southern League. Aberdeen's Pittodrie ground became an ARP post.

Rangers' first defeat in the League came on 30 November 1940 when they were beaten 1-0 by Hibs. This caused a temporary wobble at Ibrox as they lost two of their next three games. There was a recovery but not before losing 3-2 at home to Celtic in the New Year clash and Rangers also lost their last game by three clear goals at Third Lanark. There were still three points to spare over Clyde. Rangers made it a double triumph as they won the Scottish League War Cup after a replay with Hearts. The first game was drawn 1-1, Rangers winning the replay 4-2. For this tournament the 16 entries had been split into groups of four, the winners going into the semi-finals.

A Summer Cup suggested by Hibernian chairman Harry Swan was also started in June, the ties being decided on the home-and-away principle until the semi-final. This time Rangers had to acknowledge Hibs as their masters as the Easter Road side beat them 3-2 on a blazingly hot day. The Hi-Bees had occasional guest assistance from Sunderland's Alex Hall and Bob Kane of Leeds. In 1945 they introduced a 16-year-old forward called Lawrie Reilly and other wartime finds included Gordon Smith, Jock Govan and Hugh Howie.

A North-Eastern series was started in 1941–42 with the three previously named reserves making the number up to eight teams. Because of the restricted programme of games, a Second Series featured in the second half of the season with an experiment in the points system. An extra point was awarded to teams having a higher goal aggregate from their home and away games against each opponent. Rangers reserves, who had won the First Series by a point from East Fife, lost out as a result of this system of bonus points, as despite winning more games overall, they had only five bonus points compared to Aberdeen's six.

In the Southern League Rangers suffered their first defeat on 27 September 1941, losing 8-1 to Hibs, but the effect on Hibs was the more remarkable; they went a month before winning again! Earlier in the month on 1 September, Rangers won a prestige friendly with Preston, the top English side, by 3-1.

Rangers' next defeat was on 1 November, 2-1 at Morton, but Hibs clinched a home-and-away double against them on 27 December with a single goal win at Ibrox. In the Celtic match Jerry Dawson the Rangers goalkeeper saved the penalty he had conceded himself by bringing down Jimmy Delaney.

An individual highlight of the season was Albert Juliussen of Huddersfield Town scoring six of Dundee United's goals in their 7-1 win over St Bernard's in the Mitchell Cup on 15 November 1941. Aberdeen, who were back in action, beat United in the final 7-6 on aggregate after extra time. They also won a Spring competition involving United, East Fife and Rangers.

Juliussen, born in Blyth the son of a Norwegian sailor, had the unusual experience of scoring 11 goals in a match yet still finished on the losing side. Posted to the Black Watch in Perth, he played in an Army trial match. His team were leading 6-0 at half-time and he had scored all six goals. He was switched to the other side in the second half and managed only five goals so his 'second' team were beaten 6-5! For Dundee United he scored 83 goals in only 70 games.

In the Summer Cup, Hibs held Rangers to a goalless draw after extra time and since both teams had achieved two corners the game was unsatisfactorily decided in Rangers' favour by the toss of a coin.

Rangers had beaten Morton 1-0 in the Scottish Southern League Cup with a goal from Torry Gillick. An Everton player, he had missed most of the previous season with injury and went back to Rangers to race greyhounds at the track next to Ibrox. By now they had installed some new faces, notably centre-half George Young recruited from Rob Roy in September 1941 and had the assistance of

Preston's Willie McIntosh either on the left wing or at centre-forward. Gillick had suffered severe burns to his left arm and hand which necessitated skin grafting from his leg.

In 1942–43 Rangers did not sustain defeat until 3 October 1942, losing away to Queen's Park by a single goal, but Hibs were still top on 14 November despite a 7-2 reverse at Clyde. However, on 19 December Rangers claimed the leadership on goal average and suffered just one more reverse at the close of the season.

On New Year's Day Rangers had beaten Celtic 8-1. Celtic had Malky MacDonald and Matt Lynch sent off within minutes of each other for arguing when Rangers were leading 4-1. MacDonald was suspended until August and fined £10, Lynch until March and given a £5 fine.

Aberdeen won both the First and Second Series of their competition and the Mitchell Cup beating Dunfermline Athletic 9-3 on aggregate in the final. The Spring Cup tournament, enlarged to encompass eight teams, also went to Aberdeen 7-3 on aggregate over Raith Rovers. The Dons had various times had the assistance of Rangers' Sammy Cox, Alex Dyer from Plymouth, George Green of Huddersfield and Newcastle's Bobby Ancell. They had three serving in the Corps of Signals: Matt Armstrong, Billy Strauss and Andie Cowie. Archie Baird, taken prisoner at Tobruk, spent two years as a POW in Italy before escaping. He went into hiding with an Italian family and learned the language. But he returned home to play in the 1946 Southern League Cup final. Later he took a BA (Hons) degree in Italian and English at London University.

In the Southern League Cup the final between Rangers and Falkirk was drawn 1-1 and the match was decided on corners, Rangers winning 11-3. However, there was no clean sweep down south for the Ibrox brigade as St Mirren beat them with a Linwood goal in the Summer Cup final. Clyde had the leading marksman in Doug Wallace, who scored 40 of their League goals, the highest tally in Scottish wartime fare.

In 1943–44 Rangers had a 7-point margin of success over Celtic in the Southern League. In the North-Eastern League, Raith won the First Series but the second competition went to the last game before being resolved. Rangers' goalkeeper Jerry Dawson suffered a leg fracture in a collision with Hibs' Tommy Bogan and his own defender Dougie Gray in a Southern League Cup match that season.

A new system of points had been instituted: two for a home win, one for a home draw, three for an away win, two for an away draw. On the last day of the season Rangers reserves had to draw to ensure the title but were beaten 3-0 by Aberdeen. Even though Rangers had a game in hand, they had an inferior goal average and ultimately finished second.

The Ibrox 'stiffs' had a consolation having won the Autumn Cup and the Spring tournament. In the Southern League Cup, Hibs and Rangers again faced each other in a tense final which ended scoreless, Hibs winning 6-5 on corners.

Neither Rangers nor Celtic entered the Summer Cup, Dundee United and Raith taking their places. Motherwell, with a new-look team, beat Clyde 1-0 in the final, watched by some 40,000. Earlier in the war, Motherwell had had the guest services of Arsenal's Gordon Bremner and Dave Mathie, the Hibs leader. Both were subsequently signed, Bremner for £2,750.

In 1944–45 Dundee and Arbroath swelled the numbers in the North-Eastern League, Dundee edging Aberdeen out of honours by a point in the First Series with the Dons recovering to take the Second Series.

With more fixtures for the northern-based teams, the League Cup was reduced. A Supplementary Cup began in December, with just the first four to finish in the First Series of the North-Eastern League playing home and away. Aberdeen easily beat Dundee 5-0 in the final. The Mitchell Cup followed in May, involving all ten teams; a play-off after the first round reducing the number to manageable proportions. Aberdeen, winners of this extra game, were thus worthy winners, beating Hearts reserves 4-3 on aggregate.

Rangers won the Southern League Cup beating Motherwell 2-1 in the final with the partnership of Gillick and Venters scoring their goals. Celtic came back to the Summer Cup, but only 14 teams entered.

Celtic had to be content with runners-up spot in the Southern League for the second year in a row, although Morton were the surprise front runners at first, followed by Clyde. Hibs had a flutter at the top in November and Rangers only assumed their place at the head of affairs in the latter part of December, though they had had games in hand.

Two individual scoring feats of seven goals came from Inglis of Falkirk on 23 September 1944 against Hamilton in a 9-1 win and by Hearts' Kelly in a 10-3 win away to Albion Rovers on 11 November.

In 1945–46 normality had almost been restored but not quite. An A Division of 16 teams and a B Division of 14 were formed as clubs were given a year to regroup. In addition, an Eastern League initially provided seven more teams including Dundee reserves. A combined St Bernard's and Leith Athletic made an attempt to enter but failed because they could not find a ground. In the first half of the season Dundee's second string won this League convincingly with newly formed Stirling Albion finishing second. St Johnstone reserves came in for the second series.

Stirling rose from the ashes of King's Park. They had a unique headquarters: a 21-room, eighteenth-century mansion in the heart of a wooded estate which was used as dressing-room accommodation. Oak trees were cut down for the pitch and a motor lorry acted as a grandstand. Coal merchant Tom Fergusson, who had also been chairman of King's Park, was the financial backer and the name of the club, Albion, sprang from the make of his coal trucks!

Rangers won the A Division by eight points from Hibs, while Dundee had a 10-point margin over East Fife and lost only once at home. Juliussen, by now transferred to Dundee, was top scorer with 38 League and Cup goals, his total including five against Arbroath in an 8-0 win on 10 November.

The Southern League Cup embraced Stirling and was won by Aberdeen, who answered criticism that their success had merely been at the expense of Rangers and other teams' second strings by beating the Ibrox first team 3-2 in the final. Aberdeen's inside-left Archie Baird had been taken prisoner in North Africa and had spent two years in Italy on frugal fare.

A Scottish Victory Cup, open to non-league clubs as well as those in the League, replaced the Mitchell Cup. It was launched with a preliminary competition won by East Stirlingshire, who beat Clachnacuddin 5-2 after extra time on 2 January 1946. These two teams joined the 30 A and B division sides in a home-and-away knock-out tournament won 3-1 by Rangers against Hibs. Johnny Duncanson with two goals and Gillick were the scorers for Rangers, Johnny Aitkenhead replying for Hibs. Teams: Rangers: Brown; Cox, Shaw, Watkins, Young, Symon, Waddell, Gillick, Thornton, Duncanson, Caskie. Hibs: Kerr; Goven, Shaw, Howie, Aird, Finnigan, Smith, Peat, Milne, Aitkenhead, Nutley.

Internationally, the transitional season brought Scotland back to the forefront after the doldrums of the war years. The Shaw brothers, Jock of Rangers and Hibs' David, partnering each other at full-back and Frank Brennan the Airdrie pivot making an impression among the younger clan of whom goalkeeper Bobby Brown of Queen's Park, Birmingham City's Neil Dougall, Jackie Husband from Partick, Billy Campbell of Morton and Hibs's flying winger Gordon Smith were mentioned with youthful pride and without prejudice.

The youngest player to turn out in a Scottish senior game was Ronnie Simpson, who made his first team debut in goal for Queen's Park against Kilmarnock in the Southern League on 11 August 1945 at the age of 14 years 304 days.

Scottish football also attracted several leading players from the Football League. Stanley Matthews played a few games for Morton and one for Rangers, while Tommy Lawton scored for the Greenock club on his honeymoon. Matthews also turned out for Airdrie in a Scottish War Cup semi-final replay in 1940, but was on the losing side against Dundee United. His Blackpool and England colleague Stan Mortensen had a spell assisting Aberdeen, while Frank Swift turned out for Hamilton.

Dundee United could not complain about Airdrie fielding Matthews. When they lost 1-0 to Rangers in the final they had only two of their own players and nine guests. Their line-up was. Thomson (Exeter); Miller (Bristol C), Dunsmore (Hibs), Baxter (Barnsley), Littlejohn (Cowdenbeath), Robertson, Glen (Raith), Gardiner (Bristol R), Milne (Hibs), Adamson (Forfar), Fraser.

United's neighbours Dundee had opposed them in a friendly on 7 October 1939, the Dens Park side winning 4-2 on their own ground. A crowd of 4,914 paid £100 to see the game but many were turned away by the police for not carrying their gas masks. Dundee's last game on closing down was 18 May 1940 when they defeated Falkirk 4–2 and they had a chastening experience on their return – a friendly against a British Army side who beat them 7–0 on 5 August 1944. Only full-back Bobby Rennie played in both matches for Dundee.

There were some odd decisions born of necessity. In the game between Clyde and Morton to qualify for the Scottish Cup final in 1944, no midweek replay was possible. It was agreed if scores were level after extra time, corner kicks would decide. In the event the game ended 3–3 and 15–15 on corners!

The answer was provided by the goal average of the two teams throughout the competition, Clyde going through 19–4 compared with Morton's 8–5. Then there was the Scottish Second XI Cup match involving Celtic and St Mirren which was also decided after extra time by tossing a coin, Celtic calling correctly.

The 1941 Glasgow Cup 'Auld Firm' affair between Celtic and Rangers was played at Hampden Park as Parkhead was under closure through suspension. Celtic were awarded three penalties and missed two of them.

Alas, the 1940 Glasgow Charity Cup between the two clubs did not live up to its name. In the semi-final at Ibrox, Venters was sent off for dissent, Divers for a brush with Symon. After the match won 5–1 by Rangers, the Scottish FA suspended Venters, Symon, MacDonald, Divers and Lynch for a month, the punishment starting from the 1940–41 season.

Rivalry between the teams boiled over on other occasions. In September 1941 at Ibrox Jimmy Delaney and Johnny Crum were carried off, bottles were thrown and five spectators arrested. It led to Parkhead being closed for a month, a decision which enraged Celtic officials and supporters.

In the semi-final of the Victory Cup in 1945–46, 90,000 watched a goalless draw between them on 1 June. Half that number of spectators appeared for the replay on the following Wednesday. Willie Gallacher was injured and eventually went off, while Jimmy Sirrel became little more than a passenger. With 20 minutes left, Rangers leading 1–0 were awarded a penalty, vigorously disputed by Celtic players, two of whom, George Paterson and Jimmy Mallan, were sent off. Celtic thus went 2–0 in arrears with only seven effective players. Incredibly the game had been cleanly fought!

Even so, Paterson and Mallan were suspended for three months, Celtic were fined £50 and ordered to post warning notices. Moreover, Lynch was suspended for a month despite a written plea from Rangers' Duncanson on his behalf that he had been innocent. According to the *Daily Record* of 23 September 1940 the same referee, M. C. Dale, had officiated at a Rangers v St Mirren game headlined 'We Must Not Have Such Refereeing'. Rangers had won 1–0.

Celtic had 13 of their senior professionals in the Forces and had to call more and more on youth. In one game they had six youngsters only a year out of the Boys Club. Once they refused to use Matt Busby, who was available and willing.

For the second game of the 1944–45 season against Albion Rovers, Celtic introduced Bobby Evans, a promising prospect from St Anthony's, but again frequent changes upset any hope of consistency. They did manage one trophy a late-season victory in the Europe Cup, though Rangers did not take part. On 9 May Celtic beat Queen's Park by one goal and three corners to one goal and two corners.

In February 1940 ex-player Jimmy McStay succeeded Willy Maley who had had 52 years service at the club as manager of Celtic. In July 1945 the legendary Jimmy McGrory succeeded McStay. August 1945 marked the retirement of Clyde's long-serving trainer and groundsman Matta Gemmell after 47 years' service.

24 ON THE EMERALD ISLE

THE IRISH LEAGUE programme continued in 1939–40 and was won for the fifth year in succession by Belfast Celtic, who, however, in company with Distillery, Glentoran and Linfield, decided not to compete in subsequent Irish League competitions, although they were prepared to participate in a regional substitute. Thus, the Irish FA approved a new tournament, and at varying times throughout the war Belfast Celtic, Distillery, Linfield, Glentoran, Cliftonville, Portadown and Coleraine all took part.

Meanwhile, the Irish Cup continued, as did many other competitions at various levels, like the Steel and Sons Cup, the Intermediate Cup and Irish Junior Cup. After Ballymena's Irish Cup victory in 1940, Belfast Celtic and Linfield shared the honours equally in the six remaining seasons.

Representative games were also continued against the League of Ireland across the border as well as an Inter-City Cup at club level which was well received on both sides.

Players of Football League experience who found themselves posted to Ulster were able, with the usual permission, to guest for Irish clubs in the North Regional League as it became known, but it was a home-grown player who produced the highest individual scoring performance ever seen in Irish League football. In January 1944 Belfast Celtic's centre-forward Peter O'Connor scored 11 goals in the 13-0 win over Glenavon.

The period was not a barren one for players in other positions who emerged successfully. Gerry Bowler developed into a useful centre-half after joining Distillery from Derry City for £1,000. The same club made a find in Norman Lockhart, the outside-left discovered with Windsor Star. He was transferred to Linfield for £225.

Then there was inside-forward Sam McCrory, who came from East Belfast in the Minor League to Linfield, and Danny Blanchflower, who first caught attention playing for Belfast Tech in 1939–40.

At 14, Blanchflower played for Connsbrook in the Minor League and then started a team of his own called Bloomfield United in the East Berlin Summer League. In 1944 he joined the RAF and was stationed at the University of St

Andrews in Scotland. There he played not only soccer, but rugby, hockey and cricket. Later he figured in squash, badminton, table tennis and all manner of other sports before being posted to Canada for nine months.

Christmas 1945 saw him back home, where he played for Glentoran reserves against Ards. Glentoran's manager Frank Thompson signed him as a professional but the registration form had to be cancelled. His first taste of English football came guesting for Swindon in 1945–46.

It was McCrory who scored the goal by which the Irish League defeated a Combined Services team which was really the England side in thinly veiled disguise, who only a couple of days before had beaten Northern Ireland in a Victory International at Windsor Park. But this time, with 15,000 crammed into Cliftonville's tiny ground on 17 September 1945, the score was reversed.

Other well-known names who appeared at odd times for North Regional League sides included Len Townsend of Brentford who assisted Belfast Celtic. Blackburn's Bobby Langton not only guested for Glentoran after five years with the Army in India, but was chosen for the Irish League against the Combined Services. He was the only 'guest' from a Football League club in the team.

Others who figured in the League at various times included Les Bennett (Spurs), Jack Rowley, Ivor Broadis, Frank Neary and Jim Taylor (both Fulham) and the Liverpool contingent of Dick Kemp, Phil Taylor, Jimmy McInnes and Harry Eastham. Arsenal's George Drury was another from the Football League.

The League of Ireland was able to continue its domestic competition as the Republic was neutral in the war, but they played no international matches between 1939 and 1946, although the Inter-League programme with the North Regional League in Ulster was actually increased to include home and away games in the season.

In the League itself the 1939–40 winners were St James Gate but thereafter Cork United were almost untouchable except for 1943–44 when Shelbourne were the winners. In 1940–41 they were fortunate, however, to be awarded the title when level with Waterford, as their opponents failed to agree terms for a test match between the two of them.

Shamrock Rovers were the most successful team in the Cup with three wins, Drumcondra won it twice and Dundalk once, while Cork United achieved the double in 1940–41; but during these seven seasons the League shrank from twelve clubs to eleven, then ten and finally eight.

25 SERVICE GALLANTRY AND HONOUR

S OCCER HAD ITS share of heroes. They served. Most were unsung. Not all of them came back. A few won medals. They fought through the searing sands of the desert, shivered in rain, sleet and mud and sweated in the steam heat of the jungle, shoulder to shoulder with clerks, shopkeepers, factory workers and schoolteachers. They could be found in the air over homeland or foreign territory, on and even underneath the high seas. Others were captured and spent the rest of the war in POW camps. Some escaped and returned to service. Then there were those who had a quieter war, training their comrades. Many shuffled papers, filed orders and more simply obeyed them.

According to *Victory Was Their Goal*, between 3 September 1939 and the end of the war 98 men went from Crystal Palace, 91 from Wolverhampton Wanderers, 76 from Liverpool, 68 from Luton, 69 from Chester (two of whom became Bevin Boys), etc., etc.

So it went on, with every Football League club supplying most of its professional and amateur players on a manpower conveyor belt throughout the wartime seasons, replacements on the field taking their turn on the assembly line for the services.

West Ham defender Dick Walker was a sergeant with an infantry battalion. He fought from El Alamein to Italy and was several times mentioned in despatches. He turned in his stripes and volunteered for the paras, for whom he completed more than 60 jumps and he still managed a few games of football while he was in Egypt.

Abe Rosenthal, the Tranmere Rovers forward, knew all about the paras himself. He was a glider pilot. Bill Edrich, not unknown as a cricketer, was a Squadron Leader bomber pilot in the first 1,000-aircraft raid on Germany in 1941 and won the DFC. Rangers' forward Ian McPherson, who guested for Birmingham and Notts County, won the DFC and bar flying with Mosquitos.

Alf Rowland, who turned out at centre-half for Aldershot reserves in 1945–46, had served in the Green Howards in the Middle East. He was captured at Gazala and spent four years as a POW. Bristol City's Cyril Williams, who guested for Reading on a number of occasions, was in the Airborne Forces himself and was badly wounded at Arnhem. Don Dorman was a paratrooper in the same raid. His platoon defended to the last ditch. He was twice wounded. In May 1946 he joined Birmingham City. Fulham goalkeeper Larry Gage was another para. Alan Kippax the Burnley winger who was an amateur, served in the RAF as a fighter pilot and was frequently assigned to missions escorting bombers on raids to the continent.

Reading left-winger Jack Sherwood, captured at Singapore, did not arrive in Melbourne until October 1945. Those who were taken prisoner by the Japanese suffered more than most. Cardiff City had a trio of them: Billy James, Bobby Tobin and Billy Baker, who had four years of ill-treatment. James, who had been in the Royal Artillery, was near blindness through malnutrition, Cyril Thompson the Southend United forward made a successful return after forced marches during five years in their hands.

Johnny Lynas, the Blackpool trainer, was another captured at Singapore and worked in a POW hospital in Thailand. He was a qualified masseur who previously as a player had served with Bo'ness, Sunderland and Third Lanark as an inside-forward.

Chesterfield's outside-left Harold Roberts was captured in a Commando raid on St Nazaire. He was wounded in both legs and spent the rest of the war at a POW camp in Bremen after a German surgeon performed a miracle operation on him. He lost two stone in weight during his time there, but resumed his footballing career. Sheffield United inside-forward Harry Hampson, the first from the club to join the Army, died after a short illness in 1942.

Southampton goalkeeper Len Stansbridge, serving in the RAMC, was captured at Dunkirk and spent four years as a prisoner. Alf Wood, the Coventry goalkeeper, was an RASC driving instructor but also an expert in unarmed combat training.

Exeter City's Steve Walker served on the destroyer HMS *Worcester* which chased the German vessels *Scharnhorst* and *Gneisenau* when they escaped from the Channel ports. Fulham winger Ernie Shepherd assisted Bradford City as a guest but during his six years with the RAF he was in Malta during the prolonged day and night raids there. His Craven Cottage colleague Len Quested chugged around in the Navy on a tugboat in Sydney Harbour.

Torquay's Bob Keeton was in the First Paras in Sicily by mistake. As a sergeant in the APTC he should have been in Scotland, but he landed in Algiers with the First Army and worried officials unmercifully until he was transferred to active duty.

Nick Collins of Crystal Palace worked in a munitions factory before joining the Royal Navy. He served as an anti-aircraft gunner on merchant ships and later on the *Queen Mary*. His gun crew shot down an enemy plane and even tackled a U-boat with small-arms fire until a destroyer arrived to finish it off.

Aston Villa's six-foot right-back Arthur Hickman joined the Militia early on. A Bofors sergeant, he fought at Caen on D-day +6 and suffered shrapnel wounds.

After a spell in hospital he caught up with his Regiment as they crossed the Rhine. He was one of the first to enter Belsen's notorious concentration camp and was given the task of guarding Joseph Kramer, the 'Beast of Belsen'.

George Ephgrave, a goalkeeper whose early football had been played in Guernsey, signed as an Aston Villa amateur. One of the tallest in the League at nearly six feet five inches, he was captured on Crete in 1941 and taken to Odessa. Later repatriated, he played in local football in the Exeter area before joining Swindon.

Ipswich's goalkeeper Tom Brown was originally in the Commandos and parachuted into China to aid the guerrillas fighting the Japanese and assisting escapees from Singapore. Twin brothers Bill and Alf Stephens had joined Leeds United together from Cramlington. Both served in the Royal Engineers and were even POWs in the same camp.

In addition to the loss of Eric Stephenson, killed while serving with the Gurkha Rifles in Burma in 1944, Leeds also lost centre-half Leslie Thompson and centre-forward Maurice Lawn.

Liverpool full-back Ted Spicer, a lieutenant in the Marines, actually captured a German NCO who turned out to be a soccer international. A Commando, Spicer had been commissioned in May 1942 and was later promoted to captain. He was wounded at the Battle of Wesel in 1945. Jackie Bray, the Manchester City wing-half who joined the RAF in 1940, later transferred to a unit which rehabilitated wounded fighter pilots and was demobbed in 1945 having been awarded the BEM.

Two of his City colleagues had other stories to tell. While in the Army, inside-forward George Smith suffered a shotgun wound in South Africa and had his lower forearm amputated at the wrist, which affected his balance; but he was able to play again. Full-back Eric Westwood fought on the Normandy beaches and was mentioned in despatches.

Mansfield Town's Harry Oscroft volunteered for the Royal Navy at 17 in 1943 and became a telegraphist operator on a minesweeper. On dry land he managed to play representative games for the Navy. Middlesbrough's inside-forward Wilf Mannion joined the Green Howards in January 1940. He was at Dunkirk and later had two years in the Middle East. At one time he acted as company runner for Hedley Verity the England cricketer! Then in 1942 Mannion played a season in South Africa for the Peninsula Club, Johannesburg. Boro defender Harold Shepherdson also served in the Green Howards.

Newcastle's Ernie Taylor and Paddy Fitzgerald, the Queens Park Rangers wing-half, were two in the Submarine Service, while Plymouth Argyle centre-forward Tommy Briggs served on landing craft in the war and was several times under fire in the Mediterranean campaigns.

Queens Park Rangers goalkeeper Reg Allen was initially a Territorial, served in the Queen's Westminsters and became a Bren-gun expert. He also volunteered for the Commandos. He took part in several landings from submarines. He was taken prisoner in North Africa in 1942 but escaped by jumping off a train, only to be recaptured and spent three years in a Stalag where in six-a-side games he always played centre-forward. He was eventually released by the Russians in Austria.

His club colleague, Alec Stock, was in the Duke of Wellington's Regiment, later commissioned in the Northamptonshire Yeomanry with the rank of captain. He commanded a tank crew in Caen and received shrapnel wounds in his back, but was soon playing again. Danny Boxshall, another Rangers forward, was held up in London during bad weather during Army service, so was able to play for the club on New Year's Day. They signed him on. Three months later he was winning the MM in France in charge of a Bren-gun crew.

Another QPR forward Albert Bonass was something of a ju-jitsu expert. He guested for several clubs during wartime but had the misfortune to lose his life in a flying accident in August 1945.

Dennis Woodhead, a Sheffield Wednesday winger signed in 1944, flew in Lancasters and took part in more than 50 raids over Germany before being sent out East. Of Stoke City's contingent to the colours, goalkeeper Dennis Herod served in the Middle East and then, after the invasion of Europe, he survived a burnt-out tank which miraculously left him with just a scar on his left cheek.

Bob Hamilton, who joined Chester from Hearts in 1945, had been a spotter on an American liberty ship in the Normandy landings when he was only 18. His ship was blown up after striking a mine. The survivors were picked up by a Norwegian vessel.

Albert Mullard, a Stoke amateur forward and later with Walsall, was captured on Crete and spent four years as a prisoner. Harry Meakin won the MM in Normandy. Swansea's Joe Payne was another involved in the D-day operations. Bill Shorthouse of Wolves was wounded in the arm within a couple of hours of landing there. Sent back to England he soon managed to persuade the hospital authorities to allow him to use a ball in the grounds.

The Scots were well represented, too. Rangers centre-forward Willie Thornton became a wireless operator in the Artillery and won the MM at Salerno in Italy. Peter 'Ma Ba' McKennan joined the Army in September 1939. He served first with the RAs then the Royal Welch Fusiliers. He landed at Normandy two weeks after D-day and was involved in the battle for Caen. He was one of only four survivors of his section in one engagement. McKennan was mentioned in despatches for patrol work and rose to the rank of sergeant major. He, too, managed the odd game or two as a guest for Wolves and Chelsea.

Ken Chisholm of Queen's Park and Leith Athletic's John Love were RAF pilots. Love won the DFC and suffered a shrapnel wound crossing the Rhine and retained the splinters from it. Harry Bamford, the Brentford winger, became a Warrant Officer, won the MBE and was twice mentioned in despatches while serving in Italy. Fred Cutting, the Leicester City and former Norwich inside-left, won the MM with the Royal Scots.

Northampton Town's Sergeant Alex Lee was awarded the AFM while another sergeant, Tom Barkas, an RAF instructor, received the BEM for gallantry during the siege of Malta. Chelsea amateur, Flight Sergeant Pilot Leslie Chatworthy, won the DFM as did LAC Dennis Love, a Bristol City player. Arsenal trainer Tom Whittaker was also received the MBE. The Gunners' centre-half Alf Fields was awarded the BEM in Italy. QPR's Albert Smith was similarly honoured. Harold White, the West Bromwich player, won the Military Medal in March 1942 and Bill Jones, Liverpool's utility player, was another similarly honoured, rescuing wounded comrades under fire.

Those who served in the Civil Defence forces also did their share of heroic deeds. One of those War Reserve Policemen was Ernest 'Mush' Callaghan of Aston Villa. He was awarded the BEM for conspicuous bravery during the Birmingham blitz in September 1942. Tom Cheetham, who had been a professional soldier before becoming a professional footballer with Queens Park Rangers, was wounded in Normandy and Howard Girling the Palace winger was hit in both legs on the Western Front in January 1945.

Alf Barratt of Leicester and later Northampton was involved in the D-day landings on the beaches of northern France. He was with the 47th Royal Marine Commandos and had also taken part in the attacks on Walcheren Island. Tommy McKenzie had originally played for Haddington and joined Hearts in 1941 as a part-timer, being loaned out to Leith. He joined the Army in February 1943 and served mostly in the Far East, playing virtually no football. He was with the Royal Scots Fusiliers in Burma. His section was ambushed by a Japanese patrol, and the man beside him was killed. They were pinned down by machine-gun fire and one bullet whanged off the ground and whizzed past his face, missing it by inches. He spent 18 months out there and was finally sent home suffering from acne!

Billy Elliott signed amateur forms for Bradford Park Avenue in 1940. He made his debut against Rotherham at 15 and turned professional on his 17th birthday. He kept his place in the side until called up for the Royal Navy in April 1943. As an AB, he served on a frigate hunting U-boats. He played in Navy representative sides in the West Indies, Gibraltar, Northern Ireland and even in the USA.

Tragic accidents also took their toll. Liverpool's England full-back Tom Cooper was killed on 25 June 1940 near Aldeburgh. Serving as a sergeant in the Military Police he lost his life when his motor-cycle was involved in a head-on crash with a bus. Another road victim was George Bullock, the Barnsley outside-right who had assisted Portsmouth as a guest. A naval rating, he was killed on 2 June 1943. On 13 February he had scored four times for Barnsley against Fulham. Another Barnsley player, Tom Robinson lost a leg in the Normandy campaign while Rochdale's centre-half Tom Jones had both feet amputated.

The death toll was harsh enough. Arsenal alone were savaged by it. Bobby Daniel, who had played three representative games for Wales early in the war, was reported missing on 23 December 1943. A flight sergeant gunner in the RAF, he had 30 operations to his credit. Fusilier Hugh Glass of the Royal Fusiliers was drowned at sea in 1943. Harry Cook, who had come from Oxford City, was killed in a flying accident. Leslie Lack was reported missing around the same time. An RAF flight sergeant Spitfire pilot, he had been to Canada. Cyril Tooze serving in the Royal Fusiliers was killed by a sniper's bullet in Italy on 10 February 1944. The club's trainer and former centre-half Herbie Roberts, a captain in the same regiment, who had become a crack shot with a pistol, died of erysipelas in Middlesex Hospital in June 1944.

Then there was Flying Officer Sidney Pugh. He had made his Arsenal debut in April 1939 against Birmingham but had been injured and spent some months in hospital. In 1942–43 he guested for Northampton, scoring twice in a 4-2 win at Birmingham. At the time he was a sergeant pilot and captain of a bomber crew in the midlands. In April 1944 he lost his life on active service.

Other Arsenal players escaped with injuries. Private Jimmy Blakeney, signed as a centre-forward from Accrington Stanley in June 1938, was a motor-cycle despatch rider. He was involved in an accident in 1942 and suffered severe injuries which left him with his body in plaster. He spent eight months in hospital. But by 1943–44 he was working in the coal-mining industry and playing for a local club in the Durham area.

Sergeant Harry Colley was serving in the Eighth Army in North Africa in 1943 when the lorry in which he was travelling hit a land mine. He suffered severe burns to his legs, arms, body and face and rendered deaf in one ear. Len Dutton, who had been signed from the Enfield nursery and had guested for Nottingham Forest, was reported missing for a while in 1943. Goalkeeper Ted Platt was captured by the Italians in Tunisia suffering from battle fatigue, but released when the British troops re-entered Tunis.

Even two of the actors who had appeared in the 1939 cinema version of *The Arsenal Stadium Mystery* were involved. Lieutenant Richard Norris, a serving officer in a Commando unit, was killed in action in the Mediterranean. He had played the part of the Trojan player who had nursed a doll in the dressing-room at Highbury. Lieutenant Esmond Knight was blinded in the attack on the *Prince of Wales*.

Then there was Bill Dean, a goalkeeper with a works team at Stoke Newington who had had a few games for Arsenal in 1940-41 and died in action with the Royal Navy in March 1942. After his first game for the Gunners he had said: 'Well, I have fulfilled my life's ambition; I have played for Arsenal.'

Tottenham's casualties included non-fatalities. Willie Hall, who had attributed his record five goals for England against Northern Ireland in 1938 thus: 'I owed much to the unselfishness of Matthews and Lawton', retired in March 1944 at 31.

He had his left leg amputated after thrombosis and resigned as Orient manager in December 1945. He was awarded a benefit game in May 1946 when Tottenham beat an FA XI 5-1 before a crowd of 30,222.

However, Lieutenant David Bearman, younger son of the Spurs' chairman Fred J. Bearman, was killed in Italy, and Newcastle's Colin Seymour, son of the United chairman, also lost his life in an aircraft crash near Perth. Two Luton players who died were goalkeeper Joseph Coen, killed in a flying accident in the RAF in October 1941 and Sergeant Charlie Clark who died of wounds on 30 March 1943. Alan Fowler, a former schoolboy international who joined Swindon Town in 1934 from Leeds, lost his life while serving with the Dorset Regiment in August 1944. Johnny Wallis, a full-back, suffered severe shrapnel wounds while in Palestine and ended his Football League career though he played later in non-league football.

Millwall's outside-right Fred Fisher was reported missing from operations over the Continent in September 1944 while Cardiff City goalkeeper Fred Pritchard had been reported lost at sea in the Pacific in the previous January. Flight Sergeant Alfred Keeling of Manchester City was also reported missing presumed killed in early December 1942 from an operational flight. Months earlier he had brought down a Junkers 88 in the Bay of Biscay. Preston's Tommy Taylor was killed in a motor-cycle accident six days after scoring a hat-trick for Middlesbrough against Bradford on 4 April 1942. Another Preston fatality was David Willacy the previous year.

Not all those posted as missing were lost. Spurs' Albert Hall was serving as a Gunner in the RA when he was captured at Singapore in February 1942. Later he was one of 58 survivors from a Japanese transport which was sunk in the Pacific in September 1943. He returned home in November 1944 and was playing again in April 1945.

Corporal Alec Munro of Blackpool, reported missing in the Middle East in July 1942, turned up as a POW in Italy two months later. Wolves' Alec McIntosh was listed as missing believed killed in action in April 1945 but also later appeared safe as a POW.

Nottingham Forest lost Grenville Roberts, Frank Johnson and Joe Croft all killed in action, the latter who died after losing a leg. Another Forest legend died of natural causes in March 1940, the England intenational centre-forward Tinsley Lindley at the age of 75.

Bury's Eddie Kilshaw survived a tragedy himself. He was piloting a Catalina flying boat from Scotland to an Atlantic base in what could only be described as below-zero visibility. His aircraft hit a hillside on a remote Scottish island, killing three of the RAF crew. Kilshaw and the surviving members battled across icy, windswept wastes to the cottage of a fisherman who was the island's sole inhabitant. From there they were rescued by the Navy.

26 WOULD YOU BELIEVE IT?

IT WAS CHRISTMAS morning 1941 and Bristol City were due to play at Southampton. They set out in three cars. The last to leave contained two players and the team's kit. This arrived first but, although the referee delayed the kick-off, there was no sign of the missing vehicles. The crowd shuffled about trying to keep warm and interested. Eventually the referee insisted on a start.

Southampton manager Tom Parker offered City five reserves plus trainer Jimmy Gallagher, who had not played for years. With the two City players already stripped, the side was completed by a soldier, a schoolmaster and another spectator from the crowd. The match kicked off an hour late and 20 minutes after that the missing players arrived. One car had broken down and the other had stayed to render assistance, but it was too late for replacements and the nine latecomers sat and watched. Gallagher scored against his own club, but Southampton won 5-2. The teams were: Southampton: Bernard; Creecy, Malpass, Stroud, Harris, Affleck, Hassell, Bidewell, Roper, Howard, Middleton. Bristol City: Charles (Southampton); Fisher (Southampton), Preece, Messom (Southampton), Aldersea (spectator), McNess (spectator), Gallagher (Southampton), Perrett (Southampton), Bourton, Laney (Southampton), Waterman (spectator). The crowd was 2,250 and Howard scored four for the Saints.

However, many of the onlookers had missed another drama which had developed at half-time. City were three goals down and one of their volunteers was injured. Among the remaining City players recently arrived was Ernie Brinton, their left-half and captain. He changed into his strip, rubbed mud into his shorts and legs, ruffled his hair and took the injured player's place, being the nearest in size and looks to him. The referee beckoned Brinton on but almost immediately he was called upon to take a throw-in; the 'ringer' was spotted by a linesman and the referee despatched him back to the dressing-room!

On the previous Christmas morning, Brighton had travelled to Norwich with only five of their own players. They were hoping to recruit more on the way. When they arrived a call was made around the ground and the side was completed by Norwich reserves and a few soldiers who volunteered to play. The crowd was 1,419.

Goals were rattled into the Brighton net with some regularity. There were three separate hat-tricks by Norwich players, a double treble from Fred Chadwick, the Ipswich forward and even an own goal. The timing of the goals was: 3, 5, 15, 19, 23, 24, 29, 35, 40, 41, 52, 54, 69, 73, 75, 78, 80 and 83 minutes. The half-time score of ten goals was the most in one half by one team and the final score of 18-0 was the highest margin in the history of the game involving two Football League clubs.

Not that everyone managed to reach Norwich. On 15 November 1941 Nottingham Forest set off for Carrow Road but caught the wrong connection at Peterborough and headed in the other direction. The Norwich patrons had to make do with a scratch seven-a-side match.

Even earlier on 19 October 1940 the game at Norwich had been delayed for half an hour awaiting the arrival of three Southend players who had been involved in a road accident. They turned up in their badly damaged car but made a quick change and pluckily played. The trio of latecomers were Sam Bell, who scored one goal, Frank Walton and Charlie Fuller. Norwich won 8-4.

The Bristol City club were also concerned in another odd event. Leicester were the visitors to Ashton Gate, but after torrential rain, an area of the pitch near one of the corner flags resembled a small lake and in normal times the match would never have started. However, the referee, having consulted both captains, agreed to go ahead. All went well until a corner was forced on that side of the ground.

The problem was that the ball literally floated when placed on the corner segment. After three gallant attempts to centre the ball, which simply rose and flopped back onto the water, the referee ordered the kick to be taken from the other wing and continued to do this throughout the game; using his initiative to good effect.

Finances were often strained. Plymouth played both their South-West Regional League games against Newport at Somerton Park on consecutive days in June 1940 to save travelling expenses for Newport; but County owed Argyle money on this and had to play one game in 1940–41 to raise the cash against Lovell's Athletic on Christmas Day. It was their only match in five seasons!

In April 1940 Brighton were short of a player at Crystal Palace. They contacted John Clifford who had played for Northampton in the ten-goal eve-of-war debacle at Bournemouth. This ex-Crystal Palace goalkeeper lived locally. By half-time he had let in five goals and switched places with Brighton's left-winger Gordon Mee, who was actually the Albion's own goalkeeper. Mee himself conceded the same number of goals as Palace ran out 10-0 winners.

At least one player temporarily forgot that Arsenal were not playing at home during the war. Peter Trainor the Brighton centre-half was missing when the rest of the team turned up to play the Gunners at White Hart Lane on 22 February 1941. He had gone to Highbury by mistake. Fortunately Brighton had a 12th man, Jack Westby, but were beaten 3-1. Just how many would-be spectators made the same mistake at some time during the period was not recorded.

The night before Arsenal were due to play Watford, Lionel Smith travelled down from Yorkshire to play centre-half for them on 8 March 1941, but because of a mix-up in hotel booking arrangements there was no accommodation for him and he spent the night sleeping on an Underground station along with many other Londoners who did the same every night. Arsenal won 5-0.

Humour frequently surfaced. For their opening game of 1945–46 against Arsenal, West Ham's programme referred to it as the Roofless v Homeless. Superstition was still evident, war or no war. Forest manager Billy Walker discovered his players had developed a hoodoo over their change strip. He arranged for a white shirt with a single red band, results improved and everyone was happy again!

Occasionally footballers would try to pull rank to obtain an advantage over the civilians. It was Boxing Day 1944. The venue was Leeds. It was an RAF v Army representative match. It was foggy. Jock Dodds and Stanley Matthews arrived at the station five minutes before kick-off time. A large taxi queue stared at them through the mist, but taking their courage into their voices they rushed to the front shouting 'Footballers! We've got to get to the ground in five minutes!' It worked. The queue stood aside. The players changed in the taxi and arrived as nine men were standing to attention listening to the National Anthem. But they were still beaten.

In the early days of the war Dodds, who drove a tanker lorry, and Hugh O'Donnell shared digs in Blackpool. The two had been chosen for an RAF unit game but lengthy spells on duty had made both of them tired. They overslept, only to be woken by their CO banging on the door. Outside the team coach was waiting. Dodds came partly dressed, O'Donnell forgot to bring his boots, yet he played in his service issue footwear and scored a tremendous goal from 20 yards!

Despite the German occupation of the Channel Islands, relatively few incidents occurred to affect the game, which continued modestly enough, but if the Germans wanted to use the pitch they just took over even if there was a match being played at the time. Three Jersey players were deported to Germany and three players and four officials were imprisoned in the island for offences against the occupying forces. Two Channel Islanders were awarded decorations, Lieutenant H. Nicolls of Guernsey Rangers won the MC and Corporal B. G. Esnoul of Jersey the MM and a mention in despatches.

Len Duquemin was a 16-year-old working on a farm and market garden belonging to the Vimiera Monastery. He had twice played for Guernsey Schools against Jersey. A friend of his on the island was a Tottenham supporter and as soon as the British recaptured their territory he arranged for him to have a trial at Spurs. Duquemin arrived at White Hart Lane the day Joe Hulme was appointed manager in January 1946 and his first game was as a guest for Chelmsford, then managed by Arthur Rowe. Duquemin's side lost 3-1 to Swindon reserves, but he scored. He also hit three for Spurs reserves and made his senior debut while still an amateur at Fulham on 9 March 1946.

Norwich's comparative geographical remoteness or rather the problem of getting there and back in half a day resulted in some other outlandish events. In 1940–41, Brentford refused to play there because of the difficulty in collecting a team that could take a whole day off. Norwich offered to play at Brentford and said they would travel in a bus which had sleeping accommodation, but the match was cancelled because of the air raid situation. During the same season on 14 September, Queens Park Rangers had only three players available for the Norwich excursion. The remainder were in the police, on munitions or other essential work and had to get back for the night shift.

In February of the same season, the aeroplane manufacturers' team Shorts Sports of Rochester invited Norwich to play in War Weapons week guaranteeing them £50 expenses. Norwich accepted and were beaten 6-1.

There were other gestures. On 21 November 1942 Leicester arranged an all-ticket game with Forest to be played at Coalville as a treat for the local miners. A crowd of 3,200 watched City win 2-1.

Not all rules were bendable, however. On 12 December 1942 Brighton wanted to admit servicemen free of charge at Christmas games but, as this was against League rules, they overcame the problem by making them guests of the directors. On the same day police refused admittance to spectators at the Bristol City v Cardiff City game who were not carrying their identity cards. The recorded attendance was 1,500. Bristol won 5-0.

Gimmicks were often featured. Liverpool signed the World Heavyweight Boxing Champion Joe Louis, then aged 30, in 1944 although never seriously considered him to add punch to the attack. 'Pongo' Waring played for Aston Villa reserves in 1944–45 and drew a crowd of 7,000 against West Bromwich. He was in his late 30s at the time. In a friendly between Bath and an Army XI the referee wore a pedometer in his stocking and clocked six-and-a-half miles in the first half.

In a number of international and service matches involving foreign service players and broadcast to Europe, the real identity of individuals involved had to be kept secret for fear of reprisals against relatives still living on the Continent, but families invariably realised their kin were playing because the commentators would disguise reference to them in such a way that the relatives alone would recognise them.

When France played Holland at Dulwich in February 1943, Farago was a last-minute choice for the French services team. He had travelled from South America to join the Free French Forces and celebrated by scoring the five French goals in 55 minutes. Earlier when Belgium had beaten the Dutch 5-4 at Wembley, Holland's left-half Van de Bosch could not speak a word of Dutch. He had lived in Great Britain for 20 years.

The Stalag IVB POW camp in Germany was so well off for players that a complete team of those drawn from good-class amateur and professional teams could be produced: McKinnon (Hibs), McBride (Barnsley), Hall (Newhaven), Roberts (Cardiff C), Dann (Newcastle U), Miller (Hibs), Steen (Wolves), Jeffrey (Motherwell), Hanlon (Manchester U), McCall (Bradford PA) and Morgan (Scottish junior club).

Such was the drive and enthusiasm for the game that servicemen would put on a match almost anywhere at the drop of a tin hat. Crews of landing craft played against other ships on the Normandy beaches in the wake of D-day. The huge concrete installations on the Western Front which had been overrun by the Allies' advance were even marked out as pitches.

In 1944–45 the Canadian Military HQ team in England played 27 games. Their captain and centre-half was Lance Corporal Alec Archer, a pre-war member of the Wembley Lions ice hockey team.

At the start of the 1941–42 season, the Bury crowd left Gigg Lane in tears after the 4-4 draw with Bolton. Beforehand the Civil Defence Committee had warned that a gas test would be held that Saturday but times and places had not been specified. Fully half the crowd of 2,730 were caught without their gas masks.

Arsenal, whose emergence had been aided in the years before the turn of the century by being given a set of red shirts by Nottingham Forest, were themselves able to help others. They loaned the Canadian Army team a full set of red shirts, with shorts and stockings. The Canadians sewed their maple leaf crest over the field gun emblem on the shirts. Arsenal had another Canuck connection. Jack Whent, born in Darlington, went to Canada as a boy. He had stayed 20 years and joined the Army there. He came to England, signed for Arsenal and guested for Brighton.

One of the oddest events involving a red shirt occurred, however, in the pre-match 'entertainment' before the Bolton v Manchester United, North Cup final at Maine Road in 1945. A one-legged man in a red singlet and white shorts hopped around ostensibly parodying the notion that United could win on one leg. It was the second leg of the final, but United only drew 2-2 and Bolton won the cup, United having lost the first leg . . .

Early in August 1944 Stoke staged a £100 sprint contest at the Victoria Ground similar to the pre-war Powderhall Sprint. It even included Jim Harley, the Liverpool full-back who had probably been the youngest to win this event when only 18, running under the assumed name of A. B. Mitchell.

Billy Rees was the man who ended a marathon. He had played rugby at school in Wales until he was 16, but playing in a six-a-side soccer game for a local team called Bluebirds at the end of 1943–44 he was spotted and given a game with Cardiff reserves. In a 14-0 win, Rees scored six goals. Three days later he made his senior debut in a 7-1 win over Swansea. The second leg of the Cardiff v Bristol City League Cup tie on 14 April 1945 at Ninian Park was much closer and lasted 202 minutes.

'Players collapsed all over the field, positional changes were made on both sides as men were treated for cramp, exhaustion and sheer excitement,' said Rees.

'Some spectators even went off for their tea and came back to see the finish. That came when Colin Gibson crossed from the right and somehow I found enough strength to head home.'

Worse – just about 60 seconds of it – followed the next season in the Third Division (North) Cup on 30 March 1946, when Stockport's second-leg match with Doncaster lasted 203 minutes. There was 90 minutes of normal time, ten minutes of extra time each way and a further 93 minutes had been added. At this point in time, 6.43 p.m. to be precise, bad light stopped play, the aggregate still being 4-4. A replay was necessary. After consultation with the Football League, the clubs tossed for choice of ground in the replay, which Doncaster won.

Other incidents ranged from the makeshift to the bizarre. Arsenal manager George Allison converted the referee's room at Highbury into his own personal flat after his family had been bombed out, and on one occasion West Ham goalkeeper Ernie Gregory deliberately lent against a goalpost when Spurs scored two palpably offside goals.

Instant bomb disposal, however, fell into an entirely different category, not to mention crater. An unexploded bomb had holed Chelsea's terracing. A police inspector told manager Billy Birrell that the disposal brigade were so busy they would be a week before tackling it. With a match on the following day, Birrell acted quickly. He put his hand in the hole, fiddled around with something metallic and pulled out a shell cap!

Other veterans had other problems. England international Charlie Buchan, who had retired in 1928 to take up journalism, was turned down by the services on account of his age just three weeks short of his 48th birthday. He enlisted in the Home Guard but on a field exercise pulled a muscle and limped around for six weeks. It was the worst injury he had suffered!

After one game in the 1945–46 season, a small boy approached Manchester City goalkeeper Frank Swift and asked for his autograph. The admiring lad enquired how he could become as great a goalkeeper.

'Well, son,' said Swift, 'after every match in which a goal has been scored against me, I make a practice of sitting down and drawing diagrams to see where I was at fault.'

After City lost 8-2 at home to Bradford Park Avenue in the FA Cup, Swift found the same youngster and enquired whether he wanted another autograph. 'No, sir,' came the reply, 'I just came to tell you that you've got a lot of homework to do this evening!'

Arsenal's pre-war popularity showed no sign of diminishing during the period of hostilities. The club received fan mail from servicemen in all theatres of war each week and many from POW camps in Germany.

With so many foreign servicemen in the country, a number of them found their way into League teams. Queens Park Rangers had a couple of Belgians on amateur forms: Emiel De Busser and Hadelin Yielleyoye. Brighton had a Polish international goalkeeper, Stankowski, Everton signed J. Scott Lee, a Chinese graduate of Manchester University, and Wolves gave Spanish Civil War evacuee Emilio Aldecoa a chance in their team.

Prisoners of War in Allied hands also attracted attention and although none was then signed by League clubs, several made their mark with minor teams. Paratrooper Bert Trautmann was captured on the Rhine and taken to a POW camp in Ashton-in-Makerfield in April 1945. For a time he was attached to a bomb disposal squad at Huyton. Alec Eisentrager was on the books of Hamburg SV as a youngster but was called up before he was 17. After three months as a recruit and in action less than a week, he was taken captive at Breda in Holland. Early in 1945 he was brought to England and played for teams in the south-east and west country areas.

Not all friendly foreigners were what they seemed, however. Stanley Rous was presented to a Norwegian escapee who was recommended for a PT instructor's course. When the FA Secretary questioned him about Norwegian Olympic players, his answers were totally unconvincing. He passed his suspicions on to the Home Office, but these were dismissed. Then a year later Lord Haw-Haw's familiar German propaganda broadcast beginning with this narrative: 'Germany calling, Germany calling. You sports enthusiasts in Britain may like to know that the nice Norwegian who has toured so many of your military establishments is in fact an agent of ours. Two nights ago he left as he arrived by boat to a waiting submarine and is on his way now to Berlin.'

One unexplained incident involved Leeds United travelling back from Hartlepools. The coach was passing through New Park in Harrogate when a bullet shattered a window, narrowly missing the head of trainer Bob Roxburgh. Two of the players Gerry Henry and Jim Milburn, the latter recovering from a war wound, were cut by flying glass. The identity of the culprit was never discovered.

William Garbutt coached in Italy before the First World War. When hostilities broke out he returned to England and joined up. After the armistice he went back to Italy until the late 1930s when he became a coach in Spain, only just escaping when the Civil War started and losing all the family's belongings.

Back in Italy he wanted to return to England to enlist again for the Second World War but was over age and decided to stay on as he had many friends there who promised to hide him from the Axis.

He managed to avoid capture over many months, but his wife was killed in an air raid. He changed his identity to become Michele Attardo, born Syracuse, and continued to foil the enemy until one day he was caught in a check-up and lined up in a village with other suspects. It seemed inevitable that he would be arrested, but a pig escaped from a nearby farmyard and in the confusion which followed, he made off himself.

27 THE FORCES TAKE PRIORITY

WHILE IT WAS obvious that players were servicemen first and footballers second, there was a measure of cooperation at various levels between the Armed Forces, national service organisations and the civilian game. Naturally, command performances requiring personnel to undertake tours under either Army or RAF jurisdiction called for no reference back to clubs at all, but as a PR operation or propaganda exercise these exhibitions were first class. One CO from a service headquarters overseas remarked that 'one soccer party was worth five ENSA shows in battle areas'.

For the participants it was no joy-ride covering miles of territory in Army trucks which were scarcely the last word in comfort. After every stop there was the need to not only put on an exhibition but one which would have to be better than the team playing against them. Invariably, this consisted of players with League experience, anxious to put one over on the galaxy of stars in opposition. Under these conditions the tourists had to be on their best behaviour, especially as it was under these circumstances that they had to find themselves the butt of local criticism from battle-weary troops. Of course, these star names were not expected to fight, but were required to be in reasonable shape to kick a ball about.

Tommy Lawton recalled the first hostile reaction he received in the war was when he was on tour in Italy and there were cries of 'D-day Dodgers' and 'PT Commandos' among the more repeatable comments hurled at him and his comrades.

Across the various continents towards the end of the war there were other crack sides operating in a series of entertainment exercises for the troops. Probably the two most famous next to the Wanderers were Denis Compton's touring team in India and Tommy Walker's side in the Far East. There were others involved, like Harry Johnston the Blackpool half-back who captained an RAF side which made a 3,000-mile tour of the Middle East.

Jackie Pitt had joined the RAF at 18. He was stationed in India and played centre-half while captaining the Combined Services team there. He led them against Walkers touring side before returning home to guest for Bath and Aberaman, as his Bristol Rovers club did not resume until 1945–46.

Ted Ditchburn the Spurs goalkeeper was in Compton's party which in one spell was unbeaten in 50 games. Johnny Morris the Manchester United inside-forward played against Walker's team in India and was then invited to join them. In 1944–45 one of Ditchburn's tours involved 33 games in India, Assam, Burma and Ceylon in tropical heat, where only 35 minutes each way could be played.

Matches designated as 'international' were also the subject of journalistic licence. The International Soccer Match announced for Christmas Eve 1945 at the Halton Ground in Karachi, India as 'England & Wales v Scotland & Ireland' consisted of players provided from the local RAF depot! The only recognised international was the England-Wales skipper Bernard Harper of Barnsley who had played for England in 1939–40.

In India there was an Anglo-Indian team, the Indians in it playing in bare feet. Often the number of matches by service players was phenomenal. Blackpool centre-half Eric Hayward recalled that in one spell of 82 days he played in 65 games.

Tommy Walker had joined the Army in 1940, served five and a half years mostly in the Royal Corps of Signals and became a Captain in the Welfare Section in India. Doncaster Rovers discovered Paul Todd while he was serving in the RAF. He captained an All-Services team in Ceylon. He had enlisted in 1941 after trials with Leicester and Wolves.

One of the oddest of impromptu games played by the services must have been the one which took place in a mountain village in Italy, between British soldiers and a team composed of Italian civilians. One goalpost was a fruit tree, the other a side of a house. Yet for Ted Sagar, Everton's long-serving goalkeeper and a Lance-Corporal in the Royal Signals, it was a position which had to be defended!

Italy was the stamping ground for almost as many studs as Army hobnails. As a hotbed of the game it attracted many servicemen to local teams. Albert Wakefield, a Leeds United centre-forward, impressed to the extent that several offers were made to him for when the war ended. He did not stay on, but one who did was centre-forward Norman Adcock. Born in Lincolnshire in 1923 and virtually unknown as a player in England, he was a member of the liberation army in 1945 who remained and played for several first-class Italian clubs.

Many aspiring footballers shone in Italy. One was Wally Fielding, an inside-forward who could easily be picked out in a game because of the shirt sleeves flapping in the breeze. His prowess had crossed with him from the Middle East football where he had first become prominent. Jock Sharp, an Everton director, then serving as a major in the Royal Ordnance Corps in Bari, noticed 'Nobby' Fielding's cool approach, confident swagger on the ball and natural swerve.

While touring players had to enhance their reputations as best they could, several modest servicemen had the opportunity to put themselves before the critical eye of the professionals. Willie Moir was in the RAF when he was noticed by Bert Johnson the Charlton wing-half who was assisting Bolton as a guest player.

He recommended Moir to Bolton and then persuaded the CO of Moir's unit to allow him time off to play in Wanderers' trial, which he did in 1943.

Another Bolton capture was Matt Gillies who had been a pre-war Glasgow medical student. He was an RAF navigator and stationed near Blackpool. But one of the oddest and cheapest captures was arguably Angus Morrison. He was spotted playing in Scotland in an RAF inter-services game in 1945 and recommended to Derby, who presented his 'discoverer' with a box of cigars for his trouble.

George Dews was serving at Whitby in the Army when Middlesbrough manager David Jack gave him a trial in August 1945. Dews scored two goals in the first half and was promptly signed during the interval. Gordon Hurst, an outside-right and Oldham amateur, was in the Royal Marines at HMS *Robertson*, their shore establishment in Kent. His CO recommended him to Charlton.

Sid Thomas, the Fulham forward who stood five feet six inches tall and wore size four and a half boots, served in Airfield Construction in West Africa and endured its exacting climate. 'They didn't know a great deal about the game, but were terrifically fast and beat us to the ball', he commented. 'It was a little humiliating, so I concentrated on speeding up my tackles.'

Lieutenant Norman Miller, an Arbroath forward who guested for Arsenal, also recalled natives in Africa 'beating us in bare feet'.

Six years of war and seven seasons of regionalised football had changed not only the face of the domestic game but the make-up of the players themselves. Jesse Pye had been a part-timer with Sheffield United before the war. He combined his football with work as a joiner. He enlisted in the Army and was posted to a Royal Engineers battalion where he became plain, simple Sapper Pye. In the Middle East he was a member of the Eighth Army and was selected to play for their team led by Stan Cullis, whose Wolves manager Frank Buckley had moved from Molineux to Notts County in 1944. When the Allied troops invaded Italy, Pye went with them. However, at the time of a representative game he had fallen foul of the authorities and was 'confined to barracks'. He was allowed to play but was marched there and back under escort. It was worth it. He scored a goal against Swift and was subsequently signed by Notts County.

Eddie Hapgood was an established international but also found himself in the embarrassing situation of being under close arrest and actually escorted by RAF police into the tunnel at White Hart Lane for a match! It should be recorded that the charge against him was dropped.

Hapgood's first posting was graphically recalled in his autobiography *Football Ambassador* (1945):

> From Cosford I moved, a fully qualified PT Corporal to Ruislip, arriving there late one winter's afternoon, very wet, heavily laden, and, need I add, browned off.

At the guard room they told me, politely, there was no accommodation for me at the moment, but that something would be fixed up for the night and I'd have to straighten things up for myself in the morning.

Then the SP called on a Corporal Ratcliffe to show me to some temporary sleeping quarters. With Ratcliffe carrying a pile of blankets and me still loaded with kit, we ploughed through the rain, past huts, barracks and outbuildings for what seemed miles, each moment getting more miserable.

We passed one sleeping hut, with a young Erk leaning out of the window. Spotting me, he called out – is that Eddie Hapgood? I wasn't very interested, but replied it was.

'I'm Sibley of Southend,' he replied.

With which my escorting Corporal threw down the blankets into a nice healthy looking puddle and in a broad Lancashire accent shouted – 'Well, what do you know. I'm Ratcliffe of Oldham Athletic.'

Things weren't so bad, after all, I was among friends again.

But war or no war, service life intruded. Harry Clarke was stationed in the RAF at Chippenham and played for Lovell's in their 1945–46 FA Cup run. He travelled by train to Newport, changing at Bristol. Before the tie with Bath he asked for a weekend pass but it was refused. He still played, but was caught and given seven days 'confined to camp', the RAF equivalent of 'barracks' on fatigue duties.

Interest in the game in service life became ingrained in its actual roots. According to Tom Finney:

Unit and depot sides didn't go by numbers or even regiments. They named their elevens after famous League clubs back home and battled all the harder. Imagine Huddersfield, Brentford, Queen of the South, Manchester City, Arsenal, Glasgow Rangers and Millwall all playing in the same League and Cup competitions.

Having said that, Finney himself played for a team called Bovington United . . .

Of the many touring service sides the Wanderers were the most famous. They were a combined services team who would play anywhere they could find opposition. One tour of Palestine produced 13 games in 23 days in a variety of towns like Jerusalem, Haifa, Beirut and Tel Aviv. Their method of transport was train and lorry. They won eleven and drew one of their matches, scoring 81 goals and conceding 20. They reached double figures three times. Equipment such as boots and other gear often arrived in comfort parcels for the troops from home.

When the Yugoslav partisans were given material help by the Allies towards the end of the war, several teams played matches against British service sides in the Mediterranean area. Hajduk Split defeated a number of them.

Among the signing-on forms that whistled around the world in those latter stages of the conflict, one went to Len Boyd, who was signed by Plymouth in

1945 while in Malta. An Argyle fan serving there wrote home to the club for amateur forms to be sent to him. Others went to Germany, France, the Middle East and India. Stan Pearson recommended to Manchester United a centre-half called Bob Robinson, seen playing in an Army side in Bombay.

Although these footballers who entered either the Royal Navy or the Merchant Navy found fewer opportunities on the high seas for a game than their shore-based colleagues in the Army and RAF, there were the exceptions of those installed on dry land.

Jimmy Logie, a Scot, had been spotted by Arsenal playing for Lochore Welfare and signed in June 1939. He made his debut in the Gunners' third team on Enfield's ground against Worcester City in a Southern League match. Arsenal won 3-1, all their goals coming from Tom Whalley. Two months later Logie was in the Navy and at one stage of his service was playing six times a week! He guested for Dunfermline regularly and also managed to assist Plymouth at Tottenham during 1945–46, but had played comparatively few matches under the auspices of the Football League in wartime.

Volunteering for anything in services was considered the height of stupidity. Trevor Ford was posted to North Wales where he volunteered for football only to be told they already had three full-backs. A corporal shouted at him when he left: 'You're a professional footballer, Ford. You should be able to play anywhere.'

Ford nodded. 'Right. You'll turn out at centre-forward tomorrow. We haven't got one.'

Ford scored twice in this inter-unit game. He was later posted to an anti-aircraft site in Essex and guested for Orient at centre-forward. Then in 1945–46 he was the country's leading scorer at Swansea.

Inter-service rivalry finally ended when the last Army v RAF fixture was played on 14 March 1946 and resulted in another victory for the khaki-clad, this time 3-0. They had never lost one of the games in the series, having won four and drawn three of the encounters.

The 1941–42 Inter-Allied Cup competition had attracted 11 teams. The Royal Navy did not enter, but by 1943–44 all except the National Fire Service were using amateur players. Amateurs rubbed studs with professionals many times. Tich Bellamy played in the same 5th North Staffs unit as Stoke's Norman Wilkinson, Jack Challinor, Jock Kirton, George Antonio, Jim Westland and Freddie Steele.

During hostilities, the Kentish Cup tournament, a three-sided affair between the French, English and Belgian Armies was held in abeyance. Belgium had won it in 1939. But officers of the Belgian Army had the presence of mind to hide the trophy from the Germans when the invasion came.

Hiding identities was not uncommon either. Malcolm Allison, a member of Charlton's nursery team, was called up and spent three months in Austria in 1945 playing for Klagenfurt and Rapid Vienna under the assumed name of Herbert Schmidt.

28 NON-LEAGUE PROGRESS

NON-LEAGUE SEMI-PROFESSIONAL football also survived, but had probably suffered more than any other branch apart from schools football which had been unable to organise itself outside of local areas. However, in the summer of 1939 there had been the usual activity in the transfer market.

Tunbridge Wells Rangers, whose manager was Ernest Hart, former Leeds and England centre-half, recruited Herman Conway, the West Ham and former Burnley goalkeeper. Scunthorpe & Lindsey United signed John Campbell who had scored over 100 goals in five years with nearby Lincoln. Former Luton skipper Jack Nelson went to Shrewsbury Town.

Versatile Welsh international forward Charlie Phillips who had cost Aston Villa £9,000 from Wolves in January 1936 moved to Chelmsford City from Birmingham. Chelmsford had appointed Harry Warren as secretary-manager in succession to Billy Walker, who had quit in October to take over Nottingham Forest. Warren had been in charge of Folkestone and saw the 1938–39 season out on the Kent coast. Fellow Essex club Colchester United added Ken Burditt ex-Norwich, Millwall and Notts forward. Both teams were comparative newcomers to the semi-professional ranks. One interesting note: Walker turned out for Forest on the left wing in a friendly against Chelmsford!

Hereford United appointed a new player-manager in Errington Keen, former Derby and England wing-half, himself with Chelmsford in the previous season. The much travelled 'Pongo' Waring opted for Bath City. Guildford City had high hopes of their own. In 1937–38 they had finished Southern League champions, two places above Ipswich Town who had gained election to the Football League. In 1938–39, Guildford had averaged crowds of 3,500.

Newcomers to the Kent League were Shorts Sports whose manager Stan Davies had an impressive pedigree as a Welsh international with Everton, West Bromwich and Birmingham. His star capture was Ted Harston, the goal-machine from Mansfield Town and Liverpool. Even South Liverpool could claim Tom Bradshaw, former Bury and Liverpool Scottish international centre-half.

The leading semi-professional competition was the Southern League. Pre-war, players could be signed while transfer-listed by Football League clubs. From

4 November a late start was made with 13 teams operating and split into East and Western sections with respectively five and eight clubs competing. Several fixtures were unplayed, but Chelmsford and Lovell's Athletic won their respective sections. The championship play-off was drawn 3-3. Worcester City won the Southern League Cup beating Chelmsford 7-3 over two legs, but Guildford City, having lost their home semi-final to Chelmsford 5-3, were not given a second leg because of the deteriorating war situation at the time.

Yeovil & Petters United who had played in this season lost their ground initially to the War Office then the USA Army who wanted to level the sloping Huish pitch to play baseball, an offer politely turned down.

The League closed down in 1940 when Chelmsford were the only non-league club represented at an Emergency League meeting, having offered to take over the fixtures of any club forced to retire during the season. This was accepted. Wigan Athletic, Gillingham and Shrewsbury also applied to fill vacancies. Being outside the League, Chelmsford and others were not restricted to paying their players £2 per game. City arranged a number of friendlies against League teams and were quite successful. At the end of December 1939 when Chelmsford played an FA XI, the visitors were drawn almost exclusively from players with London clubs. For this match they had to pay just 30s (£1.50).

On 22 May 1940 it was believed that Chelmsford was paying Football League players as much as £4 per game and in the Southern League match with Worcester, players like Frank Broome and George Edwards from Aston Villa, Dennis Westcott the Wolves centre-forward and Ted Duggan of West Bromwich were on view.

Not that it was all 'beer and skittles' for the non-league fraternity. Wigan Athletic returned from a Lancashire League game at Bolton with a 1d stamp as their share of the gate!

Chelmsford manager Warren had been commuting from Folkestone but, when Southend became a restricted area and United were forced to abandon their ground and play home matches at Chelmsford, he was promptly offered the same post with Southend.

Folkestone, who had been in financial difficulties and had decided to revert to the Kent League, blossomed on the guest front and on various occasions had the assistance of Jack Rowley and Stan Pearson from Manchester United and Fred Ramscarr of Northampton.

The Southern League was forced to close down in 1940 and even on the resumption in 1945–46 only 11 clubs could be mustered and these included the reserve teams of Swindon and Cardiff. Again not all fixtures were completed, but Chelmsford had two in hand in finishing five points ahead of Bath. Now under the managership of Arthur Rowe, they completed a double, beating Worcester in the League Cup final 9-4 on aggregate. Guest players continued to sprout throughout, but also ex-Spurs players like Fred Sargent and Andy Duncan enlivened the City side.

Gillingham, a League club until voted out in 1938, undertook a series of friendlies late in the war. Their first game did not come until Boxing Day 1943 when they played a friendly with Ford Sports. However, in 1944–45 and again in the following season they were champions of the Kent League.

The semi-professional arena was squeezed into that no-man's-land of being neither fully professional nor amateur. Those clubs which did succeed in carrying on depended on guests just as their apparent betters had to do in completing their teams. Location was important, and those within striking distance of military camps and RAF stations found life rather easier, although top players were invariably at the call of Football League clubs unless attracted by the extra money sometimes available.

It was while playing in a friendly for Shrewsbury that Frank Swift took his only penalty kick. It was a charity match against an RAF XI and Shrewsbury were five goals ahead. Shrewsbury's captain was Bob Pryde the Blackburn centre-half and he invited Swift to take the kick which the goalkeeper did, running the length of the pitch before hitting the ball straight into the net, through it and into the face of an elderly man behind the railings, breaking his false teeth.

Yeovil's plight was not really resolved until late on, though several members of the team occasionally combined with the local police to play games at Huish. Then in 1945–46 the revival of the Southern League and the closeness of military camps like Houndstone and Yeovilton enabled them to field guests of the calibre of George Milburn and Ken Gadsby from Leeds, Leicester's George Dewis and the Doncaster discovery Bert Tindill. Before that, the intermittent nature of the war game was illustrated one Boxing Day when a fixture was arranged with a strong Exmouth Marines side. The crowd turned up but there was no opposition. An hour passed. The assembly grew more restive than festive. Those who complained were given tickets for another match and went home. According to Yeovil's *Silver Jubilee Handbook*: 'The crowd thinned; just a few optimists stayed on. A few sang Christmas carols. Others swore.' Then the missing Marines arrived, much the worse for the festive spirits and Yeovil had little difficulty in disposing of the tipsy wanderers 9-0.

However, the most significant contribution from the ranks of the non-league game came when efforts to reinforce the isolated western outposts by adding clubs from outside the Football League were made initially in the second half of the 1940–41 season. Then a Western Regional League was formed with Bristol City, Cardiff City, Aberaman Athletic, Bath City and Lovell's Athletic taking part. The latter three clubs were recruited to the League West in 1942–43 to augment the three League clubs still operating there: Bristol City, Cardiff City and Swansea Town. This unique association lasted for three seasons.

Lovell's Athletic, based in Newport and renowned as the sports section of the toffee makers, were the most successful of the trio, winning the League West in 1942–43 and 1943–44 as well as finishing runners-up in the Cup during the first of these seasons.

In the last completed season of pre-war football Lovell's had been champions of the Welsh League, finishing 11 points ahead of Cardiff City reserves, who in turn were two places ahead of Aberaman with a superior goal average. Bath had been a middle-of-the-table Southern League team averaging exactly a point a game. The wartime, single-sheet Lovell's programme extolled the virtues of its product thus: 'Make the best use of your sweet coupons and buy Lovell's Toffee Rex still the king of toffees.'

Bath won the League West Cup in 1943–44 and 1944–45, but Aberaman were often struggling throughout the period, although they improved after finishing bottom in 1942–43 to move up two places above both Bristol City and Swansea in 1943–44 and again over the latter in the following season.

All three non-League sides had to rely heavily on guest players from Football League clubs from whom permission had to be obtained. Wherever possible, they also helped each other out with available players. However, Lovell's even managed to run a junior team which in the longer days of spring kicked off after the first team's home matches.

Bath had over 50 different players on duty in 1942–43. Stan Mortensen appeared in eight consecutive games from 3 October to 21 November, which produced seven straight wins and one defeat. This was 2-1 at Lovell's in the last game and the winners finished only two points ahead of Bath. Mortensen scored goals in the first six of these matches: 1, 3, 3, 2, 3, 1. In the first game of this run Ball, a Dulwich Hamlet amateur international, scored five times in a 7-0 win at Swansea.

Other full internationals who assisted the club that season were two goalkeepers – Joe Crozier of Scotland, who played three games and Welsh goalkeeper George Poland on one occasion. Goalkeeping problems persisted and, in one of the early season games at Newport, they had to be loaned Fairfax, the Lovell's trainer, to keep goal and were beaten 2-0, a loss of two points which in the end was the difference between winning the division and finishing second. Of their four defeats, three were sustained against Lovell's.

Mortensen again turned up at Bath in 1943–44 playing in a couple of games in October and scoring once. At the end of the first championship that season the club had called up 52 different players including nine goalkeepers. Attendances were generally healthy, a 3-2 win on Boxing Day being watched by 6,500, while the average crowd was half that figure. The return at Cardiff on New Year's Day, which produced a 2-1 win, was marred when the side had to be rearranged at the last minute. Hughes had tripped over a dustbin in the blackout and injured his leg.

Bath were considerably strengthened after the turn of the year by the acquisition of another international goalkeeper, John Jackson from Chelsea plus his Scottish colleague Dave McCulloch, the Derby centre-forward. From Boxing Day they had one run of seven games without defeat punctuated by a 2-0 defeat at Lovell's and another of six matches in the Cup-qualifying competition.

Having qualified for the League Cup North, Bath drew Aston Villa in the third-round first leg, doing well to lose by just a single goal at Villa Park on 1 April before a crowd of 30,000. A week later some 20,000 crammed into Twerton Park for the second leg to see an enthralling 3-3 draw and, after losing 2-1 at Swansea on 10 April, Bath remained unbeaten until the end of the season and in successive weeks in the same month beat Aberaman 16-1 at home and 8-1 away. Leslie Howe of Spurs scored six and McCulloch five goals in the former win. They had led 10-0 at half-time. As a result of their showing in the second half of the season, Bath finished top of the Second Championship although they had played only two games both against Villa with teams outside their area! In the League West Cup final, Bath beat Cardiff 4-2 at home, McCulloch scoring three times and then drew goalless away.

Goalkeepers again flitted in and out early in 1944–45. Eight different players appeared between the sticks in the first nine games alone. Mortensen assisted rather late on, scoring a hat-trick in a 5-1 win over Plymouth in a League West Cup game. Matches against Plymouth did not count in the League North Championship as Argyle had not then officially returned to regular competition, although they were playing themselves in for the following campaign.

Bath reached the League West Cup final again, beating Bristol City 1-0 at Bath on 19 May 1945 when Abe Rosenthal of Tranmere gave them a slender lead on the first leg, and the following week they emphasised their superiority with a 4-1 win at Ashton Gate, Rosenthal scoring twice.

Lovell's had the advantage of being in an area where a League club had been operating. The nucleus of a few Newport County players upon whom to call plus the attraction of a number of other useful League guests provided a sound basis for a successful side. Outstanding guests included Doug Witcomb, the West Bromwich wing-half capped by Wales, and Berry Nieuwenhuys, the South African forward of Liverpool. Welsh international Billy Lucas also made a dramatic impact on his debut on 26 September 1942 against Cardiff, scoring four times in an 8-4 win. The following week Lovell's suffered their first defeat, going down 3-1 at Cardiff. Lucas next appeared against Bath on 21 November scoring once in a 2-1 success, but oddly enough the effect was the same seven days later as Lovell's lost 2-1 at Bath. It was their only other defeat in League games.

A settled team was the keynote of success for Lovell's. Surprisingly, only 18 different players had to be used in 18 games during the first competition of the season. In the second half Lovell's succeeded in reaching the League West Cup final only to be surprisingly beaten 4-2 at home by Swansea and, though a valiant attempt was made the following week, they could only pull back one goal overall in winning this second leg 4-3, to lose the tie 7-6 on aggregate.

Other internationals who appeared included Bert Turner of Wales while Newport's Billy Owen was a regular and effective marksman. The New Year, however, brought less impressive performances with Bath again conquering them in the League Cup North proper. Bath once more proved superior in the opening games of the 1944–45 campaign, recording home and away wins over Lovell's. Again this unimpressive opening was decisive, as both Cardiff the champions and Bristol City the runners-up on goal average finished four points ahead of Lovell's, although the Newport club also lost to these two teams in successive weeks in December.

Cardiff proved just too strong for Lovell's in the first round of the League North Cup. After taking a narrow lead at Ninian Park, a goalless draw was enough for the return at Rexville in a game watched by a 10,000 crowd. But it had been a rewarding season in other ways. Witcomb, Norman Low a Newport County player and Leslie Bye formed a consistent half-back line and Eddie Jones the Swindon forward was a useful performer on the right wing.

Aberaman, a tiny Welsh club from a mining and industrial community, often experienced problems in raising a team, sometimes having to fall back on local players. Their claim to football fame was having launched the country's most expensive player, Bryn Jones, into a Football League career. Some home games were played on opponents' grounds by arrangement. They lost their first two matches but then beat Swansea 8-4 with George Crisp from Nottingham Forest, who usually assisted Lovell's, scoring four. They won only one other League game: 3-0 also against Swansea on 19 December when guest centre-forward Trevor Ford, loaned by the opposition, scored all three against his old club!

Aberaman improved noticeably in the qualifying competition of the cup to reach the first round proper. A record crowd of 2,500 turned up for the game with Bristol City, but the visitors won 3-1. A week later at Ashton Gate, Aberaman put on a fine display and had drawn level after 90 minutes with a two-goal lead, but a Clarrie Bourton goal in extra time ended their gallant fight-back.

Twice in the second half of the season they won at Lovell's and stalwarts in the side included that stoic Welsh international centre-half Harry Hanford of Sheffield Wednesday, who also played at right-back and even led the attack in an emergency, scoring a couple of goals. Bryn Jones even made a couple of nostalgic appearances as did his club and Welsh international colleague Horace Cumner.

Occasional outings by Charlton's George Tadman and Harry Brooks of Aldershot enlivened the attack in 1943–44. Matt O'Mahoney the Ipswich Town centre-half was usually on duty as well. Full-back Sam Barkas from Manchester City and an England cap was also seen, but they failed to qualify for the cup and the team varied dramatically from match to match. On Christmas Day at Newport, Lovell's had to loan them three players. Aberaman suffered a 10-goal rout at Bristol City on 20 January 1945, but on 7 April they beat Swansea 8-1 in the League West. Their last home game to Bath was lost 4-0. The attendance was estimated at 100.

29 WITH THE AMATEURS

T HE AMATEUR GAME did survive, too, its aim the same to provide recreation for the participants and onlookers whatever obstacles presented themselves. Thanks to the dedication of the few who found time to snatch odd hours between their own jobs and either Home Guard duties, fire-watching or ARP work, those clubs who found it possible to function, did so.

Earliest casualties among the ranks of the amateur leagues in the south of England were top competitions like the Isthmian and Athenian Leagues. These ground to a halt almost as soon as war was declared, but while many clubs had to pack up for the duration, others carried on and new competitions were formed.

Late in November 1939 a Surrey Combination opened with nine teams. In north London the Herts and Middlesex Combination started, largely as a result of Barnet, members of the Athenian League, who changed their minds about folding and invited Finchley for a friendly. In 1940–41 the league became the Senior Amateur League with Barnet, Enfield, Finchley, Golders Green, Hitchin Town, Hayes, Metropolitan Police, St Albans City, Slough, Southall, Tufnell Park and Wealdstone competing.

With daylight and nightly raids now commonplace, there seemed a chance that the new league might collapse, but Barnet, for example, carried on with members financing the continuation of the club from their own pockets. They won the London Senior Cup for only the second time in the club's history.

In 1941–42 with brighter prospects, Barnet were runners-up in the London Senior Cup, won the Herts Senior Cup and also became runners-up in the league. The following season they won three cups – the Herts Charity, the Finchley Hospital and Barnet Hospital for the second year running. In 1944–45 came a further breakthrough in honours with four different cups being won on successive Saturdays – the Herts and Middlesex League, Herts Senior, Herts Charity and Finchley Hospital.

In 1945–46 the amateur game returned to almost pre-war status and the FA Amateur Cup was restored, but Barnet also enjoyed a fine run in the FA Cup reaching the first round proper where they were beaten 6-2 at home by Queens Park Rangers in the first leg and 2-1 at Loftus Road in the second.

Still, they crowned even this achievement by winning the Amateur Cup. A record crowd of 53,832 was present at Stamford Bridge on 20 April 1946 and the leading northern amateur club Bishop Auckland provided the opposition. Receipts were £4,483. On the way, Barnet had beaten Wood Green, Walton Heath, Hitchin Town, Southall and Marine (Crosby).

Barnet were full value for a 3-2 win, led by their captain Lester Finch who had distinguished himself during the war period by assisting several professional clubs and being honoured with an unofficial full international appearance. In June 1941 the FA had marked his 100th appearance in representative football on 17 May by presenting him with a letter on vellum recording the occasion. Finch had been England's first choice outside-left at amateur level from 1933 to 1939. He had also played for Great Britain in the 1936 Olympics.

He had served in the RAF as a PT Instructor and was one of Barnet's scorers in the final. Another was Dennis Kelleher, who had his own story to tell but was forbidden to reveal it until after the war. Captured at Tobruk, he succeeded in escaping from a prison camp in Germany. He arrived home one Thursday in the 1943–44 season and played for the club on the following Saturday scoring two goals. Kelleher had scored 300 goals in three seasons for St Joseph's College, Upper Norwood. He became a Barnet amateur and also signed amateur forms for Crystal Palace in 1938–39.

Just as Barnet had enjoyed the services of a first-class amateur player who had added to his experience by playing as a wartime guest in professional teams, Bishop Auckland were in a similar position with one John Roderick Elliott Hardisty. Despite the several handles to his name, he was usually picked up by another one, 'Bob'. He had gained early recognition as a 17-year-old in Bishop's cup semi-final of 1939 when he was called upon to replace his own injured schoolmaster. During the war he assisted QPR, Middlesbrough, Hibernian and Reading.

Bishops had reached the final for the 12th occasion and had won it a record seven times. They were captained by Humble who with goalkeeper Washington had both won the competition in 1939.

Only six clubs operated in the Northern League when it restarted in 1939–40. They were Bishop Auckland, Crook Town, Shildon, South Bank, West Auckland and Heaton Stannington. Shildon achieved a League and Cup double. In 1943 Crook reformed from the Hole-in-the-Wall Colliery Home Guard team at the drift mine overlooking the town. Bishops also had a good run in the 1945–46 FA Cup reaching and beating Willington in the first round proper before losing to York City.

The Hampshire League managed to maintain its presence all through the war, as did the Birmingham & District League and the Northern Combination. The Isthmian League succeeded in playing one representative game against their old Athenian rivas, who beat them 3-1 in a game for the Red Cross Fund on 6 April 1940.

Both the Middlesex Senior League and Middlesex Senior Cup continued. Sufficient entries were gathered for the latter and Hayes were 1940 winners.

Wealdstone won it for the next three years then came Finchley, Southall and Wealdstone again. Pinner were runners-up in the League for five consecutive seasons from 1941–45! The Middlesex Charity Cup was renamed the Middlesex Red Cross Cup.

Other areas carried on with familiar competitions. The Durham Junior Cup, Leicester Senior Cup and Surrey Senior Cup ran uninterrupted. Stanley United won the Durham Challenge Cup, Durham Hospital Cup, Durham Central League Cup and Crook Nursing Cup in 1941–42. They added the Northern League when it restarted in 1945–46. The Lancashire Combination was one of the first northern competitions to announce a reorganised if reduced tournament in 1939–40 which Rochdale reserves won.

To make up the numbers from the dearth of civilian clubs, works teams and service sides often added to the variety in these leagues. In the London area one region was covered by the Great Western Combination, another by the South-Combination. In the former league, several works clubs in the industrialised Slough area competed with Oxford City, Uxbridge and Yiewsley. They included Heavy Duty Alloys and Windsor Works, the playing name of a company called Jacksons. In 1942–43 Leyton played games at West Ham. They were one of only three South Essex amateur teams outside of works teams still functioning. The other two were Clapton and Walthamstow.

Hersham's ground was taken over for agriculture on the outbreak of war and the club merged with Walton in 1945, but Tooting & Mitcham United carried on somehow, despite having three bombs fall on their ground and the stand destroyed twice. They played in the newly formed South-Eastern Combination, which included clubs like Dulwich Hamlet, Erith & Belvedere, Nunhead and Wimbledon. Moreover, they had a degree of success winning the League three times plus two cups. Erith created a goalscoring record in 1941–42 totalling 253 goals in 44 matches, winning 39 of them. They won the Combination with 31 points out of a possible 32 and also added the South Combination Cup and County Cup. The East Anglian Cup was also regularly contested. Cambridge Town, who had some outstanding guests at times, won it in 1943, 1944 and 1946. Amateur and semi-professional guidelines frequently blurred.

On 29 September 1939 representatives from nine of the leading amateur clubs in South Essex had met and launched the South Essex League Combination. Teams involved were Walthamstow Avenue, Leytonstone, Clapton, Romford, Leyton, Barking, Dagenham, Grays Athletic and Tilbury. Alas the 1940–41 season was only a few weeks old when this new league was disbanded; Avenue carried on and some kind of game was played each week. With Jim Lewis as player-manager, they entered five competitions in 1941–42 and won them all: London Senior Cup, East Anglian Cup, Grays and Tilbury Cup, Herts and Middlesex League plus Herts and Middlesex League Challenge Cup.

Their League championship success in their first season in the competition was achieved by a margin of ten points. They won 22 of 24 games, one match being drawn. Their sole defeat came when needing to complete their programme they had to field two teams on the same day! The juniors were no slouches either and picked off the London Junior Cup for the fourth time in seven years. The full record for the seniors including several friendlies against professional teams was: Played 38, won 33, drawn three and lost only two. They scored 156 goals and conceded 43.

On 2 May 1942 Lewis was presented with an illuminated address on vellum in recognition of his selection for over 100 representative teams. His total at the time was 126. In company with Lester Finch, Lewis had been on the England FA tour of South Africa in 1939. As amateurs they were, of course, unpaid, but on returning the FA said they could each receive a gift to the value of £10. Finch chose a clock, Lewis a new 3-speed gear bicycle for his son.

While not so successful in 1942–43, Avenue still managed to take the League and one cup honour and in 1943–44 a reserve team was started for the first time in four years, entering the Northern (London) Alliance League, which it won. They were unbeaten and scored 187 goals against 36. Over 60 players appeared for the club that season and the seniors won the League and four cups. They also beat a team of professionals from the London area 3-0 in a friendly.

In 1944–45 the two Jim Lewis's, father and son, played together and for the fourth consecutive year Avenue won the Herts and Middlesex Shield having lost only three games during the season. The reserves suffered only one defeat in winning their competition and the Essex Junior Cup by beating Leyton 3-2 in the final.

The following season the Isthmian League was restarted and proved another triumph for Walthamstow who, despite having to play ten games in 14 days at the season's end, won the championship, scoring a record 100 goals in 26 games. Jim Lewis senior was playing in his 16th season. The club had also staged the first international between two foreign countries to be held in England. On 2 February 1941 Belgium and Holland drew 3-3 at Green Pond Lane. Prince Bernhard presented the cup to the Belgium team 'as a gesture of the goodwill of his countrymen'. A crowd of over 5,000 attended and were entertained by a Dutch military band of 35 players.

Other county leagues managed to continue on a restricted basis and there were few areas which failed to provide some kind of amateur football. The Berks and Bucks Senior Cup was won for five consecutive seasons by Windsor & Eton, setting up a record for such a tournament. In the 1945–46 season they finished runners-up.

The London Senior Cup also managed to function throughout the war years, though clubs like Leytonstone, who closed down in 1940 and did not reopen until November 1944, were notable absentees. When Leytonstone did return they found themselves playing Wealdstone in a friendly when a flying bomb dropped uncomfortably near their premises.

Wembley Stadium was used as a venue for several London area cup finals and Tufnell Park claimed to be the first Isthmian League club to appear at the Empire Stadium. They were finalists in the Middlesex Red Cross Cup in successive years – 1944 and 1945. During the war they shared Golders Green's Claremont Road ground.

Minor amateur games were harder hit than even this, although again with some ingenuity and industry by officials, who managed to find time outside war work to organise teams, they played on. In 1939–40 the talk of such circles in the East End of London were East Ham CA who won the London Labour Challenge Cup, the Manor House Hospital Charity Cup, Manor House Hospital Charity Shield, East Ham Memorial Hospital Cup and their division of the league! In all they played 30 games, won all of them and scored 101 goals while conceding 29.

The war treated all alike, triumphs and tragedies, honours and heartaches respected no one's status. Kingstonian's amateur international Lionel Thornton was commissioned in the Sherwood Foresters, rose to the rank of Major in 1030, was evacuated from Dunkirk but was subsequently killed in Burma. Leyton-stone's Leon Joseph joined the Royal Fusiliers in 1939 and assisted West Ham, Charlton and even Glentoran. Twice wounded in Italy, he was invalided out of the Army in 1944. That same year Enfield's Jack Rawlings was badly wounded in a tank in France.

Jim Paviour had joined Romford after enlisting in the Army at 17. In 1937 he was captaining the United Services team in Cairo and was due to leave the services when he was posted Athenian League forms while out there. When the war came he returned to serve in Palestine, Egypt, Iraq, Persia, Syria and Italy and in 1941 captained the Middle East services side 'The Wanderers' during their tour of Turkey.

St Albans City and later Wealdstone centre-forward Charlie Bunce died at 30 as a POW in Malaya after being captured by the Japanese. He had scored 174 goals. Dulwich Hamlet's Bill Parr, an Arsenal amateur, was killed on RAF service. Able Seaman White, an amateur international widely known as 'Knocker', a formidable stopper centre-half, played his greatest game and his last for the Navy against the Army at Villa Park in May 1939. He went down with HMS *Hood* in 1941.

Walthamstow had six players who won decorations: Lt. Cmdr. D. Skells DSC, Flt. Sgt. O. Marston DFM, Flt. Sgt. J. Fordham DFM, Sgt. G. Foreman MM and Bar, Sgt. A. Gardner MM and Flt. Sgt. S. Preston MM. Four Barnet players similarly honoured: Flt. Lt. Tolchard DFC and Bar, a Bomber Command Pathfinder who took part in 60 operational flights, J. Hill AB who also won the DSM and the Polish Cross of Honour; Lt. Dennis Kelleher MBE and Sgt. Harold Faircloth MM who was killed in action in the winter of 1943–44. Hitchin Town's F/O

Izard won the DFC, LAC T. Chellow the GM; Chesham United's Sq. Ldr S.F. Keen was awarded the DFC and Conspicuous Gallantry Medal. Bromley defender Doug Cameron, a Bomber Command pilot, won the DFM and DFC.

Cambridge University Soccer Blues sadly suffered, particularly in the 1942–43 season. On 3 November Squadron Leader Roger de W.K. Winlaw, a double Blue at soccer and cricket, was reported killed on active service. The following day Pilot Officer C. T. Ashton, a triple Blue and former Corinthian and England international, was killed at the age of 41. At the end of the month Captain Roger H.C. Human, another double Blue was reported to have died in action. It was his 26th birthday. The following month on 6 February Pilot Officer Noel G. Sprake RAFVR was also killed in action.

The Varsity Match was held far more frequently in wartime than previously. These were unofficial matches which did not count in the official Battle of the Blues, but were nonetheless eagerly anticipated and keenly fought. The first was on 7 December 1939 and finished in a 2-2 draw. That was at Oxford and a return was played at Cambridge on 28 February with the Light Blues winning 3-2. While Oxford recognised these players by giving them membership of the Centaurs FC, Cambridge awarded wartime Blues and, with the advantage of scientists in residence on war effort, the Light Blues won seven and drew three of the 12 matches played. In 1945–46 official matches resumed and the teams drew 1-1 at Champion Hill, the last pre-war venue.

30 FINANCIAL BENEFITS

THE RELATIVELY LOW overheads of wartime football enabled charity to be the chief beneficiary in the period 1939–45. This was organised quickly enough. The Red Cross and St John Appeal Sports Committee was set up as early as 10 October 1939 with Colonel the Rt. Hon. Lord Wigram as Chairman and Stanley Rous as Deputy Chairman and Secretary.

In just over four years £1 million had been raised from all sources, £67,711 of it from soccer. By the end of the war the figure had risen to nearly £3 million and other funds had also benefited under the 1940 War Charities Act. The actual figure was £2,980,938, of which Association Football contributed £119,243. Of this sum, £11,387 had been donated to Mrs Churchill's Aid to Russia Fund.

The Football Association was wholly or partly responsible for many other worthy causes of a charitable concern. They included King George's Fund for Sailors, the Forces Benevolent Funds, Civil Defence Welfare Funds, Merchant Navy Comforts Fund, Soldiers, Sailors and Airmen's Families Association, St Dunstans, YMCA Services Appeal, YMCA War Services Fund, Salvation Army, National Children's Home, Newspaper Press Fund, 'Aid to China' Fund, Wings for Victory, Spitfire Fund, and so on, and the total raised was more than £84,000. Even when the war in Europe ended, some of these charities continued to receive much-needed support. The King George's Fund for Sailors, for example, received £6,000 from the meeting of the North and South Cup winners in June 1945.

The first season of wartime football inevitably produced heavy losses for clubs in England and Scotland. Of 60 such clubs announcing figures in 1940, only five showed a profit, of which there was just one Football League club, Barrow, which reported making £81.

Rangers made £1,590 and Dundee United £764, both figures excluding their share of War Cup final receipts. The other Scottish clubs which reported profits were Alloa with £231 and Raith Rovers with £16. The only other organisation to make any money was the Football League, which made an equally modest £17.

The losses were understandably heavy. The Football Association's extensive commitments led to a deficit of £13,337, the Scottish FA lost £5,877, while losses for League clubs ranged from Wrexham who had a deficit of £178 to Wolverhampton Wanderers who lost £17,717. In contrast to Dumbarton's deficit of £19, Celtic announced a loss of £7,155 and non-league Wigan Athletic £1,135; Bradford Park Avenue, who lost £1,763, were £30,154 in debt.

In the following year, Preston's successful season turned what had been a loss of £10,981 in 1940 into a profit of £2,488. Celtic and Rangers were also in the black at, respectively, £2,365 and £2,314. The Football League was in credit for the year at just £16, £1 less than the previous year. Heavy expenditure by the FA led to another loss of £9,287, while the Scottish League was down at £3,732. Wolves again lost heavily, their deficit for the year being £4,846.

In 1942 there was some joy for two north-east clubs, Gateshead and Newcastle United, which showed profits, respectively, of £1,519 and £1,509. The League profit was slightly lower but still in the black at £14. The FA's deficit was smaller at £3,703 and the Scottish League lost £186.

Bournemouth were one of the clubs whose geographical situation caused them to miss out on several wartime seasons purely because they lacked opposition. Crowds were meagre. One game at the end of the 1939–40 season realised only 440 spectators and from a gate of 900 the income was less than £50. Fortunately Cooper Dean, the owner of the ground, had come to the rescue of the club by agreeing to reduce the rent to £100 a year and few season ticket holders asked for refunds.

Friendly matches were even less well supported. One game between an RAF XI and HMS *Majestic* was watched by 18 people who contributed just under 11s (55p).

Inevitably there were odd cases of charity not benefiting as much as it might have done. It was discovered after a Home Guard v Eastern Command match in East Anglia that only 20 per cent of the proceeds had gone to the charity involved. The regulations stipulated that only 20 per cent could be retained for expenses.

As the war continued, income tended to increase. In 1943 the Glasgow Charity Cup which was won by Celtic realised £5,130, the biggest intake of cash for this competition since 1931. Increased Entertainments Tax cut into profits, but came at a time when more clubs were reporting credit rather than debit balances. In 1943 Aston Villa made a profit of £5,838 after earlier heavy losses. Tottenham, Chelsea and Manchester City were among the leaders of the profitable clubs. Rangers made £4,479 that year and even Bath City accrued £335, but Wolves lost £1,221.

In 1944 the Molineux club lost £3,585, but neighbours Aston Villa announced a profit of £3,574. Their expenditure for the season included £3,647 for income tax, £3,522 for players' benefits, £18,437 in Entertainments Tax, £11,617 for the visitors' share of gate money and £3,781 as the League's percentage. On the credit side £44,720 came from ground admissions and £6,285 from away games. Then there was £410 from the League Cup's pool. Wages were modest, of course. Even when match fees for players were increased to £4 in 1945–46 Aldershot were paying £4,569 in wages compared with £1,884 13s.6d the previous year.

Leicester, Tottenham, Coventry, Darlington and Doncaster were among other clubs who turned in favourable balance sheets that year. Spurs' profit was £3,848. Coventry not only made a profit but overall were £11,684 in credit. Yet, Arsenal reported a loss of £4,514. Their overdraft was £25,000 and although gate receipts were £17,000 they had to pay £6,240 in interest on loans.

The 1945 South Cup final brought in £26,000 of which £12,000 went to Entertainments Tax. Each club took £4,000 and £4,000 went into the Football League pool. That left £2,000 for expenses. Players received a match fee of £2; the winners were given five National Savings Certificates, the losers three each.

Scottish football raised £177,443 from wartime matches with the Scottish branch of the Red Cross receiving £38,973 of it and the Army Welfare Fund £16,953.

On Easter Monday 1944, 17 Everton players received benefit cheques totalling £5,500. The occasion was a Lancashire Cup second-round game with Liverpool, whom they proceeded to beat 3-0. The same year the Football League agreed to the payment of benefit amounting to £3,645 to 14 Wolves players including two who had died as the result of war injury – Eric Robinson and Joe Rooney. In February 1943 the Benevolent Fund was used to pay removal expenses for effects to Sunderland of Percy Saunders, a Brentford player lost at sea escaping from Singapore.

By 1946 more announced profits. Everton's £21,557 was the highest. Villa made £18,185, Rangers £6,214 and Celtic £3,614.

Although the official view was that football pools reflected badly on soccer, there were privately held opinions that some substantial credit might be taken from them if organised for the benefit of the game itself. The war helped to change the thinking about them and a move involving FA Secretary Stanley Rous and Arthur Elvin, head of Wembley Stadium, tried to bring about the institution of a national pool.

The scheme was for a pools company to be set up independent of existing bodies with half the profits filtered off to the game, but before any further steps could be taken, the Government agreed to the amalgamation of all existing pools into one Unity Pool. It was formed from Littlewoods, Vernons, Copes, Shermans, Bonds, Jervis, Screen and Socapools. Rous was still keen to implement his ideas despite this move and approached Ernest Bevin, a member of the War Cabinet. Though it was well received, it became lost in the welter of weightier problems on the minds of the Government at the time.

Because of the paper shortage, the printing of coupons was prohibitive, but it was agreed that these should be reproduced in newspapers for the benefit of the pools punters. Littlewoods' building was used for rubber dinghy manufacture and many pools workers were switched to war work, making parachutes and barrage balloons instead of checking coupon entries. However, Littlewoods and Vernons administered the new pool. One early win produced indignation from moralists and the anti-pools lobby. On 20 January 1940 a female pools punter from Hull won a record Unity Pool dividend on the previous week with £8,059 from an outlay of 1s.6d (7p).

The FA's thoughts for after the war included revolutionary pools plans. This, in 1943, was in stark contrast to the hostility which had hitherto been attributed to this form of gambling. The recommendations were as follows:

> The use of Pools is so firmly established with such a large proportion of the population that it is suggested that the FA should approach the appropriate Government departments with a view to their devising a scheme whereby part of the proceeds of Pools should form a central fund from which the costs of the provision of grounds, gymnasia, recreation rooms, sports centres and clubs might be made. A scheme of this type has been for some years in operation in Sweden under Government control and it resulted in no less than eight million pounds being made available for health and recreation services in three years.

Before a return could be made to peacetime regulations there was a court ruling which declared newspaper coupons illegal. A suit filed by a Stockport clergyman was successful. He claimed that they violated the 1934 Betting and Lotteries Act. On 22 June 1945 Lord Goddard gave judgement in the King's Bench Divisional Court. The pools promoters appealed and at the same time took steps to introduce coupons through the mail.

Another outstanding success of the period was the League War Cup run by the League to compensate for the lack of an FA Cup competition. Despite the late start made in the 1939–40 season, each competing club received £160 from the pool. The following year they each had £150. In 1941–42 the London League was able to distribute £300 each to their clubs from their own cup competition.

In 1943 the War Cup pool share was nearly £390, the predominance of northern clubs, of which there were 54 operating, producing £17,724 and the 18 southern sides £10,316. In 1943–44 the figure went up to £410 per club. It was hoped to use the pool funds to pay off the £29,000 still outstanding by clubs in transfer fees. It was proposed that each club would loan its share of £410 from the pool to the League interest free, but the idea failed to gain sufficient support.

Though there had been a trickle of transfers, it was only after the European war ended that the market perked up. The first substantial move came at £4,500 on 22 August 1945 when West Ham transferred Len Goulden to Chelsea. The same club then signed their wartime guest centre-half John Harris from Wolves for £7,000 and Tommy Lawton from Everton in November 1945 for £11,500, the second highest transfer fee in the history of the game.

Earlier in the war many moves had been from amateur to professional ranks. Walley Barnes had been a messenger with Portsmouth and Gosport Gas Co. He could have joined either Pompey or Southampton, but chose the former as they were in the First Division. He was a Territorial and was immediately called up. He had a couple of games for Portsmouth but then joined Southampton in 1942–43, scoring 19 goals as either inside-left or left-winger before moving to Arsenal, where he became an international defender!

31 INDISCIPLINE AND MISCONDUCT

WHILE *SINE DIE* suspensions for wartime misdemeanours seemed to be handed out by the FA with the abandon of someone throwing confetti at a wedding and then just as quickly sweeping it up again, they were divorced from punishments postponed from peacetime, which produced more permanent pronouncements. In truth, the indefinite bans were lifted with relative speed.

There were prior warnings issued in several cases. On 5 June 1940 both Dudley Milligan of Chesterfield and Aston Villa's George Cummings were warned as to their future conduct. On 27 October 1942 Milligan was suspended *sine die*, Cummings followed on 18 January 1943, the latter after incidents in the Leicester v Villa game on 25 December. Cummings had his suspension lifted on 20 August and Milligan was also subsequently cleared to play again. In a little over a year, Cummings was turning out for Scotland.

As far as Milligan was concerned, in 1941 he had gone to work in the Belfast shipyards and assisted several Ulster clubs, but ran into more disciplinary trouble playing for Distillery.

In contrast, on 3 June 1940 five Leicester City directors were suspended *sine die* and four others suspended for periods up to four years. Former manager Frank Womack was suspended for one year and the club was fined £500. These findings came as a result of an investigation started before the war involving excess bonus and signing-on fees and irregular payments to amateurs. It was followed up on 6 September by the suspension for one year of 12 players.

However, not all the contemporary suspensions were dismissed as easily as those imposed on Milligan and Cummings. Charlie Napier of Sheffield Wednesday was unique in that he twice suffered *sine die* suspensions to become soccer's classic three-time loser. His first suspension occurred on 15 February 1941 while guesting for Falkirk. A month later the Scottish club appealed to the Scottish FA to intervene on behalf of Napier, but nothing happened until 8 September when the FA announced that the Disciplinary Committee had reviewed the case but were unable to change their decision. He was reprieved in August 1943 but fell out of favour again by being banned *sine die* for a second time on 11 January 1944 following an alleged remark to a Grimsby player on 23 October 1943 when he was playing for Sheffield Wednesday. That club later appealed that it had been a case of mistaken identity and eventually the player was reinstated. Then in September 1945 he played his last game for Wednesday before being transferred to Falkirk!

The deliberations over Derby County's payments in excess of those allowed dating back to the period between 1925 and 1938 did not materialise until 29 August 1941 when the FA announced that six directors and former manager George Jobey had been suspended *sine die* and the club fined £500.

Other players apparently suspended for life and then reinstated included Eddie Connelly of West Bromwich who was sent off twice and banned from 9 November only to be allowed to return on 25 October 1941, and Berry Nieuwenhuys, the South Africa-born captain of Liverpool. His case revealed a scandal which had been largely covered up or ignored during the war concerning players asking for more than the regulation £2 per game. 'Nivvy', one of the most accomplished wingers in the game, had apparently asked a certain League club for extra payment. L. V. Manning writing in the *Daily Sketch* said of the incident:

> The only surprise about this case is that a club has the courage to pass on to the League the letter written by the Liverpool captain. The exposure comes too late in the war to do much good, but it must have made many well-known players realise how lucky they have been.
> Pity the League were not in a position to expose an evil which everybody back-stage knows to have flourished all through the war seasons.

Nieuwenhuys was unlucky enough to be caught. The number of players receiving more than their statutory fee plus reasonable expenses was probably few enough, but clubs who could afford to pay over the odds, since leading players knew monetary inducement would invariably attract top guests. Charlton had been fined in November 1939 for paying players more than 30s (£1.50) in friendlies. This was later rescinded as other clubs had overpaid in error, but as early as 1940 there were hints that some clubs were paying players £3 per game. Mostly, it was not a question of players holding clubs to ransom, since it was a seller's market and the better-quality players were continually in demand.

Even so, Nieuwenhuys was not lost to the game for good; indeed it was probably felt that since his 'capture' had been almost selected by lottery for its exposure, no benefit would have derived from punishing him to the extent of taking his livelihood away. He, too, was later reinstated. Court action might well have rendered the punishment illegal anyway.

When the Crystal Palace chairman Percy Harper was given a life ban on 3 February 1945 following criticism he made of the FA Council members in the club's match programme on 30 September 1944, there was such an outcome. Harper refused to apologise for the remarks and he took out a High Court injunction against the FA. The ban was immediately lifted.

It should be mentioned that Nieuwenhuys, a flight-sergeant in the RAF, was later that season awarded the Czech Medal of Merit in recognition of services rendered to the Czech Fighter Squadron with whom he had served as an instructor. Tommy Lawton, allegedly left out of several England teams for publicly voicing his displeasure at payment for international service, was reinstated and even given the captaincy.

Instances of misbehaviour on the field were rare but not unknown. Even during the friendly matches before the start of the regional competitions, the Disciplinary Committee of the FA had expressed their concern at events. One Colchester United player was suspended for a month and following a Doncaster Rovers v Notts County friendly, several players received 14-day bans.

While teams were often short of players, trying to find referees was another problem. It was just as difficult to use qualified Football League officials for every game as it was to unearth professional footballers and those amateurs attached to League clubs. The quality of replacements varied. On 15 February 1941 in a first-round, first-leg War Cup game, Clapton Orient had to send round the ground for a referee and two linesmen. They beat Aldershot 3-2. It was one of only two games they won all season! Incidents were mercifully uncommon. Matches were generally played in an atmosphere of goodwill, but no less competitive for all that and not unnaturally there were some odd happenings.

For some reason Crystal Palace had more than their share of lively events in the 1940–41 season at Selhurst Park. Perhaps, as the eventual winners of the South League, keenness was a contributory factor, not to mention the local derby aspect. On 28 September against Millwall, the visiting players disputed a penalty and became involved in fighting a section of the crowd. The referee ordered both teams to the dressing-room and there was a 6-minute cooling off period before a resumption. Palace won 2-1. The crowd was 2,500. On 8 March Millwall returned. The referee awarded Palace a penalty, Millwall objected. Several players manhandled the official. He remained firm, the game continued and Palace won 5-3.

Two weeks later against Brentford, Palace, who were leading by four clear goals, were awarded another penalty. Harry Duke, the Norwich goalkeeper who was between the sticks for Brentford that day, quit his goal in protest. Brentford players chased after the referee who also left the field. Five minutes later both teams walked off. The game was held up for 15 minutes before they resumed. Arthur Hudgell scored from the delayed penalty; Palace won 5-0. Then, on 17 May 1941 when Southend were the visitors to Selhurst Park, a more bizarre episode took place – the mysterious case of the vanishing goalkeeper.

Nick Collins scored the fifth Palace goal which the Southend goalkeeper clearly considered offside. When it was not disallowed he walked off the pitch and into the dressing-room. The referee followed him, retrieved his jersey, which he handed to another player and the game continued. Southend lost 7-0.

It was also difficult to separate traditional rivalry which often went over the bounds of reasonable behaviour simply because circumstances had passed from peacetime to wartime conditions. The Rangers–Celtic game at Ibrox on 6 September 1941 boiled over. Rangers won 3-0 and police had to draw their batons and charge a section of Celtic supporters. Two players had been stretchered off and bottles were thrown on the pitch. Eleven days later as a result of these incidents the Celtic ground was closed until 17 October. On 25 December 1942 in the game between Hibs and Rangers, the Rangers goalkeeper Jerry Dawson was knocked out by a bottle thrown from the terraces. He was carried off and the remaining Rangers players wanted to leave with him but were persuaded to stay by their chairman.

These were isolated examples of unpleasantness. The majority of games were conducted in fine spirit and appreciated by the spectators. Indeed, the practice of players shaking hands with opponents after a match became the accepted norm, whereas in pre-war days it had been a rarity.

On 14 November 1942 in a League West game between Cardiff City and Lovell's Athletic, spectators invaded the pitch when the game turned into a rough-house. Several players needed police protection and then the remainder left the field. The referee subsequently brought them back and made them all shake hands before resuming. Lovell's won 1-0.

The practice in the north of home and away matches on alternate weeks against the same team sometimes meant that animosities which might have been dissipated over several months of a season were kept fresh. In November 1942 five players were sent off in one weekend, a cause for considerable concern at the time. On 26 October 1940 rival supporters attending the Stockport County v Liverpool match were involved in fisticuffs. Stockport won 2-0 but lost 5-0 at Anfield the following Saturday.

In February 1944 the Disciplinary Committee warned players – two in particular – to avoid 'reckless' and 'unduly robust play'. In May 1942 the FA had warned referees that the abnormal conditions were no excuse for failing to implement the laws of the game and ignoring their duties. Particular reference was made to the injury suffered by Stan Cullis while playing for Fulham, but no disciplinary action was taken at the time.

In March 1941 after a match involving Chelsea and Brentford, the Brentford captain was censured for not insisting that one of his players accept the referee's decision and resume play. The FA decided that clubs under their jurisdiction be told that 'a team captain is responsible for the collective conduct of his players and failure of this will lead to disciplinary action against the captain and the club. Clubs are to inform their captain.'

Clubs themselves had to face problems as well. Clapton Orient's wretched 1940–41 season, in which they won only twice and one of those a War Cup match which they lost over the two legs, brought more trouble. On 22 April 1941 the FA suspended them for a failure to meet 'certain obligations'. But they were reinstated four days later after apparently rectifying these. Previously, they had been chided for ignoring the regulations about obtaining players, not to mention officials, from the crowd. In 1940–41 there were other examples of amateur players being suspended for up to a year for accepting money, and professionals suspended and clubs fined for faulty registration of players.

On 13 April 1940 there was a row between the FA and Everton over the selection of Joe Mercer for an England v Wales international and at the same time being picked for Everton's Lancashire Cup semi-final derby game with Liverpool. Everton refused to release Mercer for England duty. He played for Everton wearing the number 7 shirt for the first and only time in his career – a kind of protest, figuratively speaking! An investigation afterwards cleared Sergeant Instructor Mercer of any blame in the matter, but two Everton directors were suspended by the FA.

Derby County were fined 10s (50p) for not having a result sheet in on time in 1943 and Bath City were fined two guineas (£2.10) for being late at games at Aberaman and Cardiff, both decisions apparently harsh in view of postal and travel difficulties which had become part of everyday life.

32 MANAGERIAL MOVES

THE MAJOR MANAGERIAL move ironically involved Major Frank Buckley, that mercurial Molineux manipulator of the minor whose Buckley Boys had founded a dynasty at Wolverhampton. In the First World War he had joined the Footballers' Battalion. After revolutionising Wolves' approach not only to the adoption of a strict youth policy but the manner in which they played the long-ball game, he was surprisingly allowed to join Notts County on 7 February 1944. His salary at Meadow Lane was reported at the time to have been between £4,000 and £4,500 a year, the highest paid in the game's history.

That same season it seemed Millwall managed to have more than their wartime ration of managers. They began the war with Charlie Hewitt in charge but his own involvement in the First World War caused him to be brought back into uniform. Hewitt, the Millwall secretary-manager, was called up for the Army. He had served in the Royal Navy on a destroyer in the earlier conflict and was in the reserve of officers. He was put in charge of a troopship – for once an imaginative compromise by the services.

Bill Voisey, himself a hero of the 1914–18 war, was co-opted into the chair and he gave way to Jack Cock in November 1944. That season the club almost shared bottom place in the League with Clapton Orient, but caused a sensation in London circles by reaching the final of the League South Cup. Voisey had served as a sergeant in the Royal Flying Corps, later RAF during the First World War, spending three years in Flanders. He won the DCM, MM and Croix de Guerre. During the Second World War he joined the Home Guard.

On 15 June 1942 two managers resigned: Clem Stephenson of Huddersfield Town and Spurs' Peter McWilliam. Most of the managerial changes occurred towards the second half of the war period. One of the first appointments of a new man at the helm came at Huddersfield in September 1943, when David Steele was given the job. He had previously been in charge of Bradford and 11 months earlier had made an appearance for Park Avenue during an emergency when he turned out in a game against Sheffield Wednesday. Steele was then 49 and his age exceeded by one year the combined ages of three other members of the team: Billy Elliott, Johnny Downie and Geoff Walker. He still managed to score a goal in a 3-3 draw! Bradford themselves chose Fred Emery as their replacement for Steele in October 1943. Wolves went to Ted Vizard as the man to succeed Major Buckley in April 1944.

In July of that year Frank Hill became Crewe Alexandra's boss and Harry Hibbs left his beloved Birmingham to take the reins at Walsall. On the same day Eddie Hapgood became Blackburn manager. David Jack, who had led Southend United, but retired to take up insurance work in August 1940, was persuaded back to the Middlesbrough management role in September 1944. Three years earlier some kind of a record had been established when David Bone Nightingale Jack and his son, also David aged 17, had turned out for Barclays Bank against Ealing Association.

Although Matt Busby was adopted as Manchester United's manager as early as February 1945, he was unable to take up his appointment at the club until the autumn, after being demobilised from the Army. He took up his duties on 22 October. In May of that year, Burnley put their management affairs in the hands of Everton and England international wing-half Cliff Britton, while Birmingham appointed Harry Storer, erstwhile Coventry City manager. Tom Mather became Leicester City's boss in June 1945 and Bury gave Norman Bullock his second opportunity to lead them. His first spell had been in pre-war times after he set up three records at Gigg Lane: most League goals in a season, goals in aggregate plus most League appearances. He had spent seven years in charge of Chesterfield in the interim and began the war by starting to learn German!

Steele was not the only manager to have to turn out on the playing field in a time of crisis for his club. It happened to Voisey at the tender age of 50, when he had to thrust himself into the Millwall side at outside-right. Billy Wright, the Clapton Orient head man, had to play in goal on a couple of occasions as did Billy Walker of Nottingham Forest well into his 40s when he was forced to deputise in a depleted team against Lincoln on 18 January 1941. Walker had also organised a junior knock-out competition in 1940. At Sheffield Wednesday he had discovered Robinson, Packard and Lowes in the same way. Eric Taylor was appointed secretary-manager of Wednesday in 1942 after a spell as just secretary.

Managerial devotion was unaffected. Haydn Green, Swansea's manager, was so keen to sign Trevor Ford that he gave up his Christmas dinner time for the privilege and was only to sit down for his meal at midnight. Green was constantly on the search for talent and watching a minor game one day in 1943 he suc-ceeded in snatching two players – Reg Weston and Darvel Williams.

The war also gave unexpected opportunity for players to learn the routine of management. Ted Fenton had combined soccer at West Ham with a thriving painting and decorating business employing 25 men in pre-war days. When the war came he sold up and joined the Army where he became a PT instructor. Posted to Colchester, he made guest appearances for them and was also given the chance to arrange fixtures with other teams.

Fred Howarth, the Secretary of the Football League, had been a schoolmaster like Rous at one time. Rous, educated at University College Exeter, was appointed games master at Watford Grammar School in 1921. He became a first-class referee and handled the 1934 FA Cup final. However, nobody could have had a more appropriate background for his ultimate position in the game than Howarth. He was born in 1888, the year the League was founded, in Preston, home of the Football League.

Howarth was at Winchester and trained there as a schoolmaster. In 1920 he was appointed assistant to League Secretary Tom Charnley and became Secretary himself in 1933. A man with a tidy, scholastic mind he was calm and courteous with a deep affection for the game. In his off-duty moments his hobbies were golf and croquet. His wartime application to his duties with virtually no staff was supported by the dedication of the members of the League Management Committee, whose attendance records were almost beyond criticism.

Much of this attitude stemmed from the vigorous example of the veteran Willie Cuff, who had resigned as Everton secretary when the First World War ended. He later became a director. Despite being in his 70s he maintained an authoritarian approach. Appointed President of the Football League, Cuff was impressed with the standard of play revealed during the latter stages of the emergency period and expressed the view that, given less tension on the field, football would be of higher quality.

On 27 November 1943 the Players' Union announced a new scheme for professionals. They proposed the abolition of the maximum wage, establishment of a superannuation scheme, greatly increased bonus payments in semi-final and final cup-ties and representative games, alteration of players' agreements to run from 1 August to 31 July each year, increased compensation for injured players, player representation on committees affecting their well-being and a revised transfer system. Other points included a £4 guaranteed minimum wage if the abolition was not acceptable and, if clubs could not meet these demands, a system of pooling resources should be introduced. The superannuation scheme was to be financed by receipts from practice games, plus a percentage from all gates and from players' wages and greater benefit from the Jubilee Fund.

These ideas were left in abeyance until Guy Fawkes Day 1945 when representatives of the Players' Union declared in favour of a strike unless some of their demands were met. Fifty-two clubs were represented. A postal ballot among the players of the 86 clubs operating at the time had declared in favour of a strike. It was agreed that, unless the Management Committee were prepared to meet the Players' Union, no League football would be played in England or Wales after 17 November. Agreement was reached.

Jimmy Fay, the firm but fair champion of the professional footballer, was white-haired, softly spoken and articulate. He had been a pro himself, serving Oldham for six years and Bolton for ten and missed less than half a dozen games during that time. He had been one of the first to join the Players' Union in 1907. Later he became chairman for eight years and had been appointed secretary in 1929, succeeding Harry Newbould.

Referees were not immune to the vagaries of the time. Arthur Ellis, serving in the RAF, was selected to officiate at a Cup game between Grimsby and Rotherham. He had a friend on the camp who lived in Grimsby and was invited to spend the weekend with him. They had an 80-mile journey and decided to hitch-hike. It seemed all was well when the first lift was obtained from a farmer in a car via Thorne and Scunthorpe. The farmer had had to turn off the main road shortly after passing a bus which indicated 'Grimsby' on its front. They duly presented themselves in the road ahead of the bus and waited. And waited.

A small boy passing on a bicycle told them that the bus detoured to a nearby village and only returned on the main road further on! While just starting to panic slightly they walked to a nearby railway station in time to see the train leaving. They rushed back to the main road and had given up hope of reaching their destination when a lorry came by. It stopped at their frantic signals and Ellis and friend climbed into the back to discover that their accompaniment was six cans of pig swill. The driver, having been asked to put his foot down on the gas pedal, did so to the discomfort of his two passengers who soon found themselves covered in the van's contents every time they hit a bump in the road.

Once in Grimsby they joined the lengthy queue for trolley buses in Market Place and appealed to a policeman to allow them to the front of it, but by then the two servicemen were looking like tramps in their filthy uniforms. The constable fumed: 'You RAF blokes are all alike – if you are the referee for today then I play for Arsenal. Get back to the end of the queue!' Fortunately the day ended happily as they managed to arrive in time for Ellis to change for the kick-off.

Grimsby was also the setting for another refereeing farce. In 1940–41 Barnsley were the visitors in another cup game. The first leg had ended 1-1 at Oakwell. In the second game the overall score was 3-3 when the referee, Flying Officer McKenzie, was called away on urgent RAF duties and stopped the game. The League decided there was insufficient time for a third meeting and awarded the game to Barnsley because of their higher League position at the time!

33 IN FOREIGN FIELDS

BENITO MUSSOLINI MADE the trains run on time. Adolf Hitler reorganised German football when the Nazi party came to power in 1933. Sixteen new districts or Gau were created, the champions of each one qualifying for the national play-offs. Later, more Gauliga were added and with the occupation of other European countries more were established including Wartehland, Ostmark, Alsace, Sudetenland and Bohmen-Mahren and the oddly named Generalgouvernement!

Territorial claims were realised either by force of arms or will and eighteen leading teams from these occupied areas took part in the German regional leagues. Six of these clubs were from the Sudetenland, five from Poland, four from Austria, two from Alsace and one from Luxembourg.

When the regional programme started again on 1 December 1939 these areas were sub-divided into smaller groups to save transport, petrol and energy. Districts like Schlesien were divided into two, Oberschlesien and Niederschlesien. In Nordmark there was a three-way split – Hamburg, Schleswig-Holstein and Mecklenburg. Thus, all districts were able to organise their own championships from sub-groups and complete them up to and including the 1944–45 season.

Of the Austrian clubs, Rapid Vienna became 1941 German champions while FK Austria won the Cup in 1943 beating LSV Hamburg 3-2 after extra time. That was the last German cup tournament, but the League was completed in the same season, the final play-off in Berlin being watched by 70,000. Hamburg were again the victims, losing by four clear goals to Dresdner SC for whom Helmut Schoen was a goalscorer. It was D-day plus 12.

At the height of the later pre-war period in Germany, the Schalke 04 club from the Ruhr city of Gelsenkirchen in the heartland of Hitler's Third Reich had been the dominating force. The team effectively used the WM formation which had made Arsenal the success of the 1930s.

The annexation of Austria had given Germany access to leading international players from that country who were quickly absorbed into the national side. In 1938 they had used a couple of them in the World Cup.

The German national team managed six international games after the outbreak of war. In the first they suffered a substantial 5-1 defeat in Budapest against Hungary. Three weeks later they reversed this scoreline in Belgrade against Yugoslavia, with Schoen scoring a hat-trick. Subsequent games were played against Bulgaria, Bohmen-Mahren, Italy and Slovakia. In 1940 they completed ten matches including a high-scoring 13-0 win over Finland in Leipzig on 1 September in which the Austrian Wilhelm Hahnemann scored six and Edmund Conen four goals.

In 1941 nine internationals were played and in 1942 it was ten, including two against Croatia, Germany's satellite state. Their opponents in Berlin on 12 April were Spain, who travelled to the match at the Olympic Stadium by train from Madrid through occupied France into Germany. In the crowd were members of the German Blue Division who had fought on Franco's side in the Spanish Civil War. On the way home the Spaniards went via Milan, stopping off to play the Italians there a week later. The last wartime international for the Germans was a 5-2 win in Pressburg against Slovakia.

In 1942 the Germans went to Berne and defeated the Swiss by 5-3 in front of a crowd of 34,000. The match was a personal triumph for Ernst Willimowski, scorer of four German goals. He had been Poland's leading goalscorer in the 1938 World Cup finals ...

Stuttgart played a friendly in Barcelona on 12 January 1941, drawing 3-3 before a crowd of 25,000 to mark the resumption of foreign visits after the Civil War interruption. On the same day Spain's national team played in Portugal and hosted a return two months later. The Spanish played against France in March 1942 in Seville, winning by four clear goals.

Otto, later Dr, Nerz, Professor of Medicine, who was Germany's national coach, twice visited England in the 1920s to study tactics and train with the players. Under Hitler's regime his stature increased, but when the Germans were beaten by Norway in the 1936 Olympics he was axed. Towards the end of the war he was taken prisoner by the Russians and died in February 1949 of dystrophy aged 57 at the concentration camp at Sachsenhausen.

Of all the countries occupied by the Nazis, France was in the strangest position. As far as the game was concerned the professional championship was abandoned on the outbreak of war, but a regional competition was started, split into three zones – North, South-East and South-West.

By the beginning of 1940–41 France had surrendered, though the Free French under de Gaulle carried on the fight in exile. By agreement with the Germans and the new Vichy government, a large part of the southern half of the country was unoccupied. Despite many obvious problems the professional championship was resumed, split into north and south zones, the headquarters of the unoccupied zone being Marseille. Ironically, the first cup final after the war began was between Racing Club Paris and Olympique Marseille played at the Parc des Princes and watched by 25,969. Racing won 2-1.

While the League structure carried on, the cup in 1941 was divided into three zones – the occupied, unoccupied and a free one. The Football Federation managed some form of professionalism. Teams were restricted to 16 players of whom only a maximum of 15 could be paid. Receipts were pooled and the Federation paid the players. At one time Helenio Herrera had managed to sign contracts with two different teams – Lorient and Red Star.

There was no fraternisation with the occupiers. Jean Borota, who was the French sports chief, did not feel free to direct activities. Orders went out to restrict matches to 80 minutes because of food shortages, which affected players' stamina. The Nazis realised this was a deliberate snub to them, but the players felt that if this was the case why not have a longer half-time break. The referees thought this was against the spirit of the game, so the whole idea was largely ignored with typical Gallic indifference.

Matches were remarkably well attended, many deciding to support it rather than German entertainment and propaganda. Jules Rimet himself, President of the Federation, resigned when Vichy began to influence football and he did not return to duty until France was liberated.

It was thought France had about 300,000 amateurs plus around 300 professionals paid at the same level as general civil servants, postal workers and policemen. Three internationals were also completed, at home to Portugal in Paris, against Switzerland in Marseille and against Spain in Seville.

In 1942–43 an individual scoring record was set up in France when Stefan Stanis (real name Dembicki) scored 16 of the 32 goals by which Racing Club Lens defeated Aubry-Asturies in Lens on 13 December 1942 in the French Cup. Stanis scored 44 goals in 30 matches that season and in 1943–44 he registered 41 of the 89 attributed to Lens. That same season all France's professionals were nationalised! Instead of the 32 teams, they were amalgamated into 14 regional teams like Paris-Ile-de-France, Paris-Capital, Lens-Artois, Rouen-Normandie, Marseille-Provence, etc. Mercifully, that lasted just one season.

Neutral Switzerland found a reasonable number of international opponents. They played Hungary and Germany four times each early in the war and Italy twice. They also met Spain, France and Portugal and played home and away against Sweden in the middle years of the war. Switzerland was also the headquarters of FIFA, the world governing body. It managed to keep its office open in Zurich throughout the war under Dr Ivo Schricker. Although the 1940 Congress planned for Luxembourg was postponed indefinitely, some meetings of the continental members of the executive committee were held. Resources were non-existent and without a full complement attending no resolutions could be passed, although in 1941 Germany put forward the idea that charging by players challenging for the ball should be made legal.

Italy had won the World Cup in 1938. The Jules Rimet trophy itself was the subject of considerable wartime mystery. Most of the sports officials in the Italian government were by definition Mussolini supporters, including the brothers Francesco and Giovanni Mauro, secretary Ottorino Barassi and the Head of Italian Sport, Consule-Generale Giorgio Vaccaro. Yet, all of them put sport above politics and for security decided not to trust each other too much. Thus, General Vaccaro and Giovanni Mauro smuggled the trophy from the safe of the Italian FA and deposited it in the vaults of a Swiss bank in Rome. Dr Barassi, however, fearing the Nazis would still confiscate the gold statuette, decided to find a safer hiding place for it. Thus the World Cup spent most of the war in a shoe box under his bed!

The Italians, under propaganda pressure from Mussolini, carried on with their normal League and Cup programme up to and including the 1942–43 season. In 1943 Torino achieved the 'double' with their Stadio Communale ground long since renamed 'Benito Mussolini'.

Italy managed eight wartime internationals, the last of them when Spain visited Milan in 1942. Two weeks earlier they had beaten Croatia 4-0 in Genoa. Regional reorganisation also played its role in Italian football after 1943 and certainly places like Rome went on largely unhindered. Lazio won the 1943–44 Romano championship with Roma second; in 1944–45 they swapped first and second places.

The 1943–44 season was shortened by the Allied invasion. When Mussolini was deposed and the Italians changed sides, further regional changes had to be brought in. Pre-war star Silvio Piola scored 27 goals in 1944 for the Torino club in a wartime championship; the next two years he assisted Juventus.

Since the Netherlands and Belgium respectively had enjoyed an amateur existence and modest part-time professionalism, they were able to adjust to some form of competition during the occupation. The Dutch succeeded in maintaining League football throughout the period until the tide of war swept back across their country in the 1944–45 period. In Belgium, though all League and international competitions were suspended in the spring of 1940, an official wartime League was restarted in 1941–42 until it, too, had to stand aside for the same campaign of liberation.

During the Nazi occupation of Luxembourg, Stade Dudelange who were the 1939 and 1940 champions actually played in the south-west regional league of Germany, but official domestic competition only returned in 1944–45 when Dudelange were again the masters.

The war did not prevent the Hungarian League from continuing each season and there was only slight disruption in 1944–45 while the country was in the throes of becoming a socialist state. From being an Axis ally the wheel turned full circle for them, and fashionable Ferencvaros, who represented a right-wing political faction, became distinctly unpopular. Demands on personnel were heavier. Jozsef Braun, a pre-war international right-winger on the field and one of Hungary's most accomplished forwards, lost his life in 1943 as a member of a forced labour battalion sent to the Russian front.

However, in Yugoslavia, where the war raged both internally and externally, there was no League competition after Gradjanska Zagreb won the 1939–40 championship; but under Gemany's protection, the Romanians were able to complete up to and including their 1942–43 season. Bulgaria also experienced a political swing from right to left during the period and only missed one season when the war front caught up with them.

Yet, the oddest situation in all of eastern Europe existed in the Soviet Union, where there was no official League football after Moscow Dynamo won the 1940 title and before they retained it in 1945, with an impressive record of 40 points from 22 games, losing only one and scoring 73 goals against 13 conceded. In 1940 a Bulgarian team visited Moscow to play Spartak and created such interest that many hundreds of thousands tried to buy tickets for the game. The following year the increased interest in the game was such there were a million organised players, with over 300,000 of them taking part in various competitions and at the watershed of their wartime trauma, the siege of Stalingrad. There were matches between various cities and, from the subsequent evidence of Dynamo's impressive tour of England in the early winter of 1945, there had been considerable effort put into producing well-trained and well-coached teams – all this, bearing in mind how close the Germans came to the outskirts of Moscow at one juncture!

However, no country suffered more from occupation than Poland. The Hitler pact with Stalin and subsequent invasion brought about not only defeat for the Poles but left their land equally devoured by the Germans and Russians. The 1939 championship was never even completed.

In Scandinavia the Finns became the first country to be involved when the Soviet Union declared war on them, only to be held up by the winter campaign until the spring of 1940 when Finland sued for peace. The national team was even invited to play in Germany and were heavily beaten 13-0. Wilhelm Hahnemann (an Austrian!) scored six goals and Edmund Conen four. On the domestic front only the 1943 season was disrupted. Norway was not so fortunate. Occupied in 1940 by the Germans along with Denmark, the Norwegians were unable to devote much time or resources to organised League football. In 1936 the Norwegian Olympic team had taken the bronze medal, eliminating the German team on the way in front of an infuriated Hitler. Their coach, Halvorsen, who had played soccer as a student in Hamburg, was tortured by the Gestapo for refusing to allow the Norwegian national team to play under German direction.

The Danes were less affected and organised a championship throughout the war period. Nils Middelboe, a Danish international, who had played for Chelsea around the time of the First World War, was surprised one day towards the end of the second great conflict when his son rushed in to tell him the Allied tanks were in Copenhagen. He then climbed on the leading one and had a conducted tour of his own city, while the unit themselves were persuaded to set up head-quarters in his home!

Neutral countries like Sweden and Switzerland were able to develop their game, the only problem being the scarcity of opponents at international level. In 1941 a Swedish cup competition was launched and only days after the liberation of Denmark in 1945 the Scandinavian Championship was restarted.

When the Czechs lost the Sudetenland in 1938 they also saw six of the leading clubs from this area absorbed into the Greater German League system. The other division of the country, called Slovakia, had been granted a form of political auto-nomy by the Nazis, and from 1939 organised its own semi-official national team playing several internationals chiefly against the Germans but also Bulgaria and Romania. During the occupation of the whole country, the Prague-based Czech championship continued with Slavia winning five successive titles before the 1944–45 season coincided with the winding-up of the war period.

The Germans' artificial creation of Croatia in Yugoslavia around 1942 was fol-lowed by another semi-official national team for this area which played half a dozen international games against the Axis countries, chiefly Germany, but also Italy, Bulgaria and Romania.

The Spanish Civil War had interrupted Iberian football, which was not resumed until 1939–40. The newly formed air force club Atletico Aviacion, a team created by the new Franco government from the merger of Atletico Madrid and Club Aviacion under the managership of Ricardo Zamora, the international goalkeeper, won the title two years in a row. The amalgamation suggested by Don Luis Navarro Garnica, Commander of the Air Force, was not to be a perma-nent one, though it was successful in the short term since they had been previ-ously steeped in survival struggles.

While European countries did their best to overcome day-to-day logistical problems in organising the game, South America was largely untouched by the global war. The South American Championships were held in Santiago, Chile in 1941; in Montevideo, Uruguay the following year and again in the Chilean capital in 1945. Argentina's River Plate produced in 1941 what was probably the finest team ever seen in that country, which earned its fame from a forward line nicknamed the *maquina* (machine) and read: Munoz, Moreno, Pedernera, Labruna and either Loustau or Deambrosi. The following year they discovered Alfredo di Stefano. He made his debut in the fourth amateur team and was bap-tised as a senior in 1944 aged 18.

The country's blood ties with Italy inevitably led them into sympathy with their homeland. In Brazil a different view was taken. After the country declared war on Germany in 1943, the Palestra Italia club in Sao Paulo, founded in 1914 by Italian immigrant workers, had its name changed to Palmeiras after all public references to the Axis powers were forbidden by the government.

The American Soccer League, the United States of America's professional competition, had managed to continue, relying heavily on foreign players to staff their teams. By the end of the war they were hoping to restrict the number to three per team. Earlier on, the National Challenge Cup, open to all professional and amateur teams in the States, had experienced some difficulties; the winners in 1943 and 1944 came from a single-game final resulting from the restriction on travel because of the war effort. Perhaps even more difficult to comprehend was the fact that the strong German-American League was able to flourish without apparent problems during the period of hostilities.

Still, the attraction of the game in 'Blighty' transcended all problems. A telegram received by Reuters from Malta in April 1942: 'Please repeat Saturday's football results – heavy bombing interfered with our reception.' In Malta it was not uncommon for off-duty men to be playing while enemy planes were over-head. Sometimes shell splinters would rattle on the corrugated roof of the stand.

There was, however, a darker side to the horrors of the conflict. In September 1942 the American United Press reported: 'Yugoslav patriots invaded a football ground during a match between Italians and Croats last night; the Italian referee and six Italian players were killed.'

Even more harrowing events occurred in German-occupied Ukraine in 1942. Former Dynamo Kiev and Lokomotiv players re-formed as FC Start. Several days after beating a Luftwaffe team 5-3, in a game which became known as the 'Death Match', the eleven winners were arrested by the Gestapo. One was tortured to death – the remainder being sent to a concentration camp. Six months later three more were executed. Only recapture by Soviet forces saved the others.

By contrast, in the summer of 1945 the British Services team which went to Switzerland was surprised to be entertained in Berne by over 200 young people between the ages of 12 and 20 – all apparently glowing with health – who gave a pre-match demonstration of football arts and ball control skills. Next, their seniors, coached since 1942 by Karl Rappan, managed to beat the British tourists 3-1, one of the goals being scored by Laura Amado, the Swiss captain who had played as an amateur in England for Tufnell Park from 1933–35. The second game in Zurich was played under floodlights, the Services winning 3-0, but it was just as illuminating to discover the varying degrees to which the game had survived in countries directly and indirectly affected by hostilities.

34 THE FIRST WORLD WAR

THE FIRST WORLD WAR was unique in two different aspects: it provided the only occasion when an unofficial, temporary armistice was celebrated with an impromptu football match, and a Football League player was posthumously awarded the VC.

Unlike the abandonment of the normal programme in the Second World War, the 1914–15 season was completed. The changes occurred in 1915–16. Then two groups, Lancashire and Midlands, were formed for all except five clubs in the South who combined with Southern League teams and played in a London Combination. The Football League's regional competition was also divided between a Principal Tournament and a Subsidiary Tournament. The latter competition ran towards the end of the season after the completion of the Principal Tournament. All international matches were cancelled at a conference in December 1914.

However, one was sanctioned by the FA in aid of the Lord Mayor of Liverpool's Roll of Honour Fund for widows and dependants of local servicemen killed in the war. On 13 May 1916 at Goodison Park, the English soldiers beat their Scottish counterparts 4-3. Then, in 1919, a series of Victory Internationals were staged. The Scottish FA decided to continue with their cup competition, but only by a vote of 14 to 13.

The London Combination was also split into a Principal Tournament and what was known as a Supplementary Tournament. Manchester City were the first winners of the Lancashire Section's Principal Tournament in 1915–16, followed in successive seasons by Liverpool, Stoke and Everton. However, in the Midland Section, Nottingham Forest and Leeds City shared the honours equally, Forest winning the first and last competitions and Leeds the two middle seasons. In 1917–18 and 1918–19 the champions of each section met each other at home and away, the aggregate winner being declared League Champions. Thus, in the first of these seasons Leeds beat Stoke 2-1 (2-0, 0-1) while Forest overcame Everton 1-0 (0-0, 1-0). In the London Combination Chelsea won the first and third Principal tournaments, while West Ham were successful in 1916–17 and Brentford in the last wartime campaign.

Across in France the slaughter in the trenches was halted on Christmas morning 1914. A football was produced from the German lines and a match in which several hundred opposing troops participated was unofficially won by the Lancashire Regiment against the Saxon Regiment. Other impromptu games were staged. In one of them, the Worcesters lost 2-1 to the Germans.

The East Surreys kicked a football along to the German trenches when going into action in France in the great advance of July 1916. The ball was subsequently sent home to Kingston Barracks to be retained as a regimental trophy.

It was temporary 2nd Lt. Donald Simpson Bell of the Green Howards who received the posthumous award of the Victoria Cross for 'most conspicuous bravery', capturing a German machine gun almost single-handed on the Somme. He was killed in July 1916 just five days after performing that heroic feat while again leading a charge over the top. A schoolmaster at Harrogate, he had been a full-back for Bradford Park Avenue and previously with Newcastle United and Crystal Palace.

With the outbreak of war in August 1914, the first players to be called up had been the Reservists who had previously served in the Army plus members of the TA. Hardest hit in the first week were Nottingham Forest and Crystal Palace, who each lost three men. Pressure of public opinion was immediately placed on the game to release their 7,000 fit athletes to fight the Germans and a Mr F. N. Charrington of the Mile End Mission (a notable philanthropist) attempted to form a new regiment 'The Footballers' Battalion' to answer Lord Kitchener's call for half a million men. Mr Charrington's idea was rejected by the FA, who had decided to offer the War Office support in other ways.

Mr Charrington then began speaking in condemnation of football and received a great deal of public sympathy. However, when he attempted to voice his opinion during the interval of the Fulham v Clapton Orient match on 5 September 1914, he was ejected from the ground by Mr W. G. Allen and Mr Phil Kelso, Fulham's Chairman and Secretary respectively. Mr Charrington subsequently took these individuals to court to answer a charge of assault, but he lost the case and was ordered to pay two guineas (£2.10) costs.

Before the first month of the war had elapsed, Croydon Common were said to have more players in the Services than any other – a total of 12 of their players had rallied to the colours. On the outbreak of war, the Corinthians had been about to begin a tour of Brazil with 14 players. They cancelled it, returned home and eight players immediately joined up. They had actually reached Rio but only had time to walk up to the football ground before re-embarking for home.

The uncompromising attitude by the public to the continuation of football remained throughout this season and did not really improve until later, when it was seen just how many footballers had actually joined up. One of the first professionals to be killed at the front in September 1914 was John Wilson of Vale of Leven and previously Dumbarton. He was with the Black Watch.

In December 1914 the War Office agreed to the formation of a Footballers' Battalion in which the members would be allowed absence on Saturdays to play for their clubs. This officially became the 17th Service Battalion of the Middlesex Regiment and was to be 1,350 strong. Their first HQ was at the Richmond Athletic Ground. The battalion was formed at a public meeting held at Fulham Town Hall and one of the first to join was Richard McFadden of Clapton Orient. He subsequently reached the rank of CSM, was awarded the Military Medal for gallantry and was killed in 1916.

Major Frank Buckley was, for a long time, second in command of this battalion. He was wounded in the shoulder and lung in 1916. The battalion left for the front in November 1915 and first went into action in France a month later. It was commanded by Lt. Col. H. J. Fenwick.

Before going to the front, the battalion had been engaged in many recruiting drives. For example, they paraded under the command of Lt. Frank Buckley at the Millwall v Bolton replayed cup-tie in February 1915. On another occasion they marched from Hackney Station to the Clapton Orient ground. No less than six Orient players were on parade that day. A Second Footballers' Battalion was formed in 1915 and went to France the following year. In December that year, the Footballers' Battalion beat the Royal Engineers 19-1.

During off-duty hours behind the lines, they generally swept the board in football competitions. For instance, they beat the 13th Essex 9-0 on one occasion and the 1st South Staffs 6-0. Alex Troup of Dundee and Ayr United, serving in the Royal Engineers, scored ten goals in a 12-2 win over a French team on 6 January 1918.

The Registration Act came in during 1915 and this put more pressure and difficulties on football clubs. For 1915–16 it was decided that matches could only be played on Saturdays and public holidays. No mid-week games were permitted, so as not to interfere with the making of munitions etc. It was also decided to divide the 40 leading clubs into Lancashire and Midland sections plus the London Combination. All League points were officially eliminated, although it was obvious that the press would continue to award points. There would be no cups, medals or other similar awards.

Stoke were admitted to the Football League from the Southern League, but the latter competition claimed to control the transfer of their players and to be in a position to take one-third of all transfer fees. Stoke were also fined £250 for leaving the Southern League without proper notice, originally £300, but reduced on appeal.

The League announced that there were to be no broken time payments, only genuine expenses and that all footballers would be expected to take up bona fide work for the benefit of the country. It was decided during December 1915 that all games should be reduced to 80 minutes. The referee could also dispense with the ten-minute interval. This applied in each of the following wartime seasons with the period being extended from about the middle of November to the middle of January.

Compulsory military service was introduced in 1916. Police kept close watch at football matches, trying to catch men shirking military service. All men had to carry exemption cards if they were not engaged in the armed forces.

A National Football War Fund began in 1917 to assist the bereaved and maimed among those associated with the game, and by this time the ill-feeling against football had died out.

Steve Bloomer, the former England international, had gone to Berlin in July 1914 to coach the Britannia Club for the 1916 Olympics. He was interned along with another player coaching in the German capital, John Brearley, formerly of Notts County, and Blackburn Rovers' Fred Pentland. They were interned in Ruhleben Camp. In the 1915–16 season Bloomer's team won the camp football competition winning all 13 games.

One of the first clubs to withdraw from either the Football League or Scottish League was St Johnstone in August 1914. Croydon Common went into liquidation in 1917. Two years earlier, the club had actually placed 84 players on their retain list!

In 1914–15 the Football League had asked clubs to make mutual arrangements with their players for the reduction of wages, varying from 5 per cent to 15 per cent on a scale graduated according to income, with this exception: that any player with less than £2 per week be left the whole of his living wage. The total deducted was to be forwarded with an additional 2.5 per cent of each gross home gate to the League for distribution to the poorer clubs. In addition, the League proposed that all clubs should pay the visitors 10 per cent of the admission money apart from the stands. This reduction of wages was suspended after 13 weeks (it had been backdated to the start of the season) and those who started late had to make it up to 13 weeks.

Summer wages for professionals were cancelled in April 1915 and it was announced that new players were to start the 1915–16 season at £3 per week and have a ten shilling (50p) rise after each two years' continuous service. However, in June 1915 there was a complete change of outlook and most Leagues (except the Scottish) decided that they would no longer pay professional footballers for the duration of the war. This meeting was attended by the Football, Scottish, Irish and Southern Leagues. It was the first time in history that these four had met together. The Scottish League decided to continue to pay players £1 per match, plus another £1 per week at the end of the season where funds allowed. In Scotland a First Division was maintained throughout the conflict.

Celtic played two League games in one day, during the rush to complete fixtures at the end of 1915–16. On 15 April they beat Raith Rovers 6-0 at Celtic Park and in the evening, defeated Motherwell 3-1 at Fir Park. Similarly, Queen's Park and Rangers also played twice in order to clear up their programme on 10 March 1917. Rangers lost 3-1 at Hamilton, motored back to Glasgow to meet Queen's Park, who had already played Partick and beaten them 2-0. Rangers won 1-0. When Rangers beat Partick 3-0 on 20 January 1917, they allowed Thistle to use McIntyre, a substitute for their injured winger Morrison. This aroused some interest and discussion about the use of replacements for all games.

For season 1916–17 the Football League decided on an end to pooling gates, but 1 per cent had to go to the League for management expenses and a further 5 per cent to charity. In 1917–18 it was 1 per cent of gates to the League and 4 per cent to charity – a reduction of 1 per cent. Visitors were to receive 20 per cent of the net takings after these deductions. However, in the subsidiary programme, the 20 per cent would go to a pool divided among all the clubs. Entertainments Tax was introduced on 1 October 1917.

As already mentioned, the FA forbade the paying of players' wages in July 1915 as well as the presentation of cup medals and other awards. The embargo on wages remained, but in December 1917 the FA decided that in matches and competitions for War Funds and charitable objects, cups and medals could be presented, provided they were not bought out of gate receipts of the game.

As an example of the difficulty in mustering teams and the system of guest players, Blackburn Rovers called on 95 players to complete their 36-match programme in the Lancashire Section Principal and Subsidiary competitions in 1916–17. Middlesbrough's Scottish-born, centre-forward Andy Wilson frequently assisted Hearts as a guest under several assumed names! Hearts as a club were well represented in the war, supplying the nucleus of a whole battalion in the Royal Scots. Many were killed in action and a memorial at Haymarket commemorates their gallantry and sacrifice.

The Football League investigated a report that the Manchester United v Liverpool match played on Good Friday 1915 was rigged. United had won 2-0. After a long period of investigation, the Commission agreed and various players were suspended. One of these, Enoch West, later brought action for libel against the FA and the *Athletic News*, but after losing this case, he eventually admitted the charge. His suspension was lifted in 1945!

Because of United's victory, they escaped relegation at Chelsea's expense. This was taken into consideration when normal football resumed in 1919 and Chelsea were elected to the First Division without having to be voted in.

In August 1915 Leeds City, which had been in the hands of the receiver since 1912, contemplated moving to the Leeds Cricket and Football Club Ground at Headingley from Elland Road. Suggestions that the Leeds Northern Union club should buy up Leeds City, lock, stock and barrel were made, but a new syndicate took over at Elland Road. After the migration of Arsenal from Plumstead to Highbury in 1914, the Football League introduced a rule that such moves would in future have to be sanctioned by them.

In 1916 the FA suspended indefinitely a player who had appeared under various names for several clubs. He used the name Stewart, Crockford and Hughes to play for Motherwell, Dumbarton, Newcastle, Watford, Clapton Orient, Brentford and Southampton. He was unsuccessful in obtaining a trial with either Fulham or West Ham! His suspension was eventually lifted and he played for Fulham against Queens Park Rangers on 5 January 1918 as Harrold Crockford, which was said to be his real name.

There were the usual crop of match oddities. On 10 November 1917 Stoke loaned Blackburn two players and beat them 16-0. A month later Stoke won 8-1 at Blackburn. However, the previous season Bolton had beaten Stoke 9-2 and Blackburn had had a 6-1 win over Rochdale. Joe Smith scored six in the first game, George Chapman all six in the other one. Archie Bown was another six-goal striker for Swindon against Watford in a Southern League match in April 1915.

Bobby Thomson registered 39 goals in 31 games for Chelsea in 1915–16. In 1916–17 Luton's Ernie Simms scored 40 goals in 29 matches. The following season Syd Puddefoot scored the same number out of West Ham's total of 103 goals. Another prolific goalscorer was Jimmy McIlvenny of Bradford City. In 12 consecutive games up to October 1916, excluding one in which he was injured after only 20 minutes, he scored 25 goals in total.

Preston used twelve different centre-forwards in a run of 21 matches at the start of 1915–16. Around the same time, Crystal Palace fielded 15 in the same position. When Watford defeated Arsenal 2-1 on 29 April 1916, they included three brothers, Owen, Vic and Fred Gregory.

Hartlepools' Victoria Ground was hit by two German bombs from a Zeppelin raid on 27 November 1916, which destroyed the wooden grandstand. Lengthy correspondence after the war with the German authorities failed to produce any compensation and the only material reply came in the Second World War when more bombs were dropped on the town, though they missed the ground that time.

Individual problems were also highlighted. Patrick Gallagher of Celtic was in 1916 employed as a carpenter by a shipbuilding firm on the Clyde. He was brought before the Glasgow Munitions Tribunal and fined £3 to be paid in six instalments for absenting himself from work to play for Celtic on four Saturdays. He was also subsequently suspended for a month and Celtic were fined £25 for playing him after his conviction. One of the criticisms made at the time was that, if players were not paid in Scotland (as they were not in England), then they would not choose to absent themselves from important work to play football.

Archie Rawlings was a Preston right-winger at the time. During the war he played for Rochdale. 'After all expenses had been met, the gate was shared among the players,' he said. 'It was a sight to see us all line up outside the office after the game waiting for our "bonus". Then we were paid in coppers, sixpences and threepenny bits. I was once paid 16 shillings [80p] all in coppers!'

Millwall were one of a number of clubs hit by the war. Four players were killed in action, while Jim Collins, later to become trainer, won the DCM and MM while serving in the RAMC. He stood on a grenade to save two other soldiers and had his heel blown off. Another heroic deed won Angus Seed the Military Medal when he dug Tom Ratcliffe out of debris which had buried him for two hours. Ratcliffe became Seed's trainer at Barnsley.

Billy Birrell suffered a serious left leg injury, leaving him with small pieces of shrapnel embedded. He did manage to return to League football with Middlesbrough, but had to switch to his right as the favoured foot.

RECORDS AND
STATISTICS

THE EVE OF WAR TABLES

Positions in England on the eve of the outbreak of war, 2 September 1939

1939–40

DIVISION 1

	P	W	D	L	F	A	Pts
1 Blackpool	3	3	0	0	5	2	6
2 Sheffield U	3	2	1	0	3	1	5
3 Arsenal	3	2	1	0	8	4	5
4 Liverpool	3	2	0	1	6	3	4
5 Everton	3	1	2	0	5	4	4
6 Bolton W	3	2	0	1	6	5	4
7 Derby Co	3	2	0	1	3	3	4
8 Charlton Ath	3	2	0	1	3	4	4
9 Stoke C	3	1	1	1	7	4	3
10 Manchester U	3	1	1	1	5	3	3
11 Chelsea	3	1	1	1	4	4	3
12 Brentford	3	1	1	1	3	3	3
13 Grimsby T	3	1	1	1	2	4	3
14 Aston Villa	3	1	0	2	3	3	2
15 Sunderland	3	1	0	2	6	7	2
16 Wolverhampton W	3	0	2	1	3	4	2
17 Huddersfield T	3	1	0	2	2	3	2
18 Portsmouth	3	1	0	2	3	5	2
19 Preston NE	3	0	2	1	0	2	2
20 Blackburn R	3	0	1	2	3	5	1
21 Middlesbrough	3	0	1	2	3	8	1
22 Leeds U	3	0	1	2	0	2	1

DIVISION 2

	P	W	D	L	F	A	Pts
1 Luton T	3	2	1	0	7	1	5
2 Birmingham	3	2	1	0	5	1	5
3 Coventry C	3	1	2	0	8	6	4
4 Plymouth Arg	3	2	0	1	4	3	4
5 West Ham U	3	2	0	1	5	4	4
6 Tottenham H	3	1	2	0	6	5	4
7 Leicester C	3	2	0	1	6	5	4
8 Nottingham F	3	2	0	1	5	5	4
9 Newport Co	3	1	1	1	5	4	3
10 Millwall	3	1	1	1	5	4	3
11 Manchester C	3	1	1	1	6	5	3
12 WBA	3	1	1	1	8	8	3
13 Bury	3	1	1	1	4	5	3
14 Newcastle U	3	1	0	2	8	6	2
15 Chesterfield	2	1	0	1	2	2	2
16 Barnsley	3	1	0	2	7	8	2
17 Southampton	3	1	0	2	5	6	2
18 Sheffield W	3	1	0	2	3	5	2
19 Swansea T	3	1	0	2	5	11	2
20 Fulham	3	0	1	2	3	6	1
21 Burnley	2	0	1	1	1	3	1
22 Bradford PA	3	0	1	2	2	7	1

DIVISION 3 NORTH

	P	W	D	L	F	A	Pts
1 Accrington S	3	3	0	0	6	1	6
2 Halifax T	3	2	1	0	6	1	5
3 Darlington	3	2	1	0	5	2	5
4 Chester	3	2	1	0	5	2	5
5 New Brighton	3	2	0	1	6	5	4
6 Rochdale	3	2	0	1	2	2	4
7 Crewe Alex	2	1	1	0	3	0	3
8 Wrexham	3	1	1	1	3	2	3
9 Tranmere R	3	1	1	1	6	6	3
10 Lincoln C	3	1	1	1	6	7	3
11 Rotherham U	3	1	1	1	5	6	3
12 Hull C	2	0	2	0	3	3	2
13 Carlisle U	2	1	0	1	3	3	2
14 Gateshead	3	1	0	2	6	7	2
15 Doncaster R	3	1	0	2	4	5	2
16 Southport	3	0	2	1	4	5	2
17 Barrow	3	0	2	1	4	5	2
18 Oldham Ath	3	1	0	2	3	5	2
19 Hartlepools U	3	0	2	1	1	4	2
20 York C	3	0	1	2	3	5	1
21 Bradford C	3	0	1	2	3	6	1
22 Stockport Co	2	0	0	2	0	5	0

DIVISION 3 SOUTH

	P	W	D	L	F	A	Pts
1 Reading	3	2	1	0	8	2	5
2 Exeter C	3	2	1	0	5	3	5
3 Notts Co	2	2	0	0	6	3	4
4 Ipswich T	3	1	2	0	5	3	4
5 Brighton & HA	3	1	2	0	5	4	4
6 Cardiff C	3	2	0	1	5	5	4
7 Crystal Palace	3	2	0	1	8	9	4
8 Bournemouth	3	1	1	1	13	4	3
9 Bristol C	3	1	1	1	5	5	3
10 Clapton Orient	3	0	3	0	3	3	3
11 Mansfield T	3	1	1	1	8	8	3
12 Norwich C	3	1	1	1	4	4	3
13 Southend U	3	1	1	1	3	3	3
14 Torquay U	3	0	3	0	4	4	3
15 Walsall	3	1	1	1	3	3	3
16 QPR	3	0	2	1	4	5	2
17 Watford	3	0	2	1	4	5	2
18 Northampton T	3	1	0	2	2	12	2
19 Aldershot	3	0	1	2	3	5	1
20 Swindon T	3	0	1	2	2	4	1
21 Bristol R	3	0	1	2	2	7	1
22 Port Vale	2	0	1	1	0	1	1

36 NON-PARTICIPATING CLUBS

Clubs who did not participate in Football League during wartime seasons 1939–45

1939–40
Aston Villa
Derby Co
Exeter C
Gateshead
Ipswich T
Sunderland

1940–41
Accrington S
Aston Villa
Barrow
*Blackpool
*Bolton W
Bristol R
Carlisle U
Darlington
Derby Co
Exeter C
Gateshead
Hartlepools U
Ipswich T
Newport Co
Plymouth Arg
Port Vale
Sunderland
Swindon T
Torquay U
Wolverhampton W

1941–42
Accrington S
Aston Villa
Barrow
Birmingham
Bristol R
Carlisle U
Coventry C†
Crewe Alex
Darlington
Derby Co
Exeter C
Hartlepools U
Hull C
Ipswich T
Newport Co
Notts Co
Plymouth Arg
Port Vale
Southend U
Swindon T
Torquay U

1942–43
Accrington S
Barrow
Bournemouth & BA
Bristol R
Carlisle U
Darlington
Exeter C
Hartlepools U
Hull C
Ipswich T
New Brighton
Newport Co
Norwich C
Plymouth Arg
Port Vale
Preston NE
Southend U
Swindon T
Torquay U

1943–44
Accrington S
Barrow
Bournemouth & BA
Bristol R
Carlisle U
Exeter C
Hull C
Ipswich T
New Brighton
Newport Co
Norwich C
Plymouth Arg
Port Vale
Preston NE
Southend U
Swindon T
Torquay U

1944–45
Barrow
Bournemouth & BA
Bristol R
Carlisle U
Exeter C
Ipswich T
New Brighton
Newport Co
Norwich C
Plymouth Arg
Southend U
Swindon T
Torquay U

1945–46
Hull C
New Brighton

*Played in second half of season only.
†Coventry C did not compete in second half.

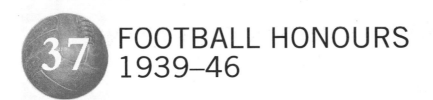

FOOTBALL HONOURS
1939–46

1939–40
South 'A'   Arsenal
South 'B'   QPR
South 'C'   Tottenham H
South 'D'   Crystal Palace
South-West   Plymouth Arg
Midland   Wolverhampton W
East Midland   Chesterfield
West   Stoke C
North-West   Bury
North-East   Huddersfield T
League Cup   West Ham U;
    runners-up Blackburn R

1940–41
North   Preston NE
South   Crystal Palace
London Cup   Reading
West Regional Cup   Bristol C
League Cup   Preston NE;
    runners-up Arsenal

1941–42
North   Blackpool
South   Leicester C
League Championship   Manchester U
League Cup   Wolverhampton W;
    runners-up Sunderland
London League   Arsenal
London Cup   Brentford;
    runners-up Portsmouth

1942–43
North   Blackpool
North (Second Championship)   Liverpool
South   Arsenal
West   Lovell's Ath
League North Cup   Blackpool;
    runners-up Sheffield W
League South Cup   Arsenal;
    runners-up Charlton Ath
League West Cup   Swansea T;
    runners-up Lovell's Ath

1943–44
North   Blackpool
North (Second Championship)   Bath C
South   Tottenham H
West   Lovell's Ath
League North Cup   Aston Villa;
    runners-up Blackpool
League South Cup   Charlton Ath;
    runners-up Chelsea
League West Cup   Bath C;
    runners-up Cardiff C

1944–45
North   Huddersfield T
North (Second Championship)   Derby Co
South   Tottenham H
West   Cardiff C
League North Cup   Bolton W;
    runners-up Manchester U
League South Cup   Chelsea;
    runners-up Millwall
League West Cup   Bath C;
    runners-up Bristol C

1945–46
North   Sheffield U
South   Birmingham C
Third Division North (West)   Accrington S
Third Division North (East)   Rotherham U
Third Division South (North)   QPR
Third Division South (South)   Crystal Palace
League Third Division North Cup
    Rotherham U; runners-up Chester
League Third Division South Cup
    Bournemouth; runners-up Walsall
FA Amateur Cup   Barnet:
    runners-up Bishop Auckland
FA Cup   Derby Co; runners-up
    Charlton Ath

FINAL LEAGUE TABLES
1939–40 to 1945–46

38

1939–40

SOUTH A 1939–40

	P	W	D	L	F	A	Pts
1 Arsenal	18	13	4	1	62	22	30
2 West Ham U	18	12	1	5	57	33	25
3 Millwall	18	8	5	5	46	38	21
4 Watford	18	9	3	6	44	38	21
5 Norwich C	18	7	6	5	41	36	20
6 Charlton Ath	18	8	1	9	61	58	17
7 Crystal Palace	18	5	3	10	39	56	13
8 Clapton Orient	18	5	3	10	28	60	13
9 Tottenham H	18	5	2	11	37	43	12
10 Southend U	18	4	0	14	30	61	8

SOUTH B 1939–40

	P	W	D	L	F	A	Pts
1 QPR	18	12	2	4	49	26	26
2 Bournemouth	18	11	2	5	52	37	24
3 Chelsea	18	9	5	4	44	37	23
4 Reading	18	10	2	6	47	42	22
5 Brentford	18	8	2	8	42	41	18
6 Fulham	18	7	4	7	50	51	18
7 Portsmouth	18	7	2	9	37	42	16
8 Aldershot	18	5	4	9	38	49	14
9 Brighton & HA	18	5	1	12	42	53	11
10 Southampton	18	4	0	14	41	64	8

SOUTH C 1939–40

	P	W	D	L	F	A	Pts
1 Tottenham H	18	11	4	3	43	30	26
2 West Ham U	18	10	4	4	53	28	24
3 Arsenal	18	9	5	4	41	26	23
4 Brentford	18	8	4	6	42	34	20
5 Millwall	18	7	5	6	36	30	19
6 Charlton Ath	18	7	4	7	39	36	18
7 Fulham	18	8	1	9	38	42	17
8 Southampton	18	5	3	10	28	55	13
9 Chelsea	18	4	3	11	33	53	11
10 Portsmouth	18	3	3	12	26	45	9

SOUTH D 1939–40

	P	W	D	L	F	A	Pts
1 Crystal Palace	18	13	1	4	64	30	27
2 QPR	18	10	3	5	38	28	23
3 Watford	18	7	7	4	41	29	21
4 Southend U	18	8	3	7	41	37	19
5 Bournemouth	18	8	2	8	40	41	18
6 Aldershot	18	7	3	8	38	36	17
7 Clapton Orient	18	7	3	8	33	45	17
8 Norwich C	18	6	4	8	33	36	16
9 Reading	18	6	2	10	31	42	14
10 Brighton & HA	18	2	4	12	30	65	8

Bournemouth 2 Norwich C 1 played out of season and not included in appearances and goals.

NORTH-EAST 1939–40

	P	W	D	L	F	A	Pts
1 Huddersfield T	20	15	4	1	54	22	34
2 Newcastle U	20	12	0	8	58	39	24
3 Bradford PA	19	10	2	7	44	38	22
4 Middlesbrough	20	9	4	7	49	42	22
5 Leeds U	18	9	3	6	36	27	21
6 Bradford C	19	9	3	7	41	36	21
7 Hull C	20	8	1	11	35	41	17
8 York C	20	8	1	11	36	51	17
9 Darlington	19	6	3	10	44	56	15
10 Hartlepools U	20	6	1	13	27	47	13
11 Halifax T	19	3	2	14	28	53	8

Bradford PA v Darlington; Bradford C v Leeds U and Leeds U v Halifax T unplayed.

EAST MIDLAND 1939–40

	P	W	D	L	F	A	Pts
1 Chesterfield	20	14	2	4	69	23	30
2 Barnsley	20	10	5	5	43	29	25
3 Sheffield U	20	12	1	7	46	34	25
4 Grimsby T	20	10	2	8	40	44	22
5 Mansfield T	20	9	3	8	49	48	21
6 Lincoln C	20	9	0	11	42	53	18
7 Doncaster R	20	7	4	9	37	45	18
8 Rotherham U	20	7	4	9	24	42	18
9 Sheffield W	20	5	5	10	33	42	15
10 Nottingham F	20	5	4	11	37	43	14
11 Notts Co	20	6	2	12	40	57	14

SOUTH-WEST 1939–40

	P	W	D	L	F	A	Pts
1 Plymouth Arg	28	16	4	8	72	41	36
2 Torquay U	28	14	6	8	73	62	34
3 Bristol R	28	9	10	9	62	55	28
4 Newport Co	28	12	4	12	70	63	28
5 Swindon T	28	10	8	10	66	63	28
6 Cardiff C	28	6	13	9	45	63	25
7 Swansea T	28	10	6	12	54	60	26
8 Bristol C	28	7	5	16	57	92	19

MIDLAND 1939–40

	P	W	D	L	F	A	Pts
1 Wolverhampton W	28	19	3	6	76	44	41
2 WBA	28	18	4	6	87	51	40
3 Coventry C	28	13	3	12	68	57	29
4 Birmingham	28	12	5	11	56	60	29
5 Luton T	28	10	4	14	76	88	24
6 Northampton T	28	7	8	13	48	59	22
7 Leicester C	28	7	6	15	51	71	20
8 Walsall	28	7	5	16	51	83	19

WESTERN 1939–40

	P	W	D	L	F	A	Pts
1 Stoke C	22	13	5	4	57	41	31
2 Liverpool	22	12	5	5	66	40	29
3 Everton	22	12	4	6	64	33	28
4 Manchester U	22	14	0	8	74	41	28
5 Manchester C	22	12	4	6	73	41	28
6 Wrexham	22	10	5	7	45	50	25
7 New Brighton	22	10	3	9	55	52	23
8 Port Vale	22	10	2	10	52	56	22
9 Chester	22	7	5	10	40	51	19
10 Crewe Alex	22	6	1	15	44	79	13
11 Stockport Co	22	4	3	15	45	79	11
12 Tranmere R	22	2	3	17	41	93	7

NORTH-WEST 1939–40

	P	W	D	L	F	A	Pts
1 Bury	22	16	2	4	64	30	34
2 Preston NE	22	15	2	5	63	27	32
3 Blackpool	22	13	6	3	73	36	32
4 Bolton W	22	13	4	5	55	30	30
5 Oldham Ath	22	11	2	9	55	61	24
6 Burnley	22	9	5	8	48	43	23
7 Barrow	22	8	4	10	54	57	20
8 Blackburn R	22	7	4	11	37	40	18
9 Rochdale	22	5	5	12	38	58	15
10 Southport	22	5	4	13	34	62	14
11 Carlisle U	22	4	4	14	38	68	12
12 Accrington S	22	2	6	14	31	78	10

1940–41

NORTH REGIONAL 1940–41

	P	W	D	L	F	A	Ave
1 Preston NE	29	18	7	4	81	37	2.189
2 Chesterfield	35	20	6	9	76	40	1.900
3 Manchester C	35	18	10	7	104	55	1.890
4 Barnsley	30	18	4	8	86	49	1.775
5 Everton	34	19	7	8	85	51	1.666
6 Blackpool	20	13	3	4	56	34	1.646
7 Halifax T	30	10	13	7	64	51	1.254
8 Manchester U	35	14	8	13	80	65	1.249
9 Lincoln C	27	13	7	7	65	53	1.226
10 Newcastle U	23	12	0	11	49	41	1.195
11 Huddersfield T	33	11	6	16	69	58	1.189
12 Middlesbrough	27	16	1	10	84	71	1.183
13 New Brighton	26	15	1	10	97	82	1.182
14 Burnley	35	17	7	11	62	53	1.169
15 Leeds U	30	13	8	9	62	54	1.148
16 Liverpool	37	15	6	16	91	82	1.109
17 Wrexham	29	15	5	9	78	71	1.098
18 Chester	35	14	6	15	94	89	1.056
19 Doncaster R	32	15	7	10	77	74	1.040
20 Oldham Ath	37	17	4	16	78	77	1.012
21 Grimsby T	27	12	2	13	60	63	0.952
22 Bradford PA	31	9	7	15	64	74	0.864
23 Rotherham U	29	12	5	12	48	57	0.842
24 Blackburn R	32	9	10	13	49	60	0.816
25 Bury	38	10	8	20	80	100	0.800
26 Bolton W	16	6	2	8	31	40	0.775
27 Tranmere R	25	9	5	11	67	90	0.744
28 Sheffield U	25	6	6	13	44	60	0.733
29 Bradford C	29	8	3	18	72	99	0.727
30 Rochdale	32	12	5	15	64	92	0.695
31 Southport	28	7	2	19	61	88	0.693
32 York C	25	7	4	14	49	71	0.690
33 Hull C	23	8	3	12	44	67	0.656
34 Sheffield W	30	9	6	15	50	78	0.641
35 Stockport Co	29	9	5	15	54	93	0.580
36 Crewe Alex	24	2	3	19	32	84	0.380

SOUTH REGIONAL 1940–41

	P	W	D	L	F	A	Ave
1 Crystal Palace	27	16	4	7	86	44	1.954
2 West Ham U	25	14	6	5	70	39	1.794
3 Coventry C	10	5	3	2	28	16	1.750
4 Arsenal	19	10	5	4	66	38	1.736
5 Cardiff C	24	12	5	7	75	50	1.500
6 Reading	26	14	5	7	73	51	1.431
7 Norwich C	19	9	2	8	73	55	1.327
8 Watford	35	15	6	14	96	73	1.315
9 Portsmouth	31	16	2	13	92	71	1.296
10 Tottenham II	23	9	5	9	53	41	1.292
11 Millwall	31	16	5	10	73	57	1.280
12 Walsall	32	14	7	11	100	80	1.250
13 WBA	28	13	5	10	83	69	1.202
14 Leicester C	33	17	5	11	87	73	1.191
15 Northampton T	30	14	3	13	84	71	1.183
16 Bristol C	20	10	2	8	55	48	1.145
17 Mansfield T	29	12	6	11	77	68	1.132
18 Charlton Ath	19	7	4	8	37	34	1.088
19 Aldershot	24	14	2	8	73	68	1.073
20 Brentford	23	9	3	11	51	51	1.000
21 Chelsea	23	10	4	9	57	58	0.981
22 Birmingham	16	7	1	8	38	43	0.883
23 Fulham	30	10	7	13	62	73	0.849
24 Luton T	35	11	7	17	82	100	0.820
25 Stoke C	36	9	9	18	76	96	0.791
26 QPR	23	8	3	12	47	60	0.783
27 Brighton & HA	25	8	7	10	51	75	0.680
28 Nottingham F	25	7	3	15	50	77	0.649
29 Bournemouth	27	9	3	15	59	92	0.641
30 Notts Co	21	8	3	10	42	66	0.636
31 Southend U	29	12	4	13	64	101	0.633
32 Southampton	31	4	4	23	53	111	0.477
33 Swansea T	10	2	1	7	12	33	0.363
34 Clapton Orient	15	1	3	11	19	66	0.287

LEAGUE SOUTH 1940–41

		P	W	D	L	F	A	Pts
1	Brighton & HA	13	8	3	2	41	25	19
2	Watford	14	8	1	5	54	33	17
3	Portsmouth	13	7	0	6	48	29	14
4	Southend U	12	6	1	5	30	35	13
5	Luton T	11	5	1	5	29	33	11
6	Bournemouth	12	5	1	6	26	39	11
7	Norwich C	6	3	0	3	17	22	6
8	Southampton	13	1	1	11	25	54	3

These results were also included in the South Regional table.

After a dispute between the clubs, Brighton & HA beat Watford 4–1 in a title decider.

1941–42

LONDON 1941–42

		P	W	D	L	F	A	Pts
1	Arsenal	30	23	2	5	108	43	48
2	Portsmouth	30	20	2	8	105	59	42
3	West Ham U	30	17	5	8	81	44	39
4	Aldershot	30	17	5	8	85	56	39
5	Tottenham H	30	15	8	7	61	41	38
6	Crystal Palace	30	14	6	10	70	53	34
7	Reading	30	13	8	9	76	58	34
8	Charlton Ath	30	14	5	11	72	64	33
9	Brentford	30	14	2	14	80	76	30
10	QPR	30	11	3	16	52	59	25
11	Fulham	30	10	4	16	79	99	24
12	Brighton & HA	30	9	4	17	71	108	22
13	Chelsea	30	8	4	18	56	88	20
14	Millwall	30	7	5	18	53	82	19
15	Clapton Orient	30	5	7	18	42	94	17
16	Watford	30	6	4	20	47	114	16

SOUTHERN 1941–42

Ending 25 December 1941

		P	W	D	L	F	A	Ave Pts
1	Leicester C	17	11	3	3	40	17	26.4
2	WBA	13	9	1	3	62	26	26.3
3	Cardiff C	15	9	1	5	43	28	22.8
4	Norwich C	8	4	2	2	20	13	22.5
5	Bournemouth	10	6	0	4	26	18	21.6
6	Bristol C	15	9	0	6	46	45	21.6
7	Walsall	18	9	1	8	49	45	19.0
8	Northampton T	16	7	2	7	39	38	18.0
9	Wolverhampton W	16	6	2	8	27	36	15.7
10	Southampton	10	4	0	6	27	32	14.4
11	Luton T	18	5	1	12	34	73	11.0
12	Nottingham F	13	2	1	10	18	39	6.9
13	Swansea T	9	1	0	8	18	39	4.0

Average points calculated on 18 matches.

NORTHERN (1st) 1941–42

		P	W	D	L	F	A	Pts
1	Blackpool	18	14	1	3	75	19	29
2	Lincoln C	18	13	3	2	54	28	29
3	Preston NE	18	13	1	4	58	18	27
4	Manchester U	18	10	6	2	79	27	26
5	Stoke C	18	12	2	4	75	36	26
6	Everton	18	12	2	4	61	31	26
7	Blackburn R	18	10	6	2	40	24	26
8	Liverpool	18	11	4	3	66	44	26
9	Gateshead	18	9	5	4	39	35	23
10	Sunderland	18	9	4	5	50	30	22
11	Huddersfield T	18	10	1	7	48	33	21
12	Bradford PA	18	8	5	5	33	28	21
13	Grimsby T	18	7	6	5	41	31	20
14	Barnsley	18	8	4	6	39	31	20
15	Newcastle U	18	7	6	5	46	39	20
16	Sheffield W	18	7	5	6	33	37	19
17	Manchester C	18	8	3	7	48	54	19
18	Sheffield U	18	7	4	7	39	38	18
19	Burnley	18	6	6	6	36	40	18
20	Halifax T	18	7	3	8	29	41	17
21	Oldham Ath	18	6	4	8	40	49	16
22	Rochdale	18	6	4	8	28	52	16
23	Chesterfield	18	5	5	8	27	31	15
24	Chester	18	6	3	9	45	53	15
25	Middlesbrough	18	6	3	9	44	56	15
26	Leeds U	18	7	1	10	36	46	15
27	Doncaster R	18	6	2	10	39	46	14
28	Bradford C	18	5	4	9	32	42	14
29	Rotherham U	18	6	2	10	33	47	14
30	New Brighton	18	4	6	8	39	75	14
31	Tranmere R	18	5	3	10	35	60	13
32	York C	18	4	4	10	41	55	12
33	Mansfield T	18	6	0	12	29	50	12
34	Bolton W	18	3	5	10	35	48	11
35	Southport	18	5	1	12	33	61	11
36	Bury	18	3	3	12	37	59	9
37	Wrexham	18	2	5	11	40	69	9
38	Stockport Co	18	2	2	14	34	73	6

Ending 25 December 1941.

NORTHERN (2nd) 1941–42

27 December 1941 to 30 May 1942.

	P	W	D	L	F	A	Ave Pts
1 Manchester U	19	12	4	3	44	25	33.89
2 Blackpool	22	14	4	4	108	34	33.45
3 Northampton T	21	14	2	5	70	31	32.85
4 Liverpool	21	14	2	5	57	39	32.85
5 Wolverhampton W	20	13	1	6	52	29	31.05
6 Huddersfield T	20	9	6	5	42	33	27.60
7 Blackburn R	22	10	6	6	40	31	27.18
8 WBA	18	9	3	6	53	43	26.83
9 Grimsby T	18	8	5	5	31	22	26.83
10 Sunderland	22	9	7	6	53	42	26.13
11 Cardiff C	20	9	4	7	59	38	25.30
12 Preston NE	19	6	7	6	41	30	23.00
13 Chesterfield	18	8	2	8	32	31	23.00
14 Middlesbrough	18	7	4	7	37	36	23.00
15 Everton	23	9	5	9	37	41	23.00
16 Stoke C	20	9	2	9	41	49	23.00
17 Leicester C	18	6	4	8	39	38	20.44
18 Bradford PA	19	5	6	8	35	40	19.36
19 Halifax T	19	4	7	8	30	40	18.15
20 Burnley	19	7	1	11	29	53	18.15
21 Chester	20	6	3	11	34	41	17.25
22 Oldham Ath	18	4	3	11	30	43	14.05

NON-QUALIFIERS (in alphabetical order)

	P	W	D	L	F	A	Pts
1 Barnsley	15	9	3	3	48	23	21
2 Bolton W	15	5	4	6	26	33	14
3 Bradford C	14	6	1	7	28	25	13
4 Bournemouth	8	2	2	4	11	21	8
5 Bristol C	17	9	3	5	55	29	21
6 Bury	15	6	2	7	46	39	14
7 Doncaster R	9	2	0	7	10	30	4
8 Gateshead	13	4	2	7	23	36	10
9 Leeds U	17	7	0	10	33	33	14
10 Lincoln C	13	7	1	5	45	33	15
11 Luton T	16	4	2	10	20	54	10
12 Manchester C	17	9	1	7	33	26	19
13 Mansfield T	11	1	2	8	15	36	4
14 New Brighton	11	5	0	6	23	38	10
15 Newcastle U	17	5	6	6	33	40	16
16 Norwich C	12	7	1	4	27	19	15
17 Nottingham F	16	8	1	7	32	30	17
18 Rochdale	13	5	0	8	23	39	10
19 Rotherham U	15	6	2	7	32	34	14
20 Sheffield U	17	8	4	5	39	33	20
21 Sheffield W	15	5	2	8	22	36	12
22 Southampton	12	6	2	5	27	32	12
23 Southport	16	6	2	8	30	38	14
24 Stockport Co	10	1	3	6	12	38	5
25 Swansea T	11	1	4	6	11	39	6
26 Tranmere R	15	4	3	8	24	55	11
27 Walsall	13	4	0	9	14	34	8
28 Wrexham	12	4	2	6	26	32	10
29 York C	17	6	7	4	39	37	19

Average points calculated on 23 matches; only those playing 18 or more qualified for the Championship. Results included ties played in qualifying competition for the League Cup knock-out games in the Cup competition proper and county and regional cup fixtures which, in some instances, also counted as League matches!

1942–43

NORTH (1st) 1942–43

Ending 25 December 1942.

	P	W	D	L	F	A	Pts
1 Blackpool	18	16	1	1	93	28	33
2 Liverpool	18	14	1	3	70	34	29
3 Sheffield W	18	12	3	3	61	26	27
4 Manchester U	18	12	2	4	58	26	26
5 Huddersfield T	18	10	6	2	52	32	26
6 Stoke C	18	11	3	4	46	25	25
7 Coventry C	18	10	5	3	28	16	25
8 Southport	18	11	3	4	64	42	25
9 Derby Co	18	11	2	5	51	37	24
10 Bradford PA	18	8	7	3	46	21	23
11 Lincoln C	18	9	5	4	58	36	23
12 Halifax T	18	10	3	5	39	27	23
13 Gateshead	18	10	3	5	52	45	23
14 Aston Villa	18	10	2	6	47	33	22
15 Everton	18	10	2	6	52	41	22
16 Grimsby T	17	8	5	4	42	31	21
17 York C	18	9	3	6	47	36	21
18 Blackburn R	18	9	3	6	56	43	21
19 Barnsley	18	8	5	5	39	30	21
20 Sheffield U	18	7	6	5	45	35	20
21 Birmingham	18	9	2	7	27	30	20
22 Sunderland	18	8	3	7	46	40	19
23 Chester	18	7	4	7	43	40	18
24 Walsall	18	6	5	7	33	31	17
25 Northampton T	18	8	1	9	38	44	17
26 Newcastle U	18	6	4	8	51	52	16
27 Chesterfield	18	5	6	7	30	34	16
28 WBA	18	6	4	8	35	43	16
29 Notts Co	18	7	2	9	34	57	16
30 Manchester C	18	7	1	10	46	47	15
31 Nottingham F	18	6	3	9	38	39	15
32 Burnley	18	5	5	8	35	45	15
33 Leicester C	18	5	4	9	32	37	14
34 Bury	18	6	2	10	53	81	14
35 Stockport Co	18	5	3	10	34	55	13
36 Rotherham U	18	4	5	9	28	48	13
37 Tranmere R	18	5	3	10	36	63	13
38 Wolverhampton W	18	5	2	11	28	41	12
39 Crewe Alex	18	5	2	11	43	64	12
40 Middlesbrough	18	4	4	10	30	50	12
41 Rochdale	18	5	2	11	34	57	12
42 Wrexham	18	5	1	12	43	67	11
43 Leeds U	18	3	4	11	28	45	10
44 Oldham Ath	18	4	2	12	29	54	10
45 Bradford C	18	4	2	12	30	63	10
46 Bolton W	18	3	3	12	31	52	9
47 Doncaster R	17	3	3	11	23	41	9
48 Mansfield T	18	2	4	12	25	65	8

NORTH (2nd) 1942–43

26 December 1942 to 1 May 1943.

	P	W	D	L	F	A	Pts
1 Liverpool	20	15	2	3	64	32	32
2 Lovell's Ath	20	11	5	4	63	32	27
3 Manchester C	19	11	5	3	43	24	27
4 Aston Villa	20	13	1	6	44	30	27
5 Sheffield W	20	9	8	3	43	26	26
6 Manchester U	19	11	3	5	52	26	25
7 York C	18	11	3	4	52	30	25
8 Huddersfield T	19	11	3	5	48	28	25
9 Coventry C	20	11	3	6	33	21	25
10 Stoke C	20	10	4	6	42	34	24
11 WBA	20	11	2	7	49	38	24
12 Notts Co	20	9	6	5	37	34	24
13 Blackpool	19	8	7	4	49	31	23
14 Newcastle U	19	10	3	6	62	42	23
15 Blackburn R	19	8	4	5	45	35	22
16 Bristol C	19	8	6	5	41	33	22
17 Chesterfield	20	9	4	7	35	30	22
18 Derby Co	20	8	5	7	41	34	21
19 Aberaman Ath	18	10	1	7	39	40	21
20 Sunderland	19	8	4	7	58	40	20
21 Rochdale	16	9	2	5	39	26	20
22 Leicester C	20	9	2	9	40	37	20
23 Sheffield U	19	8	4	7	43	42	20
24 Bradford PA	19	7	5	7	35	31	19
25 Everton	19	9	1	9	51	46	19
26 Bath C	18	7	4	7	49	46	18
27 Birmingham	20	8	2	10	32	29	18
28 Barnsley	17	8	2	7	34	37	18
29 Nottingham F	18	7	4	7	30	34	18
30 Crewe Alex	20	7	4	9	44	57	18
31 Bradford C	16	7	2	7	29	29	16
32 Wrexham	17	7	3	7	36	37	17
33 Bolton W	17	7	2	8	34	42	16
34 Tranmere R	20	6	4	10	37	48	16
35 Halifax T	18	7	2	9	30	39	16
36 Chester	20	6	3	11	40	49	15
37 Northampton T	17	6	2	9	30	37	14
38 Wolverhampton W	17	5	4	8	38	45	14
39 Swansea T	18	4	6	8	35	52	14
40 Grimsby T	13	4	5	4	30	27	13
41 Bury	16	5	3	8	44	42	13
42 Doncaster R	17	5	3	9	27	41	13
43 Rotherham U	18	4	5	9	28	43	13
44 Gateshead	13	6	0	7	29	36	12
45 Stockport Co	19	4	4	11	37	76	12
46 Southport	18	4	3	11	38	58	11
47 Leeds U	16	5	1	10	32	50	11
48 Oldham Ath	18	4	3	11	28	47	11
49 Middlesbrough	18	5	0	13	31	69	10
50 Lincoln C	10	4	1	5	23	18	9
51 Burnley	14	3	3	8	17	31	9
52 Walsall	16	3	2	11	22	35	8
53 Cardiff C	17	2	3	12	22	47	7
54 Mansfield T	10	1	1	8	12	41	3

32 clubs reached the knock-out stage of the Cup from qualifying matches included in this table.

SOUTH 1942–43

Ending 27 February 1943.

	P	W	D	L	F	A	Pts
1 Arsenal	28	21	1	6	102	40	43
2 Tottenham H	28	16	6	6	68	28	38
3 QPR	28	18	2	8	64	49	38
4 Portsmouth	28	16	3	9	66	52	35
5 Southampton	28	14	5	9	86	58	33
6 West Ham U	28	14	5	9	80	66	33
7 Chelsea	28	14	4	10	52	45	32
8 Aldershot	28	14	2	12	87	77	30
9 Brentford	28	12	5	11	64	63	29
10 Charlton Ath	28	13	3	12	68	75	29
11 Clapton Orient	28	11	5	12	54	72	27
12 Brighton & HA	28	10	5	13	65	73	25
13 Reading	28	9	6	13	67	74	24
14 Fulham	28	10	2	16	69	78	22
15 Crystal Palace	28	7	5	16	49	75	19
16 Millwall	28	6	5	17	66	88	17
17 Watford	28	7	2	19	51	88	16
18 Luton T	28	4	6	18	43	100	14

WEST 1942–43

Ending 25 December 1942.

	P	W	D	L	F	A	Pts
1 Lovell's Ath	18	14	2	2	59	21	30
2 Bath C	18	14	0	4	66	26	28
3 Cardiff C	18	8	3	7	41	45	19
4 Bristol C	17	7	3	7	59	37	17
5 Swansea T	18	3	1	14	27	77	7
6 Aberaman Ath	17	2	1	14	29	75	5

1943–44

SOUTH 1943–44

Ending 6 May 1944.

	P	W	D	L	F	A	Pts
1 Tottenham H	30	19	8	3	71	36	46
2 West Ham U	30	17	7	6	74	39	41
3 QPR	30	14	12	4	69	54	40
4 Arsenal	30	14	10	6	72	42	38
5 Crystal Palace	30	16	5	9	75	53	37
6 Portsmouth	30	16	5	9	68	59	37
7 Brentford	30	14	7	9	71	51	35
8 Chelsea	30	16	2	12	79	55	34
9 Fulham	30	11	9	10	80	73	31
10 Millwall	30	13	4	13	70	66	30
11 Aldershot	30	12	6	12	64	73	30
12 Reading	30	12	3	15	73	62	27
13 Southampton	30	10	7	13	67	88	27
14 Charlton Ath	30	9	7	14	57	73	25
15 Watford	30	6	8	16	58	80	20
16 Brighton & HA	30	9	2	19	55	82	20
17 Clapton Orient	30	4	3	23	32	87	11
18 Luton T	30	3	5	22	42	104	11

WEST 1943–44

Ending 25 December 1943.

	P	W	D	L	F	A	Pts
1 Lovell's Ath	18	12	0	6	62	30	24
2 Cardiff C	18	11	1	6	45	28	23
3 Bath C	18	9	1	8	41	42	19
4 Aberaman Ath	18	8	2	8	32	35	18
5 Bristol C	18	8	1	9	32	36	17
6 Swansea T	18	3	1	14	25	66	7

NORTH (1st) 1943–44

Ending 25 December 1943.

		P	W	D	L	F	A	Pts
1	Blackpool	18	12	4	2	56	20	28
2	Manchester U	18	13	2	3	56	30	28
3	Liverpool	18	13	1	4	72	26	27
4	Doncaster R	18	11	5	2	45	25	27
5	Bradford PA	18	11	4	3	65	28	26
6	Huddersfield T	18	12	2	4	48	25	26
7	Northampton T	18	10	5	3	43	25	25
8	Aston Villa	18	11	3	4	43	27	25
9	Sunderland	18	10	3	5	46	30	23
10	Hartlepools U	18	10	3	5	44	31	23
11	Everton	18	9	4	5	60	34	22
12	Blackburn R	18	10	2	6	47	32	22
13	Rochdale	18	10	2	6	43	41	22
14	Sheffield U	18	8	5	5	30	26	21
15	Lincoln C	18	8	4	6	51	40	20
16	Birmingham	18	8	4	6	38	31	20
17	Manchester C	18	9	2	7	38	35	20
18	Mansfield T	18	9	2	7	32	33	20
19	Derby Co	18	8	4	6	43	45	20
20	Chester	18	9	2	7	40	43	20
21	Grimsby T	18	8	3	7	32	36	19
22	WBA	18	8	3	7	42	44	19
23	Gateshead	18	8	2	8	40	51	18
24	Burnley	18	5	7	6	24	22	17
25	Walsall	18	5	7	6	27	31	17
26	Nottingham F	18	6	5	7	33	39	17
27	Leeds U	18	6	5	7	38	50	17
28	Leicester C	18	6	4	8	33	30	16
29	Darlington	18	6	4	8	49	48	16
30	Rotherham U	18	7	2	9	38	42	16
31	York C	18	7	2	9	35	40	16
32	Halifax T	18	6	4	8	27	36	16
33	Southport	18	7	2	9	33	51	16
34	Stoke C	18	6	3	9	40	35	15
35	Chesterfield	18	7	1	10	29	31	15
36	Oldham Ath	18	7	1	10	30	44	15
37	Stockport Co	18	5	5	8	24	43	15
38	Coventry C	18	4	6	8	25	23	14
39	Newcastle U	18	5	4	9	32	37	14
40	Sheffield W	18	5	4	9	29	34	14
41	Middlesbrough	18	4	6	8	35	52	14
42	Wolverhampton W	18	5	3	10	30	42	13
43	Bury	18	6	1	11	31	44	13
44	Barnsley	18	5	2	11	32	42	12
45	Bradford C	18	4	3	11	27	47	11
46	Wrexham	18	5	1	12	43	63	11
47	Notts Co	18	4	3	11	26	53	11
48	Bolton W	18	5	0	13	24	46	10
49	Tranmere R	18	4	1	13	39	71	9
50	Crewe Alex	18	4	1	13	29	62	9

NORTH (2nd) 1943–44

27 December 1943 to 6 May 1944.

		P	W	D	L	F	A	Pts
1	Bath C	21	16	2	3	78	26	34
2	Wrexham	21	15	4	2	62	29	34
3	Liverpool	21	14	2	5	71	38	30
4	Birmingham	20	12	5	3	47	19	29
5	Rotherham U	21	12	5	4	54	30	29
6	Aston Villa	21	13	3	5	50	34	29
7	Blackpool	20	12	3	5	53	27	27
8	Cardiff C	21	13	1	7	53	28	27
9	Manchester U	21	10	7	4	55	38	27
10	Bradford PA	20	11	4	5	50	30	26
11	Newcastle U	20	13	0	7	47	36	26
12	Everton	21	12	1	8	73	39	25
13	Stoke C	21	10	5	6	66	45	25
14	Leicester C	21	10	5	6	40	32	25
15	Darlington	21	11	2	8	50	30	24
16	Nottingham F	20	9	6	5	31	20	24
17	Coventry C	21	10	4	7	48	36	24
18	Sheffield U	21	11	2	8	53	35	24
19	Manchester C	21	9	6	6	42	35	24
20	Lovell's Ath	20	10	2	8	48	30	22
21	Gateshead	21	9	4	8	45	53	22
22	Doncaster R	17	9	3	5	42	33	21
23	Derby Co	21	8	5	8	33	28	21
24	Rochdale	20	8	5	7	40	36	21
25	Barnsley	17	8	4	5	34	30	20
26	Halifax T	20	8	4	8	44	42	20
27	Chester	20	9	2	9	65	65	20
28	Hartlepools U	20	8	4	8	49	50	20
29	Stockport Co	19	10	0	9	44	49	20
30	Sheffield W	20	8	4	8	32	36	20
31	Blackburn R	16	8	3	5	30	27	19
32	Huddersfield T	21	8	3	10	41	40	19
33	WBA	21	5	9	7	46	48	19
34	Bolton W	21	8	3	10	42	49	19
35	Leeds U	18	8	3	7	34	40	19
36	Northampton T	19	11	0	10	37	39	18
37	Burnley	18	6	6	6	39	42	18
38	Bristol C	20	6	5	9	38	42	17
39	York C	20	7	2	11	37	40	16
40	Middlesbrough	21	6	4	11	41	51	16
41	Swansea T	20	7	2	11	42	67	16
42	Grimsby T	15	6	3	6	23	28	15
43	Bury	20	6	3	11	38	55	15
44	Sunderland	19	6	2	11	44	58	14
45	Oldham Ath	18	5	4	9	28	36	14
46	Chesterfield	19	5	4	10	31	41	14
47	Mansfield T	14	6	1	7	23	25	13
48	Tranmere R	20	6	0	14	29	62	12
49	Wolverhampton W	20	3	6	11	28	56	12
50	Walsall	17	3	6	8	17	35	12
51	Bradford C	18	4	2	12	27	47	10
52	Southport	20	3	3	14	35	67	9
53	Lincoln C	18	3	2	13	25	56	8
54	Notts Co	20	3	0	17	23	68	6
55	Crewe Alex	18	2	1	15	31	83	5
56	Aberaman Ath	18	1	1	16	20	87	3

32 clubs reached the knock-out stage of the Cup from qualifying matches included in this table.

1944–45

NORTH (1st) 1944–45

Ending 23 December 1944.

		P	W	D	L	F	A	Pts
1	Huddersfield T	18	14	3	1	50	22	31
2	Derby Co	18	14	1	3	54	19	29
3	Sunderland	18	12	4	2	52	25	28
4	Aston Villa	18	12	3	3	54	19	27
5	Everton	18	7	2	4	58	25	26
6	Wrexham	18	11	3	4	40	18	25
7	Doncaster R	18	12	0	6	48	27	24
8	Bolton W	18	9	6	3	34	22	24
9	Bradford PA	18	10	4	4	45	31	24
10	Manchester C	18	9	4	5	53	31	22
11	Stoke C	18	9	4	5	37	25	22
12	Birmingham C	18	8	6	4	30	21	22
13	Barnsley	18	10	2	6	42	32	22
14	Rotherham U	18	9	4	5	31	25	22
15	WBA	18	9	4	5	36	30	22
16	Liverpool	18	9	3	6	41	30	21
17	Grimsby T	18	9	3	6	37	29	21
18	Halifax T	18	8	5	5	30	29	21
19	Chester	18	9	3	6	45	45	21
20	Burnley	18	8	4	6	39	27	20
21	Blackpool	18	9	2	7	53	38	20
22	Leeds U	18	9	2	7	53	42	20
23	Sheffield W	18	9	2	7	34	30	20
24	Chesterfield	18	8	3	7	30	19	19
25	Darlington	18	9	1	8	52	45	19
26	Wolverhampton W	18	7	5	6	31	27	19
27	Rochdale	18	7	5	6	35	33	19
28	Crewe Alex	18	9	1	8	43	41	19
29	Blackburn R	18	7	4	7	30	29	18
30	Manchester U	18	8	2	8	40	40	18
31	Preston NE	18	7	4	7	26	28	18
32	Walsall	18	5	6	7	27	29	16
33	Gateshead	18	7	2	9	45	53	16
34	Northampton T	18	5	6	7	30	38	16
35	Newcastle U	18	7	1	10	51	38	15
36	Sheffield U	18	6	3	9	27	25	15
37	Hartlepools U	18	7	1	10	41	47	15
38	Oldham Ath	18	7	1	10	28	36	15
39	Mansfield T	18	6	3	9	31	40	15
40	Nottingham F	18	5	5	8	22	34	15
41	Coventry C	18	6	2	10	23	42	14
42	York C	18	6	1	11	49	52	13
43	Middlesbrough	18	5	3	10	34	57	13
44	Bradford C	18	6	1	11	35	60	13
45	Accrington S	18	5	2	11	29	46	12
46	Port Vale	18	5	2	11	22	36	12
47	Bury	18	5	2	11	28	48	12
48	Stockport Co	18	5	1	12	33	70	11
49	Hull C	18	4	3	11	23	60	11
50	Southport	18	3	4	11	32	55	10
51	Lincoln C	18	4	2	12	32	56	10
52	Leicester C	18	3	4	11	23	46	10
53	Tranmere R	18	2	1	15	20	53	5
54	Notts Co	18	2	1	15	19	62	5

NORTH (2nd) 1944–45

25 December 1944 to 26 May 1945.

		P	W	D	L	F	A	Pts
1	Derby Co	26	19	3	4	78	28	41
2	Everton	27	17	3	7	79	43	37
3	Liverpool	24	16	3	5	67	26	35
4	Burnley	26	15	3	8	56	36	22
5	Newcastle U	23	15	1	7	71	37	31
6	Aston Villa	25	14	2	9	70	45	30
7	Chesterfield	24	10	9	5	40	24	29
8	Wolverhampton W	24	11	7	6	45	31	29
9	Manchester U	22	13	3	6	47	33	29
10	Darlington	24	13	3	8	61	45	29
11	Bristol C	22	13	2	7	55	33	28
12	Blackburn R	25	13	2	10	63	54	28
13	Wrexham	22	10	7	5	55	36	27
14	Bolton W	23	11	5	7	51	35	27
15	Blackpool	24	12	3	9	58	42	27
16	Stoke C	23	12	2	9	67	42	26
17	Lovell's Ath	19	12	2	5	44	27	26
18	Cardiff C	20	12	2	6	41	27	26
19	Grimsby T	21	10	6	5	51	37	26
20	Huddersfield T	26	11	4	11	47	47	26
21	Birmingham C	24	9	7	8	38	34	25
22	Crewe Alex	23	11	3	9	50	50	25
23	Doncaster R	20	11	2	7	44	26	24
24	Bradford PA	22	10	4	8	49	39	24
25	Barnsley	23	11	2	10	37	38	24
26	Accrington S	24	9	6	9	39	41	24
27	Rotherham U	20	10	3	7	41	37	23
28	Gateshead	21	9	5	7	46	42	23
29	Preston NE	25	9	4	12	41	56	22
30	Sheffield U	24	9	3	12	56	48	21
31	Sunderland	25	9	3	13	53	54	21
32	Leeds U	22	9	3	10	53	55	21
33	Sheffield W	25	8	5	12	53	56	21
34	Leicester C	21	7	6	8	40	38	20
35	Bath C	20	10	0	10	50	48	20
36	Bury	20	8	4	8	38	43	20
37	York C	22	8	4	10	48	56	20
38	Chester	22	9	2	11	49	61	20
39	Bradford C	20	8	3	9	43	46	19
40	WBA	22	6	7	9	39	44	19
41	Hartlepools U	21	8	3	10	34	54	19
42	Coventry C	21	6	6	9	36	53	18
43	Nottingham F	17	5	7	5	23	25	17
44	Tranmere R	23	8	1	14	40	56	17
45	Halifax T	18	6	5	7	22	35	17
46	Lincoln C	17	6	4	7	42	51	16
47	Manchester C	19	7	2	10	32	43	16
48	Northampton T	14	6	3	5	23	30	15
49	Oldham Ath	21	7	1	13	39	56	15
50	Stockport Co	19	7	0	12	31	50	14
51	Middlesbrough	24	6	2	16	40	72	14
52	Walsall	18	5	3	10	24	33	13
53	Swansea T	20	6	1	13	42	63	13
54	Port Vale	21	5	2	14	27	60	12
55	Mansfield T	12	5	1	6	22	38	11
56	Hull C	18	5	1	12	30	54	11
57	Rochdale	20	4	3	13	17	49	11
58	Southport	22	3	3	16	33	82	9
59	Notts Co	21	4	0	17	29	62	8
60	Aberaman	17	2	2	13	36	69	6

32 clubs reached the knock-out stage of the Cup from qualifying matches included in this table.

SOUTH 1944–45

Ending 26 May 1945.

		P	W	D	L	F	A	Pts
1	Tottenham H	30	23	6	1	81	30	52
2	West Ham U	30	22	3	5	96	47	47
3	Brentford	30	17	4	9	87	57	38
4	Chelsea	30	16	5	9	100	55	37
5	Southampton	30	17	3	10	96	69	37
6	Crystal Palace	30	15	5	10	74	70	35
7	Reading	30	14	6	10	78	68	34
8	Arsenal	30	14	3	13	77	67	31
9	QPR	30	10	10	10	70	61	30
10	Watford	30	11	6	13	66	84	28
11	Fulham	30	11	4	15	79	83	26
12	Portsmouth	30	11	4	15	56	61	26
13	Charlton Ath	30	12	2	16	72	81	26
14	Brighton & HA	30	10	2	18	66	95	22
15	Luton T	30	6	7	17	56	104	19
16	Aldershot	30	7	4	19	44	85	18
17	Millwall	30	5	7	18	50	84	17
18	Clapton Orient	30	5	7	18	39	86	17

WEST 1944–45

Ending 23 December 1944.

		P	W	D	L	F	A	Pts
1	Cardiff C	18	12	3	3	54	24	27
2	Bristol C	18	13	1	4	59	30	27
3	Lovell's Ath	18	10	3	5	40	31	23
4	Bath C	18	8	3	7	47	46	19
5	Aberaman Ath	18	3	1	14	34	72	7
6	Swansea T	18	2	1	15	32	63	5

1945–46

DIV 3 North (West) CUP 1945–46

		P	W	D	L	F	A	Pts
1	Stockport Co	10	7	1	2	26	15	15
2	Southport	10	6	2	2	20	13	14
3	Accrington S	10	6	1	3	24	17	13
4	Oldham Ath	10	4	4	2	18	15	12
5	Crewe Alex	10	3	4	3	23	27	10
6	Wrexham	10	4	1	5	21	20	9
7	Chester	10	4	1	5	26	25	9
8	Tranmere R	10	4	1	5	17	25	9
9	Rochdale	10	2	2	6	18	20	6
10	Barrow	10	1	1	8	13	29	3

First eight teams in each section qualified for knock-out competition; some of these matches were also included in the second Championship!

DIV 3 North (East) CUP 1945–46

		P	W	D	L	F	A	Pts
1	Doncaster R	10	6	3	1	24	15	15
2	Carlisle U	10	7	0	3	30	17	14
3	Bradford C	10	4	3	3	27	22	11
4	Hartlepools U	10	4	3	3	25	21	11
5	Gateshead	10	4	2	4	21	23	10
6	Darlington	10	5	0	5	26	31	10
7	Rotherham U	10	3	2	5	24	26	8
8	York C	10	2	4	4	16	18	8
9	Halifax T	10	2	4	4	15	18	8
10	Lincoln C	10	2	1	7	21	38	5

DIV 3 South (North) CUP 1945–46

		P	W	D	L	F	A	Pts
1	QPR	16	11	3	2	38	11	25
2	Walsall	16	10	4	2	34	18	24
3	Mansfield T	16	8	4	4	24	15	20
4	Southend U	16	7	5	4	22	21	19
5	Norwich C	16	7	2	7	27	25	16
6	Ipswich T	16	7	1	8	19	24	15
7	Clapton Orient	16	6	3	7	22	31	15
8	Port Vale	16	5	4	7	21	25	14
9	Northampton T	16	5	2	9	27	29	12
10	Watford	16	5	1	10	23	35	11
11	Notts Co	16	5	0	11	17	31	10

DIV 3 South (South) CUP 1945–46

		P	W	D	L	F	A	Pts
1	Bournemouth	16	8	4	4	37	20	20
2	Bristol R	16	8	3	5	27	19	20
3	Reading	16	8	2	6	46	29	18
4	Crystal Palace	16	7	4	5	37	30	18
5	Cardiff C	16	8	1	7	39	22	17
6	Bristol C	16	7	3	6	30	27	17
7	Torquay U	16	6	4	6	19	30	16
8	Exeter C	16	5	4	7	22	28	14
9	Swindon T	16	5	4	7	21	35	14
10	Aldershot	16	3	4	9	23	48	10
11	Brighton & HA	16	1	6	9	23	45	8

Positions 1 and 2 in each region qualified for the semi-finals. There was also some cross-matching between the two regions known as the South (North and South) Cup!

SOUTH 1945–46

		P	W	D	L	F	A	Pts
1	Birmingham C	42	28	5	9	96	45	61
2	Aston Villa	42	25	11	6	106	58	61
3	Charlton Ath	42	25	10	7	92	45	60
4	Derby Co	42	24	7	11	101	62	55
5	WBA	42	22	8	12	104	69	52
6	Wolverhampton W	42	20	11	11	75	48	51
7	West Ham U	42	20	11	11	94	76	51
8	Fulham	42	20	10	12	93	73	50
9	Tottenham H	42	22	3	17	78	81	47
10	Chelsea	42	19	6	17	92	80	44
11	Arsenal	42	16	11	15	76	73	43
12	Millwall	42	17	8	17	79	105	42
13	Coventry C	42	15	10	17	70	69	40
14	Brentford	42	14	10	18	82	72	38
15	Nottingham F	42	12	13	17	72	73	37
16	Southampton	42	14	9	19	97	105	37
17	Swansea T	42	15	7	20	90	112	37
18	Luton T	42	13	7	22	60	92	33
19	Portsmouth	42	11	6	25	66	87	28
20	Leicester C	42	8	7	27	57	101	23
21	Newport Co	42	9	2	31	52	125	20
22	Plymouth Arg	42	3	8	25	39	120	14

DIV 3 North (West) 1945–46

		P	W	D	L	F	A	Pts
1	Accrington S	18	10	4	4	37	19	24
2	Rochdale	18	10	2	6	43	35	22
3	Crewe Alex	18	9	3	6	43	31	21
4	Chester	18	8	5	5	44	38	21
5	Wrexham	18	8	4	6	30	25	20
6	Tranmere R	18	9	2	7	33	31	20
7	Stockport Co	18	6	3	9	38	38	15
8	Oldham Ath	18	5	5	8	29	32	15
9	Barrow	18	4	4	10	21	44	12
10	Southport	18	3	4	11	22	47	10

DIV 3 North (East) 1945–46

		P	W	D	L	F	A	Pts
1	Rotherham U	18	12	2	4	56	28	26
2	Darlington	18	12	2	4	61	36	26
3	Gateshead	18	11	2	5	51	34	24
4	Doncaster R	18	8	4	6	34	35	20
5	York C	18	6	6	6	34	34	18
6	Halifax T	18	7	4	7	39	46	18
7	Bradford C	18	6	4	8	45	40	16
8	Carlisle U	18	5	3	10	34	58	13
9	Lincoln C	18	4	2	12	34	54	10
10	Hartlepools U	18	3	3	12	22	45	9

DIV 3 South (South) 1945–46

		P	W	D	L	F	A	Pts
1	Crystal Palace	20	13	3	4	55	31	29
2	Cardiff C	20	13	2	5	69	31	28
3	Bristol C	20	11	2	7	51	40	24
4	Brighton & HA	20	10	1	9	49	50	21
5	Bristol R	20	7	6	7	44	44	20
6	Swindon T	20	8	3	9	35	47	19
7	Bournemouth	20	7	3	10	52	50	17
8	Aldershot	20	6	5	9	38	56	17
9	Exeter C	20	6	4	10	33	41	16
10	Reading	20	5	5	10	43	49	15
11	Torquay U	20	5	4	11	22	52	14

NORTH 1945–46

		P	W	D	L	F	A	Pts
1	Sheffield U	42	27	6	9	112	62	60
2	Everton	42	23	9	10	88	54	55
3	Bolton W	42	20	11	11	67	45	51
4	Manchester U	42	19	11	12	98	62	49
5	Sheffield W	42	20	8	14	67	60	48
6	Newcastle U	42	21	5	16	106	70	47
7	Chesterfield	42	17	12	13	68	49	46
8	Barnsley	42	17	11	14	76	68	45
9	Blackpool	42	18	9	15	94	92	45
10	Manchester C	42	20	4	18	78	75	44
11	Liverpool	42	17	9	16	80	70	43
12	Middlesbrough	42	17	9	16	75	87	43
13	Stoke C	42	18	6	18	88	79	42
14	Bradford PA	42	17	6	19	71	84	40
15	Huddersfield T	42	17	4	21	90	89	38
16	Burnley	42	13	10	19	63	84	36
17	Grimsby T	42	13	9	20	61	89	35
18	Sunderland	42	15	5	22	55	83	35
19	Preston NE	42	14	6	22	70	77	34
20	Bury	42	12	10	20	60	85	34
21	Blackburn R	42	11	7	24	60	111	29
22	Leeds U	42	9	7	26	66	118	25

DIV 3 North (2nd) 1945–46

		P	W	D	L	F	A	Pts
1	Rotherham U	8	5	3	0	18	7	13
2	Rochdale	8	6	0	2	17	10	12
3	Carlisle U	9	5	1	3	20	11	11
4	Crewe Alex	8	5	1	2	14	11	11
5	Chester	8	4	2	2	20	10	10
6	Gateshead	8	4	2	2	17	13	10
7	Tranmere R	8	5	0	3	16	17	10
8	Lincoln C	8	4	1	3	17	13	9
9	Hartlepools U	9	4	1	4	20	18	9
10	Stockport Co	9	3	2	4	17	17	8
11	Darlington	9	3	2	4	17	21	8
12	York C	8	3	1	4	14	17	7
13	Southport	8	3	1	4	11	14	7
14	Accrington S	8	3	1	4	13	18	7
15	Barrow	8	3	0	5	14	17	6
16	Doncaster R	8	1	4	3	12	15	6
17	Halifax T	7	1	3	3	8	10	5
18	Bradford C	8	2	1	5	12	18	5
19	Wrexham	7	1	2	4	7	14	4
20	Oldham Ath	8	1	2	5	7	20	4

DIV 3 South (North) 1945–46

		P	W	D	L	F	A	Pts
1	QPR	20	14	4	2	50	15	32
2	Norwich C	20	11	4	5	54	31	26
3	Port Vale	20	9	6	5	34	25	24
4	Watford	20	10	2	8	42	47	22
5	Ipswich T	20	8	4	8	33	36	20
6	Notts Co	20	15	4	8	39	47	20
7	Northampton T	20	8	3	9	37	34	19
8	Clapton Orient	20	5	6	9	28	42	16
9	Walsall	20	6	3	11	31	42	15
10	Southend U	20	5	5	10	33	49	15
11	Mansfield T	20	3	5	12	29	42	11

WARTIME CUP RESULTS

League War Cup results, North Cup, South Cup, London Cup, FA Cup (1945–46) for wartime period. Some qualifying results are included in League tables.

1939–40

LEAGUE WAR CUP 1939–40

PRELIMINARY ROUND

Barrow 1, Carlisle U 0
Bournemouth 5, Bristol C 1
Brighton & HA 1, Clapton Orient 2
Bristol R 2, Aldershot 0
Cardiff C 1, Reading 1
Darlington 2, Gateshead 0
Doncaster R 0, Rotherham U 0
Hartlepools U 2, Halifax T 1
Hull C 1, Lincoln C 0
Mansfield T 3, Notts Co 5
New Brighton 2, Crewe Alex 1
Northampton T 1, Watford 1
Port Vale 2, Walsall 2
Rochdale 3, Accrington S 0
Southend U 1, QPR 0
Southport 1, Oldham Ath 1
Swindon T 1, Torquay U 1
Wrexham 3, Stockport Co 0
York C 6, Bradford C 4

REPLAYS

Oldham Ath 0, Southport 1
Reading 1, Cardiff C 0
Rotherham U 1, Doncaster R 0
Torquay U 5, Swindon T 0
Walsall 6, Port Vale 0
Watford 2, Northampton T 1

FIRST ROUND, FIRST LEG

Arsenal 4, Notts Co 0
Barnsley 3, Hartlepools U 0
Barrow 2, Liverpool 0
Blackburn R 5, Bolton W 1
Blackpool 4, Southport 0
Bradford PA 2, Newcastle U 0
Chester 1, Burnley 3
Chesterfield 2, Huddersfield T 1
Coventry C 3, Luton T 0
Crystal Palace 4, Tottenham H 1
Everton 3, Preston NE 1
Fulham 4, Brentford 1
Leeds U 6, Sheffield W 3
Leicester C 5, Clapton Orient 2

Manchester U 0, Manchester C 1
Middlesbrough 4, Grimsby T 1
New Brighton 1, Stoke C 4
Newport Co 2, Birmingham 2
Norwich C 2, Millwall 1
Nottingham F 1, Charlton Ath 0
Plymouth Arg 0, Bournemouth 1
Rochdale 1, Bury 0
Sheffield U 0, Rotherham U 0
Southampton 1, Bristol R 1
Southend U 3, Watford 1
Sunderland 1, Darlington 1 (*at Newcastle*)
Swansea T 2, Walsall 0
Torquay U 2, Reading 0
WBA 3, Portsmouth 1
West Ham U 3, Chelsea 2
Wrexham 1, Wolverhampton W 1
York C 1, Hull C 1

FIRST ROUND, SECOND LEG

Birmingham 5, Newport Co 2
Bolton W 1, Blackburn R 3
Bournemouth 4, Plymouth Arg 1
Brentford 1, Fulham 2
Bristol R 3, Southampton 1
Burnley 3, Chester 0
Bury 1, Rochdale 1
Charlton Ath 1, Nottingham F 3
Chelsea 0, West Ham U 2
Clapton Orient 2, Leicester C 0
Darlington 2, Sunderland 3
Grimsby T 3, Middlesbrough 1
Hartlepools U 1, Barnsley 1
Huddersfield T 2, Chesterfield 0
Hull C 1, York C 0
Liverpool 1, Barrow 2
Luton T 2, Coventry C 1
Manchester C 0, Manchester U 2
Millwall 1, Norwich C 1
Newcastle U 3, Bradford PA 0
Notts Co 1, Arsenal 5
Portsmouth 3, WBA 2
Preston NE 2, Everton 2
Reading 3, Torquay U 0
Rotherham U 0, Sheffield U 3

Sheffield W 3, Leeds U 2
Southport 2, Blackpool 4
Stoke C 2, New Brighton 1
Tottenham H 2, Crystal Palace 1
Walsall 2, Swansea T 1
Watford 1, Southend U 3
Wolverhampton W 3, Wrexham 0

SECOND ROUND, FIRST LEG
Arsenal 3, Crystal Palace 1
Barnsley 3, Sheffield U 0
Barrow 0, Stoke C 2
Birmingham 2, Reading 0
Blackburn R 1, Manchester U 2
Bournemouth 1, WBA 2
Bristol R 6, Swansea T 0
Burnley 1, Blackpool 2
Everton 5, Rochdale 1
Huddersfield T 1, Hull C 1
Leicester C 1, West Ham U 1
Middlesbrough 2, Newcastle U 2
Norwich C 1, Fulham 1
Nottingham F 3, Southend U 1
Sunderland 0, Leeds U 0
Wolverhampton W 0, Coventry C 2

SECOND ROUND, SECOND LEG
Blackpool 3, Burnley 1
Coventry C 5, Wolverhampton W 2
Crystal Palace 0, Arsenal 2
Fulham 1, Norwich C 0
Hull C 0, Huddersfield T 1
Leeds U 0, Sunderland 1
Manchester U 1, Blackburn R 3
Newcastle U 2, Middlesbrough 1

Reading 0, Birmingham 2
Rochdale 4, Everton 2
Southend U 0, Nottingham F 1
Sheffield U 1, Barnsley 0
Stoke C 6, Barrow 1
Swansea T 3, Bristol R 0
West Ham U 3, Leicester C 0
WBA 3, Bournemouth 1

THIRD ROUND
Arsenal 1, Birmingham 2
Barnsley 0, Blackpool 1
Blackburn R 3, Sunderland 2
Coventry C 0, WBA 1
Everton 1, Stoke C 0
Fulham 2, Nottingham F 0
Huddersfield T 3, West Ham U 3
Newcastle U 1, Bristol R 0

THIRD ROUND, REPLAY
West Ham U 3, Huddersfield T 1

QUARTER-FINALS
Blackburn R 2, WBA 1
Blackpool 0, Newcastle U 2
Fulham 5, Everton 2
West Ham U 4, Birmingham 2

SEMI-FINALS
Blackburn R 1, Newcastle U 0
West Ham U 4, Fulham 3 (*at Chelsea*)

FINAL (*at Wembley*), 8 JUNE 1940
West Ham U 1, Blackburn R 0

1940–41

LEAGUE WAR CUP 1940–41

PRELIMINARY ROUND, FIRST LEG
Bolton W 6, Bradford C 0
Southport 4, Crewe Alex 1
Stockport Co 1, Blackpool 3
York C 7, Sheffield W 0

PRELIMINARY ROUND, SECOND LEG
Blackpool 9, Stockport Co 2
Bradford C 1, Bolton W 3 (*at Bolton*)
Crewe Alex 3, Southport 6
Sheffield W 2, York C 1 (*at Scunthorpe*)

FIRST ROUND, FIRST LEG
Blackpool 1, Manchester C 4

Blackburn R 2, Oldham Ath 0
Bolton W 3, Burnley 1
Brighton & HA 1, Arsenal 4
Bury 4, Preston NE 4
Cardiff C 3, Swansea T 2
Chelsea 3, Portsmouth 1
Chester 2, Tranmere R 0
Chesterfield 1, Barnsley 4
Clapton Orient 3, Aldershot 2
Crystal Palace 0, QPR 1
Grimsby T 1, Doncaster R 0 (*at Scunthorpe*)
Halifax T 2, Leeds U 3
Huddersfield T 2, Middlesbrough 2
Hull C 4, Lincoln C 1
Leicester C 3, Birmingham 3

Liverpool 2, Southport 3
Luton T 4, Northampton T 5
Manchester U 2, Everton 2
Mansfield T 6, Stoke C 1
New Brighton 2, Wrexham 1
Newcastle U 1, Rochdale 2
Norwich C 2, West Ham U 1
Notts Co 4, WBA 0
Reading 3, Bristol C 2
Sheffield U 2, Rotherham U 3
Southampton 2, Brentford 2 (*at Portsmouth*)
Southend U 3, Millwall 1
Tottenham H 4, Bournemouth 1
Walsall 3, Nottingham F 2
Watford 4, Fulham 1
York C 3, Bradford PA 2

FIRST ROUND, SECOND LEG
Aldershot 4, Clapton Orient 0
Arsenal 3, Brighton & HA 1
Bournemouth 1, Tottenham H 6
Bradford PA 3, York C 4 (*at Scunthorpe*)
Brentford 5, Southampton 2
Bristol C 1, Reading 2
Burnley 2, Bolton W 2
Cardiff C 6, Swansea T 2*
Chesterfield 2, Barnsley 5
Doncaster R 0, Grimsby T 0
Everton 2, Manchester U 1
Fulham 2, Watford 1
Leeds U 2, Halifax T 2
Leicester C 3, Birmingham 2†
Lincoln C 3, Hull C 2
Manchester C 0, Blackpool 1
Middlesbrough 4, Huddersfield T 2
Millwall 2, Southend U 1
Northampton T 5, Luton T 0
Nottingham F 8, Walsall 1
Oldham Ath 1, Blackburn R 5
Portsmouth 1, Chelsea 4
Preston NE 2, Bury 1
QPR 3, Crystal Palace 2
Rochdale 1, Newcastle U 3
Rotherham U 0, Sheffield U 3
Southport 2, Liverpool 2
Stoke C 2, Mansfield T 0
Tranmere R 9, Chester 2
WBA 5, Notts Co 0
West Ham U 4, Norwich C 1
Wrexham 5, New Brighton 8

SECOND ROUND, FIRST LEG
Aldershot 2, QPR 1
Barnsley 1, Grimsby T 1

Bolton W 1, Preston NE 4
Brentford 2, Chelsea 2
Everton 5, Southport 0
Hull C 1, Sheffield U 0
Manchester C 5, Blackburn R 2
Middlesbrough 2, Leeds U 0
Nottingham F 0, Leicester C 2
Reading 0, Cardiff C 1
Southend U 2, West Ham U 1
Tottenham H 4, Northampton T 0
Tranmere R 0, New Brighton 3
Watford 0, Arsenal 4
WBA 2, Mansfield T 3
York C 1, Newcastle U 1

SECOND ROUND, SECOND LEG
Arsenal 5, Watford 0
Blackburn R 2, Manchester C 4
Cardiff C 4, Reading 1
Chelsea 3, Brentford 1
Grimsby T 2, Barnsley 2
(*Barnsley won because of higher League place!*)
Leeds U 2, Middlesbrough 2
Leicester C 1, Nottingham F 1
Mansfield T 6, WBA 2
New Brighton 0, Tranmere R 4
Newcastle U 4, York C 1
Northampton T 1, Tottenham H 3
Preston NE 2, Bolton W 0
QPR 4, Aldershot 2
Sheffield U 3, Hull C 1
Southport 0, Everton 5
West Ham U 3, Southend U 1

THIRD ROUND, FIRST LEG
Everton 1, Manchester C 1
Leicester C 2, Mansfield T 2
Middlesbrough 0, Newcastle U 1
Preston NE 12, Tranmere R 1
QPR 2, Chelsea 0
Sheffield U 3, Barnsley 1
Tottenham H 3, Cardiff C 3
West Ham U 0, Arsenal 1

THIRD ROUND, SECOND LEG
Arsenal 2, West Ham U 1
Barnsley 1, Sheffield U 1
Cardiff C 2, Tottenham H 3
Chelsea 2, QPR 4
Manchester C 2, Everton 0
Mansfield T 1, Leicester C 2
Newcastle U 3, Middlesbrough 0
Tranmere R 1, Preston NE 8

*Both legs of tie played at Cardiff C as Swansea T's ground not available.
†Both legs of tie played at Leicester C as Birmingham's ground banned at the time.

FOURTH ROUND, FIRST LEG
Arsenal 2, Tottenham H 1
Manchester C 1, Preston NE 2
QPR 2, Leicester C 1
Sheffield U 2, Newcastle U 0

FOURTH ROUND, SECOND LEG
Leicester C 6, QPR 1
Newcastle U 4, Sheffield U 0
Preston NE 3, Manchester C 0
Tottenham H 1, Arsenal 1

SEMI-FINALS, FIRST LEG
Arsenal 1, Leicester C 0
Preston NE 2, Newcastle U 0

SEMI-FINALS, SECOND LEG
Leicester C 1, Arsenal 2
Newcastle U 0, Preston NE 0

FINAL (at Wembley), 10 MAY 1941
Preston NE 1, Arsenal 1

REPLAY, 31 MAY 1941
Preston NE 2, Arsenal 1

LONDON CUP 1940–41

LEAGUE WAR CUP 1941–42

FIRST ROUND, FIRST LEG
Barnsley 1, Grimsby T 2
Blackburn R 1, Manchester U 2
Bradford C 4, Huddersfield T 1
Burnley 0, Liverpool 3
Bury 4, Southport 4
Cardiff C 3, Southampton 1
Everton 2, Preston NE 2
Leicester C 2, Norwich C 0
Lincoln C 6, Nottingham F 5
Middlesbrough 3, Bradford PA 2
Northampton T 3, Bristol C 0
Oldham Ath 1, Sunderland 1
Rotherham U 2, Sheffield U 5
Stoke C 5, WBA 3
Wolverhampton W 3, Chester 1

FIRST ROUND, SECOND LEG
Bradford PA 2, Middlesbrough 0
Bristol C 3, Northampton T 1
Chester 0, Wolverhampton W 1
Grimsby T 1, Barnsley 1
Huddersfield T 2, Bradford C 1

Group A

	P	W	D	L	F	A	Pts
Brentford	10	4	5	1	25	20	13
Crystal Palace	10	4	4	2	25	18	12
QPR	10	5	1	4	26	26	11
Aldershot	10	4	2	4	21	24	10
Fulham	10	4	0	6	32	34	8
Chelsea	10	2	2	6	19	26	6

Group B

	P	W	D	L	F	A	Pts
Reading	10	6	4	0	29	8	16
Tottenham H	10	5	3	2	32	14	13
West Ham U	10	6	1	3	23	19	13
Arsenal	10	5	2	3	38	18	12
Millwall	10	2	1	7	13	26	5
Clapton Orient	10	0	1	9	9	59	1

SEMI-FINALS
Reading 4, Crystal Palace 1
Tottenham H 0, Brentford 2

FINAL
Reading 3, Brentford 2

1941–42

Liverpool 4, Burnley 1
Manchester U 3, Blackburn R 1
Norwich C 3, Leicester C 0
Nottingham F 4, Lincoln C 2
Preston NE 1, Everton 2
Sheffield U 3, Rotherham U 3
Southampton 1, Cardiff C 1
Southport 2, Bury 1
Sunderland 3, Oldham Ath 2
WBA 6, Stoke C 1
Blackpool withdrew v Manchester C w.o.

SECOND ROUND, FIRST LEG
Bradford PA 2, Sheffield U 0
Cardiff C 1, WBA 1
Grimsby T 3, Nottingham F 1
Liverpool 0, Everton 2
Manchester U 5, Wolverhampton W 4
Northampton T 3, Norwich C 4
Southport 1, Manchester C 4
Sunderland 1, Bradford C 2

SECOND ROUND, SECOND LEG
Bradford C 4, Sunderland 6
Everton 0, Liverpool 1

Manchester C 3, Southport 0
Norwich C 3, Northampton T 1
Nottingham F 1, Grimsby T 5
Sheffield U 2, Bradford PA 1
WBA 3, Cardiff C 2
Wolverhampton W 2, Manchester U 0

THIRD ROUND, FIRST LEG
Bradford PA 0, Sunderland 1
Norwich C 1, Grimsby T 0
WBA 3, Everton 1
Wolverhampton W 2, Manchester C 0

THIRD ROUND, SECOND LEG
Everton 1, WBA 5
Grimsby T 2, Norwich C 0
Manchester C 1, Wolverhampton W 0
Sunderland 2, Bradford PA 2

SEMI-FINALS, FIRST LEG
Sunderland 0, Grimsby T 0
WBA 0, Wolverhampton W 4

SEMI-FINALS, SECOND LEG
Grimsby T 2, Sunderland 3
Wolverhampton W 3, WBA 0

FINAL, FIRST LEG (at Sunderland)

23 MAY 1942
Sunderland 2, Wolverhampton W 2

FINAL, SECOND LEG
(at Wolverhampton)

30 MAY 1942
Wolverhampton W 4, Sunderland 1

LONDON CUP 1941–42
Group 1

	P	W	D	L	F	A	Pts
Arsenal	6	5	0	1	19	7	10
West Ham U	6	5	0	1	18	11	10
Clapton Orient	6	1	0	5	10	19	2
Brighton & HA	6	1	0	5	11	21	2

Group 2

	P	W	D	L	F	A	Pts
Brentford	6	4	2	0	17	9	10
Millwall	6	2	3	1	15	12	7
QPR	6	2	1	3	8	7	5
Aldershot	6	1	0	5	8	20	2

Group 3

	P	W	D	L	F	A	Pts
Charlton Ath	6	4	1	1	17	6	9
Tottenham H	6	3	1	2	9	11	7
Watford	6	2	1	3	10	12	5
Reading	6	1	1	4	9	16	3

Group 4

	P	W	D	L	F	A	Pts
Portsmouth	6	4	1	1	16	4	9
Fulham	6	4	1	1	14	16	9
Chelsea	6	1	3	2	8	8	5
Crystal Palace	6	0	1	5	8	18	1

SEMI-FINALS
Arsenal 0, Brentford 0
Replay: Brentford 2, Arsenal 1
Charlton Ath 0, Portsmouth 1

FINAL
Brentford 2, Portsmouth 0

1942–43

LEAGUE WAR CUP 1942–43

FIRST ROUND, FIRST LEG
Aberaman Ath 1, Bristol C 3
Aston Villa 5, Wolverhampton W 2
Barnsley 1, Sheffield U 4
Blackpool 4, Everton 1
Bradford PA 0, Huddersfield T 0
Chester 2, Stoke C 3
Coventry C 1, WBA 1
Derby Co 1, Notts Co 3
Halifax T 2, Chesterfield 1
Liverpool 1, Bury 3
Lovell's Ath 1, Bath C 2

Manchester U 0, Manchester C 1
Newcastle U 3, York C 2
Nottingham F 0, Leicester C 1
Rochdale 1, Blackburn R 2
Sheffield W 1, Bradford C 0

FIRST ROUND, SECOND LEG
Bath C 1, Lovell's Ath 1
Blackburn R 3, Rochdale 1
Bradford C 1, Sheffield W 1
Bristol C 1, Aberaman Ath 2
Bury 2, Liverpool 7
Chesterfield 2, Halifax T 0

Everton 4, Blackpool 3
Huddersfield T 2, Bradford PA 3
Leicester C 0, Nottingham F 2
Manchester C 2, Manchester U 0
Notts Co 2, Derby Co 2
Sheffield U 3, Barnsley 0
Stoke C 5, Chester 2
WBA 3, Coventry C 0
Wolverhampton W 3, Aston Villa 5
York C 2, Newcastle U 0

SECOND ROUND, FIRST LEG
Bath C 2, Bristol C 2
Blackburn R 2, Manchester C 0
Liverpool 3, Blackpool 1
Nottingham F 1, Sheffield W 0
Sheffield U 4, Notts Co 1
Stoke C 1, Aston Villa 3
WBA 2, Chesterfield 3
York C 2, Bradford PA 1

SECOND ROUND, SECOND LEG
Aston Villa 2, Stoke C 0
Blackpool 5, Liverpool 0
Bradford PA 0, York C 3
Bristol C 2, Bath C 1
Chesterfield 3, WBA 3
Manchester C 4, Blackburn R 0
Notts Co 2, Sheffield U 1
Sheffield W 5, Nottingham F 1

THIRD ROUND, FIRST LEG
Blackpool 3, Manchester C 1
Bristol C 0, Aston Villa 0
Sheffield W 3, Sheffield U 2
York C 2, Chesterfield 0

THIRD ROUND, SECOND LEG
Aston Villa 2, Bristol C 1
Chesterfield 0, York C 2
Manchester C 1, Blackpool 1
Sheffield U 0, Sheffield W 0

SEMI-FINALS, FIRST LEG
Blackpool 3, Aston Villa 1
Sheffield W 3, York C 0

SEMI-FINALS, SECOND LEG
Aston Villa 2, Blackpool 1
York C 1, Sheffield W 1

FINAL, FIRST LEG (*at Blackpool*)

1 MAY 1943
Blackpool 2, Sheffield W 2

FINAL, SECOND LEG
(*at Hillsbrough*)

8 MAY 1943
Sheffield W 1, Blackpool 2

THE LEAGUE SOUTH CUP 1942–43
Group 1

	P	W	D	L	F	A	Pts
Arsenal	6	5	0	1	21	5	11
West Ham U	6	3	2	1	19	9	7
Watford	6	1	2	3	9	12	5
Brighton & HA	6	0	5	1	4	27	1

Group 2

	P	W	D	L	F	A	Pts
QPR	6	4	1	1	16	8	9
Southampton	6	4	2	0	14	6	8
Clapton Orient	6	1	3	2	6	14	4
Brentford	6	1	4	1	7	15	3

Group 3

	P	W	D	L	F	A	Pts
Reading	6	5	0	1	24	5	11
Tottenham H	6	4	1	1	12	3	9
Chelsea	6	2	4	0	9	18	4
Millwall	6	0	0	6	4	23	0

Group 4

	P	W	D	L	F	A	Pts
Charlton Ath	6	5	1	0	20	5	10
Aldershot	6	3	2	1	12	11	7
Portsmouth	6	2	2	2	11	12	6
Fulham	6	2	2	2	12	16	6
Crystal Palace	6	1	3	2	7	9	4
Luton T	6	1	4	1	5	14	3

SEMI-FINALS
Charlton Ath 2, Reading 1
Arsenal 4, QPR 1

FINAL
Arsenal 7, Charlton Ath 1

1943–44

LEAGUE WAR CUP 1943–44

FIRST ROUND, FIRST LEG
Bath C 2, Bristol C 1
Birmingham 3, Leicester C 1
Blackpool 7, Everton 1
Bradford PA 5, Sheffield W 0
Burnley 3, Rochdale 3
Derby Co 2, Coventry C 1
Gateshead 1, Darlington 2
Hartlepools U 3, Newcastle U 1
Liverpool 8, Oldham Ath 1
Lovell's Ath 2, Cardiff C 0
Manchester C 3, Blackburn R 0
Rotherham U 2, Grimsby T 2
Sheffield U 3, Leeds U 1
Stoke C 4, Aston Villa 5
Wrexham 1, Manchester U 4
York C 4, Barnsley 1

FIRST ROUND, SECOND LEG
Aston Villa 3, Stoke C 0
Barnsley 3, York C 1
Blackburn R 4, Manchester C 2
Bristol C 1, Bath C 2
Cardiff C 1, Lovell's Ath 0
Coventry C 3, Derby Co 0
Darlington 1, Gateshead 1
Everton 1, Blackpool 3
Grimsby T 2, Rotherham U 1
Leeds U 1, Sheffield U 0
Leicester C 2, Birmingham 1
Manchester U 2, Wrexham 2
Newcastle U 3, Hartlepools U 0
Oldham Ath 1, Liverpool 0
Rochdale 2, Burnley 1
Sheffield W 1, Bradford PA 2

SECOND ROUND, FIRST LEG
Birmingham 3, Manchester U 1
Blackpool 8, Rochdale 0
Coventry C 1, Aston Villa 2
Darlington 2, Newcastle U 0
Lovell's Ath 1, Bath C 3
Manchester C 1, Liverpool 1
Sheffield U 4, Grimsby T 0
York C 1, Bradford PA 5

SECOND ROUND, SECOND LEG
Aston Villa 2, Coventry C 1
Bath C 3, Lovell's Ath 0
Bradford PA 2, York C 1
Grimsby T 0, Sheffield U 1

Liverpool 2, Manchester C 3
Manchester U 1, Birmingham 1
Newcastle U 4, Darlington 1
Rochdale 2, Blackpool 1

THIRD ROUND, FIRST LEG
Aston Villa 1, Bath C 0
Blackpool 2, Bradford PA 2
Manchester C 1, Birmingham 0
Sheffield U 4, Newcastle U 0

THIRD ROUND, SECOND LEG
Bath C 3, Aston Villa 3
Birmingham 0, Manchester C 0
Bradford PA 1, Blackpool 2
Newcastle U 3, Sheffield U 1

SEMI-FINALS, FIRST LEG
Aston Villa 3, Sheffield U 2
Blackpool 1, Manchester C 1

SEMI-FINALS, SECOND LEG
Manchester C 1, Blackpool 2
Sheffield U 2, Aston Villa 2

FINAL, FIRST LEG (at Blackpool)

29 APRIL 1944
Blackpool 2
Aston Villa 1

FINAL, SECOND LEG (at Villa Park)

6 MAY 1944
Aston Villa 4
Blackpool 2

THE LEAGUE SOUTH CUP 1943–44

Group 1

	P	W	D	L	F	A	Pts
Charlton Ath	6	3	2	1	12	11	8
Crystal Palace	6	3	1	2	16	11	7
Brentford	6	2	1	3	18	17	5
Brighton & HA	6	2	0	4	11	18	4

Group 2

	P	W	D	L	F	A	Pts
Chelsea	6	4	1	1	17	10	9
West Ham U	6	3	0	3	15	11	6
Watford	6	2	1	3	7	13	5
Southampton	6	2	0	4	12	17	4

Group 3

	P	W	D	L	F	A	Pts
Tottenham H	6	5	0	1	8	3	10
Aldershot	6	4	1	1	17	5	9
Millwall	6	1	1	4	7	15	3
Portsmouth	6	0	2	4	3	12	2

Group 4

	P	W	D	L	F	A	Pts
Reading	6	6	0	0	23	6	12
QPR	6	5	1	0	25	7	11
Arsenal	6	1	2	3	13	15	4
Fulham	6	2	0	4	15	15	4
Luton T	6	1	1	4	8	21	3
Clapton Orient	6	1	0	5	7	27	2

SEMI-FINALS

Chelsea 3, Reading 2 aet
Tottenham H 0, Charlton Ath 3

FINAL

Charlton Ath 3, Chelsea 1

1944–45

LEAGUE WAR CUP 1944–45

FIRST ROUND, FIRST LEG

Aston Villa 1, Wolverhampton W 2
Blackpool 2, Wrexham 0
Bolton W 0, Accrington S 0
Bradford PA 1, Doncaster R 1
Bristol C 5, WBA 2
Burnley 2, Manchester U 3
Bury 3, Stoke C 2
Cardiff C 1, Lovell's Ath 0
Halifax T 1, Chesterfield 1
Leicester C 2, Derby Co 1
Liverpool 1, Everton 0
Manchester C 5, Crewe Alex 1
Newcastle U 2, Darlington 1
Northampton T 0, Birmingham C 2
Rotherham U 2, Barnsley 1
Sheffield U 2, Bradford C 2

FIRST ROUND, SECOND LEG

Accrington S 0, Bolton W 4
Birmingham C 2, Northampton T 2
Barnsley 3, Rotherham U 0
Bradford C 4, Sheffield U 3
Chesterfield 3, Halifax T 1
Crewe Alex 2, Manchester C 0
Darlington 0, Newcastle U 3
Derby Co 2, Leicester C 0
Doncaster R 2, Bradford PA 0
Everton 0, Liverpool 1
Lovell's Ath 0, Cardiff C 0
Manchester U 4, Burnley 0
Stoke C 3, Bury 0
WBA 3, Bristol C 3

Wolverhampton W 1, Aston Villa 0
Wrexham 2, Blackpool 2

SECOND ROUND, FIRST LEG

Barnsley 2, Chesterfield 2
Birmingham C 0, Wolverhampton W 0
Blackpool 1, Bolton W 4
Bristol C 1, Cardiff C 2
Doncaster R 1, Derby Co 2
Liverpool 3, Manchester C 0
Manchester U 6, Stoke C 1
Newcastle U 6, Bradford C 2

SECOND ROUND, SECOND LEG

Bolton W 1, Blackpool 2
Bradford C 0, Newcastle U 1
Cardiff C 2, Bristol C 2
Chesterfield 2, Barnsley 0
Derby Co 1, Doncaster R 4
Manchester C 1, Liverpool 3
Stoke C 1, Manchester U 4
Wolverhampton W 1, Birmingham C 0

THIRD ROUND, FIRST LEG

Bolton W 3, Newcastle U 0
Doncaster R 1, Manchester U 2
Liverpool 0, Chesterfield 0
Wolverhampton W 3, Cardiff C 0

THIRD ROUND, SECOND LEG

Cardiff C 2, Wolverhampton W 1
Chesterfield 1, Liverpool 0
Manchester U 3, Doncaster R 1
Newcastle U 4, Bolton W 2

SEMI-FINAL, FIRST LEG
Manchester U 1, Chesterfield 1
Wolverhampton W 2, Bolton W 2

SEMI-FINAL, SECOND LEG
Bolton W 2, Wolverhampton W 1
Chesterfield 0, Manchester U 1

FINAL, FIRST LEG (*at Bolton*)

19 MAY 1945
Bolton W 1, Manchester U 0

FINAL, SECOND LEG (*at Maine Road*)

26 MAY 1945
Manchester U 2, Bolton W 2

THE LEAGUE SOUTH CUP
1944–45

Group 1

	P	W	D	L	F	A	Pts
Arsenal	6	5	0	1	20	8	10
Portsmouth	6	4	0	2	16	8	8
Reading	6	1	2	3	5	14	4
Clapton Orient	6	0	2	4	5	16	2

Group 2

	P	W	D	L	F	A	Pts
Millwall	6	4	1	1	12	11	9
Fulham	6	4	0	2	15	9	8
Brighton & HA	6	2	0	4	16	18	4
Brentford	6	1	1	4	13	18	3

Group 3

	P	W	D	L	F	A	Pts
West Ham U	6	4	1	1	14	6	9
QPR	6	3	2	1	7	8	8
Tottenham H	6	3	1	2	13	4	7
Aldershot	6	0	0	6	3	19	0

Group 4

	P	W	D	L	F	A	Pts
Chelsea	6	5	1	0	13	3	11
Southampton	6	4	2	0	29	11	10
Charlton Ath	6	4	1	1	16	5	9
Luton T	6	1	1	4	8	25	3
Crystal Palace	6	0	2	4	5	13	2
Watford	6	0	1	5	6	20	1

SEMI-FINALS
Arsenal 0, Millwall 1
Chelsea 2, West Ham U 1

FINAL
Chelsea 2, Millwall 0

1945–46

FA CUP 1945–46

FIRST ROUND, FIRST LEG
Barnet 2, QPR 6
Barrow 1, Netherfield 0
Bath C 3, Cheltenham T 2
Brighton & HA 3, Romford 1
Bromley 2, Slough 1 (*abandoned 80 minutes*)
Bromley 6, Slough 1
Carlisle U 5, North Shields 1
Chorley 2, Accrington S 1
Clapton Orient 2, Newport (IW) 1
Crewe Alex 4, Wrexham 2
Darlington 2, Stockton 0
Doncaster R 0, Rotherham U 1
Halifax T 1, York C 0
Hartlepools U 1, Gateshead 2
Kettering T 1, Grantham T 5
Lovell's Ath 4, Bournemouth 1
Mansfield T 3, Gainsborough Trinity 0
Marine (Crosby) 4, Stalybridge Celtic 0
Northampton T 5, Chelmsford C 1
Notts Co 2, Bradford C 2
Port Vale 4, Wellington T 0
Reading 3, Aldershot 1
Shrewsbury T 5, Walsall 0
South Liverpool 1, Tranmere R 1
Southport 1, Oldham Ath 2
Stockport Co 1, Rochdale 2
Sutton U 1, Walthamstow Avenue 4
Swindon T 1, Bristol R 0
Torquay U 0, Newport Co 1
Trowbridge T 1, Exeter C 3
Watford 1, Southend U 1
Willington 0, Bishop Auckland 5
Wisbech T 0, Ipswich T 3
Yeovil & Petters U 2, Bristol C 2
Yorkshire Amateur 1, Lincoln C 0

FIRST ROUND, SECOND LEG
Accrington S 2, Chorley 0
Aldershot 7, Reading 3
Bishop Auckland 0, Willington 2
Bournemouth 3, Lovell's Ath 2
Bradford C 1, Notts Co 2
Bristol C 3, Yeovil & Petters U 0
Bristol R 4, Swindon T 1
Chelmsford C 0, Northampton T 5
Cheltenham T 0, Bath C 2
Exeter C 7, Trowbridge T 2
Gainsborough Trinity 4, Mansfield T 2
Gateshead 6, Hartlepools U 2
Grantham T 2, Kettering T 2
Ipswich T 5, Wisbech T 0
Lincoln C 5, Yorkshire Amateur 1
Netherfield 2, Barrow 2
Newport Co 1, Torquay U 1
Newport (IW) 2, Clapton Orient 0
North Shields 2, Carlisle U 3
Oldham Ath 3, Southport 1
QPR 2, Barnet 1
Rochdale 1, Stockport Co 1
Romford 1, Brighton & HA 1
Rotherham U 2, Doncaster R 1
Slough 1, Bromley 0
Southend U 0, Watford 3
Stalybridge Celtic 3, Marine (Crosby) 3
Stockton 1, Darlington 4
Tranmere R 6, South Liverpool 1
Walthamstow Avenue 7, Sutton U 2
Walsall 4, Shrewsbury T 1
Wellington T 0, Port Vale 2
Wrexham 3, Crewe Alex 0
York C 4, Halifax T 2

SECOND ROUND, FIRST LEG
Aldershot 7, Newport (IW) 0
Barrow 4, Carlisle U 2
Bishop Auckland 1, York C 2
Bristol C 4, Bristol R 2
Bromley 1, Watford 3
Darlington 2, Gateshead 4
Grantham T 1, Mansfield T 2
Lovell's Ath 2, Bath C 1
Newport Co 5, Exeter C 1
Northampton T 3, Notts Co 1
Oldham Ath 2, Accrington S 1
Port Vale 3, Marine (Crosby) 1
QPR 4, Ipswich T 0
Rotherham U 2, Lincoln C 1
Shrewsbury T 0, Wrexham 1
Tranmere R 3, Rochdale 1
Walthamstow Avenue 1, Brighton & HA 1

SECOND ROUND, SECOND LEG
Accrington S 3, Oldham Ath 1
Bath C 2, Lovell's Ath 5
Brighton & HA 4, Walthamstow Avenue 2
Bristol R 0, Bristol C 2
Carlisle U 3, Barrow 4
Exeter C 1, Newport Co 3
Gateshead 1, Darlington 2
Ipswich T 0, QPR 2
Lincoln C 1, Rotherham U 1
Mansfield T 2, Grantham T 1
Marine (Crosby) 1, Port Vale 1
Newport (IW) 0, Aldershot 5
Notts Co 1, Northampton T 0
Rochdale 3, Tranmere R 0
Watford 1, Bromley 1
Wrexham 1, Shrewsbury T 1
York C 3, Bishop Auckland 0

THIRD ROUND, FIRST LEG
Accrington S 2, Manchester U 2
Aldershot 2, Plymouth Arg 0
Birmingham C 1, Portsmouth 0
Bolton W 1, Blackburn R 0
Bradford PA 2, Port Vale 1
Bristol C 5, Swansea T 1
Bury 3, Rochdale 3
Cardiff C 1, WBA 1
Charlton Ath 3, Fulham 1
Chelsea 1, Leicester C 1
Chester 0, Liverpool 2
Chesterfield 1, York C 1
Coventry C 2, Aston Villa 1
Grimsby T 1, Sunderland 3
Huddersfield T 1, Sheffield U 1
Leeds U 4, Middlesbrough 4
Lovell's Ath 2, Wolverhampton W 4
Luton T 0, Derby Co 6
Manchester C 6, Barrow 2
Mansfield T 0, Sheffield W 0
Newcastle U 4, Barnsley 2
Northampton T 2, Millwall 2
Norwich C 1, Brighton & HA 2
Nottingham F 1, Watford 1
Preston NE 2, Everton 1
QPR 0, Crystal Palace 0
Rotherham U 2, Gateshead 2
Southampton 4, Newport Co 3
Stoke C 3, Burnley 1
Tottenham H 2, Brentford 2
West Ham U 6, Arsenal 0
Wrexham 1, Blackpool 4

THIRD ROUND, SECOND LEG
Arsenal 1, West Ham U 0
Aston Villa 2, Coventry C 0
Barnsley 3, Newcastle U 0
Barrow 2, Manchester C 2
Blackburn R 1, Bolton W 3
Blackpool 4, Wrexham 1
Brentford 2, Tottenham H 0
Brighton & HA 4, Norwich C 1
Burnley 2, Stoke C 1
Crystal Palace 0, QPR 0 (*abandoned*)
Derby Co 3, Luton T 0
Everton 2, Preston NE 2
Fulham 2, Charlton Ath 1
Gateshead 0, Rotherham U 2
Leicester C 0, Chelsea 2
Liverpool 2, Chester 1
Manchester U 5, Accrington S 1
Middlesbrough 7, Leeds U 2
Millwall 3, Northampton T 0
Newport Co 1, Southampton 2
Plymouth Arg 0, Aldershot 1
Portsmouth 0, Birmingham C 0
Port Vale 1, Bradford PA 1
Rochdale 2, Bury 4
Sheffield U 2, Huddersfield T 0
Sheffield W 5, Mansfield T 0
Sunderland 2, Grimsby T 1
Swansea T 2, Bristol C 2
Watford 1, Nottingham F 1 (*abandoned*)
WBA 4, Cardiff C 0
Wolverhampton W 8, Lovell's Ath 1
York C 3, Chesterfield 2

THIRD ROUND, REPLAYS
Crystal Palace 0, QPR 1 (*at Fulham*)
Watford 1, Nottingham F 0 (*at Tottenham*)

FOURTH ROUND, FIRST LEG
Barnsley 3, Rotherham U 0
Birmingham C 5, Watford 0
Blackpool 3, Middlesbrough 2
Bolton W 5, Liverpool 0
Bradford PA 1, Manchester C 3
Brighton & HA 3, Aldershot 0
Bristol C 2, Brentford 1
Charlton Ath 5, Wolverhampton W 2
Chelsea 2, West Ham U 0
Derby Co 1, WBA 0
Manchester U 1, Preston NE 0
Millwall 2, Aston Villa 4
Sheffield W 5, York C 1
Southampton 0, QPR 1

Stoke C 2, Sheffield U 0
Sunderland 3, Bury 1

FOURTH ROUND, SECOND LEG
Aldershot 1, Brighton & HA 4
Aston Villa 9, Millwall 1
Brentford 5, Bristol C 0
Bury 5, Sunderland 4
Liverpool 2, Bolton W 0
Manchester C 2, Bradford PA 8
Middlesbrough 3, Blackpool 2
Preston NE 3, Manchester U 1
QPR 4, Southampton 3
Rotherham U 2, Barnsley 1
Sheffield U 3, Stoke C 2
Watford 1, Birmingham C 1
WBA 1, Derby Co 3
West Ham U 1, Chelsea 0
Wolverhampton W 1, Charlton Ath 1
York C 1, Sheffield W 6

FOURTH ROUND, REPLAY
Middlesbrough 1, Blackpool 0 (*at Leeds*)

FIFTH ROUND, FIRST LEG
Barnsley 0, Bradford PA 1
Bolton W 1, Middlesbrough 0
Brighton & HA 1, Derby Co 4
Chelsea 0, Aston Villa 1
Preston NE 1, Charlton Ath 1
QPR 1, Brentford 3
Sunderland 1, Birmingham C 0
Stoke C 2, Sheffield W 0

FIFTH ROUND, SECOND LEG
Aston Villa 1, Chelsea 0
Birmingham C 3, Sunderland 1
Bradford PA 1, Barnsley 1
Brentford 0, QPR 0
Charlton Ath 6, Preston NE 0
Derby Co 6, Brighton & HA 0
Middlesbrough 1, Bolton W 1
Sheffield W 0, Stoke C 0

SIXTH ROUND, FIRST LEG
Aston Villa 3, Derby Co 4
Bradford PA 2, Birmingham C 2
Charlton Ath 6, Brentford 3
Stoke C 0, Bolton W 2

SIXTH ROUND, SECOND LEG
Birmingham C 6, Bradford PA 0
Bolton W 0, Stoke C 0
Brentford 1, Charlton Ath 3
Derby Co 1, Aston Villa 1

SEMI-FINALS
Bolton W 0, Charlton Ath 2 (*at Villa Park*)
Derby Co 1, Birmingham C 1
  (*at Hillsborough*)

SEMI-FINAL, REPLAY
Derby Co 4, Birmingham C 0
  (*at Maine Road*)

FINAL (*at Wembley*)   98,215

27 APRIL 1946
Derby Co (0) 4, Charlton Ath (0) 1

THIRD DIVISION NORTH CUP 1945–46

FIRST ROUND, FIRST LEG
Accrington S 1, York C 0
Carlisle U 5, Tranmere R 1
Chester 3, Bradford C 0
Crewe Alex 1, Hartlepools U 2
Darlington 2, Southport 1
Doncaster R 2, Stockport Co 2
Oldham Ath 2, Gateshead 2
Rotherham U 4, Wrexham 0

FIRST ROUND, SECOND LEG
Bradford C 2, Chester 2
Gateshead 3, Oldham Ath 0
Hartlepools U 3, Crewe Alex 3
Southport 3, Darlington 1
Stockport Co 2, Doncaster R 2
Tranmere R 2, Carlisle U 1
Wrexham 0, Rotherham U 2
York C 3, Accrington S 1

SECOND ROUND, FIRST LEG
Carlisle U 1, Gateshead 2
Chester 4, York C 0
Doncaster R 0, Rotherham U 0
Hartlepools U 1, Southport 2

SECOND ROUND, SECOND LEG
Gateshead 2, Carlisle U 1
Rotherham U 2, Doncaster R 0
Southport 1, Hartlepools U 1
York C 1, Chester 0

SEMI-FINALS, FIRST LEG
Chester 3, Southport 0
Gateshead 2, Rotherham U 2

SEMI-FINALS, SECOND LEG
Rotherham U 3, Gateshead 1
Southport 2, Chester 4

FINAL, FIRST LEG
Rotherham U 2, Chester 2

FINAL, SECOND LEG
Chester 2, Rotherham U 3

THIRD DIVISION SOUTH CUP 1945–46

SEMI-FINALS
Bournemouth 1, QPR 1
Bristol R 1, Walsall 3

SEMI-FINAL, REPLAY
QPR 0, Bournemouth 1

FINAL (*at Stamford Bridge*)
Bournemouth 1, Walsall 0

40 CUP FINAL TEAMS FOR MAJOR COMPETITIONS 1939–46

LEAGUE WAR CUP FINAL 1939–40

Wembley, 8 June 1940   42,399

West Ham U 1 *(Small)*
Blackburn R 0

West Ham U: Conway; Bicknell, Walker C, Fenton, Walker R, Cockroft, Small, Macaulay, Foreman, Goulden, Foxall.
Blackburn R: Barron; Hough, Crook, Whiteside, Pryde, Chivers, Rogers, Butt, Weddle, Clarke, Guest.

LEAGUE WAR CUP FINAL 1940–41

Wembley, 10 May 1941   60,000

Preston NE 1 *(McLaren)*
Arsenal 1 *(Compton D)*

Preston NE: Fairbrother; Gallimore, Scott, Shankly, Smith, Beattie A, Finney, McLaren, Dougal, Beattie R, O'Donnell H (Blackpool).
Arsenal: Marks; Scott, Hapgood, Crayston, Joy, Collett, Kirchen, Jones, Compton L, Bastin, Compton D.

LEAGUE WAR CUP FINAL 1940–41 REPLAY

Ewood Park, 31 May 1941   45,000

Preston NE 2 *(Beattie R 2)*
Arsenal 1 *(og)*

Preston NE: Fairbrother; Gallimore, Mansley, Shankly, Smith, Beattie A, Finney, McLaren, Dougal, Beattie R, O'Donnell H (Blackpool).
Arsenal: Marks; Scott, Hapgood, Crayston, Joy, Collett, Kirchen, Jones, Drake, Bastin, Compton D.

LONDON WAR CUP FINAL 1940–41

Stamford Bridge, 7 June 1941   9000

Reading 3 *(Sherwood, Chitty, Edelston)*
Brentford 2 *(Perry 2)*

Reading: Mapson (Sunderland); McPhie (Falkirk), Fullwood, Young, Ratcliffe (Oldham Ath), Layton, Chitty, Edelston, McPhee, Bradley, Sherwood.

Brentford: Poland (Liverpool); Brown, Poyser, Mackenzie (Middlesbrough), James, Holliday, Hopkins, Townsend, Perry (Doncaster R), Wilkins, Bamford.

LEAGUE WAR CUP FINAL 1941–42 FIRST LEG

Roker Park, 23 May 1942   35,000

Sunderland 2 *(Stubbins, Carter)*
Wolverhampton W 2 *(Westcott 2)*

Sunderland: Heywood; Gorman, Eves, Housam, Hewison, Hastings, Spuhler, Stubbins (Newcastle U), Whitelum, Carter, Robinson (Charlton Ath).
Wolverhampton W: Sidlow; Dowen (Hull C), Robinson, Thornhill, Galley, Dorsett, Broome (Aston Villa), McIntosh, Westcott, Stevenson, Mullen.

LEAGUE WAR CUP FINAL 1941–42 SECOND LEG

Molineux, 30 May 1942   43,038

Wolverhampton W 4 *(Rowley 2, Westcott, Broome)*
Sunderland 1 *(Carter)*

Wolverhampton W: Sidlow; Dowen (Hull C), Taylor, Robinson, Galley, Dorsett, Broome (Aston Villa), McIntosh, Westcott, Rowley (Manchester U), Mullen.
Sunderland: Heywood; Gorman, Eves, Housam, Hewison, Hastings, Spuhler, Stubbins (Newcastle U), Whitelum, Carter, Robinson (Charlton Ath).

LONDON WAR CUP FINAL 1941–42

Wembley, 30 May 1942   72,000

Brentford 2 *(Smith L 2)*
Portsmouth 0

Brentford: Jackson (Chelsea); Brown, Poyser, Mackenzie (Middlesbrough), James, Sneddon (Swansea T), Hopkins, Wilkins, Perry, Hunt (Sheffield W), Smith L.
Portsmouth: Walker; Rookes, Rochford, Guthrie, Flewin, Wharton, Bullock (Barnsley), Griffiths, Black (Hearts), Barlow, Parker.

**CUP WINNERS PLAY-OFF
1941–42**

Stamford Bridge, 6 June 1942   20,174

Brentford 1 *(Collett)*
Wolverhampton W 1 *(Mullen)*

Brentford: Jackson (Chelsea); Brown, Poyser, Mackenzie (Middlesbrough), James, Collett (Arsenal), Hopkins, Wilkins, Perry, Hunt (Sheffield W), Smith L.
Wolverhampton W: Sidlow; Dowen (Hull C), Taylor, Robinson, Ashton, Dorsett, Broome (Aston Villa), McIntosh, Westcott, Stevenson, Mullen.

**LEAGUE SOUTH CUP FINAL
1942–43**

Wembley, 1 May 1943   75,000

Arsenal 7 *(Lewis 4, Drake 2, Compton D)*
Charlton Ath 1 *(Green)*

Arsenal: Marks; Scott, Compton L, Crayston, Joy, Male, Kirchen, Drake, Lewis, Bastin, Compton D.
Charlton Ath: Hobbins; Cann, Shreeve, Phipps, Oakes, Davies (Barrow), Green, Mason (Third Lanark), Welsh, Brown, Revell.

**LEAGUE NORTH CUP FINAL
1942–43 FIRST LEG**

Bloomfield Road, 1 May 1943   28,000

Blackpool 2 *(Finan, Burbanks)*
Sheffield W 2 *(Cockroft, Robinson)*

Blackpool: Savage (Q of S); Pope (Hearts), Jones S, Farrow, Johnston, Powell (QPR), Matthews (Stoke C), Dix (Tottenham H), Dodds, Finan, Burbanks (Sunderland).
Sheffield W: Morton; Ashley, Catlin, Russell, Millership, Cockroft (West Ham U), Reynolds (Rochdale), Robinson, Melling, Thompson J, Swift.

**LEAGUE NORTH CUP FINAL
1942–43 SECOND LEG**

Hillsborough, 8 May 1943   42,657

Sheffield W 1 *(Robinson)*
Blackpool 2 *(Dodds, Gardner)*

Sheffield W: Morton; Ashley, Gadsby (Leeds U), Russell, Millership, Cockroft (West Ham U), Reynolds (Rochdale), Robinson, Melling, Thompson J, Swift.

Blackpool: Savage (Q of S); Pope (Hearts), Hubbick (Bolton W), Farrow, Hayward, Johnstone, Gardner (Burnley), Dix (Tottenham H), Dodds, Finan, Burbanks (Sunderland).

**CUP WINNERS PLAY-OFF
1942–43**

Stamford Bridge, 15 May 1943   55,195

Blackpool 4 *(Dix, Burbanks, Dodds, Finan)*
Arsenal 2 *(Lewis, Compton D)*

Blackpool: Savage (Q of S); Pope (Hearts), Hubbick (Bolton W), Farrow, Hayward, Johnstone, Matthews (Stoke C), Dix (Tottenham H), Dodds, Finan, Burbanks (Sunderland).
Arsenal: Marks; Scott, Compton L, Crayston, Joy, Male, Kirchen, Drake, Lewis, Bastin, Compton D.

**LEAGUE SOUTH CUP FINAL
1943–44**

Wembley, 15 April 1944   85,000

Charlton Ath 3 *(Revell 2, Welsh)*
Chelsea 1 *(Payne (pen))*

Charlton Ath: Bartram; Shreeve, Jobling, Smith, Oakes, Chilton (Manchester U), Robinson, Brown, Revell, Welsh, Duffy (Leith Ath).
Chelsea: Woodley; Hardwick (Middlesbrough), Westwood (Manchester C), Russell (Airdrieonians), Harris (Wolverhampton W), Foss, Ashcroft (Tranmere R), Fagan (Liverpool), Payne, Bowie, Mitten (Manchester U).

**LEAGUE NORTH CUP FINAL
1943–44 FIRST LEG**

Bloomfield Road, 29 April 1944   28,000

Blackpool 2 *(Dodds 2)*
Aston Villa 1 *(Goffin)*

Blackpool: Savage (Q of S); Pope (Hearts), Kinsell (WBA), Johnstone, Hayward, Jones S, Matthews (Stoke C), Dix (Tottenham H), Dodds, Finan, Pearson (Newcastle U).
Aston Villa: Wakeman; Potts (Doncaster R), Cummings, Massie, Callaghan, Iverson, Broome, Edwards, Parkes, Starling, Goffin.

LEAGUE NORTH CUP FINAL 1943–44 SECOND LEG

Villa Park, 6 May 1944   54,824

Aston Villa 4 *(Broome 2, Edwards, Iverson)*
Blackpool 2 *(Dix, Pearson)*

Aston Villa: Wakeman; Potts (Doncaster R), Cummings, Massie, Callaghan, Starling, Broome, Edwards, Parkes, Iverson, Houghton.
Blackpool: Savage (Q of S); Pope (Hearts), Kinsell (WBA), Johnstone, Hayward, Jones S, Matthews (Stoke C), Dix (Tottenham H), Dodds, Finan, Pearson (Newcastle U).

CUP WINNERS PLAY-OFF 1943–44

Stamford Bridge, 20 May 1944   38,540

Aston Villa 1 *(Houghton)*
Charlton Ath 1 *(Revell)*

Aston Villa: Wakeman; Potts (Doncaster R), Cummings, Massie, Callaghan, Starling, Broome, Edwards, Parkes, Iverson, Houghton.
Charlton Ath: Bartram; Shreeve, Jobling, Smith, Oakes, Chilton (Manchester U), Robinson, Brown, Revell, Welsh, Duffy (Leith Ath).

LEAGUE SOUTH CUP FINAL 1944–45

Wembley, 7 April 1945   90,000

Chelsea 2 *(McDonald, Wardle)*
Millwall 0

Chelsea: Black (Aberdeen); Winter (Bolton W), Hardwick (Middlesbrough), Russell, Harris (Wolverhampton W), Foss, Wardle (Exeter C), Smith L (Brentford), Payne, Goulden (West Ham U), McDonald (Bournemouth).
Millwall: Bartram (Charlton Ath); Dudley, Fisher G, Ludford (Tottenham H), Smith E, Tyler, Rawlings, Brown R (Charlton Ath), Jinks, Brown T, Williams (Aberdeen).

LEAGUE NORTH CUP FINAL 1944–45 FIRST LEG

Burnden Park, 19 May 1945   40,000

Bolton W 1 *(Lofthouse)*
Manchester U 0

Bolton W: Fielding; Threlfall, Hubbick, Taylor, Hamlett, Murphy, Woodward, Hunt, Lofthouse, Barrass, Butler.

Manchester U: Crompton; Walton, Roughton, Warner, Whalley, Chilton, Chadwick, White (Tottenham H), Bryant, Sloan (Tranmere R), Wrigglesworth.

LEAGUE NORTH CUP FINAL 1944–45 SECOND LEG

Maine Road, 26 May 1945   57,395

Manchester U 2 *(Wrigglesworth, Bryant)*
Bolton W 2 *(Barrass 2)*

Manchester U: Crompton; Walton, Roughton, Warner, Whalley, White (Tottenham H), Bryant, Astbury (Chester), Sloan (Tranmere R), Glidden (Tranmere R), Wrigglesworth.
Bolton W: Fielding; Threlfall, Hubbick, Taylor, Hamlett, Murphy, Woodward, Hunt, Lofthouse, Barrass, Butler.

CUP WINNERS PLAY-OFF 1944–45

Stamford Bridge, 2 June 1945   35,000

Bolton W 2 *(Hunt, Hamlett)*
Chelsea 1 *(Rooke)*

Bolton W: Fielding; Threlfall, Hubbick, Taylor, Hamlett, Murphy, Woodward, Hunt, Lofthouse, Barrass, Moir.
Chelsea: Black (Aberdeen); Cowan (Rangers), Hardwick (Middlesbrough), Russsell, Harris (Wolverhampton W), Foss, Wardle (Exeter C), Machin, Rooke (Fulham), Goulden (West Ham U), Bain.

FA CUP FINAL 1945–46

Wembley, 27 April 1946   98,215

Derby Co (0) 4 *(Turner H (og), Doherty, Stamps 2)*
Charlton Ath (0) 1 *(Turner H)*

Derby Co: Woodley; Nicholas, Howe, Bullions, Leuty, Musson, Harrison, Carter, Stamps, Doherty, Duncan.
Charlton Ath: Bartram; Phipps, Shreeve, Turner H, Oakes, Johnson, Fell, Brown, Turner A, Welsh, Duffy.

DIV 3N CUP FINAL 1945–46 FIRST LEG

Millmoor, 27 April 1946   12,000

Rotherham U 2 *(Shaw J 2)*
Chester 2 *(Bett, Hamilton)*

Rotherham U: Warnes; Selkirk, Hanson, Edwards, Williams H, Mills, Guest, Shaw J, Ardron, Burke (Luton T), Dawson.
Chester: Scales; James (Bradford PA), McNeil, Marsh, Walters, Lee, Bett (Sunderland), Leahy, Burden (Wolverhampton W), Astbury, Hamilton.

DIV 3N CUP FINAL 1945–46 SECOND LEG

Sealand Road, 4 May 1946   12,650

Chester 2 *(Leahy, Bett)*
Rotherham U 3 *(Dawson, Burke, Shaw J)*

Chester: Scales; James (Bradford PA), McNeil, Marsh, Walters, Lee, Bett (Sunderland), Leahy, Burden (Wolverhampton W), Astbury, Hamilton.
Rotherham U: Warnes; Selkirk, Hanson, Mills, Williams H, Williams D, Wilson (Crystal Palace), Shaw J, Ardron, Burke (Luton T), Dawson.

DIV 3S CUP LEAGUE CUP FINAL 1945–46

Stamford Bridge, 4 May 1946   19,715

Bournemouth 1 *(McDonald)*
Walsall 0

Bournemouth: Bird; Marsden, Sanaghan, Woodward, Wilson, Gallacher, Currie, Paton, Kirkham, Tagg, McDonald.
Walsall: Lewis; Methley, Shelton, Crutchley, Foulkes, Newman, Hancocks, Talbot, Mullard, Wilshaw (Wolverhampton W), Alsop.

41 LEAGUE APPEARANCES AND GOALSCORERS 1939–46

Players' appearances and goals have been compiled from official records and contemporary newspaper reports. Because of the difficulties experienced in fielding teams and identifying names of players, the correct line-ups for many matches may never be known. In 1939–40, it was the intention of the Football League to use the League War Cup as a replacement for the FA Cup. As such, appearances have not been included for these games, although goalscorers are provided. However, from 1940–41 onwards, the League War Cup was used as a supplement to League games and appearances and goals have been combined. In 1940–41, the London Cup was not recognised by the Football League and appearances and goals for this have been added under the appropriate season. Although the 1941–42 season saw 16 London area clubs expelled by the Football League, a complete record does appear in this book. In many instances, county cup competitions also doubled for League games, but where matches were decided in extra time, only the score after 90 minutes counted in the League table. Extra-time goals have been included in the relevant totals. In a few cases, the second leg of cup ties were not included in the table at all, but the goalscorers for these matches have been added as a footnote. In 1945–46, goalscorers only have been given for FA Cup matches. Guest players, where known, are designated thus ★. There were a number of guest players who subsequently signed for the club they were assisting. In these instances, the asterisk was removed for the appropriate season.

Accrington Stanley

1939–40

Ainsworth A★ 4	Hall G 1	Moir J 1	Seddon H★ 4
Ainsworth F 6	Hargreaves T★ 2	Morgan R 19	Smith WS 1
Ash JW 20	Harker W★ 1	Mortimer R★ 2	Sutherland HR★ 2
Aspin A★ 2	Higham N★ 3	Owens CL 16	Swinden SA 18
Bargh GW★ 1	Jackson H★ 1	Parr JE★ 2	Walton G★ 7
Barker W 1	Johnson JC 23	Pollard H★ 1	Ward F 4
Conroy M 11	Jones T★ 9	Reeday M★ 21	Webster R★ 18
Dooley TE 19	Kearney SF 13	Robbins P 3	Wightman JR★ 1
Dyson J★ 5	Mauchline R 7	Robinson JJ★ 7	
Gale A 1	McShane W★ 6	Sams A 12	

Goals (37): Morgan 5, Swinden 5, Conroy 4, Higham 4, Dooley 3, Johnson 2, Kearney 2, Robbins 2, Sams 2, Ainsworth A 1, Dyson 1, Harker 1, Jones 1, McShane 1, Moir 1, Sutherland 1, Webster 1.

1940–41

Blackburn Combination.

1941–42

Lancashire Combination.

1942–43

Did not compete.

1943–44

Did not compete.

1944–45

Ainsworth F   1
Ardron W*   2
Ash JW   15
Baldwin H   1
Briggs F*   2
Briggs JC*   21
Burrows A*   2
Capstick A   1
Clark GV*   2
Clark H   26
Cockburn H*   12
Conroy RM   36
Cook L*   1
Curran F*   9

Duckworth J   2
Eastwood R*   16
Fogg J   1
Gibson F   1
Holdcroft GH*   19
Holt G   2
Hutton T   4
Jessop W*   1
Johnson J*   1
Johnson JC   15
Jones W   1
Kearney SF   2
Keeley L   1
Keeley W   19

Livingstone A*   2
Malcolm JM   37
Male CG*   2
Maudsley RC   6
Mercer S*   21
Molloy P*   25
Mutch G*   1
Mycock A*   1
Porter W*   1
Reeday M*   28
Reid JM*   1
Roach JE*   5
Rotherham E   6
Rothwell G   36

Rudd J*   3
Seddon H   1
Shaw K*   1
Simpson J*   1
Snowden R*   1
Topping H*   1
Tyson W*   6
Waddington J   11
Walmsley J*   22
Whittle A   1
Wilson JH*   24
Wilson R*   1
Winterburn E   1

Goals (68): Mercer 23, Conroy 12, Keeley W 6, Curran 5, Clark H 4, Rothwell 4, Malcolm 2, Maudsley 2, Capstick 1, Cockburn 1, Cook 1, Eastwood 1, Kearney 1, Rudd 1, Siddon 1, Tyson 1, Waddington 1, Whittle 1.

1945–46

Ash JW   3
Briggs JC   34
Cain D   8
Clark H   29
Conroy RM   29
Cornwell E   24
Dooley TE   3
Eastwood R*   9

Hacking J   34
Haworth WE   1
Hudson CA   14
Hutton T   12
Kearney SF   9
Keeley W   35
Lythgoe A   8
Malcolm JM   34

Mauchline R   5
Mercer S*   3
Moir J   4
Molloy P*   1
Morgan R   2
Morris E   5
Rose J   2
Rotherham E   7

Rothwell G   35
Seatree F   1
Smith H   1
Thomas DSL*   6
Webster R*   35
Wilson JH*   2
Wood C   1

Goals (74): Keeley 20, Rothwell 12, Cain 8, Hudson 8, Kearney 6, Conroy 5, Mauchline 3, Clark 2, Morris 2, Rotherham 2, Lythgoe 1, Mercer 1, Moir 1, Morgan 1, Thomas 1, own goal 1.

FA Cup goals (10): Hudson 3, Keeley 3, Rothwell 2, Conroy 1, own goal 1.

Aldershot

1939–40

Anderson DN★ 1
Bargh GW★ 2
Beattie A★ 3
Beauchamp H 1
Betmead H★ 3
Bigg RJ 3
Bott W★ 1
Briggs CE★ 13
Britton CS★ 4
Brolly T★ 3
Brook L★ 2
Brooks H 29
Browne RJ★ 2
Buchanan PS★ 4
Burke JJ★ 1
Burnicle WF 4
Chalmers W 27
Clark C★ 12

Clarke RL 1
Compton DCS★ 1
Cook W★ 6
Copping W★ 5
Crook W★ 5
Cross T 1
Cullis S★ 3
Cunliffe AJ★ 4
Dawes AG 2
Diaper B★ 2
Dixon WH 6
Duns L★ 2
Eastwood R 3
Egan GD 4
Fagan W★ 1
Fitzgerald AM★ 3
Gray A★ 2
Greaves G 15

Griffiths R★ 3
Hagan J★ 18
Hold O 4
Holley T★ 3
Holston R★ 1
Horton JC 31
Hurst SC 1
Jackson J★ 1
Kelly L 9
Lawton T★ 2
Lowe HP★ 2
Mahon J★ 3
Middleton J 1
Nash FC★ 4
Palmer RW 32
Pattison JM★ 11
Proud J 8
Pryde RI 2

Ray CH 5
Raynor G 30
Ridyard A★ 12
Sheppard HH 21
Sproston B★ 1
Stephenson JE★ 4
Summerbee GC 17
Swift FV★ 2
Sykes J★ 6
Taylor G★ 2
Thomson JR★ 1
Thorogood J★ 1
Townsend D 1
Upperton RT 1
Wilson J★ 1
Yorston BC★ 1

Goals (79): Brooks 24, Hagan 14, Chalmers 8, Palmer 7, Pattison 5, Lawton 4, Raynor 4, Clark 2, Beauchamp 1, Bigg 1, Britton 1, Brook 1, Buchanan 1, Compton 1, Cunliffe 1, Duns 1, Holston 1, Hurst 1, Sheppard 1.

War Cup goals (0).

1940–41

Alder W★ 1
Bamford HFE★ 21
Beattie A★ 2
Bentley G★ 2
Betmead H★ 1
Briggs CE★ 10
Britton CS★ 10
Brolly T★ 1
Brooks H 2
Buckley A★ 5
Campbell J 3
Campbell J (3rd Lanark) 1
Cann ST★ 1
Chalmers W 23
Compton DCS★ 2
Coulston DW 2
Crook W★ 3
Cross T 1

Cullis S★ 1
Cunliffe AJ★ 2
Darvill G★ 2
Dawes AG 9
Denby S★ 1
Diaper B 4
Dixon WH 2
Duns L★ 5
Edelston M★ 1
Egan GD 3
Foster T★ 19
Gallacher P★ 6
Geldard A★ 1
Goldberg L★ 1
Green G★ 1
Griffiths WM★ 2
Hagan J★ 17
Hobbs RG 4

Hold O 1
Holwill DJ 1
Hopper LR 1
Horton JC 11
Jardine I 2
Kelly L 19
Lawton T★ 8
Lloyd C★ 1
Lowe HP★ 1
Martin CS 1
Maskell LJ★ 1
McCulloch D★ 1
McMillan –★ 1
Middleton J 2
Morgan R★ 1
Palmer RW 4
Powell A★ 1
Proud J 20

Pryde RI★ 2
Putt C 7
Ray CH 3
Raynor G 12
Robinson S★ 4
Rolls G★ 1
Shepherdson H★ 2
Sheppard HH 7
Simpson J★ 1
Stephens A★ 3
Stephenson JE★ 2
Swift FV★ 3
Walters TB★ 4
Welsh D★ 2
Wilson J★ 4
Wright H★ 1
Wright HE★ 1

Goals (83): Chalmers 18, Hagan 14, Lawton 13, Proud 9, Compton 4, Britton 3, Dawes 3, Duns 3, Bamford 2, Stephens 2, Brooks 1, Cunliffe 1, Gallacher 1, Green 1, Edelston 1, Egan 1, Martin 1, Pryde 1, Welsh 1, own goals 3.

London Cup

Alder 2, Anderson DN★ 2, Bamford 9, Bentley 2, Britton 7, Briggs 4, Brooks 2, Campbell 2, Chalmers 6, Dawes 4, Dixon 1, Egan 1, Fagan W★ 1, Foster 6, Gallacher 3, Geldard 1, Hagan 5, Hardwick GFM★ 1, Holley T★ 2, Keeton A★ 5, Kelly 7, Lawton 2, Morgan 1, Putt 4, Proud 3, Ray 5, Raynor 9, Sheppard 5, Smith GC★ 1, Taylor G★ 3, Walters TB★ 4.

Goals: Bamford 5, Hagan 4, Dawes 3, Brooks 2, Raynor 2, Britton 1, Chalmers 1, Gallacher 1, Morgan 1, Ray 1.

1941–42

Alder W★   2
Alsford W★   5
Anderson DN★   2
Bamford HFE★   1
Bargh GW★   1
Blackman JJ★   1
Blair Doug★   8
Bonass AE★   5
Boulton FP★   1
Briggs CE★   12
Britton CS★   23
Brooks H   3
Browne RJ★   1
Campbell J   1
Campbell J (Celtic) ★   1
Chalmers W   6
Court HJ★   1
Craig B★   5
Cunningham E★   1

Davidson D★   1
Dawes AG   4
Dixon WH   4
Egan GD   2
Foster T★   2
Gardiner –★   1
Geldard A★   2
Glasby H   6
Goldberg L★   1
Grant AF   2
Gray R★   1
Griffiths R★   1
Hagan J★   16
Halton RL★   15
Holliday JW★   2
Hunt DA★   1
Jefferson A★   3
Johnson R★   12
Jones GH★   14

Keeton A★   3
Kelly L   11
Kinnear D★   1
Lawton T★   16
Lester FC★   15
Loughran J★   2
Mahon J★   1
Marsden F★   3
Martin JR★   1
Maskell LJ★   2
McCall AJ★   1
Miles RI   1
Monk LSF   2
Neill –★   1
Palmer RW   11
Pescod G★   11
Preskett F★   1
Putt C   18
Ray CH   3

Raynor G   31
Richardson JR★   1
Sabin G★   1
Sheppard HH   25
Sibley A★   1
Simpson J★   2
Smeaton J★   2
Smith GC★   3
Smith JF★   1
Stewart G★   12
Swift FV★   2
Taylor F★   1
Taylor G★   20
Walters TB★   16
Webb –★   1
Wiggins –★   1
Wright H★   2

Goals (93): Lawton 16, Hagan 15, Raynor 10, Halton 9, Britton 5, Jones 5, Blair 4, Geldard 3, Glasby 3, Martin 3, Palmer 3, Holliday 2, Maskell 2, Pescod 2, Ray 2, Smeaton 2, Wright 2, Campbell J (Celtic) 1, Hunt 1, Mahon 1, Neill 1, Taylor G 1.

1942–43

Alder W★   1
Bonass AE★   15
Briggs CE★   1
Britton CS★   21
Broome –★   1
Clayton S★   2
Cook W★   2
Copping W★   2
Coulston WB★   1
Cullis S★   17
Cunliffe AJ★   15
Dixon WH   7
Duke GE★   4
Duns L★   4
Fitzgerald AM★   2

Gallacher P★   21
Geldard A★   2
Glasby H   8
Hagan J★   20
Halton RL★   18
Herod DJ★   9
Hinchliffe T★   1
Hold O   5
James T★   2
Jones GH★   4
Jordan C★   2
Joslin PJ★   2
Keeton A★   4
Kelly L   5
Kinnear D★   2

Lawton T★   15
Macaulay AR★   1
Marsden F★   24
Martin DK★   1
McCulloch D★   17
Miller AG★   18
Muttitt E★   2
Palmer RW   13
Pescod G★   1
Putt C   7
Raynor G   15
Royston R★   28
Shepherdson H★   1
Sheppard HH   1
Smart AD   1

Smith GC★   1
Summerbee GC   2
Swift FV★   3
Taylor G★   9
Tootill A★   4
Wakefield AJ★   1
Walker J★   2
Wardle G★   1
Webb R   1
White AL   1
Wiles WA   1
Wilson A★   1
Winning A★   1
Wright H★   1

Goals (99): Lawton 25, McCulloch 17, Hagan 13, Bonass 6, Britton 6, Gallacher 6, Glasby 6, Halton 4, Clayton 3, Cunliffe 3, Jordan 3, Muttitt 2, Dixon 1, Duns 1, Palmer 1, Raynor 1, own goal 1.

1943–44

Allsopp W★   1
Antonio GR★   1
Bell E   3
Black A★   6
Boyes W★   2
Briggs CE★   18
Britton CS★   23
Brooks H   14
Butt L★   3
Clayton S★   1
Compton DCS★   1
Cullis S★   17
Cunliffe AJ★   19
Davie J★   7
Davies DD★   4
Davis RD★   1
Devlin J★   1
Dorling GJ★   1
Duke GE★   12
Duns L★   2
Egan H★   1

Evans HA★   3
Fagan W★   1
Gage A★   1
Galley T★   2
Hagan J★   21
Hall G★   1
Halton RL★   12
Harris F★   1
Harvey John★   2
Hobbs RG   1
Hold O   5
Horton JC   12
Jones G★   1
Jones GH★   16
Jordan W★   2
Keeton A★   1
Kelly L   1
Kinnear D★   1
Langstone G   2
Lawton T★   2
Leyfield C★   1

Liddell J   1
Little G★   1
Lloyd C★   1
Lucas WH★   2
Marsden F★   23
Marshall E★   9
Martin J★   1
Maskell LJ★   1
McCulloch D★   11
Mercer J★   13
Miller A★   5
Milton GW★   1
Moore NW★   1
Morris J★   17
Murphy F★   6
Oldham G★   1
Pescod G★   3
Powell A★   3
Richmond G★   1
Royston R★   28
Sabin G★   6

Salmon L★   2
Shearer J★   2
Sinclair T★   3
Smith –★   1
Stewart G★   1
Storey WCG★   1
Stroud RW★   1
Summerbee GC   7
Swift FV★   1
Tennant AE★   1
Thorley GT   1
Trigg SA★   1
Wales H★   1
Wardle G★   1
Watson JF★   1
Westby JL★   1
White FRH★   4
Williams E★   2
Wilson A★   1
Younger A★   1

Goals (81): Hagan 16, McCulloch 11, Lawton 8, Brooks 7, Cunliffe 5, Davie 5, Jones GH 3, Morris 3, Clayton 2, Marshall 2, Mercer 2, Murphy 2, Powell 2, Sabin 2, Black 1, Britton 1, Compton 1, Devlin 1, Duns 1, Jordan 1, Sinclair 1, Smith 1, Thorley 1, White 1, own goal 1.

1944–45

Anderson – 1
Antonio GR★ 17
Armstrong M★ 2
Asterbury –★ 1
Ayres J 1
Baird A★ 1
Bartlett FL★ 1
Bower RWC★ 1
Boyes W★ 1
Briggs CE★ 5
Brooks H 26
Cawdell L★ 1
Chapman E★ 1
Clapton G★ 1
Clark TH★ 1
Collingridge EW 2
Conroy M★ 1
Cox WE 1
Cross T 3
Cunliffe AJ★ 19
Daniels G★ 3
Davie J★ 1
Davies DD★ 4
Denby S 2

Dixon WH 1
Dodds C 3
Duke GE★ 9
Durrant FH★ 3
Evans HA★ 1
Fidler F★ 1
Fiore F 1
Gadsby KJ★ 4
Glidden GS★ 1
Halton RL★ 12
Harvey Joe★ 5
Hawkes DC 3
Hewitt J★ 1
Hobbs RG 6
Hold O 1
Horton JC 30
Ireland R★ 1
Jones GH★ 9
Jordan W★ 3
Joslin PJ★ 8
Kiernan T★ 5
Knight AW★ 4
Lawrence W★ 5
Longmuir J★ 1

Lucas WH★ 1
Lumby WCW★ 1
Machin AH★ 1
Marsden F★ 7
Marshall E★ 9
McCulloch D★ 2
McPheat J★ 6
Mercer J★ 11
Miller AG★ 3
Monk LSF 1
Morris J★ 20
Niblett V★ 1
O'Callaghan E★ 2
O'Connor A 6
Osborne RJ 1
Paice CR 1
Parlane J★ 1
Perry E★ 1
Pescod G★ 2
Pond H★ 1
Prett J 4
Proud J 1
Pryde RI★ 1
Purvis B★ 1

Ray CH 1
Robinson P★ 14
Rose FA 5
Rowley JF★ 1
Royston R★ 27
Russo J 1
Salmon L★ 1
Sargent F★ 2
Shufflebotham FC★ 1
Sinclair TM★ 1
Smith GC★ 1
Stewart T 1
Suart R★ 1
Summerbee GC 15
Swift FV★ 1
Tapken N★ 3
Taylor G★ 1
Thorley GT 1
Toser EW★ 1
Wallace J★ 7
White FRH★ 3
Wilson A 1
Wright H★ 1
Yeomanson J★ 5

Goals (47): Brooks 12, Antonio 7, Cunliffe 5, O'Connor 3, Armstrong 2, Halton 2, Hobbs 2, McPheat 2, Mercer 2, Longmuir 1, Lucas 1, McCulloch 1, Machin 1, Marshall 1, Pond 1, Pryde 1, Rowley 1, Sargent 1, Stewart 1.

1945–46

Bartlett FL★ 2
Beauchamp H 1
Bell E 11
Bewley D★ 1
Bradley J★ 1
Brooks H 32
Brown H★ 3
Carr L★ 1
Collins RD★ 1
Cunliffe AJ★ 4
Dimmer H★ 1
Evans HA★ 2
Fairclough –★ 1
Fitzgerald AM 24
Fulton J★ 3
Gleave C★ 1

Hassell TW★ 5
Hindle FJ★ 1
Hobbs RG 24
Hold O 7
Hope R★ 1
Horton JC 24
Hullett W★ 1
Hunter J★ 2
Hurst SC 1
Iddon H★ 1
Jones EN★ 1
Kernick DHG★ 1
Lewin D★ 1
Liddell J 3
Lyman CC★ 1
Lyon ER 1

Marshall E★ 5
McCormack CJ★ 4
Medley LD★ 1
Morris J★ 14
Palmer RW 21
Prett J 1
Price AJW★ 5
Pritchard HJ★ 3
Rampling DW★ 2
Ray CH 17
Raynor G 1
Reynolds RSM 31
Richardson EW 1
Robinson P★ 6
Rogers A★ 30
Rose FA 1

Sargent F★ 5
Sheppard HH 21
Sinclair T 3
Smith –★ 1
Somerfield A★ 7
Stevens L★ 3
Summerbee GC 13
Timlin WJ 1
Warrington H★ 5
Watson –★ 1
White AL 1
White J 25
Wilson R★ 3

Goals (61): Brooks 23, Hold 6, Fitzgerald 5, Price 4, Bell 3, Hassell 3, Hobbs 3, Somerfield 3, Hullett 2, Palmer 2, Cunliffe 1, Iddon 1, Kernick 1, McCormack 1, Medley 1, Richardson 1, Summerbee 1.

FA Cup goals (24): Brooks 13, Fitzgerald 3, Hobbs 2, Hold 2, Ray 1, Summerbee 1, White J 1, own goal 1.

Arsenal

1939–40

Bastin CS 27	Drake EJ 8	Lewis R 30	Pryde D 10
Bremner GH 7	Drury GB 2	Logie JT 1	Scott L 9
Carr EM 1	Hapgood EA 30	Male CG 37	Smith EF 1
Collett E 13	Holmes E★ 1	Marks GW 22	Swindin GH 5
Compton DCS 19	Jones B 9	Morgan AS 1	Wilson A 5
Compton LH 35	Jones LJ 31	Nelson D 19	
Crayston WJ 24	Joy B 37	Parr WW 1	
Curtis GF 13	Kirchen AJ 24	Platt EH 7	

Goals (111): Compton L 28, Lewis 20, Kirchen 13, Compton D 10, Crayston 9, Drake 8, Bastin 7, Nelson 4, Jones L 3, Drury 2, Carr 1, Curtis 1, Hapgood 1, Jones B 1, Logie 1, Morgan 1, own goal 1.

War Cup goals (15): Compton L 7, Kirchen 4, Lewis 2, Drake 1, Jones L 1.

1940–41

Bastin CS 30	Dean WB 3	Joy B 20	Pryde D 4
Beasley A★ 4	Dobson J 1	Kirchen AJ 24	Rigg T★ 4
Boulton FP★ 3	Drake EJ 16	Lewis R 7	Scaife G★ 1
Collett E 31	Fisher AN 5	Male CG 15	Scott L 30
Compton DCS 20	Hapgood EA 15	Marks GW 16	Smith EF 1
Compton LH 28	Henley L 21	Mills GR★ 2	Smith L 1
Crayston WJ 10	Jobson TH★ 3	Nelson D 9	Wilson A 2
Curtis GF 7	Jones LJ 7	Platt EH 1	

Goals (93): Compton L 25, Kirchen 24, Drake 10, Bastin 8, Compton D 7, Crayston 3, Fisher 3, Nelson 3, Curtis 1, Jobson 1, Jones L 1, Henley 1, Lewis 1, Mills 1, own goals 4.

London Cup

Alsford WJ★ 1, Beattie A★ 1, Bastin 9, Beasley 5, Blakeney J 1, Boulton 7, Collett 10, Compton DCS 6, Compton LH 8, Crayston 1, Curtis 4, Drake 8, Hapgood 2, Henley 9, Jones LJ 2, Joy 8, Kirchen 4, Lewis 1, Male 5, Marks 2, Nelson 5, Pryde 2, Rigg 1, Scott 6, Smith L 1, Waller H 1.

Goals: Compton L 17, Drake 6, Bastin 4, Compton D 2, Henley 2, Kirchen 2, Blakeney 1, Crayston 1, Curtis 1, Jones L 1, Nelson 1.

1941–42

Bastin CS 38	Curtis GF 5	Jones LJ 4	Platt EH 24
Beasley A★ 2	Drake EJ 19	Joy B 29	Pryde D 2
Blakeney J 1	Drury GB 1	Kirchen AJ 22	Scott L 30
Collett E 35	Goldberg L★ 2	Lewis R 28	Smith L 2
Compton DCS 21	Hapgood EA 24	Male CG 27	Tweedy GJ★ 6
Compton LH 23	Henley L 10	Marks GW 6	Waller H 1
Crayston WJ 17	Hobbins SG★ 1	Miller N 7	Young AE 1
Cumner RH 5	Hooper PG★ 1	Nelson D 24	

Goals (128): Lewis 45, Kirchen 14, Compton D 13, Bastin 12, Drake 11, Miller 7, Nelson 7, Compton L 4, Henley 4, Crayston 3, Cumner 2, Beasley 1, Male 1, own goals 4.

1942–43

Bastin CS 32	Cumner RH 4	Joy B 27	Pryde D 2
Briscoe J★ 3	Drake EJ 19	Kelly P★ 3	Scott L 26
Collett E 11	Fields A 1	Kirchen AJ 27	Shankly W★ 11
Colley H 3	Hapgood EA 11	Lewis R 30	Strauss W★ 1
Compton DCS 19	Henley L 15	Male CG 33	Swindin GH 5
Compton LH 16	Johnston D★ 1	Marks GW 19	Tweedy GJ★ 4
Copping W★ 3	Jones B 12	McKillop T★ 1	Watson-Smith N★ 2
Crayston WJ 21	Jones LJ 2	Morgan AS 1	Winter D★ 3
Crozier J★ 1	Joslin P★ 1	Nelson D 20	Young AE 6

Goals (134): Lewis 47, Compton D 18, Drake 16, Kirchen 16, Bastin 11, Crayston 5, Henley 4, Jones B 4, Briscoe 2, Compton L 2, Nelson 2, Colley 1, Cumner 1, Male 1, Morgan 1, own goals 3.

Additional goalscorers in Cup-Winners' Cup: Lewis, Compton D.

1943–44

Alexander T 2	Cumner RH 2	Hamilton W★ 8	Marks GW 25
Barnes W 25	Curtis GF 7	Henley L 3	McLennan J★ 4
Bastin CS 29	Delaney L 1	Hooper PG★ 1	Nelson D 15
Briscoe J★ 21	Dingwall GH★ 1	Hughes W★ 2	Scott L 24
Bryant B★ 1	Drake EJ 23	Jones A (Frickley)★ 2	Smith C★ 1
Buckby MJ 1	Duke GE★ 4	Jones A (Shorts)★ 1	Stroud RW 3
Cabrelli P★ 3	Edington J 8	Jones EN★ 3	Swindin GH 1
Collett E 29	Farquhar D 4	Jones JT★ 1	Thomas RA★ 1
Compton DCS 19	Flack WLW★ 1	Joy B 31	Young AE 3
Compton LH 3	Flavell R★ 11	Kirchen AJ 3	
Crayston WJ 10	Gillies M★ 2	Lewis R 25	
Crozier J★ 1	Goulden LA★ 1	Male CG 30	

Goals (85): Lewis 24, Compton D 13, Drake 13, Bastin 12, Briscoe 6, Flavell 4, Barnes 3, Nelson 3, Crayston 2, Curtis 2, Alexander 1, Kirchen 1, Thomas 1.

1944–45

Barnes W 14	Edelston M★ 1	Joy B 21	Scott L 17
Barr J★ 1	Farquhar D 32	Kelly P★ 1	Smith C 4
Bastin CS 34	Ferrier H★ 3	Male CG 10	Southam J★ 1
Beasley A★ 1	Gallimore L★ 1	Marks GW 14	Stanley EAW 1
Bowden J 1	Griffiths WR★ 2	Matthews S★ 1	Steele FC★ 11
Bowden NH 2	Griggs CC 1	McFarlane DL★ 1	Stevens L★ 1
Bradley G★ 5	Hall FW★ 7	Mennie F★ 2	Swindin GH 15
Bremner GH 1	Hamilton W★ 17	Mitchell FR★ 1	Taylor E★ 1
Briscoe J★ 2	Harris K★ 2	Moody R★ 9	Taylor V 2
Collett E 25	Henley L 19	Morrad F★ 2	Tunnicliffe G 3
Cumner RH 1	Hodges C 1	Mortensen SH★ 17	Wade JS 3
Davis S★ 1	Holland EJ 3	Nelson E 18	Ward RA★ 1
Dawes AG★ 1	Horsman L★ 5	Orr T★ 1	Wrigglesworth W★ 27
Drake EJ 28	Jones A (Frickley)★ 5	Paton J★ 1	
Duke GE★ 3	Jones T★ 1	Ratcliffe B★ 1	

Goals (97): Mortensen 25, Drake 23, Farquhar 10, Wrigglesworth 9, Bastin 8, Steele 6, Horsman 3, Nelson 3, Gallimore 2, Beasley 1, Bowden N 1, Briscoe 1, Holland 1, Matthews 1, Paton 1, own goals 2.

1945–46

Barnard CH 10	Fields A 1	Joy B 17	Patterson G★ 6
Barnes W 1	Fisher F★ 1	Lewis R 2	Roberts F★ 1
Bastin CS 29	Griffiths WR★ 16	Lillie D 1	Roffi G 4
Beasley A★ 5	Griggs CC 4	Little A★ 2	Russell D 1
Bowden NH 2	Hall FW★ 1	Logie JT 5	Scott L 35
Bremner GH 14	Halton RL★ 1	Mackenzie P★ 2	Smith A★ 1
Cartwright S 3	Hamilton W★ 2	Male CG 13	Smith L 11
Chenhall J★ 3	Hapgood EA 5	Marks GW 5	Stanley EAW 1
Collett E 24	Henley L 13	McPherson I★ 6	Swindin GH 16
Compton DCS 11	Hitchen J★ 1	Mercer S★ 1	Wade JS 19
Compton LH 5	Hodges C 5	Moody K★ 4	Waller H 9
Cross A★ 1	Holland EJ 5	Morgan AS 4	Wilson J 2
Cumner RH 12	Horsfield A 7	Mortensen SH★ 2	Wrigglesworth W★ 3
Curtis GF 7	Jones B 1	Nelson D 39	Young AE 1
Delaney L 1	Jones LJ 9	Nieuwenhuys B★ 2	
Drury GB 14	Jones S 1	O'Flanagan K 18	
Farquhar D 12	Joslin P★ 1	Ollerenshaw J 1	

Goals (76): O'Flanagan 11, Drury 9, Bremner 6, Compton D 6, Bastin 5, Farquhar 5, Henley 5, Hodges 3, Jones L 3, Morgan 3, Barnard 2, Cumner 2, Horsfield 2, McPherson 2, Nelson 2, Roffi 2, Bowden 1, Holland 1, Lewis 1, Mercer 1, Wilson 1, Young 1, own goals 2.

FA Cup goals (1): Cumner 1.

Aston Villa

1939–40

Allen JP 3	Cummings G 3	Martin JR 3	Starling RW 2
Broome FH 3	Edwards GR 3	Massie A 3	
Callaghan E 3	Haycock F 1	O'Donnell F 3	
Carey WJ 1	Iverson RT 3	Rutherford J 2	

Goals (3): Cummings 1, Edwards 1, Martin 1.

1940–41

Birmingham & District League.

1941–42

Birmingham & District League.

1942–43

Bate J 3	Edwards GR 25	Iverson RT 31	Shell FH 4
Billingsley G 2	Godfrey LL 4	Kerr AW 7	Starling RW 31
Broome FH 30	Goffin WC 6	Martin JR 6	Wakeman A 36
Callaghan E 32	Gutteridge R 16	Massie A 32	
Cummings G 22	Haycock F 22	Parkes H 27	
Davis RD★ 15	Houghton WE 33	Potts VE★ 34	

Goals (91): Houghton 20, Davis 18, Broome 17, Edwards 10, Haycock 9, Parkes 8, Iverson 3, Kerr 3, Callaghan 1, Cummings 1, Goffin 1.

1943–44

Billingsley G 3	Edwards GR 14	Iverson RT 39	Potts VE★ 40
Broome FH 40	Godfrey LL 2	Martin JR 6	Starling RW 38
Callaghan E 19	Goffin WC 5	Massie A 35	Wakeman A 37
Canning L 2	Gutteridge R 9	Morby JH 20	
Cummings G 36	Haycock F 23	O'Donnell F 14	
Davis RD★ 5	Houghton WE 36	Parkes H 17	

Goals (93): Broome 30, Houghton 21, Iverson 8, O'Donnell 7, Edwards 4, Haycock 4, Parkes 4, Starling 4, Goffin 3, Canning 2, Martin 2, Davis 1, Gutteridge 1, own goals 2.

Additional scorer in Cup-Winner' Cup: Houghton. Addtional appearances also included in this summary.

1944–45

Broome FH 20	Godfrey LL 4	Iverson RT 36	Morby JH 3
Callaghan E 38	Goffin WC 18	Latham L 1	Parkes H 26
Canning L 1	Gutteridge R 9	Martin JR 1	Potts VE★ 41
Cummings G 40	Haycock F 34	Massie A 34	Starling RW 42
Edwards GR 37	Houghton WE 43	McConnoy JE 2	Wakeman A 43

Goals (124): Edwards 33, Houghton 28, Iverson 21, Haycock 10, Parkes 10, Goffin 9, Broome 7, Massie 3, own goals 3.

1945–46

Beresford RM 1	Godfrey LL 3	Lowe E 24	Rutherford J 9
Broome FH 27	Goffin WC 17	Martin JR 25	Scott RA★ 2
Callaghan E 26	Graham J 4	Massie A 3	Shell FH 4
Carey WJ 1	Haycock F 1	Morby JH 9	Smith LGF 22
Cummings G 42	Houghton WE 14	Moss F 11	Starling RW 28
Dixon JT 5	Iverson RT 41	Parkes HA 30	Wakeman A 30
Edwards GR 35	Kerr AW 9	Potts VE 39	

Goals (106): Edwards 39, Iverson 16, Broome 14, Martin 9, Goffin 7, Kerr 4, Dixon 3, Parkes 3, Smith 3, Houghton 2, Cummings 1, Graham 1, own goals 4.

FA Cup goals (22): Broome 6, Goffin 5, Edwards 4, Smith 4, Iverson 2, Parkes 1.

Barnsley

1939–40

Adey W* 1
Allison JJ 5
Asquith B 7
Bennett WH 1
Binns CH 23
Bokas F 20
Bramham A* 1
Bray E 2
Brunskill N 3

Bullock GF 19
Deakin J* 2
Dodd RI* 1
England AA 8
Everest J 3
Gallagher F 1
Gladwin G* 2
Glover A 1
Harper B 19

Harper K* 16
Harston JC 1
Hubbard C* 1
Hydes A 3
Jones W 1
Lang J 3
Logan JW 21
Maxwell JM 3
McGarry D 3

Pallister G 1
Robinson TW 3
Robinson W* 2
Shotton R 21
Smith G 17
Steele J 23
Thorogood J* 12
Woffinden RS 1
Wright T* 2

Goals (50): Smith 10, Steele 9, Shotton 5, Thorogood 4, Maxwell 4, Asquith 3, England 3, Allison 2, Bullock 2, Deakin 2, Gallagher 1, Hubbard 1, Hydes 1, McGarry 1, Robinson T 1, own goal 1.

War Cup goals (7): Calder 2, Bullock 1, Lang 1, Smith 1, Steele 1, Woffinden 1.

1940–41

Asquith B* 24
Bennett WH 1
Binns CH 29
Bokas F 33
Bray E 4
Bullock GF 33
Clegg H 1
Fisher FW* 1

Glover A 2
Greaves G* 2
Gregory FC* 5
Harper B 27
Harper K* 27
Harston JC 9
Hold O* 1
Jones W 4

King J* 1
Logan JW 33
McGarry D 4
Pallister G 2
Richardson G* 1
Sagar E* 2
Shotton R 36
Smith G 35

Steele J 33
Thorogood J 32
Whitelum C* 1
Wilkinson C* 2
Woffinden RS 11

Goals (100): Steele 24, Smith 23, Bullock 16, Thorogood 8, Asquith 7, Gregory 5, McGarry 4, Shotton 4, Bray 2, Clegg 1, Fisher 1, Logan 1, Woffinden 1, own goals 3.

1941–42

Allott JV 1
Arran F* 1
Asquith B* 30
Barclay R* 1
Binns CH 26
Bokas F 29
Burton S* 1
Davis R* 1
Fleetwood ED 15

Gibson F* 1
Gregory FC* 3
Harper B 12
Harper K* 30
Harston JC 21
Henry GR* 2
Hubbard C* 9
Hullett W* 2
Jones W 5

Kilpatrick W* 4
Lacey E 4
Logan JW 32
McGarry D 2
Nicholls J* 4
Robinson TW 1
Robledo GO 1
Settle A* 1
Shotton R 31

Smith G 32
Spence A 1
Steele J 26
Styles W* 1
Thorogood J* 29
Wesley JC* 1
Wipfler CP* 1
Woffinden RS 2

Goals (87): Smith 20, Steele 18, Asquith 13, Thorogood 10, Fleetwood 8, Hubbard 3, Hullett 3, Lacey 2, Bokas 1, Davis 1, Gregory 1, Harston 1, Henry 1, Logan 1, McGarry 1, Wipfler 1, own goals 2.

1942–43

Asquith B* 31
Barlow H* 1
Binns CH 31
Bokas F 29
Bray E 6
Brunskill N 6
Bullock GF 2
Burton S* 3
Clegg H 7

Cooling R 4
Coulston W* 1
Dawson WR 1
Fenton R 2
Fisher FW* 1
Fleetwood ED 30
Forster JW* 1
Griffiths JS* 2
Harper B 30

Harper K* 10
Harston JC 22
Henry GR* 1
Hold O* 2
Jones W 14
Lacey E 1
Logan JW 30
Marsh R* 2
McGarry D 6

Myers JH* 2
Oldroyd K 1
Pallister G 3
Shotton R 34
Smith G 35
Steele J 11
Thorogood J* 20
Woffinden RS 3

Goals (73): Fleetwood 17, Smith 14, Thorogood 11, Steele 10, Asquith 6, Harston 4, McGarry 3, Bray 2, Griffiths 2, Bullock 1, Clegg 1, Harper 1, Hold 1, Logan 1, Myers 1, own goal 1.

Includes three County Cup goals.

1943–44

Armeson LR★ 6	Fisher FW★ 1	Pallister G 24	Spence R★ 2
Asquith B 33	Fisher S 1	Pond H★ 1	Stabb GH★ 1
Barlow H★ 1	Fleetwood ED 27	Robledo GO 21	Steele J 7
Binns CH 27	Harper B 14	Rogers W★ 2	Stevens W★ 1
Bokas F 21	Harston JC 31	Rymer GH 8	Walker GR★ 1
Boocock – 1	Hold O★ 1	Shotton R 22	Williams R★ 1
Brown AW★ 5	Logan JW 35	Sinclair TM★ 11	Willingham CK★ 5
Burkenshaw GA 4	Makepeace – 1	Sloan J★ 18	Woffinden RS 2
Cooling R 2	McGarry D 13	Smith G 34	

Goals (66): Asquith 16, Smith 16, Fleetwood 8, Robledo 7, McGarry 4, Shotton 2, Sinclair 2, Sloan 2, Walker 2, Barlow 1, Logan 1, Rogers 1, Stabb 1, Steele 1, own goals 2.

1944–45

Asquith B 41	Fleetwood ED 23	Logan JW 37	Shotton R 20
Barlow H★ 22	Flood T 1	McGarry D 35	Smith G 40
Binns CH 37	Glover A 1	Nicholson L 2	Smith J★ 1
Bokas F 1	Harper R★ 2	Pallister G 36	Steele J 2
Burkenshaw GA 39	Harston JC 22	Rimmington N 3	Taylor J★ 3
Cooling R 32	Horbury K 1	Robledo GO 38	Thorogood J★ 4
Fisher S 4	Kitchen J 3	Rymer GH 1	

Goals (79): Robledo 23, Cooling 13, McGarry 12, Smith G 9, Barlow 7 Asquith 3, Logan 3, Fisher 2, Pallister 2, Shotton 2, Fleetwood 1, Flood 1, own goal 1.

1945–46

Asquith B 34	Cunningham L 25	Jackson E★ 1	Pallister G 34
Baxter JC 25	Fenton WH 1	Kelly JC 24	Robledo GO 36
Bennett WH 9	Ferrier H 3	Kitchen J 2	Rymer GH 18
Binns CH 10	Fisher S 11	Logan JW 39	Shanks R★ 1
Brunskill N 3	Glover A 6	Mansley CV 23	Shotton R 2
Burkenshaw GA 6	Gray H 14	McGarry D 15	Smith G 39
Clayton L 2	Harper K★ 12	Morgan – 1	Thorogood J★ 1
Cooling R 20	Harston JC 11	Mount G 1	Wilson J 15
Cox AEH★ 1	Holdcroft GH 14	Nicholson L 3	

Goals (76): Robledo 15, Smith 13, Cooling 10, Fisher 9, Baxter 5, Gray 5, Asquith 4, Bennett 3, Kelly 3, Logan 2, McGarry 2, Pallister 2, Fenton 1, Wilson 1, own goal 1.

FA Cup goals (10): Pallister 2, Robledon 2, Smith 2, Baxter 1, Kelly 1, Wilson 1, own goal 1.

Barrow

1939–40

Allcock CW   18
Baker A   3
Cargill J   23
Chalmers WR   3
Davies CJ   15
Hall L   25

Hamilton S   1
Harris T   24
Hartley S   10
Hollingsworth H   24
Kilduff G   16
King HJ   2

Lapham H   15
McCormick P★   6
McIntosh RJ   4
Phillipson WE   22
Randle HC   14
Rutherford J   3

Samuel DJ   23
Scott A   1
Simpson S   23

Goals (58): Harris 21, Kilduff 13, Lapham 7, Cargill 5, Davies 5, McCormick 2, Chalmers 1, McIntosh 1, Samuel 1, own goals 2.

War Cup goals (6): Harris 5, McIntosh 1.

1940–41

Did not compete.

1941–42

Did not compete.

1942–43

Did not compete.

1943–44

Did not compete.

1944–45

Did not compete.

1945–46

Batey R★   1
Birch H   23
Bond A★   5
Burgess S   1
Caine W   17
Carr SR★   1
Clarke K   26
Clarkson C   22
Collings W   11
Conway E   4
Davies CJ   1

Dougall P★   1
Dunnigan J   17
Fenney S   24
Forbes G★   5
Goodwin R★   1
Hall L   32
Harris T   3
Hartley S   10
Hilliard WR★   4
Houldsworth J   1
Hull W   3

Key J   2
Kilduff G   4
Livingstone W   3
McGrath J   27
McIntosh RJ   23
Miller E   16
Mullen JW   20
O'Connor J   4
Ogilve H   4
Pearson H   4
Phillipson WE   30

Phoenix J   1
Pitt L   4
Quigley G   12
Shanks J   14
Simpson S   5
Simpson T   1
Smith W   1
Urmston JR   4
Wilding F   2
Woodcock A★   2

Goals (48): Clarke 14, Clarkson 7, McIntosh 6, Miller 5, Harris 4, Mullen 3, Hull 2, Shanks 2, Dunnigan 1, Kilduff 1, Livingstone 1, Urmston 1, own goal 1.

FA Cup goals (15): Clarke 9, McIntosh 3, Clarkson 1, Dunnigan 1, Hull 1.

Birmingham

1939–40

Allen JP★ 1	Deakin FA★ 3	Harris F 22	Merrick GH 1
Bate J★ 1	Dearson DJ 22	Hibbs HE 12	Morris S 1
Bellamy SC 4	Devey R 3	Hughes WM 20	Moss F★ 2
Bodle H 17	Duckhouse E 9	Iverson RT★ 7	Moss FW 1
Broome FH★ 7	Edwards GR★ 10	Jennings DB 8	Quinton W 18
Brown E 1	Farrage TO 3	Jones CW 15	Rowley DW 1
Brown J 18	Foulkes RE 7	Jones WT 2	Shaw R 13
Bye JH 22	Gardner FC 2	Kernick DHG★ 1	Trigg C 19
Craven C 9	Godden AE 5	Martin JR★ 2	Turner A 20
Cummings G★ 4	Guest WF★ 6	Massie A★ 4	Wheeler WJ 18

Goals (61): Jones 10, Bodle 9, Brown J 6, Duckhouse 6, Broome 5, Trigg 5, Dearson 4, Edwards 4, Guest 2, Bye 1, Farrage 1, Gardner 1, Godden 1, Harris 1, Jennings 1, Turner 1, own goals 3.

War Cup goals (15): Trigg 6, Godden 4, Bodle 3, Jones 1, Turner 1.

1940–41

Batty SG★ 1	Eastham GR★ 6	Jennings DB 12	Shaw R 3
Bodle H 1	Foulkes RE 14	Jones CW 12	Thayne W★ 1
Brown J 7	Galley DS 1	Kernick DHG★ 4	Trigg C 12
Bye JH 6	Gardner FC 12	Merrick GH 13	Turner A 3
Craven C 4	Gill JD 5	Morris S 1	Wheeler WJ 5
Deakin FA 7	Godden AE 6	Moss FW 1	
Dearson DJ 14	Harris F 13	Pearce H 2	
Devey R 4	Hughes WM 12	Quinton W 16	

Goals (43): Trigg 20, Dearden 6, Gardner 3, Jones 3, Harris 2, Bodle 1, Bye 1, Craven 1, Eastham 1, Gill 1, Godden 1, Jennings 1, Shaw 1, own goal 1.

1941–42

Played friendlies only.

1942–43

Acquroff J★ 31	Dearson DJ 23	King SH 1	Romp LW 1
Ainsley GE★ 1	Devey R 2	Lewis CJ 6	Shaw J 1
Bartram S★ 1	Dolphin LG 2	McCormick J★ 28	Shaw R 31
Bate J★ 1	Eden E 7	McEwan W★ 3	Shelton JBT★ 1
Batty SG★ 2	Finan RJ★ 1	Merrick GH 35	Sibley E★ 1
Bellamy SC 1	Freeman W 1	Middleton N 2	Smith TW 1
Bodle H 1	Gill JD 7	Millichap E 2	Sweeney F 1
Bray J★ 1	Goffin WC★ 1	Mitchell FR★ 16	Tranter GH 2
Brown J 3	Guest WF★ 2	Moss FW 1	Trickett JE 1
Butter DJ 1	Hapgood EA★ 1	Ottewell S★ 13	Trigg C 5
Bye JH 3	Hardwick GFM★ 1	Pears WT 2	Turner A 32
Chapman S★ 1	Harris F 4	Pearson TU★ 2	Vause PG★ 1
Collins GE★ 3	Hughes WM 1	Pope J 1	Watton GD 15
Craven C 24	Jenkins PJ 1	Quinton W 30	Watts FJ 1
Davy H 4	Jennings DB 37	Richards E 3	Webber W 1
Deakin FA 1	Jones CW 6	Robinson GH★ 2	

Goals (59): Acquroff 8, Dearson 7, Ottewell 7, Jones 6, Craven 5, McCormick 5, Watton 5, McEwan 2, Bate 1, Brown 1, Eden 1, Gill 1, Harris 1, Lewis 1, Richards 1, Romp 1, Shaw R 1, Trickett 1, Turner 1, own goals 3.

1943–44

Acquroff J★   13
Barnett RH   4
Bodle H   4
Bright RL★   27
Bye JH   4
Craven C   6
Day EF   1
Dearson DJ   30
Doherty PD★   4
Dolphin LG   1
Faulkner R★   1
Gee H   2

Godden AE   2
Green K   7
Hackett J   1
Harris F   4
Hayward LE★   2
Hinsley G★   5
Hughes WM   5
Jennings DB   26
Jones WVA   1
McKillop T★   1
Merrick GH   38
Middleton N   2

Mitchell FR   11
Montgomery JD   1
Morgan LD★   1
Morris S   2
Mulraney A★   33
Ottewell S★   1
Peacock T★   1
Quinton W   24
Redwood H★   1
Revell C★   1
Roberts NE   2
Roberts TD   16

Shaw R   32
Sibley TI   2
Sinclair M★   1
Stanton SH   7
Stanton T   1
Trickett JE   1
Trigg C   30
Turner A   32
Turner H★   27

Goals (85): Trigg 35, Mulraney 14, Bright 10, Dearson 5, Roberts T 4, Hinsley 3, Shaw 3, Acquroff 2, Bodle 1, Bye 1, Doherty 1, Faulkner 1, Gee 1, Godden 1, Jennings 1, Mitchell 1, Morris 1, Revell 1.

Includes one extra-time goal.

1944–45 (as Birmingham City)

Adams HS   1
Ball RT   1
Barnett RH   1
Berry JR   2
Bodle H   4
Booth WS★   6
Bright RL★   19
Clements AB   1
Craven C   12
Dearson DJ   38
Elliott JM   1
Faulkner KG   14
Fenton JW   1

Garrett AA★   1
Greatrex J   1
Harris F   6
Harris W   1
Hicklin WA   11
Hikins D   10
Hughes WM   7
Jenks N   2
Jennings DB   40
Jordan C★   1
Kernick DHG★   3
King SH   3
Lewis R   3

Marriott AHP   4
Martin GBH   1
Massart DL   9
Matthews JB   2
Merrick GH   38
Metcalf WF★   5
Mitchell FR   7
Mitcheson F★   1
Morris S   3
Mulraney A★   37
Murrell RE   2
O'Donnell H★   3
Pope AL★   1

Quinton W   12
Roberts TD   2
Shaw R   30
Sibley TI   2
Small SJ★   24
Smith SR   1
Stanton SH   14
Trentham DH★   1
Trigg C   22
Turner A   39
Turner H★   1
White FRH★   10
Williams I   1

Goals (68): Trigg 22, Massart 9, Mulraney 7, Bright 4, White 4, Small 3, Bodle 2, Dearson 2, Faulkner 2, Kernick 2, Lewis 2, Craven 1, Harris F 1, Hikins 1, Matthews 1, Shaw 1, Turner A 1, own goals 3.

1945–46

Bodle H   40
Dearson DJ   34
Ditchburn EG★   1
Dougall C   38
Duckhouse E   26
Edwards G   38

Harris F   39
Hughes WM   4
Jenks N   2
Jennings DB   41
Jones CW   27
King SH   2

Laing RS   2
Massart DL   11
McPherson I★   1
Merrick GH   39
Mitchell FR   26
Mulraney A   38

Owen SW   5
Shaw R   2
Stanton SH   1
Trigg C   1
Turner A   40
White FRH★   4

Goals (96): Jones 20, Bodle 16, Edwards 13, Mulraney 13, Dougall 10, Massart 9, Duckhouse 6, Harris 2, Turner 2, White 2, Dearson 1, Laing 1, Mitchell 1.

FA Cup goals (19): Mulraney 7, Jones 5, Bodle 3, Dougall 3, own goal 1.

Blackburn Rovers

1939–40

Aspden T   2
Asquith B★   6
Bargh GW   2
Barron J   4
Bray J★   1
Brindle J★   1
Briscoe J★   1
Brown AW★   2
Butt L   14
Cahill R   5
Chew J   8

Chivers FC   21
Clarke A   3
Cook L   1
Crook W   15
Davison D   1
Dickie P   4
Doherty PD★   2
Fairbrother J★   11
Glaister G   4
Greenhalgh H   2
Hargreaves T   11

Higham N★   8
Hough W   24
Hulbert R★   2
Jones T★   3
Lanceley E   10
Langton R   3
Lee WR   1
McShane H   7
Miller D★   3
Mulraney A★   1
Pryde RI   18

Robinson JJ★   7
Rogers W   17
Rose J★   1
Smith J★   1
Weddle J   18
Whiteside A   22
Wightman JR   7
Young –   1

Goals (40): Hargreaves 7, Rogers 7, Weddle 6, Higham 5, Asquith 4, Doherty 4, Cahill 2, McShane 2, Butt 1, Chew 1, Langton 1.

War Cup goals (18): Clarke 6, Butt 5, Weddle 3, Guest 2, Hargreaves 1, own goal 1.

1940–41

Anderson DN★   18
Atkinson J★   1
Barron J   4
Bentley G★   2
Brindle J   1
Butt L   21
Cahill R   8
Carter K   6
Chew J   15
Chivers FC   35
Clarke A   2
Cook L   4
Crook W   13
Cross G   3

Davison D   1
Dickie P   19
Fairbrother J★   2
Farrow GH★   2
Forbes GP   2
Glaister G   7
Goodall EI★   1
Greenhalgh H   11
Guest WF   9
Hallam –   1
Hargreaves T   18
Hopwood KE★   1
Hough W   6
Hubbick H★   1

Jones HJ★   7
Lanceley E   28
Lomax G   3
Mann D★   1
Marshall G★   1
McNeil J★   1
Miller J★   1
Owen CL★   9
Pearson TU★   6
Pryde RI   29
Reeday M★   6
Rilet E★   2
Robinson JJ★   2
Rogers W   17

Roxburgh A★   9
Shankley R★   3
Stanfield D   1
Ward –   1
Watson A   1
Watson J★   1
Webster R★   1
Weddle J   15
Westby JL   1
Whiteside A   13
Wightman JR   18
Wilson R   4
Wright A★   1

Goals (60): Butt 20, Hargreaves 10, Rogers 8, Chivers 3, Pryde 3, Carter 2, Pearson 2, Weddle 2, Cahill 1, Chew 1, Clarke 1, Glaister 1, Greenhalgh 1, Guest 1, Jones 1, McNeil 1, Shankley 1, own goal 1.

1941–42

Ancell RFD★   9
Anderson DN★   3
Aspden T   4
Barron J   1
Bremner GH★   5
Bryson W   1
Butt L   17
Carter K   6
Chivers FC   27
Conway H   39
Cook L   5
Crawshaw P★   6
Currier J★   1
Dawson J   6

Dickie P   3
Fairclough WT   1
Forbes GP   31
Gardner T★   2
Glaister G   30
Greenhalgh H   1
Hall FW   2
Halsall WG★   2
Hargreaves T   2
Higham N★   2
Hough W   5
Johnson WH★   1
Jones C★   2
Lanceley E   1

Lomax G   1
Maudsley RC★   15
McLean A   1
McShane H   5
Mortimer R   6
Mulligan E   1
Ottewell S★   1
Pearson TU★   31
Percival J★   10
Pryde RI   36
Reeday M★   2
Rilet E★   11
Robinson J★   8
Rogers W   18

Smith R   1
Soo F★   1
Stephan H   1
Taylor W   30
Watkins –   1
Weddle J   3
Westby JL   7
Whalley H★   2
Whiteside A   29
Wightman JR   2
Wilde E   1
Woodruff A★   1

Goals (80): Butt 13, Pearson 10, Robinson 10, Glaister 8, Rogers 6, McShane 4, Rilet 4, Carter 3, Maudsley 3, Mortimer 3, Pryde 3, Bremner 2, Crawshaw 2, Weddle 2, Anderson 1, Bryson 1, Dawson 1, Forbes 1, Gardner 1, Hargreaves 1, Lomax 1, Whalley 1.

Includes one extra-time goal.

1942–43

Ancell RFD★ 2	Forbes GP 31	Mansley C★ 1	Smith J 1
Anderson DN★ 29	Glaister G 2	Martindale L★ 2	Stephan H 9
Aspden T 6	Guest WF 7	McLaren A★ 13	Syme C★ 1
Beardshaw EC★ 2	Hall J★ 1	McShane H 2	Taylor W 10
Bradford L★ 1	Hayhurst S 4	Melia J 9	Tomlinson RW 2
Bruton J 1	Hindle FJ 7	Miller W★ 4	Weddle J 1
Butt L 5	Hough T★ 1	O'Donnell H★ 5	Westby JL 1
Coates F 6	James G 7	Pearson TU★ 24	Wharton J★ 6
Conway H 25	John WR★ 5	Powell IV★ 1	Whiteside A 31
Cook L 7	Johnston J 4	Pryde RI 33	Wightman JR 3
Dougal J★ 32	Jones S★ 1	Riddiough HH 3	Wilson A★ 1
Entwistle D 4	Latham G 1	Robertson WJT★ 26	
Fairbrother J★ 1	Lucas WH★ 13	Rogers W 1	

Goals (101): Dougal 29, Pearson 16, McLaren 11, Melia 4, Robertson 4, Butt 3, Coates 3, Guest 3, Lucas 3, Stephan 3, Bruton 2, McShane 2, Miller 2, O'Donnell 2, Wightman 2, Wilson 2, Ancell 1, Aspden 1, Cook 1, Martindale 1, Pryde 1, Rogers 1, Syme 1, Tomlinson 1, Weddle 1, own goal 1.

1943–44

Allen FS 1	Cook L 4	Hunter J 1	Taylor W 12
Anderson DN★ 4	Crook W 34	Lucas WH★ 6	Webster R★ 1
Aspden T 1	Dougal J★ 29	Marshall D★ 1	Wharton JE★ 24
Barron J 4	Egerton F 1	McShane H 2	Whiteside A 32
Barton – 1	Fairweather W 1	Pearson TU★ 16	Wightman JR 1
Bibby JJ 11	Forbes GP 23	Pryde RI 29	Woods C★ 1
Butt L 10	Graham J 7	Robertson WJT★ 31	Woodward V★ 6
Chappell FC★ 1	Grant JA★ 1	Rogers W 9	Wyles TC★ 1
Coates F 8	Guest WF 9	Smith H 1	
Conway H 28	Hindle FJ 4	Stephan H 18	

Goals (77): Stephan 14, Dougal 12, Lucas 10, Pearson 6, Bibby 5, Butt 5, Rogers 5, Woodward 4, Guest 3, Pryde 3, Wharton 3, Aspden 1, Cook 1, Graham 1, Grant 1, McShane 1, Smith 1, own goals 2.

Includes one extra-time goal.

1944–45

Anderson DN★ 1	Crossland B★ 1	Hindle FJ 25	Smith D 1
Attwell RF★ 3	Daniels D 1	Kinghorn WJD★ 1	Smith G★ 4
Bibby JJ 18	Durrant FH★ 17	Laing FJ★ 4	Smith H 22
Bradford L★ 1	Egerton F 37	Langton R 11	Smith JJ★ 9
Brain H★ 3	Entwistle D 1	McShane H 2	Stephan H 24
Brocklebank R★ 1	Fairweather W 6	Mutch G★ 2	Tattersall A 1
Burgess J 1	Forbes GP 41	Paynter F★ 1	Taylor W 8
Cater R★ 1	Gardner T★ 3	Porter W★ 1	Walsh W★ 1
Chappell FC 1	Glaister G 10	Pryde R 4	Westby JL 9
Coates F 33	Graham J 4	Robertson WJT★ 1	White – 1
Conway H 40	Green A 13	Rooke RL★ 2	Whiteside A 24
Cook L 30	Guest WF 1	Rudman H★ 1	Wightman JR 3
Crook W 36	Hargreaves T 1	Simpson JT 5	Woodcock E 1

Goals (93): Durrant 18, Coates 17, Stephan 10, Langton 9, Cook 7, Smith J 5, Bibby 4, Smith H 3, Brocklebank 2, Fairweather 2, Laing 2, McShane 2, Rooke 2, Simpson 2, Smith G 2, Brain 1, Gardner 1, Graham 1, Robertson 1, own goals 2.

1945–46

Baldwin JJ 13	Crook W 14	Hall WW★ 3	Smith H 2
Barron J 19	Dailey H 1	Hapgood EA★ 2	Smith J★ 1
Bell JE 37	Dellow RW★ 2	Hayhurst S 5	Smith Jack 9
Bibby JJ 4	Egerton F 19	Hindle FJ 2	Stephan H 28
Boothway J★ 1	Fairweather W 5	Langton R 21	Tattersall A 2
Bowden NH★ 2	Flinton W★ 2	Mansley EH★ 1	Taylor W 2
Boydell R 1	Forbes GP 25	Morson M 1	Tomlinson RW 5
Butt L 2	Glaister G 16	Patterson JG 15	Whiteside A 19
Campbell JJ 20	Godwin V 17	Peters J 3	Wightman JR 22
Chapman E★ 1	Green A 23	Pryde RI 25	Wyles TC★ 22
Coates F 18	Hacking R★ 1	Rawcliffe F★ 1	
Cook L 14	Hall FW 6	Rogers W 8	

Goals (60): Wyles 16, Langton 7, Stephan 7, Coates 5, Glaister 5, Smith Jack 5, Baldwin 4, Fairweather 3, Campbell 2, Bowden 1, Butt 1, Hall W 1, Pryde 1, Rawcliffe 1, Rogers 1.

FA Cup goals (1): Wyles 1.

Blackpool

1939–40

Ainsley GE★ 7	Cardwell L★ 2	Johnston H 18	O'Donnell H 3
Ashworth JJ 4	Dodds E 20	Jones S 22	Oakes T 1
Astley DJ 8	Eastham GW 20	Lawrence C 1	Roxburgh AW 22
Blair D 11	Farrow GH 25	Lewis TH 7	Sibley ES 22
Buchan WRM 7	Finan RJ 23	Munro AD 22	Suart R 1
Butler MP 3	Hayward LE 22	O'Donnell F 1	Wallace JM 3

Goals (78): Dodds 33, Finan 8, Astley 6, Eastham 5, Ainsley 4, Buchan 4, Ashworth 3, Farrow 3, Hayward 3, Munro 3, Lewis 2, O'Donnell F 2, Blair 1, own goal 1.

War Cup goals (14): Dodds 8, Astley 2, Eastham 1, Finan 1, Jones 1, Munro 1.

1940–41

Ainsley GE 1	Finan RJ 1	Lowe J 4	Pugh SJ★ 2
Boulton LM★ 4	Hughes WM★ 8	MacFadyen W★ 1	Rist FH★ 1
Buchan WRM 20	Johnson JW★ 14	Murphy G★ 4	Russell DW★ 22
Burbanks WE★ 22	Johnston H 21	O'Donnell H 1	Stevenson AE★ 1
Deverall HR★ 9	Jones CW 10	Ottewell S★ 1	Strong GJ★ 4
Dodds E 15	Jones P 2	Pope AL★ 18	Trigg C★ 8
Fiddes J 2	Jones S 19	Powell IV★ 4	Whittaker W 23

Goals (70): Dodds 28, Jones CW 9, Buchan 7, Burbanks 6, Trigg 6, Deverall 3, Boulton 2, Johnson 2, Murphy 2, Johnston 1, O'Donnell H 1, Pope 1, Russell 1, Stevenson 1.

1941–42

Ancell RFD★ 1	Dykes J★ 2	Lewis TH 3	Powell IV★ 12
Barker J★ 16	Eastham GR 1	Matthews S★ 30	Roxburgh AW 22
Buchan WRM 4	Farrow GH 28	McEwan W★ 2	Savage R★ 18
Burbanks WE★ 27	Finan RJ 16	McShane H★ 1	Stevenson AE★ 1
Critchley G★ 1	Hayward LE 6	Mortensen SH 10	Suart R 21
Cuthbertson JH★ 1	Johnston H 33	Mountford GF★ 1	Whittaker W 13
Dix RW★ 33	Jones CW★ 29	O'Donnell H 7	Williams G★ 3
Dodds E 32	Jones S 29	Pope AL★ 37	

Goals (183): Dodds 65, Jones CW 31, Dix 32, Mortensen 13, Burbanks 11, Finan 8, Farrow 5, Buchan 2, Johnston 2, Matthews 2, McEwan 2, O'Donnell H 2, Whittaker 2, Cuthbertson 1, Lewis 1, Pope 1, own goals 3.

1942–43

Atkinson JE★ 4	Finan RJ 34	Lomax J★ 1	Powell IV★ 18
Barker J★ 6	Gardner T★ 4	Matthews R 3	Roxburgh AW 31
Beattie R★ 2	Hargreaves WJ 2	Matthews S★ 24	Savage R★ 8
Buchan WRM 3	Hayward LE 30	McEwan W★ 2	Shaw C★ 3
Burbanks WE★ 36	Horton JC★ 2	Miller W★ 1	Shields J★ 3
Colquhoun DM★ 1	Hubbick H★ 3	Mortensen SH 5	Williams G★ 23
Dix RW★ 34	Johnston H 33	Murphy G★ 1	Withington RH 1
Dodds E 29	Jones CW★ 3	O'Donnell H 4	
Farrow GH 34	Jones S 11	Pope AL★ 30	

Goals (142): Dodds 45, Dix 29, Finan 26, Burbanks 13, Farrow 6, Johnston 5, Mortensen 4, Buchan 2, Gardner 2, Jones CW 2, Matthews S 2, O'Donnell H 2, Colquhoun 1, Shields 1, Withington 1, own goal 1.

Additional goalscorers second leg North Cup Final and Cup-Winners' Cup: Dodds 2, Burbanks 1, Dix 1, Finan 1, Gardner 1. Additional appearances also included in this summary.

1943–44

Beattie R★ 8	Farrow GH 12	Lawrence C 1	Powell HL 6
Bradley J★ 1	Finan RJ 31	Matthews S★ 23	Roxburgh AW 2
Brand MR★ 1	Garrett T 1	Maudsley RC 3	Savage R★ 35
Burbanks WE★ 9	Gibbons W★ 1	McEwan W★ 3	Sibley ES 3
Butler MP 1	Hayward LE 15	McGahie J 1	Suart R 1
Clements BA 1	John WR★ 1	Mortensen SH 18	Tapping FH 7
Cregan JP 1	Johnson JW★ 4	O'Donnell F★ 2	Watkin D 1
Cutting SW★ 1	Johnston H 33	O'Donnell H 19	Williams G★ 2
Davies RG★ 8	Jones S 21	Paterson G★ 2	Williams K 3
Dix RW★ 30	Kinsell TH★ 31	Pearson TU★ 11	Withington RH 1
Dodds E 25	Kirkham F 2	Pope AL★ 37	

Goals (109): Dodds 23, Mortensen 21, Dix 20, Beattie 9, Finan 9, O'Donnell H 7, Farrow 5, McEwan 4, O'Donnell F 2, Pearson 2, Bradley 1, Hayward 1, Johnson 1, Kirkham 1, Matthews 1, Tapping 1, own goal 1.

1944–45

Bailey A★ 3	Finan RJ 18	McLaren M 1	Sibley ES 14
Blair JA★ 1	Forster LJ 1	Miller H 8	Slater WJ 4
Bradley J★ 1	Franklin ST 3	Mortensen SH 10	Suart R 8
Cardwell L★ 3	Gallimore L★ 3	Munro AD 1	Tapping FH 10
Cregan JP 1	Garrett T 1	O'Donnell F★ 17	Theurer W 1
Crook W★ 3	Halliwell JA 1	O'Donnell H 23	Thomas DSL★ 1
Cross J 4	Johnson JW★ 16	Oakes J★ 1	Thorpe WF 19
Davies RG★ 28	Johnston H 2	Paterson G★ 25	Todd J 13
Dix RW★ 3	Jones S 23	Pearson TU★ 9	Tweedie JJ 6
Dodds E 5	Kilgallon J 1	Pope AL★ 25	Walsh W★ 4
Eakins D 2	Kirby N★ 17	Revell C★ 3	Withington RH 1
Eastham H★ 15	Laing FJ★ 16	Rogerson J 2	Worrall F★ 8
Edwards CI★ 1	Larner L 3	Rosser PGJ 1	
Farrow GH 29	Manley T★ 3	Roxburgh AW 14	
Fenton M★ 12	Matthews S★ 5	Savage R★ 9	

Goals (111): Mortensen 14, Farrow 13, Finan 11, Fenton 9, Laing 9, O'Donnell F 9, Walsh 5, Worrall 5, Dodds 4, O'Donnell H 4, Johnson 3, Matthews 3, Pearson 3, Tweedie 3, Eastham 2, Jones 2, Todd 2, Davies 1, Dix 1, Eakins 1, Larner 1, Paterson 1, Slater 1, Tapping 1, Theurer 1, own goals 2.

1945–46

Astley DJ 1	Finan RJ 2	Laing F★ 1	Roxburgh AW 26
Blair JA 28	Forster LJ 1	Larner L 1	Sibley ES 6
Buchan WRM 19	Franklin ST 3	Lewis WA 41	Suart R 33
Burke R 11	Harper K 1	Matthews S★ 5	Tapping FH 11
Butler MP 12	Hesford RT★ 1	McLaren M 2	Thorpe WF 11
Cowell A 1	Hobson A 16	Mortensen SH 33	Todd J 10
Dodds E 22	Johnston H 9	Munro AD 7	Wallace JM 4
Eastham GR 8	Jones S 19	O'Donnell F★ 2	Withington RH 11
Farrow GH 27	Kelly HT 19	O'Donnell H 40	
Fenton M★ 9	Kennedy GM 2	Paterson G★ 7	

Goals (94): Mortensen 34, Dodds 14, O'Donnell H 14, Fenton 9, Blair 8, Farrow 6, Buchan 3, Eastham 1, Finan 1, Tapping 1, Withington 1, own goals 2.

FA Cup goals (13): Dodds 5, Mortensen 4, O'Donnell H 2, Blair 1, Buchan 1.

Bolton Wanderers

1939–40

Atkinson JE 18	Forrest E 1	Howe D 4	Sidebottom W 22
Burgess AC 11	Geldard A 3	Hubbick H 24	Taylor G 6
Butler T★ 4	Goodall EI 20	Hunt GS 24	Walton G★ 1
Chadwick C★ 5	Goslin H 4	Hurst J 5	Westwood WR 3
Connor J 19	Graham RE 4	Jones WEA 10	Whalley H★ 19
Cunliffe JN★ 20	Hanks CW 1	Richardson N★ 3	Winter DT 4
Eastwood E★ 21	Hanson S 5	Rothwell E 8	Woodward T 6

Goals (61): Hunt 16, Sidebottom 9, Burgess 6, Cunliffe 5, Chadwick 4, Connor 4, Howe 4, Rothwell 4, Butler 2, Hubbick 2, Jones 2 , Walton 1, Westwood 1, Woodward 1.

War Cup goals (2): Hanks 1, Hunt 1.

1940–41

Atkinson JE 19	Cunliffe JN★ 7	Houghton W 1	O'Neill W 1
Banks R 19	Eastham GR★ 3	Howe D 2	Pearson TU★ 3
Barker H 1	Eastwood E★ 7	Hubbick H 22	Platt E 1
Berry J 2	Finan RJ★ 7	Hunt GS 19	Pryde RI★ 1
Bolton R 9	Gallon JW★ 1	Hurst J 2	Pugh SJ★ 1
Burgess AC 1	Goodall EI 2	Johnson WH★ 6	Richardson A 1
Butler S★ 8	Goslin H 3	Knight J 1	Rothwell E 2
Chadwick C★ 10	Gosling G 1	Leyland EC 1	Ryder R 1
Clancy D★ 1	Grainger D★ 2	Lofthouse N 11	Sidebottom W 15
Cload H 6	Grimsditch SW 7	Mann D 1	Smith JD 1
Connor J 20	Hanson S 1	Martindale L★ 2	Taylor G 1
Cooper JE 1	Heslop N 3	Morrison ER 3	Winter DT 2

Goals (46): Hunt 12, Lofthouse 11, Chadwick 4, Sidebottom 4, Howe 3, Cunliffe 3, Butler 2, Eastham 2, Finan 2, Johnson 2, Cload 1, Connor 1, Goslin 1, Grainger 1, Knight 1.

Includes four extra-time goals.

1941–42

Atkinson JE 18	Forrest E 1	Knight J 30	Schofield W 2
Banks R 22	Foster R 3	Lofthouse N 12	Shields J★ 1
Beardshaw EC★ 1	Gallon JW★ 5	Mangham W 1	Shore J★ 2
Boulter LM★ 1	Goslin H 6	Marsh R 2	Shuttleworth J 1
Breedon J★ 1	Grimshaw SW 11	Martindale L★ 2	Smith JD 5
Brown J 4	Hanks CW 4	Mawdsley LAC★ 3	Speak K 2
Brown W 6	Hanson S 1	McCormick JM 7	Steen AW★ 2
Burgess AC 3	Haslam AD 8	McEwan W★ 1	Swinburne TA★ 4
Catterall G 1	Howe D 1	Morris J★ 4	Walker E 1
Chadwick C★ 20	Hubbick H 32	Morrison ER 2	Whalley H★ 1
Cload H 3	Hunt GS 31	Myers J 5	Whitehead GK 2
Connor J 21	Hurst J 2	Newton RR 1	Winter DT 1
Cross RM★ 2	Jackson J 4	Platt E 1	Wright H 6
Eastham GR★ 5	Johnson JW★ 6	Robinson JJ★ 1	Wright J 1
Eastham H★ 2	Johnson WH★ 19	Rothwell E 3	
Eastwood E★ 1	Jones WEA 9	Russell DW★ 3	

Goals (61): Hunt 20, Knight 8, Chadwick 7, Lofthouse 6, Wright H 4, Morris 3, Myers 2, Burgess 1, Gallon 1, Goslin 1, Johnson J 1, Johnson W 1, Jones 1, Eastham G 1, Rothwell 1, Speak 1, own goals 2.

1942–43

Atkinson JE 10	Davies JK 1	Hughes GE 5	Moir W 1
Banks R 2	Finney T★ 1	Hunt GS 31	Murphy D 7
Beardshaw EC★ 1	Gallon JW★ 2	Ithell WJ 2	Parker LT★ 3
Bolton R 1	Gee H 4	John WR★ 5	Power GF 16
Bray J 1	Geldard A 1	Johnson JW★ 6	Rothwell E 4
Briddon S★ 2	Gillies MM 23	Johnson WH★ 25	Russell DW★ 3
Burgess AC 1	Gorman WE★ 28	Knight J 4	Savage RG 1
Chadwick C★ 31	Grimsditch S 1	Lievesley L★ 2	Stephan H 1
Charlesworth S★ 3	Gunner R★ 3	Lofthouse N 25	Tate N 3
Colclough W★ 2	Hall J★ 2	Longman FH 4	Taylor G 9
Connor J 3	Harker J 2	Marsh R 1	Watson J★ 6
Cross RM★ 2	Haslam AD 1	Maudsley RC 8	West FW 1
Crossley J 1	Hopkins RW★ 3	McCormick JM 1	Wharton JE★ 26
Crozier J★ 3	Hubbick H 35	Middleton T 2	Wright H 13

Goals (65): Hunt 17, Chadwick 15, Lofthouse 14, Johnson W 3, Wharton 3, Colclough 2, Gee 2, Gillies 2, Harker 1, Hughes 1, Knight 1, Rothwell 1, Tate 1, Watson 1, Wright 1.

1943–44

Anderson J 2	Harrison FH 1	McClelland C 6	Speak K 3
Berry J 10	Higham H 1	Middlebrough A 6	Sullivan A 1
Carter DF★ 1	Hubbick H 39	Murphy D 24	Taylor G 27
Chadwick C★ 19	Hughes AL 1	Owens JG 1	Watson A★ 1
Connor J 2	Johnson WH★ 33	Rigby E 6	Whalley H★ 4
Currier J 35	Knight J 4	Rimmer J 3	Windsor F 1
Foxton JD 3	Lancaster JN★ 2	Rothwell E 2	Winter DT 3
Gillies MM 3	Liddle J★ 2	Shankly W★ 2	Woodburn J★ 2
Gorman WC★ 34	Lofthouse N 24	Smith G★ 1	Woodward T 35
Grimsditch SW 1	MacFarlane R★ 1	Smith JR 1	Wright H 23
Hall HHC 30	Marsh R 1	Smith K 2	
Hamlett TL 17	Marshall D★ 8	Smith RAG 1	

Goals (66): Currier 17, Lofthouse 15, Woodward 8, Middlebrough 5, Hamlett 3, Chadwick 2, Johnson 2, McClelland 2, Wright 2, Berry 1, Carter 1, Gorman 1, Knight 1, Marshall 1, Rothwell 1, Shankly 1, Smith R 1, Taylor 1, own goals 2.

Includes one extra-time goal.

1944–45

Barrass MW 39	Hall HHC 8	Koffman SJ 2	Rigby E 1
Berry J 1	Hamlett TL 41	Lofthouse N 30	Rothwell E 4
Butler S★ 9	Hanson AJ★ 5	McClelland C 16	Taylor G 29
Connor J 6	Hubbick H 41	McCormick JM 2	Threlfall JR 13
Daily H 1	Hunt GS 40	Middlebrough A 9	Topping H★ 12
Fielding W 33	Johnson WH★ 11	Milne JL★ 3	Whalley H★ 2
Foxton JD 5	Jones S 1	Moir W 5	Winter DT 6
Gillies MM 2	Knight J 1	Murphy D 32	Woodward T 41

Goals (85): Lofthouse 30, Barrass 22, Hunt 10, Middlebrough 5, Woodward 5, Hamlett 3, Murphy 3, McClelland 2, Moir 2, Butler 1, Hanson 1, Johnson 1, Rothwell 1.

Includes one extra-time goal. Additional goalscorers in Cup-Winners' Cup: Hunt, Hamlett.

1945–46

Aspinall J 1	Hanks CW 2	Moir W 32	Taylor G 6
Atkinson JE 7	Hanson S 27	Murphy D 35	Threlfall JR 34
Barrass MW 28	Howe D 29	Neal C 1	Tomlinson F 2
Fielding W 14	Hubbick H 42	Roberts JH 6	Westwood WR 13
Forrest E 8	Hunt GS 29	Rothwell E 2	Woodward T 26
Geldard A 19	Hurst J 23	Sinclair TM 3	
Hamlett TL 38	Lofthouse N 34	Sullivan A 1	

Goals (67): Lofthouse 20, Moir 9, Barrass 8, Hamlett 7, Hunt 7, Howe 6, Westwood 3, Woodward 3, Geldard 2, Roberts 1, Sullivan 1.

FA Cup goals (13): Westwood 8, Hunt 2, Lofthouse 2, Moir 1.

Bournemouth & Boscombe Athletic

1939–40

Banks R 12	Foss F* 1	McDonald JC 34	Smith W 3
Bigg R* 1	Gallacher P 30	Millar NH 5	Stone JSG 3
Bird KB 26	Gardener C* 1	Monaghan P 3	Swinfen R* 1
Brewer F* 1	Hitchmough HR* 4	Paton TG 31	Tennent C* 1
Bright P* 1	Kelly J* 1	Pincott F 3	Tunnicliffe WF 3
Bungay E* 1	Kirkham J 23	Redfern R 26	Twiss R* 28
Burke C 34	Langley WE 10	Rowe T 14	Wilkinson EC 1
Cole C* 2	Lowery H* 3	Sanaghan J 34	Wilson FC 27
Cowan A^ 3	Malton A* 1	Schofield A* 4	
Edrich WJ* 1	Marsden F 38	Sellars W 3	

Goals (103): Paton 26, Kirkham 20, Gallacher 12, Redfern 12, McDonald 9, Burke 7, Marsden 5, Langley 4, Banks 3, Millar 1, Monaghan 1, Tunnicliffe 1, Twiss 1, own goal 1.

Bournemouth 2 Norwich C 1 played out of season – included in the table but not in appearances and goals; scorers were Burke, Paton.

War Cup goals (12): Kirkham 4, McDonald 3, Gallacher 2, Marsden 1, Paton 1, Redfern 1.

1940–41

Archibald –* 1	Dent –* 1	Lomas – 1	Rowell JF 1
Ashall –* 1	Dixon S* 12	Longdon CW* 2	Sibley ES* 2
Barrowman W* 2	Flint HG* 2	Malton A* 1	Siddall – 3
Bartram S* 5	Freeman – 1	Mannion W* 2	Smith AW 22
Blackadder F* 1	Gale –* 1	Mason J* 1	Spencer DH* 2
Brunton H* 10	Gray H* 4	Matthews R* 12	Stuttard JE* 7
Bungay E* 2	Green LF* 2	McDonald JC 25	Tebbutt –* 1
Burke C* 22	Hitchmough HR 12	Millar NH 6	Trim RF* 4
Burns L* 5	Jefferies – 1	Okin F* 1	Tunnicliffe WF 1
Chapman – 1	Johnson – 1	Paton TG 1	Watson W* 15
Clark C* 1	Jourdan – 1	Phipps H* 1	Westlake FA* 1
Cooke WH 1	Kelly JE* 8	Priestley M* 6	Whitelaw D* 1
Cowan SA* 29	King AE 3	Raynor G* 1	Whittingham A* 7
Dando – 1	Kirkham J 1	Reid EJ* 2	Wilson FC 7
Dann S* 2	Knight – 1	Robinson TW* 14	Wright – 1
Day – 1	Levitt GR 14	Rothery H* 2	Young RG 16

Goals (61): Matthews 14, Cowan 10, McDonald 9, Burke C 7, Whittingham 4, Brunton 2, Gray 2, Kirkham 2, Smith A 2, Spencer 2, Barrowman 1, Bungay 1, Clark 1, Reid 1, Sibley 1, Tunnicliffe 1, own goal 1.

1941–42

Bartram S* 2	Halliday T* 1	Riches W* 5	Tidman O* 2
Brook L* 4	Hinchliffe T* 2	Rigg T* 5	Tweedy GJ* 2
Cawthrone W 12	Holland – 1	Robinson TW* 8	Veal WO 2
Cowan SA 16	Layton WH 1	Rose NJ 2	Waller H* 2
Deakin G* 1	Lindley WM* 1	Rothery H 2	Watson W* 10
Delaney – 1	Marsden F 7	Rowell JF 11	Weare AJ 6
Dixon S* 14	McCulloch D* 2	Simpson J* 4	Westlake FA* 5
Gallacher P 1	McDonald JC 2	Smith W 4	Whitehead GK* 1
Gray H* 1	Morrison JA* 6	Spencer DH 1	Whittingham A* 18
Griffiths H* 3	Picton H* 1	Stapleton A* 1	Wilson FC 1
Griffiths MW* 3	Platt EH* 1	Sweeney – 1	Woodward L 7
Gunn GD* 1	Ray CH* 1	Tarrant – 2	Young RG 11

Goals (37): Whittingham 9, Rowell 5, Morrison 4, Brook 3, Cowan 3, Griffiths H 2, Hinchliffe 2, McCulloch 2, Tidman 2, Cawthrone 1, Deakin 1, Gray 1, Griffiths M 1, Watson 1.

1942–43

Did not compete.

1943–44

Did not compete.

1944–45

Did not compete.

1945–46

Bird KB 37	Jones NG★ 3	Preece JC★ 1	Tagg E 15
Bretherton T★ 2	King AE 2	Raybould ME★ 1	Taylor –★ 1
Burke C 30	Kirkham J 15	Redfern R 12	Taylor J★ 2
Busby M★ 2	Liddle TB★ 1	Robinson J★ 6	Thomas J 24
Cothliff HT★ 15	Mallern R★ 2	Rose J 2	Thomas SE★ 1
Currie JE 10	Marsden F 35	Ross –★ 1	Tootill GA★ 2
Darling HL★ 1	Martin E★ 1	Salter RJ 2	Trim RF★ 1
Dixon S★ 8	Mayers T★ 7	Sanaghan J 19	Troke F★ 11
Fielding WA★ 2	McDonald JC 35	Simpson J★ 12	Wilkinson E 1
Finch LC★ 5	Olver WE★ 2	Squires A★ 5	Wilson FC 11
Gallacher P 26	Paton TG 39	Stocker TM★ 1	Woodward L 3
Grant –★ 1	Pincott F 1	Summerbee GC★ 7	Young RG 6

Goals (92): Thomas J 27, McDonald 22, Paton 12, Kirkham 7, Burke 5, Finch 4, Cothliff 2, Currie 2, Mayers 2, Redfern 2, Busby 1, Dixon 1, Fielding 1, Gallacher 1, Summerbee 1, Tagg 1, own goal 1.

FA Cup goals (4): Thomas J 3, Paton 1.

Bradford City

1939–40

Beardshaw EC 1	Foulkes J* 10	Lovery JB 3	Scaife G* 2
Beresford FE 1	Goodyear G 2	Mahon J* 2	Scrimshaw S 1
Brown WW 2	Hall AF* 1	Matthews W 1	Smailes J 21
Buck T* 1	Hall AG 1	McDermott C 19	Stephenson JE* 1
Calverley A* 1	Harvey J 5	McGraw J* 1	Thompson L* 1
Charlesworth S* 1	Hastie A 15	McPhillips WP 22	Vincent NE* 1
Colquhoun DM 1	Hinsley G 20	Milburn John* 1	Ward RA* 9
Deakin J 1	Hydes A* 1	Molloy P 17	Whittingham A 21
Douglas JS* 1	Jones TC 1	Moore C 22	Woffinden RS* 1
Everest J* 1	Keeling AJ* 5	Murphy G 20	
Farrington R 1	Killourhy M* 2	Peel H* 1	

Goals (44): Whittingham 13, Smailes 12, Hinsley 10, Farrington 2, Hastie 2, Keeling 2, Foulkes 1, Harvey 1, Mahon 1.

War Cup goals (4): Hinsley 1, Killourhy 1, Smailes 1, Moore 1.

1940–41

Bailey G* 2	Farrington R 1	Jones TC 16	Powell S 4
Beardshaw EC 20	Firth JW* 3	Kaye G* 1	Pugh S* 1
Beresford FE 5	Fowler HN* 2	McDermott C 3	Richardson D 1
Blenkinsop E 7	Gallon JW* 1	McGraw J* 6	Rist FH* 6
Burdett T* 1	Gilroy WG* 9	McKellor WH* 13	Shackleton LF* 2
Calverley A* 1	Gregory FC* 2	McPhillips WP 7	Smailes J 28
Clapham H 8	Grimshaw R 1	Mills H 1	Spivey R* 1
Clegg N 1	Ham HS 1	Milnes W 1	Stabb GH* 1
Cochrane T* 1	Harvey J 22	Molloy P 17	Thompson G* 15
Cowell J* 1	Hastie A 6	Moore C 2	Vaughan JH* 1
Dalton J* 1	Henry GR* 1	Murphy G 21	Watson J* 8
Davies W* 2	Hinsley G 16	Norton JG* 1	Watts V 1
Deakin J 4	Hodgson LB 1	Ottewell S* 7	Wesley JC* 5
Douglas T 1	Hutchinson JA* 1	Pickles FW 1	Westgarth ER 2
Everest J* 4	Huwaert M 13	Powell IV* 6	Whittingham A 4

Goals (73): Hinsley 16, Harvey 12, Murphy 12, Smailes 9, Whittingham 5, McKellor 3, McGraw 2, Shackleton 2, Beresford 1, Clapham 1, Deakin 1, Farrington 1, Gregory 1, Ham 1, Molloy 1, Norton 1, Ottewell 1, Powell I 1, Stabb 1, own goal 1.

1941–42

Anderson N 12	Fisher GA 2	Malpass ST* 3	Rist FH* 13
Bailey G* 1	Gallon JW* 3	Mantle J* 1	Shackleton LF* 1
Barron J* 1	Gledhill S* 1	McDermott C 4	Smailes J 32
Beardshaw EC 8	Gregory FC* 18	McGarry T* 1	Smith AS 3
Beresford FE 1	Ham HS 1	McGraw J* 2	Spelman I* 1
Bradley CJ* 1	Harvey J 26	McKellor WH* 3	Toser EW* 2
Broad RR 2	Hastie A 12	Molloy P 24	Waddell W* 1
Calvert GV 2	Hesford RT* 1	Moore C 1	Watson T* 10
Clegg N 1	Hinsley G 17	Murphy G 27	Westgarth ER 1
Cochrane T* 1	Jones D* 1	Ottewell S* 17	Wharton F* 1
Duffy R* 1	Jones G 1	Patrick R 1	Whittingham A 8
Dunn WC 21	Jones TC 2	Powell S 3	Woodhouse – 1
Farr WF* 1	Kidd WE* 7	Reid JDJ* 11	
Farrington R 9	Lee AH* 9	Richardson D 17	

Goals (60): Smailes 14, Anderson 8, Hinsley 7, Ottewell 6, Reid 6, Harvey 4, Gregory 3, Hastie 2, Murphy 2, Farrington 1, Jones T 1, Malpass 1, McGraw 1, Moore 1, Whittingham 1, own goals 2.

1942–43

Adams W★   21
Alldis GJ★   2
Amos R   1
Anderson N   4
Baker G   2
Barrett J★   11
Bartram S★   1
Beardshaw CE   1
Beresford FE   1
Bokas F★   1
Boothroyd G★   1
Bray E★   1
Buck T★   2
Calverley A★   1
Calvert G   5
Clegg D★   3
Cochrane T★   2
Conroy M★   6
Corvan J   1

Coulston W★   1
Cowan J   1
Farrington R   6
Flatley AA★   3
Fleetwood ED★   2
Goodyear G   2
Gregory FC★   25
Hall AG   2
Harston JC★   4
Harvey J   11
Hastie A   2
Hawthorn W★   10
Hinsley G   20
Hodgson L   2
Isaac J★   19
Jones S★   2
Keeley A★   1
Kidd WE★   9
Lewin RD   6

Lindley WM★   17
Logan J   2
Malpass ST★   3
McDermott C   4
McKellor WH★   1
Millman C   3
Molloy P   6
Moore K   11
Moralee M★   2
Morgan SS★   2
Murphy G   8
Pickles FW   1
Poole J★   1
Powell S   1
Powell WH   1
Reid JDJ★   7
Richardson D   14
Rogers W★   3
Scrimshaw S   12

Shafto J★   1
Shotton R★   1
Smailes J   11
Smith S★   4
Steele J★   1
Stone J★   9
Stoney J   1
Swindin GH★   3
Teasdale K   13
Trigg SA   9
Trodden J★   1
Tweedy GJ★   1
Waller H★   1
Watson J★   3
Wesley JC★   3
Westlake FA★   13
Whittingham A   2
Wilson A★   3

Goals (59): Murphy 7, Reid 7, Isaac 6, Adams 5, Gregory 4, Hinsley 4, Lewin 3, Smailes 3, Barrett 2, Calvert 2, Farrington 2, Fleetwood 2, Scrimshaw 2, Stone 2, Beresford 1, Harvey 1, Molloy 1, Malpass 1, Rogers 1, Steele 1, Trigg 1, own goal 1.

1943–44

Barrett P★   1
Beardshaw EC   28
Beattie W★   8
Bokas F★   2
Braine J   1
Bray E★   1
Cartwright S★   3
Conroy M★   8
Davidson RT★   7
Deakin J   2
Deplidge W★   1
Dryden H★   1
Duffy R   3
Duggan JP★   2
Eggleston P   5
Farrington R   4
Flatley AA★   9
Gibbons W★   2

Gibson S   5
Gillegan A   1
Goodyear G   6
Grierson A   1
Haddington R★   1
Harston JC★   2
Harvey J   28
Hastie A   2
Hatfield B★   1
Hodgson JV★   1
Isaac J★   17
Jackson AG   2
Jones TC   2
Keating E   5
Kelly D   8
Kilshaw EA★   3
Lewin RD   15
Lewis W★   2

Lindley MW★   32
Logan JW★   1
Malcolm W   1
McDermott C   4
McGinn F   6
McKellor WH★   1
McSpadyen A★   1
McTavish H★   1
Miles V   1
Miller J★   1
Miller JW   1
Moffatt J   1
Molloy P   1
Moore K   5
Murphy G   24
Page AE★   5
Pallister G★   1
Powell WH   1

Pridmore AJ★   6
Rae R   11
Richardson   7
Rodgers AW★   4
Royston R★   1
Rozier AT★   2
Scrimshaw S   8
Shotton R★   1
Smith G★   2
Stone J★   2
Teasdale K   31
Thain W   1
Thompson A★   1
Tyrell D   1
Walker CH★   4
Westlake FA★   18
Woffinden RS★   9
Woodward V★   9

Goals (54): Harvey 17, Murphy 8, Davidson 3, Isaac 3, Lindley 3, Woodward 3, Gibson 2, Haddington 2, Rozier 2, Scrimshaw 2, Beattie 1, Farrington 1, Jackson 1, Pridmore 1, Rodgers 1, Stone 1, Walker 1, Woffinden 1, own goal 1.

1944–45

Anderson N   2
Barclay R★   6
Bartram S★   1
Battye JE★   1
Beardshaw EC   5
Birch A   1
Boothroyd G★   1
Burke T   3
Burton S★   14
Cabrelli P★   5
Cheetham TM★   2
Cockroft H★   1
Conroy M★   1
Coulthread G   1
Courtier L   1
Davidson RT★   17
Deplidge W★   1

Downie JD★   3
Duggan J★   3
Ellis JS   6
Farrar W   2
Gibson S   1
Gisbourne H   6
Glover A★   1
Gregory FC★   6
Haddington R★   1
Harrison G   1
Harston JC★   11
Harvey J   25
Hatfield B★   1
Heywood J   1
Hinsley G   2
Hold O★   10
Hollis H★   3

Horsfield J★   29
Isaac J★   32
Jales R   12
James JS★   2
Kelly D   1
Kirkham N★   1
Lenton L★   1
Lovery JB   1
Mackie W   4
McGraw J★   8
Miles L   1
Morrison J   2
Murphy G   2
Noble N★   6
Randell W   1
Richardson D   8
Robinson JN★   1

Robson AP★   1
Rozier AT★   32
Rutherford E★   3
Schofield E★   16
Scrimshaw S   3
Serpel W   1
Shepherd E★   29
Shreeve JTT★   12
Smith A★   1
Spacey PB★   1
Strong R   1
Swindin GH★   2
Teasdale K   27
Westlake FA★   28
Whittingham A   1
Wood WM   2

Goals (78): Shepherd 27, Hold 14, Isaac 8, Schofield 7, Barclay 3, Gisbourne 3, Harvey 3, Davidson 2, Gibson 2, Rozier 2, Boothroyd 1, Burton 1, Coulthread 1, Downie 1, Gregory 1, Hinsley 1, Whittingham 1.

1945–46

Adams W* 2	Daniels J 16	Horsfield A* 3	Pickergill F 1
Beardshaw EC 1	Davies H 2	Isaac J 35	Pickles FW 19
Beattie A* 1	Diamond S 11	Jales R 9	Rozier AT* 11
Brookham G 1	Ellis JS 1	Joyce E 15	Schofield E 10
Broughton E 10	Gibson S 2	Kaye G* 1	Scrimshaw S 7
Brown W 2	Goodyear G 1	Leech F 16	Seagrave J 1
Bryant W 22	Halliday G 10	Lovery JB 1	Smailes J 1
Burkenshaw GA* 1	Harper K 13	Matier G 17	Tomlinson J 2
Carroll T 2	Harston JC* 1	McDermott C 1	Webb J 4
Cockroft H* 19	Harvey J 8	Milburn John* 17	Westlake FA* 4
Conroy R 3	Hastie A 13	Mosby A 1	Whitehead S 1
Cooke TV 1	Hays CJ* 1	Murphy G 27	Whittingham A 1
Cooling R* 1	Hinsley G 4	Neary W 1	
Dailey A* 1	Hirst K 6	Newey JH 12	
Dalton J 9	Hold O* 1	Noble N 12	

Goals (84): Isaac 15, Leech 14, Murphy 13, Diamond 11, Milburn 6, Newey 4, Pickles 4, Broughton 2, Bryant 2, Cockroft 2, Hastie 2, Brown 1, Conroy 1, Harvey 1, Hinsley 1, Hold 1, Horsfield 1, Rozier 1, Webb 1, Whittingham 1.

FA Cup goals (3): Murphy 2, Pickles 1.

Bradford Park Avenue

1939–40

Bailey G★   3
Barton H★   7
Blenkinsop E   1
Brown J   1
Carr J★   6
Cochrane T   8
Coxon G★   1
Curry R★   5
Dann RW   1
Danskin R   21
Davidson DBL   1

Davis H★   17
Farr TF   11
Gilroy WG   11
Gordon RH★   1
Hallard W   1
Hepworth R   4
Hughes JH   3
Hutchinson JA★   3
Johnstone R   10
Juliussen AL★   5
Kaye G   14

Martin WJ   3
McCall J   1
McGarry T   13
McKenzie CL   1
Norton JG   2
Offord ST   1
Page E   1
Palmer W   1
Shackleton LF   2
Sheen J★   5
Smith FA   5

Smith FH   1
Smith G   5
Spivey R★   1
Stabb GH   20
Stephen JF   20
Stephenson GH★   3
Ward RA★   1
Watson E   4
Wesley JC   16
Wharton L   1

Goals (46): McGarry 13, Davis 7, Wesley 7, Sheen 5, Curry 3, Barton 2, Juliussen 2, Stabb 2, Cochrane 1, Hutchinson 1, Shackleton 1, Smith FA 1, Watson 1.

War Cup goals (2): Davis 1, Milne 1.

1940–41

Baines R★   1
Baker H   1
Bannister J   3
Barton H★   6
Brook F   1
Carr EM★   20
Carte R   26
Cochrane H   1
Conroy M★   1
Cross B   1
Danskin R   31
Davis H★   2

Dodd RI★   5
Dodds L★   1
Elliott WH   1
Farr TF   28
Farrell A   10
Firth JW   27
Futter A   2
Gilroy WG   1
Goslin H★   1
Greaves SW   2
Harrison H   6
Hastie A★   1

Kaye G   1
Keeling AH★   2
Kelly G★   2
Laycock K   1
McCall J   3
McGarry T   1
Miller J   7
Murphy G★   1
Nicholls J   4
Offord SJ   8
Palmer W   18
Paton HM   1

Prior FE   4
Shackleton LF   33
Smailes J★   1
Stabb GH   25
Steele DM   1
Stephen JF   33
Stokes A   1
Tomlinson CC   16
Wesley J   19
Wharton L   2

Goals (69): Shackleton 19, Carr 16, Stabb 14, Tomlinson 7, Danskin 2, Wesley 2, Cochrane 1, Dodd 1, Farrell 1, Futter 1, Greaves 1, Hastie 1, McCall 1, Miller 1, own goal 1.

1941–42

Baird H   1
Bedford E   1
Brenen A★   1
Carr EM★   33
Coxon A★   1
Crowther R   1
Danskin R   33
Davis H★   5
Deplidge W   30
Elliott WH   25

Farr TF   36
Farrell A   16
Geldard A★   1
Gibson S   1
Gill L   1
Green GF   14
Harvey J★   1
Lee G★   5
Lewis TH★   4
McCall J   1

McGarry T   4
McKenzie CL   1
Miller JW   6
Mills GR★   1
Moore K   17
Nicholls J   1
Offord SJ   3
Palmer W   31
Prestley M   2
Shackleton LF   34

Stabb GH   33
Steele DM   1
Stephen JF   35
Tomlinson CC   1
Walker GR   3
Walker J   1
Wesley JC   14
Wharton F   2
Wharton L   6

Goals (68): Shackleton 24, Carr 15, Green 5, Stabb 5, Deplidge 4, McGarry 3, Lee 2 , Miller 2, Wesley 2, Baird 1, Bedford 1, Danskin 1, Farrell 1, Lewis 1, Palmer 1.

1942–43

Anderson W★   1
Asquith B★   1
Bannister J   1
Barclay R★   2
Brophy HF★   3
Cabrelli P★   3
Carr EM★   3
Danskin R   37
Davis H★   1
Dawson J★   2
Deplidge W   14
Devlin E★   1

Dickie P★   4
Dobson J   1
Doran S★   1
Downie JD   4
Elliott WH   19
Farr TF   35
Farrell A   30
Firth JW   2
Flatley AA★   9
Green GF   24
Hatfield B   7
Hawksworth D   1

Hirst H   18
Johnson A★   14
Knight JE   1
McGarry T   17
McKellor WH★   1
Miller JW   3
Moore K   3
Palmer W   1
Shackleton LF   36
Short JD★   1
Simpson R★   6
Smith JW★   5

Stabb GH   33
Steele DM   1
Steele FC★   5
Stephen JF   19
Walker GR   35
Walker J   1
Walker T★   1
Warburton A★   1
Williamson J★   1

Goals (81): Shackleton 36, McGarry 7, Green 6, Johnson 6, Steele F 5, Hatfield 4, Walker G 4, Simpson 3, Flatley 2, Stabb 2, Barclay 1, Brophy 1, Carr 1, Deplidge 1, Steele D 1, Walker T 1.

1943–44

Ainsley GE★ 29	Elliott WH 1	Hodgson S★ 5	Shotton R★ 1
Asquith B★ 1	Farr TF 38	Horsman L 3	Smith FH 2
Baird H★ 2	Farrell A 38	Jones G★ 1	Smith JW 37
Carr EM★ 32	Firth JW 5	Jones TC★ 1	Stabb GH 37
Compton LH★ 13	Green GF 4	Knight JE 11	Stephen JF 33
Danskin R 37	Haddington R 1	Logan JW★ 2	Stirland CJ★ 3
Davidson DBL 1	Haines JWT★ 1	Offord SJ 1	Taylor DH 3
Dobson J 2	Henry GR★ 1	Palmer W 1	Thorogood J★ 1
Downie JD 5	Hepworth R 1	Shackleton LF 28	Walker GR 36

Goals (115): Shackleton 34, Ainsley 27, Carr 21, Walker 7, Farrell 5, Smith J 5, Stabb 4, Compton 3, Horsman 3, Downie 1, Henry 1, Offord 1, Smith F 1, Stephen 1, own goal 1.

1944–45

Britton J 3	Dobson J 3	Hawksworth D 10	Noble M★ 1
Broadis IA★ 1	Downie JD 26	Horsman L 1	Rodgers AW★ 2
Clarke A 3	Elliott WH 2	James JS 6	Shackleton LF 39
Conway A 1	Farr TF 37	Kendall A★ 2	Shotton R★ 3
Cummins JWH 2	Farrell A 39	Knight JE 1	Smith JW 27
Danskin R 36	Flatley AA 19	Leonard H★ 1	Stabb GH 38
Dawson T★ 1	Flynn J 1	McGarry T 1	Stephen JF 35
Deplidge W 4	Gibbons AH★ 6	McTaff S 9	Walker GR 33
Dickens L 1	Haddington R 2	Miller JW 1	Willingham CK★ 2
Dickinson P★ 1	Hallard W 21	Murphy W 7	
Dix R 8	Hatfield B 1	Naylor E 3	

Goals (94): Shackleton 40, Downie 11, Walker 7, Farrell 6, Gibbons 5, Smith 5, Stabb 5, Murphy 3, Dix 2, Naylor 2, Broadis 1, Cummins 1, Flatley 1, Hallard 1, Hawksworth 1, Horsman 1, McTaff 1, Rodgers 1.

1945–46

Britton J 5	Flatley AA 4	Kaye G 5	Shirley H★ 1
Chisholm K★ 1	Gibbons AH 21	Knott H 8	Smith G★ 1
Colley JH★ 3	Glasby H 4	Leonard H 3	Smith JW 30
Danskin R 30	Greenwood R★ 32	McCall J 13	Sperrin W 1
Dix R 7	Haddington R 1	McTaff S 19	Stabb GH 16
Dobson J 4	Hallard W 13	Offord SJ 1	Stephen JF 19
Downie JD 33	Hawksworth D 5	Poole J★ 1	Walker GR 31
Farr TF 42	Hepworth R 35	Rodi J★ 1	White R★ 8
Farrell A 24	Horsman L 5	Ruecroft J★ 2	Whittingham A 1
Firth JW 1	James JS 1	Shackleton LF 30	

Goals (71): Downie 16, Shackleton 12, Gibbons 8, Walker 8, Smith J 6, Farrell 3, Knott 3, McCall 3, Hawksworth 2, Horsman 2, Rodi 2, Stabb 2, Colley 1, Hepworth 1, Smith G 1, own goal 1.

FA Cup goals (16): Gibbons 8, Dix 3, Downie 1, Farrell 1, Hallard 1, Knott 1, Shackleton 1.

Brentford

1939–40

Aicken AV 1	Doherty PD★ 3	Kay J 3	Scott AT 6
Anderson DN 1	Gaskell E 20	Manley T 18	Scott WR 2
Anderson J 3	Gorman WC 38	McCulloch D★ 5	Smith LGF 27
Boulter LM 14	Hilliam CE★ 1	McKenzie D★ 34	Stephens HJ★ 1
Brown W 29	Holliday JW 26	Muttitt E 6	Thomas RA 3
Burgess H★ 1	Hopkins I 36	Poyser GH 32	Townsend LF 8
Cheetham TM 3	Hunt DA★ 11	Reay EP★ 3	Wilkins GE 27
Clack FE 3	Jackson J★ 6	Saunders AHR 1	Woodley VR★ 4
Crozier J 4	James J 33	Saunders P 8	Yorston BC★ 8

Goals (87): Holliday 17, Wilkins 10, Hunt 9, Boulter 7, Hopkins 7, McKenzie 7, Townsend 6, Manley 5, Yorston 5, Brown 2, Burgess 2, Doherty 2, Smith 2, Gorman 1, James 1, McCulloch 1, Saunders P 1, own goals 2.

War Cup goals (2): Brown 1, Smith 1.

1940–41

Aicken AV 6	Duke GE★ 22	Hunt DA★ 20	Scott AT 2
Bamford HFE 1	Eastham GR★ 2	Jackson J★ 2	Shepherdson H★ 2
Beasley SJ 2	Ferris R 1	James J 27	Smith LGF 22
Boulter LM 2	Gaskell E 1	McKenzie D★ 23	Thomas RA 1
Brown C 1	Gibbons AH★ 1	Mills GR★ 1	Townsend LF 11
Brown W 22	Gilson F 1	Muttitt E 15	Wilkins GE 16
Cheetham TM 1	Holliday JW 23	Perry E★ 11	Wrigglesworth W★ 2
Cousins ST 1	Hopkins I 27	Poland G★ 2	
Davie J★ 2	Houghton WE★ 1	Poyser GH 23	

Goals (61): Hopkins 11, Hunt 11, Perry 11, Townsend 7, Wilkins 5, Holliday 4, McKenzie 4, Muttitt 2, Bamford 1, Boulter 1, Cheetham 1, Ferris 1, James 1, Smith 1.

London Cup

Bamford 2, Beasley A 1, Boulter 1, Brown W 12, Davie 2, Duke 5, Holliday 12, Hopkins 11, Hunt 7, Jackson 2, James 12, McKenzie 12, Muttitt 3, Perry 6, Poland 5, Poyser 12, Smith LGF 10, Smith T 1, Townsend 4, Wilkins 12.

Goals: Perry 10, Hopkins 6, Smith L 4, Muttitt 2, Townsend 2, Boulter 1, Davie 1, Hunt 1, McKenzie 1, Wilkins 1.

1941–42

Aicken AV 7	Duncan A★ 1	Manley T 1	Smale DM★ 3
Anderson DN 5	Duns L★ 7	McCulloch D★ 1	Smith J★ 1
Bartram S★ 1	Harrison – 2	McKenzie D★ 36	Smith LGF 30
Bonass AE★ 1	Holliday JW 18	Muttitt E 13	Smith W★ 1
Brown HT★ 2	Hopkins I 38	Peacock T★ 1	Sneddon WC★ 16
Brown W 39	Hunt DA★ 33	Perry E★ 27	Townsend LF 13
Cheetham TM 2	Jackson J★ 12	Poland G★ 19	Whittaker W 2
Collett E★ 1	James J 38	Poyser GE 33	Wilkins GE 25
Davidson D★ 1	Jones E★ 4	Purdie JJ★ 2	
Duke HP★ 1	Kiernan T★ 1	Rickett HF★ 2	

Goals (101): Perry 20, Hunt 18, Smith L 13, Hopkins 12, Townsend 9, Wilkins 8, Cheetham 3, Holliday 3, McKenzie 3, Duns 2, Duncan 1, James 1, Muttitt 1, Smale 1, Smith J 1, Sneddon 1, own goals 4.

1942–43

Aicken AV 2
Armstrong M★ 3
Bonass AE★ 1
Boyes W★ 2
Brown W 34
Cheetham TM 2
Collett E★ 3
Cunningham E★ 1
Dooley H 3
Driver A★ 1
Duke GE★ 1

Finch J★ 2
Foss SR★ 1
Gallacher P★ 1
Groves K★ 1
Henley L★ 1
Hillman S 1
Holliday JW 6
Hopkins I 28
Hunt DA★ 29
Jackson J★ 29
James J 33

Kiernan T★ 10
Mason WS★ 1
McCulloch D★ 2
McKenzie D★ 29
Milton GW★ 2
Muir A★ 2
Muttitt E 10
O'Donnell F★ 1
Perry E★ 18
Poyser GH 31
Pugh R★ 1

Saphin RF 2
Scott WR 2
Smith LGF 26
Sneddon WC★ 18
Townsend LF 20
Vidler HG★ 1
Whittaker A★ 9
Wilkins GE 4

Goals (71): Townsend 19, Hunt 14, Kiernan 9, Hopkins 5, Perry 5, Holliday 3, McKenzie 3, McCulloch 2, Smith 2, Aicken 1, Armstrong 1, Henley 1, James 1, O'Donnell 1, Sneddon 1, Wilkins 1, own goals 2.

1943–44

Baynham J 2
Bentley G★ 7
Briggs CE★ 1
Brown W 35
Cowan R★ 1
Crozier J 16
Davis RD★ 2
Deakin J★ 1
Driver A★ 1
Duke HP★ 3
Durrant FH 1
Flavell R★ 1
Floodgate B★ 1

Girling HM★ 1
Holliday JW 3
Hopkins I 14
Houldsworth FC★ 1
Hunt DA★ 30
James J 23
Jenner F★ 1
Jones JT★ 2
Jones L★ 1
Kiernan T★ 4
Lester F★ 1
Leyfield C★ 1
Little G★ 2

Manley T 4
Mason WS★ 1
McKennan P★ 20
McKenzie D★ 18
Muttitt E 11
Nelson D★ 4
Poyser GE 30
Richfield M 1
Roxburgh AW★ 1
Saunders AHR 4
Shepherd E★ 2
Smith LGF 25
Soo F★ 15

Stevens AH★ 1
Stewart G★ 28
Taylor JG★ 1
Thomas RA 8
Thompson H★ 1
Townsend LF 15
Watson J★ 20
Watson JF★ 1
Westcott D★ 5
Whittaker W 24

Goals (89): Hunt 18, Townsend 15, McKennan 14, Smith 13, Stewart 8, Westcott 6, Baynham 2, Hopkins 2, Thomas 2, Watson J 2, Driver 1, Duncan 1, Holliday 1, Little 1, Shepherd 1, Soo 1, Stevens 1.

1944–45

Ballard EA 2
Banner A★ 2
Baynham J 12
Boulter LM 12
Boyd J 2
Briddon S★ 5
Brown C 4
Brown HT★ 1
Brown W 35
Busby M★ 1
Cheetham TM 2
Collett E★ 6
Cowan R★ 3

Croker PH★ 1
Dawes FW★ 1
Edelston MJ★ 1
Fullwood J★ 1
Goldberg L★ 1
Gorman WC 6
Hammond AW 1
Hobbis HHF★ 1
Hopkins I 34
Hunt DA★ 26
Jackson J★ 18
Jales R★ 1
Jobling J★ 1

Jones JT★ 12
Livingstone A★ 1
Lloyd C★ 2
Manley T 13
McKenzie D★ 4
Mountford RC★ 1
Muttitt E 18
O'Callaghan E★ 1
Oakes John★ 2
Poyser GE 26
Russell RI★ 1
Saunders AHR 3
Scott WR 3

Sheldon PJ 1
Smith LGF 21
Soo F★ 10
Stephens HJ★ 1
Tadman M★ 1
Thomas DWJ★ 10
Thomas RA 33
Townsend LF 28
Tunnicliffe W★ 1
Whittaker W 23

Goals (100): Townsend 30, Thomas R 26, Hunt 13, Smith 7, Boulter 5, Thomas D 5, Baynham 4, Hopkins 3, Brown C 2, Soo 2, Cheetham 1, Manley 1, own goal 1.

1945–46

Bamford HFE 1
Baynham J 7
Boulter LM 1
Brown W 41
Coulson R 1
Crozier J 35
Durrant FH 27
Edelston MJ★ 1
Fenton EBA★ 1
Ferrier H★ 2

Gaskell E 1
Gorman WC 42
Gotts JA 4
Hammond AW 1
Hopkins I 36
Hunt DA★ 12
Jones EN 20
Keene DC 2
Manley T 2
Mapson J★ 6

McAloon G 20
Munro RA 5
Muttitt E 1
Oliver HS 7
Phillips W★ 8
Poyser GE 26
Roberts JH★ 1
Scott WR 31
Sloan JW★ 6
Smith GH 25

Smith LGF 9
Stroud R 4
Sutton JB 1
Thomas RA 33
Townsend LF 18
Watson W★ 1
Whittaker W 19
Wilkins GE 3
Wilson R★ 1

Goals (82): McAloon 17, Thomas 17, Townsend 14, Durrant 13, Scott 4, Sloan 4, Hunt 2, Wilkins 2, Bamford 1, Edelston 1, Gotts 1, Hopkins 1, Jones 1, Roberts 1, Smith G 1, Watson 1, own goal 1.

FA Cup goals (17): McAloon 6, Durrant 4, Hopkins 3, Scott 1, Thomas 1, Townsend 1, own goal 1.

Brighton & Hove Albion

1939–40

Abel S★   1
Austin H★   2
Baldwin H   1
Bott W★   14
Briggs W★   5
Broomfield D★   2
Butler MP★   1
Chase C   2
Chesters A★   7
Clarkson G★   2
Clifford J★   1
Collins H★   1
Cothliff HT★   1
Court R   1

Cowan S   2
Darling HL   37
Davie J   34
Day A   3
Devine JS★   1
Duke GE★   2
Evans T   25
Farrell R★   27
Flack DW★   1
Francis V★   1
Goffey HH   1
Grundy JA   1
Harman C   2
Harris J   3

Hickman S★   2
Hindley F   2
Isaac WJ   4
Kay J★   3
Keen ERL★   1
Kelly JG★   1
Kelly L★   1
Layton WH★   1
Longdon CW   19
Lowe HP★   1
Marriott E   30
Martin E   35
Mee G   26
Packham W★   2

Poulter J★   1
Risdon S   24
Spencer G   3
Stephens HJ   24
Stevens J   38
Swinfen R★   1
Tait T★   1
Trainor P   1
Watts R★   2
Wilson A   1
Wilson JA   24

Goals (77): Davie 24, Stephens 14, Farrell 11, Risdon 6, Wilson J 6, Bott 3, Collins 1, Cothliff 1, Darling 1, Goffey 1, Harman 1, Hindley 1, Isaac 1, Kay 1, Kelly J 1, Marriott 1, own goals 3.

War Cup goals (1): Stephens 1.

1940–41

Austin H   4
Balmer J★   7
Barber –   1
Bartram A★   1
Bird S★   1
Briggs W   1
Burtenshaw CE   3
Bush TW★   1
Chase C   13
Christie –   1
Colborn H   3
Darling HL   25
Davie J   6

Devenport G   5
Dye D   1
Eastham H★   4
Farrell R   8
Felton R★   1
Goffey HH   1
Gunn A   10
Harman C   16
Hickman S   10
Isaac WJ   10
Ithell WJ★   1
Jones EL   1
Jones R★   1

Kinghorn WJD★   1
Laney L★   1
Longdon CW   2
Marriott E   2
Martin E   16
McCoy W   7
McDermott J   1
McInnes JS★   5
McNaughton J   6
Mee G   26
Pinchbeck F★   1
Ramsden B★   3
Risdon S   26

Slater –   1
Smith A★   1
Spry –   1
Stacey WA★   1
Stephens HJ   15
Taylor PH★   3
Trainor P   2
Watts R   4
Welsh D★   7
Westby JL★   4
Willemse S   5
Wilson FC★   7
Wilson JA   13

Goals (53): Welsh 15, Stephens 12, Balmer 7, Harman 3, Davie 2, Isaac 2, Risdon 2, Willemse 2, Wilson J 2, Devenport 1, Colborn 1, Gunn 1, Jones R 1, Laney 1, own goal 1.

1941–42

Ball JA   3
Balmer J★   6
Bowles RF   2
Browning GC   8
Buckell –   1
Burdett T   1
Burgess R   4
Bush TW★   2
Chapman A   1
Chase C   4
Clatworthy L   1
Cunliffe AJ★   18
Curtis GF★   3
Darling HL   5
Davie J   26
Day A   1
Dugnolle JH   1

Easdale J★   2
Eastham G★   3
Eastham H★   8
Ford FG★   9
Goffey HH   2
Gregory F   1
Griffin ARC   2
Gunn A   2
Hart A   14
Haworth –   3
Henley L★   1
Jones S   9
Kelly L★   2
Kyle –   1
Lancelotte EC★   1
Lane W   1
Lewis WA★   1

Longdon CW   12
Malpass ST★   13
Marriott E   4
Martin E   5
McInnes JS★   5
Mee G   33
Moores P   1
Morgan SS★   20
Mulraney A★   1
Nixon –   1
Owens –   1
Patterson GL★   2
Pearson SC★   3
Peters K★   1
Pryde RI★   1
Ramsden B★   5
Risdon S   34

Scrimshaw CT★   1
Shafto J★   1
Simmons L★   1
Stephens HJ   10
Taylor PH★   8
Thew –   1
Thorne AG   1
Tooze CE★   17
Tunnicliffe WF★   5
Waller H★   6
Welsh D★   2
Westby JL★   13
Williams S★   6
Wilson FC★   5
Wilson JA   26
Woodley VR★   1
Woods –   1

Goals (82): Davie 27, Cunliffe 11, Balmer 7, Morgan 7, Wilson J 6, Stephens 3, Day 2, Hart 2, Tunnicliffe 2, Welsh 2, Chase 1, Easdale 1, Griffin 1, Gunn 1, Jones 1, Lancelotte 1, Lane 1, Pearson 1, Peters 1, Ramsden 1, Risdon 1, Shafto 1, Taylor 1.

1942–43

Ball JA 29
Blackman JJ* 1
Bojar F 10
Bowles RF 4
Bunyon W* 1
Cameron J 1
Cater R* 1
Cook P* 1
Darling HL 12
Davie J 8
Day A 2
Easdale J* 20
Eastham H* 20
Ford FG* 1
France E 1
Gillespie IC* 1
Gore L* 2
Griffin ARC 2
Griffiths WM* 5
Harlock DS* 1
Jones S* 11
Kinghorn WJD* 17
Kirkman N* 1
Longdon CW 29
Malpass ST* 16
Marriott E 3
McInnes JS* 5
Mee G 5
Moore BJ 1
Morgan SS* 12
Mountford GF* 1
O'Donnell F* 1
Ohlens P 1
Pearson SC* 5
Reid EJ* 29
Richmond G* 1
Risdon S 34
Shafto J* 18
Stephens HJ 29
Stevens J 1
Taylor PH* 11
Thorne AG 2
Tully FA* 1
Walker C* 1
Watson JF* 2
Wilson JA 12
Woodward L* 2

Goals (69): Shafto 16, Stephens 10, Morgan 9, Kinghorn 7, Davie 5, Darling 3, Eastham 3, Griffiths 3, Reid 2, Risdon 2, Pearson 2, Wilson J 2, Gore 1, Malpass 1, O'Donnell 1, Ohlens 1, Thorne 1.

1943–44

Anderson JC* 3
Ball JA 6
Bell – 1
Bentley G* 1
Boyd JM* 1
Cocker J* 1
Darling HL 13
Davie J 2
Dooley A* 1
Driver A* 1
Easdale J* 15
Eastham H* 18
Edington J* 1
Fairhurst WG* 7
Fox D 4
France E 1
Grainger J* 2
Grier – 1
Griffiths WM* 7
Hassell TW* 23
Hickman S 1
Hillman D 9
Hollis H* 1
Hooper PG* 1
Ithell WJ* 1
Kemp DJ* 13
Kinghorn WJD* 2
Lawrence – 1
Longdon CW 13
Lowrie G* 1
Mackenzie D* 8
Malone R 1
Marriott E 15
Martin E 6
Matthewson G* 1
McInnes JS* 14
McNeill HJ* 2
Mee G 3
Moore BJ 7
Muttitt E* 2
Newman – 1
Pointon WJ* 1
Reid EJ* 25
Richardson D* 1
Risdon S 35
Sanderson – 1
Shafto J* 9
Sperrin W* 2
Stankowski S 1
Stephens HJ 27
Taylor PH* 16
Tootill A* 1
Ward J* 2
Wassall JV* 4
Weaver S* 1
Wilson FC* 12
Wilson JA 32
Woodward L* 4
Wright TB* 9
Younger – 1

Goals (66): Hassell 11, Stephens 11, Wilson J 9, Reid 6, Shafto 6, Moore 4, Taylor 4, McNeill 3, Hillman 3, Davie 2, Griffiths 2, Driver 1, Eastham 1, Longdon 1, Malone 1, Wright 1.

1944–45

Adams W 1
Ball JA 4
Barlow H* 1
Bratley GW* 14
Briscoe J* 3
Brown J* 1
Brown JR 15
Cook R* 9
Cornish D* 4
Crawford E* 6
Croft C* 1
Day A 4
Fairhurst WG* 26
Farmer A* 1
Frost AD* 3
Gregory JL* 1
Groves K* 1
Hancock J 1
Hassell TW* 7
Hodges CL* 19
Hodgson S* 9
Jackson L* 1
Lewis D* 1
Lobb FJ 1
Longdon CW 1
Lyle – 1
Mackenzie D* 4
Marriott E 1
Martin E 3
McDermott J* 16
McFarlane D* 1
Moore BJ 28
Muir R* 2
Needham FR* 3
O'Donnell F* 14
Offord SJ* 1
Pinkerton H* 3
Reece TS* 26
Reid EJ* 31
Risdon S 34
Ross T* 1
Stear JA* 1
Stephens HJ 28
Tapken N* 2
Townsend LF* 1
Wallis J* 3
Weir J* 3
Whent J* 3
Wilson JA 34
Winning A* 17

Goals (82): Hodges 15, Stephens 15, Moore 13, Wilson J 6, McDermott 5, Reid 5, Day 4, Cook 3, Cornish 3, O'Donnell 3, Crawford 2, Briscoe 1, Frost 1, Hassell 1, Offord 1, Reece 1, Risdon 1, Townsend 1, Weir 1.

1945–46

Alexander FR★　1
Baldwin H　32
Ball JA　4
Broomfield D　2
Chase C　3
Cowan S　1
Curtis J　1
Darling HL　23
Davie J　10
Day A　6
Dugnolle JH★　1
Ford FG★　3
Green F　9

Gunn A　3
Hart A★　1
Hassell TW★　9
Hillman D　3
Hindley F　2
Hughes H　2
Longdon CW　24
Louden D　1
Marriott E　14
Martin E　2
Martindale L★　4
McDermott J★　1
McNaughton J　1

Miles –　1
Millbank JH★　1
Moore BJ　26
Moore JFB★　1
Munro AD★　6
O'Donnell F★　11
Parr C　1
Philbin J　8
Pugh J　1
Reece TS★　4
Reid EJ★　2
Risdon S　27
Robson AP★　1

Rowley GA★　5
Sage F　1
Sheppard R　5
Stephens HJ　29
Trainor P　15
Watson J★　14
Wharton F★　1
Whent J　32
Willemse S　3
Williams W★　1
Wilson A★　1
Wilson JA　36

Goals (72): Moore B 27, Stephens 11, O'Donnell 8, Davie 4, Darling 3, Hassell 3, Gunn 2, Watson 2, Wilson J 2, Broomfield 1, Day 1, Longdon 1, Philbin 1, Reece 1, Robson 1, Rowley 1, Sheppard 1, Trainor 1, Whent 1.

FA Cup goals (23): Davie 10, Stephens 5, Chase 2, Longdon 2, Hindley 1, Moore B 1, Willemse 1, Wilson J 1.

Bristol City

1939–40

Armstrong RJ 17	Curran F 7	Maggs P* 15	Skinner F* 1
Booth L 16	Dawson E 4	Millar A 3	Stock AWA* 2
Bourton CFT 27	Dix RW* 16	Milsom J* 13	Turner JR 3
Brain J 4	English J 1	Mizen R* 2	Vidler HJ 29
Bridge CJ 15	Fitz D 1	Morgan CI 22	Watts RE 12
Brook R 3	Gallacher F 1	Morgan MM 1	Williams C* 3
Butterworth A* 12	Hathway EA* 4	Pincott F* 16	Williams S* 14
Caple HE 4	Jones EJ 1	Preece JC* 14	
Carr LL* 1	Kelso J* 11	Robbins D* 2	
Clark DF 8	King ET* 11	Roberts D 25	

Goals (62): Bourton 14, Dix 11, Armstrong 10, Williams S 7, Booth 6, Milsom 4, Vidler 4, Clark 1, Curran 1, Gallacher 1, Morgan C 1, Turner 1, Williams C 1.

War Cup goals (1): Bourton 1.

1940–41

Armstrong RJ 1	Dix RW* 5	Lowe –* 1	Quick E 3
Bentley RTF 20	English J 2	Maggs P* 19	Roberts D 17
Booth L 2	Gibson –* 1	McPherson –* 2	Roberts E* 13
Bourton CFT 5	Goddard R* 3	Mitchell W* 11	Robinson TW* 5
Bowers CH 5	Gregg I 2	Mizen RV 1	Shankley R* 2
Brinton EJ* 2	Iles AK* 2	Morgan CI 19	Tadman GH* 4
Carr LL* 14	King E 4	O'Mahoney M* 4	Talbot L* 1
Clark DF 19	Kingston – 1	Paisley R* 1	Warren RR* 2
Collis R 1	Lewis JW 1	Preece JC* 17	Whitfield W* 4
Cousins K 3	Low NH* 1	Prescott –* 1	Williams S 21

Goals (58): Roberts E 16, Williams 8, Carr 7, Bourton 6, Bentley 3, Bowers 3, Tadman 3, Dix 2, Goddard 2, Clark 1, Gregg 1, Iles 1, Lewis 1, Quick 1, Prescott 1, Roberts D 1, Talbot 1.

1941–42

Aldersea –* 1	Cousins K 9	Jefferies JT 1	Preece JC* 32
Arnold –* 2	Dumble HE 2	Laney L* 1	Rew RE 1
Bedford JE 14	Duns L* 1	Maggs P* 4	Roberts D 25
Bentley RTF 30	Fairhurst WG* 2	Mardon WJ 1	Roberts E* 16
Billington F* 3	Fisher KW* 1	McNess –* 1	Rogers E* 1
Bourton CFT 16	Gallagher –* 1	Messom G* 1	Tadman GH* 26
Bowers CH 15	Garrett A* 8	Mills M 1	Warren R* 3
Brinton EJ* 21	Graham DR* 1	Mitchell W* 20	Waterman –* 1
Brown WH* 6	Hall AE* 1	Morgan CI 23	Williams C 5
Carr LL* 21	Hargreaves J* 2	Painter EG* 1	
Charles R* 1	Harris T 1	Perrett RF* 1	
Clark DF 26	Hesford –* 1	Perry C* 1	

Goals (101): Tadman 41, Bentley 16, Roberts E 12, Carr 9, Garrett 9, Bowers 2, Duns 2, Bourton 1, Brinton 1, Dumble 1, Gallagher 1, Mills 1, Mitchell 1, Perrett 1, Warren 1, Williams 1, own goal 1.

1942–43

Artus K 2	Chilcott K 4	Hyslop A* 5	Moore JFB* 4
Beckett H 3	Clark DF 27	Jeffries JT 1	Morgan CI 24
Benjamin J 3	Davis – 1	Lambert C 1	Newman – 1
Bentley RFT 15	Dumble HE 3	Maggs P* 10	Preece JC* 33
Bourton CFT 28	Fitz D 10	Mardon HJ 2	Roberts D 32
Bowers CH 1	Ford V* 1	Mardon WJ 10	Roberts E* 22
Bradshaw GF* 15	Fox D* 7	Mather H* 2	Scott WJ* 1
Brinton E* 27	Garrett A* 1	McDonald JC* 2	Southcombe – 1
Buchan W* 1	Hargreaves J* 32	McLaren A* 5	Tadman GH* 20
Butterworth – 1	Hayward DS* 6	Millar A 2	Warren RR* 5
Carney S* 1	Hobbis HHF* 3	Mitchell W* 16	Williams Cyril 5

Goals (100): Tadman 21, Hargreaves 16, Roberts E 16, Bentley 15, Bourton 10, Clark 4, Chilcott 3, Hayward 3, Williams 3, Moore 2, Beckett 1, Benjamin 1, Buchan 1, Dumble 1, McLaren 1, Marden HJ 1, Warren 1, own goal 1.

Includes one extra-time goal.

1943-44

Armstrong RJ 1	Collis R★ 1	Hyslop A★ 1	Preece JC★ 28
Artus KG 1	Corry S★ 1	Jennings R★ 1	Rees TW★ 1
Bedford JE 6	Cousins K 31	Jones –★ 1	Rich L★ 2
Bentley RFT 4	Dawson E 1	Longdon CW★ 1	Roberts D 34
Bishop GJ 1	Dumble HE 2	Mardon HJ 1	Roberts E★ 3
Bourton CFT 23	Edwards D★ 3	Markey JF 3	Scott WJ★ 1
Brinton EJ★ 34	Evans –★ 1	McPhie J★ 1	Stoles A 2
Brooks H★ 1	Fitz D 1	Melville J★ 1	Stuart RW★ 3
Butler – 1	Fitz O 1	Milton GW★ 10	Thomas WG 8
Cann ST★ 21	Garrett A★ 1	Mitchell W★ 26	White AS★ 3
Carter DF★ 1	Graham G★ 7	Morgan CI 35	Williams R 1
Chilcott K 24	Hargreaves J★ 35	Morton – 1	
Clark DF 25	Haydon TJ 1	Norcott AC 5	
Collins RD 6	Holmes WA 9	Phillips R 1	

Goals (70): Hargreaves 13, Bourton 6, Chilcott 6, Clark 5, Morgan 5, Thomas 5, Holmes 4, Mitchell 4, Bentley 3, Collins 3, Norcott 3, Brinton 2, Milton 2, Roberts D 2, Carter 1, Dumble 1, Edwards 1, Garrett 1, Jennings 1, Roberts E 1, own goal 1.

1944-45

Bailey EJ 4	Fitz O 1	Mitchell W★ 12	Scrimshaw S★ 3
Bentley RFT 4	Fox GR 2	Morgan CI 35	Stock AWA★ 1
Brinton EJ★ 19	Guy I 33	Nutt I 1	Thomas WG 34
Chilcott K 22	Hargreaves J★ 37	Owen W★ 39	Williams Cyril 4
Clark DF 36	Hayward DS★ 5	Preece JC★ 34	
Collins RD 33	Jenkins C 1	Reilly LH★ 4	
Ferguson A★ 40	McPhie J★ 1	Roberts D 35	

Goals (114): Clark 29, Hargreaves 22, Thomas 21, Collins 12, Owen 12, Chilcott 7, Morgan 5, Bentley 2, Williams 2, Brinton 1, own goal 1.

1945-46

Artus KG 1	Clark DF 24	Guy I 33	Preece JC★ 11
Ashton E 3	Collins RD 15	Hancock G 1	Roberts D 36
Bailey EJ 34	Cousins KF 12	Hargreaves J 27	Silcocks L 5
Bentley RFT 19	Curran F 15	Hayward D 8	Sperring G 5
Booth L 1	Dymond WH 3	Howarth S★ 2	Sutton JB★ 2
Brinton EJ★ 1	Eddolls JD 9	Jones EJ 6	Thomas WG 24
Carter J 1	Fairhurst WG 7	Lovering W 3	Wedlock D 1
Chilcott K 24	Gadsby KJ★ 1	Morgan CI 32	Williams Cyril 30

Goals (81): Clark 21, Curran 10, Williams 10, Hargreaves 8, Bentley 7, Chilcott 6, Collins 5, Thomas 5, Lovering 4, Hayward 2, Guy 1, Roberts 1, own goal 1.

FA Cup goals (20): Clark 5, Chilcott 4, Williams 3, Curran 2, Morgan 2, Artus 1, Bentley 1, Hargreaves 1, Thomas 1.

Bristol Rovers

1939–40

Angus J*	1	Feebery A	3

Angus J* 1
Barber AW* 3
Booth L* 1
Britton CS* 3
Butterworth A 3
Buttery A 3
Caldwell R 21
Crack FW* 4
Curran F* 1

Feebery A 3
Fletcher AF 3
Forster WB 3
Gardiner R 3
Giles A 7
Iles AK 29
Kirby J* 20
Maggs P* 2
McArthur WJ 27

McNeil J* 1
Mitchinson F* 1
Morgan CI* 1
Nicholls JH 3
O'Mahoney M* 24
Smith HS 10
Smith WV 24
Tadman GH* 6
Talbot FL* 19

Taylor PH* 5
Topping H 26
Turner A* 1
Warren RR 10
Watson J 2
Watts R* 2
Weare AJ* 24
Whitfield W 27
Woodward W 18

Goals (64): Iles 14, Tadman 9, Talbot 9, Whitfield 7, Caldwell 4, O'Mahoney 4, Woodward 4, Barber 3, Crack 3, Curran 2, Warren 2, Kirby 1, McArthur 1, own goal 1.

War Cup goals (12): Woodward 4, Whitfield 3, Iles 2, Talbot 2, O'Mahoney 1.

1940–41

Did not compete.

1941–42

Did not compete.

1942–43

Did not compete.

1943–44

Did not compete.

1944–45

Did not compete.

1945–46

Baldie DW 5
Bamford HC 19
Binham C 1
Burgess RJ 1
Butterworth A 26
Clarke R 25
Davis R 10
Dixon W 1
Firth JW* 3

Gardiner R 3
Giles A 5
Gingell C 3
Hargett H 2
Hibbs L* 5
Lambden VD 35
Long C 7
McCourt F 3
McGahie J 13

Mills TJ 10
Morgan WJ 4
Petherbridge GE 19
Robbins D 1
Russell JS 6
Skinner G* 2
Smith HS 13
Smith WV 8
Studley E 5

Talbot FL* 10
Topping H 28
Warren RR 33
Watkins RB 34
Weare AJ 29
Whitfield W 37
Williams S* 1

Goals (72): Lambden 21, Clarke 15, Long 4, Petherbridge 4, Warren 4, Bamford 3, Butterworth 3, Talbot 3, Whitfield 3, Baldie 2, Hibbs 2, Morgan 2, Davis 1, Gardiner 1, Giles 1, McGahie 1, Mills 1, Russell 1.

FA Cup goals (6): Butterworth 2, Mills 2, Clarke 1, Whitfield 1.

Burnley

1939–40

Adams EF 11	Gardner T 23	Marshall JG 18	Smith GB★ 1
Bentley G 6	Hays CJ 3	Martindale L 8	Smith TS 14
Bray G 18	Hetherington TB★ 1	Mather H 22	Spencer H 1
Brocklebank RE 23	Hornby R 23	McIntosh JM★ 1	Taylor F 12
Clayton JG 6	Hulbert R★ 1	Moir J★ 1	Wood J★ 6
Dougall C★ 4	Kippax FP 1	Morton H 6	Woodruff A 22
Dryden J 2	Knight GR 22	Nuttall F★ 2	
Emptage AG★ 1	Lomax J 3	Robinson A 2	

Goals (49): Knight 12, Hornby 9, Brocklebank 8, Wood 6, Clayton 5, Taylor 5, Nuttall 2, Gardner 1, Moir 1.

War Cup goals (8): Hornby 3, Morris 3, Billingham 1, Brocklebank 1.

1940–41

Adams EF 6	Fairbrother J★ 6	Kirkman N 2	Potts H 1
Bentley G 3	Gardner T 36	Knight GR 19	Robinson A 14
Bray G 2	Holdcroft GH★ 5	Lomax J 14	Snowden R 13
Bright RL 17	Hornby R 36	Loughran J 17	Taylor F 1
Brocklebank RE 36	Jackson H 3	Marsden N★ 1	Wilkinson E 3
Coates F 14	Jackson P 1	Marshall JG 20	Woodruff A 36
Conway H★ 15	Jeavons WH★ 1	Martindale L 3	
Cooke W★ 5	Johnson REO 2	Mather H 35	
Dougall C 13	Kippax FP 25	Nuttall S★ 2	

Goals (65): Brocklebank 17, Kippax 16, Bright 6, Coates 6, Knight 6, Hornby 5, Cooke 4, Martindale 2, Wilkinson 2, Gardner 1.

1941–42

Bentley G 4	Harrison H 6	Lomax J 15	Snowden R 30
Bray G 4	Holdcroft GH★ 27	Marsden N 6	Strong GJ★ 2
Bright RL 12	Hornby R 29	Martindale L 3	Sutcliffe TC 4
Brocklebank RE 37	Jackson H 8	Mather H 1	Taylor F 3
Clayton JG 1	Jackson P 1	Prest TW★ 1	Waddington RH 9
Coates F 2	Johnson REO 3	Readett H★ 4	Ward F 9
Crossland B 1	Jones D★ 1	Richmond G 2	Whalley H 17
Deverall HR★ 1	Kippax FP 22	Robinson A 20	Woodruff A 36
Gardner T 36	Kirkman N 25	Sagar WH★ 1	
Gastall JWH★ 1	Knight GR 1	Salmon L 19	
Gibson S★ 1	Lawson J 1	Smith TS 1	

Goals (65): Brocklebank 19, Kippax 13, Gardner 10, Hornby 5, Whalley 4, Jackson H 5, Waddington 3, Bright 2, Clayton 1, Salmon 1, own goals 2.

1942–43

Allen BJ★ 1	Dougall C 1	Manning J★ 7	Shields T★ 1
Bannister JA 2	Gardner T 31	Marsden N 1	Shorthouse WH★ 1
Barker J★ 1	Holdcroft GH★ 31	Martindale L 1	Smith TS 1
Bentley G 1	Holden JK 1	Mather H 3	Snowden R 19
Birch HJ★ 1	Hornby R 12	McEwan W★ 1	Taylor F 1
Bray G 3	Horton JC★ 1	Newsome R★ 2	Taylor W★ 1
Bright RL 18	Jackson H 9	O'Donnell H★ 17	Waddington RH 14
Brindle J 2	Keighley G 9	Readett H 7	Ward F 1
Brocklebank RE 20	Kippax FP 4	Riddiough HH★ 1	Watson WT★ 13
Carter DF★ 1	Kirkham N 4	Roach JE★ 1	Webster R★ 19
Crawshaw C★ 5	Knight GR 1	Robinson A 24	Wigglesworth E 3
Crossland B 1	Lomax J 8	Rudman H 15	Woodruff A 30

Goals (52): Bright 8, Gardner 7, Jackson 6, Waddington 6, Crawshaw 4, O'Donnell 4, Kippax 3, Robinson 3, Brocklebank 2, Hornby 2, McEwan 2, Manning 2, Brindle 1, Webster 1, own goal 1.

1943–44

Batley CF★ 1	Hargreaves H 1	Mather H 16	Slingsby GE★ 1
Bentley G 2	Holden JK 3	McGahie J★ 3	Smith TS 5
Bray G 3	Hornby R 7	McNee C★ 1	Snowden R 5
Bright RL 2	Horner L★ 1	Potts H 3	Spencer H 2
Brindle J 1	Jackson H 6	Reeday M★ 3	Strong GJ★ 30
Brocklebank RE 33	Johnson REO 4	Reid JM 19	Taylor JG★ 5
Burns OH 1	Keighley G 3	Reynolds J★ 1	Walmsley J★ 2
Clayton JG 1	Kippax FP 8	Robinson A 21	Ward F 1
Cook L★ 1	Kirby N★ 1	Rose NJ★ 1	Watson WT★ 23
Dougall C 3	Knight GR 2	Rudman H 28	Webster R★ 25
Edwards G★ 1	Loughran J 1	Russell DW★ 3	Williams R★ 1
Gallon JW★ 2	MacFarlane R★ 2	Sargent F★ 21	Woodruff A 36
Gardner T 36	Mansley C★ 2	Scott W★ 1	
Geddes A★ 6	Marshall JG 4	Sibley ET★ 1	

Goals (63): Brocklebank 16, Gardner 12, Jackson 7, Watson 5, Reid 3, Robinson 3, Bright 2, Hornby 2, Potts 2, Rudman 2, Sargent 2, Snowden 2, Burns 1, Kippax 1, MacFarlane 1, own goals 2.

1944–45

Bradford L★ 12	Dryden J 5	Makin G★ 3	Smith J 3
Bray G 10	Edwards WJ★ 1	Marshall JG 3	Spencer H 1
Brereton GA★ 1	Gallimore L★ 25	Martindale L 44	Strong JG★ 41
Bright RL 3	Gardner T 38	Mather H 16	Taylor K★ 2
Brocklebank RE 38	Henderson T 3	McCavana T 1	Tonge J★ 2
Brooks W 18	Hodgeon J 1	Mignot N★ 1	Watson WT★ 2
Burns OH 5	Holden JK 6	Moss L★ 2	Webster R★ 36
Clarkson RV★ 1	Holdsworth R★ 1	Patterson GL★ 21	Whittaker W★ 3
Conway H★ 1	Jackson H 10	Potts H 4	Woodruff A 39
Crossland B 2	Kinghorn WJD★ 12	Reid JM 1	Wyles TC★ 2
Crowther K 1	Kippax FP 13	Robinson A 17	
Dougall C 1	Kirkman N 7	Rudman H 14	
Drury GB★ 6	Loom B★ 2	Salmon L 3	

Goals (95): Gardner 15, Brocklebank 14, Brooks 11, Jackson 9, Martindale 9, Patterson 8, Kinghorn 6, Dryden 4, Potts 3, Rudman 3, Burns 2, Drury 2, Kippax 2, Bright 1, Mignot 1, Reid 1, Salmon 1, Smith 1, Webster 1, Wyles 1.

1945–46

Ancell R★ 2	Foxcroft G★ 1	Kippax FP 24	Roach JE★ 1
Attwell RF★ 15	Gardner T 14	Knight J 2	Rudman H 18
Bowden NH★ 1	Haigh G 20	Loughran J 11	Shreeve JTT★ 7
Bray G 19	Harrison RW 2	Martindale L 2	Sidlow C★ 2
Breedon J 4	Hays CJ 23	Mather H 35	Sneddon D★ 2
Brooks W 1	Hobson A★ 5	McBain – 2	Soo F★ 3
Bunter – 1	Hodgson J 2	Meek J★ 3	Spencer H 7
Burns OH 5	Hold O★ 8	Milner P★ 3	Strong GJ 24
Campbell R★ 1	Hornby R 3	Morris W 22	Taylor F 1
Chew JE 25	Innard D★ 3	Mulraney D★ 3	Wigglesworth E 4
Crowther K 7	Jackson H 29	Owens JE 2	Wilson C★ 15
Drury GB★ 9	Johnson R 26	Potts H 1	Woodruff A 42

Goals (63): Jackson 18, Morris 12, Kippax 9, Hays 8, Hold 4, Chew 2, Crowther 2, Drury 2, Attwell 1, Brooks 1, Haigh 1, Hornby 1, own goals 2.

FA Cup goals (3): Jackson 1, Kippax 1, Morris 1.

Bury

1939–40

Bradshaw GF   22
Burdett T   21
Carter DFA   19
Davies G   10
Dougal P   22
Fairhurst WG   3

Gemmell J   25
Griffiths W   3
Halton RL   25
Hart JL   4
Hulbert R   13
Jones D   22

Kelly J   3
Kilshaw EA   3
Livingstone A   25
Matthewson G   4
McGowan J   17
McNeill HJ   3

Olsen TB   3
Roberts F   3
Robinson A★   22
Wood JH   3

Goals (68): Burdett 20, Carter 10, Davies 8, Halton 6, Livingstone 6, Jones 5, Dougal 3, Hulbert 3, Wood 2, Kelly 1, Kilshaw 1, McNeill 1, Roberts 1, own goal 1.

War Cup goals (1): Carter 1.

1940–41

Anderson RJ   1
Aston WV   3
Atkinson JE★   10
Bradshaw GF   22
Burdett T   10
Burnham W   6
Carter DFA   36
Chadwick RA   2
Clarke R   1
Dalton RT   1
Davies G   34

Dougal P   23
Fairhurst WG   4
Filbey A   1
Goodall EI★   6
Gorman WC★   14
Griffiths G   6
Griffiths W   33
Halton RL   4
Hart JL   20
Holdcroft GH★   1
Hornby R   4

Hubbick H★   17
Hulbert R   10
Jones D   36
Jones WEA★   3
Kilshaw EA   1
Knight J★   1
Livingstone A   23
Matthewson G   1
McNeill HJ   10
Murray J   1
Newton F★   1

Olsen TB   2
Pollard F   3
Quigley E   10
Robbie DM   1
Roberts F   5
Robinson A★   22
Slack L   8
Walton J   5
Watson JF   31
Whitfield W   7

Goals (85): Davies 39, Carter 14, Burdett 6, Dougal 6, Jones D 6, Livingstone 6, Hulbert 2, Chadwick 1, McNeill 1, Olsen 1, Slack 1, Watson 1, own goal 1.

1941–42

Ashworth JS   2
Atkinson JE★   1
Ayres D   2
Bacuzzi J★   5
Bebb D   10
Bell A   1
Bradshaw GF   3
Burdett T   3
Burnham W   5
Carlisle E   6
Carter DFA   16
Clark R★   1

Davies G   32
Davies J★   1
Dougal P   25
Dykes L   2
Evans K   7
Fairhurst WG   1
Gemmell J   17
Graham W★   1
Griffiths G   22
Griffiths W   33
Halton RL   4
Hart JL   17

Jenkinson F   1
Jones D   24
Livingstone A   12
Marshall A★   1
Marshall GB   3
Mather H   1
Matthewson G   3
Middleham RA   8
Olsen TB   4
Pollard F   1
Poole WG   2
Prescott J★   1

Quigley E   30
Rawlings JSD★   2
Roberts F   5
Robinson A★   1
Robinson L   4
Russell DAP★   4
Self RE★   1
Urmston TK   8
Waters W   8
Watson JF   6
Whitworth H   2
Worsley H★   14

Goals (83): Davies G 35, Carter 14, Urmston 9, Livingstone 5, Jones 4, Olsen 3, Burdett 2, Roberts 2, Bebb 1, Dougal 1, Evans 1, Gemmell 1, Griffiths W 1, Middleham 1, Robinson L 1, Self 1, Worsley 1.

1942–43

Berry N   3
Birch N★   1
Black W   10
Bradshaw GF   3
Burdett T   6
Carter DFA   27
Carver –   1
Charlton JW   2
Davies G   33
Davies P   1
Dougal P   8
Duncan J   7

Gemmell J   10
Griffiths G   22
Griffiths W   33
Halton RL   4
Hart JL   28
Hill F   1
Horsfield A★   6
Jones D   22
Jordan W★   1
Lawrence –   1
Lewis P   6
Livingstone A   1

Matthewson G   20
Maudsley J★   2
Middleham RA   3
Moss J   7
Murphy D★   2
Olsen TB   1
Potts HJ   16
Quigley E   18
Redpath J   1
Riddiough HH★   1
Roberts F   3
Robinson A★   1

Robinson L   20
Roby S★   1
Smith J   5
Smith R★   1
Taylor F★   1
Taylor LT★   3
Tomlinson RW★   1
Urmston TK   3
Watson JF   1
Whitehead GK★   25
Whitworth H   1

Goals (97): Davies G 40, Carter 16, Robinson L 11, Black 5, Quigley 5, Griffiths W 3, Burdett 3, Urmston 2, Roberts 2, Dougal 1, Halton 1, Horsfield 1, Jones 1, Lewis 1, Moss 1, Potts 1, Roby 1, Whitworth 1, own goal 1.

1943–44

Ainsworth A★   3
Anderson C   3
Anderson RA   4
Berry N   3
Birch NJ   1
Black W   19
Bradshaw GF   27
Brocklebank R★   1
Brooks G★   1
Burdett T   1
Burnham W   4
Burtenwood –★   1
Caldicott R   14
Carter DFA   28
Cheetham TF   4

Davies G   17
Duncan J   5
Eastwood J★   1
Gemmell J   1
Graham W★   1
Griffiths G   34
Griffiths W   33
Hallam J   9
Halton RL   4
Hamilton W★   28
Hammond WE★   1
Hardman J   3
Hart JL   36
Holland KA   2
Hopkins F★   1

Horsfield A★   4
Hulbert R   1
Jones D   14
Jones J★   1
Lewis P   2
Maculey J★   1
Mather H   1
Matthewson G   4
Meaney T   2
Moss J   18
Potts HJ   4
Quigley E   5
Ranson G   1
Redpath J   1
Revell C★   12

Roberts F   3
Robinson L   19
Smethurst J   4
Smith J   3
Snowden A★   2
Swift A   1
Topping H★   1
Walmsley J★   1
Watson JF   9
White G   1
Whitworth H   8
Windle C★   4
Wright HT★   1

Goals (69): Carter 12, Revell 12, Robinson L 9, Berry 6, Davies G 6, Griffiths W 6, Black 5, Ainsworth 2, Anderson 2, Caldicott 2, Moss 2, Potts 2, Horsfield 1, Meaney 1, Ranson 1.

1944–45

Berry N   16
Black W   2
Blunt E★   27
Bradshaw GF   24
Burdett T   1
Burrows A★   7
Caldicott R   1
Carter DFA   15
Collier AJ   5
Cornthwaite T   1

Davies G   26
Drury GB★   35
Edwards –★   1
Gemmell J   7
Gorman WC★   29
Greenhalgh F   1
Griffiths G   32
Griffiths W   36
Halton RL   6
Hamilton W★   9

Hart JL   24
Hayward DS   1
Holland KA   14
Horsfield A★   2
Ingham D   1
Jenkins A   9
Jones D   13
Livingstone A   9
Lyons AE   4
McFeat –★   9

Meaney T   8
Potts HJ   4
Renshaw C   3
Roberts F   2
Rowland –   1
Stott S   5
Watson JF   3
Whitworth H   3
Wilde RP   7
Worsley H★   15

Goals (66): Drury 16, Davies 14, Berry 9, Livingstone 7, Griffiths W 6, Carter 4, Halton 3, Blunt 2, Gemmell 1, Greenhalgh 1, Meaney 1, Stott 1, Wilde 1.

1945–46

Aston WV   11
Berry N   26
Bickerstaffe J   1
Black W   1
Blunt E★   8
Bradshaw GF   39
Carter DFA   1
Davies G   27
Fairclough C   10
Graham W★   1
Greenhalgh F   9

Hart JL   37
Griffiths G   39
Griffiths W   24
Halton RL   32
Herbert F   12
Howarth S   11
Hulbert R★   3
Jenkins A   3
Jones D   22
Kilshaw EA   13
Littler J★   2

Quigley E   8
Livingstone A   19
Lyons AE   5
Makin G★   1
McGill J   2
Meaney T   1
Moss J   31
Roberts F   7
Robinson A★   1
Taylor A   2
Tompkin M   19

Van Gelden J★   1
Warburton G   1
Watson JF   15
Whitehead G   1
Whitworth H   13
Wood A★   1
Yates –★   2

Goals (60): Berry 14, Davies 9, Moss 6, Halton 5, Livingstone 4, Blunt 3, Greenhalgh 3, Whitworth 3, Jones 2, Quigley 2, Griffiths G 1, Herbert 1, Hulbert 1, Kilshaw 1, Tompkin 1, Watson 1, Yates 1, own goals 2.

FA Cup goals (13): Davies 3, Roberts 3, Halton 2, Jones 2, McGill 1, Moss 1, Tompkin 1.

Cardiff City

1939–40

Anderson RS   2
Baker WG   8
Ballsom WG   23
Booth WS   27
Boulter LM★   2
Britton CS★   1
Clark TG★   9
Collins JH   12
Cope JJ★   10
Corkhill WG   4
Court HJ   12
Cringan JA   3
Cumner RH★   2
Egan H   4

Fielding W   3
Ford L   4
Forse T   1
Granville A   27
Green –   1
Griffiths W   1
Hill CJ   1
Hogg G★   5
James WJ   20
Jones B★   10
Kelso J   2
Lewis AC★   3
Marshall E   30
McPhillips L   3

Meades R   1
Mitchell JW   1
Moore JFB   5
Morrelli –   1
Morris T   3
Myers JH   3
Nicholson WE★   1
Owen WM★   2
Parker G★   5
Poland G★   2
Pritchard FJ★   1
Prosser C   2
Pugh JHB   1
Pugh R   24

Reid CH   9
Rooney J★   5
Sabin G   12
Scott W   2
Smith JA★   1
Steggles J★   4
Sykes EA   3
Tobin R★   3
Tucker –   1
Wilkinson R★   15
Williams TD   2
Wood TL   1
Woodward L★   1

Goals (50): Collins 7, Marshall 7, Court 6, Pugh R 5, James 4, Sabin 3, Boulter 2, Egan 2, Meades 2, Moore 2, Parker 2, Tobin 2, Anderson 1, Baker 1, Corkhill 1, Morris 1, Owen 1, own goal 1.

War Cup goals (1): Mitchell 1.

1940–41

Allen J   2
Baker WG   22
Barry P★   1
Burns JC   10
Butler SJ   1
Charlesworth S★   1
Court HJ   1
Dodge J   1
Forse T★   1
Glass FW   1
Goddard R★   3

Granville A   19
Griffiths KJ   1
Hall FN   2
Hart PJ   1
Hollyman KC   5
Hyman R   1
James WJ   29
Jones E   1
Jones HA   13
Joy H   3
Meades R   1

Moore JFB   30
Morgan GW   1
Morris AD★   2
Parker LT   30
Phillips RJ   2
Pritchard FJ   27
Pritchard GC   1
Pugh JHB   29
Pugh R   11
Reid CH   1
Rooney J★   2

Scott W   3
Smith CE   1
Springthorpe TA★   1
Steggles EJ   14
Stitfall AE   1
Tobin R   26
Williams JA   1
Wood TL   25
Wrigglesworth W★   2

Goals (94): Moore 32, James 29, Parker 16, Baker 2, Hollyman 2, Morris 2, Pugh J 2, Burns 1, Joy 1, Scott 1, Steggles 1, Tobin 1, Williams 1, Wood 1, Wrigglesworth 1, own goal 1.

1941–42

Baker WG   2
Butler SJ   3
Carey JJ★   1
Carter HS★   1
Chilton A★   3
Clarke AW★   1
Dare R   14
Dunstan R   1
Fenton BRV★   5
Griffiths KJ   14
Griffiths WR   20
Gristock FC   1
Hargreaves J★   1
Hollyman KC   34

Hustwick DC   1
James WJ   7
Jarman WJ   2
Jones EN★   1
Jones HA   22
Jones JA   2
Lewis I★   5
Lewis W   11
Macaulay JAR★   1
Marshall E   8
McKenzie J★   1
McLoughlin KJA   3
Mitten C★   1
Moore JFB   35

Morgan GW   2
Morris T   11
Owen IJ   3
Parker LT   25
Parr J★   1
Parry DJ   4
Paul R★   1
Phillips JRW   34
Presdee HG   1
Pritchard GC   1
Pugh JHB   34
Sabin G   2
Sargeant G   1
Shelley A★   1

Sheppard S   1
Sherwood AT   2
Steggles EJ   9
Stitfall AE   2
Stuart D   1
Thomas RA★   1
Tobin R   6
Tomkin AH★   1
Weir A★   11
Whatley WC   1
Wood TL   18
Wright GA   10

Goals (102): Moore 28, Parker 28, James 8, Weir 8, Wood 6, Wright 4, Fenton 3, Hollyman 3, Dare 2, Lewis 2, Shelley 2, Butler 1, Griffiths K 1, Lewis I 1, Morgan 1, Morris 1, Parr 1, Steggles 1, Thomas 1.

1942–43

Artus K★ 1
Bewley R 1
Bird FHW 10
Bradshaw GF★ 2
Chedgzoy S★ 2
Clarke AW★ 1
Clarke R 28
Collis R 3
Conway G 7
Corbett W★ 1
Courtier L 1
Daly J 2
Dare R 1
Davies DT 1
Devonshire KA 2
Downs R 1
Drury S 1
Edwards WJ 9

Ford L 5
Fursland S★ 1
Gilchrist M 1
Gilthrow – 1
Gregory F 1
Griffiths KJ 21
Griffiths WR 27
Gristock FC 1
Grocott T 1
Hollyman KC 7
Hustwick DC 1
Jenkins FAV 1
Jones HA 30
Jones JA 24
Kinsey N 1
Lester LJ 2
Lewis W 1
Macaulay JAR★ 3

Mackay R★ 1
McDonald JC★ 2
McLoughlin KJA 6
Mitchell JW 1
Moore JFB 32
Morgan CS 9
Morgan D 1
Murphy J★ 2
Nairn J★ 1
Orphan LJ 1
Owen IJ 3
Palfrey VN★ 1
Parker LT 23
Phillips JRW 6
Pugh JHB 9
Rees N 2
Richards TJ 2
Sargeant G 1

Shankly W★ 1
Sherwood AT 32
Sneddon W 1
Sparshott G 2
Stitfall AE 2
Stitfall RF 2
Tame A 1
Thomas WP 1
Turner H★ 2
Turner ML 1
Vrapehart W★ 2
Welsh ME 3
Williams AC 1
Willicombe WT 2
Wood TL 1
Wright GA 25

Goals (63): Clarke 20, Moore 12, Griffiths K 5, Morgan 5, Wright 4, Daly 2, Grocott 2, Macaulay 2, Nairn 2, Parker 2, Sparshott 2, Evans 1, Murphy 1, Pugh 1, Willicombe 1, own goal 1.

1943–44

Bufton T 1
Carless E 15
Chew J★ 13
Clarke R 28
Court HJ 2
Dare R 1
Davies DT 2
Gibson TH 9
Griffiths KJ 2

Griffiths WR 23
James KHL 1
Jones HA 22
Jones JA 3
Kinsey N 1
Lester LJ 3
Lever AR 39
McIntosh A 7
McLoughlin KJA 2

Moore JFB 39
Parker LT 1
Parker WE★ 1
Phillips JRW 2
Pugh JHB 15
Raybould ME 29
Rees W 19
Richards TJ 1
Rowlands V 1

Sherwood AT 38
Smith AOS 5
Stansfield F 39
Steggles EJ 4
Williams W 31
Wood TL 28
Wright GA 2

Goals (98): Moore 19, Rees 16, Williams 14, Clarke 12, Gibson 7, Raybould 7, Carless 5, Wood 5, Sherwood 4, Steggles 3, Court 1, Dare 1, Griffiths K 1, Lester 1, own goals 2.

1944–45

Allen BW★ 1
Booth WS 1
Brain H★ 4
Brooks H★ 1
Cain G★ 1
Canning D 1
Carless E 8
Clarke R 36
Crisp GH★ 1
Davies DT 1

Day GE 2
Evans LT 1
Forse T 1
Foxey –★ 1
Gibson CH 36
Griffiths KJ 1
Griffiths WR 1
Hill C 1
Hollyman KC 3
Jones HA 2

Lester LJ 36
Lever AR 38
Lewis LC★ 1
Lewis T 1
McLoughlin KJA 2
Moore JFB 32
Moore R 2
Phillips JRW 19
Pollard J 1
Raybould ME 4

Rees W 38
Rowlands V 7
Sherwood AT 37
Smith AOS 34
Stansfield F 37
Steggles EJ 1
Tennant DW 2
Wood TL 22

Goals (95): Rees 34, Wood 18, Clarke 14, Moore B 12, Gibson 6, Carless 4, Lester 3, Hollyman 2, Lever 1, Moore R 1, Raybould 1.

Includes one extra-time goal.

1945–46

Allen BW 18
Baker WG 5
Canning D 9
Carless E 11
Clarke R 36
Foulkes WI 5
Gibson CH 25
Griffiths WR 1

Haddon HL 2
Hill C 2
Hollyman KC 32
Jones R 1
Lester LJ 19
Lever AR 26
Lewis W 1
Marshall E 2

McLoughlin KJA 9
Moore JFB 8
Phillips JRW 3
Raybould ME 25
Rees W 25
Richards SV 11
Rowlands TL 1
Sherwood AT 30

Smith AOS 17
Stansfield F 32
Tennant DW 1
Tobin R 3
Wager L 1
Wood TL 24
Wright GA 11

Goals (108): Rees 25, Clarke 23, Allen 12, Wood 7, Gibson 6, Richards 6, Hollyman 5, Wright 5, Carless 4, Moore 4, Hill 2, Lever 2, Haddon 1, Lester 1, Tennant 1, own goals 4.

FA Cup goals (1): Allen 1.

Carlisle United

1939–40

Adamson RM　2
Adey W*　4
Allison JJ*　1
Ancell RFD*　1
Annables W　2
Armstrong T　1
Baxendale F　1
Bickerstaffe J*　4
Blackadder L*　1
Blackshaw HK*　3
Bradford L*　1
Burgon FA　2
Clarke B　2
Curry RV　1
Dellow RW　2

Douglas W*　1
Fairbairn GH*　1
Finlay J*　4
Gallagher –　1
Gibson G*　6
Gorman J*　13
Hamilton S　4
Howshall JH　5
Hunt SW　9
Jones D　3
Kerr TM　19
Knox T*　3
Laidler JR*　12
Mansley C*　1
Maxfield J　2

McAlister J　6
McGuinness L　16
McLaren A*　1
Middleton MY*　8
Mills H　23
Moir J*　4
Pallister GJ*　2
Patrick JC*　13
Pond H　2
Pratt J*　6
Russell JW*　16
Sanderson JR*　6
Savage RE*　1
Scholfield –*　5
Smith JT*　2

Smith W*　1
Spuhler JO*　2
Steele E*　2
Sullivan –*　6
Taylor A　9
Thompson C*　9
Torney –*　2
Trainor P*　1
Wallbanks WH　3
Weston RP*　1
Wharton JE*　1
Wilson A*　4

Goals (41): Mills 10, Moir 7, Patrick 5, Russell 5, Hunt 3, Smith J 2, Thompson 2, Blackshaw 1, Dellow 1, Gibson 1, Kerr 1, Laidler 1, Sullivan 1, own goal 1.

War Cup goals: 0.

1940–41

Did not compete.

1941–42

Did not compete.

1942–43

Did not compete.

1943–44

Did not compete.

1944–45

Did not compete.

1945–46

Adams W*　20
Armstrong T　2
Binns C　9
Bokas F　23
Bowes S　1
Broadis IA*　20
Cape J　24
Clark T　8
Connor JT*　25
Dellow RW　28
Douglas D　10
Edwards CI*　6

Elliott E*　11
Elliott G　1
Gallagher –*　5
Hamilton S　5
Hayton E　9
Hendon –*　1
Higgins F*　6
Hindmarsh E　34
Holden GL*　6
Horrigan K　6
Howe J*　1
Jones D　12

King D　20
Kirkpatrick J　10
Lawson R　4
Leicester J　7
Lomas W*　1
Maxfield J　1
McBride W　9
McGorrighan F　2
McKeown J*　1
McKerrell D　12
Meredith R　7
Monk T　5

Pond H　4
Pridmore AJ*　2
Reay L　9
Russell J*　1
Russell JW*　2
Sanderson JR*　2
Taylor A　24
Tweedie J　2
Vetch DD*　3
Woolacott H　6

Goals (84): Connor 28, Cape 17, Broadis 10, Dellow 6, Kirkpatrick 4, Adams 3, McKerrell 3, McKeown 2, Clark 1, Douglas 1, Gallagher 1, Hayton 1, Howe 1, Leicester 1, Lomas 1, Meredith 1, Russell JW 1, own goals 2.

FA Cup goals (13): Cape 3, Clark 3, Hamilton 3, Adamson R 2, Dellow 1, Douglas 1.

Charlton Athletic

1939–40

Astley DJ★   4
Bartram S   27
Brown ARJ   39
Calland R★   1
Cann ST   2
Casserley W   1
Dawson T   2
Dryden JG   1
Etherton PR   1
Ford FGL   12

Furmage E   3
Gillespie IC★   1
Green GH   23
Hall SA★   3
Hammond WE   2
Hicks G   1
Hobbins SG   7
Hobbis HHF   34
Jobling J   12
Lancelotte EC   1

Lawton T★   2
Mordey HV   1
Oakes James   5
Oakes John   33
Owens TL★   2
Revell C   9
Robinson GH   29
Sanders JA   1
Shreeve JTT   1
Smith GC   11

Swift FV★   1
Tadman GH   13
Tann BJ   8
Thomas RA★   10
Tully FA★   1
Turner HG   32
Welsh D   30
Whittaker WP   8
Wilkinson JM   16
Wright RCA   39

Goals (103): Welsh 33, Brown 18, Tadman 14, Robinson 8, Hobbis 5, Thomas 4, Revell 4, Smith 3, Wilkinson 3, Oakes John 2, Wright 2, Astley 1, Dawson 1, Gillespie 1, Green 1, Tann 1, Turner 1, own goal 1.

War Cup goals (1): Smith 1.

1940–41

Brown ARJ   1
Dryden JG   5
Etherton PR   4
Ford FGL   1
Furmage E   1
Gibbs SG   1
Green GH   15

Hammond WE   11
Hobbins SG   18
Hobbis HHF   16
Jobling J   19
Kurz FJ★   9
Lancelotte EC   17
Oakes John   16

Owens TL★   4
Revell C   17
Robinson GH   19
Smith GC   5
Turner HG   2
Walker J★   1
Watts R★   1

Welsh D   2
Whittaker WP   17
Wilkinson J   2
Wright RCA   4

Ten players 30.11.40 v West Ham U

Goals (37): Kurz 9, Revell 7, Hobbis 6, Robinson 6, Lancelotte 2, Welsh 2, Dryden 1, Etherton 1, Gibbs 1, Green 1, Smith 1.

1941–42

Bartram S   15
Baxter AG★   10
Beasley A★   1
Brown ARJ   5
Cann ST   32
Catlin AE★   3
Croom W★   1
Dryden JG   5
Dykes J★   1
Etherton PR   1

Ford FGL   5
Foxall JS★   1
Gee H   1
Geldard A★   13
Gibbs SG   3
Green GH   27
Hammond WE   1
Hobbins SG   19
Hobbis HHF   31
Jobling J   10

Lancelotte EC   7
Lewis E★   1
Mason J★   13
Mordey HV   3
Muttitt E★   1
Oakes John   32
Phipps HJ   15
Revell C   26
Sanders JA   3
Shreeve JTT   6

Smith GC   31
Tadman TH   9
Turner HG   6
Watson G★   1
Weightman E★   15
Welsh D   19
Whitfield R   1
Whittaker WP   33

Goals (89): Revell 16, Welsh 16, Hobbis 12, Green 10, Tadman 9, Smith 6, Baxter 3, Lancelotte 3, Mason 3, Brown 2, Dryden 2, Geldard 2, Ford 1, Gibbs 1, Oakes 1, Watson 1, Whittaker 1.

1942–43

Barnes JB★   1
Bartram S   2
Blackman JJ★   1
Brown ARJ   6
Calland R★   1
Cann ST   28
Davies CJ★   16
Delaney L★   3
Dryden JG   15
Duffy C★   20
Dugnolle JH★   1
Etherton PR   6
Fenton BRV★   1
Ford FGL   1

Geldard A★   1
Gibbs SG   1
Giddings P★   1
Green GH   22
Hanks J★   1
Hobbins SG   34
Hobbis HHF   21
Holland FC★   1
Hooper M★   9
Hunt JK★   3
Jobling J   21
Kinnell R★   2
Kippax FP★   1
Lancelotte EC   2

Mason J★   19
Mellish R   1
Money A★   1
Mulraney A★   6
Nash LD   1
Oakes John   30
Phipps HJ   20
Purvis B★   1
Revell C   22
Reynolds GAC★   4
Richardson JR★   1
Robinson GH   4
Shaw R★   1
Shreeve JTT   5

Sinclair MJ★   1
Smith C★   13
Smith GC   13
Stewart G (Dundee)★   1
Stewart G (Hamilton)★   3
Tadman GH   2
Tadman MR   1
Tann BJ   1
Thompson A★   1
Turner HG   6
Wales H★   4
Welsh D   9
Whittaker WP   3

Goals (91): Revell 21, Dryden 11, Green 11, Smith G 8, Welsh 8, Duffy 5, Hobbis 4, Hooper 4, Mason 4, Delaney 3, Mulraney 3, Brown 2, Kinnell 2, Davies 1, Etherton 1, Smith C 1, Stewart G (Hamilton) 1, Tadman G 1.

1943–44

Bartram S 6
Bray G* 1
Brown ARJ 27
Callegari S 4
Cann ST 7
Cassidy J* 1
Chilton A* 21
Croker PH 3
Davie J* 4
Davies CJ* 6
Davies JW* 1
Duffy C* 27
Embleton E* 2
Etherton PR 1
Furmage E 1
Gallacher P* 1

Gay A 1
Gibbs SG 1
Green GH 6
Hall C 3
Hobbins SG 23
Hobbis HHF 14
Jobling J 29
Keen ERL* 3
Kernick DG* 1
Kerr AW* 1
Law A* 1
Liddle J* 2
Mather H* 4
McFarlane W* 1
McSpadyen A* 1
McTavish – 1

Moore NW* 4
Mulvaney J* 1
Oakes John 31
Pearson CF 5
Phipps HJ 2
Revell C 11
Reynolds GAC* 1
Robinson W* 20
Rogers J 1
Ross J* 1
Sanders JA 9
Sargeant CA 1
Scott FH* 13
Shreeve JTT 23
Shrimpton HG 3
Skinner G* 1

Smith GC 21
Tann BJ 2
Thomas RA* 1
Turner AA 3
Turner HG 3
Ubee J* 1
Wales H* 15
Warboys AG 2
Welsh D 7
Whittaker WP 12
Wilson C 1
Wilson R* 10
Woodcock A* 4
Wright RCA 4

Goals (75): Revell 15, Robinson 12, Brown 10, Scott 8, Welsh 6, Duffy 4, Shrimpton 2, Smith 2, Turner A 2, Woodcock 2, Davie 1, Embleton 1, Furmage 1, Gallacher 1, Jobling 1, Law 1, Liddle 1, Moore 1, Oakes 1, Ross 1, Thomas 1, Wilson R 1.

Additional goalscorer in Cup-Winners' Cup: Revell.

1944–45

Bartram S 4
Broome FH* 1
Brown ARJ 24
Callegari S 3
Campbell J 2
Clarke EJ 1
Crack FW* 4
Crisp AJ 14
Croker PH 33
Curzon WA 1
Dawson T 1
Eden E* 1
Etherton PR 9
Farmer A* 1

Fell LJ 20
Fenton BRV* 10
Ford FGL 1
Furmage E 3
Gallacher P* 1
Gilberg H* 1
Graham J 1
Green GH 1
Hall C 6
Hammond CS 1
Hobbis HHF 33
Hollis H* 1
Hubble L* 3
Jennings J 2

Jobling J 34
Johnson WH 4
Mellish R 1
Morris J* 4
Oakes John 30
Revell C 10
Rothery H* 1
Salmon L* 4
Sanders JA 32
Shreeve JTT 2
Smith GC 23
Stevens LWJ 1
Tadman GH 3
Tadman MR 16

Tann BJ 2
Taylor JR 1
Thomas KC 2
Turner AA 20
Turner HG 1
Wales H* 5
Welsh D 6
Whitchurch CH* 1
Whittaker WP 7
Williams TG* 1
Yates R* 2

Goals (88): Turner A 17, Revell 14, Tadman M 9, Hobbis 8, Brown 6, Fell 6, Welsh 5, Crisp 4, Fenton 4, Green 3, Crack 2, Etherton 2, Smith 2, Callegari 1, Ford 1, Hubble 1, Johnson 1, Taylor 1, Yates 1.

1945–46

Bartram S 41
Brown ARJ 31
Cann ST 1
Croker PH 36
Dawson T 8
Duffy C 33

Fell LJ 35
Hobbis HHF 13
Jobling J 9
Johnson WH 37
Oakes John 31
Phipps HJ 6

Revell C 9
Rist FH 16
Robinson GH 12
Sanders JA 1
Shreeve JTT 30
Smith GC 7

Tadman GH 5
Tadman MR 7
Turner AA 33
Turner HG 25
Welsh D 36

Goals (92): Turner A 27, Welsh 26, Duffy 17, Fell 7, Revell 4, Tadman M 4, Brown 3, Johnson 2, Robinson 1, Smith 1.

FA Cup goals (29): Duffy 10, Turner A 7, Welsh 4, Fell 3, Brown 1, Robinson 1, Tadman M 1, Turner H 1, own goal 1.

Chelsea

1939–40

Abel S★ 1	Crook W★ 1	Mayes AJ 18	Smale DM 2
Alexander DB 25	Dickie M 2	Mills GR 22	Smith AJ 19
Argue J 1	Farmer A★ 2	Mitchell W 2	Smith JF 25
Barber GF 33	Foss SR 13	O'Hare J 19	Spence R 33
Bott W★ 1	Griffiths R 10	Payne J 33	Strauss W★ 2
Brown ARJ★ 1	Hanson AJ 3	Pugh SJ★ 1	Tennant AE 2
Buchanan PS 15	Jackson J 20	Reay EP★ 1	Vaux E 3
Burgess H 8	James D 3	Ridyard A★ 1	Weaver S 36
Busby M★ 4	Kiernan T★ 7	Salmond RC 32	Woodley VR 19
Butler MP★ 1	Lowe HP★ 2	Sherborne JL 6	

Goals (81): Payne 34, Mills 8, Spence 7, Buchanan 6, Smith JF 5, Weaver 5, Alexander 3, Sherborne 3, Strauss 3, Burgess 2, Foss 2, Brown 1, James 1, Kiernan 1.

War Cup goals (2): Hanson 1, Kiernan 1.

1940–41

Alexander DB 1	Galloway JA★ 14	Kilduff G★ 8	O'Hare J 12
Barber GF 24	Greenwood R 1	Kurz FJ★ 10	Salmond RC 13
Bedford G★ 1	Griffiths R 22	Lyon W 7	Smith AJ 13
Chalkley AG★ 1	Hardwick GFM★ 2	Macaulay JAR 15	Smith GC★ 4
Clatworthy L 3	Hipkin RW★ 1	March R★ 1	Smith JF 8
Clifton H★ 1	Jackson J 20	Mercer J★ 3	Spence R 28
Etherton RP★ 1	James D 1	Mills GR 14	Tennant AE 20
Foss SR 15	Jones EN★ 11	Milton GW★ 1	Weaver S 18
Friend AF 2	Kiernan T★ 13	Molloy P★ 1	Woodley VR 9

Goals (71): Spence 15, Galloway 9, Foss 7, Kurz 7, Mills 7, Jones 5, Kiernan 5, Kilduff 5, Smith JF 3, Tennant 2, Weaver 2, Griffiths 1, James 1, Macaulay 1, Smith G 1.

London Cup

Barber 8, Cronk FJ 2, Ferguson W 1, Foss 2, Galloway 4, Griffiths 7, Hardwick 2, Hurley C 1, Jackson 7, Kiernan 4, Kilduff 1, Kurz 9, Lyon 3, Macaulay 4, Milburn G 2, Mills 5, O'Hare 3, Revell C★ 1, Salmond 3, Smith AJ 2, Smith GC 6, Smith JF 4, Spence 10, Tennant 8, Weaver 8, Woodley 3.

Goals: Kurz 5, Spence 5, Galloway 3, Kiernan 2, Hurley 1, Mills 1, Tennant 1, own goal 1.

1941–42

Aicken AV★ 1	Finch LC★ 1	Kurz FJ★ 16	Smith AJ 4
Anderson DN★ 3	Foss SR 3	Lewis FA 1	Smith C 10
Attwell RF★ 1	Galloway JA★ 21	Little G★ 3	Smith JF 11
Bacon CW 7	Gibbons AH★ 1	Macaulay JAR 3	Spence R 29
Barber GF 4	Goslin H★ 1	Malpass ST★ 1	Tennant AE 31
Bearryman HW 13	Griffiths MW★ 2	Mayes AJ 5	Thomas DWJ★ 1
Boulton FP★ 1	Griffiths R 10	McCulloch D★ 1	Townsend LF★ 5
Clatworthy L 13	Hardwick GFM★ 25	Mills GR 1	Tweedy GJ★ 1
Clements BA 2	Jackson J 25	Muttitt E★ 1	Vause PG★ 4
Compton LH★ 1	Jefferson A★ 1	Payne J 2	Weale J★ 23
Craig D★ 10	Johnson J 2	Peacock J★ 4	Weaver S 30
Croom W★ 1	Joyner F★ 2	Salmond RC 19	Winterbottom W 7
Dixon WH★ 1	Kiernan T★ 13	Sibley A★ 1	Woodley VR★ 9
Dykes J★ 4	Kilpatrick W 1	Smale DM 1	Wrigglesworth W★ 2

Goals (64): Galloway 13, Weale 8, Smith JF 6, Townsend 6, Weaver 6, Kurz 5, Spence 4, Tennant 3, Payne 2, Thomas 2, Bearryman 1, Foss 1, Gibbons 1, Joyner 1, Kiernan 1, Peacock 1, Smith C 1, Wrigglesworth 1, own goal 1.

1942–43

Abel S★ 1	Davies E★ 1	Jones LJ★ 1	Sinclair A★ 1
Airlie S★ 5	Deverall HR★ 1	Kurz FJ★ 1	Smith AJ 1
Allen JP★ 25	Duke GE★ 1	Liddell WB★ 5	Smith LF 1
Bearryman HW 22	Farmer A★ 2	Mahon J★ 1	Soo F★ 5
Bidewell SH 18	Fiddes J★ 1	Mathie D★ 4	Spence R 29
Birkett RJE★ 8	Fitzgerald AM★ 1	McKennan P★ 25	Tennant AE 18
Brown WH★ 2	Foss SR 33	Mills GR 10	Weaver S 4
Bryant BL 14	Greenwood R 3	Moseley WA 1	White A 6
Buchanan PS 2	Hall AE★ 1	Mountford RC★ 22	Whittaker W★ 4
Butt L★ 1	Hapgood EA★ 1	Muttitt E★ 2	Winterbottom W 19
Campbell J★ 2	Hardwick GFM★ 21	Palmer RW★ 2	Woodley VR 33
Collett E★ 1	Hold O★ 1	Payne J 8	
Cothliff HT★ 1	Jefferson A★ 1	Savage RE★ 1	

Goals (61): McKennan 13, Foss 11, Bryant 10, Spence 9, Payne 5, Mills 4, Liddell 2, Airlie 1, Bidewell 1, Deverall 1, Hardwick 1, Mathie 1, Soo 1, Tennant 1.

1943–44

Ashcroft LL★ 9	Gilberg H★ 1	Malpass ST★ 1	Sinclair MJ★ 1
Bacon CW 3	Greenwood R 5	Marsden F★ 1	Smith JCR★ 1
Barlow H★ 1	Hapgood EA★ 1	Martin JD★ 3	Smith JF 1
Bentley G★ 7	Hardwick GFM★ 24	Mayes AJ 1	Spence R 30
Bidewell SH 1	Harris J★ 37	McKennan P★ 1	Sperrin W★ 3
Bowie JD 12	Hinchcliffe T★ 1	Millar J 2	Stewart G★ 1
Campbell A 1	Humphreys JV★ 1	Milton GW★ 1	Swindin GH★ 1
Curtis GF★ 3	Jackson J 7	Mitten C★ 29	Tennant AE 17
Dagley VA 1	James D 2	Morgan L 1	Wales H★ 2
Devlin J★ 1	Jefferson A★ 1	Mountford RC★ 3	Weaver S 1
Dimond S 1	Latimer JE 2	Muttitt E★ 1	Westwood E★ 25
Dyer JB★ 2	Law J★ 1	Newbold J 1	White A 1
Effern A 2	Lloyd C★ 1	Payne J 35	Whittingham A★ 6
Fagan W★ 22	Lowes AR★ 1	Purvis RB★ 1	Williams C★ 1
Foss SR 37	Ludford G★ 1	Riley ER 1	Woodley VR 20
Friend AF 1	Machin AH 1	Russell RI★ 30	Young AE★ 1
Fullwood J★ 1	Mackay J 1	Sanders JA★ 1	

Goals (100): Payne 50, Mitten 9, Spence 9, Fagan 7, Ashcroft 4, Effern 3, Russell 3, Tennant 3, Whittingham 3, Foss 2, Barlow 1, Bowie 1, Harris 1, Milton 1, Sperrin 1, Weaver 1, own goal 1.

1944–45

Anderson A★ 8	Foss SR 37	Machin AH 16	Spence R 8
Bacon CW 4	Franks DJ 2	McDonald JC★ 10	Stevens L★ 3
Bain JA★ 1	Gillies MM★ 1	McDonald P★ 2	Tennant AE 19
Bearryman HW 1	Gingell CS★ 1	Mills GR 1	Toop RW 1
Bidewell SH 4	Goulden LA★ 1	Mitten C★ 17	Walker T★ 6
Black H★ 12	Hapgood EA★ 15	Muttitt E★ 1	Wallis J★ 1
Bowie JD 1	Hardwick GFM★ 12	Payne J 28	Wardle G★ 27
Buchanan PS 17	Harris J★ 32	Prentice JW★ 1	Whittingham A★ 5
Cowan RM★ 11	Hassell TW★ 2	Purvis RB 10	Williams EC 1
Dawes FW★ 1	Herd A★ 5	Roper DG★ 3	Williams RF★ 1
Dodgin W★ 1	Hickman JF 1	Russell RI 32	Winter DT★ 21
Evans CJ★ 1	Hurrell W★ 12	Saunders D 1	Woodley VR 17
Fisher FT★ 1	Jones LJ★ 1	Smith LGF★ 1	

Goals (117): Payne 40, Wardle 16, Mitten 9, Walker 9, Machin 7, Buchanan 6, Hurrell 6, Bacon 3, Herd 3, Russell 3, Foss 2, McDonald J 3, Roper 2, Spence 2, Whittingham 2, Hapgood 1, Hardwick 1, Hassell 1, Tennant 1.

Additional goalscorer in Cup-Winners' Cup: Rooke (Fulham).

King George VI shaking hands with Scotland's Bobby Flavell while Archie Macaulay and Jimmy Cowan await their turn before losing 6-2 to England at Wembley in February 1944.

D.C. Thomson

The King chats informally to Stan Cullis and England captain Eddie Hapgood (3) before the match with Scotland. Members of royalty were frequent visitors to Wembley internationals.

Getty Images

Jimmy Stephen had the traditional baptism of fire on his international debut for Scotland at 21, trying to cope with the maestro Stanley Matthews. Here he attempts a friendly hug.

General Eisenhower greets Chelsea players before the 1944 South Cup final with D-Day thoughts in his mind perhaps. Bobby Russell receives the handshake and the American admitted he rooted for one side then the other during the game.

Chelsea captain John Harris (5) greets his Charlton opposite number Don Welsh before the start of the 1944 South Cup final. Charlton won 3-1.

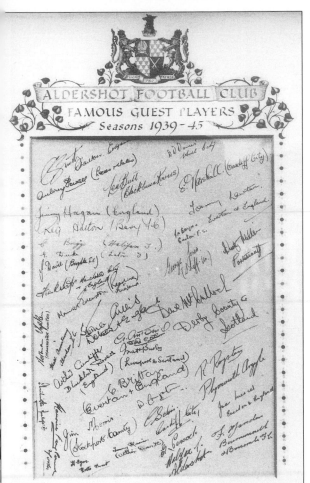

Aldershot produced a special scroll with autographs of some of the famous guest players who assisted them during the war years. They included Tommy Lawton, Jimmy Hagan and Dave McCulloch. Matt Busby signed it, though he could not get a game.

Topical Press

'England' half-back line of Cliff Britton (Everton), Stan Cullis (Wolves) and Joe Mercer (Everton) were among the 49 different international players who wore the red and blue.

In 1944–45 Aldershot were skippered by Joe Mercer. Back row left to right: Jim Horton, Bob Royston (Plymouth), Mercer (Everton), Fred Rose, Fred Marsden (Bournemouth), Reg Halton (Bury). Front: Harry Brooks, George Antonio (Stoke), Dave McCulloch (Derby), Jock McPheat (Guildford), George Jones (Sheffield Utd).

Moscow Dynamo made a tremendous impact during their visit to Britain in November 1945. The players initially trained at the White City Stadium.

Graphic Photo Union

Getty Images

Tiger Khomich, the Dynamo goalkeeper, was only briefly troubled in the match against Cardiff City. Most of the action was at the other end as the Russians won 10-1.

Getty Images

Chelsea players looking distinctly embarrassed having been presented with bunches of flowers by their Dynamo opponents. Chelsea had to wear red shirts for the occasion – the Russians were in their traditional club blue.

Estimates of the crowd for the Chelsea v Moscow Dynamo match varied. Officially 85,000, it was more likely closer to 100,000.

Khomich makes a spectacular save during the Chelsea game which finished in a thrilling 3-3 draw after the Dynamos had trailed 2-0 at half-time.

From army service in the heat of India to the mud of the training ground: Matt Busby introduces himself to his Manchester United players after taking over as manager of the Old Trafford club in 1945. Stan Pearson shakes his hand while (left to right) Billy Redman, Johnny Hanlon, Allenby Chilton, Johnny Carey, John Aston, Jack Warner, Norman Tapken and Ted Buckle look on.

The return of the FA Cup in 1945–46 was marred by the Burnden Park disaster when Bolton endured its darkest day.

The transitional season of 1945–46 brought something like normality back to regional football. Charlie Wilson-Jones scores for Birmingham City in their 3-0 win against Arsenal at Highbury on 2 February 1946. Birmingham went on to win the League South.

After suffering at the hands of the English for much of the war, Scotland gained revenge in 1946 at a packed Hampden Park with its record 139,468 crowd. Jimmy Delaney divides the teams with the only goal, leaving Frank Swift beaten.

Tommy Lawton, often at odds with the FA over payment of match fees for internationals, was forgiven and rewarded with the captaincy against Switzerland at Stamford Bridge in May 1946. England won 4-1.

Getty Images

The first post-war FA Cup final and Charlton Athletic centre-forward Arthur Turner (9) is caught in a *pas de trois* (?) with Derby's Leon Leuty and goalkeeper Vic Woodley.

Getty Images

TopFoto.co.uk

Jubilant Derby County players carry skipper Jack Nicholas on high after the 4-1 win against Charlton. But before the encounter he had to have a curse removed from the club . . .

1945–46

Argue J 4	Dawes FW★ 1	Harris J 39	Russell RI 22
Armstrong K 5	Dickie M 3	Humphreys JV★ 1	Scott L★ 1
Ashcroft LL★ 2	Dolding DL 19	James D 10	Smith GC★ 1
Bain JA 25	Ferrier H★ 1	Lawton T 20	Spence R 15
Bidewell SH 1	Foss SR 31	Lewis FA 6	Tennant AE 38
Bowie JD 1	Galloway JA★ 2	Machin AH 17	White A 3
Brindle J 2	Gingell CS★ 2	McCall W★ 6	Williams BF★ 2
Brown H (Partick) ★ 1	Goulden LA 35	Payne J 7	Williams RF 42
Brown H (Queen's P)★ 1	Hall FW★ 1	Phipps HJ★ 1	Winter DT 36
Brown R★ 1	Hanlon W★ 1	Ridley D★ 1	Woodley VR 11
Buchanan PS 8	Hanson AJ 3	Robertson W 27	Woodward T★ 2
Chisholm K★ 1	Hardwick GFM★ 2	Robson AP★ 1	

Goals (92): Lawton 19, Goulden 16, Williams R 16, Dolding 5, Machin 5, Payne 5, James 4, Bain 3, Foss 3, Spence 3, Buchanan 2, Galloway 2, McCall 2, Argue 1, Brindle 1, Brown H (Partick) 1, Chisholm 1, Hanson 1, own goals 2.

FA Cup goals (5): Goulden 1, Lawton 1, Machin 1, Spence 1, Williams R 1.

Chester

1939–40

Astbury TA 20	Forgham N 1	Law A 2	Sanders RM 14
Booth GV 1	Gregg W 3	Leyfield C★ 7	Shortt WW 22
Brown VC 22	Griffiths GE 2	Marsh FK 3	Simms HA★ 1
Butcher R 15	Hobson A 3	McGough J 10	Stubbs EPC★ 3
Chiverton GF 2	Hollis H 6	McIntosh JM★ 3	Walters TB 20
Cole GD 10	Hollis K 4	McMahon D★ 5	Warburton G 2
Common EW 12	Horsman W 19	McNeil D 1	Williams A 6
Cook W★ 1	Howarth H 25	Park JB★ 1	Worswick R 1
Devlin J★ 1	Hughes JH★ 3	Pendergast WJ 6	Yates R 13
Dickinson A★ 1	Keeley A 1	Rogers JH 3	

Goals (45): Yates 9, McMahon 8, Astbury 6, Sanders 4, McGough 3, Horsman 2, Pendergast 2, Dickinson 1, Howarth 1, Law 1, Leyfield 1, McIntosh 1, Rogers 1, Simms 1, Warburton 1, own goals 3.

War Cup goals (1): Yates 1.

1940–41

Astbury TA 35	Goodall EI★ 1	McNeil D 17	Shortt WW 24
Boswell J 1	Hollis H 7	Mercer J★ 1	Tunnicliffe WF★ 1
Bremner GH★ 25	Hollis K 2	Owen AA★ 1	Turnbull J 10
Brigham H★ 1	Horsman W 2	Pearson H★ 7	Vose G★ 3
Brown VC 12	Howarth H 37	Pendergast WJ 26	Walters TB 14
Cairns WH★ 1	Jones JE★ 5	Quinton W★ 2	White FRH★ 8
Cole GD 36	Jones L★ 2	Reay EP★ 3	Williams DH 26
Coley WH★ 1	Jones WEA★ 2	Redfern WJ★ 1	Yates R 37
Davies B★ 1	Lanceley ER 5	Rigby W 12	Young W 1
Dix RW★ 2	Manley T★ 3	Roberts F★ 12	
Glaister G★ 4	McIntosh JM★ 15	Sanders RM 1	

Goals (98): Yates 29, Pendergast 24, Bremner 9, Astbury 8, Roberts 6, Glaister 5, Cole 4, McIntosh 4, White 4, Howarth 2, Brigham 1, Lanceley 1, Pearson 1, Redfern 1, own goals 2.

Includes three extra-time goals.

1941–42

Alderton JH★ 1	Glaister G★ 5	Marsh FK 2	Shortt WW 16
Armeson LR★ 5	Graham W★ 2	McIntosh JM★ 6	Spedding JJ★ 1
Astbury TA 37	Gregg W 2	McNeil D 36	Stubbs EPC★ 4
Bates H 9	Griffiths AG 10	Moore J★ 1	Swain JS 2
Bazley J 18	Guest R 1	O'Neill G 4	Tagg E★ 3
Birkett RJE★ 2	Hastings P 2	Payne EGH★ 4	Turnbull JA 8
Breeze JT 1	Hickman AH★ 1	Pendergast WJ 9	Vasey R★ 1
Brooks H★ 2	Hollis H 2	Piercy R 1	Veacock J 3
Brown VC 1	Horsman W 1	Polk S★ 3	Walters TB 8
Bryant W★ 1	Howarth H 34	Redfern WJ★ 3	Wharton G★ 1
Chadwick T★ 2	Iddon H★ 4	Rigby W 21	Williams DH 27
Chambers J 1	Jackson G★ 11	Roberts F★ 18	Yates R 35
Cole GD 29	Lanceley ER 2	Sanders RM 1	
Currier J★ 1	Leyfield C★ 5	Sharp NW★ 5	
Fisher LP★ 1	Lucas WH★ 1	Shepherd JE 1	

Goals (79): Yates 32, Roberts 10, Astbury 7, Bazley 3, Glaister 3, McIntosh 3, Currier 2, Lanceley 2, Brooks 1, Bryant 1, Chambers 1, Fisher 1, Howarth 1, Iddon 1, Leyfield C 1, Lucas 1, McNeil 1, Pendergast 1, Piercy 1, Redfern 1, Sharp 1, Stubbs 1, Swain 1, own goals 2.

1942–43

Astbury TA   25
Atherton JG   1
Bates H   16
Bird G   8
Booth GV   21
Boswell J   1
Bremner GH★   2
Brookbank JA   5
Brown R★   2
Clarke R   10
Cole GD   7
Collins GE★   1
Compton LH★   9
Dutton R   28

Fairbrother J★   3
Glaister G★   3
Hallard W★   4
Harris F★   8
Hollis H   6
Hughes WM★   12
Iddon H★   16
Jones C★   1
Jones HE   1
Jones JL   1
Keeley A★   1
Kelly J   6
Kirby E   1
Lacey DP   5

Lucas WH★   1
McIntosh JM★   29
McNeil D   37
McPeake M   3
Mercer J★   2
O'Neill G   1
Ottewell S★   1
Payne J   2
Rawcliffe F★   2
Riddiough HH★   1
Roberts F★   8
Sharp NW★   22
Shortt WW   26
Taylor T★   1

Thorpe S   1
Thow LK★   4
Turner JT★   3
Turner P   1
Veacock J   17
Walters TB   6
Weight W   1
Welsh D★   3
Wilkie F   1
Williams DH   32
Yates R   9

Goals (83): McIntosh 18, Sharp 9, Yates 8, Compton 7, Veacock 6, Astbury 5, Kelly 3, McNeil 3, Hallard 2, Harris 2, Rawcliffe 2, Thow 2, Turner J 2, Booth 1, Bremner 1, Clarke 1, Glaister 1, Hughes 1, Iddon 1, Lacey 1, Lucas 1, Payne 1, Roberts 1, Taylor 1, Welsh 1, own goals 2.

1943–44

Adams EF★   1
Astbury TA   36
Atherton JG   1
Bates H   16
Black A★   6
Booth GV   3
Boswell J   1
Brinton JV★   7
Brookbank JA   8
Brown R★   2
Browne JH★   1
Bryan EN   3
Butler T★   4
Childs F★   1
Clarke R   10
Cole GD   12
Corkhill WG★   2

Cothliff HT★   4
Coupland R★   1
Davies TA   3
Dutton R   8
Dwyer F   1
Essex JR★   1
Gillies MM★   3
Hancocks J★   1
Harris F★   6
Hartley J   1
Hewitt H★   1
Housam A★   4
Hughes WM★   30
Hulligan MJ★   1
Ithell WJ★   1
Jones H   1
Jones L   1

Kirby E   1
Lanceley ER   1
Lee G★   3
Leigh JF   3
Leyfield C★   1
Leyfield JG   1
Loxham W   32
Makin G★   2
Mann A   1
Matthews W   1
McDonnell M★   2
McNeil D   37
Millar D★   1
Mills J   2
Molloy P   1
Moore N★   23
Newsome R★   16

O'Neill G   7
Piercy R   2
Pincott F★   11
Rigby W   1
Roberts F★   7
Scales G★   27
Slater R   2
Smith H   1
Spendlove D★   2
Tagg E★   29
Tilston TA   1
Veacock J   4
Walton R★   6
Wheatman JR★   2
Williams DH   3
Yates R   3

Goals (105): Loxham 20, Hughes 16, Moore 11, Newsome 10, Astbury 8, Brinton 5, Yates 5, Black 4, Harris 4, O'Neill 4, McNeil 3, Lee 2, Spendlove 2, Veacock 2, Browne 1, Butler 1, Davies 1, Leigh 1, Mann 1, Matthews 1, Piercy 1, Roberts 1, own goal 1.

1944–45

Armstrong M★   8
Astbury TA   36
Bainbridge KV★   6
Bett F★   6
Black A★   20
Brinton JV★   2
Brookbank JA   11
Brown R★   7
Bryan EN   3
Burden TD★   14
Butler T★   1
Campbell J★   2
Corkhill WG★   18
Cothliff HT★   1
Derrick A★   4
Dewar J★   3

Dutton R   11
Dyer JB★   17
Edwards D★   4
Ellis K   3
Gorner N   2
Hamilton R★   11
Hanson AJ★   2
Harris F★   14
Hollis H   3
Housam A★   8
Howshall T★   1
Hughes WM★   8
King R★   10
Kirby D★   13
Lee G★   1
Lewis TG★   3

Leyfield JG   1
Lunn G★   4
McCormack CJ★   1
McCormick JM★   2
McNeil D   35
Mills J   5
Naylor E★   2
Neary HF★   13
Newsome R★   13
Pidcock E   1
Piercy R   4
Pincott F★   21
Pitts H★   1
Preskett F★   2
Radcliffe B★   1
Reeve A   1

Rhodes A   3
Sargeant C★   2
Scales G   16
Shortt WW   1
Skinner D★   1
Suart R★   3
Tapken N★   1
Tilling HK★   4
Tucker C★   10
Turner P   3
Warburton G   5
Webb F   2
Wheatley J★   1
Williams DH   8
Yates R   19

Goals (94): Astbury 18, Black 17, Yates 16, Armstrong 7, Burden 7, Neary 4, Bainbridge 3, Hamilton 3, McNeil 3, Hanson 2, Hughes 2, Newsome 2, Derrick 1, Dewar 1, Kirby 1, Lee 1, Leyfield 1, Piercy 1, Preskett 1, Rhodes 1, Sargeant 1, Turner 1.

1945–46

Astbury TA 33	Cole GD 11	Long J 1	Stubbs EPC 19
Bainbridge KV★ 9	Corkhill WG★ 7	Lunn G★ 3	Tilston TA 1
Baninck R 1	Dewar J★ 4	Marsh FK 26	Turner P 8
Bennett W★ 1	Dutton R 3	McCormack CJ★ 1	Walters TB 16
Bett F★ 21	Dyer JB★ 6	McNeil D 32	Warburton G 2
Black A★ 9	Ellis K 1	Mills J 11	Whitelaw D★ 1
Breeze JT 1	Ferguson I 1	Mills W★ 1	Williams DH 4
Brookbank JA 5	Hamilton RM 30	Pendergast WJ 2	Woof N 1
Bryan EN 3	Isherwood D 1	Piercy R 2	Yates R 16
Burden TD★ 23	James J★ 6	Scales G 19	
Butcher R 5	Leahy T 13	Shortt WW 10	
Campbell R 1	Lee J 16	Skinner D 9	

Goals (90): Yates 17, Bett 13, Burden 12, Hamilton 12, Black 11, Astbury 8, Leahy 8, Bainbridge 5, Dewar 1, Lee 1, Turner 1, own goal 1.

FA Cup goals (1): Astbury 1.

Chesterfield

1939–40

Bargh GW 2	Jessop F 1	Miller LR 12	Sutherland AG 21
Barton H★ 1	Jones T 20	Milligan D 17	Thompson J★ 5
Booker K 21	Kidd WE 22	Myers JH★ 1	Turner R 1
Burbanks WE★ 1	Lyon TK 2	Pringle A 21	Watson W 4
Cornwell J 2	Machent SC★ 3	Revill JA 1	
Garrett A★ 5	Middleton R 20	Seagrave J★ 1	
Hartley TW 20	Milburn GW 22	Sinclair RD 16	

Goals (71): Milligan 16, Hartley 9, Jones 8, Milburn 8, Sinclair 5, Miller 4, Sutherland 4, Machent 3, Pringle 3, Burbanks 2, Revill 2, Watson 2, Barton 1, Garrett 1, Lyon 1, Thompson 1, own goal 1.

War Cup goals (2): Hartley 1, Jones 1.

1940–41

Alderson WS 20	Crooks SD★ 4	Middleton R 37	Sinclair T★ 1
Asquith B★ 1	Devine J 5	Milburn GW 37	Smith G★ 1
Betmead HE★ 2	Hartley TW 37	Milligan D 34	Stamps JD★ 1
Bird RE 1	Holmes J★ 2	Montgomery P★ 1	Steele J★ 1
Booker K 3	Hunt H 11	Pringle A 37	Sutherland AG 14
Boswell L★ 3	Johnson T★ 1	Regan RH 12	Taylor TA 1
Broome FH★ 2	Jones T 33	Robinson – 1	Thomson CM★ 3
Bullock N★ 1	Kidd WE 37	Ryan – 1	Turner R 3
Cockroft J★ 4	Lucas WH★ 1	Shaw EW 1	White R 5
Collingdridge C★ 1	Lyman CC★ 5	Simmons S★ 1	Whittaker W 8
Courts F★ 1	Machent SC★ 7	Sinclair RD 25	

Goals (79): Milligan 33, Hartley 10, Alderson 4, Hunt 4, Jones 4, Milburn 4, Sinclair R 4, Regan 3, Machent 2, Bird 1, Boswell 1, Broome 1, Crooks 1, Kidd 1, Lyman 1, Pringle 1, Robinson 1, Turner 1, own goals 2.

1941–42

Alderson WS 31	Harkin J★ 4	Lawrance MA 1	Revill JA 2
Barrand TF 2	Harper D 1	Linacre W 16	Sinclair RD 7
Bateman EA 4	Hartley TW 36	Lyman CC★ 18	Southall R 1
Bokas F★ 1	Hill A 5	Machent SC★ 2	Steele E★ 4
Booker K 6	Hill DGD 1	Mackie J 5	Sutherland AG 12
Bullock RS 3	Hulme W★ 8	Middleton R 36	Taylor H 1
Collins AD 12	Hunt H 8	Milburn GW 36	Whittaker W 34
Darwin GO 1	Jeffries A★ 5	Miller LR 31	Wills REJ 2
Devine J 8	Jones T 21	Mills GR★ 2	Windle C★ 2
Dewis G★ 2	Kidd WE 5	Ottewell S 5	
Goodfellow S 3	Laird W★ 1	Pringle A 8	
Hall JT 1	Latham H★ 1	Regan RH 1	

Goals (59): Lyman 9, Linacre 8, Milburn 7, Miller 7, Jones 5, Sinclair 4, Collins 3, Hartley 3, Hulme 3, Bateman 2, Machent 2, Hunt 1, Mackie 1, Steele 1, Windle 1, own goals 2.

1942–43

Alderson WS 31	Devine J 1	Levene DJ 1	Revill JA 1
Bateman EA 1	Gaucher TW 2	Linacre W 8	Sinclair TM★ 1
Bennie L 1	Gregg W★ 12	Lyon TK 1	Southall R 13
Bicknell J★ 5	Halcrow RJ 2	Machent SC★ 1	Stanton TJ 2
Booker K 9	Hall JT 4	Matthews R 2	Tapping FH 1
Bullions JL 1	Hanson F★ 4	Middleton R 38	Tomlinson CG★ 4
Bullock KS 1	Harper D 11	Milburn GW 27	Turner G 2
Burgin M★ 1	Harston JC★ 3	Miller LR 24	Whitfield W★ 3
Burton S★ 23	Hartley TW 34	Nightingale A★ 1	Whittaker W 27
Cairns WH★ 4	Hill A 4	Ottewell S 2	Wills REJ 1
Clegg H★ 1	Hulme W★ 6	Poole C★ 3	Woffinden RS★ 18
Cocker RJ★ 1	Jeffries A★ 1	Pringle A 35	
Collins AD 12	Jones T 18	Ranshaw JW★ 5	
Darwin GO 1	Kidd WE 1	Reed HD 2	

Goals (65): Hartley 11, Burton 8, Pringle 8, Jones 4, Machent 4, Collins 3, Hall 3, Miller 3, Alderson 2, Bicknell 2, Booker 2, Burgin 2, Harper 2, Linacre 2, Milburn 2, Cairns 1, Hulme 1, Matthews 1, Ottewell 1, Southall 1, Stanton 1, Tomlinson 1, own goal 1.

Includes one extra-time goal.

1943-44

Alderson WS   8
Baker GS★   4
Birch A   1
Booker K   5
Bullions JL   21
Coe L   1
Collins AD   18
Davies AM   1
Dooley GW   6
Egan H★   11
Fretwell LDJ   1
Gilmour T   1

Gregg W★   4
Hale D   1
Harper D   30
Hartley TW   14
Hawkeswell JS   6
Hill DGD   1
Hogg F★   5
Jay H   1
Jones C★   1
Jones T   17
Kidd WE   21
Linacre W   20

Longdon CW★   1
Middleton R   35
Milburn GW   30
Miller LR   6
Oakley JC   2
Ottewell S   3
Pringle A   37
Ramsbottom W   1
Reed HD   1
Rhodes A★   1
Rickards CT★   2
Rickett W★   1

Sinclair RD   4
Southall R   34
Taylor H   1
Watford A   13
Watson W   1
Whitfield W★   6
Whittaker W   24
Wills REJ   1
Woffinden RS★   4

Goals (60): Linacre 10, Egan 9, Hawkeswell 6, Pringle 6, Milburn 5, Collins 3, Harper 3, Jones T 3, Hogg 2, Sinclair 2, Whitfield 2, Alderson 1, Baker 1, Davies 1, Dooley 1, Hartley 1, Kidd 1, Miller 1, Ottewell 1, Southall 1.

1944-45

Allport CE   7
Booker K   5
Carlile GR   3
Clarke JH   10
Collins AD   15
Coombes JR   1
Davie J★   14
Derbyshire W   1
Dooley GW   1
Harper D   11
Hart WR   1

Hartley TW   13
Hawkeswell JS   6
Herbert F★   12
Hewitt H   1
Hill DGD   10
Hill H   6
Hobson L   21
Iddon H★   4
Johnson J★   2
Jones T   24
Kidd WE   41

Linacre W   39
Lyman CC★   1
Middleton R   42
Milburn GW   42
Miller LR   4
Nelson D★   2
Nightingale A★   1
Payne J★   1
Peters J★   18
Powell T★   1
Pringle A   39

Rawding H★   1
Roberts H   1
Simpson J   1
Southall R   21
Sutherland AG   1
Watford A   4
White R   1
Whittaker W   33

Goals (70): Linacre 12, Davie 10, Milburn 7, Collins 6, Herbert 6, Jones 4, Payne 3, Peters 3, Pringle 3, Clarke 2, Hawkeswell 2, Iddon 2, Nelson 2, Allport 1, Harper 1, Hartley 1, Hewitt 1, Hill D 1, Hobson 1, Kidd 1, Miller 1, Southall 1, own goal 1.

Includes two extra-time goals.

1945-46

Ainscough S   2
Bennie L   5
Booker K   5
Collins AD   21
Davie J★   14
Dooley GW   14
Goodfellow S   20
Hart WR   22

Hobson L   30
Jones T   8
Kidd WE   42
Linacre W   18
Mather JB   1
Middleton R   42
Milburn GW   27
Miller LR   2

Milligan D   4
Ottewell S   7
Pringle A   26
Roberts H   26
Simpson J   10
Sinclair RD   24
Southall R   4
Swinscoe TW   8

Tapping F★   3
Watford A   1
Watson W   16
Whittaker W   41
Wilson J   19

Goals (68): Davie 10, Milburn 9, Linacre 8, Swinscoe 6, Roberts 5, Wilson 5, Sinclair 4, Dooley 3, Goodfellow 3, Hart 3, Southall 3, Collins 2, Simpson 2, Tapping 2, Milligan 1, Ottewell 1, own goal 1.

FA Cup goals (3): Roberts 2, Dooley 1.

Clapton Orient

1939–40

Allum LH 1	Fletcher CA★ 30	Mulraney A★ 1	Thomas DWJ★ 4
Astley DJ★ 11	Forder JL★ 1	Perry E★ 1	Toser EW★ 1
Barnes SC 1	Gage A★ 1	Pitts H★ 1	Tully FA 32
Bartlett FL 34	Gore LF 6	Pryde D★ 1	Vaux E★ 2
Black RW 32	Hall SA 30	Rist FH★ 31	Whittaker W★ 1
Bungay RH 4	Hann L 2	Rumbold G 34	Williams R 3
Chadwick FW★ 1	Hobbins SG★ 2	Sargent C★ 1	Willshaw G 29
Collier H★ 1	Ingle A★ 1	Shankley R 24	Wilson A★ 1
Dawes FW★ 3	Jobling J★ 19	Smith IIM 32	Wright RCA★ 2
Devine JS★ 4	Layton WH★ 1	Swinfen R 1	
Ellis J 3	Macfadyen W 3	Tanner S★ 2	
Flack DW★ 2	McNeil JL 3	Taylor H 29	

Goals (64): Shankley 23, Willshaw 9, Smith 7, Fletcher 6, Astley 5, Thomas 4, Tully 3, Perry 2, Williams 2, Devine 1, Gore 1, own goal 1.

War Cup goals (6): Smith 3, Willshaw 2, Shankley 1.

1940–41

Armstrong M★ 1	Diaper B★ 1	Levey F 1	Sargent C 5
Astley DJ★ 8	Fieldus S★ 1	Lunn G★ 6	Shankley R 3
Baines L★ 1	Fisher AN★ 2	McNeil J 1	Sidness F★ 1
Barraclough A★ 1	Fletcher A★ 2	Montgomery SW 2	Silver H★ 4
Bartlett F L 16	Fletcher CA★ 12	Muttitt E★ 1	Skeggs C 2
Bates –★ 1	Galley –★ 1	Nelson –★ 1	Smith F 5
Bell R★ 1	Ghost – 1	Payne – 1	Smith HM 5
Black RW 11	Gillespie IC★ 1	Pemberton –★ 1	Spears G 1
Burnett – 1	Gregory G★ 1	Perry E★ 1	Sperrin J★ 1
Butterworth –★ 1	Hall SA 4	Phypers E★ 2	Tully FA 15
Collier H★ 2	Houston – 1	Raven –★ 1	Wade R 2
Collin HH★ 2	Hyatt G 1	Rawlings J 6	Weightman E★ 2
Cousins ST★ 1	Jobling J★ 2	Reeves KE★ 1	Williams –★ 1
Davie J★ 1	Jones L 1	Rist FH★ 1	Willshaw G 7
Devine JS★ 2	Levene D★ 10	Rumbold G 2	Wright WP 13

Ten players only v Tottenham H 21.12.40.

Goals (22): Astley 3, Fletcher 3, Shankley 3, Smith H 3, Houston 2, Willshaw 2, Fisher 1, Gillespie 1, Gregory 1, Muttitt 1, Rawlings 1, Tully 1.

London Cup

Allum LH 1, Astley 4, Barnes SC 1, Bartlett 10, Birdseye –★ 1, Black 3, Brooks CE 1, Collier 1, Crawford E 2, Eaton –★ 1, Fisher 8, Fletcher CA★ 8, Gibson –★ 1, Goodwin –★ 1, Hall 6, Hillam CE★ 2, Jenkins –★ 1, Jobling 6, Jobson –★ 1, Johnson –★ 1, Levene 1, Lunn 1, MacIlroy –★ 1, McNeil 3, Muller –★ 1, Rawlings 9, Reeves 1, Ross –★ 1, Sargent 1, Silver 1, Smith F 1, Tully 10, Wade 10, Weightman 5, Wright W 1, Wright WP 3.

Goals: McNeil 4, Fletcher 2, Rawlings 2, Fisher 1.

1941–42

Aicken AV★ 14	Crawford E 34	Kelly L★ 6	Silver H★ 1
Allum LH 18	Curtis GF★ 1	Levene D 1	Strauss W★ 2
Armstrong M★ 22	Dryden JG 15	Lucas E 2	Summerbee G★ 1
Austin –★ 1	Ellis J 2	McDonald – 1	Thorogood J★ 9
Barford – 1	Fisher AN★ 1	Nicholls – 1	Tully FA 24
Barnes SC 31	Fletcher CA★ 28	Odell WR 21	Willshaw GJ 16
Bartlett FL 35	Griffin A 7	Parry O★ 1	Woodroffe – 2
Bestwick –★ 6	Hall SA 33	Phillips – 1	Wright WP 2
Black RW 17	Hedges –★ 1	Rankin – 1	
Brooks CE 30	Jobling J★ 1	Reynolds – 1	
Brown – 1	Jones EN★ 1	Rumbold G 3	

Goals (52): Armstrong 13, Willshaw 9, Crawford 6, Fletcher 6, Dryden 5, Odell 5, Tully 4, Barnes 2, Bestwick 1, own goal 1.

1942–43

Aicken AV★ 1	Dodgin W★ 26	Kelly L★ 22	Smith HM 4
Allum LH 34	Dryden JG★ 11	Lucas E 4	Summersett D 10
Armstrong M★ 18	Fieldus S 1	McLuckie JS★ 5	Swindin GH★ 1
Barnes SC 20	Fletcher A 9	Odell WR★ 15	Tully FA 2
Bartlett FL 33	Gage A★ 3	Rickett H 13	Waller H★ 2
Black RW 21	Hall SA 16	Rumbold G 2	Warnes J★ 1
Boyes W★ 5	Hewett J 28	Saul AW★ 1	Williams R 1
Campbell J★ 5	Iceton J 1	Scott J★ 1	Williamson J★ 2
Chitty W★ 1	Irving A 1	Shankley R★ 1	Willshaw GJ 20
Crawford E 15	Jobson TH★ 1	Shufflebottom F★ 8	Young CR★ 1
Curtis GF★ 6	Juby –★ 1	Smith C★ 1	

Goals (60): Armstrong 14, Hewett 14, Willshaw 8, Summersett 5, Dryden 4, Odell 3, Crawford 2, Dodgin 2, Barnes 1, Black 1, Fletcher 1, Lucas 1, McLuckie 1, Saul 1, Tully 1, own goal 1.

1943–44

Aicken AV★ 10	Crawford E 2	Kirkham R★ 1	Robinson P★ 1
Allum LH 29	Curtis GF★ 1	Lambert ESG★ 1	Robson AP★ 3
Andrews F 3	Daniels J★ 3	Lane W★ 1	Rumbold G 4
Ayres H 18	Dreyer G★ 6	Liddell J★ 19	Salmon L★ 1
Baines H 10	Dugnolle JH★ 5	Lowes AR★ 1	Saul AW 10
Bartlett FL 29	Ford T 9	Lucas E 1	Saunders W 1
Blackman JJ★ 2	Fullwood J★ 1	Ludford G★ 6	Seddon A★ 1
Boyd JM★ 1	Gage A 4	Malloy P★ 2	Sharp HG 5
Boyd W★ 2	Gallacher P★ 2	McLuckie JS★ 18	Shufflebottom F★ 1
Brophy H★ 1	Gillespie IC★ 13	Muttitt E★ 2	Simpson J★ 1
Bryant BL★ 16	Hall SR★ 1	Oakes John★ 1	Smith C★ 30
Campbell J★ 1	Hewitt J 12	Odell WR★ 15	Stewart J★ 1
Chalkley AG★ 1	Jones F★ 1	Parry O★ 1	Summersett D 11
Clarke RL★ 2	Kelly G★ 4	Perkins C★ 1	Weaver S★ 2
Cothliff HT★ 1	Kelly L★ 30	Rickett H 31	Wilkinson J 3

Goals (39): Bryant 8, Ford 5, Smith 5, Odell 3, Saunders 2, Ayres 1, Blackman 1, Clarke 1, Crawford 1, Gillespie 1, Kelly G 1, Liddell 1, Lowes 1, Lucas 1, Parry 1, Robson 1, Saul 1, Sharp 1, Summersett 1, own goals 2.

1944–45

Allum LH 21	Ford T★ 24	Lucas GR 4	Rothery H★ 1
Antonio GR★ 2	Foreman GA★ 1	Ludham F★ 1	Rumbold G 24
Barnes SC 1	French RA 1	Morrad FG★ 13	Sharp HG 2
Bartlett FL 26	Gillespie IC★ 14	Nairn J★ 1	Smith HM 1
Beattie A★ 1	Hall SA 17	Needham FR★ 5	Somerfield A★ 1
Blackman JJ★ 6	Harrison AV 3	Odell WR★ 19	Stewart A★ 9
Boyd – 1	Jameson J★ 1	Parry W 32	Walsh RP 1
Browne JH★ 3	Kelly G 5	Pond H★ 1	Walters H★ 18
Colloff BD 15	Kelly L★ 3	Pritchard AV★ 1	Whitfield W★ 1
Cross F 3	Kitching G 1	Pulfrey VN★ 2	Wright W 1
Daniels J★ 23	Kurz FJ★ 1	Purvis B★ 2	Younger A★ 8
Dawes AG★ 1	Liddell J 24	Richardson JR★ 2	
Dugnolle JH★ 27	Love ES 2	Rickett H 19	

Goals (44): Ford 9, Daniels 7, Odell 5, Younger 4, Blackman 2, Colloff 2, Kelly G 2, Liddell 2, Parry 2, Pond 2, Browne 1, Cross 1, Dugnolle 1, Foreman 1, Morrad 1, Walters 1, own goal 1.

1945–46

Allum LH   6
Astley DJ★   1
Ballard EA   5
Barnard CH★   1
Barnes SC   11
Bartlett FL   34
Baynham J★   9
Beer R   1
Blain J★   4
Buchanan PS★   1
Calverley A★   1
Campbell WB   3
Clark JT   12
Collins W★   1
Cumner RH★   1
Dinnern M   6
Dobson L   1

Dugnolle JH★   5
Farley A   11
Ferrier H★   1
Fletcher CA   2
French RA   1
Froom B   8
Fullbrook JFA   5
Georgson –   2
Goodyear GW★   1
Gore LF   20
Griffiths G   1
Hall SA   27
Howshall T★   12
Hunt DA   5
Jobling J★   1
Kirby G   1
Knott H★   1

Lewis E   7
Liddell J   18
Love ES   1
Lucas GR   1
Marriott G   6
McMurdo A   2
Medley LD★   2
Merrett G   6
Morrad FG★   3
Moss A★   3
Oldham G★   1
Owens J   9
Palmer L   1
Parr H   21
Pullen WE   20
Rampling DW★   4
Ringrose A★   13

Ritson L   5
Robson AP★   4
Rowlinson WA★   1
Rumbold G   20
Saunders W★   1
Slade E   5
Smith F★   2
Smith J★   4
Somerfield A★   2
Stock AWA★   13
Taylor J★   2
Tidswell A   1
Walters H★   12
Watley G   2
Wilson C★   1
Young AW★   1

Goals (50): Parr 8, Pullen 6, Gore 5, Robson 5, Stock 5, Campbell 4, Dinnern 3, Medley 2, Smith J 2, Somerfield 2, Baynham 1, Fletcher 1, Froom 1, Howshall 1, Hunt 1, Merrick 1, Morrad 1, Taylor 1.

FA Cup goals (2): Gore 1, Parr 1.

Coventry City

1939–40

Armeson LR 3	Davidson RT 17	Lewis IS 10	Smith B 6
Ashall GH 5	Elliott CS 12	Lowrie G 14	Smith N 1
Astley J 23	Frith W 23	Mason GW 25	Snape J 15
Barratt H 7	Green T 24	Metcalf WF 24	Taylor GT 19
Boileau HA 25	Harris A 1	Mitchell F 1	Warner LH 14
Coen L 3	Lager EW 3	Morgan W 17	Wood AR 14
Crawley T 27	Lauderdale JH★ 4	Murray D 4	

Goals (76): Crawley 23, Davidson 11, Green 11, Lowrie 6, Frith 5, Murray 5, Taylor 5, Barratt 4, Lager 2, Lauderdale 2, Lewis 1, Mason 1.

War Cup goals (11): Davidson 4, Lowrie 4, Taylor 2, Crawley 1.

1940–41

Armeson LR 2	Elliott CS 9	Lowrie G 7	O'Brien RV★ 7
Ashall GH 4	Frith W 8	Mason GW 10	Taylor GT 10
Boileau HA 9	Jones LJ★ 1	Metcalf WF 10	Wood AR 3
Crawley T 10	Lauderdale JH★ 3	Morgan W 7	
Davidson RT 8	Lewis IS 1	Murray D 1	

Goals (28): Crawley 7, Lowrie 7, Frith 3, Ashall 2, Lauderdale 2, O'Brien 2, Taylor 2, Davidson 1, Elliott 1, Mason 1.

1941–42

Did not compete.

1942–43

Abrahams L 1	Elliott CS 29	Lee J 2	Shaw R★ 1
Armeson LR 7	Evans JT 1	Lewis IS 7	Simmons CK 17
Ashall GH 2	Frith W 21	Lowrie G 33	Simpson DR 21
Bainbridge G 1	Gardner R 1	Mason GW 35	Smith SW 6
Barratt H 17	Greenway NR 6	Merrick GH★ 1	Snape J 10
Batchelor E 1	Grubb KH 2	Metcalf WF 13	Taylor GT★ 1
Bennett SL 2	Hartopp RK 1	Mitchell F 1	Thacker J 1
Boileau HA 23	Humphries CWH 1	Morgan W 5	Walker JL★ 1
Bolan LA★ 9	Kelley SR 1	Murray D 5	Whitecroft T 1
Bond WA 3	Kelly – 3	O'Brien RV★ 30	Wood AR 30
Chapman SA 3	Lager EW 4	Quinton W★ 1	Young C 1
Coen L 8	Lapworth D★ 1	Roberts E 1	
Craven C★ 1	Lauderdale JH★ 1	Ryan RA 2	
Crawley T 29	Laurie J 1	Setchell AS 12	

Goals (61): Lowrie 23, Crawley 11, Simmons 8, Simpson 4, Coen 2, Lager 2, Armeson 1, Ashall 1, Barratt 1, Bolan 1, Lee 1, Mason 1, Murray 1, O'Brien 1, Setchell 1, Taylor 1, Young 1.

1943–44

Armeson LR 2	Edwards G★ 25	Mason GW 35	Simmons CK 4
Astley J 1	Elliott CS 33	McKeown J 23	Simpson DR 10
Barratt H 34	Frith W 1	Metcalf WF 30	Smith N 1
Boileau HA 22	Gardner F★ 10	Miles JP 1	Smith SW 3
Bond WA 2	Garner R 9	Morgan W 22	Snape J 2
Chapman SA 2	Green KL 1	Murphy P 5	Vinall EJ★ 3
Coen L 22	Grubb KH 1	Nash WG 2	Ward R 1
Cornwell SH 9	Hale H 1	Newbold A 2	Warner LH 4
Crawley T 34	Harris A★ 1	O'Brien RV★ 25	Watkins KC 2
Cryer A 1	Keeble F★ 1	Pritchard HJ★ 2	Wood AR 7
Dougall T 2	Lewis IS 5	Quinney H★ 1	Wright WC 2
Doyle P 1	Lowrie G 19	Setchell AG 3	

Goals (73): Crawley 20, Lowrie 13, Barratt 10, McKeown 9, Edwards 4, Gardner 3, Simpson 3, Coen 2, Mason 2, Vinall 2, Boileau 1, Newbold 1, Pritchard 1, Setchell 1, own goal 1.

1944–45

Armeson LR   5
Barratt H   10
Boileau HA   8
Bowles JC★   13
Brown T   1
Carey WJ★   8
Cook J   4
Copson F   2
Crawley T   34
Currie A   6
Dougall C★   18
Dougall T   1
Douglas FL   1

Edwards G   32
Elliott CS   30
Evans JT★   3
Faulkner K★   13
Fitzpatrick J   1
Frith W   16
Garner R   14
Green T   15
Hall –   2
Jarvis JH★   1
Jones LJ★   7
Kelley SR   1
Kendall JT   10

Kerry D   7
King J★   3
Lewis G★   2
Lewis IS   5
Lowrie G   1
Mason GW   33
Matthews H   4
McKeown A   1
McKeown J   14
Metcalf WF   18
Morton A   1
O'Brien RV★   28
Paul RG   10

Robinson FH   1
Ryan RA   4
Simmons CK   3
Simpson DR   4
Smith C★   1
Snape J   3
Taylor FW   4
Ward RA   10
Warner.LH   1
Watkins KC   4

Goals (59): Crawley 9, Paul 8, Dougall C 7, Edwards 7, Elliott 7, Currie 3, Faulkner 3, Barratt 2, Lewis I 2, McKeown J 2, Frith 1, Jarvis 1, Jones 1, Kerry 1, Lowrie 1, O'Brien 1, Smith 1, own goals 2.

1945–46

Aldecoa E   30
Ashall GH   1
Barratt H   42
Bilbao J   5
Calverley A★   1
Crawley T   39
Davidson RT   4
Dougall T   1
Eggleston T★   1
Elliott CS   31
Gardner FC★   16

Goddard R★   1
Harris A★   1
Houghton WE★   1
Johnson D★   2
Jones LJ★   2
Kelley SR   17
Kelly D   1
Kendall JT   1
Lewis IS   2
Loughran J★   1
Lowrie G   21

Lyman CC★   1
Mason GW   33
Matthews H   5
McKeown A   2
McKeown J   1
Metcalf WF   35
O'Brien RV★   9
Owens TL★   2
Pritchard HJ★   7
Roberts E   14
Setchell AG   3

Simpson DR   24
Small SJ★   9
Smith C★   2
Snape J   21
Ward RA   1
Warner LH   22
Watkins KC   8
Wood AR   42

Goals (70): Barratt 26, Lowrie 11, Aldecoa 6, Simpson 5, Crawley 4, Roberts 4, Small 4, Owens 2, Bilbao 1, Gardner 1, Matthews 1, Metcalf 1, O'Brien 1, Pritchard 1, Warner 1, own goal 1.

FA Cup goals (2): Barratt 1, Simpson 1.

Crewe Alexandra

1939–40

Basford S 2
Bradbury T 4
Chandler FEG 2
Cobourne E 17
Cooke WH 1
Cooper J 8
Cope G 22
Davies SR★ 1

Dyer JA 16
Essex JK★ 1
Foreman JJ★ 3
Gilchrist G 11
Hill RA★ 4
Johnson MH 16
Kneale CH 16
Lewis J 2

Matthews S★ 1
McArdle P 1
Picton H 2
Poskett TW 21
Rice A 23
Rigsby W 3
Smith C★ 7
Stevens GL 23

Still RA 19
Tagg E★ 1
Trentham DH★ 1
Turner A★ 2
Tutin A★ 12
Waring J 22

Goals (47): Stevens 21, Rice 8, Cobourne 7, Waring 3, Chandler 2, Smith 2, Cooper 1, Dyer 1, Kneale 1, own goal 1.

War Cup goals (1): Rice 1.

1940–41

Aldersey E 2
Anthony H 1
Basford S 21
Bourne J 3
Cobourne E 10
Cooke WH★ 1
Cooniham H 5
Cope G 25
Davies S 1
Devlin J★ 1
Dyer JA★ 2
Egerton H 2

Essex JR★ 9
Foster TC 1
Geoghans J 1
Gibson D 4
Gilchrist G 2
Gourlay T 16
Harding C 3
Hayes AC★ 1
Hill RA★ 1
Hollinshead F 1
Ingham J 2
Le Clere J 5

MacLean A 3
Maddocks A 1
Major A 7
McNeill HJ★ 5
Nokes G 1
Poskett TW 20
Rice A 8
Rowe J★ 1
Rugman K★ 1
Russon K 4
Smith C★ 8
Stevens GL 15

Still RA 12
Tagg E★ 11
Trentham DH★ 1
Triner DA★ 3
Turner A★ 15
Turnock C 3
Tutin A★ 18
Waring J 20
Wilson J 9

Goals (36): Stevens 9, Turner 4, Gibson 3, McNeill 3, Waring 3, Cobourne 2, Essex 2, Tagg 2, Cooke 1, Devlin 1, Ingham 1, Le Clere 1, MacLean 1, Russon 1, Smith 1, Tutin 1.

1941–42

Did not compete.

1942–43

Aldersey E 11
Anderson AJ 12
Bartholomew R★ 8
Basnett AE★ 1
Bateman A 26
Blunt E★ 4
Boothway J★ 15
Bray J★ 1
Caffrey J 3
Chandler FEG 35
Cobourne E 1
Collantine J 1
Cope G 2
Currier J★ 1

Dickenson A★ 1
Dyer JA★ 3
Eden W 1
Egerton H 1
Essex JR★ 13
Fawthrop F 1
Gaffney J★ 1
Gallagher P★ 7
Gibson D 1
Glover S★ 27
Gourlay T★ 1
Gray M 7
Griffiths A★ 3
Griffiths P 1

Hewitt H 3
Hibbs L 5
Isherwood D 4
Jones R 4
Kahn H 1
Kinnear D★ 1
Lewis TH★ 4
Major A 3
Malam A★ 24
Poskett TW 37
Prince J 1
Rawcliffe F★ 2
Roberts S★ 2
Sharpe C 1

Stevens GL 2
Still RA 32
Tagg E★ 38
Thompson D 1
Trentham DH★ 3
Tutin A★ 7
Underhill CR 1
Wardell A 2
Waring J 1
Waring T★ 22
Wheatley F 2
Williams E★ 25
Wright G★ 1

Goals (87): Boothway 13, Malam 11, Waring 8, Gray 6, Bateman 5, Chandler 5, Dyer 4, Tagg 4, Anderson 3, Essex 3, Gallagher 3, Hibbs 3, Aldersey 2, Caffrey 2, Currier 2, Griffiths A 2, Still 2, Wardell 2, Bartholomew 1, Cobourne 1, Hewitt 1, Isherwood 1, own goals 3.

1943–44

Aldersey E   12
Anderson HA   3
Bailey A*   3
Basnett AE*   8
Bateman A   20
Bettany G   5
Black A*   8
Blake G   1
Blunt E*   35
Boothway J*   1
Bradbury G   1
Chandler FEG   0
Cochrane D   2

Cope G   17
Cox F   1
Daniel R*   1
Davies A   3
Derrick A*   1
Dyer JA*   2
French AJ   7
Glover S*   19
Gregory M*   6
Hancocks J*   2
Hayward EJ   6
Hill FR*   1
Hopley D   8

Hughes S*   11
Inskip FC   28
Jones E   23
Lewis R   1
Malam A*   9
McCormick J*   20
Morris S   3
Parker WD*   20
Poskett TW   20
Rawcliffe F*   1
Roberts R   18
Samson R*   1
Scott W*   6

Simms H   1
Simpson J   3
Slater J*   6
Smallwood K   2
Smith G   1
Stevens GL   5
Still RA   25
Tagg E*   2
Talbot FL*   2
Turner A*   3
Tutin A*   1
Underhill CB   1
Woodcock E   1

Goals (60): Roberts 12, Inskip 11, Blunt 9, Basnett 3, Black 3, Cochrane 3, McCormick 3, Malam 3, Hancocks 2, Aldersey 1, Anderson 1, Bailey 1, Bateman 1, Boothway 1, Jones 1, Smallwood 1, Tagg 1, own goals 3.

1944–45

Ainsley GE*   2
Aldersey E   1
Almond J   13
Barclay R*   1
Barlow H   3
Bartram S*   1
Basnett AE*   22
Bateman A   8
Boothway J   32
Bray J*   6
Bridges H*   1
Brinton JV*   5
Buckingham VF*   1
Chandler FEG   31
Cope G   1
Cowden T*   11

Currier J*   1
Derrick A*   2
Dowey WL   3
Dyer JA*   4
Essex JR*   3
Ferris R   1
Franklin ST*   1
Gilchrist G   1
Gleave JR   1
Graham DR*   29
Haining J   6
Hall WW*   5
Hancocks J*   3
Hanson AJ*   1
Hayward EJ   4
Heath G   8

Hill F   31
Howe LF*   2
Hughes S   37
Jackson A   4
Jones E   6
Jones T*   1
Jones TW*   3
Kerr J*   1
Kettle F   1
Machin AH*   1
Makin G*   1
Marsh F   1
McCormick J*   28
Miller AG*   2
Mountford GF*   3
Pearson H*   1

Poskett TW   1
Powell E   1
Prince R*   1
Rawcliffe F*   14
Rickards CT*   3
Robinson GH*   2
Sellars J*   4
Shaw A   10
Shaw J*   2
Smedley C*   1
Still RA   36
Streten BR*   3
Tagg E*   38

Goals (93): Boothway 29, Basnett 13, McCormick J 9, Rawcliffe 6, Shaw A 5, Chandler 4, Heath 3, Jones E 3, Sellars 3, Almond 2, Brinton 2, Hall 2, Howe 2, Bridges 1, Hancocks 1, Hayward 1, Kettle 1, Powell 1, Rickards 1, Robinson 1, Shaw J 1, Tagg 1, own goal 1.

1945–46

Bainbridge A   4
Barlow H   3
Basnett AE*   2
Bateman A   30
Berley H   8
Boothway J   35
Bray E*   1
Brayley F   3
Chandler FEG   35
Clancey P   1
Cooke WH   12
Cooper J   1
Cope G   18

Franklin ST*   2
Corkan L   3
Dyer JA*   4
Essex JR*   1
Gilchrist G   4
Glidden GS*   8
Haining J   2
Hayward EJ   13
Hill F   12
Insley D   7
Johnson JA*   9
Jones A*   1
Jones E   1

Roberts R   5
Kelly E*   1
Kelly MJ   19
Mawson R   34
Metcalf J   3
Palmer FW   21
Ray CH*   2
Scott R*   3
Sellars J*   2
Shaw A   26
Smith K   2
Soo F*   1
Stevens GL   2

Still RA   14
Tagg E*   4
Thomson M   3
Waddington A   10
Walker D   8
Willis G*   1
Wood JV   1
Wood T   9
Worrall FJ   5

Goals (80): Boothway 36, Shaw 10, Chandler 5, Kelly M 5, Bateman 4, Glidden 2, Insley 2, Johnson 2, Roberts 2, Stevens 2, Basnett 1, Brayley 1, Dyer 1, Hill 1, Soo 1, Thomson 1, Waddington 1, Willis 1, own goals 2.

FA Cup goals (4): Boothway 2, Hayward 1, Shaw 1.

Crystal Palace

1939–40

Bark WH 25	Gillespie IE 20	Lievesley L 3	Smith JT 36
Bigg R 1	Gregory FC 34	Millbank JH 30	Steele E 3
Blackman JJ 24	Gregory M 4	Milligan GH 1	Taylor H★ 2
Chesters A 7	Hudgell AJ 35	Owens E 31	Tootill A 32
Collins N 35	James AE 3	Reece TS 2	Waldron E 3
Dawes AG★ 11	Joy B★ 1	Robson AP 36	Wilson A 32
Dawes FW 12	Lewis J 2	Shanks R 4	

Goals (111): Robson 26, Smith 18, Bark 13, Blackman 13, Gregory F 13, Wilson 9, Dawes A 8, Waldron 5, Gillespie 3, Owens 1, Steele 1, own goal 1.

War Cup goals (6): Robson 3, Wilson 2, Bark 1.

1940–41

Bark WH 7	Gillespie IC 20	Millbank JH 20	Tootill A 29
Blackman JJ 26	Gregory FC 2	Revill J 2	Waite EA 11
Collins N 28	Gregory M 29	Ridley TR 2	Wilson A 14
Dawes AG★ 18	Halliday WJ 3	Robson AP 29	Wilson RA 1
Dawes FW 27	Hudgell AJ 23	Smith JT 16	
Eastman DJ 2	Lievesley L 3	Taylor H 7	

Goals (88): Robson 25, Dawes A 20, Blackman 12, Wilson A 7, Gillespie 5, Hudgell 5, Smith 5, Bark 3, Gregory M 2, Waite 2, Collins 1, Gregory F 1.

London Cup

Bark 1, Blackman 11, Collins 11, Dawes AG 5, Dawes FW 11, Gillespie 6, Gregory M 11, Halliday 2, Hudgell 9, Jackson J★ 1, Lievesley 1, Millbank 8, Revill 2, Ridley 1, Robson 11, Smith 10, Tootill 10, Waite 2, Wilson A 7, Wilson RA 1.

Goals: Robson 11, Dawes AG 7, Blackman 4, Smith 2, Wilson A 2.

1941–42

Bark WH 19	Geldard A★ 1	Lewis G 1	Scaife G★ 1
Bartram S★ 2	Gillespie IC 26	Lewis J 1	Sibley A★ 1
Blackman JJ 18	Gregory FC 1	MacPhee MG★ 1	Smith JF★ 1
Boulton FP★ 1	Gregory M 24	Mather H★ 1	Smith JT 22
Catlin AE★ 1	Halford D★ 1	Millbank JH 11	Tootill A 29
Chilvers GT 1	Hawke –★ 2	Morris RW★ 23	Tweedy GJ★ 1
Collins N 36	Henley L★ 3	Mulligan GH★ 1	Weale J★ 1
Dawes AG 23	Hitchins AW★ 1	Muttitt E★ 2	Wilson A 29
Dawes FW 30	Hobbins SG★ 2	Oakes John★ 1	Young AA★ 1
Duncan A★ 1	Hooper P★ 1	Raynor G★ 1	
Forder JL 2	Hudgell AJ 35	Reece TS 2	
Fuller – 1	Lester FC★ 1	Robson AP 32	

Goals (78): Robson 22, Dawes A 13, Bark 10, Gillespie 7, Smith JT 6, Blackman 4, Collins 3, Wilson 3, MacPhee 2, Geldard 1, Gregory M 1, Hawke 1, Henley 1, Hudgell 1, Lewis G 1, Smith JF 1, own goal 1.

1942–43

Allen JP★ 2	Farmer A★ 1	Lewis G 6	Spencer H★ 7
Bark WH 12	Fenton BRV★ 1	Lewis J 9	Tootill A 12
Barnes S★ 1	Finch J★ 4	Lowe HP★ 1	Turner M 1
Bassett WEG 14	Fletcher H 1	Lowes AR★ 6	Walker –★ 1
Bastin FW 5	Ford WH 4	Mennie R★ 1	Walker CJ★ 1
Batey R★ 2	Gillespie IC 16	Millbank JH 3	Waller H★ 5
Blackman JJ 22	Girling HM 1	Milton GW★ 1	Ward TA★ 4
Bratley GW 2	Gregory FC 1	Morris RW 6	Ware H★ 3
Briscoe JE★ 2	Gregory M 6	Poland G★ 9	Williams CE 1
Brown HS★ 4	Harding EJ 6	Porritt W★ 1	Williams EE 3
Buckley A★ 1	Hawkes DC 1	Potts H★ 1	Wilson A 26
Collins N 1	Henley L★ 3	Reece TS 10	Winter DT★ 1
Davie J★ 1	Hobbins SG★ 1	Robson AP 24	Wright EV 5
Dawes AG 28	Hudgell AJ 7	Scaife G★ 2	Young AE★ 6
Dawes FW 24	Johnston I★ 4	Smith C★ 3	
Delaney L★ 1	Joslin PJ★ 3	Smith JGH 1	
Driver A★ 2	Kirk J★ 1	Smith JT 29	

Goals (56): Dawes A 10, Smith JT 10, Robson 9, Bark 7, Wilson 5, Bastin 2, Gillespie 2, Lowes 2, Ward 2, Wright 2, Blackman 1, Gregory M 1, Potts 1, Ware 1, own goal 1.

1943–44

Allen KG 2	Dawes AG 31	Lewis J 3	Smith JT 30
Bassett WEG 6	Dawes FW 12	Malpass ST★ 1	Somerfield A★ 1
Biggs A★ 1	Embleton E★ 1	McCrae A★ 2	Spencer H★ 28
Blackman JJ 9	Ferrier RJ★ 25	Millbank JH 2	Tennant AE★ 3
Bray G★ 1	Flavell R★ 3	Mountford RC★ 30	Thompson D★ 1
Briscoe J★ 1	Franks J 1	Muttitt E★ 1	Tootill A 29
Brophy H★ 2	Gallagher P★ 3	Nunn AJ 2	Tunney E★ 4
Brown ARJ★ 1	Gilbert AV 1	Page AE★ 3	Ward TA★ 2
Brown J★ 1	Girling HM 8	Pond H★ 1	Williams EE 6
Bryant BL 4	Grogan J★ 1	Redfern R★ 5	Wilson A 29
Cabrelli P★ 19	Henley L★ 1	Robinson J★ 2	Wilson FC★ 1
Collins L 1	Humphreys JV★ 8	Robinson P★ 4	Young AA★ 17
Compton LH★ 1	Lambert ESG 1	Robson AP 30	
Cuthbertson JG★ 2	Lewis G 11	Russell RI★ 1	

Goals (91): Ferrier 21, Dawes A 15, Wilson A 15, Smith 11, Robson 10, Girling 4, Allen 2, Bryant 2, Spencer 2, Biggs 1, Briscoe 1, Cuthbertson 1, Lewis G 1, Lewis J 1, Redfern 1, Robinson P 1, Somerfield 1, Ward 1.

1944–45

Barrett JW★ 1	Driver A★ 2	Lowes AR★ 4	Spence – 4
Betts E 4	Ferrier H★ 22	McCormack JT★ 1	Spencer H★ 21
Blackman JJ 10	Ferrier RJ★ 1	McFarlane DL★ 17	Stanley EAW 1
Blair J★ 1	Foreman GA★ 1	Millbank JH 3	Stephens R 3
Bradshaw R 1	Geddington – 1	Moore NW★ 3	Stevens L★ 4
Briscoe JER★ 5	Gillespie IC 2	Morrad F★ 2	Stewart J★ 1
Brown HT★ 2	Gregory E★ 1	Mountford RC★ 31	Stock AWA★ 1
Buchanan P★ 1	Harding EJ 5	Muir M★ 1	Storey WCG★ 1
Burke C★ 2	Horn –★ 1	Parlane J★ 5	Taylor GE★ 1
Burley B★ 1	Hudgell AJ 28	Paton JA★ 1	Tickridge S★ 1
Challis SMD 4	Hurrell W★ 1	Phillips W★ 14	Tootill A 14
Cheetham TM★ 7	Jackman DC 1	Rampling DW★ 1	Townsend HRJ 3
Clarkson HC 1	Jones EN★ 13	Redfern R★ 1	Wales H★ 1
Connor JT★ 1	Kurz FJ★ 20	Reece TS 3	Ward LA 1
Cruickshanks J★ 1	Lewis G 10	Robson AP 12	Wilson A 26
Dawes AG 19	Lewis J 8	Scarr R 1	Young GM 1
Dawes FW 8	Lievesley L 4	Somerfield A★ 22	

Goals (79): Kurz 15, Somerfield 14, Wilson 9, Dawes A 6, Blackman 5, Robson 4, Cheetham 3, Driver 3, Ferrier R 3, Jones 3, Betts 2, Mountford 2, Stevens 2, Connor 1, Dawes F 1, Lewis G 1, Parlane 1, Spencer 1, Stock 1, own goals 2.

1945–46

Addinall AW★ 2	Fagan W★ 3	Humphreys JV★ 15	Robson AP 9
Allen KG 1	Ferrier RJ★ 1	Jackman DC 1	Smith JT 15
Bark WH 8	Ford WH 11	Kurz FJ 30	Stamps JD★ 5
Bassett WEG 14	Forder JL 2	Lewis G 15	Stevens L★ 2
Blackman JJ 12	Girling HM 6	Lewis J 33	Stewart J★ 1
Burrell LF 4	Graham DR 23	Lievesley L 9	Surtees J★ 1
Chilvers GT 1	Gregory FC 22	Male G 5	Waldron E 2
Collins N 2	Harding EJ 3	Matthewson G★ 2	Wilson A 26
Corbett J★ 1	Henley L★ 1	McFarlane DL★ 1	Winter DT★ 1
Dawes AG 8	Hindle FJ★ 1	Millbank JH 3	Woodward V★ 1
Dawes FW 31	Hudgell AJ 33	Morris RJ 3	
Eastman DJ 3	Hughes WH★ 1	Reece TS 22	

Goals (92): Kurz 32, Reece 8, Lewis G 7, Blackman 6, Lievesley 5, Robson 5, Addinall 4, Wilson 4, Bark 3, Dawes A 3, Stamps 3, Smith 2, Stevens 2, Dawes F 1, Fagan 1, Ferrier 1, Girling 1, Hudgell 1, Lewis J 1, Surtees 1, Waldron 1.

FA Cup goals (0).

Darlington

1939–40

Annables W★ 1	Foulkes HE 15	Loughran J★ 3	Smith W 15
Ashley H 3	Frost J 1	Milburn J★ 5	Spedding JJ 15
Birkett RJE★ 10	Fuller RJ 3	Odell WR 3	Stephenson GH★ 2
Brown W 3	Hodgson D★ 2	Pallister A 6	Stuart RW★ 1
Calverley A★ 1	Hodgson J 16	Park W 2	Surtees J 16
Cartwright G★ 1	Hodgson S 3	Reeve KE★ 1	Theaker CA★ 5
Charlesworth S★ 1	Hogg F 13	Richardson J★ 7	Thomson CM★ 1
Cochrane T★ 6	Hughes WA★ 1	Riches W★ 1	Todd A 13
Deacon R★ 13	Jameson P 2	Robinson J★ 1	Wallace JW★ 1
Dinsdale M★ 1	Johnson WT 3	Scott WR★ 8	Wardle GW★ 1
Dyson G★ 1	Kelly D 5	Simpson R 20	Woodward W★ 2
Forrest W★ 1	Kelly TW 6	Smith S 1	

Goals (49): Surtees 11, Simpson 6, Hogg 5, Cochrane 3, Reeve 3, Kelly TW 2, Loughran 2, Odell 2, Park 2, Robinson 2, Stephenson 2, Ashley 1, Birkett 1, Deacon 1, Johnson 1, Spedding 1, Stuart 1, Wardle 1, Woodward 1, own goal 1.

War Cup goals (5): Hogg 2, Odell 1, Simpson 1, Surtees 1.

1940–41

Did not compete.

1941–42

Did not compete.

1942–43

Did not compete.

1943–44

Barron J★ 2	Dodds R★ 1	Makepeace R★ 1	Tapken N★ 32
Billingham J★ 13	Dodds TB★ 2	McKillop J★ 1	Taylor F★ 10
Birse CV★ 12	Dorsett R★ 1	McMahon H★ 2	Thyne RB 26
Browne CJ★ 37	Dowen JS★ 15	Mullen J★ 13	Todd AC 2
Burchell GS 10	Forster LJ★ 2	Pickering B 2	Tooze DG★ 29
Cadman J 1	Forster WB★ 1	Rudkin TW★ 20	Towers J 10
Carr EM★ 2	Hamilton S 2	Saunders H★ 1	Treanor J★ 1
Cheyne A 2	Hays CJ★ 9	Shergold WR★ 1	Tudor W★ 2
Christie I★ 12	Hetherington TB★ 2	Simpson R 22	Varty T 1
Clarke JH★ 2	Jameson B★ 1	Smith S★ 8	Wharton G★ 29
Crack FW★ 1	Kelly J★ 18	Spelman I★ 2	Wright TB★ 1
Cuthbert ED 1	Kelly TW 31	Stobbart GC★ 3	Young R 1
Deacon R 5	Knight AW★ 5	Stubbs CF 19	

Goals (99): Browne 37, Billingham 9, Simpson 9, Kelly J 5, Stobbart 5, Stubbs 5, Rudkin 4, Birse 3, Thyne 3, Christie 2, Kelly T 2, Wharton 2, Birchall 1, Cadman 1, Cheyne 1, Clarke 1, Dodds T 1, McKillop 1, Mullen 1, Tooze 1, Towers 1, own goals 4.

1944–45

Beaumont R★ 2
Blythe J 5
Brown C★ 12
Burchell GS 21
Cassidy W★ 11
Chapman W★ 1
Clarke JH 32
Cochrane J★ 3
Colley JH★ 1
Connor JT★ 8
Craig J★ 2
Davidson RT★ 7
Deacon R 1

Dodds R 4
Dowen JS★ 6
Everitt R 9
Gordon J★ 2
Hallam J★ 11
Harper JJ★ 1
Hetherington TB★ 15
Hutchinson K 1
Inglis J★ 18
Kelly J★ 12
Kelly TW 5
Kilcram J 1
Knight AW★ 1

Leonard H 5
Liddle J 2
Logan JW★ 1
Middleton MY★ 1
Mullen J★ 14
Nicholson WE★ 20
Parsley WN 11
Paton W★ 1
Rojan OW★ 4
Rudkin TW★ 17
Samuelson F★ 1
Shergold WR★ 11
Sidlow C★ 20

Simpson R 23
Stubbs CF 29
Sykes K 1
Syles J★ 1
Tapkin N★ 6
Taylor F★ 1
Thomas A 1
Thompson G 1
Thyne RB 13
Towers J 32
Varty T 20
Ward TA★ 6
Wharton G★ 28

Goals (113): Clarke 25, Inglis 23, Brown 11, Varty 9, Wharton 6, Rudkin 5, Ward 5, Sykes 4, Connor 3, Kelly J 3, Simpson 3, Davidson 2, Liddle 2, Mullen 2, Shergold 2, Stubbs 2, Beaumont 1, Gordon 1, Kelly T 1, Samuelson 1, Thyne 1, own goal 1.

1945–46

Birkett RJE★ 5
Blythe J 7
Burchell GS 6
Clarke JH 35
Coxon J 2
Davidson RT★ 19
Dodds R 9
Dunn W 27

Everitt R 6
Govan R 4
Harrison R 14
Hutchinson K 23
Kelly J★ 2
Kelly TW 28
Langston G★ 3
Liddle J 6

Lyons W★ 2
McCue JW★ 1
Mullen J★ 3
Parsley WN 21
Simpson R 30
Stephenson H 4
Stubbs CF 9
Tapken N★ 6

Thyne RB 21
Towers J 32
Varty T 30
Warburton G★ 3
Whaley G 1
Wharton G★ 26
Williams S 15
Wort JF 7

Goals (104): Clarke 46, Simpson 12, Varty 9, Davidson 7, Williams 5, Govan 3, Harrison 3, Parsley 3, Stubbs 3, Warburton 3, Wharton 2, Dodds 1, Liddle 1, Mullen 1, Stephenson 1, Thyne 1, own goals 3.

FA Cup goals (10): Harrison 4, Clarke 2, Towers 2, Sykes K 1, Varty 1.

Derby County

1939–40

Barker JW 3	Howe JR 3	Stamps JD 3	Wilson J 1
Boulton FP 3	McCulloch D 3	Walsh W 3	
Duncan D 3	Nicholas JT 3	Ward TV 2	
Hann R 2	Redfern WJ 2	Wilcox GE 2	

Goals (3): Duncan 1, Nicholas 1, Redfern 1.

1940–41

Did not compete.

1941–42

Played friendly games only.

1942–43

Attwood E 5	Delaney L★ 7	McCulloch D 5	Sinclair T★ 1
Bacuzzi J★ 2	Duncan D 31	McDonald R★ 1	Smith D 3
Bailey L 3	Eggleston T 1	Musson WU 1	Smith S 1
Baxter WE★ 1	Fisher FW★ 1	Nicholas JT 25	Smith TM★ 16
Beattie A★ 10	Gardener S★ 1	Pallett KW 1	Stamps JD 3
Bivens TA 7	Grace A 2	Parr J 33	Townsend W 37
Boulton FP 1	Griffiths FS★ 1	Pithie W★ 5	Trim RF★ 11
Butler G 3	Hann R 12	Powell T 29	Tunstall RE 5
Challenger W 6	Hibbs L 5	Ramage PMF 11	Vose C★ 5
Challinor J★ 1	Jones H 1	Rawcliffe F★ 1	Ward TV 4
Collins A★ 1	Leuty LH★ 3	Richardson WG★ 2	Weaver S★ 25
Collins Alex★ 1	Lyman CC★ 35	Rickards CT★ 1	Webber EV★ 1
Corkhill WG★ 1	Marriott GW 1	Riddell GE 3	Westland J★ 10
Crooks SD 31	McCormick J★ 1	Shaw A 1	Wilcox GE 2

Goals (92): Lyman 22, Duncan 17, Crooks 12, Powell 10, McCulloch 6, Attwood 4, Nicholas 4, Weaver 3, Challenger 2, Ramage 2, Sinclair 2, Westland 2, Beattie 1, Bivens 1, Fisher 1, Smith D 1, own goals 2.

1943–44

Airlie S★ 1	Firth JW★ 2	Jones TA 24	Riddell GE 1
Ancell RFD★ 3	Fisher F★ 2	Knight JW 7	Rodgers AW★ 2
Attwood E 2	Grace A 8	Knott H★ 1	Slack L 4
Bivens TA 5	Griffiths J★ 1	Lambert EV 3	Smith D 1
Boulton FP 4	Hann R 14	Leuty LH 37	Spacey PB 1
Bowyer F★ 3	Harrison RF 1	Lyman CC★ 4	Stamps JD 2
Brigham H★ 11	Heydon C 1	Mackay GDF★ 2	Swindin GH★ 14
Carter HS★ 14	Hibbs L 1	McCulloch D 2	Tapping FH★ 4
Challenger W 11	Hinchliffe T 5	Mountford F★ 2	Thompson A 1
Conway J★ 4	Hold O★ 1	Musson WU 11	Townsend W 19
Crooks SD 28	Howell JR 1	Nicholas JT 27	Trim RF 23
Delaney L★ 6	Jeffrey R 1	Parr J 22	Vose G★ 10
Duncan D 33	John WR★ 2	Pithie DS★ 1	Ward TV 15
Egan H★ 2	Jones H 1	Powell T 19	Woodward V★ 2

Goals (76): Carter 13, Duncan 9, Nicholas 9, Crooks 6, Powell 4, Bowyer 3, Grace 3, McCulloch 3, Stamps 3, Woodward 3, Conway 2, Hinchliffe 2, Jones T 2, Knight 2, Attwood 1, Bivens 1, Challenger 1, Harrison 1, Hold 1, Mackay 1, Mountford 1, Musson 1, Rodgers 1, Slack 1, Spacey 1, own goal 1.

1944–45

Baird H★   3
Baxter WE★   5
Bilton DH   5
Bolton FP   2
Brown ARJ★   1
Bullions JL   41
Butler G   1
Carter HS★   28
Crooks SD   26
Doherty PD★   29

Duncan D   41
Eccles WR   1
Grant AF★   3
Harrison RF   3
Johnston GT★   1
Jones TA   9
Jordan C★   3
Kinnerlay F   1
Knight JW   2
Lambert EV   1

Leuty LH   43
Lyman CC★   25
Marshall JG★   2
Morrison AC   7
Musson WU   38
Nicholas JT   17
Parr J   42
Powell T   22
Savage R★   27
Slack L   1

Smith C★   8
Stephen JH★   1
Tapping FH★   9
Townsend W   1
Trim RF   27
Vanham SC   2
Wainwright A   3
Ward TV   1
Williams BF★   2

Goals (132): Doherty 35, Carter 29, Lyman 18, Duncan 11, Tapping 10, Crooks 9, Powell 5, Wainwright 3, Smith 2, Baird 1, Bullions 1, Harrison 1, Jones 1, Jordan 1, Leuty 1, Morrison 1, Slack 1, own goals 2.

1945–46

Allsopp W★   2
Beasley A★   1
Bilton DH   2
Bolton FP   24
Brinton JV   2
Bullions JL   33
Carter HS   21
Crooks SD   18

Doherty PD   32
Duncan D   35
Eggleston T   8
Griffiths W   1
Hann R   6
Harrison RF   27
Howe JR   11
Leuty LH   37

Lyman CC★   4
McCulloch D   7
Morrison AC   29
Musson WU   31
Nicholas JT   42
Parr J   31
Powell T   14
Price AJW★   2

Savage R★   5
Shearer JM   1
Simpson J★   1
Slack L   1
Stamps JD   16
Trim RF   5
Ward TV   5
Woodley VR   8

Goals (101): Doherty 23, Morrison 19, Carter 13, Stamps 12, Duncan 10, Harrison 7, Musson 3, Powell 3, Price 3, Lyman 2, McCulloch 2, Simpson 1, own goals 3.

FA Cup goals (37): Carter 12, Doherty 10, Stamps 9, Crooks 3, Harrison 1, Morrison 1, own goal 1.

Doncaster Rovers

1939–40

Barraclough A 17	Gold W 23	Malam A 3	Raynor F 4
Bell F 2	Heavey JW★ 1	McFarlane RR 3	Shaw W 20
Beresford FE 19	Henry GR★ 4	Millership W★ 1	Sinclair TM★ 2
Burbanks WE★ 15	Jordan C 2	Mitchell A 17	Stirland CJ 14
Burton S★ 4	Killourhy M 16	Myers JH★ 1	Thompson L★ 1
Bycroft S 21	Kirkaldie J 3	Owens TL 7	Vincent E 1
Casson JW 1	Kuhnel D★ 1	Perry E 4	Walker A 23
Deakin – 3	Leyfield C 3	Phypers E 12	
Dodd RI★ 1	Lievesley L★ 2	Potts VE 2	

Goals (41): Killourhy 9, Barraclough 7, Burbanks 4, Bycroft 4, Beresford 3, Henry 3, Owens 3, Leyfield 2, Mitchell 2, Perry 2, Jordan 1, Sinclair 1.

War Cup goals (0).

1940–41

Asquith B★ 3	Coulston W★ 2	Lievesley L★ 5	Phypers E 14
Barraclough A 6	Forde S★ 8	Mayberry S★ 22	Shaw W 2
Beckwith – 1	Gledhill S★ 2	McLean J 1	Sinclair TM 12
Bodle H★ 32	Gold W 12	Meens H★ 2	Stirland CJ 20
Bray E★ 1	Henry GR★ 15	Mills J★ 1	Vincent E 1
Burbanks EW★ 1	Johnson H 10	Mitchell A 23	Walker A 31
Burton S★ 30	Jones G★ 1	Moralee M★ 1	Wooldridge J 18
Bycroft S 33	Jones W★ 2	Morris A★ 2	
Carte R★ 1	Jordan C 9	Nightingale S 23	
Copping W★ 9	Killourhy M 9	Oram DC 9	

Goals (77): Bodle 23, Henry 19, Nightingale 6, Burton 5, Jordan 5, Killourhy 4, Johnson 3, Oram 3, Sinclair 3, Shaw 2, Burbanks 1, Bycroft 1, Jones G 1, Mitchell 1.

1941–42

Bailey L★ 7	Fuller RJ 8	Jordan C 9	Poxton W 2
Barber AW★ 5	Gibson F 5	Killourhy M 3	Rogers W★ 3
Barraclough A 4	Gladwin G★ 1	Lievesley L★ 4	Shaw W 1
Beresford FE★ 1	Gold W 2	Little G 2	Sinclair TM 4
Bodle H★ 19	Grainger D★ 1	Marshall CR★ 1	Stirland CJ 8
Brough GT 17	Harston JC★ 6	Mayberry S★ 4	Swallow E 2
Burton S★ 26	Head BJ★ 9	Meens H★ 5	Vaux E★ 1
Bycroft S 10	Hindmarsh JW★ 4	Mitchell A 19	Wadsworth CE★ 1
Daniels J★ 3	Hubbard C★ 12	Nicholls J★ 1	Walker A 19
Dodd RI★ 1	Johnson H 1	Nightingale S 25	Walker CH 1
Drury GB★ 1	Jones G 3	Oram DC 1	Wooldridge J 18
Ferguson A 10	Jones S★ 1	Owens TL 6	

Goals (49): Bodle 13, Nightingale 7, Burton 6, Hubbard 6, Fuller 4, Owens 3, Jordan 2, Rogers 2, Bailey 1, Barber 1, Barraclough 1, Brough 1, Killourhy 1, Mitchell 1.

1942–43

Alsford W★ 3	Ferguson A 11	Laking GE★ 19	Steele FC★ 5
Atter AM 22	Gladwin G★ 5	Leeman AT 5	Stirland CJ 26
Attwell RF★ 4	Grainger D★ 3	Little G 1	Sutherland HR★ 5
Banner A★ 2	Gregory M★ 4	Lunn G★ 1	Swallow E 4
Barraclough A 1	Haines JTW★ 2	McDermott C★ 1	Thorogood J★ 14
Bodle H★ 26	Hardy JH★ 5	Mitchell A 5	Walker A 12
Brader FW★ 1	Harkin J★ 14	Nightingale S 4	Walker CH 4
Brough GT 10	Head BJ★ 1	Poxton W 21	Westland J★ 4
Burton S★ 4	Henry GR★ 1	Shaw W 1	Wildman FR★ 1
Bycroft S 16	Hubbard C★ 28	Sherwood GW★ 2	Wilkinson N★ 1
Challinor J★ 10	Jordan C 4	Sinclair TM 29	Wilson R★ 1
Drury GB★ 10	Killourhy M 1	Somerfield A★ 2	Wooldridge J 18

Goals (50): Hubbard 15, Bodle 6, Harkin 5, Jordan 4, Steele 4, Drury 3, Sutherland 3, Sinclair 2, Thorogood 2, Burton 1, Gladwin 1, Gregory 1, Walker 1, Westland 1, own goal 1.

1943–44

Atter AM   1
Attwell RF★   19
Banner R★   24
Beresford FE★   1
Bodle H★   31
Brough GT   4
Bycroft S   28
Carte R★   1

Courtier L★   1
Gregory FC★   30
Hartley TW★   7
Jones G   2
Jones T★   1
Jordan C   13
Kirkaldie J   1
Laking GE★   30

Macaulay AR★   9
Malam A   1
Massarella L★   27
Mitchell HV   16
Poxton W   6
Quinn T   2
Robinson JJ★   29
Sinclair TM   12

Steele FC★   15
Stirland CJ   12
Thorogood J★   32
Walker CH   2
Westland J★   19
Wooldridge J   9

Goals (87): Bodle 18, Massarella 13, Steele 12, Thorogood 12, Sinclair 7, Westland 7, Hartley 5, Jordan 4, Gregory 3, Attwell 2, Brough 1, Macaulay 1, Stirland 1, own goal 1.

1944–45

Alberry WE   3
Attwell RF★   12
Banner A★   2
Beedall BB   2
Bodle H★   34
Britton CS★   16
Brough GT   5
Bycroft S   37

Every C   1
Heydon C★   6
Jordan C   32
Lightfoot AJ   1
Marriott J   3
Massarella L★   4
Mitchell HV   12
Mitcheson F   26

Peters T   3
Potts VE   1
Poxton W   13
Quinn T   5
Robinson JJ★   25
Stevenson A   12
Stirland CJ   26
Swallow E   2

Thorogood J★   34
Tindill H   36
Tomlinson H   25
Williams A★   5
Woodburn J★   1
Wooldridge J   34

Goals (92): Bodle 27, Jordan 27, Tindill 13, Thorogood 10, Mitcheson 7, Massarella 2, Alberry 1, Attwell 1, Heydon 1, Marriott 1, Quinn 1, own goal 1.

1945–46

Archer WH   28
Attwell RF★   4
Baynham D   3
Burditt G   1
Bycroft S   5
Cork J   1
Eades C   9
Ferguson A   4
Gregory FC   3

Hardwick K   25
Heydon C   24
Jordan C   33
Killourhy M   3
Kirkaldie J   9
Lightfoot AJ   1
Little G   6
Maddison R   17
Marriott J   16

McFarlane RR   19
Mitcheson F   24
Owen TL   1
Robinson JJ★   7
Roby H   1
Staniforth H   7
Starbuck J   1
Stevenson A   6
Stirland CJ   17

Swallow E   27
Thorogood J★   8
Tindill H   14
Todd PR   33
Tomlinson H   1
White L   2
Wooldridge J   36

Goals (70): Jordan 20, Todd 16, Marriott 7, Mitcheson 4, Thorogood 4, Archer 3, Kirkaldie 3, Maddison 3, Tindill 3, Gregory 2, Killourhy 2, Heydon 1, McFarlane 1, Stirland 1.

Div 3N goals (4): Maddison 3, Todd 1.

Match not included in final table.

FA Cup goals (1): Todd 1.

Everton

1939–40

Barber E 1	Davies JW 1	Jones TG 19	Sharp NW 1
Bell RC 6	Gee CW 2	Lawton T 17	Simmons S 2
Bentham SJ 22	Gillick T 7	Lindley WM 14	Stevenson AE 23
Boyes W 25	Greenhalgh N 24	Lyon J 1	Sumner W 2
Burnett GG 2	Jackson G 21	Mercer J 17	Sweeney FT 4
Catterick H 4	Johnson A 1	Sagar E 23	Watson TG 24
Cook W 3	Jones JE 1	Saunders GE 1	Wyles TC 7

Goals (69): Lawton 16, Stevenson 15, Bentham 8, Boyes 6, Bell 4, Gillick 3, Jones TG 3, Mercer 3, Simmons 3, Sweeney 2, Wyles 2, Catterick 1, Davies 1, Greenhalgh 1, Johnson 1.

War Cup goals (15): Lawton 6, Jones TG 2, Stevenson 2, Bentham 1, Boyes 1, Gillick 1, Sumner 1, Wyles 1.

1940–41

Arthur J 13	Finnis HA 2	Lewis C 5	Sagar E 24
Bailey G 2	Greenhalgh N 40	Lindeman HF 1	Simmons S 15
Barber E 1	Hankin N 2	Lindley WM 1	Stevenson AE 28
Bell RC 3	Hill M 4	Lovett PR 15	Sumner W 2
Bentham SJ 38	Jackson G 18	Lyon J 18	Thomson JR 1
Boyes W 13	Johnson A 1	Mercer J 26	Trentham DH 1
Britton CS 6	Jones JE 8	Owen W 4	Watson TG 29
Catterick H 21	Jones TG 33	Penlington A 4	Wyles TC 8
Cook W 31	Lawton T 21	Powell J 1	

Goals (100): Lawton 30, Catterick 17, Stevenson 11, Bentham 8, Jackson 5, Lyon 5, Mercer 5, Simmons 5, Boyes 4, Jones TG 2, Wyles 2, Arthur 1, Bailey 1, Bell 1, Britton 1, Cook 1, Owen 1.

1941–42

Anderson EW★ 34	Curwen G 7	Kinnell R★ 1	Soo F★ 1
Bailey G 1	Greenhalgh N 32	Lawton T 11	Stevenson AE 35
Barber E 1	Higham N★ 1	Lovett PR 3	Thomson JR 3
Bentham SJ 40	Hill M 6	Lyon J 18	Waring T★ 2
Boyes W 13	Ireland R 1	Mercer J 23	Watson TG 9
Burnett GG 29	Jackson G 17	Mutch G★ 3	Williams A 3
Caskie J 2	Jones HJ★ 26	Owen W 21	Wyles TC 1
Catterick H 1	Jones JE 5	Sagar E 8	
Cook W 39	Jones TG 23	Seddon EA 1	
Cunliffe JN 3	Keen ERL★ 26	Sharp NW 1	

Goals (98): Lawton 14, Stevenson 12, Jones H 10, Cook 8, Mercer 8, Owen 8, Jones TG 7, Lyon 6, Anderson 5, Bentham 5, Jackson 4, Boyes 3, Soo 2, Catterick 1, Cunliffe 1, Kinnell 1, Mutch 1, Waring 1, Wyles 1, own goal 1.

Includes one extra-time goal.

1942–43

Anderson EW★ 7	Curwen G 9	Jones HJ★ 20	Mercer J 12
Ashcroft LL★ 1	Dellow RW★ 13	Jones JE 10	Mutch G★ 33
Beattie R★ 1	Dunkley R★ 1	Jones TG 8	Owen W★ 1
Bentham SJ 31	Fairfoull T 3	Lawton T 12	Rosenthal A★ 1
Birkett W 11	Fowler T 17	Linaker JE 1	Stevenson AE 35
Boyes W 5	Grant JA 2	Lowe W 2	Urmston TK★ 2
Burnett GG 24	Greenhalgh N 34	Lyon J 3	Watson TG 22
Carey JJ★ 2	Higham N★ 2	Makin G★ 1	Williams E★ 1
Cook W 23	Humphreys JV 15	McDonnell M 3	Wyles TC 6
Curran F★ 7	Jackson G 24	McIntosh JM★ 2	

Goals (103): Mutch 16, Lawton 15, Curran 10, Stevenson 10, Fowler 8, Jones H 8, Wyles 6, Bentham 5, Dellow 5, Jackson 5, Anderson 3, Cook 2, Urmston 2, McIntosh 2, Mercer 2, Curwen 1, Grant 1, Higham 1, own goal 1.

1943–44

Astbury TA*   1
Bentham SJ   22
Boothway K*   3
Boyes W   3
Britton CS   1
Burnett GG   40
Caskie J   1
Catterick H   2
Doyle RL   1
Gillick T   1
Glidden GS*   1
Grant JA   36

Greenhalgh N   36
Hall WW*   1
Hallard W*   5
Higgins WC   1
Humphreys JV   2
Jackson G   33
Jones F   1
Jones JE   26
Jones S*   7
Jones TG   33
Lawton T   25
Lee JS*   2

Linaker JE   2
Low N*   1
Lowe W   3
Makin G   1
McDonnell M   3
McIntosh JM*   40
Mercer J   7
Morley J   1
Murphy G*   1
Mutch G*   2
Roberts F*   1
Rogers E*   1

Sharp NW   1
Smith A*   1
Steele EC*   2
Stevenson AE   27
Tatters C   2
Turner P*   2
Wainwright EF   22
Watson TG   23
Wootton L   1
Wyles TC   12

Goals (133): Lawton 40, McIntosh 29, Stevenson 22, Wainwright 9, Wyles 9, Bentham 8, Jones TG 5, Grant 3, Jackson 3, Boothway 2, Catterick 1, Mutch 1, own goal 1.

Appearances include County Cup final second leg match.

1944–45

Ashley A   2
Bentham SJ   23
Boyes W   17
Burnett GG   45
Catterick H   15
Curwen G   1
Doyle RL   2
Dugdale G   1
Gillick T   2

Grant JA   44
Greenhalgh N   44
Heath C*   1
Hedley JR   1
Hill M   2
Humphreys JV   11
Jackson G   44
Jones F   1
Jones TG   12

King TH   1
Lawton T   17
Lindley WM   22
Logan JW*   1
Makin G   15
McDonnell M   1
McIntosh JM*   10
Mercer J   5
Morris J*   1

Peters T*   3
Rawlings JSD*   28
Sharp NW   5
Stevenson AE   36
Wainwright EF   17
Watson TG   43
Wootton L   2
Wyles TC   20

Goals (137): Lawton 28, Wyles 26, Stevenson 17, Bentham 14, Rawlings 11, Catterick 10, Wainwright 10, Jones TG 8, Makin 4, Boyes 3, McIntosh 2, Grant 1, Jackson 1, Mercer 1, Peters 1, own goal 1.

Includes one extra-time goal.

1945–46

Bell RC   5
Bentham SJ   32
Bond T*   1
Boyes W   42
Burnett GG   42
Catterick H   28
Cookson J   1

Elliott T   4
Fielding WA   34
Grant JA   10
Greenhalgh N   41
Higgins WC   4
Humphreys JV   22
Jackson G   42

Johnson A   2
Jones TG   10
Lawton T   5
Lowe W   3
Makin G   5
McIlhatton J   1
Mercer J   25

Rawlings JSD   17
Stevenson AE   18
Wainwright EF   27
Watson TG   37
Wyles TC   4

Goals (88): Catterick 25, Wainwright 17, Boyes 12, Bentham 5, Jones 4, Fielding 3, Lawton 3, Mercer 3, Rawlings 3, Bell 2, Higgins 2, Stevenson 2, Wyles 2, Elliott 1, Grant 1, Greenhalgh 1, Watson 1, own goal 1.

FA Cup goals (3): Catterick 1, Elliott 1, Mercer 1.

Exeter City

1939–40

Angus J   3
Blood JF   3
Bowl HT   3
Ebdon R   1

Fellowes WJ   3
Freeman RH   1
Little J   1
Riley H   2

Speed F   2
Sutherley C   3
Thomson C   3
Walker S   3

Wardle G   3
Windle C   2

Goals (5): Ebdon 2, Riley 2, Bowl 1.

1940–41

Did not compete.

1941–42

Did not compete.

1942–43

Did not compete.

1943–44

Did not compete.

1944–45

Did not compete.

1945–46

Angus J   14
Attwood E★   1
Baxter G   1
Blood JF   31
Bowden AJ★   10
Boye-Karlsen H   1
Brown JB   7
Casey D   2
Challis SMD   18
Coles A   15
Crawshaw C   1
Cutting SW   8
Dalgliesh G★   1
Davison AE★   1

Eastham S   5
Ebdon R   31
Elliott EW   1
Franklin JL★   1
Gadsby KJ★   8
Gallagher J   2
Goodfellow DO★   12
Haddington R★   2
Haddock H   4
Harris J★   2
Hydes A   5
Jones EN★   1
Jones T★   1
Jordan W   27

Joslin PJ★   1
Kernick DHG★   8
Lambton WE   3
Langford W   1
Latham L★   2
Lewis G   6
Long JW   2
Mitcheson F★   9
Murray J   25
Perkins LA   1
Petherbridge GE   1
Purvis R★   1
Regan DJT   9
Rich L★   2

Roughton GW★   10
Singleton B   13
Staveley W   1
Sutherley C   2
Thomson C   6
Tickell R   9
Topsham C★   3
Walker S   31
Wardle G   28
Warren C   2
Wright H   7

Goals (55): Ebdon 15, Challis 8, Walker 8, Kernick 5, Wardle 5, Casey 2, Mitcheson 2, Regan 2, Wright 2, Blood 1, Bowden 1, Haddington 1, Jones E 1, Tickell 1, Warren 1.

FA Cup goals (12): Walker 5, Challis 2, Crawshaw 1, Ebdon 1, Gallagher 1, Tickell 1, own goal 1.

Fulham

1939–40

Arnold J 29
Bacuzzi J 18
Boulton FP★ 4
Burgess H★ 7
Cann H 19
Chesters A★ 1
Cothliff HT★ 1
Cox FJA★ 4
Cranfield HR 3
Dennison RS 1
Evans JL 35
Finch J 27

Fisher LP 2
Flack DW 7
Freeman HG 7
Green GH★ 2
Griffiths J★ 7
Higgins D 2
Hiles EC 33
Jones LJ★ 1
Keeping AEM 37
Mason WS★ 1
McCormick J★ 6
McCormick R 4

Mills GR★ 4
Muttitt E★ 1
O'Callaghan E 3
Ottewell S★ 5
Perry E★ 5
Pitts H 1
Reay EP★ 3
Rooke RL 28
Rozier AT 1
Scott HS 1
Shepherd E 1
Smith J★ 1

Stuart R 2
Taylor JG 35
Thomas DS 4
Thomas DWJ★ 3
Tompkins JJ 22
Turner H 3
Weaver S★ 2
Whatley WJ★ 1
Wilkins GE★ 2
Woodward V 37
Worsley H 6

Goals (91): Rooke 27, Woodward 19, Arnold 10, Ottewell 5, Perry 5, McCormick J 3, Burgess 2, Cranfield 2, Finch 2, Fisher 2, Mills 2, Taylor 2, Thomas DS 2, Muttitt 1, Thomas DWJ 1, Tompkins 1, Wilkins 1, own goals 4.

War Cup goals (18): Rooke 6, Woodward 4, Arnold 3, McCormick J 2, Jones 1, Thomas DS 1, own goal 1.

1940–41

Arnold J 2
Bacuzzi J 10
Bastin CS★ 1
Birkett RJE★ 3
Bonass AE★ 1
Boulton FP★ 12
Briggs F★ 5
Buckham K★ 1
Cardwell L★ 3
Collett E★ 1
Cranfield HR 2
Cullis S★ 9
Duke GE★ 1
Evans JL 7
Finch J 17

Fisher LP 11
Flack DW 7
Freeman HG 7
Griffiths WM★ 1
Grundy JA★ 5
Halton RL★ 3
Hammond RAC 1
Hiles EC 31
Hobbins SG★ 4
Hughes WM★ 2
Jobling J★ 1
Joslin PJ★ 8
Kay W★ 1
Keeping AEM 2
Lunn G★ 1

Malpass ST 7
Matthewson G★ 5
McCormick J★ 2
McCormick R 2
Miller JW 6
Morris R 5
Muttitt E★ 10
O'Callaghan E 9
O'Leary V★ 15
Osborne J 2
Pavitt WE 1
Penn F 1
Poulter J★ 1
Revell C★ 14
Richfield M 2

Robinson GH★ 2
Rodger R★ 2
Rooke RL 27
Rozier AT 1
Scaife G★ 14
Smith JT★ 2
Spence R★ 3
Taylor JG 7
Thomas DWJ★ 14
Thomson JR★ 1
Trewick G★ 1
Weaver SA 3
Whittaker W★ 3
Wilson J 1
Woodward V 29

Goals (65): Rooke 25, Thomas 9, Woodward 8, Revell 5, Miller 3, Finch 2, Fisher 2, Halton 2, O'Callaghan 2, Birkett 1, Hiles 1, McCormick J 1, Osborne 1, Richfield 1, Robinson 1, Taylor 1.

London Cup

Bacuzzi 4, Beasley A★ 2, Chalkley AG★ 1, Cullis 6, Evans 4, Frewick – 1, Griffiths R★ 2, Griffiths WM★ 1, Hiles 10, Hobbins 9, Howe LF★ 1, Joslin 1, Keeping 2, McCormick J★ 1, Mahon J★ 1, Matthewson 2, Muttitt 2, O'Callaghan 6, O'Leary 5, Read – 1, Revell 10, Robinson 7, Rooke 9, Scaife 3, Smith 1, Taylor 1, Tomkins JJ 2, Whittaker 7, Woodward 8.

Goals: Rooke 10, O'Callaghan 4, Woodward 4, Revell 3, Beasley 2, Keeping 2, Robinson 2, Cullis 1, Evans 1, Frewick 1, Smith 1, own goal 1.

1941–42

Abel S★   1
Bacuzzi J   10
Beasley A★   1
Bonass AE★   2
Briggs CE★   1
Briggs F★   1
Buckingham VF★   1
Compton LH★   1
Conley JJ★   20
Cranfield HR   6
Cullis S★   9
Cumner RH★   2
Dean CG★   14
Duffy J★   6
Duke HP★   25
Evans JL   3
Finch J   10
Ford FG★   1
Foxall JS★   5

Freeman HG   13
Gallacher P★   29
Gibbons AH★   1
Griffiths WM★   2
Hamilton W★   1
Hiles EC   24
Holley T★   1
Holliday J★   2
Howe LF★   1
Jones EN★   7
Jones L★   24
Joslin PJ★   4
Keen ERL★   2
Kelly L★   1
Kiernan T★   5
Lester FC★   2
Lodge –★   1
Ludford G★   1
Mackie J★   1

Malpass ST   7
Marsden F★   1
Matthewson G★   18
McCormick J★   6
Milsom J★   1
Milton GW   1
Morgan –★   1
Muttitt E★   7
Neary HF   1
Nichols E   1
Parry O★   1
Poland G★   1
Pryde RI★   2
Rampling DW   4
Richardson JR★   6
Rooke RL   25
Scaife G★   2
Sharp –★   3
Sibley A★   12

Skinner G★   1
Smith C★   1
Smith E★   2
Sneddon WC★   1
Stevens AH   1
Swift FV★   5
Taylor F★   4
Thomas DWJ★   4
Tickridge S★   1
Tompkins JJ   10
Tuckett EW   1
Wallbanks H   1
Walsh W★   1
Ward RA★   1
Whatley WJ★   11
Whitfield W★   6
Wilson J   1
Woodward V   2
Young AA★   1

Goals (93): Rooke 30, Conley 18, Gallacher 12, Dean 7, Finch 5, Hiles 3, Woodward 3, Cranfield 2, Kiernan 2, Foxall 1, Freeman 1, Jones E 1, Jones L 1, McCormick 1, Morgan 1, Muttitt 1, Rampling 1, Richardson 1, Sibley 1, Thomas 1.

1942–43

Arnold J   1
Bacuzzi J   13
Broadhurst R★   1
Buckley A★   6
Bush TW★   12
Conley JJ★   32
Conway J★   1
Copping W★   2
Costello W   1
Davie J★   1
Dean CG★   14
Drake EJ★   2
Driver A★   5
Duke HP★   34
Evans JL   19
Farmer A★   1

Ferrier H★   1
Finch J   18
Freeman HG   20
Gallacher P★   3
Hiles EC   3
Hobbis HHF★   1
Holley T★   20
Holliday JW★   2
Jones L★   29
Kirkman N★   1
Kurz FJ★   1
Lester FC★   5
Leyfield C★   7
Lloyd C★   5
Ludford G★   1
Malpass ST   7

Martin DK★   1
McCulloch O★   1
McInnes JS★   4
Merrett GE   1
Milton GW   5
Muir A★   3
Muttitt E★   6
Neary HF   2
Nicholson WE★   1
O'Donnell F★   3
Ottewell S★   9
Palmer RW★   1
Pilkington SH   1
Pitts H   1
Rampling DW   1
Rooke RL   26

Rozier AT   2
Salmon L★   1
Savage RE★   1
Smith C★   1
Smith JT★   2
Sneddon WC★   2
Sperrin W★   1
Stevens AH   2
Thomas DWJ★   10
Thomson JR★   3
Tompkins JJ   4
Tuckett EW   4
Watson JF★   1
Whitfield W★   2
Wilson J   2
Woodward V   1

Goals (81): Rooke 23, Conley 16, Dean 7, Thomas 6, Leyfield 4, Broadhurst 3, Driver 3, Jones 3, Ottewell 3, Finch 2, Freeman 2, Arnold 1, Gallacher 1, Hobbis 1, Holley 1, Holliday 1, Martin 1, Muttitt 1, Neary 1, Tompkins 1.

1943–44

Allen JP★   2
Bowpitt T   3
Brophy HF★   1
Brown J★   8
Buchan WRM★   7
Chick W   1
Cobley WA★   1
Conley JJ★   30
Copping W★   2
Cowan RM★   7
Cox AEH★   18
Dean CG★   3
Devlin J★   4
Duggan EJ★   1
Duke HP★   23
Evans JL   11
Flack WLW★   6
Freeman HG

Fuller C★   1
Halton RL★   1
Henley L★   1
Hickman AH★   3
Hiles EG   1
Holley T★   20
Horton JC★   1
Humphreys J★   1
Humphreys PR★   2
James J★   1
Jones L★   31
Jones VC   2
Joslin PJ★   5
Kiernan T★   11
Kinnear D★   1
Laing FJ★   1
Lester FC★   8
Leyfield C★   15

Lloyd C★   16
Lumby WCM★   1
Malpass ST   7
Mangnall D★   1
Manley T★   6
Millbank JH★   2
Milton GW   2
Muttitt E★   3
O'Callaghan E   10
Phipps H★   1
Quested WL   1
Rampling DW   4
Rooke RL   32
Royston R★   1
Sears DR★   1
Shepherd E   3
Stamps JD★   15
Stevens AH   8

Summers J   4
Taylor JG   1
Taylor TE   8
Thomas DWJ★   11
Thomas RA★   2
Tompkins JJ   4
Wallbanks H   1
Wallbanks J★   1
Ward TA★   1
Watson J★   1
Watson JF★   3
Weaver S★   1
Whittaker W★   2
Wilson J   3
Woodward V   1

Goals (95): Rooke 32, Kiernan 14, Stamps 14, Conley 7, Thomas DWJ 5, Devlin 3, Leyfield 3, Duggan 2, Jones L 2, Holley 2, Quested 2, Stevens 2, Dean 1, Flack 1, Malpass 1, Muttitt 1, O'Callaghan 1, Rampling 1, Taylor TE 1.

1944–45

Abel S★   1
Adams BK   1
Arnold J   7
Bacuzzi J   18
Bewley DG   2
Blair J★   1
Borrows JE★   1
Boulter LM★   6
Bowpitt T   1
Briggs F★   2
Briscoe JER★   1
Buchanan PS   1
Buckingham VF★   7
Buckton T   1
Cheetham TM★   6
Chitty W★   1
Conley JJ★   3
Cowan RM★   15
Cox FJA★   1
Cunliffe AJ★   2
Dawes AG★   1
Dawes FW★   3
Dodds E★   9

Duke HP★   18
Flack WLW★   10
Freeman HG   20
Gage A   2
Gallacher P★   2
Gibson WG★   3
Hamilton DS★   1
Hiles EC   1
Hollis H★   2
Hopkins I★   2
Hudgell AJ★   1
Hunt DA★   1
Jarvis DH   2
Jessop W★   8
Jones C★   1
Jones EN★   2
Jones F★   2
Jones GH★   1
Jones L★   33
Jones S★   3
Jones VC   1
Jordan J★   1
Kiernan T★   1

Kippax FP★   5
Laws WC   1
Leyfield C★   9
Livingstone A★   4
Lloyd C★   12
Lowes AR★   20
Mallett J★   1
McClusky II★   1
McCormick J★   3
Meadows JR   1
Millbank JH★   2
Miller JW   3
Moody KG★   1
Moore NW★   1
Morris J★   1
Muir MR★   1
Muttitt E★   3
Neary HF   2
O'Callaghan E   10
Potts H★   10
Preskett J   2
Rampling DW   2
Redfern R★   1

Rickett HF   10
Robson AP★   1
Rooke RL   15
Shepherd E   1
Sloan JW★   11
Smith J★   3
Smith LGF★   1
Squires A★   1
Steele FC★   1
Taylor JG   3
Tennant AE★   1
Thomas DWJ★   2
Thomas RA★   4
Toser E★   1
Tunnicliffe G★   2
Wallbanks H   1
Watson JF★   26
Weston AL   1
White R★   1
Whittaker W★   1
Wilson J   3
Wright H★   1

Goals (94): Rooke 27, Dodds 11, Potts 11, Lowes 6, Sloan 6, Cheetham 3, Kippax 3, O'Callaghan 3, Thomas RA 3, Arnold 2, Conley 2, Jones L 2, Leyfield 2, Livingstone 2, Steele 2, Flack 1, Gallacher 1, Jessop 1, Watson 1, Weston 1, Wilson 1, own goals 3.

1945–46

Bacuzzi J   35
Beasley A   22
Dewley DG   12
Bremner GH★   1
Brown AW★   1
Buchanan PS   25
Chisholm J★   2
Collins W★   1
Evans JL   8
Evans O   13
Ferrier H★   4
Freeman HG   40

Frost GC   2
Gage A   4
Hiles EC   1
Hindle FJ★   1
Holben G   2
Hunt DA★   1
Jarvis D   7
Jessop W★   1
Jones EN★   9
Little A★   1
Lloyd C   13
Lowes AR★   1

Machin AH★   1
Malpass ST   4
McCormick J   31
McDermott J★   3
Miller JW   4
Morris J★   1
O'Callaghan E   1
Rampling DW   13
Rickett HF   15
Rooke RL   39
Sanders JA★   1
Sargent F★   1

Shepherd E   33
Stevens AH   1
Taylor JG   35
Thomas DS   1
Wallbanks H   26
Wardle C★   4
Watson JF★   25
Wilkins GE★   1
Woodward V   14
Worsley H   1

Goals (93): Rooke 31, Shepherd 16, Buchanan 9, Woodward 8, Beasley 6, McCormick 5, Rampling 4, Freeman 3, Taylor 3, Wardle 2, Collins 1, Frost 1, Jessop 1, Miller 1, Sargent 1, own goal 1.

FA Cup goals (3): Rooke 2, Rampling 1.

Gateshead

1939–40

Birtley R 3	Cassidy W 3	Gallacher HK 3	McLaughlin J 3
Brown A 1	Conroy T 3	Inskip JB 3	Miller EC 2
Callender J 3	Dudgeon A 3	Livingstone A 3	Spooner PG 3

Goals (6): Birtley 2, Callender 2, Spooner 2.

War Cup goals (0).

1940–41

Did not compete.

1941–42

Agar W 3	Curry R★ 2	Lansbury R★ 1	Scott WR★ 4
Barron J★ 31	Devlin E 1	Livingstone A 31	Spelman I★ 26
Black WF★ 5	Dudgeon A 28	Makepeace R★ 3	Spooner PG 13
Bohills J 1	Forster LJ★ 23	McCormack CJ 25	West N★ 5
Cairns JG 1	Gale T 5	Musgrove TD 1	Wilbert GN★ 14
Callender TS★ 6	Glease R 2	Nesbit A 1	Wilson J★ 12
Cassidy W 26	Harrison R 6	Oxley A 4	
Conroy T 12	Johnson T 26	Park W★ 2	
Coyde N★ 2	Lamb GH 1	Scott FH★ 18	

Goals (62): McCormack 20, Johnson 12, Scott F 7, Forster 6, Agar 4, Wilbert 4, Wilson 3, Spelman 2, Cassidy 1, own goals 3.

1942–43

Agar W 3	Dryden H 2	Livingstone A 27	Simpson R★ 2
Barrett P 22	English A★ 1	Makepeace R★ 1	Smith R★ 1
Callender J 13	Farrington R★ 2	McCormack CJ 29	Spelman I★ 19
Callender TS★ 26	Forster LJ★ 15	Mills H 1	Wands A 10
Cassidy W 26	Forster WB★ 5	Oxley A 4	Wilbert GN 24
Casson J 3	Gale T 13	Park W★ 2	Young G 3
Clarke JH 1	Gray R 1	Ross J★ 1	
Dawson E★ 30	Harrison R 11	Scott FH★ 4	
Devlin E 16	Johnson T 22	Shanks R★ 1	

Goals (81): McCormack 23, Forster L 12, Johnson 12, Barrett 9, Callender J 7, Wilbert 7, Cassidy 2, Ross 2, Scott 2, Agar 1, Harrison 1, Oxley 1, Park 1, Spelman 1.

1943–44

Barrett P 7	Dryden H 5	Hetherington TB★ 7	Tulip J★ 1
Barron J★ 1	Easten W 5	Johnson J 1	Turnbull FE 18
Batey R★ 2	Embleton E 1	Johnson T 35	Wands A 21
Bohills J 3	Forster LJ★ 6	Lancaster W 18	West N★ 1
Callender J 13	Forster WB★ 25	Livingstone A 25	Wilbert GN 2
Callender TS★ 38	Gale T 17	McConnoy JE★ 4	Wilson JJ 1
Cassidy W 24	Gibson W 7	McCormack CJ 29	Wort JF 15
Clarke JH 5	Gray R 21	Middleton W 1	
Dawson E★ 4	Harper A 3	Park W★ 2	
Devlin E 35	Harrison R 24	Robson R 2	

Goals (85): McCormack 25, Johnson T 20, Forster W 9, Harrison 6, Livingstone 6, Barrett 4, Harper 3, Lancaster 3, Turnbull 3, Forster L 2, Devlin 1, Dryden 1, Turnbull 1, Wands 1.

1944–45

Bell JH   2
Bohills J   4
Cairns WH   25
Callender J   34
Callender TS★   37
Carr GM★   1
Cassidy W   21
Casson J   1
Clark J★   10
Devlin E   31
Down G   9
Dryden H   4
Dudgeon A   36
Farrington R★   1
Forster A   2
Forster LJ★   13
Gale T   2
Gascoigne W   1
Gray R   22
Hays CJ★   36
Howden J   5
Johnson T   36
Lancaster W   2
Livingstone A   1
McCormack CJ   34
Nesbit A   3
Park W★   8
Thompson W   21
Turnbull FE   1
Tweedie J★   1
Wands A   12
Wilbert GN   3
Wilson A   7
Wort JF   3

Goals (91): McCormack 38, Cairns 14, Thompson 10, Johnson 9, Hays 5, Forster L 4, Bohills 2, Callender J 2, Cassidy 2, Dudgeon 2, Dryden 1, Howden 1, Tweedie 1, own goal 1.

Includes one extra-time goal.

1945–46

Atkinson FJ   11
Bell JH   18
Bentley RFT★   1
Bircham B★   3
Brown R   4
Cairns WH   24
Callender J   30
Callender TS★   30
Cant E   11
Cassidy W   20
Clark H★   1
Cowell GR★   1
Dawson E★   3
Devlin E   30
Dryden H   8
Dudgeon A   24
Forster LJ★   27
Gallon JW   11
Gray R   7
Hays CJ★   5
Howden S   26
Johnson T   27
Lancaster W   1
McCormack CJ   18
McDermott J   1
Oxley A   2
Render J   1
Robinson E   9
Rutherford R   3
Thompson W   16
Wilson A   23

Goals (91): Cairns 35, McCormack 12, Forster L 8, Howden 7, Johnson 7, Callender T 6, Thompson 4, Cant 3, Atkinson 2, Callender J 1, Cassidy 1, Dryden 1, Gallon 1, Lancaster 1, Oxley 1, own goal 1.

Includes two extra-time goals.

FA Cup goals (15): Cairns 5, McCormack 5, Atkinson 1, Callender J 1, Howden 1, Rutherford 1, Thompson 1.

Grimsby Town

1939–40

Bartholomew R   6
Beattie JM   6
Bestall J*   2
Betmead HE   11
Boyd JM   1
Buck T   16
Burton S   1
Charlesworth S   11
Collins A*   2

Crack FW   3
Dodd RI   5
Hall AF   19
Hillard JG   2
Hodgson JV   22
Holmes MM*   6
Howe F   8
Johnson JW   12
Jones TW   4

Kurz FJ   1
Little –   2
Lumby WCW*   11
Moralee W*   5
Neish J*   2
Pearson S*   3
Ponting W*   7
Pridmore AJ   5
Reeve FW   2

Reeve K   7
Roberts J   4
Robinson –   1
Taylor RE   4
Tweedy GJ   19
Vincent NE   23
Ward TCG*   3
Wardle W   3
Wattam F   14

Goals (42): Hall 6, Howe 6, Bartholomew 3, Dodd 3, Reeve K 3, Vincent 3, Beattie 2, Crack 2, Johnson 2, Lumby 2, Moralee 2, Pearson 2, Betmead 1, Buck 1, Holmes 1, Kurz 1, Ponting 1, Roberts 1.

War Cup goals (4): Howe 3, Moralee 1.

1940–41

Allen S   11
Annables W*   1
Bainbridge R   1
Betmead HE   9
Buck T   29
Chadwick H*   1
Charlesworth S   1
Crack FW   2
Fields GE   3
Fleetwood ED   3
Flowers IJ*   13

Frost J   2
Gorman JH   2
Gott JH   1
Hall AF   30
Hodgson JV   31
Holland C   2
Holmes MM   9
Howshall T*   1
Jennings HW*   19
Johnson H*   20
Johnson JW   1

Joyce E*   1
Kurz FJ   1
Logie JT*   5
Marlow G*   4
Maw A*   3
Middleton F   2
Millington M   19
Moulson GB   1
Nightingale S*   2
Reeve K   19
Rudkin TW   1

Scrimshaw S*   19
Swinburne TA*   1
Syred T   2
Tweedy GJ   21
Vincent NE   31
Ward CW   2
Wattam F   6
Wilkin LC   1
Witcomb DF*   8

Goals (64): Johnson H 18, Jennings 10, Reeve 9, Flowers 7, Betmead 3, Rudkin 3, Scrimshaw 3, Hall 2, Syred 2, Annabels 1, Buck 1, Crack 1, Gorman 1, Nightingale 1, Wattam 1, Witcomb 1.

1941–42

Buck T   35
Butler MP*   1
Crack FW   2
Davies W*   22
Dodds LS*   11
Doherty PD*   14
Ferguson A*   3
Ferrier RJ*   26
Fleetwood ED   1
Flowers IJ*   6
Hall AF   35

Harris JB*   1
Hodgson JV   34
Hullett W*   1
Iggleden H*   1
Jennings HW*   10
Johnson H*   17
Johnson JW   2
Jones W   1
Kurz FJ   1
Lumby WCW*   1
Marsh FK*   1

Meek J*   1
Middleton F   2
Millington M   36
Moody KG   1
Moore NW   3
Moore TR   1
Murphy JJ   1
Nightingale S*   8
Platts L*   1
Pridmore AJ   1
Robertson LV   6

Rudkin TW   15
Stocks H   3
Thomas DWJ*   27
Tweedy GJ   22
Vincent NE   34
Wardle W   1
Wildman FR*   5
Wilson CM   2

Goals (72): Ferrier 15, Doherty 11, Rudkin 9, Johnson H 6, Thomas 6, Davies 5, Nightingale 5, Buck 2, Hall 2, Jennings 2, Thomas 2, Vincent 2, Flowers 1, Hodgson 1, Hullett 1, Marsh 1, Stocks 1.

1942–43

Allard H   1
Archer GW   1
Black A*   9
Blenkinsopp TW   1
Bradley G*   3
Brain H*   1
Browning F   2
Buck T   30
Butler MP*   4
Chamberlain –   1
Clewlow SJ*   2
Crack FW   2

Davies W*   21
Doherty PD*   12
Eastham J   12
Ely GBV   2
Ferrier RJ*   1
Fields GE*   1
Frost J   1
Gilchrist M*   1
Grenfield H   1
Hall AF   27
Hodgson JV   30
Johnson H*   5

Kippax FP*   4
Kurz FJ   4
Lilley J   3
Marsh FK*   1
McKenzie R   4
Miller WH   2
Millington M   29
Moody KG   4
Moore NW   3
Moralee M*   22
Moulson GB   2
Pearson WGA   1

Platts L*   2
Pridmore AJ   2
Ranshaw JW   27
Raynor F*   2
Reeve KE   1
Sackett G   1
Slear –   1
Smith J*   15
Squires F*   1
Vincent NE   27
White F*   1

Goals (72): Moralee 14, Ranshaw 13, Doherty 9, Black 6, Davies 4, Kurz 4, Browning 3, Vincent 3, Johnson 3, Moore 3, Clewlow 2, Eastham 2, Allard 1, Butler 1, Crack 1, Hall 1, Kippax 1, own goal 1.

1943–44

Arthur G 1	Eastham J 3	Kurz FJ 3	Ranshaw JW 32
Baines PC★ 10	Ewing WF 2	Lowrey JE★ 1	Reeve FW 1
Brain H★ 14	Ferrier RJ★ 1	Major BB 1	Roberts – 1
Browning F 4	Forsyth J★ 18	Millington M 33	Rook L 14
Buck T 31	Gibson R★ 3	Moody KG 2	Rudkin TW 4
Bytheway G 2	Glaister G★ 1	Moore NW 2	Sears DR 5
Canning L★ 2	Hall AF 25	Moulson C★ 1	Sweeney FT★ 2
Courtier LJ 1	Hodgson JV 32	Moulson GB 33	Vincent NE 32
Dorsett R★ 13	Hodgson S 3	Pearson WGA 5	Vinson SR 2
Dunderdale WL★ 12	Johnson H★ 9	Pridmore AJ 2	

Goals (55): Dorsett 9, Ranshaw 7, Dunderdale 6, Brain 5, Forsyth 4, Vincent 4, Johnson 3, Rook 3, Sears 3, Hall 2, Pridmore 2, Rudkin 2, Vinson 2, Baines 1, Eastham 1, Pearson 1.

1944–45

Atkinson WH★ 1	Darley R 2	Johnson R 1	Reeve KE 2
Bainbridge R 1	Dolan P 2	Jones S★ 1	Robertson L 2
Bateman A 6	Dunderdale WL★ 15	Kurz FJ 4	Rodi J 10
Beattie JM 6	Foulston JG 1	Lamb HE★ 24	Rook L 1
Bellamy R 2	Fraser HGD 1	Lewis G★ 11	Rudkin TW 2
Bellas WJ★ 1	Glass FW 15	Matthewson G★ 2	Sampson HM 1
Birch A★ 1	Gray R 7	Millington M 32	Stevenson – 1
Blenkinsopp TW 1	Green SS 7	Minto J 1	Tallant EV 3
Blewitt R 1	Grogan J★ 5	Moody KG 1	Taylor WB 1
Brown J★ 2	Hall AF 34	Moore NW 1	Vincent NE 37
Browning F 1	Harvey W★ 1	Moore TR 2	Wallbanks A★ 5
Buck T 28	Hodgson JV 39	Moulson GB 37	Williams A★ 3
Chadwick H★ 4	Horden L 1	Pashley E 2	Wood D★ 3
Charlesworth S 1	Hurley J 2	Pearson WGA 7	
Corbett – 1	Huxford H 7	Pridmore AJ 1	
D'Arcy W★ 1	Johnson JW 4	Ranshaw JW 30	

Goals (88): Rodi 13, Hall 9, Lamb 9, Ranshaw 9, Dunderdale 8, Huxford 6, Vincent 5, Johnson JW 3, Kurz 3, Lewis 3, Reeve 3, Beattie 2, Hodgson 2, Pearson 2, Bainbridge 1, Bateman 1, Chadwick 1, Foulston 1, Glass 1, Green 1, Moore NW 1, Wallbanks 1, own goals 3.

1945–46

Baines PC★ 7	Clifton H 13	Johnson J 14	Robertson L★ 2
Baird H★ 4	Crack FW 2	Johnson JW 1	Rodi J 22
Bateman A 1	Davies W★ 10	Jones TW 15	Rook L 1
Bell E★ 3	Fisher FT 2	Kurz FJ 3	Rudkin TW 1
Betmead H 20	Glass FW 3	Lamb HE★ 6	Temple W 1
Blenkinsopp TW 5	Hall AF 11	Lewis G★ 9	Tweedy GJ 8
Browning F 2	Harris JB★ 12	Moody KG 5	Vincent NE 33
Buck T 34	Harvey W 2	Moore NW 27	Vinson SR 2
Candice – 1	Hodgson JV 42	Moulson GB 34	Wardle W 18
Chadwick H 20	Hodgson S 18	Mouncer FE 2	
Charlesworth S 23	Howe F 11	Pearson WGA 12	

Goals (61): Rodi 7, Moore NW 6, Chadwick 5, Clifton 5, Baines 4, Jones 4, Vincent 4, Buck 3, Davies 3, Johnson J 3, Howe 2, Kurz 2, Lamb 2, Wardle 2, Betmead 1, Blenkinsopp 1, Charlesworth 1, Hodgson JV 1, Lewis 1, Pearson 1, Temple 1, own goals 2.

FA Cup goals (2): Moore 1, Rodi 1.

Halifax Town

1939–40

Allsop WH 22	Clark SJH 8	Hargreaves J★ 1	Short JD★ 1
Baines R 15	Craig E 15	Henry GR★ 1	Thompson L★ 1
Barkas T 17	Davidson DBL★ 5	Hodgson J★ 1	Turner H 5
Blenkinsop E★ 4	Davies E★ 1	Hutton H 5	Widdowfield E 18
Briggs CE 16	Doran S 2	Jackson H 6	Wood S 21
Brown AW★ 4	France J 1	Lee AH★ 1	Worthington E 4
Bruce W 3	Graham W 3	Mahon J★ 2	Wrigglesworth JL 1
Chapman W★ 4	Green H 20	Ruecroft EJ 3	
Chester TH 3	Griffiths JS 10	Ruecroft J 18	

Goals (34): Widdowfield 10, Baines 7, Wood 6, Allsop 1, Barkas 1, Bruce 1, Davies 1, Doran 1, Graham 1, Griffiths 1, Hargreaves 1, Hutton 1, Mahon 1, Ruecroft J 1.

War Cup goals (1): Baines 1.

1940–41

Allsop WH 32	Fallaize RA 6	Kelly L★ 1	Rayner E 16
Barkas T 26	Gilbert E 2	Laidler JR★ 1	Ruecroft J 30
Binns CH★ 1	Greaves G★ 10	Malpass S★ 1	Smith C★ 2
Chester TH★ 9	Green H 32	McDernard W★ 1	Stephen JF★ 1
Connor R 1	Hamilton G 2	Moncrieff JC 1	Wardle G★ 30
Craig E 29	Hanna S 3	Orton V 4	Widdowfield E 26
Dempsey A★ 2	Hastings P★ 1	Palmer W★ 1	Wilson S★ 2
Dennis J 1	Hogg F★ 29	Pollard F★ 1	Wood S 31
Doran S 1	Hunter S 1	Pope A 4	
Elliott WG 2	Jackson H 8	Prior FC★ 1	

Goals (68): Widdowfield 27, Wardle 16, Barkas 11, Wood 4, Hogg 3, Fallaize 2, Pope 2, Smith 1, own goals 2.

1941–42

Allsop WH 37	Greaves G★ 31	MacFadyen W 7	Shotton R★ 1
Barkas T 3	Green H 36	Manning J★ 1	Smith C★ 2
Booth PH 2	Green L 11	McGarry T★ 6	Waddell W★ 1
Chester TH★ 26	Hanna S 10	McKellor WH★ 9	Walker GR★ 5
Craig E 35	Hastie A★ 1	Nicholls JH★ 6	Wardle G★ 27
Davidson RT★ 22	Hogg F★ 27	Nicholson S★ 1	Wesley JC★ 1
Davies G★ 3	Isaac J★ 1	Offord SJ★ 1	Whitehouse J 2
Doran S 3	Jackson H 8	Parker RW 3	Widdowfield E 1
Dunn L 3	Kershaw G 4	Robinson G 1	Wood S 36
Elliott WG 1	Knott H★ 1	Ruecroft J 30	Worthington E 1

Goals (63): Wood 13, Wardle 9, McGarry 6, Hogg 5, Davidson 4, Green L 4, Davies 3, Doran 2, Jackson 2, Kershaw 2, McKellor 2, Walker 2, Green H 1, Hanna 1, Knott 1, Manning 1, Parker 1, Ruecroft J 1, Smith 1, Waddell 1, own goal 1.

Includes four extra-time goals.

1942–43

Allsop WH 36	Findlay W★ 2	Jones D★ 2	Trodden JJ 6
Bell JG★ 2	Greaves G★ 18	Kershaw G 1	Wesley JC★ 14
Briggs CE 17	Green H 35	McGarry T★ 1	Widdowfield E 2
Brown W★ 2	Hall SR 1	Millar D 1	Wildman WA★ 1
Cabrelli P★ 2	Hiftle WA 2	Niblo A 15	Williams D★ 2
Craig E 29	Highmoor GW 3	Ruecroft EJ 26	Wilson R★ 4
Crowther K 6	Hogg F★ 33	Ruecroft J 33	Wood S 35
Davidson RT★ 33	Jackson H 31	Taylor LT★ 1	

Goals (69): Davidson 14, Niblo 11, Hogg 10, Wood 9, Ruecroft E 5, Jackson 3, Wesley 3, McGarry 2, Trodden 2, Wilson 2, Millar 1, Ruecroft J 1, Widdowfield 1, Wildman 1, Williams 1, own goals 3.

1943–44

Allsop WH   38
Baines –*   2
Barkas T   11
Barrett J   1
Bell W*   20
Birkett E   1
Boothroyd G*   1
Bratley GW*   1
Briggs CE   5
Burns OH*   1
Coyle O   1
Craig E   7
Davidson RT*   17
Duffy A   1
Dunn L   1

Edington J*   1
Elvy R   2
Fisher FW*   1
Flatley AA*   26
Fleetwood ED*   3
Garner G   1
Green H   34
Grummett J*   19
Hamilton G*   2
Heavey J*   1
Hicks S*   1
Hiftle WA   2
Hitchen T   2
Hogg F*   4
Humphreys PR   6

Jackson AG*   1
Jackson H   9
Johnston A*   11
Jones WM   22
Jones WR   1
McMenemy H*   5
Miller JW*   1
Morrison M*   1
Niblo A   2
Poxton W*   1
Robinson L*   1
Ruecroft J   38
Rymer GH*   4
Smith FH*   4
Stewart J*   2

Storey S*   1
Strike H   9
Sykes H   1
Taylor G   3
Taylor JT*   3
Topping H*   24
Trodden J   2
Wallace J*   18
Walmsley J*   2
Wesley JC*   5
Widdowfield E   15
Wilkinson K   1
Woffinden RS*   12
Wood S   5
Woodhead D*   1

Goals (71): Jones WM 18, Wallace 13, Smith 7, Davidson 6, Barkas 5, Flatley 3, Widdowfield 3, Green 2, Morrison 2, Robinson 2, Taylor 2, Fisher 1, Fleetwood 1, Humphreys 1, Jackson H 1, Storey 1, own goals 3.

1944–45

Allsop WH   35
Ardron W*   1
Baird H*   1
Barclay C*   1
Barkas T   28
Battye JE*   2
Birch N   1
Boothroyd G*   16
Briggs CE   11
Clarke A*   1

Elvy R   4
Flatley AA*   16
France J   10
Gorman WC*   1
Green H   36
Grummett J*   26
Haddington R*   2
Harvey W   6
Henry GR*   1
Hogg T*   3

Isitt D   1
Jackson H   20
Lodge JT*   4
Niblo A   1
Riddle H*   5
Ruecroft EJ   5
Ruecroft J   36
Senior C   3
Smith C*   25
Stewart A   6

Tate W   12
Thompson J*   1
Thurlow ACE*   3
Topping H*   5
Widdowfield E   18
Woffinden RS*   31
Wood S   4
Worboys R   1
Worthington E   12
Young A*   1

Goals (52): Widdowfield 14, Smith 10, Worthington 7, Barkas 4, Grummett 4, Flatley 3, Harvey 2, Ardron 1, Haddington 1, Jackson 1, Riddle 1, Senior 1, Tate 1, Wood 1, own goal 1.

1945–46

Allsop WH   33
Barkas T   23
Bimms E   4
Briggs CE   24
Brook L*   1
Burrows A*   1
Butler A   1
Chapman L   3
Doran S   15

England F   3
Flately AA*   1
France J   34
Gordon L   22
Graham W*   4
Green H   33
Harvey W*   2
Haughey F   1
Hazeldine GV   23

Jackson H   17
Killarney A   2
Merron J   10
Millar D   7
Moncrieff JC   8
Morefield W   2
Oliver G   15
Rayner E   12
Ruecroft EJ   1

Ruecroft J   34
Shirley A   9
Smith C*   27
Turner E   3
Widdowfield E   1
Wild J   1
Woffinden RS*   1
Wood S   2
Worthington E   5

Goals (62): Smith 15, Gordon 12, Barkas 7, Hazeldine 5, Jackson 3, Millar 3, Oliver 3, Brook 2, France 2, Harvey 2, Chapman 1, Doran 1, Green 1, Merron 1, Moncrieff 1, Ruecroft J 1, own goals 2.

FA Cup goals (3): Barkas 2, Gordon 1.

Hartlepools United

1939–40

Agar W★   1
Armes GW★   2
Blenkinsopp TW★   8
Brown CM   1
Carr D★   1
Carter HS★   6
Copping W★   1
Daniels G   1
Dawson T★   1
Deacon J   3
Docking SH★   6
Dodds LS   4
Douglas JS   3
Earl S   6
Fairhurst DL   3
Finlay J★   1
Foreman JJ   3

Fowler HN★   3
Gallon JW   1
Glassey RJ   6
Gorman J★   1
Hall J★   3
Hall JL★   13
Hastings A★   4
Hepplewhite G★   4
Heslop E   1
Heywood AE★   2
Hodgson G★   1
Howe JR★   13
Isaac J★   2
Johnston R★   16
Laidler JR★   6
Laurence A★   1
Leadman F★   1

Logan JW★   2
Love RW   2
Maguire JE★   3
Mantle J   2
Marshall JG★   5
McDermott C★   1
McMahon W★   6
McPhillips WP★   1
Middleton J   5
Molloy P★   1
Mordue GA★   8
Morton JE★   1
Nealle J★   1
Neowe R★   3
Nicholson WE★   1
Price J   1
Robinson J   2

Robinson J★   1
Scrimshaw S★   3
Shanks R★   1
Smailes J★   1
Smith J★   6
Spuhler J★   2
Stephens JW★   6
Thomas E   16
Turner C   3
Wallace J   1
Wardle W★   13
West N   19
Wilson JB   4
Wright J   3

Goals (28): Stephens 9, West 5, Carr 2, Maguire 2, Middleton 2, Armes 1, Glassey 1, Howe 1, Mantle 1, Marshall 1, Morton 1, Scrimshaw 1, Wilson 1.

War Cup goals (3): Dawson 1, Gallon 1, Heslop 1.

1940–41

Did not compete.

1941–42

Did not compete.

1942–43

Did not compete.

1943–44

Adams W★   12
Atkinson A   10
Baines PC★   7
Bamford T★   13
Barrett JW★   19
Batey R★   1
Beresford J   1
Corbett J   3
Cox R★   1
Daniels G   4
Dawes FW★   5
Deacon R★   1
Delaney L★   1
Drake W   5

Farrington R★   16
Forde S★   9
Frazer N★   1
Gledson R   1
Hamilton M★   4
Harrison H★   1
Heal W   1
Heywood AE★   38
Hipkin R★   1
Howe JR★   2
Hyslop A★   2
Johnston R   3
Levitt J   1
Makepeace R★   23

Malpass ST★   4
Martin J★   1
Milne W   3
Mitchell JF   3
Mullen W   20
Nettleton E★   2
Phillips W★   20
Robinson GH★   31
Rookes PW★   5
Rudkin TW★   1
Scott WR★   38
Scrimshaw S★   2
Short JD★   31
Skinner G★   21

Slack T   3
Smallwood F★   8
Tabram P★   11
Thomas G   1
Tootill GA★   3
Tracey CP★   1
Tunney E★   16
Ward J   1
Wardle W★   2
Wilson A★   2
Woodgate TJ★   1
Woods PB★   1

Goals (93): Short 22, Robinson 10, Adams 8, Baines 7, Bamford 6, Scott 6, Farrington 5, Johnston 4, Skinner 4, Mullen 3, Barrett 2, Corbett 2, Drake 2, Nettleton 2, Smallwood 2, Hamilton 1, Phillips 1, Scrimshaw 1, Ward 1, Wardle 1, own goals 3.

1944–45

Adams W★ 7	Forde S★ 36	Morris D 3	Shore J★ 1
Atkinson A 25	Harrison RF★ 22	Mullen W 6	Short JD★ 24
Bainbridge T 1	Harvey J★ 2	Murphy G★ 1	Skinner G★ 22
Bainbridge W★ 3	Havlin W 6	Nesbit A★ 1	Smallwood F★ 4
Barrett J★ 14	Hetherington TB★ 1	Nettleton E 12	Spelman I★ 10
Birse F★ 1	Horton L★ 12	Porter W 5	Tabram W★ 6
Brown C★ 14	Jackson J 1	Price J 1	Tomlinson J 7
Catterick H★ 1	James JS★ 2	Purvis B★ 1	Tootill GA★ 8
Chilton A★ 13	Keeys F 5	Robertson L 4	Troman B★ 1
Cochrane T★ 11	Lilley J★ 1	Robinson GH★ 3	Turney JA 4
Copeland E 16	Lloyd WL★ 6	Robinson J 2	Wardle W★ 2
Coughlan J 2	Lyon S 3	Rutherford TV★ 30	West N 7
Cross T★ 6	Makepeace R★ 5	Saxton A 2	Wharton A 1
Douglas JS 6	Male L 1	Scott F★ 1	Williams R 1
Dunn R★ 2	Mitchell JF 1	Scott WR★ 33	

Goals (75): Brown 14, Short 9, Horton 8, Cochrane 7, Harrison 6, Nettleton 5, Copeland 3, Lyon 3, Scott W 2, Skinner 2, Smallwood 2, West 2, Williams 2, Adams 1, Bainbridge W 1, Barrett 1, Catterick 1, Douglas 1, Robertson 1, Robinson G 1, Turney 1, Wardle 1, own goal 1.

1945–46

Baines PC★ 3	Harrison RF★ 3	Morris D 13	Scott WR★ 3
Barkas T★ 1	Hesford RT★ 6	Moses J 3	Short JD★ 12
Beardshaw EC★ 1	Heywood AE 25	Mullen W 1	Sidlow C★ 3
Brunskill N★ 1	Holland J 2	Mulroy J 1	Simpson J★ 1
Copeland E 23	Hooper HR★ 2	Nash FC★ 1	Skinner G★ 4
Daniels G 3	Howe JR★ 1	Nettleton E★ 1	Spelman I★ 34
Dryden H 6	Jarrie F 2	Newton J★ 1	Tabram W 8
Fenton WH★ 1	Johnson M 11	Oakes J★ 1	Tootill GA★ 17
Flatley AA★ 1	Johnstone R 1	Parker T★ 1	Troman JV 6
Flinton W★ 2	Jones H★ 1	Porter W 24	Turney JA 5
Flood G 1	Keeys F 26	Price J 11	Weir A★ 1
Flynn J 1	Lloyd WL★ 10	Roberts E 1	West N 4
Forde S★ 8	Makepeace R 4	Robertson L 14	Wheatman L 4
Foreman JJ 1	Mason – 1	Robinson GH★ 4	Willetts J 20
Gorman J 2	McKinley J 1	Russell W★ 3	Woods PB 9
Harden LS 5	McMahon H 27	Scott S 12	Woollett C★ 1

Goals (68): Johnson 13, McMahon 11, Short 11, Price 8, Copeland 5, Robertson 4, Harden 2, Morris 2, Spelman 2, Tabram 2, Baines 1, Dryden 1, Harrison 1, Moses 1, Oakes 1, Robinson 1, Scott 1, Woollett 1.

Includes one extra-time goal.

FA Cup goals (3): McMahon 2, Holland 1.

Huddersfield Town

1939–40

Asquith B★   1
Bailey G   4
Baird H   1
Barclay R   18
Beasley AP   18
Birch JW   1
Boot E   20
Brook L   2
Brown AW   6

Calverley A   4
Carter HS   10
Danskin R★   1
Gordon RH   2
Hastie A★   1
Hayes WE   21
Hepplewhite G   1
Hesford RT   23
Hobson J   1

Hodgson D   1
Isaac J   20
Juliussen AL   5
Mahon J   1
McKellor WH   1
Metcalfe V   1
Mills W   4
Mountford RC   20
Price AJW   8

Shepherd E★   1
Smailes J   1
Smith FA   1
Watson W   15
Whittingham A   3
Willingham CK   16
Young A   20

Goals (56): Barclay 11, Beasley 7, Price 7, Carter 6, Brook 5, Isaac 5, Watson W 5, Juliussen 3, Boot 2, Smailes 1, Smith 1, Whittingham 1, own goals 2.

War Cup goals (9): Barclay 2, Baird 1, Barkas 1, Brook 1, Hagan 1, Isaac 1, Juliussen 1, Mountford 1.

1940–41

Bailey G   15
Barclay R   23
Bell D   1
Boot E   32
Boothroyd G   11
Brook L   2
Brophy HF★   1
Brown AW   10
Butt L★   2
Chivers FC★   2
Clark J   2
Clegg D   4

Danskin R★   1
Gilroy WG★   2
Hanks ET★   2
Hayes WE   32
Henry GR★   1
Hepplewhite G   1
Hesford RT   13
Hodgson D   6
Holley T★   1
Isaac J   23
Jones TB★   2
Juliussen AL   1

Lodge JT   20
Mahon J   2
Makinson J★   1
Manning J   1
McGraw J★   1
McKellor WH   6
McKerren DF★   5
Metcalfe V   30
Mountford RC   15
Neil T   8
Nicholls JH★   1
Price AJW   31

Priestley T   1
Rogers W★   1
Shackleton LF★   1
Stewart A   8
Townend A   1
Turner H★   2
Watson W   4
Wesley JC★   1
Wilkinson K   3
Willingham CK   30
Young A   22

Goals (73): Price 17, Metcalfe 10, Lodge 8, Barclay 7, Isaac 6, McKerren 5, Hayes 4, Neil 3, Boot 2, McKellor 2, Mountford 2, Brook 1, Brown 1, Butt 1, Henry 1, Wilkinson 1, Willingham 1, own goal 1.

1941–42

Ainsley GE★   1
Bailey G   31
Baird H   17
Barclay R   27
Barker H★   1
Biggs G   1
Bokas F★   3
Boot E   34
Boothroyd G   6
Brown ARJ★   3
Brown AW   14
Burgess JW★   1
Butt L★   3
Carter HS★   4
Clegg D   2
Cockroft J★   1
Croft C   8
Curnow J★   20

Danskin R★   1
Davis H★   1
Duffy R★   1
Elliott WH★   1
England FW   1
Hardwick K   1
Harper F★   1
Hepplewhite G   1
Hesford RT   8
Hodgson D   2
Hornby R★   1
Isaac J   6
Juliussen AL   3
Kidd WE★   1
Lancaster JM   1
Lodge JT   6
Logan JW★   1
MacFadyen W★   1

Mahon J   4
Manning J   4
McEwan W★   2
McKellor WH   5
Metcalfe V   13
Mortensen SH★   1
Mountford RC   3
Nevin W   1
North E   1
Perry RA   1
Price AJW   31
Robinson E★   1
Roughton WG★   1
Scott D   1
Scrimshaw S★   1
Shakleton LF★   1
Smailes J★   1
Smith G★   2

Stabb GH★   2
Stewart A   27
Swinfen R★   1
Thompson A   25
Thorogood J★   2
Waddell W★   4
Watson W   4
Whittingham A   3
Whittingham H★   1
Wilkinson E   1
Wilkinson K   7
Willingham CK   31
Wipfler CJ★   2
Wood HM   1
Wood J   1
Wood S★   1
Young A   15

Goals (90): Price 22, Barclay 13, Baird 8, Carter 6, Wilkinison K 6, Willingham 5, Thompson 4, Juliussen 3, Metcalfe 3, Butt 2, Mahon 2, Robinson 2, Ainsley 1, Biggs 1, Boot 1, Burgess 1, Cockroft 1, Davis 1, Lodge 1, McKellor 1, Manning 1, Mortensen 1, Mountford 1, Shackleton 1, Stabb 1, Whittingham A 1.

1942–43

Bailey G   36
Baird H   25
Barclay R   33
Barker J★   3
Beardshaw EC★   1
Boot E   33
Boothroyd G   16
Brown AW   25
Copeland E   1
Crack FW★   2

Craig AP   2
Croft C   1
Curnow J★   20
Duffy R★   1
England FW   1
Hardwick K   1
Howe G   1
Isaac J   3
Juliussen AL   2
Lodge JT   5

Manning J   2
McKellor WH   2
Mortensen SH★   1
Mountford RC   5
Naylor TW   1
Poole J   15
Price AJW   30
Robledo GO   1
Simpson John   1
Stabb GH★   1

Stewart A   26
Storey S   2
Thompson A   36
Watson W   28
Wilkinson K   8
Willingham CK   35
Windle R   1

Goals (100): Price 38, Watson 17, Barclay 15, Baird 7, Boot 5, Juliussen 3, Poole 3, Thompson 3, Wilkinson 3, Mortensen 2, Willingham 2, Duffy 1, Isaac 1, McKellor 1, Rickett 1, own goals 2.

Includes four goals in Combined Counties final second leg v Sunderland.

1943–44

Bailey G   36
Baird H   26
Barclay R   17
Barker J★   16
Bateman A   17
Battye JE   17
Birch JW   5
Boot E   32
Boothroyd G   3

Brown AW   17
Calverley A   4
Clegg D   12
Curnow J★   21
Dring R   2
Ellis N   4
Glazzard J   23
Howe G   3
Hubbard C★   4

Hughes WA   1
Isaac J   14
Jepson H   1
Johnson A★   11
Lodge JT   3
Mahon J   4
Male CG★   1
Noble N   4
Poole J   23

Price AJW   39
Sibley ET★   3
Smith G★   1
Steele DM★   1
Stewart A   23
Storey S   2
Thompson A   2
Watson W   7
Willingham CK   30

Goals (89): Price 46, Baird 8, Barclay 7, Isaac 6, Glazzard 5, Calverley 4, Watson 4, Poole 3, Boot 2, Bateman 1, Storey 1, Thompson 1, own goal 1.

1944–45

Asquith B★   1
Bailey G   44
Baird H   20
Barkas T★   2
Barker J★   30
Bateman A   33
Battye JE   7
Beasley AP   1
Boot E   42
Boothroyd G   1
Brooke S★   1

Brown AW   40
Bywater NL   2
Calverley A   1
Clegg D   25
Danskin R★   1
Dyer JA★   4
Farr TF★   5
Farrell A★   4
Glazzard J   42
Green GF   6
Howe G   5

Hurst H   1
Isaac J   1
Juliussen AL   1
Milburn JET★   2
Mosby H   2
Noble N   1
Perry RA   1
Poole J   35
Price AJW   39
Radford A   2
Rodgers AW   14

Rusdale C   1
Shackelton LF★   3
Smith G★   1
Stabb GH★   1
Stephen JF★   1
Stewart A   1
Thompson GH   1
Thurlow ACE   10
Watson W   13
Willingham CK   33
Yates H   3

Goals (97): Price 40, Glazzard 18, Rodgers 8, Watson 8, Bateman 7, Poole 6, Baird 3, Boot 2, Shackleton 2, Green 1, Mosby 1, own goals 2.

Includes one extra-time goal.

1945–46

Bailey G   41
Barker J   37
Bateman A   37
Baxter JC★   1
Boot E   41
Briggs TR   4
Brook L   10
Brown AW   17

Carr EM   33
Clegg D   13
Glazzard J   32
Green GF   3
Hesford RT   22
Howe G   14
Hurst H   1
McManus B   6

Metcalfe V   12
Morton A   8
Newbold A   1
Noble N   1
Poole J   28
Price AJW   26
Radford A   1
Rodgers AW   14

Simpson James   1
Simpson John   17
Tanner JD   1
Thurlow ACE   1
Watson A   10
Watson W   13
Willingham CK   16

Goals (90): Price 22, Carr 18, Rodgers 13, Glazzard 10, Boot 5, Watson 5, Brook 4, Poole 4, Bateman 3, Barker 1, Baxter 1, Green 1, Willingham 1, own goals 2.

FA Cup goals (1): Price 1.

Hull City

1939–40

Anderson N 18
Bly W 1
Clubley RT 1
Crawford E* 1
Cunliffe AJ 11
Curnow J 21
Davies DD 17

Dawson D* 3
Dyer RH 1
Gilmore HP 20
Lowe RE 2
Meens H 21
Prescott JR 16
Quigley D 2

Reeves EP 1
Richardson EW* 9
Richardson G 2
Riches W 2
Robinson C 4
Robinson J 17
Smith TF 21

Spivey R* 3
Stephenson JE* 1
Watson A 22
Woodhead C 20
Woods C 4
Young H 1

Goals (38): Prescott 15, Anderson 9, Davies 4, Meens 3, Cunliffe 2, Lowe 2, Dawson 1, Richardson E 1, Woods 1.

War Cup goals (4): Cunliffe 2, Davies 1, Prescott 1.

1940–41

Anderson N 18
Barraclough W 19
Bly W 17
Bradley GJ* 11
Bratley G 12
Bratton W 1
Burdett T* 7
Butcher R* 2
Cottam A 2
Cunliffe AJ 16

Curnow J 7
Davies DD 17
Dawson D 6
French J 1
Gowdy W 3
Green R 1
Heelbeck L 3
Herdman H* 1
Hewick A 1
Knott H 19

Lucas WH* 6
McCurdie J 1
Meens H 24
Neary J* 2
Porteus JW* 1
Pritchard TH 1
Raynor G* 1
Reeves EP 1
Robinson J 23
Rogers W 1

Ross A* 16
Selby WA 1
Sherwood GW* 6
Spivey R 13
Sullivan M* 1
Twells D 1
Wilson D 2
Woodhead C 26

Goals (52): Knott 19, Anderson 11, Cunliffe 6, Burdett 5, Davies 3, Barraclough 2, Dawson 2, Spivey 2, Bratley 1, own goal 1.

1941–42

Did not compete.

1942–43

Did not compete.

1943–44

Did not compete.

1944–45

Adams C 3
Archer JW* 5
Armeson LR* 7
Beardshaw EC* 14
Beeson G* 20
Bell E* 26
Bircham B* 1
Brailsford T 1
Brewer C 3
Brown G 1
Bunting A 1
Clark S 1
Collier T 5
Crofts E 2
Cunliffe AJ 2
Curnow J 24
Dickinson P 4
Dixon JT* 1
Dowen JS* 1
Dowling J 1
Downie J* 1

Drummond A 1
Eatherington H 2
Finch R* 3
Flinton W 16
Galloway A 1
Gilmore P 1
Glaister G* 19
Gobey E 1
Greaves S 1
Harnby DR* 1
Harris JB* 34
Harvey G 6
Hewick A 4
Hollis H* 8
Hope C 1
Howe LF* 9
Hubbard C* 6
Hutchinson JA* 1
Huxford H* 3
Johnson J* 10
Johnson K 1

Jones JT* 1
Kingswell L 2
Knott H 3
Lamb G 2
Landles J 1
McDowell C 5
Meese A 1
Miller D* 15
Montgomery S 10
Moore TR* 1
Neary J* 1
Prescott JR* 4
Read S 1
Rhodes B 1
Richardson G 11
Riches W 1
Robinson J 1
Rothery H* 3
Sargent F* 2
Shephard G* 1
Sherwood GW* 1

Singleton EA* 1
Skidmore W* 1
Smith J 2
Spencer E 1
Stokes F* 10
Stone J* 7
Sykes H 1
Symons J 12
Talbot F* 7
Thomas R 8
Vaughan E 9
Vaux E* 2
Walker F 4
Ward TEG* 1
Waters D 1
Whitchurch S 4
White L 3
Wilkinson N* 1

Goals (53): Glaister 6, Knott 6, Howe 5, Bell 4, McDowell 4, Montgomery 4, Flinton 3, Talbot 3, Finch 2, Sargent 2, Armeson 1, Beeson 1, Brailsford 1, Dixon 1, Eatherington 1, Harris 1, Johnson J 1, Rothery 1, Smith J 1, Smith K 1, Spencer 1, Sykes 1, Vaughan 1, own goal 1.

1945–46

Did not compete.

Ipswich Town

1939–40

Bell D 3	Dale W 3	Hick J 2	Mitcheson F 3
Burns M 3	Fletcher CA 3	Little JA 3	Mulraney A 3
Chadwick FW 3	Harris WHG 1	McLuckie JS 3	O'Mahoney M 3

Goals (5): Chadwick 2, Little 1, Mitcheson 1, Mulraney 1.

1940–41

Did not compete.

1941–42

Did not compete.

1942–43

Did not compete.

1943–44

Did not compete.

1944–45

Did not compete.

1945–46

Antonio GR★ 3	Forder JL★ 1	McNally M 1	Ross AB 1
Baird H★ 1	Fox GR 15	Mitcheson F 2	Roy JR 12
Bell D 36	Gillespie IC★ 26	Mulraney A 1	Saphin R 27
Biggs A★ 5	Harris WHG★ 12	Newman E 1	Sayers D 2
Burns M 4	Hick J 1	Noonan EJ 2	Smythe R 7
Coleman E★ 1	Hobbis HHF★ 1	O'Mahoney M 36	Somerfield A★ 1
Combe R★ 1	Hornby R 1	Parker T 12	Southam J★ 11
Connor JT 1	Jones S★ 1	Parlane J★ 3	Stow AC 8
Day A★ 21	Little JJ 25	Parry O 31	Tadman GH★ 1
Edwards D 11	Maskell LJ★ 1	Perrett GR 14	Tootill A★ 4
Fitzsimmons M 1	McCormack CJ★ 2	Price GB 10	Trenter R 15
Fletcher CA 3	McLuckie JS 17	Robinson J★ 1	Wardlaw JC 2

Goals (52): Day 16, Little 6, Trenter 6, Gillespie 4, Parker 4, Edwards 3, O'Mahoney 3, Roy 2, Biggs 1, Hornby 1, McCormack 1, Parlane 1, Smythe 1, Stow 1, own goals 2.

FA Cup goals (8): Parker 3, Little 2, Price 2, Fletcher 1.

Leeds United

1939–40

Ainsley GE 2	Gadsby KJ 17	Makinson J 16	Stephens A 2
Brown JM 8	Goldberg L 14	McGraw J 12	Stephens JW 4
Browne RJ 6	Hargreaves J 7	Milburn James 2	Stephenson JE 8
Buckley A 3	Henry GR 14	Milburn John★ 6	Swindin GH★ 9
Cochrane D 13	Hodgson G 11	Murgatroyd AL 3	Thompson L 15
Copping W 6	Holley T 15	Powell A 14	Twomey JF 1
Dunderdale WL 1	Kane R 1	Saxon – 1	Wharton C 2
Edwards W 2	Lee AH 9	Short JD 7	

Goals (36): Cochrane 7, Henry 6, Hodgson 6, Powell 4, McGraw 3, Short 3, Brown 2, Stephens A 2, Stephenson 2, Holley 1.

War Cup goals (8): Stephens A 3, Hargreaves 2, Hodgson 1, Powell 1, Thompson 1.

1940–41

Ainsley GE 3	Gadsby KJ 25	Howitt H 4	Powell A 14
Baird M★ 2	Goldberg L 1	Jacketts S★ 1	Short JD 12
Baker H★ 1	Goslin H★ 3	Lee AH 24	Spike S★ 1
Brown JM 1	Hargreaves J 17	Mahon J★ 6	Stacey A 1
Burditt GL★ 9	Heaton WH 2	Makinson J 34	Stephenson JE 27
Copping W 14	Henry GR 17	McGraw J 10	Sutherland HR 2
Daniels J 9	Hodgson G 21	McTavish H 1	Thompson L 10
Dempsey A 3	Hodgson J 1	Meens H★ 1	Townsend LF★ 12
Edwards W 19	Holley T 25	Milburn James 9	
Farrage TO★ 3	Houldershaw R 4	Milburn John★ 25	

Goals (69): Townsend 14, Hargreaves 7, Hodgson G 7, Short 7, Stephenson 5, Henry 4, Powell 4, Burditt 3, Milburn John 3, Edwards 2, Lee 2, Mahon 2, McGraw 2, Mackinson 2, Ainsley 1, Bair d 1, Milburn James 1, Sutherland 1, own goal 1.

1941–42

Adam C★ 23	Goldberg L 3	Makinson J 33	Spike S★ 5
Ainsley GE 9	Haddow JB 6	McClure J★ 3	Spink K 1
Asquith B★ 2	Hargreaves J 19	McGraw J 10	Stanton RW 3
Attwell RF★ 1	Harvey P 1	Milburn James 14	Stephenson JE 4
Bratley GW 2	Heaton WH 2	Milburn John★ 4	Taylor LT 3
Brown JM 2	Henry GR 33	Murgatroyd AL 3	Turner JT 2
Burton S★ 1	Holley T 22	Powell A 31	Vickers H 5
Bush TW★ 4	Keeping AEM★ 2	Ramsay T★ 2	Warburton G★ 2
Clarke RL★ 1	Kidd WE★ 1	Ramsden B★ 8	Watson G 1
Copping W 11	Knight AW 13	Scaife G 1	Wesley J★ 1
Daniels J 28	Lee AH 8	Seller RK 1	Williams WJ 1
Eastham H★ 3	Litchfield EB★ 15	Shafto J 1	
Fowler HN★ 14	Livingstone AHD 2	Shanks R★ 6	
Gadsby KJ 5	Maddison R 1	Short JD 6	

Goals (69): Henry 28, Hargreaves 8, Adam 6, Powell 5, Short 4, Knight 3, Ainsley 2, McGraw 2, Asquith 1, Holley 1, Litchfield 1, Milburn James 1, Milburn John 1, Shanks 1, Stephenson 1, Turner 1, own goals 3.

1942–43

Ainsley GE   12
Anson S   1
Argue J★   4
Bedford H   1
Binns CH★   2
Bokas F★   1
Boyes W★   2
Brown JM   3
Bush TW★   2
Butterworth FC   22
Campbell R★   1
Clutterbuck J   1
D'Arcy L   1
Dainty A★   1
Daniels J   32
Dunn W   1
Eastham H★   3
Edwards W   1

Fallaize RA   3
Fowler HN★   3
Gadsby KJ   7
Goldberg L   1
Hargreaves J   1
Harper B★   3
Harris W★   2
Harston JC★   2
Henry GR   27
Hick J★   1
Holley T   10
Houldershaw H   2
Houldershaw R   13
Jones W★   2
Jones WH★   2
Kinghorn WJD★   2
Kirby D   1
Knight AW   26

Lawn M   2
Limbert R   3
Marshall D   1
McGraw J   19
McInnes JS★   3
Milburn James   10
Milburn John★   6
Moss A★   8
O'Farrell J   1
Patterson GL★   3
Powell A   32
Poxon J   4
Pyke RD★   1
Rhodes A   4
Robbins H   1
Rutherford E★   20
Scaife G   1
Short JD   8

Simpson J★   2
Smith G★   2
Sturrock W★   2
Taylor PH★   2
Taylor W★   2
Tindall J   1
Vickers H   1
Wakefield AJ   21
Warren R★   7
Wheeler G★   1
Whittle R★   1
Wilcox GE★   2
Wildon N   1
Wilkinson K★   1
Williams D★   1
Woffinden RS★   1

Goals (60): Powell 16, Henry 9, Wakefield 9, Short 7, Rutherford 6, Houldershaw R 3, Ainsley 2, Argue 1, Brown 1, Fallaize 1, Hargreaves 1, Lawn 1, Milburn James 1, Smith 1, Williams 1.

1943–44

Ainsley GE   1
Antonio GR★   10
Attwell RF★   1
Boyes W★   28
Brown JM   1
Butterworth FC   32
Challinor J★   14
Corbett NG★   1
Curry R★   1
Daniels J   25
Davie J★   5
Davies CJ★   6
Dewis G★   2
Dorling GJ★   4
Dowen JS★   1
Dutchman JA   1
Fallaize RA   2

Farrell A★   1
Gadsby KJ   10
Galley T★   4
Glover A★   1
Goldberg L   4
Goodburn H   1
Henry GR   33
Hindle T   25
Hirst H★   1
Hodgson JP   1
Holley T   3
Houldershaw H   1
Jameson P   1
Jones S★   3
Jordan C★   1
Kirby D   3
Kirton J★   6

Knight AW   18
Lawn M   1
Lindley WM★   1
Mahon J★   5
Makinson J   17
McGraw J   18
McKellor WH★   1
Milburn GW★   3
Milburn James   7
Milburn John★   5
Moule J   2
O'Neil TH★   1
Padgett H   1
Paton TG★   1
Poland G★   10
Powell A   22
Rhodes A   2

Rogers W★   2
Rozier AT★   3
Sharp NW★   1
Short JD   5
Steele FC★   2
Stevens T   1
Stokes E★   5
Tatton JW   5
Thompson L   3
Tremelling J   2
Wakefield AJ   1
Walker JE   2
Ward TV★   4
Wilcox GE★   2
Williams C★   1
Wright H★   3
Yeomanson JW   5

Goals (72): Henry 16, Boyes 8, Knight 6, Powell 6, Antonio 5, Hindle 5, Davie 4, Tremelling 4, Short 3, Curry 2, Steele 2, Tatton 2, Brown 1, Davies 1, Dorling 1, Fallaize 1, Gadsby 1, Jameson 1, Mahon 1, Stevens 1, Wakefield 1.

1944–45

Ainsley GE   10
Benn A   1
Birch JW★   1
Bokas F★   4
Booth WS★   2
Burbanks WE★   12
Butterworth FC   36
Byrom T★   4
Calverley A★   2
Campbell R★   19
Cherry D   1
Coyne C   29
Crookes G   3
Daniels J   27

Downing H★   1
Dunderdale WL   4
Dutchman JA   1
Duthoit J   4
Fearnley HL   6
Forde S★   2
Gadsby KJ   13
Gleave C★   2
Glover A★   1
Goldberg L   2
Hardaker NG   2
Hargreaves J   1
Harper K★   1
Henry GR   31

Hindle T   38
Hodgson JP   2
Houldershaw R   5
Howe AKB   2
Hulbert J★   1
James S★   1
Kirby D   5
Knight AW   19
Mahon J★   22
McGraw J   13
Milburn James   1
Milburn John★   14
Morton W★   1
Moule J   16

Normanton S   2
Paton JA★   4
Pickering WH★   2
Powell A   1
Ruecroft J★   2
Sharples K★   1
Short JD   9
Shotton R★   5
Stephens JW   1
Sutherland HR   3
Twomey JF   5
Ward TV   1
Weaver S★   27
Yeomanson JW   15

Goals (106): Hindle 26, Henry 20, Ainsley 10, Coyne 9, Short 8, Mahon 7, Moule 7, Knight 3, Burbanks 2, Dunderdale 2, Milburn John 2, Sutherland 2, Weaver 2, Campbell 1, Milburn James 1, Morton 1, Ward 1, Yeomanson 1, own goal 1.

1945–46

Ainsley GE   28
Alberry WE★   1
Barton E   4
Batey R   8
Blair Doug★   1
Browne RJ   4
Buckley A   1
Burbanks WE★   2
Butterworth FC   18
Chew J★   6
Collier A★   2
Coyne C   24
Crookes G   1

Duffy R★   15
Dutchman JA   3
Duthoit J   17
Fearnley HL   4
Gadsby KJ   6
Glackin T   1
Goldberg L   7
Grainger D   35
Heaton WH   19
Henry GR   30
Hindle T   33
Hodgson JP   36
Holley T   28

Hudson GW★   7
Iceton OL★   2
Jones E★   1
Jones S★   11
Knight AW   6
Laidman F   3
Laking G   1
McGraw J   5
Milburn James   10
Milburn John★   3
Moule J   3
Oliver HS★   1
Parker W★   2

Pogson D   1
Pope AL★   1
Powell A   12
Price A   21
Short JD   11
Skidmore W★   2
Smith J   11
Stephens A   1
Stephens JW   11
Walker J   1
Westlake FA★   1

Goals (66): Ainsley 20, Henry 11, Grainger 9, Hindle 8, Short 4, Heaton 3, Dutchman 2, Powell 2, Chew 1, McGraw 1, Price 1, Stephens J 1, own goals 3.

FA Cup goals (6): Ainsley 2, Grainger 1, Henry 1, Short 1, own goal 1.

Leicester City

1939–40

Ansell T 1	Griffiths MW 1	King FAR★ 2	Rochester A★ 1
Barron W★ 6	Grogan J 12	Kinghorn WJD★ 2	Sansome F 4
Beattie A★ 4	Grosvenor P 6	Lawton T★ 3	Sharman F 20
Bedford G 13	Haycock F 10	Liddle D 7	Shell FH★ 1
Bowers JW 25	Heywood R 2	Logan S★ 1	Smith AH 2
Calvert JWH 3	Houghton WE 12	McLaren A 26	Smith JD 5
Coutts WF 10	Howe HE 16	Osborne J 1	Smith SC 28
Dewis G 15	Iverson RT★ 7	Pritchard HJ★ 10	Stubbs PEG 3
Eastham H★ 6	Jayes AG 7	Queenborough A 2	Thompson T 15
Frame WL 22	Jones DO 27	Reeday MJ 3	

Goals (57): Bowers 13, Dewis 10, Smith S 7, Lawton 5, Houghton 2, Jayes 2, Smith AH 2, Smith JD 2, Barron 1, Griffiths 1, Haycock 1, Jones 1, King 1, Kinghorn 1, Liddle 1, Logan 1, Pritchard 1, Sharman 1, Stubbs 1, Thompson 1, own goals 2.

War Cup goals (6): Haycock 2, Smith S 2, Bowers 1, Dewis 1.

1940–41

Adams C 3	Frear W 1	Lyman CC★ 4	Springthorpe TA★ 1
Bowers JW 1	Frith W★ 16	Mullin J★ 25	Steele FC★ 7
Burditt K★ 4	Frost SD 3	Paterson G★ 10	Thornhill D★ 3
Calvert JWH 38	Grogan J 2	Rochester A 21	Towers WH 5
Chapman VW 2	Harrison JC 5	Roome RG 1	Ward E★ 1
Cheney D 4	Heywood R 37	Sanderson D 5	Wilson FC★ 1
Chesters A★ 4	Howe HE 40	Sharman F 4	Witcomb DF★ 1
Cunningham E★ 1	Jayes AG 10	Sheard F 6	Wright D★ 1
Dewis G 30	Johnston H★ 4	Smith AE 21	Wright W★ 33
Fagan W★ 1	Jones DO 2	Smith JD 11	Wyles H 1
Foster WL 1	Lee J 19	Smith LG★ 4	
Frame W 43	Liddle D 35	Smith SC 1	

Goals (108): Dewis 24, Mullin 15, Smith AE 14, Lee 13, Wright W 12, Liddle 8, Jayes 5, Steele 5, Heywood 2, Howe 2, Wright D 2, Bowers 1, Chapman 1, Foster 1, Sanderson 1, Smith JD 1, own goal 1.

1941–42

Adam C 4	Dewis G 3	Howe HE 35	Parker H 2
Barnes WP 2	Drake EJ★ 1	Iggleden H 3	Paterson G 20
Barratt H★ 30	Frame W 35	Jayes AG 32	Rochester A 4
Bowers J 1	Frith W★ 26	Jones DO 1	Sanderson D 10
Buchan WRM★ 4	Frost SD 4	Jones LJ★ 1	Sheard F 6
Bulger CG★ 1	Graham DR 1	Lee J 5	Smith AE 27
Calvert J 6	Grant AF 9	Liddle D 12	Smith LGF★ 2
Chapman VW 3	Grogan J 1	Mansfield R 4	Smith SC 32
Cheney D 24	Harrison JC 1	Morgan W★ 17	Taylor G★ 2
Crawley T★ 4	Hernon J 4	Mulvaney A★ 1	Wyles H 5

Goals (79): Cheney 15, Jayes 14, Barratt 8, Dewis 7, Smith AE 7, Smith S 6, Sanderson 5, Liddle 4, Chapman 3, Buchan 2, Howe 2, Paterson 2, Frost 1, Smith L 1, Taylor 1, own goal 1.

1942–43

Barratt H★ 15	Frost SD 2	King SH 4	Sharman F 13
Bedford G★ 1	Gallagher P★ 2	Kirkaldie J★ 3	Sheard F 5
Betteridge RM 1	Gardiner C★ 2	Lewis J★ 1	Smith AE 10
Birks –★ 1	Gemmell J★ 21	Liddle D 11	Smith JD 2
Bradley G 3	Grant AF 31	Longland –★ 1	Smith SC 37
Browne JH★ 1	Hamilton W★ 4	McAskill A★ 2	Snape J★ 6
Buchan WRM★ 1	Harrison JC 7	McCormick J★ 3	Staples LG 1
Burdett T★ 1	Hernon J 18	Paterson G★ 1	Steele E★ 5
Carver –★ 1	Hilliard JG 4	Phillips RGT 6	Steele FC★ 11
Chapman VW 4	Howe HE 34	Plummer NL 22	Thompson T 2
Cheney D 9	Hughes TG 10	Pritchard HJ★ 1	Walton H 1
Dewis G 6	Jayes AG 8	Robertson JH★ 1	Walton R 28
Dunkley ME★ 7	Johnston TD★ 10	Rochester A 1	Wyles H 12
Flint K 4	Jones LO 2	Rutherford W 2	
Frame W 7	Kendall JT 5	Sanderson D 4	

Goals (72): Steele FC 13, Smith S 9, Barratt 8, Plummer 6, Cheney 5, Dewis 4, Harrison 3, Johnston 3, Chapman 2, Dunkley 2, Hernon 2, Howe 2, Liddle 2, Smith AE 2, Carver 1, Frost 1, Gardner 1, Hughes 1, Jayes 1, Phillips 1, Rutherford 1, Sanderson 1, Steele E 1.

1943–44

Alsop GA★ 8	Frost SD 2	Liddle D 20	Sharman F 13
Becci A★ 8	Gemmell J★ 30	Little G★ 11	Sheard F 22
Bowden NH★ 9	Goffin WC★ 4	Lycett T 13	Smith AE 4
Bradley G 2	Grant AF 34	Major LD 3	Smith SC 35
Bulger CG★ 9	Grant RA 1	McNeil –★ 1	Sparrow T 2
Campbell J 24	Harrison JC 1	Middleton W 1	Staples LE 4
Chapman G 2	Hilliard JG 4	Morton A 1	Steward – 1
Cheney D 2	Howe HE 22	Muncie W 1	Sutton A★ 1
Cronin DL 11	Jayes AG 1	North TW 1	Walton R 3
Crossland B★ 1	Jones DO 1	Phillips RGT 11	Wattie JH★ 3
Davidson DBL★ 1	Jones LJ★ 4	Plummer NL 1	Windle E★ 1
Dewis G 7	Kendall JT 1	Reeday M 1	Wyles H 1
Dickie P★ 26	Kilshaw F 1	Rickards CT★ 1	
Dimond S★ 2	King JC 7	Roberts GD★ 1	
Frame W 38	Knott H★ 8	Sanderson D 1	

Goals (73): Bowden 11, Dewis 8, Campbell 7, Knott 6, Smith S 6, Smith AE 5, Phillips 4, Alsop 3, Lycett 3, Cronin 2, Jones L 2, Sanderson 2, Sheard 2, Bulger 1, Dickie 1, Howe 1, Little 1, Muncie 1, Staples 1, Wattie 1, Windle 1, own goals 4.

1944–45

Baxter WE★ 2	Frame W 36	Kilshaw F 5	Rickards CT★ 12
Bowden NH★ 13	Frost SD 1	King JC 17	Riley RJ 4
Bradley G 1	Gemmell J★ 2	Leitch W★ 12	Sanderson D 2
Brown ARJ★ 1	Graham DR 6	Liddle D 13	Sheard F 36
Buckby MC 2	Grant AF 7	Lindley WM★ 2	Smart –★ 1
Campbell J 12	Grogan J 1	Long –★ 1	Smith AE 2
Chapman VW 2	Hanford N 2	Major LD 25	Smith C★ 1
Cheney D 3	Harrison JC 1	McCall RH★ 2	Smith SC 37
Clare J★ 1	Howe HE 32	Mercer S 6	Stephan H★ 4
Cobley W★ 3	Hubble L★ 3	Morby JH★ 1	Tapping F★ 7
Cronin DL 6	Iddon H▲ 11	Morrison AC★ 2	Thompson R★ 3
Dewis G 7	Johnston TD▲ 2	Muncie W 1	Towers WH 15
Dickie P★ 5	Jones LJ★ 13	Paterson G★ 1	Woodvine A 3
Douglas DN 3	Jones R 2	Phillips RGT 1	Wyles H 5
Dunkley ME★ 13	Jones T★ 5	Plummer NL 1	
Elliott BH★ 3	Kelly DJ 4	Revie D 2	

Goals (63): Leitch 12, Smith S 12, Rickards 7, Dewis 5, Bowden 3, Liddle 3, Mercer 3, Campbell 2, Cheney 2, Dunkley 2, Iddon 2, Phillips 2, Tapping 2, Cronin 1, Douglas 1, Kelly 1, Kilshaw 1, Stephan 1, own goal 1.

1945–46

Adams C 1	Frame W 35	Lee J 2	Sheard F 9
Aldecoa EG★ 4	Goffin WC★ 1	Letters WJ★ 1	Sinclair TM★ 1
Anderson R 5	Graham DR 11	Liddle D 17	Small SJ★ 1
Ashton D★ 1	Graham J 1	Lycett T 6	Smith AE 10
Attwood A 1	Grant AF 16	McInally J★ 2	Smith ETH 13
Bowden NH★ 1	Griffiths MW 10	Mercer S 21	Smith SC 39
Calvert J 15	Grogan J 19	Middleton W 1	Soo F 14
Campbell J 10	Harrison JC 2	Osborne J 12	Stubbs EPG 1
Chisholm KM★ 3	Heathcote W★ 1	Peace HJ★ 1	Sutton L 1
Cronin DL 1	Hernon J 3	Pimbley DW 8	Towers WH 24
Cutting F 3	Howe HE 30	Poulton W★ 1	Watts R 2
Davies RG★ 2	Iggleden H 3	Revie D 31	Weatherston A 3
Dewis G 10	Johnson JA★ 1	Riley RJ 1	Woodvine A 1
Edwards GR★ 1	Jones DO 20	Robinson P★ 2	
Foster WL 9	King JC 16	Russell RI★ 1	

Goals (57): Mercer 10, Smith S 6, Foster 4, Pimbley 4, Revie 4, Smith AE 4, Dewis 3, Liddle 3, Soo 3, Campbell 2, Griffiths 2, King 2, Towers 2, Aldecoa 1, Chisholm 1, Cronin 1, Heathcote 1, Jones 1, Harrison 1, Lycett 1, Osborne 1.

FA Cup goals (1): Adam 1.

Lincoln City

1939–40

Askew W 3	Clayton R 3	Hardy JH 19	Moulson C 14
Bailey L★ 1	Connor J 1	Hartshorne J 3	Moulson GB 17
Bean AS 21	Cooper S★ 17	Hetherington G★ 1	Musson WU★ 1
Bell T★ 1	Deacon R 3	Hodgson JV★ 1	Ponting WT 5
Bett F★ 19	Dunderdale WL★ 17	Holmes MM 1	Riley H★ 1
Callender J 3	Eggleston T★ 1	Hoyland E 15	Rix J 4
Callender TS 3	Gormlie WJ 3	Jessop FS★ 20	Seagrave J★ 3
Campbell J 11	Hall G★ 17	McCall RH★ 1	
Clare J 21	Hann R★ 1	Mellors RD★ 1	

Goals (48): Dunderdale 20, Clare 8, Bett 7, Campbell 4, Cooper 3, Ponting 3, Clayton 1, Hoyland 1, McCall 1.

War Cup goals (0).

1940–41

Barton H★ 3	Dickie P★ 1	Hullett W★ 1	Moulson GB★ 29
Bean AS 28	Doherty PD★ 1	Jessop FS★ 8	Smith EF★ 4
Bell T 2	Dunderdale WL★ 20	Johnston R★ 20	Towler BE★ 27
Bett F★ 9	Edrich WJ★ 1	Jones LJ★ 2	Turner AW★ 1
Brelsford JP 3	Forman RG 2	Lascelles RP 3	Wheat JH 1
Broadhurst J 1	Fox F 1	Marlow GA 10	Wightman JR★ 1
Campbell J★ 1	Hall BAC 23	Marsh FK★ 1	
Clare J 29	Hall G★ 26	Meek J★ 2	
Dean CG★ 3	Hardy JH 27	Moulson C★ 28	

Goals (69): Towler 24, Dunderdale 9, Hall A 9, Clare 8, Bett 5, Doherty 4, Hardy 2, Meek 2, Barton 1, Bell 1, Hall G 1, Jones 1, Wightman 1, own goal 1.

1941–42

Anderson RS★ 1	Dickie P★ 8	Jones LJ★ 1	Nicholson S★ 16
Barber A★ 1	Doherty PD★ 2	Knott H★ 23	Parr J 1
Bean AS 31	Farrell DO★ 2	Marlow GA 15	Ross W★ 13
Bett F★ 7	Hall BAC 4	Marsh FK★ 3	Towler BE★ 28
Cheetham TM★ 13	Hardy JH 30	Meek J★ 18	Turner H 1
Clare J 28	Hullett W★ 5	Moulson C★ 30	Watson F★ 1
Day A★ 1	Johnston R★ 24	Moulson GB★ 31	Wightman JR★ 3

Goals (99): Towler 26, Knott 23, Cheetham 12, Hullett 11, Clare 8, Meek 8, Marlow 4, Doherty 3, Bett 1, Johnston 1, Jones 1, Moulson C 1.

1942–43

Bean AS 27	Dorsett R★ 1	Marsh FK★ 16	Theaker CD★ 1
Bett F★ 24	Dryden JG★ 2	Moulson C★ 24	Thompson A 7
Bly W★ 1	Dunderdale WL★ 2	Moulson GB★ 22	Towler BE★ 28
Brown W 2	Hardy JH 28	Nicholson S★ 3	Tyson WG★ 2
Cheetham TM★ 9	Johnston R★ 15	Osborne CW 1	Wardle G★ 18
Clare J 28	Knott H★ 2	Platts L★ 4	Wightman JR★ 11
Cooper W 1	Lewis G★ 3	Rogers P 1	Winslow G 1
Dickie P★ 15	Makinson J★ 2	Stillyards G 4	Yorston BC★ 3

Goals (81): Towler 23, Bett 11, Wardle 11, Cheetham 10, Clare 9, Knott 3, Dickie 2, Stillyards 2, Yorston 2, Brown 1, Dryden 1, Hardy 1, Lewis 1, Moulson C 1, Wightman 1, own goals 2.

1943–44

Adkins E   3
Barton R   1
Bean AS   32
Bellis A★   4
Bett F★   30
Binns CH★   1
Bradley G★   5
Bray NG   11
Burton J★   1
Buttery E★   1
Cartwright B   1
Clare J   30
Clewson –   1
Corkhill WG★   3
Curry R★   1
Darley J★   1
Dawson E★   1
Douglas JE★   6
Green H★   1

Green SS★   1
Grummett J   6
Haines JWT★   6
Hall A★   1
Hardy JH   36
Hatfield B★   3
Hepworth R★   1
Hollis KB★   4
Holmes MM   2
Johnston R★   32
Jones HH★   1
Jones LJ★   1
Keen ERL★   3
Keggans H★   2
Knott H★   5
Lee G★   2
Lello CF   14
Lewis G★   15
Lowrey JE   5

Lowrie G★   2
Lyon J★   1
Marlow GA   2
Marsh FK★   28
Mason S   1
McDermott J★   2
McGinn F★   1
Mellors RD   1
Millington M★   2
Moulson C★   1
Moulson GB★   4
O'Donnell H★   4
Oakley JC★   2
Page AE★   1
Parker H   1
Parker LT★   1
Parkin FW★   1
Parr J   4
Platts L★   5

Ranshaw JW★   1
Readett H★   1
Robledo GO★   1
Rudkin TW★   1
Rutherford E★   5
Rutherford J★   1
Shimwell E★   1
Smith –   1
Smith J★   11
Stillyards G   3
Taylor L   2
Thomas GS★   1
Thompson A   7
Thompson D★   8
Topping H★   7
Towler BE★   5
Warburton A★   1
Williams G★   1

Goals (76): Lello 21, Bett 11, Clare 8, Lewis 8, Bray 4, O'Donnell 3, Thompson D 3, Haines 2, Knott 2, Marsh 2, Rutherford E 2, Bellis 1, Grummett 1, Hatfield 1, Lee 1, Lowrey 1, Lowrie 1, Parker 1, Ranshaw 1, Stillyards 1, Warburton 1.

1944–45

Acton N★   1
Bean AS   33
Beaumont L★   5
Bett F★   2
Boyes L   4
Callender TS   1
Cartwright B   12
Cheetham TM★   2
Clare J   13
Collindridge C★   1
Collins AD★   2
Cooper F   2
Davidson A★   5

Douglas JS★   14
Drysdale J★   1
Dulson RE★   1
Finan RJ★   1
Flack WLW★   2
Gillan J★   1
Gordon D   5
Grainger D★   1
Groves K★   14
Grummett J   11
Haines JWT★   31
Hall G★   5
Hardy JH   35

Harper D★   1
Hutchinson JA★   23
Jessop FS★   1
Johnson GE★   1
Johnston R★   30
Laing FJ★   1
Lello CF   2
Liddell J★   1
Manning D   1
Marlow GA   14
Marsh FK★   25
McCormick J★   1
Metcalfe L   1

Mills E★   1
Pawlaw M   8
Ravenscroft AG   19
Rossington K★   15
Rowley GA★   1
Russell G   2
Rutherford E★   11
Sleight F★   1
Stillyards G   3
Walker H   1
Watford A★   11
Williams W★   1
Worthington E★   4

Goals (74): Haines 21, Hutchinson 13, Marlow 10, Clare 3, Marsh 3, Rowley 3, Boyes 2, Cheetham 2, Collindridge 2, Gordon 2, Pawlaw 2, Rossington 2, Rutherford 2, Acton 1, Beaumont 1, Bett 1, Douglas 1, Grainger 1, Grummett 1, McCormick 1.

1945–46

Archer W   6
Bean AS   34
Callender TS   1
Cartwright GL   16
Cheetham TM★   28
Collins AD★   1
Daniels L★   1
Davies AM   25
Emery A   8
Franklin N★   3
Gadsby S   7
Grainger D★   2
Grant C   10

Grummett J   32
Haines JWT★   4
Hann R★   1
Hardy JH   24
Hartshorne J   1
Hellings D   4
Hepple A   2
Howarth S   2
Hoyland E   2
Hutchinson JA★   4
Johnson A   1
Johnson T   12
Keen ERL   2

Lello CF   1
Lumsden J   4
Marlow GA   28
Marsh FK★   8
Parkin F   15
Parkinson K   1
Powell T★   1
Ranshaw JW   7
Ravenscroft AG   3
Raynor E★   1
Rossington K★   1
Ruecroft J★   1
Settle A   12

Skelton G   2
Smedley L   9
Smith C★   4
Stillyards G   14
Tench J   2
Thompson A   12
Walker H   11
Wilkinson H   8
Wilson J★   1
Woodbridge G   3
Wroe E   14

Goals (72): Cheetham 23, Marlow 12, Grummett 9, Davies 5, Bean 3, Grant 3, Smedley 3, Ranshaw 2, Stillyards 2, Wilkinson 2, Haines 1, Hellings 1, Howarth 1, Hutchinson 1, Smith 1, Thompson 1, own goals 2.

FA Cup goals (7): Marlow 3, Cheetham 2, Wroe 1, own goal 1.

Liverpool

1939–40

Balmer J   10
Brown AW★   4
Busby M   17
Bush TW   10
Carney LF   13
Cole GD★   1
Cooper T   9
Doherty PD★   1
Done CE   5
Easdale J   3

Eastham S   9
Fagan W   15
Guttridge R★   3
Halsall W★   2
Hanson AJ★   2
Harley J   8
Kemp RJ   7
Kinghorn WJD   1
Lambert R   5
Leadbetter G   4

Liddell WB   14
Mansley EH   6
McInnes JS   14
Murphy G★   3
Nieuwenhuys B   23
Paisley R   5
Paterson GL   1
Polk S   2
Ramsden B   14
Riley AJ   10

Rogers F   5
Spicer EW   1
Stuart RW★   1
Swift FV★   2
Taylor PH   13
Tennant JW★   15
Vandenberg HC   16
Walton J★   1

Goals (72): Nieuwenhuys 18, Fagan 14, Liddell 9, Balmer 6, Carney 5, Done 5, Vandenberg 4, Doherty 2, Taylor 2, Busby 1, Eastham S 1, Hanson 1, Leadbetter 1, McInnes 1, Murphy 1, Tennant 1.

War Cup goals (1): Fagan 1.

1940–41

Balmer J   2
Bartram S★   16
Batey R★   12
Britton CS★   1
Bush TW   2
Cairns WH★   1
Carney LF   2
Carter G★   1
Collister GB   4
Cook W★   1
Cooke DF   13
Cullis S★   8
Done CE   17
Dorsett R★   6
Drury GB★   4

Eastham S   7
Fagan W   20
Fairhurst WG★   1
Farrow GH★   1
Fazackerley C   2
Grosvenor A★   1
Grundy JA★   5
Hanson AJ★   3
Harley J   6
Hobson A★   10
Hunt GS★   7
Iceton OL★   1
Jackson G★   13
Kaye GH   15
Kinghorn WJD   1

Lambert R   39
Lewis CR★   1
Liddell WB   37
Longdon CW★   1
Loran J   1
Lyon J★   1
Mansley EH   6
Massey AW★   1
Nieuwenhuys B   21
O'Donnell F★   2
Owens RT   4
Paisley R   27
Paterson GL   1
Pickstock S   3
Polk S   21

Ramsden B   1
Robinson JJ★   2
Search J   1
Seddon KJ   8
Shafto J   2
Spicer EW   31
Stuart RW★   15
Teasdale WR★   2
Turner N★   11
Westcott D★   3
Woodburn J★   3
Yoxon A   1

Goals (95): Nieuwenhuys 15, Done 13, Liddell 12, Paisley 10, Dorsett 8, Fagan 6, Westcott 6, Hunt 5, Carney 3, Drury 3, Grundy 2, Collister 1, Cooke 1, Eastham S 1, Lyon 1, O'Donnell 1, Pickstock 1, Polk 1, Search 1, Shafto 1, own goals 3.

1941–42

Ainsley GE★   10
Balmer J   12
Batey R   1
Busby M   1
Bush TW   9
Carney LF   13
Cooke DF   11
Doherty PD★   1
Done CE   30
Dorsett R★   15
Eastham H   1
Eastham S   7

Fagan W   3
Fazackerley C   11
Finney F   7
Grainger J★   1
Guttridge R★   26
Hall WW   3
Harley J   4
Haycock F★   15
Hobson A★   39
Hulligan M   1
Jones WH   5
Kaye GH   39

Lambert R   36
Liddell WB   35
McDonald J   1
McInnes JS   5
McIntosh JM★   6
McLaren A★   2
Mutch G★   1
Nieuwenhuys B   16
O'Donnell H★   2
Owen AA★   3
Owens RT   1
Paterson GL   1

Polk S   19
Pryde RI★   1
Ramsden B   2
Seddon KJ   1
Shafto J   3
Shankly W★   1
Spicer EW   9
Taylor PH   8
Wharton JE★   1
Whittaker W★   9
Woodruff A★   1

Goals (123): Done 40, Liddell 21, Dorsett 13, Polk 8, Balmer 7, Carney 6, Nieuwenhuys 6, Ainsley 5, McIntosh 3, Cooke 2, Fagan 2, Taylor 2, Bush 1, Hall 1, Haycock 1, Jones 1, McLaren 1, Mutch 1, Shafto 1, Wharton 1.

1942–43

Balmer J 16	Harley J 2	Low NH* 1	Seddon KJ 6
Bush TW 5	Haycock F* 9	Mather H* 1	Shafto J 1
Campbell J 4	Hobson A 40	McInnes JS 3	Shepherd AL 1
Carney LF 3	Hughes L 2	Mills GR* 9	Spicer EW 2
Charlesworth S* 9	Hulligan M 31	Murphy G* 1	Taylor PH 5
Done CE 39	Jackson G* 7	Nieuwenhuys B 7	Welsh D* 1
Dorsett R* 14	Jones W 5	Paterson GL 2	Westby JL* 19
Eastham H 1	Kaye GH 38	Pearson TU* 1	Williams F* 5
Edelston M* 3	Keen ERL* 17	Pilling J 36	Wood J* 1
Fagan W 28	Kirby NR* 1	Polk S 2	Woodruff A* 1
Finney F 1	Lambert R 10	Pope AL* 1	
Guttridge R* 20	Liddell WB 15	Rawlings JDS* 1	
Hall WW 4	Livingstone A* 1	Rist FH* 8	

Goals (134): Done 37, Fagan 19, Hulligan 16, Balmer 14, Dorsett 14, Mills 9, Liddell 6, Nieuwenhuys 3, Hall 2, Paterson 2, Welsh 2, Kaye 2, Campbell 1, Carney 1, Harley 1, Haycock 1, Edelston 1, Pearson 1, Pilling 1, Polk 1, Shafto 1, Shepherd 1, own goal 2.

Includes four County Cup final goals and appearances for these two matches.

1943–44

Balmer J 28	Gulliver J* 37	Kaye GH 19	Shafto J 2
Beattie R* 25	Guttridge R* 2	Lambert R 3	Shepherd AL 7
Black A* 2	Hall WW 7	Liddell WB 6	Taylor PH 4
Busby M 4	Hanson AJ* 11	McCormick J* 2	Thorpe S* 2
Butler S* 4	Harley J 3	McDonald J 1	Welsh D* 18
Campbell J 25	Hobson A 40	Nieuwenhuys B 10	Westby JL* 29
Done CE 34	Hughes L 39	Paterson GL 1	Whiteside A* 1
Dougal J* 1	Hulligan M 40	Pilling J 40	
Fagan W 1	Johnstone –* 1	Polk S 17	
Gorman WC* 1	Jones WH 3	Seddon KJ 4	

Goals (146): Done 45, Balmer 21, Welsh 16, Beattie 12, Campbell 10, Shepherd 10, Nieuwenhuys 6, Hulligan 5, Liddell 4, Polk 4, Hanson 2, Harley 2, Taylor 2, Black 1, Fagan 1, Gulliver 1, Hall 1, Hughes 1, McCormick 1, own goal 1.

Includes three goals in second leg Lancs Cup final and appearances for this match.

1944–45

Baines PC* 1	Garner T 1	Kemp DJ 5	Shannon L 4
Balmer J 3	Gulliver J* 40	Kinghorn WJD 10	Shepherd AL 3
Blood JF* 5	Hall HHC* 1	Liddell WB 15	Smith J* 2
Busby M 5	Hall WW 2	McInnes JS 8	Spicer EW 1
Bush TW 3	Harley J 14	McIntosh JM* 1	Taylor PH 36
Campbell J 30	Hinsley G* 3	Mulvaney J* 1	Thorpe S* 1
Cumner RH* 15	Hobson A 37	Nieuwenhuys B 28	Welsh D* 21
Dix RW* 6	Hughes L 39	Paterson GL 3	Westby JL* 17
Done CE 4	Hulligan M 7	Pilling J 36	Whalley H* 1
Eastham H 6	Jones R 2	Rawcliffe F* 1	
Fagan W 6	Kaye GH 32	Seddon KJ 6	

Goals (108): Welsh 26, Taylor 17, Liddell 13, Nieuwenhuys 10, Campbell 7, Fagan 5, Done 4, Shannon 4, Cumner 3, Hulligan 3, Kinghorn 3, Dix 2, Pilling 2, Smith 2, Baines 1, Eastham 1, Hinsley 1, Paterson 1, Shepherd 1, Westby 1, own goal 1.

1945–46

Ashcroft C 5	Finney F 1	Kippax FP* 1	Ramsden B 18
Balmer J 36	Gulliver J* 16	Lambert R 18	Sanders JA* 3
Baron K 8	Hall HHC 7	Liddell WB 26	Shannon L 11
Burke RJ* 1	Harley J 22	McInnes JS 6	Sidlow C 9
Bush TW 5	Hobson A 6	Nickson H 10	Spicer EW 9
Campbell J 2	Hughes L 33	Nieuwenhuys B 29	Taylor PH 33
Done CE 8	Hulligan M 2	Paisley R 25	Welsh D* 2
Easdale J 8	Jones WH 4	Paterson GL 2	Westby JL 13
Eastham H 3	Kaye GH 27	Pilling J 4	
Fagan W 36	Kemp DJ 2	Priday R 11	

Goals (80): Fagan 20, Balmer 18, Liddell 18, Done 4, Priday 4, Nieuwenhuys 3, Taylor 3, Jones 2, Kaye 2, Baron 1, Burke 1, Kippax 1, Paisley 1, Shannon 1, own goal 1.

FA Cup goals (6): Fagan 3, Balmer 1, Liddell 1, Nieuwenhuys 1.

Luton Town

1939–40

Biggs AG★ 19
Billington HJR 24
Burgess WW 1
Burgwin WD★ 1
Carroll J 10
Chambers J★ 6
Chew J 3
Coen JL 14
Cunningham E★ 2
Currant F 1

Dowers JA★ 5
Dreyer G 18
Duggan EJ 23
Duke GE 17
Dunsmore TH 17
Emmanuel L★ 1
Finlayson J 25
Forsyth J 9
Fowler JA 2
Gager HE 8

Gardiner D 6
Kerr AW★ 1
King TP 3
Lutterloch BR 30
Moore AB★ 1
Payne J★ 1
Perrins DJ 4
Pugh SJ★ 1
Ramsey J 1
Randle L★ 2

Roberts D★ 1
Roberts F 29
Robinson W★ 7
Sherborne JL★ 1
Smith TS★ 2
Stephenson GH 16
Stockill RR 3
Tennant AE★ 1
Vinall EJ 20
Young RH★ 5

Goals (83): Billington 42, Vinall 12, Duggan 6, Biggs 5, Robinson 3, Dowers 2, Stephenson 2, Stockill 2, Carroll 1, Cunningham 1, Finlayson 1, Gager 1, Kerr 1, Perrins 1, Roberts F 1, Sherborne 1, Smith 1.

War Cup goals (2): Duggan 2.

1940–41

Armes S★ 7
Bates WH 4
Billington HJR 6
Cahill R★ 3
Cambell R 21
Chew J 19
Clark PE 1
Coen JL 37
Day A★ 1

Dowers JA★ 29
Dreyer G 10
Duggan EJ 37
Dunsmore TH 33
Farrage TO★ 5
Finlayson J 1
Forsyth J 34
Gager HE 25
Goodyear GW 9

Hunt GH★ 23
Hutchinson DC★ 1
Kirkham J★ 1
Laing JF 29
Lake LE 5
Lutterloch BR 21
Mackey TS 2
Marsden S 2
Payne J★ 8

Pembleton A 1
Perrins RJ 20
Redfern R★ 4
Shepherson H★ 2
Smith AE 5
Smith JCR★ 1
Stephenson EN 1
Vinall EJ 1

Goals (86): Duggan 21, Laing 14, Dowers 8, Billington 5, Payne 5, Perrins 5, Dunsmore 4, Lutterloch 4, Campbell 3, Day 3, Gager 3, Goodyear 2, Cahill 1, Chew 1, Farrage 1, Kirkham 1, Marsden 1, Mackey 1, Redfern 1, Smith A 1, own goal 1.

1941–42

Alsop G★ 6
Ball JT 15
Barron W★ 7
Bates WH 8
Batty SG★ 1
Billington HJR 9
Burgess WW 6
Burke RJ 2
Campbell R 9
Carte R★ 1
Chew J 16
Clark PE 5

Coen JL 2
Cook F★ 1
Cook PA★ 1
Dowers JA 33
Dreyer G 8
Duggan EJ 27
Duke GE 24
Fellowes N★ 4
Finlayson J 1
Forsyth J 14
Gager HE 1
Goodyear GW 8

Haddow J★ 1
Hogg F 1
Hunt GH★ 8
Jover TR 1
Laing JF 23
Lake LE 25
Lorton R 4
Lowcock RL 3
Lutterloch BR 10
Martin GS 1
McArthur WJ★ 1
Mills GR★ 1

Pacey HJ 6
Roberts F 26
Ruffett R 19
Sanderson D★ 1
Saunders W★ 2
Shepherdson H★ 16
Smith TS★ 1
Stearn AD 1
Stephenson EN 11
Stephenson GH 1
Tomkin AH★ 1
Wellington H★ 1

Goals (54): Billington 11, Duggan 11, Laing 8, Ball 7, Dowers 2, Goodyear 2, Hunt 2, Alsop 1, Barron 1, Bates 1, Burgess 1, Burke 1, Campbell 1, Jover 1, Roberts 1, Sanderson 1, Stephenson E 1, Tomkin 1.

1942–43

Bates WH   1
Beresford FC*   1
Billington HJR   7
Bonass AE*   1
Bradley J*   4
Browne RJ*   7
Burke RJ   7
Burns J   1
Chew J   23
Clark C   9
Cook PA   2
Creecy A*   1
Crossland B*   3
Dowers JA   16
Dreyer G   20
Duggan EJ   8

Duke GE   22
Dunkley S   12
Edwards RF   6
Evans FW   1
Forsyth J   16
Gager HE   6
Goodyear GW   32
Griffiths R*   2
Hall SL*   8
Halliday A   1
Hayward LE*   1
Heslam JW*   1
Hoar JL   16
Hope JG*   1
Hudson LA   1
Hunt GH*   3

Hunter GH*   1
Kinnell R*   2
Laing JF   17
Lake LE   1
Layton W*   4
Mackey TS   1
Marshall E*   2
McInnes JS*   2
Neil J   9
Purdie W*   4
Redfern R*   2
Richardson D*   2
Richardson HW   1
Roberts F   21
Roberts GB   7
Robertson J   1

Ruffett R   1
Ruthven J*   2
Shepherdson H*   1
Smith D*   3
Stephenson EN   13
Stevens RF*   1
Stockley KS   2
Tweed GE*   2
Wade GRW   1
Walker CJ*   1
Watt-Smith DS*   1
Wilkins GH   2
Wilkinson J   4
Wilson R*   1
Woolhead AW   2
Young RH*   20

Goals (48): Stephenson 5, Billington 4, Laing 4, Clark 3, Duggan 3, Hoar 3, Neil 3, Bradley 2, Burke 2, Crossland 2, Dunkley 2, Forsyth 2, Goodyear 2, Woolhead 2, Young 2, Bonass 1, Chew 1, Dowers 1, Dunkley 1, Edwards 1, Roberts F 1, Ruthven 1.

1943–44

Alexander F*   1
Allen JP*   1
Anderson JC*   1
Bates WH   12
Billington HJR   2
Bishop RA   2
Bott VE*   2
Bradley J*   12
Brown R*   5
Brown W*   1
Browne RJ*   2
Burdett T*   1
Burke RJ   6
Burns J   1
Cawdell HA   1

Chew J   3
Coleman R*   2
Duggan EJ   22
Duke GE   7
Dunkley S   7
Forse D*   1
Gager HE   15
Gallacher P*   9
Goodyear GW   7
Grogan J*   20
Hall LF   25
Hall SR   4
Hapgood EA*   30
Harris N*   12
Hoar JL   2

Hunt GH*   7
Jones TC*   4
Laing JF   8
Lake LE   1
Loughram J*   3
Marshall E*   15
Milton GW*   2
Neil J   16
Ordish CS   3
Poole B*   2
Readett H*   1
Shankly W*   5
Sperrin JR   4
Stearn AD   1
Stockley KS   17

Stuttard JE*   10
Taylor GE*   8
Taylor H   2
Thomas G   2
Tranter AR*   2
Wales H*   2
Ward TA*   1
Watson JF*   8
Wilkinson J*   24
Williams S*   6
Williamson J   1
Woolhead AW   8
Young RH*   17

Goals (50): Duggan 15, Harris 5, Neil 4, Billington 3, Bradley 3, Grogan 3, Woolhead 3, Gallacher 2, Marshall 2, Stockley 2, Gager 1, Goodyear 1, Hunt 1, Laing 1, Thoms 1, Watson 1, Young 1, own goal 1.

1944–45

Archer JW*   12
Ball JT   4
Barker H   1
Bates WH   1
Bilbao J*   1
Billington HJR   1
Blackman JJ*   1
Blair J*   1
Bradley J*   21
Brice GHJ   3
Burke C*   1
Capron FE   3
Cawdell HA   14
Chalkley AG*   1
Chambers J   1
Chambers KA   2
Collins GE*   6
Cooke WH*   13
Daniel M   30
De-La-Hay RJ*   1

Dempsey AJ*   1
Duggan EJ   1
Duke GE   13
Dunkley S   9
Elliott BH*   1
Forsyth J   4
Gager HE   25
Gallacher P*   7
Garner CH   1
Goodyear GW   14
Grogan J*   3
Hacking R   2
Hall AE*   5
Hapgood EA*   2
Holliday J   1
Jones CN   1
Jones T*   1
Kettley SC   8
Kirkby AW   1
Laing JF   1

Lake LE   1
Marks WG*   3
Marshall E*   11
Maudsley J*   1
Miller FD*   2
Mogford R*   1
Moore NW*   3
Moorton SR   1
Morrice J*   1
Morris T*   1
Muller W*   9
Neil J   7
O'Neill D   1
Prentice J*   1
Purvis B*   1
Roberts F*   1
Robinson P*   1
Scott L*   1
Sharpe GA   6
Singfield J*   1

Smith A   2
Smith RK   1
Stephenson GH   1
Stockley KS   3
Symons J*   1
Taylor E   4
Thomas RA*   1
Tunney E*   28
Wainwright J   1
Wallbanks WH*   2
Waugh WL   20
Weir J   1
Whittle J*   1
Wilkinson J   16
Wilmot JA   1
Woolhead AW   30
Young RH*   10

Goals (64): Woolhead 18, Bradley 14, Daniel 10, Ball 2, Cawdell 2, Dunkley 2, Gallacher 2, Goodyear 2, Neil 2, Brice 1, Marshall 1, Muller 1, Stockley 1, Wallbanks 1, Waugh 1, Weir 1, own goals 3.

1945–46

Ashton D★   1
Ball JT   6
Bates WH   1
Batty SG★   1
Beach DF   27
Bellis TG★   2
Billington HJR   20
Blackshaw HK★   1
Brice GHJ   4
Burke C★   1
Bywater L★   13
Campbell R   11
Capron FE   1
Carroll L   1
Clarke J   1
Connelly E★   8
Cooke WH   24

Crossley A   1
Daniel M   32
Dare W   2
Duggan EJ   4
Duke GE   26
Dyke H   4
Edelston M★   1
Edwards RC   5
Finch R★   1
Fletcher HH   1
Gager HE   40
Gardiner D   30
Goodyear GW   27
Hall LF   1
Hassell TW   2
Henderson G★   3
Hobbis HHF★   1

Hogg F   3
Isaacs FC   13
Jackman W★   1
Jarman W   1
Jones E★   1
Kennedy L   1
Laing JF   11
Lake LE   21
Lee H   4
Leek P★   1
Lutterloch BR   6
Marshall E★   1
McVety A   11
Morrison M   2
Morton RH   2
Muttitt E★   1
Needham D   11

Rist FH★   4
Sharpe GAT   1
Stead C★   3
Stephens JW★   1
Stephenson EN   2
Steven A★   1
Tracey C   1
Tunney E★   13
Vinall EJ   13
Waugh WL   22
Wilkinson J   1
Wilson R★   1
Woolhead AW   3
Wright H★   1

Goals (60): Billington 20, Needham 8, Daniel 7, Waugh 5, Duggan 3, Dyke 3, Henderson 3, Gardiner 2, Isaacs 2, Brice 1, Connelly 1, Hall 1, Laing 1, Lee 1, McVety 1, Vinall 1.

FA Cup goals (0).

Manchester City

1939–40

Barkas S   8
Blackshaw W   8
Bray J   22
Brook EF   7
Burdett T*   1
Cardwell L   24
Clark GV   15
Currier J*   4

Davenport J*   1
Doherty PD   21
Dunkley M   3
Emptage AT   9
Heale JA   15
Herd A   24
McDowall LJ   3
McIntosh JM*   1

Milsom J   1
Neilson R   2
Percival J   19
Pritchard HJ   11
Robinson JJ   3
Rudd J   6
Smith GB   2
Smith LGF*   1

Sproston B   13
Swift FV   22
Tilson SF*   1
Toseland E*   1
Walsh W   9
Westwood E   15
Wright TB   3

Goals (79): Herd 19, Doherty 15, Currier 11, Heale 11, Pritchard 4, Brook 3, Rudd 3, Blackshaw 2, Bray 2, Emptage 2, Milsom 2, Burdett 1, Dunkley 1, Percival 1, Westwood 1, Wright 1.

War Cup goals (1): Worsley 1.

1940–41

Barkas S   7
Beaumont L*   1
Boothway J   12
Boulter L*   1
Bray J   38
Breedon J*   1
Brooks H*   1
Brown ARJ*   14
Cardwell L   2
Carey JJ*   3
Clark GV   21

Currier J*   42
Davenport J   1
Dickie P*   1
Doherty PD   25
Dunkley M   7
Eastwood E   23
Emptage AT   11
Fagan J   5
Henry GR*   1
Herd A   22
Jackson L   5

Keeling AJ   1
McShane H*   23
Mulraney A*   6
Mutch G*   4
Neilson R   21
Nuttall E   1
Pearson S   2
Percival J   11
Pritchard HJ   30
Reid JDJ*   1
Robinson JJ   17

Robinson P   1
Rudd J   4
Sproston B   18
Swift FV   25
Thomson J*   1
Turner H*   11
Vose G*   1
Walker CE*   6
Walsh W*   41
Watt A   3
Westwood E   1

Goals (121): Currier 47, Doherty 18, Herd 17, Brown 6, Boothway 5, Pritchard 5, Bray 4, Mulraney 3, McShane 2, Reid 2, Sproston 2, Walsh 2, Brooks 1, Carey 1, Dunkley 1, Emptage 1, Mutch 1, Pearson 1, Percival 1, own goal 1.

1941–42

Bacuzzi J*   1
Bardsley L   5
Barkas S   10
Boothway J   32
Bray J   26
Brown ARJ*   1
Butt L*   1
Carey JJ*   1
Carey WJ*   9
Charlesworth S*   17
Clark GV   22
Crompton J   1
Currier J*   30

Davenport DW   2
Davenport J   1
Dellow RW*   8
Devlin J*   1
Dodd L   2
Doherty PD   5
Dunkley M   13
Eastwood E   27
Emptage AT   1
Fenton BRV*   11
Goddard WG   1
Goodall EI*   1
Hall BAC*   2

Herd A   1
Hogan WJJ   3
Jones LJ*   1
Kinghorn WJD*   1
Kirton TW   7
Malam A*   2
McDowall LJ*   1
Neilson R   1
O'Donnell H*   1
Parlane J   4
Pearson S   1
Percival J   2
Pritchard HJ   4

Robinson JJ   17
Robinson P   9
Rudd J   2
Rudman K*   1
Scales G   3
Smith GB   10
Sproston B   6
Stuart D   1
Swift FV   3
Walker CE*   27
Walsh W   28
Westwood E   3
Wild A   11

Goals (81): Boothway 34, Currier 10, Fenton 7, Dunkley 6, Barkas 3, Bray 3, Dellow 3, Smith 3, Walsh 3, Herd 2, Malam 2, Doherty 1, Emptage 1, O'Donnell 1, Parlane 1, Stuart 1.

1942–43

Barclay CE   2
Bardsley L   4
Barkas S   16
Bellis A*   1
Boothway J   11
Bray J   26
Cardwell L   2
Cassidy L   1
Charlesworth S*   12
Clark GV   35

Clark H   6
Cox FJA*   9
Currier J*   36
Dellow RW*   5
Doherty PD   8
Eastwood E   35
Grant W   6
Herd A   10
Hogan WJJ   2
Jackson L   5

Jones CW*   8
Kenny F   1
King FAB*   13
Malam A*   12
McDowall LJ   6
Paton TG*   1
Pearson S   2
Pritchard HJ   1
Robinson JJ   17
Robinson P   15

Scales G   14
Setters WE   1
Stuart D   26
Swift FV   6
Taylor J   1
Walsh W   35
Welsh D*   1
Westwood E   3
Williamson WMJ*   12

Goals (89): Currier 26, Boothway 11, Malam 7, Herd 6, King 6, Stuart 6, Williamson 6, Jones 3, Cox 2, Dellow 2, Doherty 2, Robinson P 2, Welsh 2, Bardsley 1, Bray 1, Clark H 1, Hogan 1, Pearson 1, Walsh 1, own goals 2.

1943–44

Baker HV★ 1
Barclay CE 16
Bardsley L 10
Beattie A★ 2
Bentham S★ 1
Boothway J 21
Bootle W 9
Bray J 31
Brown E 2
Burke RJ★ 4
Butler MP★ 1
Carter DF★ 1
Chappell FG 7

Chisholm KM★ 1
Clark GV 28
Clark H 2
Cox FJA★ 4
Dodd L 1
Doherty PD 26
Dunkley M 1
Eastwood E 37
Eastwood R★ 2
Emptage AT 1
Fagan J 1
Grant W 2
Hanson AJ★ 1

Heale JA 20
Herd A 2
Iddon H★ 1
Jackson L 9
King FAB★ 18
Leech F 3
McDowall LJ 33
Neilson R 1
Paton J★ 3
Pearson S 1
Percival J 5
Poole B★ 1
Porter W★ 2

Powell IV★ 1
Robinson JJ 3
Robinson P 2
Scales G 4
Sproston B 7
Swift FV 25
Taylor J 7
Thomson A★ 1
Walsh W 37
Westwood E 3
Williams J★ 1
Williamson WMJ★ 24
Worrall J 2

Goals (80): Doherty 23, Williamson 16, Heale 15, Boothway 7, King 4, McDowall 4, Barclay 3, Burke 3, Herd 2, Leech 2, Baker 1, Bardsley 1, Bootle 1, Percival 1.

Includes three extra-time goals.

1944–45

Baillie M★ 1
Barber E 3
Bardsley L 2
Barkas S 1
Bootle W 22
Bray J 31
Breedon J★ 1
Brown E 3
Cardwell L 1
Clark GV 31

Doherty PD 6
Dunkley M 10
Eastwood E 33
Emptage AT 1
Grant W 5
Heale JA 9
Herd A 3
Hodgson R 3
Jackson L 1
Jones JT★ 2

King FAB★ 18
Linaker JE 2
McDowall LJ 34
McMillan J 8
Meiklem RC 1
Ollerenshaw J 1
Owen EL 9
Robinson JJ 3
Robinson P 3
Roxburgh AW★ 3

Rudd J 2
Smith GB 36
Sproston B 9
Swift FV 18
Taylor J 23
Thorpe WF★ 2
Walsh W 37
Westwood E 1
Williams E 2
Williamson WMJ★ 26

Goals (85): Smith 22, Williamson 17, King 9, Heale 7, Owen 6, Bootle 5, McDowall 4, Doherty 3, Herd 3, Taylor 3, Dunkley 2, Sproston 2, Bray 1, Walsh 1.

1945–46

Barkas S 33
Bootle W 1
Bray J 4
Brown E 2
Campbell J★ 1
Capel TA 1
Cardwell L 17
Clark GV 26
Constantine J 34
Cunliffe RA 1
Daniels D 3
Dunkley M 29

Eastwood E 8
Emptage AT 12
Fagan J 4
Gemmell E 2
Hart JP 4
Herd A 29
Hilton J 1
Hodgson R 2
Hope JG 1
King FAB★ 2
Laing R★ 1
Linaker JE 4

McCormack CJ★ 1
McDowall LJ 40
Moore B★ 3
Murray W★ 4
Pearson WG★ 14
Pimbley D 2
Pritchard HJ 1
Robinson P 2
Roxburgh AW★ 2
Smith GB 41
Sproston B 22
Swift FV 35

Taylor J 3
Thorpe WF★ 1
Toseland E★ 1
Walker S 3
Walsh W 40
Westwood E 5
Wild A 5
Williams E 8
Wilson F★ 1
Woodroffe LC 6

Goals (78): Constantine 25, Smith 20, Herd 11, Dunkley 6, Pearson 6, Wild 2, Woodroffe 2, Emptage 1, Gemmell 1, Hart 1, King 1, Sproston 1, Walsh 1.

FA Cup goals (13): Constantine 4, Herd 4, Smith 3, Dunkley 1, Hart 1.

Manchester United

1939–40

Anderson J   1
Asquith B   6
Breedon J   21
Briggs C★   2
Bryant W   4
Burdett T★   2
Butt L★   11
Carey JJ   20
Carter DF★   1
Chilton A   1

Doherty PD★   1
Dougal P★   1
Fairhurst WG★   2
Gemmell J★   2
Goodall EI★   2
Griffiths J   3
Hanlon J   10
Herd A★   1
Jones D★   3
Kilshaw E★   6

Manley T★   9
Matthews S★   1
McKay W   21
Mitten C   3
Nicholson WE   4
Pearson SC   21
Porter W   2
Redwood H   24
Roberts F★   3
Roughton WG   19

Smith J   19
Toseland E★   1
Vose G   7
Warner J   19
Wassall JV   1
Watson R★   1
Whalley H   3
Woodward T★   1
Wrigglesworth W   16

Goals (79): Pearson 16, Smith 16, Butt 8, Wrigglesworth 8, McKay 5, Hanlon 4, Carey 3, Roughton 3, Asquith 2, Bryant 2, Burdett 2, Jones 2, Manley 1, Roberts 1, Vose 1, Warner 1, Whalley 1, own goals 3.

War Cup goals (5): Carey 2, Pearson 1, Smith 1, Wrigglesworth 1.

1940–41

Ainsley GE★   1
Asquith B   4
Aston J   11
Bagley TH★   1
Bartholomew R★   3
Bellis A★   4
Breedon J   35
Briggs C   1
Brown A★   13
Bryant W   22
Buchan WRM★   2
Burbanks WE★   1

Burrows A★   5
Butt L★   2
Carey JJ   34
Carey WJ★   1
Chorley J   1
Couser HM   2
Dodds E★   4
Emptage AT★   1
Farrow G★   3
Gemmell J★   1
Gorman WC★   2
Griffiths J   2

Johnson R★   2
Jones B★   1
Jones S★   1
McKay W   19
McPhillips L★   1
Mears S   4
Mitten C   21
O'Donnell H★   5
Olsen TB★   1
Pearson SC   5
Porter W   21
Redwood H   26

Roughton WG   28
Rowley GA   1
Rowley JF   13
Smith J   34
Stock H★   1
Topping HW   2
Vose G   3
Warner J   36
Watkins T   1
Whalley H   22
Wrigglesworth W   2
Wyles TC★   1

Goals (83): Smith 26, Rowley J 19, Carey J 12, Dodds 5, Pearson 4, Aston 3, Butt 3, Bryant 2, Mears 2, Mitten 2, Warner 2, Buchan 1, Burrows 1, Farrow 1, McKay 1, Whalley 1.

Includes two extra-time goals.

1941–42

Breedon J   36
Bryant W   34
Carey JJ   35
Catterick H★   10
Chilton A   1
Dougal J★   1
Dougal T   1
Emptage AT★   1

Fidler F   1
Griffiths J   9
Holdcroft G★   1
Hornby R★   1
Lee JS   3
Mitten C   13
Morris J   25
Pearson SC   7

Porter W   36
Redwood H   17
Roach JE   7
Robinson A★   1
Robinson P   1
Roughton WG   27
Rowley GA   1
Rowley JF   23

Shore J   7
Smith J   33
Taylor EW   1
Waddington A   3
Warner J   30
Whalley H   37
Worrall H   1
Wrigglesworth W   3

Goals (123): Rowley J 42, Carey 24, Smith 18, Morris 12, Catterick 7, Bryant 5, Mitten 5, Whalley 4, Warner 3, Worrall 2, Pearson 1.

1942–43

Anderson W 1
Asquith B 1
Barkas S* 1
Bellis A* 26
Black W* 1
Breedon J 33
Broadis IA* 2
Brocklebank R* 1
Bryant W 34
Buchan WRM* 7
Burnett GG* 1
Byrom W* 2
Carey JJ 23
Catterick H* 5
Chadwick C* 1

Chilton A 1
Dainty A* 1
Dimond S 2
Dougan T 2
Eastwood E* 3
Griffiths G* 2
Griffiths J 25
Griffiths W* 2
Haigh G* 1
Hall JL 1
Harrison H* 1
Hyde EW* 2
King FO* 1
Kippax F* 1
Kirkman N* 1

Lee JS 4
Martindale L* 1
McKay W 14
Mitten C 8
Morris J 10
Newsome R* 1
Pearson S* 1
Pearson SC 15
Porter W 26
Radcliffe B* 2
Roach JE 4
Robinson JJ* 1
Roughton WG 33
Rowley GA 4
Rowley JF 6

Scales G* 1
Shore J 2
Smith J 31
Smith TM* 1
Vose G 8
Walsh W* 2
Walton J 2
Warner J 28
Westwood E* 1
Whalley H 34
White R* 1
Williams WJH 1
Woodruff A* 1
Worrall H 1

Goals (116): Smith J 38, Bryant 11, Bellis 10, Pearson SC 10, Carey 8, Rowley J 8, Mitten 5, Buchan 4, Morris 4, Catterick 3, Roughton 3, Broadis 2, Hyde 2, McKay 2, Griffiths W 1, own goals 4.

Goals total includes six in the Lancashire Cup Final over two legs and appearances for this match.

1943–44

Bailey A* 1
Barker L 1
Bellis A* 16
Black W* 1
Bootle W* 1
Breedon J 31
Brierley GN 1
Broadis IA* 2
Brook H* 16
Bryant W 35
Cochrane AM 1
Cockburn H 1
Dimond S 1

Ferrer D* 6
Gallon JW* 3
Gardner T* 1
Gibson R 1
Griffiths J 20
Grundy T 2
Hacking J 1
Hyde EW* 1
Liddell J* 3
McDonald JC* 8
McKay W 32
Mitten C 4
Morris J 17

Norris F 6
Pearson L 1
Pearson SC 16
Porter W 36
Roughton WG 29
Rowley GA 1
Rowley JF 5
Rudman H* 1
Sloan JW* 1
Smith J 33
Tilling HK* 1
Tomlinson F 1
Tyrell L 1

Vose G 1
Walmsley J* 2
Walton JA 25
Warner J 35
Watson WT* 1
Watton GD* 1
Whalley H 20
Williams WJH 1
Wilson JH 2
Wood D* 1
Woodruff H* 1

Goals (111): Smith 35, Bryant 15, Pearson S 12, Brook 8, Bellis 6, McDonald 6, Morris 6, Rowley J 6, McKay 5, Mitten 4, Broadis 1, Norris 1, Roughton 1, Rowley GA 1, Sloan 1, Warner 1, own goals 2.

1944–45

Astbury TA* 1
Bainbridge W 4
Bartholomew R* 3
Bellis A* 6
Bowden NH* 2
Boyes W* 1
Breedon J 14
Briggs C 8
Bryant W 35
Capper G 3
Chadwick C* 25
Chilton A 7

Cockburn H 8
Crompton J 26
Currier J* 3
Dougan T 3
Freer C 1
Gallon JW* 1
Glaister G* 1
Glidden GS* 1
Hession T 1
Ireland HW* 1
Johnson AA 1
Jones A 1

Keeley W* 2
Makin G* 1
McCulloch WD* 3
McDonald H 1
McDowell J* 1
McInnes JS* 2
McKay W 21
Mercer S* 1
Mitten C 6
Morris J 11
Mycock A 25
Porter W 6

Roach JE 18
Robinson P* 1
Roughton WG 29
Rowley JF 3
Sloan JW* 2
Smith J 26
Walton J 36
Warner J 32
Whalley H 35
White R* 3
Woodcock A* 7
Wrigglesworth W 11

Goals (87): Mycock 16, Bryant 13, Smith 10, Wrigglesworth 7, Chadwick 6, Morris 6, Rowley 5, Mitten 4, Bainbridge 2, Bellis 2, Woodcock 2, Bowden 1, Cockburn 1, Currier 1, Dougan 1, Freer 1, Ireland 1, Keeley 1, McCulloch 1, McDowell 1, Mercer 1, Walton 1, Whalley 1, own goals 2.

1945–46

Aston J   5
Bainbridge W   7
Bryant W   8
Buckle EW   6
Carey JJ   27
Chilton A   31
Cockburn H   38
Comer D   1
Crompton J   30
Davie J*   1

Delaney J   15
Dimond S   1
Gallacher J*   1
Hamlett TL*   1
Hanlon J   24
Hullett W   5
Keeley W*   1
Koffman S   2
Landers T   1
Langford L   1

McKay W   1
Mitten C   4
Mycock A   3
Pearson SC   12
Reid DJ*   1
Rhodes D   1
Roach JE   14
Roughton WG   4
Rowley JF   28
Smith J   22

Tapken N   12
Vose G   1
Walton J   36
Warner J   33
Whalley H   38
Wilson JH   3
Worrall F*   7
Wrigglesworth W   36

Goals (98): Rowley 20, Smith 17, Hanlon 11, Pearson 9, Wrigglesworth 9, Hullett 6, Buckle 4, Carey 4, Delaney 4, Bainbridge 3, Aston 2, Worrall 2, Bryant 1, Davie 1, Cockburn 1, Koffman 1, Mitten 1, Reid 1, Warner 1.

FA Cup goals (9): Rowley 3, Wrigglesworth 2, Bainbridge 1, Hanlon 1, Smith 1, own goal 1.

Mansfield Town

1939–40

Akers W   3
Bailey L★   3
Barke JL   20
Barsby A★   1
Beaumont L★   11
Bedford G★   7
Biddlestone TF   3
Borrows JE   2
Bramley E   3
Carr –   1
Clarke J   1
Corkhill WG★   9
Downham J★   1
Egan H★   4
Fillingham T★   2
Flowers IJ   1
Glassey RT   3
Gregg W★   7
Harkin J   23
Hillard J★   3
Hubbard C★   19
Hunt AK★   3
Hunter JB★   4
Lucas WH★   8
Matthews E★   2
Moody J★   16
Moore W   1
Nelson WF   2
Paterson W   2
Poole CJ   1
Rickards CT★   13
Robertson JH★   18
Robinson J★   5
Simms T   6
Smith E★   8
Speed F★   1
Stephenson JE★   1
Stimpson GH   23
Sullivan M   3
Turner JK★   3
Wainwright –★   2
Ward TEG   4

Goals (57): Hubbard 15, Lucas 7, Robertson 7, Rickards 4, Smith 4, Akers 3, Matthews 3, Ward 3, Beaumont 2, Hillard 2, Borrows 1, Flowers 1, Glassey 1, Harkin 1, Hunter 1, Robinson 1, own goal 1.

War Cup goals (3): Hubbard 2, Rickards 1.

1940–41

Akers W   1
Allen J   5
Ashton P★   18
Barke JL   34
Barsley C   3
Beaumont L★   34
Briggs R   1
Corkhill WG★   12
Downham J   3
Egan H★   31
Flowers IJ   3
Gilmour T   7
Hall G★   1
Hardwick H   1
Harkin J   34
Hays CJ★   1
Hesford RT★   4
Hillard J★   1
Hubbard C★   27
Hunt AK★   5
Hunter JB★   11
Jackson –   1
Johnstone R★   21
Lucas WH★   7
Marshall E★   10
Mayfield G★   1
McCall RH★   31
McDonald G★   1
Mills –   1
Poyser GH★   1
Richards S★   2
Rickards CT   31
Rigby W★   1
Robertson JH★   27
Simms T   9
Stimpson GH   4

Goals (95): Rickards 38, Egan 14, Beaumont 10, Hubbard 10, Robertson 10, Harkin 6, Lucas 2, Akers 1, Barke 1, Flowers 1, Hunter 1, Simms 1.

1941–42

Ashton P★   11
Barke JL   29
Beaumont L★   18
Butler H   3
Butler J★   6
Cairns WH★   5
Corkhill WG★   4
Cross B★   3
Egan H★   21
Galley DS★   3
Garnham –   1
Harkin J   27
Hazard H   3
Hillard J   2
Hindley F★   4
Hodgetts JH   3
Hunter JB★   13
Ithell WJ★   2
Jeffries A★   17
Johnstone R★   6
Jones SH   1
Keeton A★   1
Kingwell LE   5
Kinsell TH★   3
McCall RH★   18
Musson WU★   8
Owen WE★   1
Parr J★   11
Platts L★   11
Rich L   1
Richards S★   9
Rickards CT   27
Robertson JH★   20
Ross L   1
Siviter E   1
Somerfield A★   2
Townsend R★   1
Ward TEG   1
Webber EV★   15
Wolfe ER★   1

Goals (44): Rickards 12, Harkin 10, Beaumont 4, Barke 3, Hunter 3, Jeffries 2, Robertson 2, Somerfield 2, Cairns 1, Egan 1, Hazard 1, Hindley 1, Owen 1, Rich 1.

1942–43

Allen J   6
Barke JL   28
Bedford G   1
Benner R★   1
Bicknell J   24
Bradshaw W   2
Bramley E   3
Chessell S   11
Cooke E   15
Dunderdale WL★   2
Edwards AJS   12
Egan H★   5
Everett H   8
Findlay W   3
Flowers IJ   2
Hannah GL★   6
Harkin J   11
Hazard H   2
Hunter JB★   7
Jeffries A★   4
Jones –   4
Lievesley L★   4
Little –   2
Marlow GA★   22
Marsh T   3
Marsh W   6
Mills PC★   2
Oakley J   26
Owen WE★   2
Platts L★   2
Poole CJ   6
Pritchard R★   1
Richards S★   5
Rickards CT   16
Robertson JH★   15
Sidley –   1
Siviter E   1
Smith –   6
Taylor –   1
Walters H   1
Ward TEG   1
Webber EV★   23
Wilson –   1
Winslow –   2
Winstanley D★   2

Goals (37): Bicknell 9, Edwards 4, Marlow 4, Rickards 4, Robertson 2, Barke 1, Chessell 1, Dunderdale 1, Egan 1, Flowers 1, Hannah 1, Hunter 1, Owen 1, Siviter 1, Ward 1, Wilson 1, own goals 3.

1943–44

Akers W   1
Allen J   1
Barke JL   31
Bramley E   17
Callender J*   2
Chessell S   18
Clack FE*   23
Clarke JH*   5
Collins AD*   2
Davidson DBL*   1
Dickinson N   2
Egan H*   2

Ellis S   2
Flowers IJ   1
Galley DS*   5
Gascoigne W   3
Greaves –   1
Hamilton G   1
Harkin J   27
Hazard –   1
Hinton E   1
Hogg F*   14
Holling –   2
Hubbard C*   8

Jagger –   1
Jones DO   3
Laing FJ*   3
Leeming –   1
Marlow GA*   28
Owen WE   4
Pilcher E   5
Poole CJ   32
Rickards CT   30
Rutherford J*   1
Shadwell J*   3
Smith –   1

Smith K*   23
Sullivan M   8
Tapping FH*   25
Taylor –   1
Wall –   1
Walsh W*   1
Warburton G*   1
Weaver S*   1
Wilkinson J*   1
Wood AR*   3
Wooldridge J*   4

Goals (55): Marlow 15, Chessell 9, Smith K 6, Rickards 5, Tapping 4, Hubbard 3, Owen 3, Barke 2, Akers 1, Clarke 1, Collins 1, Gascoigne 1, Jagger 1, Laing 1, Sullivan 1, own goal 1.

1944–45

Akers W   13
Allison –   1
Alsop G*   10
Armeson LR*   5
Atter AM*   2
Barke JL   30
Baxter WE*   1
Bradley DJ*   2
Bramley E   28
Brown G*   1
Butler J   3
Christopher JW*   1
Collins AD*   2
Cooke E   9

Curry R*   13
Davie J*   1
Duffield SC*   1
Everett H   1
Flewitt S*   1
Flint K   1
Gardner JL   4
Gillan –   1
Grant AF*   19
Griffin R   1
Harkin J   28
Hartley TW*   3
Hewitt J*   7
Hogg F*   6

Hughes A*   1
Jones LJ*   13
Jones SH*   1
Kirk –   1
Liddle D*   19
Long A*   2
Marlow GA*   20
Millington –   2
Moulson C*   2
Owens MR*   1
Poole CJ   26
Poole G*   2
Ranshaw JW*   4
Richman R   1

Rickards CT   5
Rickett W*   2
Rossington K*   2
Somerfield A*   1
Tapping FH*   9
Ward TEG   2
Wheat J*   1
White F*   4
Wilcoxon GH*   5
Wilkinson J*   1
Williams FA*   8

Goals (53): Alsop 7, Cooke 6, Curry 6, Marlow 6, Hewitt 5, Akers 4, Bramley 4, Gardner 2, Tapping 2, Wilcoxon 2, Baxter 1, Davie 1, Harkin 1, Liddle 1, Owens 1, Poole C 1, Rickards 1, Ward 1, own goal 1.

1945–46

Akers W   9
Alderson WS*   4
Allen J   2
Baker A   5
Barke JL   36
Betts E   11
Bowles JC*   3
Bramley E   25
Brinton JV*   1
Carter S   10
Chessell S   33
Copestake OFR   16
Cromack V   15

Everett H   17
Ferguson J*   1
Fretwell LD   6
Grant AF*   1
Harkin J   28
Hartley TW*   1
Hawkins A   1
Hewitt H   15
Hogg F*   23
Jeffries WA   2
Kelk H   1
Lappage W   1
Longdon CW*   1

Mackay JM   1
Mallinder D   4
Marsh W   5
Martin R   1
Miller LR*   11
Naylor A   1
Oakley JC*   12
Peacock T*   5
Poole CJ   1
Pulfrey VN*   1
Richmond R   2
Rickett W*   2
Robinson R*   1

Smith E*   5
Smith L   31
Smith W   7
Thorpe L   12
Townsend JA   1
Uren P   4
Ward TA*   2
Weaver S*   1
Wombwell D   17
Woolhead AW*   1

Goals (53): Hogg 11, Wombwell 10, Carter 5, Copestake 4, Harkin 4, Hewitt 3, Barke 2, Betts 2, Miller 2, Smith E 2, Akers 1, Brinton 1, Everett 1, Jeffries 1, Marsh 1, Peacock 1, Smith W 1, Thorpe 1.

FA Cup goals (9): Wombwell 5, Harkin 1, Hogg 1, Poole C 1, Thorpe 1.

Middlesbrough

1939–40

Ainsworth W★ 1	Cumming DS 22	Mannion W 15	Murphy GJ 3
Armes S 2	Fenton M 22	Martin J 17	Murphy TE 18
Baxter RD 3	Forrest W 21	McKenzie D 4	Robinson JN 14
Brown WH 16	Fowler H 10	McMahon H★ 7	Shepherdson H 8
Camsell GH 11	Hardwick GFM 3	Miller D 3	Stobbart GC 4
Chadwick C 12	Heywood AE★ 1	Milne JV 10	Stuart RW 19
Copping W★ 1	Laking GE 3	Murphy DA 1	Yorston BC 2

Goals (52): Fenton 25, Camsell 5, Mannion 5, Stobbart 5, Forrest 3, McMahon 3, Murphy TE 3, Chadwick 2, Murphy G 1.

War Cup goals (8): Fenton 4, Milne 1, Murphy DA 1, Murphy TE 1, Stobbart 1.

1940–41

Baker F 2	Forrest W 28	McCabe JJ 2	Robinson J★ 5
Bray E★ 1	Fowler HN 2	McMahon H★ 1	Russell JW★ 4
Brown WH 18	Gilbraith RE 2	Meek J★ 1	Shepherdson H 3
Busby M★ 19	Gillies J 3	Mould W★ 15	Simpson R★ 30
Butler F★ 4	Gorman J★ 27	Munro AD★ 2	Smith H 5
Camsell GH 7	Hardisty JRE★ 16	Murphy DA 2	Spuhler JO★ 1
Clayton S★ 2	Hardwick GFM 1	Murphy TE 13	Stobbart GC 33
Cochrane T★ 6	Hepworth AW 1	Nevins L★ 1	Stuart RW 1
Cumming DS 28	Johnson A★ 13	Ormston A★ 2	Wilson A 1
Fenton M 10	Mannion W 17	Pearson SC★ 1	Woffinden RS★ 1
Ferrier H★ 1	Martin J 19	Peppitt S★ 12	

Goals (94): Stobbart 30, Fenton 9, Simpson 9, Forrest 8, Camsell 7, Peppitt 5, Busby 4, Robinson 4, Gillies 3, Cochrane 2, Mannion 2, Murphy TE 2, Nevins 2, Baker 1, Clayton 1, Hardisty 1, Ormston 1, Russell 1, Shepherdson 1, own goal 1.

1941–42

Arran R 3	Fowler HN 3	Laking GE 3	Shepherdson H 4
Baxter RD 3	Gilbraith RE 5	Mannion W 11	Sherwood HW★ 5
Birkett RJE★ 1	Graham D★ 1	Martin J 27	Simpson R★ 30
Blenkinsopp TW★ 12	Gray H★ 1	McCabe JJ 17	Smith H 1
Boyes W★ 2	Hardisty JRE★ 2	McKerrell D★ 1	Stephenson G★ 1
Brown WH 3	Hardwick GFM 2	McLean WK 1	Stobbart GC 19
Butler T 1	Hepplewhite G★ 2	Middleton MY★ 14	Stuart RW 2
Camsell GH 15	Johnson A★ 16	Morris RB 1	Taylor PT★ 8
Cochrane T★ 27	Johnson T 1	Mulroy T 1	Towers J★ 19
Cumming DS 18	Jones RG★ 1	Murphy DA 6	Warburton A★ 3
Dawson T★ 17	Kelly TW★ 2	Price WB★ 2	Weston RP★ 2
Denmark J★ 1	Kinnear D★ 5	Reid JDJ★ 3	Wright RCA★ 2
Ferrier H★ 16	Kirk J★ 7	Rickaby S 1	Yeats J★ 1
Forrest W 31	Knight G★ 5	Robinson J★ 8	

Goals (81): Stobbart 12, Dawson 11, Taylor 10, Camsell 9, Robinson 9, Cochrane 7, Towers 6, Kinnear 4, Forrest 3, Reid 2, Simpson 2, Warburton 2, Johnson A 1, Laking 1, McCabe 1, Mannion 1.

1942–43

Arran R 5	Douglass PG 2	Johnson T★ 5	Park W★ 20
Bowers P 4	Farrage TO★ 1	Kearney SF★ 4	Rickaby S 1
Brown WH 4	Farrington R★ 4	Laking GE 3	Rudkin TW★ 2
Buckley F★ 1	Forrest W 16	Livingstone A★ 1	Sargent F★ 5
Burchell GS 5	Franklin JL 14	Martin J 29	Shepherdson H 4
Carey JJ★ 1	French JW 6	McMahon H★ 4	Simpson R★ 22
Carr EM★ 1	Gilbraith RE 6	Middleton MY★ 30	Stobbart GC 18
Cassidy W★ 5	Goldsborough E 1	Mordue GA★ 1	Stuart RW 17
Connor J★ 2	Hardisty JRE★ 12	Murphy DA 5	Towers J★ 27
Craddock RCR 1	Hardwick GFM 1	Nicholson WE★ 2	Warburton A★ 6
Dawson T★ 24	Harrington DJA 13	Oliver J★ 1	Wharton G★ 21
Dent JA 6	Hirst H★ 1	Osborne F★ 1	Wilson K 10
Dicks RW 1	Johnson A★ 6	Owen W★ 4	Wright RCA★ 10

Goals (61): Stobbart 11, Wharton 8, Dawson 7, Bowers 6, Simpson 5, Farrington 3, Franklin 3, Wilson 3, Carr 2, Kearney 2, Laking 2, Dicks 1, Hardisty 1, Harrington 1, Johnson A 1, Owen 1, Rudkin 1, Towers 1, Warburton 1, own goal 1.

1943–44

Barber E★ 2	Farrington R★ 12	Laking GE 3	Stephen JF★ 1
Birse CV★ 5	Forrest W 5	Lyon TK★ 7	Stevens RF★ 3
Blenkinsopp TW★ 19	Franklin JL 3	Martin J 27	Stobbart GC 26
Brown WH 2	French JW 20	McGorrighan FO 3	Stuart RW 20
Brunskill N★ 29	Gallagher DE 9	Middleton MY★ 29	Towers J★ 15
Cassidy W★ 2	Gilbraith RE 28	Murphy TE 19	Walton R★ 1
Crack FW★ 5	Hardisty JRE★ 3	Oakes J★ 14	Warburton G★ 4
Cumming DS 8	Hardwick GFM 1	Parlane J★ 23	Weir A★ 1
Davies WC 2	Harrington DJA 4	Robinson JN 4	Wilson K 14
Dicks RW 22	Hodgson S★ 17	Shepherdson H 2	Wright RCA★ 7
Evans FM★ 1	Hubble L★ 1	Skinner G★ 2	
Fallaize RA★ 2	Kerr AW★ 1	Steele EC★ 1	

Goals (76): Stobbart 23, Parlane 11, Oakes 6, Lyon 5, Farrington 4, Dicks 3, Hodgson 3, Murphy 3, Gallagher 2, Harrington 2, Martin 2, Stevens 2, Wilson 2, Brunskill 1, Forrest 1, Hardisty 1, McGorrighan 1, Skinner 1, Warburton 1, Wright 1, own goal 1.

1944–45

Adams W★ 1	Forster LJ★ 3	Mahon L 1	Shreeve JTT★ 2
Barnes PC★ 1	Franklin JL 5	Martin J 7	Simpson R★ 1
Bell HD★ 2	French JW 18	McArthur WJ★ 2	Sinclair T★ 1
Bicknell R★ 1	Gallagher DE 1	McCabe JJ 1	Sloan J★ 2
Blenkinsopp TW★ 4	Gilbraith RE 4	McGorrighan FO 8	Stenson T 7
Borrowman W 2	Hardisty JRE★ 2	Methley I★ 1	Stevenson J★ 2
Bowes W★ 1	Hardwick GFM 4	Middleton MY★ 33	Stobbart GC 41
Bowie JD★ 11	Harnby DR★ 6	Miller D 1	Stuart RW 42
Brown WH 7	Harrington DJA 9	Moody J 14	Sutherland A★ 1
Chilton A★ 1	Heweston K 15	Murphy TE 2	Temple W★ 1
Cross T★ 1	Howe LF★ 1	Nash FC 5	Thompson KH 11
Cumming DS 3	Johnson T 28	Nevins L★ 1	Wainwright EF★ 10
Davies WC 1	Johnson WH^ 2	Porter L★ 1	Warburton G★ 2
Davison J 1	Kerr AW★ 1	Robinson JN 11	Wass W 14
Dean WHG★ 4	Kinsell TH★ 3	Robinson R 7	Wilson K 17
Dixon JT★ 7	Laking GE 1	Rowley GA★ 1	Woollett C★ 7
Fenton M 7	Larner L★ 2	Sales RD★ 6	
Ferguson C★ 2	Lilley J★ 1	Shepherdson H 7	
Forrest W 23	Long HR 5	Short JD★ 1	

Goals (74): Stobbart 33, Fenton 5, Long 4, Moody 4, Stuart 3, Bowie 2, Dixon 2, Johnson T 2, Wainwright 2, Wass 2, Wilson 2, Dean 1, Bowes 1, Forrest 1, Harrington 1, Larner 1, McGorrighan 1, Murphy 1, Nevins 1, Robinson R 1, Rowley 1, Sloan 1, Warburton 1, own goal 1.

1945–46

Attwell RF★ 1	Fenton M 30	Malan NF 2	Shepherdson H 18
Bambrough N 2	French JW 2	Mannion W 6	Spuhler JO 27
Barclay R★ 1	Gordon J 21	Mattinson H 3	Stobbart GC 25
Bell HD 36	Hardwick GFM 27	McCabe JJ 9	Stuart RW 27
Bowes W 2	Hepple G 5	McCormack CJ★ 1	Wainwright EF★ 2
Brown J 1	Herd A★ 1	Morris RB 1	Wallbanks H★ 1
Brown WH 3	Heweston K 5	Mullen J★ 1	Wass W 7
Butler T 5	Jameson P 2	Murphy TE 20	Watson R 5
Chadwick C 6	Johnson T 10	Nash FC 2	Wharton G^ 1
Cumming DS 38	Jones S★ 1	Price AJW★ 1	Wilson K 1
Dews G 37	Laking GE 16	Robinson JN 1	
Douglas J 22	Maddison J 6	Robinson R 21	

Goals (75): Fenton 20, Spuhler 12, Murphy 11, Stobbart 10, Dews 9, Stuart 3, Gordon 2, Hardwick 2, Maddison 2, Butler 1, Chadwick 1, Robinson R 1, Wass 1, own goal 1.

FA Cup goals (18): Fenton 7, Spuhler 3, Dews 2, Douglas 1, Gordon 1, Hardwick 2, Murphy 1, own goal 1.

Millwall

1939–40

Barker D 33	Fenton BRV 3	Mills GR★ 1	Thorogood J 1
Beattie JF 3	Fisher FW 39	Oakes John★ 1	Toser EW 21
Bower RW 1	Forsyth J 32	Osman HJ 8	Walsh W 4
Brolly T 34	Howe LF★ 1	Pearson HF 2	Wilkins GE★ 1
Brown ARJ★ 1	Jinks JT 30	Richardson JR 32	Williams G 35
Burke JJ 34	Lea GI 1	Smith EJ 38	Wright RCA★ 1
Chiverton EJ 8	McLeod JS 8	Smith JCR 31	Yuill D 3
Dudley RA 5	McMillen W 3	Sykes J 14	

Goals (87): Jinks 32, Barker 12, Fisher 11, Richardson 10, McLeod 6, Osman 5, Brolly 3, Smith E 2, Smith JCR 2, Beattie 1, Dudley 1, Williams 1, own goal 1.

War Cup goals (2): Fisher 1, Jinks 1.

1940–41

Bartlett FL★ 3	Evans RL 3	Johnson HG 1	Smith EJ 29
Birdseye F★ 1	Fenton BRV 2	Lancelotte EC★ 1	Smith JCR 31
Broadis IA 14	Fisher FW 28	Lievesley L★ 1	Sykes J 3
Brolly T 1	Ford FG★ 2	Mansfield RW 4	Tickridge S★ 13
Buchanan A 3	Forsyth J 30	Osborne J★ 2	Wallbanks J★ 12
Burke JJ 33	Gillespie IC★ 1	Pennington AB 4	Walsh W 1
Button R 16	Hammond WE★ 1	Read SG 2	Ward HA 1
Chaney FG 2	Jinks JT 26	Reeve FW★ 3	Williams G 22
Daniels J 5	Jobling J★ 8	Reid EJ★ 3	
Downer F 2	Jobson F★ 1	Richardson JR 24	
Dudley RA 18	Johnson CH★ 4	Ross GA★ 2	

Goals (76): Jinks 24, Fisher 15, Smith JCR 8, Broadis 6, Forsyth 4, Read 3, Richardson 5, Johnson CH 2, Mansfield 2, Reid 2, Daniels 1, Fenton 1, Jobling 1, Osborne J 1, Reeve 1.

London Cup

Bartlett 1, Burke 10, Button 3, Chaney 1, Chapman – 1, Davidson – 1, Dudley 8, Fisher 8, Ford 1, Forsyth 9, Grant –★ 1, Hammond 1, Jinks 4, Jobling 1, Johnson 1, Lancelotte 4, Mansfield 1, Oakes John★ 5, Osborne G 1, Osborne J★ 1, Pennington 1, Reeve 3, Reid 2, Richardson 4, Ross 4, Smith E 9, Smith JCR 10, Tickridge 5, Voisey W 1, Warnes –★ 1, Williams 7.

Goals: Reeve 3, Fisher 2, Jinks 2, Reid 2, Dudley 1, Forsyth 1, Johnson 1, Osborne J 1.

1941–42

Anderson RJ★ 1	Dudley RA 11	Malpass ST★ 1	Read SG 1
Bell S★ 29	Eastham GR★ 2	Mansfield RW 9	Reid JDJ★ 7
Blackman JJ★ 1	Fisher FW 32	Marsden F★ 2	Richardson JR 3
Brolly T 1	Forsyth J 20	Matthewson G★ 5	Scaife G★ 8
Brown T★ 3	Gibson SF 1	McCabe JJ★ 1	Sibley A★ 1
Burke JJ 28	Gillespie IC★ 2	McClure J★ 1	Sliman A 4
Burley B★ 16	Gray R★ 6	Morrison JA★ 1	Smith EJ 24
Burrows H★ 16	Groves K★ 2	Muir R★ 2	Smith JCR 10
Butcher R★ 3	Halton RL★ 3	Muttitt E★ 1	Soo F★ 4
Butler MP★ 2	Harrison II 2	Needham F★ 1	Sproston B★ 3
Button R 2	Heathcote W★ 8	O'Beirne – 1	Sykes J 1
Calland R★ 22	James F 2	Osborne J 18	Thomas – 1
Cardwell L★ 19	Johnson H★ 1	Osman HJ 3	Vickers W★ 2
Croom B★ 1	Jones S★ 7	Packard E★ 5	Warboys G★ 1
Dolding DL★ 2	Killourhy M★ 2	Patterson JM★ 3	Watmough – 1
Downer F 1	Lawton T★ 1	Preskett F★ 1	Woodburn W★ 3
Driver A★ 3	Ludford G★ 1	Purdie JJ★ 8	Wright EV★ 6

Goals (68): Bell 15, Osborne 12, Fisher 9, Heathcote 7, Reid 3, Smith JCR 3, Driver 2, Mansfield 2, Soo 2, Wright 2, Burley 1, Burrows 1, Dolding 1, Eastham 1, Harrison 1, Lawton 1, Richardson 1, Smith E 1, Sproston 1, own goals 2.

1942–43

Airlie S★ 1
Baines LJ 8
Barley R★ 1
Bell S★ 2
Boyes W★ 1
Brolly T 25
Bumstead CH 4
Burke JJ 23
Calland R★ 4
Cardwell L★ 4
Cutting SW★ 1
Dainty A★ 2
Davie J★ 2
Davies C★ 1
Davies JW★ 24
Davies SW 1
Dean CG★ 3
Delaney L★ 2
Dempster A★ 1
Driver A★ 1
Duffy C★ 2

Farmer A★ 1
Fenton BRV 19
Fisher FW 15
Fletcher AF★ 4
Forsyth J 6
Gibson SF 1
Gillespie IC★ 2
Grainger D★ 23
Green GH★ 1
Harrison II 5
Heathcote W 20
Holliday A★ 1
Horsfield A★ 1
Hutchinson RC 1
Johnstone D★ 3
Jones G★ 1
Jones S★ 2
Jordan W★ 1
Keen ERL★ 9
Kennedy WL★ 16
Knott H★ 2

Litchfield EB★ 1
Loom B★ 6
Lowe HP★ 1
Lowes AR★ 1
Mangnall D★ 1
Mansfield RW 1
Martin T★ 1
Maudsley RC★ 1
McCall –★ 1
McInnes JS★ 2
Mobie G★ 2
Muller H★ 1
Oakes John★ 1
Packard EG★ 7
Parr H 1
Purdie JJ 1
Rampling DW★ 1
Reynolds A 1
Saunders –★ 1
Scaife G★ 5
Sloan J★ 1

Smith C★ 1
Smith EJ 30
Smith JCR 8
Sproston B★ 7
Stewart G★ 1
Toser EW 1
Tyler LDV 7
Wallbanks J★ 4
Wardle A★ 1
Watson W★ 1
Weir A 7
Welsh D★ 1
Westwood EW★ 2
Whitfield W★ 7
Wilson CM★ 1
Winning G★ 1
Wood WE 2
Woodcock A★ 2
Wright Harry★ 1
Wright Henry★ 4

Goals (70): Heathcote 12, Grainger 11, Fenton 6, Sproston 6, Loom 4, Dainty 3, Dean 3, Weir 3, Davie 2, Davies S 2, Fisher 2, Jones G 2, Airlie 1, Bell 1, Baines 1, Brolly 1, Calland 1, Davies J 1, Green 1, Lowe 1, Mangnall 1, Smith JCR 1, Whitfield 1, Wood 1, own goals 2.

1943–44

Agnew J★ 10
Batey R★ 2
Birch J★ 1
Brandon J★ 1
Brolly T 12
Buckingham VF★ 2
Bumstead CH 27
Cardwell L★ 23
Cooke WH★ 1
Davies JW 20
Dean CG★ 25
Dearden A★ 1
Downer F 5
Driver A★ 14
Dunkley GA 4

Fenton BRV 4
Ferrier H★ 17
Fisher FW 4
Fisher GS 1
Gallacher P★ 1
Gledhill F 1
Grainger D★ 29
Greenwood R★ 2
Groves K★ 2
Hamilton W★ 1
Jinks JT 2
Jones DLG 1
Kurz FJ★ 14
Law J★ 4
Leyfield C★ 1

Lowes AR★ 3
Mahon J★ 1
Massey AW★ 1
Matthewson G★ 13
O'Connell T 9
Ormston A★ 5
Peppitt S★ 4
Pescod G★ 1
Powell A★ 1
Robinson A★ 5
Salmon L★ 19
Savage RE★ 1
Silk GH★ 3
Smeaton J★ 2
Smith EJ 21

Smith JCR 24
Smith JF★ 1
Somerfield A★ 6
Sperrin JR★ 1
Sperrin WT★ 1
Sproston B★ 1
Thow L★ 1
Tyler LDV 17
Voisey HA 1
Wallbanks J★ 1
Warfield JM 1
Watkins EJ 2
Whitfield H★ 1
Winter DT★ 15
Wright H★ 2

Goals (77): Dean 13, Kurz 13, Driver 10, Smith JCR 8, Peppitt 6, Agnew 3, Law 3, Cooke 2, Downer 2, O'Connell 2, Powell 2, Brolly 1, Fenton 1, Fisher F 1, Grainger 1, Jinks 1, Leyfield 1, Ormston 1, Salmon 1, Smeaton 1, Thow 1, own goals 3.

1944–45

Adams W★　2
Alexander FR★　2
Anderson N★　1
Bacon CW★　1
Banner A★　10
Bartram S★　2
Bennett KE★　4
Bradley J★　2
Briscoe J★　6
Brown ARJ★　2
Brown TL★　22
Buchanan PS★　2
Buckingham VF★　1
Bumstead CH　22
Burgess R★　2
Burke C★　3
Cardwell L★　2
Chalkley AG★　1
Chisholm J★　1
Cothliff HT★　3
Daniels J　1

Davies JW★　2
Dimmock EC　2
Dolding DL★　1
Downer F　3
Dudley RA　22
Dunkley G　4
Dunkley M★　4
Evans JA　17
Evans RL　5
Fagan W★　1
Fenton BRV　11
Fisher GS　15
Gordon RB　1
Grainger D★　6
Gregory E★　3
Gregson A　1
Guest R★　1
Hall AE★　1
Hassell TW★　1
Heathcote W★　1
Hurrell W★　2

Jinks JT　28
Jones S★　2
Kelly L★　3
Laidman F★　5
Lawton T★　1
Lello CF★　2
Lowe E　2
Ludford G★　11
Medley LD★　2
Miller WR★　2
Muir R★　1
Newby JJ★　1
O'Connell T　7
Oakes John★　1
Phillips RGT　17
Pinkerton H★　3
Prentice JW★ 1
Quinton W★　3
Rawlings JSD　6
Reay T★　9
Richardson JR　6

Ridley DG　4
Robinson A★　2
Round N　1
Salmon L★　2
Scrimshaw S★　3
Smith EJ　34
Smith JCR　6
Spence R★　1
Stephenson TB★　3
Stevens LW★　1
Taylor GE★　7
Thorogood J　1
Toser EW　1
Tunnicliffe G★　2
Tyler LDV　25
Voisey HA　1
Wallbanks J★　1
Walters WE★　1
Whittingham A★　5
Williams AS★　7
Willis A★　1

Goals (63): Jinks 15, Brown 7, Whittingham 6, Phillips 5, Stephenson 4, O'Connell 3, Fenton 2, Hurrell 2, Jones 2, Reay 2, Ridley 2, Adams 1, Buchanan 1, Burgess 1, Dudley 1, Evans J 1, Grainger 1, Hall 1, Heathcote 1, Ludford 1, Richardson 1, Smith JCR 1, Williams 1, own goal 1.

1945–46

Anderson JE　1
Anderson WR　10
Armstrong F　15
Brolly T　21
Brown TL　37
Bumstead CH　6
Calland R★　2
Dudley RA　39
Dunkley G　28
Evans JA　5
Fenton BRV　17
Fisher EA　4

Fisher GS　27
Ford FG　19
Gordon RB　3
Hall AE★　1
Hardy G　2
Howe LF★　1
Hurrell W　35
Hutton J　2
Jeffery G★　2
Jinks JT　21
Johnson J　24
Ludford G★　3

Medley LD★　1
Millbank JH★　1
Murphy P★　7
O'Kamback J　2
Osman HJ　17
Paton JA　22
Phillips RGT　6
Purdie JJ　8
Rawlings JSD　7
Reay T　1
Richardson JR　3
Ridley DGH　1

Ross GA　1
Smith EJ　11
Smith JCR　12
Soo F★　3
Spence R★　2
Stevens L★　1
Tadman GH★　1
Thorogood J　3
Toser EW　2
Tyler LDV　24
Williams C　1

Goals (79): Hurrell 16, Jinks 16, Brown 14, Osman 6, Anderson WR 5, Johnson 5, Fenton 4, Phillips 3, Thorogood 2, Dudley 1, Evans 1, Ford 1, Hutton 1, Jeffrey 1, Murphy 1, Paton 1, Rawlings 1.

FA Cup goals (8): Smith JCR 3, Jinks 2, Phillips 1, Ridley 1, own goal 1.

New Brighton

1939–40

Ainsworth A   5
Anderson A★   2
Bullock HC   3
Buxton A   21
Chedgzoy S★   1
Davies J   17
Davis E   4
Dodd RI   3

Eastham H★   2
Frost AD★   22
Hanson AJ★   21
Hawthorn W   25
Hughes S   25
Main R   7
Malam A★   19
Montgomery JJ   1

Morris GE   2
Mottram W★   1
Murphy DA★   13
Newcomb LR★   1
Ratcliffe B★   21
Rawcliffe H   1
Richardson N   2
Small HH   12

Smith CJ★   1
Smith W   2
Steen AW★   1
Stein J   3
Stevens JN★   1
Turner LA   3
Waring T★   22
Wright W   11

Goals (61): Frost 18, Waring 14, Hanson 11, Malam 5, Dodd 3, Small 3, Ainsworth 2, Wright 2, Bullock 1, Davies 1, Main 1.

War Cup goals (4): Frost 3, Malam 1.

1940–41

Anderson EW★   2
Anderson J★   1
Ashurst H★   1
Banks E★   1
Bower R★   2
Brown VC★   1
Burnett GG★   14
Buxton A   1
Cartwright W★   4
Chedgzoy S★   12

Cook S★   17
Davis E   21
Dellow RW★   24
Dooley TE★   2
Doyle T★   1
Frost AD★   30
Gregson W   5
Griffiths HS★   2
Hanson AJ★   28
Hawthorn W   16

Hill M★   10
Hughes S   10
Jones D★   1
Kelsall C★   1
Kieran G★   2
Lambert R★   1
Longdon CW★   20
Lowe H★   3
Major W   1
Malam A★   30

Morris GE   19
Price JT★   4
Ratcliffe B★   1
Rawcliffe F★   5
Rawcliffe H   3
Roberts T★   1
Sloan JW★   1
Surgery J   1
Waller T★   1
Waring T★   30

Goals (110): Frost 30, Hanson 26, Waring 26, Malam 16, Dellow 6, Chedgzoy 3, own goals 3.

1941–42

Adams EF★   12
Bennett JR   5
Brand N★   15
Burnett GG★   4
Caffrey J★   6
Campbell C   1
Castle IW   5

Chedgzoy S★   12
Davis E   3
Dellow RW   28
Eden W   8
Fenton W   1
Frost AD★   29
Gregson WB   20

Hill M★   21
Hughes S   7
Leyfield C^A   6
Lowe H★   23
Malam A★   29
Parker H★   13
Parker WD   10

Pilling JJ★   28
Redwood H★   1
Vose J   2
Waring T★   28
Woods S   2

Goals (62): Waring 21, Malam 15, Frost 14, Dellow 5, Caffrey 2, Pilling 2, Brand 1, Eden 1, own goal 1.

1942–43

Did not compete.

1943–44

Did not compete.

1944–45

Did not compete.

1945–46

Did not compete.

Newcastle United

1939–40

Ancell RFD 17	Gallacher P* 1	Law JA 1	Robson R 1
Birkett RJE 2	Gilhome A 1	Litchfield EG 1	Scott W 8
Blackburn M 1	Gordon J 19	MacVay TL 1	Seymour C 1
Bowden ER 3	Graham D 1	Meek J* 1	Stubbins A 14
Bradley GJ 8	Gray R 1	Mooney T 1	Swinburne TA 21
Cairns WH 13	Green S 1	Moses G 8	Taylor J 1
Clifton H 15	Hamilton DS 4	Nevins L 1	Thompson M 1
Craig B 22	Hart WR 1	Park J 5	Westwood WR* 1
Denmark J 14	Howe D* 1	Pearson TU 21	Woodburn J 6
Dodgin N 2	Hudson J 1	Price A 2	Wright JD 8
Duns L* 7	Kelly D 8	Richardson J 5	Yeats J 1

Goals (66): Cairns 12, Stubbins 9, Pearson 7, Clifton 5, Howe 5, Moses 5, Scott 4, Bowden 3, Westwood 3, Duns 2, Gordon 2, Park 2, Taylor 2, Blackburn 1, Bradley 1, Gilhome 1, Hamilton 1, Meek 1.

War Cup goals (10): Clifton 6, Cairns 2, Gordon 1, Stubbins 1.

1940–41

Ancell RFD 28	Deswert W 1	Hutton TO 3	Salthouse W 1
Anderson RJ* 1	Dodgin N 28	Lockie AJ* 1	Short JD* 4
Billington HJR* 4	Duns L* 12	McIntosh A* 3	Smirk AH* 1
Birkett RJE 23	English A 16	Milburn JN 1	Stubbins A 19
Blackburn M 11	Gilhome A 17	Myers J 1	Swinburne TA 2
Bradley GJ 2	Gordon J 20	Nevins L 30	Theaker CD 31
Cairns WH 3	Graham D 9	Osborne F* 1	Thompson M 1
Clifton H 1	Hart WR 1	Pearson TU 2	Thompson WN 1
Craig B 20	Herd A* 4	Price A 14	Woodburn J 4
Denmark J 26	Hudson J 2	Richardson J 12	Yeats J 2

Goals (66): Stubbins 21, Birkett 9, Duns 6, Gordon 6, Nevins 5, English 4, Billington 3, Herd 3, Gilhome 2, McIntosh 2, Short 2, Dodgin 1, Graham 1, Myers 1.

1941–42

Anderson RJ* 2	Graham D 35	Pearson TU 1	Surtees J* 2
Balmer J* 6	Hart WR 22	Peppitt S* 2	Taylor PH* 7
Birkett RJE 15	Howden S 7	Price A 23	Theaker CD 34
Boyes W* 2	Hubble L 1	Richardson J 24	Varty TH 1
Craig B 2	Hunter JD* 8	Robinson JA* 1	Walker TJ 15
Denmark J 7	King R 1	Robson R 4	Walshaw K* 4
Dixon JT 4	Kinghorn WJD* 2	Short JD* 20	Watson JT* 1
Dodgin N 14	McInnes JS* 1	Simpson TG 2	Watters J* 2
Donaldson RS 5	McKerrell D* 2	Smith T 30	Wayman C 12
Duns L* 1	McQuade G* 1	Soo F* 2	Willetts J 1
Eastham H* 1	Meek J* 1	Spike S 3	Woodburn J 1
Gilhome A 3	Nevins L 2	Stell – 1	Woollett C 13
Gordon J 2	Pearson SC* 5	Stubbins A 26	Yeats J 1

Goals (79): Stubbins 33, Short 17, Woollett 5, Wayman 4, Birkett 3, Dixon 2, Surtees 2, Woodburn 2, Anderson 1, Balmer 1, Donaldson 1, Hart 1, Howden 1, Meek 1, Price 1, Robson 1, Walker 1, Watters 1, own goal 1.

1942–43

Ancell RFD 1
Batey R★ 8
Bell W★ 2
Bradley GJ 3
Broady PK 1
Calder NA 1
Carr EM★ 31
Chilton A★ 2
Connor J★ 2
Coyde N★ 7
Diamond S★ 1
Dixon JT 10
Dodgin N 1
Donaldson RS 12

English A 7
Fagan W★ 2
Finney T★ 6
Forster LG★ 3
Garnham A 1
Gordon J 18
Graham D 23
Hamilton DS 4
Hart WR 14
Highmoor GW 3
Hindmarsh E 6
Howden S 2
Hughes J 2
King R 8

Litchfield EB 1
McCormack JH 2
Mortensen SH★ 1
Moses G 1
Mullen J★ 11
Nicholson WE★ 3
O'Neil TH 1
Parker W 1
Porter W 5
Price A 1
Richardson J 29
Rutherford TV 17
Sales RD 25
Scarr R 2

Seymour C 2
Short JD★ 19
Simpson T 2
Smallwood F★ 2
Smith T 11
Stubbins A 29
Tapken N★ 9
Taylor E 9
Walker TJ 4
Wallace J★ 1
Woodburn J 11
Woollett C 22
Wright JD 5

Goals (113): Stubbins 42, Carr 28, Short 16, Dixon 4, Mullen 4, Finney 3, Taylor 3, English 2, McCormack 2, Mortensen 2, Coyde 1, Diamond 1, Gordon 1, Moses 1, Walker 1, Woollett 1, own goal 1.

1943–44

Bainbridge R★ 1
Bradley GJ 3
Copeland E 20
Corbett R 6
Cowell GR 18
Cumming D★ 25
Dixon JT 24
Donaldson A 4
Donaldson RS 30
Glassey RJ★ 2
Gordon J 17

Graham D 2
Henderson HB 5
Hope G 1
Howden S 1
Juliussen AL★ 1
King R 3
Lee R 2
Lewis DG★ 1
Lightfoot L 10
Milburn JET 24
Mullen J★ 4

Nicholson WE★ 16
Parr J★ 1
Porter L 3
Price A 2
Richardson J 30
Rutherford R 14
Rutherford TV 8
Sales RD 6
Scarr R 5
Smith T 32
Spuhler JO★ 2

Stewart A★ 2
Stubbins A 32
Taylor E 7
Walker TJ 7
Woodburn J 11
Woods PB 10
Woollett C 24
Wright JD 2

Goals (79): Stubbins 43, Milburn 12, Dixon 7, Woollett 4, Copeland 3, Rutherford R 2, Taylor 2, Donaldson 1, Porter 1, Spuhler 1, Woodburn 1, own goals 3.

Includes one extra-time goal.

1944–45

Barron J★ 1
Carr EM★ 39
Corbett R 21
Cowell GR 41
Crowe CA 1
Cumming DS★ 31
Donaldson A 4
Donaldson RS 35
Duffy R★ 21

Golding W 2
Gordon J 21
Gray R★ 1
Gray TD★ 1
Hair G 16
Harnby DR 7
King R 1
McCormack CJ★ 1
Milburn JET 32

Pearson TU 9
Porter L 7
Richardson J 14
Rutherford R 5
Sales RD 3
Scott FH★ 6
Sloan J 4
Smith T 38
Stubbins A 31

Taylor E 2
Wayman C 29
Whittle E 1
Wood GA 5
Woods PB 5
Woollett C 16

Goals (122): Stubbins 43, Carr 29, Wayman 17, Milburn 12, Gordon 8, Hair 4, Woollett 3, Donaldson A 2, Pearson 1, Porter 1, Scott 1, Taylor 1.

1945–46

Batty RR 1
Brown EC 12
Clifton H 20
Corbett R 35
Cowell GR 22
Craig B 4
Crowe CA 23
Dodgin N 1
Donaldson A 4

Donaldson RS 5
Garbutt J 1
Gordon J 8
Graham D 20
Hair G 35
Hamilton DS 2
Harnby DR 1
Harvey J 33
Hubble L 1

King R 18
Milburn JET 39
Pearson TU 11
Porter L 1
Rushton G 1
Sales RD 8
Scott W 2
Sloan J 3
Smith T 34

Stubbins A 31
Swinburne TA 21
Taylor E 8
Walker TJ 3
Wayman C 30
Wood GA 2
Woodburn J 13
Woods PB 1
Wright JD 8

Goals (106): Stubbins 39, Clifton 16, Milburn 14, Wayman 14, Hair 10, Brown 4, Pearson 2, Crowe 1, Donaldson A 1, Hamilton 1, Harvey 1, Taylor 1, Woodburn 1, own goal 1.

FA Cup goals (4): Milburn 2, Hair 1, Stubbins 1.

Newport County

1939–40

Appleby T★ 10	Ford L★ 1	Low NH 27	Richards LG 22
Ballsom W★ 1	Granville A★ 1	Mead T 3	Robbins W★ 22
Brinton EJ 24	Hares W 5	Mogford RWG 4	Webb JA 30
Carr LL 13	Hickman JAE 11	Newall DJ 11	Wilcox R 7
Clark F★ 4	Higgins A★ 8	O'Reilly T 2	Williams SA 1
Duggan HA 13	Hydes AJE 11	Owen WE 28	Wood T 3
Ferguson A 31	Lawrence RS 6	Owen WM 31	Wookey K 11

Goals (75): Robbins 17, Appleby 16, Wookey 9, Carr 6, Owen WE 5, Brinton 4, Hydes 4, Hickman 2, Lawrence 2, Newall 2, Owen WM 2, Mogford 1, Webb 1, own goals 4.

War Cup goals (4): Brinton 1, Egan 1, Robbins 1, Wookey 1.

1940–41

Did not compete.

1941–42

Did not compete.

1942–43

Did not compete.

1943–44

Did not compete.

1944–45

Did not compete.

1945–46

Appleby T 5	Edwards T 1	Lucas WH★ 3	Thomas W 11
Avery A 1	Ferguson A 35	McNab A 7	Turner C 5
Avery R 15	Goldstraw A 9	Mead T 1	Warhurst F★ 12
Batty S 21	Granville N 19	Mogford RWG 7	Wayt R 2
Boatwright F 5	Hares W 1	Newcombe G 9	Webb JH 8
Brinton EJ 28	Harris B★ 2	Owen WE 3	Wilkins R 15
Brinton JV 3	Howarth S★ 1	Owen WM 41	Williams R 3
Cabrie D★ 2	Hydes AJE 2	Peacock G 3	Witcomb DF★ 1
Carr LL 30	Jones J★ 1	Pollard J 2	Wood T 3
Clarke W 3	Kinnell R★ 1	Rawcliffe F★ 1	Wookey K 34
Clifford J 1	Lawrence RS 1	Roberts B 20	
Dearnley B 1	Leamon FW 16	Shergold E 2	
Derrick A 20	Low NH 42	Southam J★ 3	

Goals (52): Derrick 12, Leamon 11, Carr 6, Batty 4, Granville 4, Wilkins 3, Wookey 3, Brinton E 2, Mogford 2, Avery R 1, Lucas 1, Newcombe 1, Owen WM 1, Rawcliffe 1.

FA Cup goals (14): Derrick 6, Hydes 2, Wookey 2, Brinton E 1, Carr 1, Granville 1, Owen WM 1.

Northampton Town

1939–40

Armeson LR 5	Cummings G★ 3	Heywood R★ 21	Miller HS 3
Baines SN 2	Dennison RS★ 20	Howe H★ 11	Moss F★ 12
Barron W 12	Dunkley M★ 25	Inwood R★ 1	Parris JE 5
Billingham J★ 17	Edwards GR★ 7	Iverson RT★ 1	Pritchard HJ★ 1
Blunt E 1	Ellwood RJ 3	Jennings HW 3	Shaw R★ 5
Broome FH★ 2	Garvey J 1	Jones JT 2	Shell F★ 12
Calvert J★ 19	Gormlie WJ★ 7	King FAR 1	Shipton R 1
Clifford J 3	Grogan J★ 10	Liddle D★ 23	Simons RR 15
Coley WE★ 6	Grosvenor P★ 4	Lyman CC★ 13	Smith B★ 1
Coutts S 11	Hewitt C★ 1	McCullough K 24	Starling RW★ 2
Crick A 4	Hewson R★ 13	Melaniphy EM 3	Strathie WJ 3

Goals (50): Billingham 14, Hewson 5, Liddle 5, Dunkley 4, Lyman 4, Shell 4, Barron 2, Edwards 2, Parris 2, Broome 1, Coutts 1, Ellwood 1, Hewitt 1, Howe 1, Melaniphy 1, Moss 1, Pritchard 1.

War Cup goals (2): Coutts 1, Liddle 1.

1940–41

Allen R★ 1	Cornish JA 1	Hinson R★ 3	Shankly W★ 9
Alsop G★ 17	Cummings G★ 11	Hunter R 20	Shaw R★ 5
Armeson LR★ 10	Curtis FH★ 5	Kerr AW★ 1	Smalley T★ 31
Ashall GH★ 3	Dearson DJ★ 4	King A 17	Smith J★ 1
Barratt AG 1	Dennison RS★ 28	Littledyke R★ 1	Towl –★ 1
Barron W 19	Dunkley M★ 24	Mitchell F★ 1	Ware H★ 9
Basnett AE★ 1	Earl-Chater R 1	Morgan W★ 3	Watson E★ 1
Beattie A★ 2	Fagan W★ 5	Newton B 2	Wharton G★ 12
Beattie R★ 11	Frost SD 1	Ormerod J 1	Willmott P★ 1
Bedford G 17	Hart R 1	Pryde D★ 1	Wood AR★ 31
Billingham J 28	Haycock F★ 26	Pursglove –★ 1	Young RH★ 2
Coley WE★ 1	Hewitt J★ 1	Salt J 1	

Goals (95): Billingham 23, Alsop 14, King 11, Ware 10, Beattie R 8, Barron 7, Dunkley 5, Haycock 3, Armeson 2, Smalley 2, Wharton 2, Basnett 1, Curtis 1, Cummings 1, Dearson 1, Dennison 1, Newton 1, own goals 2.

1941–42

Alsop G★ 18	Dearson DJ★ 8	King FAB 21	Shepherdson H★ 9
Attwell RF★ 1	Dennison RS★ 34	Lowrie G★ 23	Smalley T★ 37
Barron W 3	Fagan W★ 28	Lunn G★ 1	Steele FC★ 4
Beattie R★ 12	Harris A★ 28	Lyman CC★ 2	Ware H★ 18
Bedford G 11	Haycock F★ 15	Macaulay AR★ 5	Wellington H 1
Boileau HA★ 1	Hunter R 13	Muncie W 4	Wood AR 37
Cummings G★ 2	Johnston TD 4	Pritchard HJ★ 26	Woodburn J★ 12
Curtis FH 2	King A 1	Shaw R★ 22	Young RH★ 4

Goals (109): Lowrie 23, Fagan 21, Alsop 11, Pritchard 11, Dearson 9, Ware 6, King F 5, Smalley 4, Harris 3, Beattie 2, Bedford 2, Haycock 2, Hunter 2, Johnston 2, Steele 2, own goals 4.

1942–43

Alsop G★ 25	Dennison RS★ 30	King S★ 4	Pugh SJ★ 28
Baldwin H★ 6	Ellwood RJ 5	Labrum T 1	Purdie W 2
Banner A★ 1	Fagan W★ 3	Lane H★ 7	Quinney HJ 1
Barron W 20	Gardner FC★ 2	Lowe S 1	Scrimshaw S★ 2
Bedford G 2	Gregory E★ 1	Macaulay AR★ 16	Shepherdson H★ 22
Bliss L 1	Halliwell AD★ 3	Martin R 1	Smalley T★ 35
Bolan LA★ 16	Harris A★ 33	Metcalf WF★ 5	Tweed G★ 1
Bosse PL 2	Hillard J★ 4	Mulraney A★ 4	White H★ 1
Brownlie J★ 1	Hinsley G★ 1	Muncie W 3	Wood AR★ 5
Coley WE★ 3	Hunter R 5	Nicholls H 7	Woodgate JT★ 2
Cooper RC★ 15	Johnston TD 18	Peacock T★ 1	
Dean WHG 4	King FAB★ 1	Pritchard HJ★ 34	

Goals (68): Alsop 14, Johnston 9, Barron 6, Macaulay 5, Nicholls 5, Pritchard 5, Bolan 4, Harris 3, Pugh 3, Fagan 2, Hinsley 2, Scrimshaw 2, Hillard 1, Lowe 1, Mulraney 1, Peacock 1, own goals 4.

1943–44

Barron W 4	Fagan W★ 3	Jennings J★ 16	Pugh SJ★ 11
Bilton DH★ 14	Fenton EBV★ 2	King A 1	Shepherdson H★ 15
Bolan LA★ 13	Freeman HG★ 12	Kinnear D★ 22	Smalley T★ 37
Brolly T★ 2	Gardner FC★ 9	Lane H★ 1	Smith D 29
Brookes D 2	Harris A★ 31	Litchfield EC★ 9	Tidman OE 1
Coley WE★ 19	Haycock F★ 1	Maund JH★ 10	Tobin RF 1
Cooper RC★ 23	Henley L★ 2	Nicholls H 1	Wilson J 4
Dean WHG 6	Hess J 1	Parkes H★ 9	Wood T★ 5
Dennison RS★ 30	Hornby R★ 1	Perry E★ 26	
Denton AJ 1	Hulme J★ 4	Pritchard HJ★ 29	

Goals (80): Perry 17, Litchfield 11, Kinnear 8, Pritchard 8, Wilson 7, Barron 3, Bolan 3, Gardner 3, Smith 3, Brolly 2, Fagan 2, Fenton 2, Hulme 2, Parkes 2, Brookes 1, Coley 1, Dean 1, Henley 1, Jennings 1, own goals 2.

1944–45

Barron W 1	Gardner FC★ 20	Jones GT★ 1	Roberts DG★ 7
Billingham J★ 1	Garrett A★ 13	Lee AH 18	Shepherdson H★ 20
Brown J★ 4	Greenway M★ 2	Macaulay AR★ 1	Smalley T★ 29
Coley WE★ 21	Harris A★ 30	Morrall AD 28	Sparshott G★ 1
Cransfield W 2	Hughes TG 19	Neal G 1	Stephens V★ 9
Crawford GR 1	Hurrell W★ 4	O'Neill W 1	Syme C★ 1
Dennison RS★ 23	Hustwait GA 1	Perry E★ 14	Welsh A 22
Dixon J 2	James GC★ 1	Phillips N★ 5	Wood HE★ 15
Fagan W★ 4	Johnson J★ 1	Pringle ER 4	
Fowler T 3	Jones EN★ 1	Pritchard HJ★ 21	

Goals (53): Morrall 13, Garrett 8, Perry 6, Gardner 5, Smalley 4, Hughes 3, Pritchard 3, Fagan 2, Harris 2, Cransfield 1, Dixon 1, Fowler 1, Phillips 1, Syme 1, Welsh 1, own goal 1.

1945–46

Allen R 6	Ellwood RJ 4	Maskell LJ★ 2	Scott DP 8
Barron W 32	Fowler T 29	McGregor D★ 1	Shepherdson H★ 2
Bates ET★ 1	Gillespie J 13	McNab A★ 2	Skelton G 3
Blunt E 19	Haycock F★ 3	Morrall AD 29	Smalley T 32
Bosse PL 1	Heaselgrave SE 11	Neal G 16	Smith D 9
Coley WE★ 1	Hughes TG 23	Pringle ER 2	Welsh A 11
Collins MJ 1	Jennings HW 3	Pritchard HJ★ 2	Wilson J 7
Dean WHG 1	Jones – 8	Roberts DG 24	Wood W★ 3
Dennison RS★ 26	Lee AH 11	Sankey J 15	Worrall D★ 1
Dixon J 12	Lowery H★ 17	Saunders W★ 1	Yarker L 4

Goals (64): Morrall 15, Roberts 12, Dixon 7, Hughes 5, Heaselgrave 4, Fowler 3, Jones 3, Barron 2, Blunt 2, Lowery 2, Smalley 2, Sankey 2, Bates 1, Haycock 1, Jennings 1, own goals 2.

FA Cup goals (15): Morrall 6, Hughes 3, Roberts 2, Black 1, Blunt 1, Fowler 1, Smith 1.

Norwich City

1939–40

Acquroff J 37	Edwards GR★ 1	Little JA★ 6	Rist FH★ 2
Bartlett FL★ 1	Fenton BRV★ 4	Lochhead D 1	Robinson BC 32
Brain A 3	Furness WI 34	Manders F 29	Rodger – 1
Brain J★ 5	Gill FC 3	McLuckie JS★ 1	Rose JW 1
Brown R★ 1	Graham W 3	Milburn J 10	Smalley T 3
Burns M★ 31	Hall AE★ 7	Morris R★ 1	Taylor J 33
Chadwick FW★ 29	Hall F 3	Needs W★ 1	Ware H 17
Church J 3	Hannant LM★ 5	Parry O 5	Wilkinson P★ 1
Dale W★ 21	Housego H 1	Plunkett SE★ 33	Williams – 1
Duke HP 3	Jobling J★ 2	Proctor MH 28	Wright RCA★ 2
Edney E★ 1	Johnson A 2	Reilly LH 10	

Goals (77): Chadwick 20, Furness 13, Plunkett 13, Acquroff 10, Manders 7, Hall A 2, Little 2, Proctor 2, Robinson 2, Taylor 2, Brain A 1, Brain J 1, Church 1, Ware 1.

Bournemouth 2 Norwich C 1 played out of season – included in the table but not in appearances and goals; scorer was Brain J.

War Cup goals (4): Acquroff 1, Chadwick 1, Furness 1, Manders 1.

1940–41

Acquroff J 2	Gill FC 2	McClure J★ 3	Sinclair TM★ 5
Ashmore A★ 3	Hall F 12	McLuckie JS★ 8	Smith T★ 1
Ball W★ 1	Hannant LM 10	Moule R★ 1	Taylor J 12
Bird AS 2	Hanson S★ 2	Needs WJ 4	Thompson JV★ 2
Brain J★ 5	Hoggard AB★ 1	Nicklen C★ 2	Thornton LC★ 1
Brooks H★ 3	Housego H 1	Parry O★ 4	Turton J★ 1
Burley B★ 1	Howe D★ 4	Plunkett SE★ 17	Vanham SC 6
Chadwick FW★ 5	Hurst J★ 5	Proctor MH 19	Ware H 2
Claridge R★ 1	Joyner F★ 5	Ramsbottom AE★ 2	Westwood E★ 3
Coats A★ 1	Lello C★ 5	Reeve RA★ 1	Wharton G★ 1
Curtis GF★ 11	Little JA★ 1	Roberts JH★ 5	Whittingham A★ 2
Darvill G★ 1	Lochhead D★ 2	Robinson BC 5	Winter DT★ 3
Furness WI 19	Marshall J★ 5	Rolls G★ 3	
Geldard A★ 1	Maskell LJ 4	Shepherdson H★ 3	

Goals (76): Chadwick 12, Plunkett 9, Roberts 8, Joyner 6, Furness 5, Maskell 5, Brooks 4, Ashmore 3, Howe 3, Marshall 3, Brain 2, Hurst 2, Proctor 2, Sinclair 2, Ware 2, Curtis 1, Housego 1, Lello 1, McLuckie 1, Needs 1, Westwood 1, Whittingham 1, own goal 1.

1941–42

Ashmore A★ 3	Graham DR★ 1	McClure J★ 5	Smale DM★ 1
Brain J★ 2	Hanson S★ 12	Mountford RC★ 1	Stamps JD★ 1
Burditt FCK 1	Hesford RT★ 1	Mulraney A★ 10	Sutherland A★ 1
Chadwick FW★ 1	Howe D★ 9	Murphy DA★ 1	Taylor J 19
Curtis FH★ 1	Hurst J★ 5	Nicholson S★ 6	Thompson JV★ 2
Curtis GF★ 4	Johnstone D★ 3	Plunkett SE★ 5	Thornton W★ 5
Flack WLW 1	Jones J★ 4	Proctor MH 16	Tierney E★ 1
Flowers IJ★ 3	Knott H★ 1	Roberts JH★ 6	Tracey T★ 2
Forrest E★ 6	Longdon H★ 2	Robinson BC 15	Turner AW★ 9
Furness WI 18	Manders F 1	Saunders H★ 2	
Gee –★ 1	Manley T★ 1	Scrimshaw S★ 6	
Goslin H★ 6	Maskell LJ 14	Sinclair TM★ 2	

Goals (47): Maskell 12, Howe 6, Roberts 5, Mulraney 4, Furness 3, Manley 3, Plunkett 3, Scrimshaw 3, Thornton 3, Proctor 2, Flowers 1, Sinclair 1, own goal 1.

1942–43

Played friendly games only.

1943–44

Played friendly games only.

1944–45

Played friendly games only.

1945–46

Acquroff J 2	Davis DE 20	Jones S 29	Reid EJ 36
Antonio GR★ 2	Duffield SC★ 4	Liddell J★ 1	Reilly LH 15
Armes IW 2	Duke HP 3	Maskell LJ 7	Robinson BC 19
Chambers J★ 1	Flack WLW 34	Moore NW★ 11	Russell JW 12
Chapman G★ 2	Frost G★ 1	Newsome R★ 13	Shaw K 2
Church J 10	Furness WI 18	Pickwick D 1	Taylor J 33
Coleman E 3	Graham W 6	Plunkett SE 31	Ware H 5
Collins G★ 1	Hall F 12	Proctor MH 34	Youngs RA 1
Davies – 1	Johnson V 23	Rackham D 1	

Goals (81): Plunkett 13, Jones 12, Furness 11, Newsome 11, Johnson 10, Church 6, Moore 4, Antonio 2, Coleman 2, Graham 2, Robinson 2, Russell 2, Duffield 1, Liddell 1, Maskell 1, Taylor 1.

FA Cup goals (2): Graham 1, Ware 1.

Nottingham Forest

1939–40

Antonio GR★ 3	Crisp GH 3	Lager EW★ 1	Pritty G 3
Ashton P 13	Davies RG 20	MacKenzie P★ 1	Rawson K 3
Barks E 9	Drury GB★ 19	Martin JR★ 1	Richards S 1
Beaumont L 3	Graham T 14	Massie A★ 2	Richardson G 1
Bramley T★ 5	Haycock F★ 1	Maund JH 16	Roulston C★ 2
Brierley B 1	Hinchliffe T★ 12	McCall AJ 7	Smith –★ 1
Brook R★ 11	Houghton WE★ 1	McCall RH 9	Starling RW★ 5
Challenger J 6	Hunt AK 3	Mills P★ 1	Surtees J 3
Childs EJ 1	Hunter JB★ 16	Moon F 1	Trim RF 7
Clark TG 8	Hydes A★ 1	Munro JS 12	Walker WH★ 1
Corkhill WG★ 1	Kirton J★ 7	Peacock T 6	Westland DG★ 5
Coutts G★ 1	Knight F 1	Perry C 3	

Goals (42): Drury 17, Hinchliffe 7, Peacock 4, Starling 3, Perry 2, Graham 1, Hunter 1, MacKenzie 1, Maund 1, McCall A 1, McCall R 1, Roulston 1, Surtees 1, Walker 1.

War Cup goals (8): Armstrong 2, Crisp 2, Broome 1, Drury 1, McCall R 1, Starling 1.

1940–41

Antonio GR★ 7	Davies RG 11	Kirton J★ 14	Pimbley D 1
Arnold D★ 1	Dearson DJ★ 2	Knight F 3	Platts L 2
Barks E 22	Drury GB★ 1	Lane H★ 1	Pritty G 3
Bird R★ 1	Edwards GR★ 7	Langton E 4	Rawson K 5
Brook R★ 21	Elliott CS★ 1	Lewis J★ 1	Robinson –★ 1
Broome FH★ 1	Fillingham J★ 1	Lowrie G★ 4	Roebuck N★ 1
Brown J★ 3	Finch LC★ 6	Mason GW★ 13	Rutherford J★ 6
Burgess R★ 2	Fryer JL 1	Maund JH 6	Seagrave JW★ 1
Challinor J★ 14	Graham T 2	McNab A★ 1	Smith EF★ 12
Clarke I★ 1	Hinchliffe T★ 1	Merrick GH★ 2	Trigg C★ 1
Clements E★ 2	Hollis KB 1	Metcalf WF★ 12	Tudor W★ 1
Collins A 5	Houghton WE★ 4	Mills PC★ 1	Vose C★ 1
Copping W★ 2	Hughes –★ 1	Mitchell –★ 1	Wakeman A★ 3
Crawley T★ 7	Hunt AK 1	Moon F 9	Walker WH★ 2
Cressey W★ 1	Hunter JB★ 8	Morgan W★ 12	Ward J 1
Crisp GH 13	Iverson RT★ 14	Norris EJ 1	Ware H★ 1
Cummings G★ 1	Jennings DB★ 2	Patten –★ 1	Westland D★ 2
Curtis GF★ 1	Jones LJ★ 3	Peacock T 5	Wood HL 12

Goals (61): Smith 7, Barks 5, Broome 4, Crisp 4, Crawley 4, Lowrie 4, Wood 4, Antonio 3, Peacock 3, Brown 2, Clarke 2, Collins 2, Edwards 2, Hunter 2, Iverson 2, Jennings 2, Lane 2, Maund 2, Clements 1, Dearson 1, Jones 1, Langton 1, Norris 1.

1941–42

Aldred A 1	Collins A 7	Lambert E 2	Riley H 1
Antonio GR★ 1	Corkhill WG★ 4	Lane H★ 2	Rutherford J★ 5
Ashley H★ 1	Crawley T★ 1	Lewis J★ 1	Sadler GH★ 1
Astley J★ 11	Crooks SD★ 13	Lyman CC★ 5	Shaw J★ 1
Baldwin H★ 1	Cummings G★ 1	MacFadyen W★ 1	Slack L★ 8
Barke L★ 2	Davies RG 1	Mason W★ 10	Smith J 5
Beaumont L 13	Duncan D★ 15	Massey AW★ 13	Smith T★ 2
Bedford G★ 1	Edwards GR★ 1	Matthews RJ★ 3	Starling RW★ 12
Bowers J★ 2	Elliott CS★ 1	Maund B★ 1	Steele FC★ 1
Bray J★ 2	Finch R★ 1	Maund JH 1	Surtees J 2
Brook R★ 1	Flint HG★ 1	McCall RH 16	Townsend R 7
Broome FH★ 11	Freeman WJ 3	Mee GE 8	Trim RF 1
Brown AW★ 4	Graham T 1	Meek J★ 1	Vause PG★ 2
Buck GR 2	Hardwick GFM★ 1	Merrick GH★ 1	Wakeman A★ 1
Burgess R★ 8	Houghton WE★ 1	Metcalf W★ 12	Walker WH★ 1
Butler J 5	Howe LF★ 2	Morgan W★ 4	Ward J 9
Buttery L★ 1	Hullett W★ 2	Pallister G★ 1	Wheatley R 3
Bye JH★ 1	Iverson RT★ 7	Peacock T 1	Whitham R★ 1
Cairns WH★ 2	Johnson F 4	Potts VE★ 1	Wilkinson N★ 8
Chadwick C★ 1	Jones LJ★ 6	Quinton W★ 1	
Challinor J★ 9	Kirton J★ 9	Rawson K 1	

Goals (50): Collins 9, Broome 4, Hullett 4, Beaumont 3, Bowers 3, Smith J 3, Starling 3, Crooks 2, Iverson 2, Lyman 2, Mee 2, Surtees 2, Ward 2, Buck 1, Buttery 1, Duncan 1, Houghton 1, McCall 1, Slack 1, Smith T 1, Steele 1, own goal 1.

1942–43

Aldred A★ 1	Crofts J 34	Lambert E 1	Simpson NH 3
Baldwin H★ 2	Dulson R 1	Lane H★ 11	Slack L★ 2
Barks E 2	Egan GD★ 1	Massey AW★ 10	Smith J 1
Barratt H★ 1	Egan H 28	Maund JH 15	Smith W★ 24
Baxter WE 23	Grant AF★ 1	McCall RH 36	Southwell A 2
Bean AS★ 4	Hannah GL★ 1	Mee GE 1	Surtees J 1
Beaumont L 36	Hiatt GA 1	Moulson GB★ 1	Taylor ER 2
Bee FE 1	Hindley F★ 8	Oakley JC★ 2	Townsend R 2
Beswick J 1	Hollis KB 3	Pawlaw M 2	Trim RF 1
Blagg EA 26	Hughes TG 1	Peacock T 4	Wheatley R 17
Butler J 8	Jeffries A★ 15	Richards S 1	Wightman JR★ 5
Cairns WH★ 4	Jenkinson F★ 1	Richardson G 1	Young JFH 1
Chapman G★ 1	Jepson A★ 19	Riley H 2	
Clare J★ 4	Johnson C 3	Robertson J★ 4	
Collins A 3	Knott B★ 1	Shufflebottom F 9	

Goals (68): Egan H 20, Beaumont 17, Wheatley 5, Hindley 4, Maund 4, Jeffries 3, Cairns 2, Lane 2, McCall 2, Mee 2, Clare 1, Collins 1, Robertson 1, own goals 4.

1943–44

Airlie S★ 1	Dulson RE 25	Jones SH 7	Shufflebottom F 2
Allen R★ 1	Egan H 6	Kilshaw – 1	Smith W★ 3
Ashton P 2	Elliott BH 19	Lightfoot – 1	Steele FC★ 1
Baxter WE 36	Flewitt S 29	Long D★ 1	Thomas GS 2
Bean AS★ 2	Gardiner C 1	Maund JH 8	Trim RF 1
Beaumont L 34	Harrison C 1	McCall RH 37	Walker V 20
Bee FE 1	Hepworth R★ 1	Middleton R★ 1	Watson W★ 1
Beswick J 17	Hiatt GA 1	Oakley JC★ 1	Wattie J★ 3
Betts E 1	Hindley F★ 4	Parr J★ 2	Wheatley R 10
Blagg EA 34	Hogg F★ 2	Platts L 24	Wilkinson N★ 1
Carter HS★ 1	Hollis KB 4	Poole CJ★ 1	Wyles H★ 1
Crofts J 6	Hubbard C★ 1	Rhodes A★ 2	
Davies HJ 1	Hutchinson JA 20	Riley C 2	
Drury GB★ 3	Johnston TD 30	Robertson J★ 1	

Goals (65): Dulson 16, Flewitt 12, Johnston 11, Beaumont 9, Walker 3, Wheatley 3, Hindley 2, Maund 2, Beswick 1, Drury 1, Rhodes 1, Steele 1, Wattie 1, own goals 2.

Includes one extra-time goal.

1944–45

Allen HA 2	Edwards J 1	Kaile GW 1	Powell T★ 1
Barks E 2	Elliott BH 15	Leverton R 4	Rawson K 15
Baxter WE 33	Firth JW★ 7	Linacre W★ 1	Simpson NH 5
Beaumont L 9	Flewitt S 3	Martin FA 2	Smith J★ 2
Beswick J 10	Foreman D★ 1	Maund JH 3	Stevenson HWH 3
Betts A★ 2	Godfrey LL★ 1	McCall RH 27	Styles W★ 1
Blagg EA 34	Goffin WC★ 3	McPherson T★ 2	Taylor PD 2
Blenkinsop TW★ 4	Griffin S 1	Mee GE 1	Thomas GS 28
Brown GS 1	Guttridge R★ 4	Morris – 1	Thorpe L 3
Coen L★ 1	Hepworth R★ 1	Mozley H 1	Townsend R 2
Crisp GH 1	Hindley F★ 1	North TW 12	Walker V 7
Cronkshaw JH 2	Hutchinson JA 3	Oxley R★ 1	Waring T★ 1
Cunningham T★ 1	Iceton OL★ 1	Paul R 5	Wheatley R 10
Davie J★ 7	Inskip FC 14	Payne F 4	Wilkinson J 3
Drury GB★ 1	Johnson F 2	Peace RS 1	Williams BF★ 1
Dulson RE 13	Johnston TD 33	Platts L 20	Wright – 1

Goals (45): Johnston 9, Elliott 5, Dulson 4, Beaumont 3, Blenkinsop 3, Davie 2, Inskip 2, Leverton 2, North 2, Simpson 2, Wheatley 2, Barks 1, Baxter 1, Beswick 1, Betts 1, Martin 1, Mee 1, Peace 1, Rawson 1, Stevenson 1.

1945–46

Allen HA 12	Dulson RE 5	McPherson I★ 1	Simms T★ 1
Barks E 38	Egan H 1	Mee GE 25	Simpson NH 29
Baxter WE 41	Grant AF★ 4	Morgan C 1	Surtees J 1
Betts E 6	Hall J★ 1	Morley W 7	Thomas GS 39
Blagg EA 21	Hancocks J★ 1	North TW 34	Trim RF 1
Blenkinsop TW★ 4	Hinchliffe T★ 3	O'Donnell F 11	Walker A★ 9
Brown G 3	Johnston TD 41	Paul R 1	Weston T★ 1
Canning L★ 1	Jones E★ 1	Peacock T 1	White F★ 2
Carter HS★ 1	Ledger J 10	Pimbley D★ 2	Williams A 1
Clark TG 1	Leverton R 2	Platts L 15	Woodman D★ 1
Crofts J 1	Long B 1	Rawson C 4	
Cronkshaw JH 1	Maund JH 1	Savage R 19	
Davies RG 12	McCall RH 41	Shufflebottom F 2	

Goals (72): Johnston 26, North 11, Mee 10, Barks 7, O'Donnell 7, Betts 2, Simpson 2, Allen 1, Blenkinsop 1, Brown 1, Jones 1, Ledger 1, Long 1, Pimbley 1.

FA Cup goals (2): Allen 1, Barks 1.

Notts County

1939–40

Bailey L* 2
Barker JW* 6
Bartram S* 2
Baxter WE* 1
Beattie A* 7
Brookbanks E 2
Buckley FL 1
Chester TH 1
Clayton S 5
Coleman E* 1
Cooper S 3
Corkhill WG* 12
Coulston W 2

Crooks SD* 18
Davies RG* 1
Duncan D* 19
Flower T 3
Glover EM* 3
Griffiths J* 1
Groves A* 5
Hague JK* 3
Hall H* 10
Hann R* 9
Harrison R* 4
Hatton C 5
Hilliard C* 1

Jones B 1
Jones H* 2
Knox JP 1
Mackenzie J 13
Martin DK 2
Mason J 5
McNaughton GN 1
Mills A* 1
Mills PC 13
Moss G 4
Moulson C 2
Munks JA 4
Nicholas JT* 17

Rayner F 3
Read CW 4
Ringrose A 1
Steele FC* 2
Towler BE 8
Waite JH 1
Walsh W* 4
Ward TV* 8
Waterall K 2
Weightman E 2
Wilcox GE* 8
Wilkinson N* 6

Goals (46): Towler 8, Crooks 6, Mackenzie 6, Duncan 4, Hatton 3, Martin 3, Clayton 2, Groves 2, Harrison 2, Moss 2, Beattie 1, Buckley 1, Corkhill 1, Glover 1, Mills P 1, Nicholas 1, Read 1, Steele 1.

War Cup goals (6): Hatton 2, Crooks 1, Duncan 1, Mills P 1, O'Donnell 1.

1940–41

Beattie A* 13
Beattie R* 1
Berry – 1
Bingham – 1
Boileau HA* 4
Brook R* 2
Broome FH* 20
Buckley FL 12
Butler S* 2
Carter HS* 1
Clements – 1
Cooper E 6
Corkhill WG* 1
Crisp GH* 1
Crooks SD* 15

Davidson RT* 2
Duncan D* 15
Edwards GR* 6
Elliott CS* 4
Ellmer FB 4
Fenton M* 2
Finlow PA 1
Gallacher P* 2
Gilson H 1
Green T* 3
Griffiths J* 6
Harrison R* 1
Hinsley C* 5
Iverson RT* 5
Jackson H 4

Johnson JT* 9
Johnson JW* 4
Keen ERL* 1
Lamb W 1
Lyman CC* 2
Massie A* 8
McEwan W* 1
Middleton L 2
Mills PC 6
Moss G 4
Munks JA 1
Musson WU* 2
Nicholas JT* 21
Padman – 1
Parr J* 2

Sidlow C* 7
Smallwood E 1
Smith JT* 4
Sneddon T* 1
Steen AW* 3
Streten BR 13
Swinburne TA* 1
Taylor GT* 5
Vallance –* 4
Vause PG* 1
Warburton G* 3
Wilcox GE* 1
Wright – 2

Goals (46): Broome 15, Crooks 8, Duncan 5, Moss 3, Buckley 2, Edwards 2, Hinsley 2, Fenton 1, Johnson JW 1, Lyman 1, McEwan 1, Nicholas 1, Vallance 1, Warburton 1, own goals 2.

1941–42

Did not compete.

1942–43

Antonio GR* 19
Ashton P* 3
Bacuzzi J* 2
Barke JL* 10
Barsby CF 1
Bell T* 1
Benner R 20
Blood JF* 1
Booth LJ 7
Bowers J* 16
Brader FW 4
Brown E 2
Brown M 1
Burgess R* 13
Cairns WH* 3
Challinor J* 1
Clarke GA 13
Clayton S 1

Clift BC* 3
Collindridge C* 14
Corkhill WG* 28
Coulston W 4
Davies W* 4
Drury GB* 1
Duns L* 5
Ellmer FB 2
Fell J* 1
Flower T 1
Grant EA 1
Haines JWT* 4
Hall B 1
Hann R* 4
Hatton C 1
Hinchliffe T* 1
Hodgkins JS 1
Hollis KB* 1

Hughes S* 11
Jessop W* 3
Jones DO* 11
Jones LJ* 31
Kirton J* 18
Lawton T* 1
Leuty LH* 12
Liddle D* 12
Lilley K 1
Marsh JK 4
Marshall JG* 5
Martin EJ 1
Maund JH* 2
Moss G 2
Parker A 1
Parkin FW 4
Ramage PMF* 5
Rawcliffe F 8

Rickards CT* 18
Rigby N 1
Robinson GH* 1
Robinson P 1
Sharman F* 21
Stancer BL 2
Steele FC* 5
Stillyards G* 1
Towler BE 7
Trim RF* 1
Tweed GE* 1
Vincent NE* 2
Weaver S* 1
Wilkinson N* 28
Wright WA 1

Goals (71): Jones L 11, Collindridge 10, Bowers 8, Rickards 8, Antonio 5, Marsh 5, Liddle 4, Rawcliffe 3, Towler 3, Booth 2, Brader 2, Steele 2, Clarke 1, Clift 1, Duns 1, Haines 1, Hatton 1, Maund 1, Robinson G 1, Weaver 1.

1943–44

Alderton JH★ 1	Everett HP 4	Kirkpatrick S 2	Roberts H 1
Allen W 2	Fletcher – 1	Kirton J★ 7	Rollinson – 1
Anderson J★ 1	Flint K 7	Knott H★ 1	Ross J★ 1
Antonio GR★ 5	Flintson – 1	Lager EW★ 2	Rothwell E★ 2
Ashworth – 1	Gardner – 1	Lane H★ 4	Russell D★ 1
Ball WJE 1	Gascoigne D 2	Ledger JK 16	Sharman F★ 1
Barke JL★ 3	Godfrey LL★ 10	Major LD★ 1	Simpson NH 2
Barton – 3	Graham DR★ 1	Marsh JK 1	Skidmore W★ 1
Becci A★ 1	Gray R★ 25	Marshall JG★ 9	Slack L★ 1
Benner R 2	Greaves – 1	Martin DK 1	Smeaton J 1
Bloomfield W 1	Gregory H 3	Martin FA 1	Smith J 4
Brader FW 1	Griffiths K 1	Melling F 1	Smith L^ 3
Bradley G★ 2	Guttridge R★ 5	Moran A 2	Somerfield A★ 1
Bridges 1	Hann R★ 1	Morduc J 1	Southwell AA 4
Brown E 2	Hatfield B★ 3	Morgan – 1	Stancer BL 8
Brunt GR 2	Haycock F★ 1	Morley J 3	Streten BR 2
Burgess R★ 3	Hazell – 1	Murphy G★ 2	Taylor JL 1
Bye JH★ 1	Hepworth R 5	Musson WU★ 3	Thorpe WF 4
Challinor J★ 6	Hewitt – 1	Nicholas JT★ 1	Towler BE 12
Clack FE★ 1	Higson G 1	Nicholls H★ 13	Tyroll – 1
Clarke GA 1	Hinton E 1	Nugent GE 1	Unwin SH 5
Collindridge C★ 13	Hogg – 1	Oakley JC★ 1	Van Gelden J 1
Collins AD★ 3	Houghton WE★ 1	Openshaw – 1	Vincent NE★ 1
Corkhill WG★ 15	Hunter JB★ 3	Parr J★ 1	Walker E 2
Davidson DBL★ 15	Iddon H★ 1	Pettitt – 1	Walsh W★ 8
Davis RD★ 2	James J 1	Potts – 1	Walters H★ 8
De Lisle – 1	Jepson A★ 4	Pritchard RT★ 1	Whitehead JW 2
Dimond S★ 5	Johnson J★ 1	Rawcliffe F 8	Wilkinson N★ 5
Donaldson HA 6	Jones DO★ 2	Renshaw – 1	Wilson – 1
Drinkwater – 1	Jones JT★ 2	Rickards CT★ 2	Wright J 2
Drury GB★ 1	Jones LJ★ 19	Rigby N 8	
Drysdale J★ 1	Keen ERL★ 2	Rist FH★ 1	
Edwards GR★ 10	Kirkham R 1	Roberts D★ 2	

Goals (49): Collindridge 5, Edwards 4, Ledger 4, Dimond 3, Wright 3, Antonio 2, Davis 2, Drury 2, Gascoigne 2, Gray 2, Hunter 2, Lager 2, Rawcliffe 2, Walsh 2, Allen 1, Anderson 1, Flint 1, Hatfield 1, Knott 1, Lane 1, Martin F 1, Rickards 1, Simpson 1, Towler 1, Walker 1, Wilson 1.

1944–45

Airlie S★ 1	Corkhill WG★ 1	Knowles C 1	Shell FH★ 2
Akers W★ 1	Davie J★ 13	Lamb HE★ 1	Siddons F 2
Allen RHW 6	Dixon P 1	Lewis G★ 6	Skidmore W★ 1
Andrews G 1	Duggan EJ★ 1	Long D 3	Southwell AA 27
Bacuzzi J★ 2	Edwards WJ 3	Marshall JG★ 6	Sparrow – 2
Baker GS★ 2	Everett HP 9	McMullan –★ 2	Stancer BL 7
Ball E 1	Flaherty E 2	McPherson IB★ 14	Stanowski – 1
Barte JL★ 8	Flint K 7	Morby JH★ 8	Stephenson R 7
Barton P 5	Foster J 1	Morrad FG 13	Strain N 9
Bellis A★ 1	Gallego – 1	Moulson C 10	Streten BR 4
Benner R 1	Gascoyne L 1	Mowl JW 10	Summers – 1
Bicknell R★ 5	Goodwin FW 1	Mynard LD★ 1	Taylor J★ 3
Blood JF★ 2	Griffiths J★ 2	O'Neill T 6	Tootill R 2
Bradshaw – 2	Hepworth R★ 31	Oakley JC★ 3	Towler BE 12
Bramley E★ 4	Hogg F★ 19	Parker FW 5	Townrow RF★ 1
Brooks –★ 5	Holmes E 2	Pawlaw M★ 1	Unwin SH 1
Carrick R★ 1	Hoyle D 2	Peacock E 2	Van Gelden J 1
Carter – 1	Hubbard J 5	Piercy R★ 5	White A 3
Carter J 2	Hughes A★ 1	Pidrie D3^ 1	Wildgoose C 1
Chapman RFJ★ 1	Huntley – 1	Pomphrey EA 10	Windle R 5
Clack FE★ 4	Hutchinson J 2	Probert – 1	Wiseman G 8
Coen L★ 15	Johnstone J★ 1	Rigby N 2	Wood CC 1
Collindridge C★ 8	Kingwell –★ 1	Rollett E 2	Wright H★ 5
Connor – 1	Kirby A 1	Sewell J 21	

Goals (48): Davie 6, Sewell 6, Collindridge 5, McPherson 5, Morrad 5, Strain 4, Coen 2, Hepworth 2, Lewis 2, Towler 2, Airlie 1, Flaherty 1, Holmes 1, Knowles 1, Parker 1, Siddons 1, Southwell 1, Toothill 1, Wright 1.

1945–46

Airlie S★   1
Alexander T   3
Allen RHW   15
Bagnall R   3
Baker D   3
Barnard CH★   2
Beresford R   28
Blagg EA★   1
Bland P★   1
Briggs R   1
Brown AW★   4
Brown HT   10
Clover G   1
Corkhill WG   24
Dean –   1
Dickson W   1
Ellmer FB   1
Flower T   1

Girdham A   3
Goodman –   1
Goodwin F   1
Grant AF★   1
Haines JWT★   5
Harris K   18
Hatton C   6
Howard –   1
Howarth G   2
Hoyle D   1
Hubbard J   22
Hutchinson J   2
Iceton OL★   1
Jones A   1
Kirby A   8
Lovering W★   2
McPherson IB   27
Meredith R   10

Morrad FG   7
Moss G   1
Page D   1
Parker A   2
Parks A   15
Peacock E   13
Pye J   30
Ratcliffe PC   19
Read CW   1
Rhodes K   1
Robinson GF   5
Rollett E   1
Rossington K★   1
Rowley W   1
Ruecroft EJ★   1
Sail GH   1
Sewell J   7
Sheen J★   4

Smith L★   2
Smith R   1
Southwell AA   35
Stancer LB   2
Stewart R★   1
Strain N   5
Sweet –   2
Tapping FH★   4
Taylor WB★   1
Thorne –   1
Tootill R   2
Wilkinson N★   1
Wiseman G   12
Woodcock E   2
Woolacott H★   1

Goals (56): Pye 17, Beresford 10, McPherson 8, Hubbard 4, Hatton 2, Meredith 2, Parks 2, Sewell 2, Briggs 1, Haines 1, Harris 1, Lovering 1, Rowley 1, Sheen 1, own goals 3.

FA Cup goals (6): McPherson 3, Hubbard 1, Martin 1, Parker 1.

Oldham Athletic

1939–40

Bailey A 19	Cornock WB 3	Milligan GH★ 3	Walsh W★ 2
Blackshaw HK 3	Ferrier RJ 24	Newton F★ 1	Whalley H★ 2
Bradshaw GF★ 1	Halford D 2	Nicholson G 2	Williamson T 23
Buckley A★ 19	Hampson T 17	Paterson A 10	Worrall F★ 18
Butler T★ 16	Hayes W 3	Porter W★ 20	Wright E 8
Caunce L 20	Hilton WA 11	Ratcliffe B 3	
Chadwick C★ 6	Jones T 8	Shipman TER 24	
Chapman E 3	Ludlam W 2	Valentine AF 2	

Goals (58): Ferrier 19, Worrall 11, Buckley 7, Bailey 6, Butler 4, Valentine 2, Wright 2, Blackshaw 1, Chadwick 1, Hampson 1, Hilton 1, Porter 1, Walsh 1, Williamson 1.

War Cup goals (1): Dyson 1.

1940–41

Bailey A 32	Dougall C★ 5	Lomax J★ 1	Thomas WE 4
Blackshaw HK 18	Eaton C 2	Ludlam W 1	Valentine AF 1
Bowden J 5	Eaves TA 20	Millward AE 1	Walsh W★ 1
Buckley A★ 2	Ferrier RJ 27	Nicholson G 3	Whalley H★ 20
Butler T★ 4	Glynn KT 2	Porter W★ 20	Williamson T 36
Caunce L 16	Gosnell GL 6	Readett H★ 7	Worrall F★ 27
Chadwick C★ 17	Gray M 6	Shipman TER 39	Wright E 2
Chapman E 1	Hampson T 32	Swindin GH★ 14	
Cornock WB 6	Hilton WA 19	Taylor JT 28	
Couser H★ 1	Lewis C 1	Taylor R 2	

Goals (79): Ferrier 20, Bailey 13, Worrall 8, Blackshaw 6, Whalley 6, Chadwick 5, Taylor JT 5, Gosnell 3, Williamson 3, Gray 2, Hampson 2, Butler 1, Eaton 1, Porter 1, Shipman 1, Walsh 1, own goal 1.

1941–42

Bailey A 30	Eaves TA 12	Holmes G 1	Smith GW 1
Blackshaw HK 6	Ferrier RJ 7	Hurst G 11	Stokes J 1
Buckley A★ 3	Furness W 5	Jump F 6	Swindin GH★ 25
Butler T★ 2	Gosnell GL★ 1	Keating R 13	Taylor F 9
Carter DF★ 1	Gray M 32	Kibble G 3	Taylor JT 35
Chadwick T 10	Hall J★ 3	Price AJW★ 1	Williamson T 35
Chapman E 14	Hampson T 32	Rabey SK 5	Windson – 1
Davies G★ 1	Hilton WA 28	Ratcliffe B 1	Worrall F★ 26
Eaton C 1	Holdcroft GH★ 1	Shipman TER 33	

Goals (70): Bailey 18, Chapman 13, Hampson 8, Worrall 8, Taylor JT 5, Ferrier 4, Keating 4, Blackshaw 2, Gray 2, Taylor F 2, Hilton 1, Hurst 1, Smith 1, Stokes 1.

1942–43

Ainsworth A 24	Gray M 25	Meecham W 1	Spencer K 2
Ashworth J 1	Gregory H 1	Milligan GH★ 3	Stokes J 2
Bailey A 22	Hampson T 5	Ogden F 5	Taylor JT 33
Birch N 1	Hayes W 4	Percival J★ 1	Thomas WE 1
Buckley A★ 2	Herrod F 5	Phipps J 1	Tilling HK 31
Buckley F 5	Hilton WA 30	Radcliffe M 24	Waite W 26
Catterick H★ 1	Hurst C 16	Readett H★ 1	Whalley H★ 1
Chapman E 6	Hurst G 4	Riley T 1	Williams K 3
Eastwood R★ 5	Keating R 2	Saunders R 1	Williamson T 32
Eaton C 1	Lawrence R 3	Shipman TER 36	Worrall F★ 21
Furness W 1	Martin RO 4	Southern SC 2	

Goals (57): Waite 16, Tilling 8, Worrall 7, Bailey 6, Taylor 5, Hilton 3, Ainsworth 2, Buckley A 2, Buckley F 2, Chapman 2, Hampson 1, Hurst C 1, Hurst G 1, Williams 1.

1943–44

Ainsworth A 3
Bailey A 23
Bohan TW 1
Bowden J 6
Bratley GW* 11
Butler T* 3
Chapman E 15
Cottrill WH 10
Crawshaw H* 5
Crossley J 1

Curran F* 2
Dunning H 1
Ferrier RJ 1
Gray M 33
Hamilton W* 1
Hilton WA 5
Horton L 7
Hough T* 2
Hurst C 28
Hurst G 3

Jackson J 1
Jerram G 1
Keating R 5
Martin RO 11
Milligan GH* 1
Radcliffe M 27
Roxburgh AW* 9
Samuels G 17
Shipman TER 36
Stevens GL* 2

Stokes J 2
Taylor JT 28
Tilling HK 36
Topping H* 1
Wilkinson H 1
Williamson T 33
Worrall F* 24

Goals (58): Bailey 9, Chapman 8, Cottrill 7, Tilling 6, Worrall 5, Crawshaw 4, Taylor 3, Bowden 2, Keating 2, Martin 2, Stokes 2, Ainsworth 1, Curran 1, Hilton 1, Horton 1, Hurst C 1, Hurst G 1, Stevens 1, own goal 1.

1944–45

Adams K 1
Bailey A 15
Birch JW* 6
Bohan TW 28
Bowden J 8
Brierley K 3
Butler T* 5
Chapman E 21
Cottrill WH 4
Eastwood R* 5

Eaton C 1
Eaves TA 35
Farrington J 1
Goodman L 34
Herrick R 1
Hilton WA 1
Horton L 14
Hurst C 37
Ibbotson R 2
Keating R 6

Lawton W 8
Loveless W 1
MacMillan J 1
Marrs B 1
Martin RO 3
Mellor J 3
Ogden F 4
Phipps J 2
Porter W* 15
Radcliffe M 34

Samuels G 2
Shipman TER 20
Smith JB* 1
Smith M 7
Standring N 16
Taylor JT 26
Tiers J 3
Tilling HK 1
Williamson T 29
Worrall F* 34

Goals (67): Standring 14, Chapman 10, Worrall 9, Horton 7, Bowden 6, Shipman 4, Cottrill 3, Hurst C 3, Bailey 2, Goodman 2, Bohan 1, Brierley 1, Butler 1, Eaves 1, Tilling 1, own goals 2.

1945–46

Barclay R* 4
Blackshaw HK 6
Bohan TW 5
Boothman J 14
Bowden J 5
Brierley K 15
Buckley A* 4
Butler T* 23
Chapman E 27
Collindridge C* 2

Crookes A 2
Dixon M 1
Docherty R 1
Eaves TA 12
Ferrier RJ 10
Goodwin L 23
Hayes W 3
Herrick R 3
Hobson J 2
Horton L 36

Hurst C 1
Hurst G 1
Keating R 4
Lawton W 32
Marlor A 30
Radcliffe M 3
Rookes PW* 1
Sawbridge J 14
Schofield M 6
Shipman TER 15

Standring N 11
Taylor JT 2
Tilling HK 2
Turner H* 13
Wagstaffe E 4
Waite WJ 3
West T 20
Williamson T 36

Goals (54): Chapman 14, West 13, Brierley 4, Butler 3, Collindridge 3, Ferrier 3, Standring 3, Goodwin 2, Keating 2, Barclay 1, Blackshaw 1, Bohan 1, Crookes 1, Horton 1, Wagstaffe 1, Waite 1.

FA Cup goals (8): Chapman 2, Standring 2, West 2, Ferrier 1, Lawton 1.

Plymouth Argyle

1939–40

Archer JW   29
Clark JMC   16
Dixon S   4
Dugnolle JH   14
Fellowes WJ   5
Glover EM   9
Gorman A   30
Harper W   3

Hurst WR   1
Jones L   1
Kirkwood SJ   16
Lane H   12
Lewis AC   1
McDonald W   25
McNeil JL★   1
Middleton MY   17

Mitcheson J★   3
Olver WE   3
Parnaby TW   8
Rae J   23
Rich L★   2
Rosenthal A★   1
Royston R   2
Sargeant C   29

Silk GH   28
Simpson W★   1
Smith J   27
Stuttard JE   5
Thomas DWJ   6
Townsend LF★   7
Williams W★   1
Wright GW   11

Goals (76): Sargeant 12, Smith 12, Townsend 10, Archer 9, McDonald 8, Glover 6, Thomas 5, Rich 4, Fellowes 3, Lane 3, Olver 2, Dugnolle 1, Stuttard 1.

War Cup goals (1): Smith 1.

1940–41

Did not compete.

1941–42

Did not compete.

1942–43

Did not compete.

1943–44

Did not compete.

1944–45

League West Cup only.

1945–46

Adams WV   14
Beeson A   4
Brown Bobby★   3
Brown D   4
Brown Ron   24
Butler HE   5
Came A   4
Carless E★   11
Carter J   1
Case D   1
Clark R   1
Cole GD★   1
Court HJ★   3
Cumner RH★   2
Dixon S   28
Dryden JG★   1
Dugnolle JH   6
Dyer JA   10

Ferrier RJ★   1
Fullbrook J   8
Gallagher M   1
Gardiner J★   8
Gibson R   16
Gorman A   16
Griffiths KG★   2
Haddington R★   3
Harris T   1
Haycock F★   1
Hazlett G   3
Hodge J   1
Howshall T★   4
Hunter JB★   1
Hurst WR   6
Jenkins G   1
Jones L   29
Kerr AW★   3

Kirkham J★   1
Latham L★   1
Loft A   1
Logie J★   1
Middleton MY   14
Northover S   1
Olver WG   1
Poyser GH   3
Prescott J★   5
Rae J   2
Roberts W   3
Royston R   13
Rundle S   5
Sargent F★   1
Scrine F★   2
Shortt WW   18
Silk GH   41
Sinclair RD★   1

Smale DM★   3
Smith E   8
Smith J   2
Smith WH   5
Squires A★   2
Stephenson K   17
Stuttard JE   1
Swinscoe TW★   1
Taylor E★   2
Thomas DWJ   16
Thomas RA   3
Tinkler L   30
Tivendale J★   9
Tomlinson RW★   7
Tugwell S   4
Warren RE   2
Whittaker W★   1
Wright GW   7

Goals (39): Brown Ron 17, Thomas D 9, Tinkler 4, Hurst 2, Brown D 1, Carless 1, Prescott 1, Smith W 1, Swinscoe 1, Thomas R 1, own goal 1.

FA Cup goals (0).

Portsmouth

1939–40

Allen JP★   7
Anderson JC   34
Bagley W   28
Barlow H   37
Barnes W   2
Briggs F★   1
Bryan EC   2
Buchanan PS★   1
Bushby TW   20
Cadnam R   1
Candy R   5

Cothliffe HT★   1
Cross E★   3
Emery EJ   1
Flewin R   31
Gilchrist –   1
Guthrie JA   30
Harris J★   2
Hassell TW★   1
Hutchinson F   1
Jackson J★   1
Jones EN★   1

Layton WH★   1
Lovery J★   1
Mason J   4
McAlinden J   3
Miller AG★   7
Mills DJ   1
Morgan L   32
Parker C   37
Rochford W   37
Rowe T   3
Royston R★   2

Saunders P★   3
Smith A   27
Summerbee G   11
Tann BJ★   2
Walker GH   38
Wattie JH   1
Wharton G   3
Wilbert G★   1
Wilkinson J★   1
Worrall F   3

Goals (66): Barlow 18, Parker 12, Anderson 11, Bagley 8, Mason 3, Miller 3, Bushby 2, Emery 2, Candy 1, Guthrie 1, Harris 1, Rochford 1, Saunders 1, Wilkinson 1, Worrall 1.

War Cup goals (4): Anderson 2, Barlow 1, Worrall 1.

1940–41

Anderson JC   1
Bagley W   6
Barlow H   27
Black A★   16
Blakeney J★   1
Buchanan PS★   2
Burke R★   1
Cavell FE   2
Else SO   1
Emery EJ   16
Emptage AT★   6

Ferguson T   7
Flack DW★   3
Flewin R   28
Gardener HN   7
Grace RA   1
Guthrie JE   33
Hart A   4
Higgins HC   2
Hooper HR★   3
Hutchinson F   2
King AE★   1

Lacey A★   3
Littlewood FC   4
McIntosh JM★   2
Mills DJ   8
Moffatt R   1
Morgan L   31
Parker C   30
Rochford W   24
Rowe T   3
Smith CS   2
Summerbee G★   29

Taylor JG★   1
Walker GH   23
Walker S★   1
Walters TB★   1
Ward TA★   6
Wharton G   1
Wilkes GA★   18
Wilkins GE★   2
Winch JP   3

Goals (94): Wilkes 26, Barlow 18, Black 12, Emery 7, Parker 7, Ward 6, Guthrie 3, McIntosh 3, Cavell 2, Gardener 2, Summerbee 2, Bagley 1, Blakeney 1, Buchanan 1, Hutchinson 1, own goals 2.

1941–42

Aston J★   4
Barlow H   35
Black A★   30
Bullock GF★   11
Burke R★   2
Court HJ★   2
Emery EJ   7
Flewin R   35

Gregory FC★   2
Griffiths JS   23
Guthrie JE   37
Harrigan D★   1
Laney LC★   1
Martin JR★   1
McIntosh JM★   9
Moores PR   14

Morgan L   32
Parker C   36
Platt EH★   1
Ranner –   1
Rochford W   37
Rookes PW   5
Slater J★   2
Summerbee G★   25

Sykes J★   1
Walker GH   36
Ward TA★   16
Wharton G   11
Worrall F   1

Goals (122): Black 46, Barlow 26, Griffiths 11, Bullock 6, Moores 6, Parker 6, Guthrie 5, Ward 5, Court 3, Emery 2, Aston 1, McIntosh 1, Rochford 1, own goals 3.

1942–43

Anderson JC   3
Arnold F   1
Barlow H   31
Biggs A★   6
Black A★   4
Brown R★   1
Buchanan PS★   4
Bullock GF★   27
Bushby TW   9
Crowther J   1

Davie J★   4
Fagan J★   1
Flewin R   33
Griffiths JS   18
Guthrie JE   34
Mackintosh HF★   2
Martin W★   4
McKillop J★   3
Moores PR   6
Morgan L   34

Parker C   30
Pointon WJ★   9
Pond H★   1
Rochford W   33
Ross J★   2
Scrimshaw CT★   1
Speak K★   1
Summerbee G★   26
Swindin GH★   1
Tomlinson RW★   1

Tweedy GJ★   1
Walker GH   28
Ward TA★   4
Westland D★   3
Whitchurch CH   2
Wilkes GA★   4
Wilson R★   1

Goals (77): Bullock 20, Barlow 14, Griffiths 6, Parker 6, Pointon 5, Black 4, Guthrie 4, Mackintosh 3, Martin 3, Ward 3, Bushby 2, Davie 2, Tomlinson 2, Anderson 1, Biggs 1, Wilkes 1.

1943–44

Anderson JC   3
Barlow H   27
Black J*   3
Buchanan PS*   21
Buckingham VF*   10
Bushby TW   21
Cook R*   1
Cumner RH*   9
Dent D   1
Dickinson JW   18

Emptage AT*   2
Flewin R   22
Guthrie JE   27
Kerr AW*   3
Langley WG*   1
Lucas DJ   1
Mackintosh HF*   5
Martin E*   3
Mason J   1
McArdle P*   3

McLeod D*   6
Mills DJ   4
Mitchell FR*   2
Morgan L   31
Parker C   32
Pinkerton H*   1
Quigley E*   2
Robertson AC   7
Rochford W   21
Saunders SG   1

Sears DG*   11
Storey WCG   2
Stubbings S   2
Summerbee G*   27
Tann BJ*   5
Thomas RA*   5
Walker GH   36
Ward TA*   9
Whitchurch CH   8
Wilkes GA*   2

Goals (71): Barlow 13, Parker 11, Bushby 6, Ward 6, Buckingham 3, Mackintosh 3, Quigley 3, Sears 3, Thomas 3, Buchanan 2, McArdle 2, Rochford 2, Whitchurch 2, Wilkes 2, Anderson 1, Cook 1, Cumner 1, Emptage 1, Guthrie 1, Kerr 1, Lucas 1, McLeod 1, Mason 1, Storey 1.

1944–45

Anderson JC   27
Ashmore AJ   1
Barlow H   4
Bell KW   4
Black J*   5
Buckingham VF*   7
Bushby TW   18
Clements SFT*   2
Crossley J   2
Dempsey AJ*   1
Dickinson JW   8

Drake EJ*   1
Drummond I*   2
Emptage AT*   10
Evans FJ   5
Flewin R   19
Forrester J   4
Gardener HN   1
Grant B*   1
Gunn –*   1
Guthrie JE   33
Halton RL*   2

Harris PP   27
Hudson GW   2
Jamieson DS   1
Jeffries A*   5
Kerr AW*   7
Lonnon C*   1
Mackie J   1
Massie J*   6
McLeod D*   12
Monk LSF*   2
Morgan L   32

Offord SJ*   1
Parker C   31
Rochford W   28
Salter J*   1
Short CG   1
Speed L   1
Storey WCG   2
Summerbee G*   26
Walker GH   35
Wayman C*   7
Whitchurch CH   9

Goals (72): Parker 15, Harris 14, Anderson 8, Evans 7, Wayman 6, Buckingham 4, Drake 4, Kerr 3, Bushby 2, Black 1, Emptage 1, Guthrie 1, Gunn 1, Halton 1, McLeod 1, Massie 1, Monk 1, Whitchurch 1.

1945–46

Anderson JC   21
Barlow H   31
Bell KW   7
Bowe J   7
Bushby TW   8
Butler EAE   1
Chisholm K*   1
Crossley J   5
Dickinson JW   5
Edwards A   2

Evans FJ   22
Ferrier H   11
Flewin R   30
Foxton JD   19
Froggatt J   20
Goodwin J*   1
Guthrie JE   19
Haddington R*   3
Halton RL*   3
Harris PP   33

Henderson G*   1
Hopkins JJ   4
Hudson GW   3
Humpston R   1
Kerr AW*   1
Morby J*   1
Morgan L   30
Parker C   32
Paterson E   3
Phillips L   10

Reid DJ   11
Richards S   1
Rochford W   23
Rookes PW   13
Scoular J   20
Stott AG   6
Walker GH   40
Wharton G   6
Worrall F   7

Goals (66): Evans 12, Harris 10, Froggatt 9, Barlow 8, Parker 6, Reid 5, Stott 4, Haddington 3, Worrall 3, Anderson 2, Paterson 2, Edwards 1, Guthrie 1.

FA Cup goals (0).

Port Vale

1939–40

Bellis A 7
Blunt E★ 9
Cumberlidge AL 17
Dickie MM 2
Flatley AA 2
Griffiths HS 18
Griffiths J★ 1

Griffiths PH 22
Hannah GL 5
Higgins D 18
Jepson A 23
Moore JA 1
Morrey GA 1
Nolan TG 8

Oakes GA 7
Obrey A★ 10
Purcell RW 13
Roberts JE 18
Rowe J 17
Sanderson J 2
Scrimshaw CT 7

Smith W 24
Sproson J 4
Triner DA 5
Tunnicliffe J 17
Ware H★ 6

Goals (52): Roberts 13, Tunnicliffe 10, Griffiths P 9, Higgins 7, Griffiths H 3, Nolan 3, Bellis 2, Triner 2, Blunt 1, Cumberlidge 1, Sproson 1.

War Cup goals (2): Griffiths HS 1, Roberts 1.

1940–41

Did not compete.

1941–42

Did not compete.

1942–43

Did not compete.

1943–44

Did not compete.

1944–45

Allen R 3
Bailey A★ 2
Banks K 2
Bateman A★ 13
Bellis A 25
Betmead H★ 6
Birks WJ 3
Blunt E★ 6
Booth C 4
Bray J★ 1
Buckley WJ 4
Cardwell L★ 8
Clunn J 15
Cooper A 26
Dickie MM 2
Doherty PD★ 2
Duffy R★ 2
Fenton M★ 1

Gallon JW★ 1
Gregory RJ 1
Griffiths HS 29
Griffiths J★ 10
Griffiths PH 5
Hall AE★ 1
Hankey AE★ 4
Hannah GL 3
Howell L 1
Hughes S★ 1
Isherwood D★ 1
Jepson A 1
Jervis H 1
Johnson H 1
Kirkcaldie L★ 5
Lane H★ 21
Lowe L★ 2
Marsh FK★ 2

Martin JA 3
Maudsley RC★ 3
Maund JH★ 1
Mawson R 1
McDowell I 22
McKay W★ 1
McShane H★ 3
Mee JH 1
Meiklen RC★ 1
Meredith R 2
Mills J★ 1
Morrey GA 2
Moses G★ 1
Muir DB 3
Musgrove J 4
Nutting E 3
Pepper RF 1
Pointon F 14

Pointon WJ 8
Prince CS 1
Prince E 21
Prince H 33
Purcell RW 9
Roberts R★ 2
Roden J 6
Sanderson J 1
Smith W 10
Spender D 1
Sproson J 32
Tunnicliffe J 2
Ware H★ 2
Wheatley J 3
Wilshaw DJ★ 1
Wright GA★ 14
Yates R★ 1

Goals (49): Bellis 10, Prince E 6, McDowell 5, Pointon W 5, Clunn 3, Griffiths P 3, McShane 3, Booth 2, Kirkcaldie 2, Pepper 2, Cardwell 1, Gregory 1, Griffiths H 1, Hall 1, Isherwood 1, Musgrove 1, Pointon F 1, Ware 1.

1945–46

Allen R 18	Felton R 10	Lowndes J 1	Simpson DR★ 1
Bellis A 27	Gardner FC★ 3	Lyman CC★ 4	Smith W 29
Birchall EW 2	Gould G 3	McDowell I 13	Soo F★ 1
Buckley WJ 1	Gregory RJ 8	McGarry WH 2	Sproson J 2
Byrne W 1	Griffiths HS 26	Nutting E 2	Triner DA 3
Cheadle T 9	Heppell G 10	Oldfield JE 13	Walkins K★ 1
Clunn J 1	Hutchinson JA★ 1	Pointon F 8	Whittle R 2
Cooper A 35	James G 1	Pointon WJ 26	Willett E 1
Cumberlidge AL 2	Jepson A 14	Potts R 4	Willis G★ 1
Cumner RH★ 7	Jervis H 4	Prince E 2	Wootton L 23
Davies E 8	Johnson H 1	Prince H 12	Wright B★ 1
Dickie MM 1	Jones FA 5	Purcell RW 25	
Faulkner N★ 1	Kelly L★ 1	Shore E 19	

Goals (55): Pointon W 18, Bellis 13, Gregory 5, Davies 3, McDowell 3, Shore 3, Allen 2, Jones 2, Cheadle 1, Cooper 1, Cumner 1, Gardner 1, Wootton 1, own goal 1.

FA Cup goals (12): Bellis 3, McDowell 3, Allen 2, Gregory 2, Pointon W 1, own goal 1.

Preston North End

1939–40

Bargh GH★   2
Batey R   24
Beattie A   3
Beattie R   25
Dougal J   17
Fairbrother J   2
Finch R   1

Gallimore F   22
Groves K   1
Holdcroft GH   22
Hunter JB   3
Iceton OL   2
Maxwell JM★   1
McIntosh JM   9

Milne JL   7
Mutch G   15
O'Donnell F★   14
O'Donnell H★   13
Rawlings JSD★   2
Rookes P★   8
Scott W   2

Shankly W   23
Smith TM   18
Standing JS   2
Summerbee G   2
Wharton JE   17
White FRH   4
Williams E   14

Goals (63): O'Donnell F 15, Dougal 13, Beattie R 10, Wharton 5, Batey 4, Mutch 4, Standing 4, McIntosh 2, Milne 2, O'Donnell H 2, Bargh 1, own goal 1.

War Cup goals (3): Dougal 3.

1940–41

Beattie A   5
Beattie R   15
Dougal J   40
Fairbrother J   27
Finch R   15
Finney T   41
Gallimore F   38

Gore E   1
Holdcroft GH   14
Horton JK   2
Hough T   5
Jessop W   25
Mansley C   37
McLaren A   39

McPhie J★   1
Mutch G   17
Nuttal W   1
O'Donnell H★   10
Owens J   3
Robertson WJT   2
Scott W   38

Seed T   2
Shankly W   25
Smith TM   38
Taylor PT   4
Wharton JE   6

Goals (123): Dougal 32, McLaren 31, Beattie R 11, Mutch 11, Finney 10, Shankly 7, O'Donnell H 6, Jessop 4, Wharton 4, Hough 2, Mansley 2, Owen 2, Taylor 1.

1941–42

Batey R   6
Beardwood G   2
Beattie A   17
Beattie R   5
Bradford L   17
Bremner GH★   8
Bright R★   1
Dougal J   34
Fairbrother J   32

Finch R   1
Finney T   33
Gallimore F   13
Gardner T★   1
Gooch JA   3
Gore E   1
Holdcroft GH   2
Horton JK   13
Iddon H   1

Jessop W   1
Mansley C   13
McDougal L+   1
McIntosh JM   2
McLaren A   37
Mutch G   32
Robertson WJT   3
Scott W   32
Seed T   1

Shankly W   25
Smith TM   32
Snowden R★   1
Taylor PT   1
Wharton JE   35
White FRH   2

+ *Played first half for Beattie A v Newcastle U 21.3.42.*

Goals (99): Dougal 23, Wharton 21, McLaren 18, Mutch 16, Finney 6, Beattie R 4, Shankly 4, Beardwood 1, Bremner 1, Gore 1, Horton 1, Taylor 1, own goals 2.

1942–43

Did not compete.

1943–44

Did not compete.

1944–45

Anders H   4
Attwell RF★   1
Bond A   15
Boyes W★   1
Bradford L   27
Bradshaw GF★   1
Bryant A   1
Cater R★   11
Dainty A   2
Darley J   2

Dougal J   28
Dunn R★   12
Fairbrother J   9
Griffiths G★   1
Griffiths W★   1
Groves K   1
Hamilton W   30
Hesketh A   5
Holdcroft GH   16
Horton JK   6

Hough T   2
Iceton OL   2
Iddon H   9
Kiely T   2
Livesey J   16
McIntosh JM   23
Milne JL   23
Mutch G   22
Robertson WJT   40
Scott W   21

Seddon H   7
Simpson R   8
Smith TM   32
Squires A   2
Strachan D   9
Urquhart W★   2
Walmsley J   11
Watson WT   24
Wharton JE   43
Willingham CK★   1

Goals (67): Dougal 13, McIntosh 13, Mutch 8, Dunn 5, Livesey 5, Wharton 5, Iddon 4, Strachan 4, Bond 3, Seddon 2, Dainty 1, Horton 1, Hough 1, Robertson 1, Watson 1.

1945–46

Anders H 15	Fairbrother J 37	Iddon H 12	Simpson R 20
Anders J 1	Finney T 5	Livesey J 12	Squires A 1
Batey R 8	Groves K 1	Mansley C 2	Summerbee G 28
Beattie A 25	Hamilton W 35	McIntosh JM 42	Walmsley J 3
Beattie R 15	Holdcroft GH 1	Mutch G 42	Watson WT 15
Bradford L 2	Horton JK 13	Robertson WJT 1	Wharton JE 30
Brown W 2	Hunter JB 1	Scott W 23	Williams E 19
Dougal J 35	Iceton OL 2	Shankly W 14	

Goals (70): Mutch 18, McIntosh 15, Dougal 12, Iddon 7, Beattie R 5, Finney 4, Wharton 4, Shankly 2, Anders H 1, Livesey 1, own goal 1.

FA Cup goals (8): Livesey 2, McIntosh 2, Shankly 2, Wharton 1, own goal 1.

Queens Park Rangers

1939–40

Abel S 29	Devine JS 2	Mallett J 33	Pattison JM 3
Allen RA 5	Farmer A 28	Mangnall D 35	Powell IV 25
Barr JM 8	Fitzgerald AM 6	March R 22	Reay EP 18
Bonass AE 34	Francis ET 1	Mason WS 34	Reid JM 2
Bott W 2	Jefferson A 30	McCarthy LD 30	Ridyard A 12
Byrom W 1	Kelly JG 7	McColgan J 2	Stock AWA 2
Daniels HAG 1	Lowe HP 16	McEwan W 35	Swinfen R 6

Goals (91): Mangnall 40, McEwan 19, Mallett 11, McCarthy 10, Bonass 5, March 3, Swinfen 1, own goals 2.

War Cup goals (0).

1940–41

Abel S 30	Dumsday J 1	Ling LL 5	Pattison JM 1
Adam C* 6	Edwards EJ 1	Lowe HP 29	Powell IV 1
Armstrong RJ 1	Farmer A 20	Mahon J* 1	Reay EP 1
Bacon SG 2	Fitzgerald AM 1	Mallett J 14	Ridyard A 27
Bonass AE 16	Fowler A* 2	Mangnall D 24	Scott L* 1
Bott W 16	Griffiths R* 1	March R 23	Smith JF* 1
Campbell R* 1	Halford D* 3	Mason WS 30	Swinfen R 18
Compton LH* 1	Jackson J* 1	McCarthy LD 11	Webb JV 12
Daniels HAG 10	Jefferson A 13	McEwan W 5	Whitfield W* 4
Davie J* 4	Lievesley L* 1	Mills GR* 1	Wilson KA 1

Goals (65): Mangnall 23, Lowe 6, Swinfen 6, Bott 5, Mallett 5, Ling 4, Daniels 3, Compton 2, Ridyard 2, Adam 1, Bonass 1, Davie 1, Halford 1, McCarthy 1, Mills 1, Webb 1, own goals 2.

London Cup

Abel 7, Adam 3, Allen R 1, Armstrong 1, Bonass 3, Bott 4, Daniels 1, Davie 3, Edwards 2, Farmer 8, Fitzgerald 3, Halford 3, Hillard –* 1, Jefferson 3, Lowe 10, Mallett 1, Mangnall 8, March 10, Mason 9, McEwan 1, Mortimer –* 1, Pattison 1, Reay 3, Ridyard 10, Swinfen 5, Webb J 8.

Goals: Mangnall 9, Davie 3, Bott 2, Lowe 2, McEwan 2, Mallett 2, March 2, Adam 1, Bonass 1, Daniels 1, Fitzgerald 1.

1941–42

Abel S 20	Eastham GR* 9	Libby J 1	Paton TG* 3
Armstrong RJ 12	Edwards EJ 2	Ling LL 2	Pattison JM 18
Blizzard LWB 14	Edwards R 1	Lowe HP 12	Reay EP 8
Bonass AE 8	Farmer A 26	Mahon J* 14	Ridyard A 32
Brown B 1	Gibbs-Kennett R 1	Mallett J 20	Sibley A* 8
Brown HT 13	Gunner RV 4	Mangnall D 28	Smale DM* 1
Campbell – 5	Halford D* 6	March R 15	Smith AW 8
Cheetham TM* 1	Harris N 1	Mason WS 23	Stock AWA 5
Cottam – 1	Hatton C* 9	McEwan W 4	Swinfen R 12
Dale A* 1	Heath W 6	McNickle – 1	
Davie J* 2	Jefferson A 21	Moore – 1	
Delaney L 1	Kirkham J* 13	Painter – 2	

Goals (60): Mangnall 12, Hatton 10, Pattison 5, Mahon 4, Armstrong 3, Davie 3, Kirkham 3, Mallett 3, Eastham 2, Halford 2, Heath 2, Lowe 2, McEwan 2, Stock 2, Abel 1, Farmer 1, Harris 1, Moore 1, own goal 1.

1942–43

Abel S 25	Gadsden RF 3	Lowe HP 10	Powell IV 3
Barkas S* 1	Gunner RV 9	Mallett J 30	Reay EP 12
Beadell RC 1	Hatton C* 15	Mangnall D 25	Ridyard A 30
Blizzard LWB 2	Heath W 1	McEwan W 4	Rose J 14
Brown HT 35	Heathcote W* 10	McInnes JS* 1	Sibley A* 26
Burley B 31	Henley L* 2	Mills GR* 1	Smith AW 27
Farmer A 5	Horsfield A* 6	Parkinson A 3	Stock AWA 4
Fitzgerald AM 1	Jefferson A 15	Pattison JM 10	Swinfen R 23

Goals (81): Swinfen 16, Burley 13, Mangnall 11, Hatton 9, Heathcote 8, Sibley 5, Mallett 4, Pattison 4, Stock 3, McEwan 2, Ridyard 2, Abel 1, Parkinson 1, Reay 1, Smith 1.

1943–44

Abel S 31	Gadsden RF 7	Lowes AR★ 9	Ridyard A 20
Alexander FR 1	Gillies MM★ 5	Mallett J 35	Rose J 30
Bacon SG 1	Golding DL 1	Mangnall D 18	Roxburgh AW★ 5
Blizzard LWB 1	Greenwood R★ 1	Martin J★ 1	Shaw A 1
Brown HT 26	Griffiths J 3	Mason WS 3	Sheen J★ 8
Burley B 30	Hardy E★ 1	McEwan W 4	Sibley A★ 4
De Busser E 3	Heathcote W 33	McLuckie JS★ 2	Smith AW 31
De Lisle – 1	Hughes WA★ 1	Parkinson AA 2	Somerfield A★ 10
Dean WHG★ 1	Hutchinson R★ 1	Parry O★ 1	Swinfen R 18
Duke HP★ 1	Jefferson A 11	Pattison JM 9	Webb RCT 5
Evans F★ 1	Jones EN★ 5	Pearson SC^A 4	Yielleyoye H 1
Fowler A★ 1	Little C★ 4	Ramscar F★ 4	

Goals (94): Heathcote 36, Swinfen 13, Burley 6, Lowes 5, Somerfield 5, Jones 4, Sheen 4, Mangnall 3, Pattison 3, Dean 2, McEwan 2, Ramscar 2, Sibley 2, De Busser 1, De Lisle 1, Griffiths J 1, Little 1, Mallett 1, Pearson 1, own goal 1.

1944–45

Abel S 28	Dawes FW★ 11	Henley L★ 1	Rose J 31
Addinall AW 5	Dean WHG★ 1	Jefferson A 5	Shaw A 10
Alexander RF 1	Duke GE★ 2	Jones EN★ 9	Sibley A★ 18
Attwell RF★ 12	Duke HP★ 1	King PH 2	Smith AW 7
Bain W★ 5	Farmer A 2	Knight AW★ 1	Smith EWA 2
Brook H★ 1	Farrow DA 2	Laidman F★ 1	Somerfield A★ 1
Brown HT 9	Ferrier H★ 1	Lowes AR★ 2	Stock AWA 1
Burley B 17	Fitzgerald AM 10	Ludford G★ 1	Swinfen R 1
Chalkley AG★ 1	Forsyth J★ 3	Mallett J 36	Taylor GE★ 3
Cheetham TM★ 5	Gillies MM★ 24	Nevins L★ 2	Tennant AE★ 1
Cruikshank J★ 1	Gregory E★ 20	Phillips W★ 1	
Daniels HAG 22	Gunner RV 1	Ridyard A 33	
Darragon W 11	Heathcote W 29	Robinson P★ 2	

Goals (77): Heathcote 23, Daniels 8, Mallett 7, Shaw 5, Addinall 4, Fitzgerald 4, Jones 4, Sibley 4, Abel 3, Burley 2, Darragon 2, Gillies 2, Ridyard 2, Attwell 1, Bain 1, Cheetham 1, Lowes 1, Somerfield 1, Smith E 1, own goal 1.

1945–46

Abel S 8	Farrow DA 26	Mangnall D 1	Smith AW 2
Addinall AW 5	Gillies MM★ 2	McEwan W 10	Smith E 1
Alexander FR 2	Hamilton DS★ 3	Neary HF 23	Smith LGF★ 1
Allen RA 36	Hatton C 5	Parkinson AA 4	Somerfield A★ 8
Blizzard LWB 3	Heath WJ 13	Pattison JM 17	Stock AWA 10
Boxshall D 3	Heathcote W 22	Peppitt S★ 1	Swinfen R 4
Brown HT 2	Hibbs R 1	Powell IV 6	Webb RCT 1
Chapman RFJ 7	Jefferson A 22	Reay EP 7	Whitehead WG 4
Compton LH★ 1	Johnson J★ 1	Ridyard A 35	Wrigglesworth W★ 1
Crack FW★ 3	Jones G 1	Rose J 34	
Daniels HAG 37	Lennon J 2	Salmon L★ 4	
Darragon W 1	Mallett J 37	Shaw A 1	

Goals (89): Heathcote 20, Neary 18, Mallett 10, Heath 9, Pattison 6, McEwan 4, Stock 4, Crack 3, Hatton 3, Ridyard 3, Abel 1, Addinall 1, Boxshall 1, Chapman 1, Salmon 1, Somerfield 1, Whitehead 1, own goals 2.

FA Cup goals (21): Addinall 8, Neary 5, Mallett 2, Stock 2, Daniels 1, Heathcote 1, Pattison 1, Swinfen 1

Reading

1939–40

Abery LA   1
Burgess H★   6
Chitty WS   36
Cothliff HT★   4
Cox FJA★   7
Crooks SD★   1
Dawes FW★   1
Deverall HR   21
Dougall R   39
Duncan D★   1
Edelston M   17

Edwards L   1
Fenwick AL   1
Flack DW★   1
Fullwood J   35
Gale GW   2
Gaskell E★   1
Glidden GS   1
Hayhurst A   1
Holmes J   36
Houldsworth FC   1
Ireland H★   1

Kelsey H★   1
Layton WH   19
Lewis HH★   1
Ludford GA★   1
MacPhee MG   28
Mapson J★   32
McCarthy B   3
O'Hare J★   1
Sheppard HH★   1
Sherwood HW   11
Smallwood F   28

Tait T★   1
Taylor A   8
Wallbanks J   34
Whittam EA   1
Wilkins GE★   2
Wilson JW   3
Yorston BC★   1
Young LA   38

Goals (86): MacPhee 20, Deverall 15, Smallwood 12, Edelston 8, Layton 8, Sherwood 6, Chitty 4, Burgess 2, Cox 2, Dougall 2, Taylor 2, Cothliff 1, Kelsey 1, Lewis 1, Ludford 1, Wilkins 1.

War Cup goals (5): MacPhee 2, Young 2, own goal 1.

1940–41

Aicken AV★   1
Aird –   1
Bacuzzi J★   2
Bartlett FL★   2
Bates WH★   1
Bradley J★   5
Brooks NH   5
Chitty WS   24
Cothliff HT★   12
Cox FJA★   2
Davie J★   3
Dougall R   14
Edelston M   16
Ednay C   2

Flack DW★   2
Fullwood J   21
Geldard A★   4
Gibbons AH★   1
Gill D   2
Glidden GS   7
Hampshire F   2
Harwood RW   6
Hayhurst A   4
Holmes J   1
Hopper AH   1
Houldsworth FC   1
Howe LF★   3
Hurst J★   5

Ithell WJ★   1
James –   1
Johnston H★   2
Kelsey H   1
Kilkenny JC   5
Knott H★   1
Layton WH   30
MacPhee MG   30
Mahon J★   3
Mapson J★   25
McCarthy B   1
McPhie J   9
Millington –   1
Nelson –   3

Perry E★   1
Peters P   3
Ratcliffe B★   25
Roberts JH★   1
Sherwood HW   9
Sinclair TM★   2
Smallwood F   5
Taylor A   4
Walker D★   1
Watts –   1
Westwood E★   2
Wicks LR   3
Winter DT★   5
Young LA   5

Goals (79): MacPhee 30, Chitty 8, Edelston 8, Layton 7, Sherwood 4, Brooks 3, Bradley 2, Gibbons 2, Glidden 2, Howe 2, Sinclair 2, Taylor 2, Cothliff 1, Hurst 1, Neilson 1, Roberts 1, Smallwood 1, own goals 2.

London Cup

Bacuzzi 1, Bradley 4, Brooks 4, Chitty 12, Collingham – 1, Cothliff 9, Deverall 1, Dougall 5, Eastham GR★ 2, Edelston 6, Fullwood 11, Glidden 1, Hopper 1, Ireland 1, Layton 12, MacPhee 12, McColl – 2, McPhie 7, Mapson 10, Oxberry 1, Penny 1, Ratcliffe 11, Sherwood 7, Swift 1, Tait T★ 1, Warburton G★ 1, Westwood 2, Wilkins GE★ 1, Young 4.

Goals: MacPhee 15, Edelston 5, Chitty 3, Cothliff 3, Layton 3, Bradley 2, Brooks 2, Sherwood 2, Deverall 1.

1941–42

Allum LH★   1
Beasley A★   12
Bradley J★   14
Brooks NH   1
Burchell GS★   1
Chapman E   1
Chitty WS   36
Cook S   1
Cothliff HT★   32
Court JH★   9

Davidson D★   2
Davie J★   1
Deverall HR   4
Duns L★   9
Edelston M   22
Edwards L   1
Fullwood J   33
Goldberg L★   14
Hall AE★   4
Henley L★   4

Hopper AH   5
Howe LF★   7
Lane W★   1
Layton WH   18
MacPhee MG   33
Mapson J★   34
McPhie J   22
Muttitt E★   1
Oxberry J   1
Ratcliffe B★   33

Sanders –   2
Sherwood HW   3
Stephenson JE★   2
Taylor A   4
Tennant AE★   1
Wilson J   1
Wright RCA★   3
Young LA   23

Goals (85): MacPhee 23, Edelston 17, Bradley 13, Chitty 8, Cothliff 8, Henley 4, Sherwood 3, Beasley 2, Deverall 2, Court 1, Davie 1, Hall 1, Stephenson 1, Taylor 1.

1942–43

Aicken AV★   3
Allen R   1
Bartlett FL★   1
Beebe RC   1
Birkett RJE★   2
Bishop RJ   9
Bradley J★   13
Brooks NH   1
Burchell GS   1
Busby M★   3
Chitty WS   25
Clayton S★   1
Collier A★   2
Cothliff HT★   10
Cunliffe AJ★   2

Deverall HR   4
Edelston J   1
Edelston M   10
Ferrier R★   1
Fuller C   1
Fullwood J   28
Goldberg L★   20
Gorrie W   5
Hinchliffe T★   5
Hopper AH   2
Jones WH★   20
Joslin PJ★   2
Laird JH★   2
Layton WH   17
Litchfield ER★   1

MacPhee MG   34
Mapson J★   26
Mayes AJ★   1
McCormick JM★   2
McShane H★   1
Mercer J★   6
Milligan GH★   15
Mitchell –★   1
Mogford R★   13
Mullen J★   2
Painter EG★   15
Patterson GL★   21
Penny HC   1
Pescod G★   1
Ratcliffe B★   20

Ross R★   3
Sainsbury WH★   1
Sheppard HH★   1
Simpson –   1
Soo F★   3
Strauss W★   1
Swift FV★   4
Taylor A   1
Tunnicliffe WF★   3
Waller H★   1
Williams S★   6
Young LA   7

Goals (92): MacPhee 35, Chitty 7, Bradley 6, Layton 6, Edelston M 5, Painter 5, Mogford 4, Patterson 4, Cothliff 3, Williams 3, Clayton 2, Cunliffe 2, Deverall 2, Hinchliffe 2, Birkett 1, Busby 1, Laird 1, Mercer 1, Milligan 1, Mitchell 1.

1943–44

Adams W★   5
Ashton –   1
Bishop RJ   2
Bradley J★   16
Burgess R★   1
Busby M★   16
Chitty WS   34
Cox FJA★   2
Dreyer G★   1
Edelston M   20
Fullwood J   27
Goldberg L★   28
Gorrie W   1
Groves –   1

Hardisty JRE★   13
Harrison JC★   12
Hayhurst A   1
Hedley F★   4
Hodgson S★   2
Holliday JW★   1
Hopper AH   6
Iddon H   1
Ireland HW   1
Johnston ACM★   1
Jones WH★   2
Knight J★   1
Lambert R★   7
Layton WH   26

Little –   1
Mackinnon C★   1
MacPhee MG   37
Malcolm AM★   1
Mapson J★   36
Martin EA   1
McFarlane DC★   1
Miller AG★   3
Mogford R★   10
Morris R★   5
Muttitt E★   2
Niblett V   4
Painter EG★   3
Patterson GL★   13

Rojahn OW   2
Rollinson L   1
Smith –   1
Smith EJ★   1
Smith JCR★   1
Soo F★   1
Townend –   1
Watson –   1
Williams C★   17
Williams S★   2
Young LA   28

Goals (98): MacPhee 35, Edleston 14, Williams C 9, Bradley 8, Chitty 6, Layton 5, Patterson 4, Mogford 3, Hardisty 2, Hopper 2, Iddon 2, Ireland 2, Williams S 2, Adams 1, Busby 1, own goals 2.

1944–45

Adams W★   3
Allum LH★   2
Brooks NH   1
Burgess PM   1
Busby M★   13
Chisholm R★   4
Chitty WS   34
Davies DD★   1
Edelston M   20
Fagan W★   14
Fisher F   10
Fisher FT★   19

Fullwood J   28
Garrie D   1
Gillespie –   1
Glidden GS   1
Goldberg L★   19
Hamilton W★   1
Hardisty JRE★   13
Hardwick GFM★   2
Hill R   1
Holton –   1
Howshall T★   2
Ireland HW   3

Langton –   1
Layton WH   27
Lewis D★   1
MacPhee MG   29
Mapson J★   34
McCrohan FAT   1
Niblett V   32
Padgett H   8
Pattison JWP   4
Pond H★   7
Purvis B★   3
Ratcliffe B★   2

Sarney PJ   1
Schwabt H   1
Smith GC   1
Smith R★   1
Wick CJ   1
Williams C★   22
Williams S★   8
Yardley RJ   1
Yates R★   9
Young LA   7

Goals (83): MacPhee 28, Edelston 18, Layton 6, Chitty 4, Fagan 4, Padgett 4, Yates 4, Williams C 3, Chisholm 2, Hardisty 2, Williams S 2, Davies 1, Fisher F 1, Fullwood 1, Hamilton 1, own goals 2.

1945–46

Bishop RJ   3
Bowers F   1
Burgess PM   1
Busby M★   5
Campbell J★   3
Chilton A★   3
Chitty WS   33
Clover W   19
Day A★   1
Deverall HR   7
Duke GE★   9
Edelston M   29
Evans L   1

Fisher F   15
Fisher FT★   3
Fullwood J   1
Galloway J★   7
Glidden GS   27
Gulliver J   12
Hall AE★   1
Hardwick GFM★   2
Heathcote W★   1
Henley L★   3
Higgins C★   1
Houldsworth FC   4
Howshall T★   1

Iddon H★   1
Lane D   4
Lawrence W   9
Layton WH   32
Livingstone A   1
MacPhee MG   35
Marks WG★   12
Marshall E★   3
McCrohan AFT   15
Niblett V   10
Oakes T   1
Pattison JWP   22
Peters P   2

Purvis R★   8
Ratcliffe B   2
Sheppard HH★   1
Sherwood HW   2
Sturgess M   1
Summerfield A   12
Taylor A   2
Todd J★   5
Wallbanks J   14
Williams W   1
Young LA   8

Goals (89): Edelston 28, MacPhee 28, Chitty 6, Glidden 5, Layton 5, Marshall 3, McCrohan 3, Summerfield 3, Fisher F 2, Henley 2, Campbell 1, Galloway 1, Heathcote 1, own goal 1.

FA Cup goals (6): MacPhee 2, Summerfield 2, Edelston 1, Layton 1.

Rochdale

1939–40

Ainsworth R★ 4	Earl S★ 1	Livingstone A★ 2	Richardson A 14
Anderson A★ 10	Eastwood J★ 22	McGowan J★ 1	Robertson P 3
Baird T 1	Ellis J★ 2	Neary J 2	Robinson A★ 3
Burdett T★ 2	Ferguson A 1	Nevin GW 1	Robson E 2
Byrom W 7	Hall J★ 6	Olsen TB★ 13	Shadwell J★ 1
Carey WJ★ 12	Halton RL★ 1	Pearce J 17	Smith T★ 4
Carter DFA★ 3	Harker W 8	Pollard H 2	Sneddon T 7
Chadwick C★ 1	Haworth R 1	Prest TW 4	Steele EC★ 3
Chester T★ 5	Hunt SW★ 2	Rawlings JSD★ 3	Taylor J 7
Colquhoun DM 5	Jones GT★ 1	Redwood DJ 1	Vause PG 7
Duff J 25	Keenan W 3	Reynolds W 2	Warburton A★ 17
Dutton T 13	Kilsby R 3	Rhodes R 3	Wynn J 17

Goals (40): Richardson 14, Wynn 5, Duff 3, Dutton 3, Ainsworth 2, Burdett 2, Hunt 2, Livingstone 2, Anderson 1, Carter 1, Harker 1, Olsen 1, Rawlings 1, Reynolds 1, Vause 1.

War Cup goals (10): Duff 4, Colquhoun 1, Eastwood 1, Pearce 1, Prest 1, Redwood 1, Richardson 1.

1940–41

Ainsworth A★ 3	Farrow GH★ 1	Isherwood D★ 1	Sidebottom W★ 17
Bellis A★ 8	Fenton M★ 1	Johnson J★ 1	Smith TS★ 19
Byrom W★ 2	Graham W★ 2	Jones T★ 18	Sneddon T 6
Carey WJ★ 5	Hall J★ 28	Keen ERL★ 19	Sutherland HR★ 1
Chew J★ 1	Harker W 3	Kershaw V 5	Taylor JT★ 4
Clarke – 1	Harrison J 1	Kirkham N★ 5	Taylor P 11
Colquhoun DM★ 1	Haworth R 2	Mountford RC★ 4	Turner LA★ 4
Connor J★ 17	Heyes K 1	Neary J 4	Vause PG 6
Cunliffe JN★ 11	Horrabin W 9	Rawlings JSD★ 19	Walkden F 1
Duff J 26	Horton L 6	Reeday M★ 1	Warburton A★ 7
Dutton T 21	Hughes A★ 1	Robinson JJ★ 1	Wood J 3
Eastwood E★ 3	Hunt GS★ 5	Rothwell B★ 1	Wynn J 2
Eastwood J 30	Hunt SW★ 18	Seddon H 7	

Goals (67): Sidebottom 11, Horrabin 9, Hunt S 9, Duff 7, Cunliffe 6, Rawlings 5, Dutton 3, Taylor P 3, Bellis 2, Ainsworth 1, Eastwood J 1, Harrison 1, Haworth 1, Jones 1, Kershaw 1, Seddon 1, Taylor J 1, Vause 1, Wood 1, Wynn 1, own goal 1.

1941–42

Ainsworth A★ 2	Duff J 26	Jones J★ 2	Swinburne TA★ 5
Ancell RFD★ 1	Dutton T 1	Jones V★ 9	Taylor P 15
Barker J★ 1	Eastwood J 3	Kirkman R 1	Thorpe JA 5
Bartholomew W★ 6	France F 1	Mangham W★ 2	Toser EW★ 1
Bellis A★ 1	Gorman W★ 8	McFadyen W★ 2	Treanor J★ 30
Boulter LM★ 1	Hall J★ 4	Middleton – 1	Walsh W★ 3
Byrom W★ 4	Hanna S★ 1	Neary J 16	Webster R★ 7
Chesters A★ 2	Haworth R 1	Patton SA 3	Whittaker W★ 3
Colquhoun DM★ 23	Horrabin W 8	Pitt C 6	Whitworth H★ 1
Cunliffe JN★ 24	Horton J★ 9	Richmond G★ 5	Wood J 2
Cutting SW 6	Horton L 3	Robson E 10	Wood R 2
Davenport A 5	Hunt SW 1	Shields J★ 3	Wright F★ 3
Davies A★ 1	John WR★ 2	Smith F 11	
Delaney R 1	Jones D 9	Smith J 1	
Dooley TD★ 15	Jones DOE[A] 1	Sneddon T 21	

Goals (51): Cunliffe 13, Jones D 7, Colquhoun 5, Duff 5, Jones V 5, Bartholomew 4, Dooley 2, Taylor 2, Ancell 1, Cutting 1, Horrabin 1, Hunt 1, Smith F 1, Treanor 1, Webster 1, Wright 1.

1942–43

Barker J* 2	Curran F* 1	Horton L 3	Smith TM* 2
Bartholomew R* 5	Cutting SW* 7	Hunt SW* 4	Sneddon T 11
Bebb D 5	Dooley TE* 4	Jones A* 1	Strong JG* 28
Blood JF 3	Duff J 16	Jones DLG 15	Sweeney FT* 1
Bradford L* 34	Duffy R 11	Jones T* 12	Taylor P* 1
Breakwell T 17	Eastwood J 3	Jones V* 4	Thompson – 1
Brown – 2	Folds W 1	Manning J* 1	Thorpe J 1
Burnicle WF 1	France F 1	Marsh F* 2	Treanor J* 2
Byrom W* 8	Gallimore F* 6	Miller N* 1	Walton G* 5
Chesters A 2	Garfoot A 1	Murphy G* 4	Webb – 1
Cload H 8	Gee H* 19	Neary J 8	Whalley – 1
Collinge A 1	Goodall EI* 3	Palfreman H 3	Wildsmith T 7
Colquhoun DM* 8	Harker J 13	Richmond G* 9	Wood E 26
Cornwell E* 1	Hornby R* 1	Richmond N 1	
Cunliffe JN* 31	Horrabin W 3	Shaw – 1	

Goals (73): Cunliffe 20, Harker 13, Wood 12, Gee 7, Cload 4, Murphy 3, Bartholomew 2, Duff 2, Eastwood 2, Jones D 2, Jones T 2, Bebb 1, Colquhoun 1, Duffy 1, Jones A 1.

1943–44

Banner JE 1	Duff J 35	Joseph AE 1	Redwood DJ 2
Bradford L* 38	Eastwood J 2	Lievesley L* 1	Rudd W 2
Breakwell T 3	Fielding W* 12	Macauley J* 1	Sibley TI* 3
Byrom W* 36	Gallon JW* 1	Maudsley RC 4	Taylor P 9
Carrick R 1	Gee H* 25	McGaitie –* 1	Treanor J* 5
Chesters A* 26	Haigh G 33	Miller W* 7	Warburton A 1
Connor S* 1	Harker J 22	Milligan E 3	Wharton JE* 3
Cornwell E 3	Harrison J 17	Morris E 11	Wildsmith T 14
Cunliffe JN* 21	Horton L 2	Murphy G* 1	Windle C* 1
Davies R* 1	Jones J* 1	Neary J 3	Wood E 37
Dooley TE* 3	Jones T 21	O'Mahony M 3	

Goals (83): Harker 25, Wood 14, Gee 11, Cunliffe 9, Duff 5, Harrison 5, Morris 4, Sibley 3, Haigh 2, Taylor 2, Mulligan 1, Redwood 1, Wharton 1, Windle 1.

Includes one extra-time goal.

1944–45

Acton H 2	Cornwall E 29	Higham J* 1	Pearce J 1
Ainsworth A* 7	Cunliffe AJ* 3	Hughes AL* 1	Pickstock S* 1
Ainsworth W* 6	Cunliffe JN* 3	Hunt SW* 1	Reid J 12
Atkinson K 2	Davies R* 1	Jones G* 3	Reynolds W 18
Bailey A* 1	Duff J 38	Jones J* 15	Roberts S* 3
Banner JE 1	Eastwood J 3	Jones T 8	Seddon H* 1
Bate J* 1	Foxton JD* 1	Keenan W 1	Strachan D* 6
Bradley J* 1	Gallon JW* 22	Lowe H* 6	Taylor J* 1
Bradshaw J 2	Gastall J 2	Lyons G* 5	Taylor P 2
Brinton JV* 2	Gemmell J* 3	Macaulay J 1	Thorpe W* 1
Byrom W* 18	Griffiths A 1	Makin S 11	Treanor J* 7
Chambers J* 1	Grimsditch W 7	Malam A* 2	Whittaker F* 7
Chaney A 1	Haigh G 24	Maugham W 1	Whittle W* 1
Chesters A* 26	Hall HHC* 2	Morris E 9	Wilson CM* 1
Cochrane D 2	Hanson AJ* 4	Muir M 15	Wood E 4
Cochrane T 4	Harker J 4	Mycock A* 2	Woods W* 2
Cole GD* 1	Harrison J 4	Neary J 24	Wotherspoon J 1
Constantine J 10	Hesketh –* 1	Olive F* 1	Young J 2

Goals (52): Reid 6, Gallon 5, Morris 5, Hanson 4, Ainsworth W 3, Constantine 3, Duff 3, Jones J 3, Reynolds 3, Wood 3, Makin 2, Acton 1, Brinton 1, Cochrane D 1, Cochrane T 1, Haigh 1, Hunt 1, Pickstock 1, Roberts 1, Taylor P 1, Young 1, own goals 2.

1945–46

Ashbridge K 3	Hanson AJ⋆ 13	Lunn G⋆ 1	Richardson –⋆ 1
Bawn S 1	Hargreaves J 23	Makin S 19	Robert WE 5
Birch JW 11	Harker J 1	McCormick JM 28	Rodi J 7
Breedon J⋆ 4	Higham J 1	Meek J⋆ 4	Smith T⋆ 1
Brindle J 17	Howshall J 1	Molloy P⋆ 4	Sneddon T 15
Byrom W⋆ 5	Hurst C⋆ 5	Muir R 1	Taylor F 1
Chesters A 13	Jackson L 5	Neary J 6	Toseland E 3
Constantine J 3	Jones A 12	Neilson R⋆ 3	Walmsley J⋆ 1
Cunliffe A 29	Jones G⋆ 4	Nuttall H 1	Whittle W 4
Dobson J 5	Jones JT⋆ 2	Olive F 3	Wood E 25
Duff J 18	Keddie J⋆ 1	Partridge D 14	Woods W 12
Griffiths R 1	Kindred J⋆ 1	Pearce J 16	Yates R 1
Haigh G 3	Kirk J 5	Pomphrey EA 29	
Hamilton W⋆ 2	Livesey J⋆ 1	Reid J 1	

Goals (78): Hargreaves 18, Wood 9, Brindle 8, Hanson 7, Cunliffe 5, Makin 5, Rodi 5, Constantine 4, Duff 4, Jones A 3, Toseland 2, Livesey 1, McCormick 1, Meek 1, Reid 1, Taylor 1, Woods 1, own goals 2.

FA Cup goals (12): Hargreaves 6, Brindle 1, Cunliffe 1, Makin 1, Reynolds 1, Wood 1, Woods 1.

Rotherham United

1939–40

Armitage LG★ 1	Clarke JH 11	Hooper M 19	Sleight H 17
Barlow H★ 1	Cook S 19	Killourhy M★ 1	Stanbridge G 5
Bastow R 18	Courts F 23	Mills J 22	Tootill GA★ 1
Birkett WC 17	Dawson JR 3	Murray W 3	Wadsworth CE 2
Bramham A 19	Greaves G★ 1	Newton H 2	Westley CT 23
Brotherton G 6	Hainsworth L 9	Oxborough R 1	White F★ 1
Charnley J 1	Hanson F 22	Reid JF 1	Wilkinson C 4

Goals (29): Bramham 8, Bastow 5, Hanson 4, Hooper 3, Brotherton 2, Hainsworth 2, Wadsworth 2, Armitage 1, Barlow 1, Mills 1.

War Cup goals (1): Brotherton 1.

1940–41

Armitage LG 3	Challinor J★ 1	Mills J 30	Stamps JD★ 10
Barlow H★ 1	Charnley J 27	Montgomery P 1	Stanbridge G 1
Barnes J 30	Clarke JH 5	Morris A★ 1	Wadsworth CE 8
Bastow R 6	Courts F 28	Murray W 12	Westley CT 27
Bradford D 1	Gold W★ 5	Myers JH★ 6	Westwood HJ 16
Bramham A 24	Hainsworth L 7	Newton H 7	Wilkinson C 3
Brotherton G 3	Hanson F 24	Purdy W 17	
Buckley K 1	Hooper M 3	Sleight H 21	
Carr FJ 5	Mills B 6	Sobkowiak F 1	

Goals (51): Bramham 15, Westwood 10, Hanson 5, Wadsworth 5, Stamps 4, Mills J 3, Myers 2, Purdy 2, Armitage 1, Brotherton 1, Carr 1, Newton 1, own goal 1.

1941–42

Ardron W 14	Clarke JH 18	Mills J 32	Stamps JD★ 16
Barrett JA 3	Courts F 27	Morris A★ 1	Styles W 20
Bastow R 5	Dillon FR★ 1	Morton A★ 1	Turner BA 1
Bodle H★ 3	Gold W★ 7	Myers JH★ 33	Wadsworth CE 8
Bramham A 1	Guest G 1	Newton H 3	Wale J 7
Brown W 5	Haigh KJ 25	Quinton W★ 1	Wilcox GE★ 15
Burns – 1	Hainsworth L 17	Roberts J 1	Wilson A★ 1
Carr FJ 23	Hanson F 32	Robinson J★ 1	
Catlin S★ 1	Hooper M 2	Shaw W★ 2	
Charnley J 27	Larkin JP 4	Sleight H 3	

Goals (65): Ardron 16, Myers 8, Hainsworth 7, Hanson 7, Clarke 6, Stamps 4, Wadsworth 4, Carr 3, Haigh 2, Hooper 2, Mills 2, Brown 1, Burns 1, own goals 2.

1942–43

Ardron W 28	Dixon E 1	Mills J 34	Tomlinson CC★ 28
Armitage LG 1	Forde J 5	Moralee M★ 3	Turton C 4
Bastow R 2	Forde S★ 6	Myers JH★ 4	Wadsworth CE 1
Beighton E 1	Gadsby KJ★ 1	Nairn J★ 1	Westley CT 3
Boulton E 2	Haigh KJ 29	Owens MR★ 1	Wilcox GE★ 4
Burke R★ 1	Hainsworth L 17	Raynor F★ 19	Wilkinson C 36
Carr FJ 30	Hanson F 34	Shaw W★ 1	Williams HO 16
Charnley J 6	Healey JR 1	Shepherd C 1	Woffinden RS★ 5
Clarke JH 29	Hooper M 2	Smith H 2	Wright S 1
Cocker J★ 1	Humphries H 1	Stanbridge G 1	
Courts F 24	Johnson GE★ 2	Thompson D★ 1	
Dawson JR 3	Larkin JP 2	Tighe A 1	

Goals (56): Ardron 14, Hainsworth 8, Raynor 6, Carr 5, Clarke 5, Mills 4, Hanson 3, Tomlinson 2, Burke 1, Dawson 1, Haigh 1, Hooper 1, Myers 1, Owens 1, Shepherd 1, own goals 2.

County Cup final second leg scorers Ardron 3, Forde S 1 and Mills 1.

1943–44

Ardron W 38	Cocker J★ 1	Hogg F★ 2	Waller H 17
Asquith B★ 1	Cook S 16	Hurd H 2	Webster H 4
Austin R 1	Courts F 28	Makey JW 1	Wildman FR★ 2
Barton H★ 19	Epworth J★ 1	McDonald JC★ 2	Wilkinson C 7
Bastow R 6	Forde J 7	Mills J 33	Williams DT 33
Bodle H★ 2	Grainger D★ 1	Moralee M★ 33	Williams HO 37
Bradley GJ★ 1	Guest G 1	Nightingale K 7	Williams J 4
Brown G 2	Haigh KJ 8	Quinton W★ 1	Wilson A★ 2
Carr FJ 4	Hainsworth L 1	Sleight H 23	
Clarke JH 4	Hanson F 38	Tomlinson CC★ 39	

Goals (92): Ardron 37, Moralee 16, Tomlinson 12, Barton 8, Waller 4, Mills 3, Wilson 3, McDonald 2, Nightingale 2, Austin 1, Bastow 1, Hanson 1, Williams D 1, own goal 1.

1944–45

Ardron W 38	Dawson JR 10	Lennon AV 4	Walker A★ 1
Austin R 5	Edwards JF 7	McDonald JC★ 1	Ward H 2
Barton H★ 30	Fletcher RA 1	Mills J 34	Warnes G 5
Bolton R 6	Forde J 3	Moralee M★ 11	Westley CT 3
Bradley J★ 1	Grainger D★ 4	Shaw JS 4	Wilcox GE★ 1
Bramley E★ 1	Gregory FC★ 27	Shaw R 1	Williams DT 37
Carr FJ 10	Hanson F 38	Sinclair TM★ 24	Williams HO 38
Chafer J 16	Hargreaves WO 1	Sleight H 24	Williams J 4
Courts F 6	Howe LF★ 1	Smith C★ 6	
Cowles J 3	Kearney P 9	Stamps JD★ 1	

Goals (72): Ardron 29, Barton 12, Hanson 5, Shaw J 5, Chafer 4, Moralee 3, Dawson 2, Sinclair 2, Smith 2, Austin 1, Carr 1, Cowles 1, Grainger 1, Gregory 1, Kearney 1, Lennon 1, Mills 1.

1945–46

Ardron W 31	Gregory FC★ 5	Mills J 34	Whittam E 4
Armitage LG 1	Guest G 8	Moore HA 1	Wildman FR★ 4
Burke RJ★ 16	Hainsworth L 5	Nightingale K 21	Williams DT 25
Courts F 4	Hanson F 36	Selkirk J 22	Williams HO 35
Dawson JR 32	Hargreaves WO 1	Shaw JS 28	Williams J 3
Edwards JF 10	Hooper M 4	Shaw R 17	Wilson A★ 1
Forde J 2	Kearney P 17	Warnes G 29	

Goals (98): Ardron 27, Shaw J 15, Burke 13, Kearney 8, Williams D 8, Shaw R 7, Nightingale 6, Dawson 5, Mills 5, Guest 1, Hainsworth 1, Hooper 1, own goal 1.

FA Cup goals (12): Ardron 3, Kearney 2, Nightingale 2, Shaw J 2, Dawson 1, Shaw R 1, own goal 1.

Sheffield United

1939–40

Atkin WH 3	Hagan J 15	King J 1	Smith J 17
Barton H 7	Hampson H 2	Latham H 3	Thompson CM 3
Carr J 5	Henson GH 4	Marsden A 2	Tootill GA 4
Chafer J* 1	Hutchinson JA 1	Pickering J 17	Watt-Smith DS 1
Collindridge C 18	Jackson E 21	Reid R 3	White F 2
Cox AEH 15	Jeffries A 14	Rickett W 5	Windle W 4
Eggleston A 11	Jenkinson F* 7	Settle A 22	Young RH 15
Fulford JH 2	Johnson T 19	Sheen J 9	

Goals (49): Pickering 12, Collindridge 10, Hagan 8, Sheen 4, Jeffries 3, Henson 2, Barton 1, Eggleston 1, Hampson 1, Jackson 1, Marsden 1, Rickett 1, Thompson 1, own goals 3.

War Cup goals (4): Collindridge 1, Jackson 1, Rickett 1, Thompson 1.

1940–41

Archer W 7	Jackson E 18	Pickering J 33	Thompson CM 3
Boot E* 1	Jeffries A 31	Rickett W 29	Tootill GA 1
Brook H 2	Jenkinson F* 20	Settle A 29	Watt-Smith DS 1
Butcher L* 1	Johnson T 26	Sheen J 1	White F 18
Collindridge C 22	Latham H 30	Shimwell E 1	Whitham F 1
Eggleston A 10	Lord G 1	Shirtliff N 1	Windle W 1
Epworth J 1	Machent SC 28	Smith J 15	Wright R 1
Furniss F 1	Marsden A 6	Steele FC* 1	Young RH 18
Hagan J 2	Nightingale A 1	Stevens H 1	

Goals (58): Pickering 9, Machent 8, Collindridge 6, Eggleston 6, Jackson 5, Jeffries 5, Rickett 5, Thompson 5, Hagan 3, Settle 2, Steele 1, Watt-Smith 1, Young 1, own goal 1.

1941–42

Archer W 34	Jackson E 2	Nightingale A 13	Stone J 1
Barker TG 19	Jeffries A 3	Owens MR 1	Thompson CM 10
Barton H 32	Jenkinson F* 20	Parkin HB 1	Thompson D 4
Brook H 1	Keeton F 6	Pickering J 34	Watt-Smith DS 2
Churchill T 1	King J 1	Reid R 1	Webster R 5
Eggleston A 6	Laking GE* 1	Rickett W 31	White F 29
Froggatt AG 1	Latham H 35	Rossington K 3	Winstanley DA 6
Furniss F 5	Machent SC 32	Settle A 3	Young RH 18
Hagan J 3	Marsden A 2	Sheen J 1	
Hampson H 14	Millership W* 1	Smith J 3	

Goals (78): Rickett 15, Pickering 14, Thompson C 11, Barton 8, Hampson 5, Machent 5, Young 4, Keeton 3, Watt-Smith 3, Winstanley 3, Nightingale 2, Hagan 1, Jeffries 1, Sheen 1, own goals 2.

1942–43

Archer W 33	Hagan J 4	Nightingale A 28	Smith H 1
Barker TG 4	Jackson E 29	Owens MR 2	Smith J 5
Barton H 30	Jeffries A 3	Parkin HB 28	Staniforth H 1
Bradley G* 2	Jenkinson F* 13	Pickering J 27	Stone J 4
Brook H 2	Latham H 32	Rhodes P 2	Thompson CM 28
Churchill T 2	Lee K 1	Rickett W 35	Thompson D 2
Collindridge C 2	Machent SC 3	Rossington K 4	Watt-Smith DS 12
Eggleston A 5	Marsden A 1	Settle A 4	White F 28
Furniss F 6	Marshall E* 2	Sheen J 20	Young RH 2

Goals (88): Thompson C 19, Barton 14, Nightingale 14, Pickering 11, Rickett 9, Stone 6, Watt-Smith 3, Collindridge 2, Jackson 2, Machent 2, Brook 1, Jeffries 1, Owens 1, Sheen 1, own goals 2.

1943–44

Archer W 34	Curry R 6	Nelson G 1	Smith J 2
Baker GS 17	Eggleston A 1	Nettleship R 1	Stone J 1
Barker TG 3	Furniss F 28	Nightingale A 35	Thompson CM 18
Barton H 9	Hagan J 2	Parkin FW 2	Thompson D 3
Brook H 3	Hooper HR 1	Parkin HB 27	Watt-Smith DS 1
Buckley WE 1	Jackson E 23	Pickering J 34	White F 35
Burton E 1	Jones GH 1	Rickett W 36	Young RH 4
Christopher JW 4	Latham H 36	Rossington K 7	
Collindridge C 5	Machent SC 6	Sheen J 12	
Cox AEH 9	Matthews JB 13	Shephard G 7	

Goals (83): Thompson C 18, Nightingale 17, Pickering 12, Baker 6, Rickett 6, Collindridge 5, Barton 4, Jackson 3, Matthews 3, Brook 1, Christopher 1, Curry 1, Furniss 1, Hagan 1, Jones 1, Parkin H 1, Sheen 1, Thompson D 1.

1944–45

Archer W 33	Gadsby KJ★ 1	Nettleton E 4	Shephard G 16
Barclay R★ 8	Grainger D★ 1	Newton W 2	Shepherd H★ 1
Bower K 4	Hewitt R 2	Nightingale A 34	Smith J 24
Braddock J 1	Hunt H 4	Owens MR 2	Smith J★ 1
Brook H 5	Hutchinson JA 3	Parkin H 2	Swift HM★ 1
Buckley WE 1	Jackson E 26	Parkin HB 3	Thompson CM 6
Calverley A★ 2	Johnston FJ★ 1	Pickering J 23	Thompson D 1
Colley D 1	Jones GH 3	Poole CJ★ 1	Thorpe S 2
Collindridge C 7	Latham H 35	Poole G 2	Tootill GA 11
Cox AEH 1	Lemons CF 1	Pridmore WH 5	Warhurst R 9
Curry R 13	Machent SC 2	Regan RH 1	Whitaker W★ 1
Dale C 8	Matthews JB 2	Rickett W 30	White F 16
Dewis G★ 3	McClelland ML 1	Rossington K 4	Young RH 1
Forbes AR 21	Milburn JET★ 1	Scott L★ 2	
Furniss F 42	Nelson G 22	Shaw J 2	

Goals (83): Nightingale 16, Pickering 13, Forbes 10, Rickett 6, Barclay 5, Curry 5, Brook 4, Jones 4, Dewis 3, Furniss 3, Thompson C 3, Dale 2, Hunt 2, Warhurst 2, Bower 1, Collindridge 1, Grainger 1, Thompson D 1, own goal 1.

1945–46

Brook H 16	Hutchinson JA 10	Pickering J 11	Thompson CM 15
Collindridge C 19	Jackson E 20	Reid R 16	Thompson D 1
Cox AEH 4	Jones GH 26	Rickett W 39	Tootill GA 9
Forbes AR 33	Knott H★ 5	Sheen J 3	Troth J 1
Furniss F 38	Latham H 40	Shephard G 1	Warhurst R 1
Hagan J 12	Machent SC 19	Shimwell E 34	White F 1
Hooper HR 6	Nightingale A 41	Smith J 41	

Goals (112): Nightingale 22, Rickett 15, Jones 13, Collindridge 12, Thompson C 9, Hutchinson 9, Reid 6, Hagan 5, Knott 5, Brook 4, Pickering 3, Machent 2, Cox 1, Forbes 1, Hooper 1, Shimwell 1, Thompson D 1, own goals 2.

FA Cup goals (6): Collindridge 4, Brook 1, Jones 1.

Sheffield Wednesday

1939–40

Ashley JA   23
Burrows H   17
Catlin AE   11
Collett E★   9
Dillon FR   3
Driver A   8
Ellison R★   1
Fallon WJ   2

Hanford H   7
Hoyle G★   6
Hunt DA   12
Lester FC   6
Lewis I   2
Lowes AR   7
Massarella L   13
Millership W   16

Morton A   8
Mulraney A★   4
Napier CE   3
Packard E   8
Pickering WH   6
Robinson J   4
Rogers A   2
Russell DW   20

Schofield E   2
Smith RL   15
Thompson J   8
Toseland E   7
Walker F   5
Ward TA   18

Goals (36): Millership 8, Ward 6, Driver 4, Thompson J 4, Hoyle 3, Hunt 3, Massarella 2, Napier 2, Burrows 1, Dillon 1, Lowes 1, Schofield 1.

War Cup goals (6): Napier 3, Hunt 2, Massarella 1.

1940–41

Ashley JA   22
Burgin M★   5
Burrows H   29
Catlin AE   1
Cockroft J★   15
Curry R   7
Davis A   4
Driver A   2

Drury GB★   12
Gill L   15
Herbert F   7
Johnson T★   1
Lowes AR   2
Massarella L   16
Millership W   27
Morton A   25

Packard E   3
Pickering WH   29
Robinson J   10
Roebuck N   12
Rogers A   10
Russell DW   2
Schofield E   27
Smith A   1

Smith RL   2
Starling RW★   2
Thompson J   24
Thompson R   9
Turner B   5
Ward TA   19
Westlake FA   5
Wynn J★   2

Goals (52): Thompson J 16, Ward 9, Robinson 8, Schofield 4, Drury 2, Massarella 2, Starling 2, Thompson R 2, Burgin 1, Curry 1, Lowes 1, Millership 1, Rogers 1, Wynn 1, own goal 1.

1941–42

Armeson LR★   1
Ashley JA   13
Burgin M★   11
Burrows H   1
Catlin AE   3
Cockroft J★   33
Driver A   5
Drury GB★   18
Gill L   4

Hanks CW★   3
Herbert F   29
Howsam AD   6
Jones TB★   1
Laking GE★   24
Lane REL   1
Lowes AR   6
McCabe G   6
Melling F   24

Millership W   31
Morton A   21
Nelson B   5
Packard E   3
Padgett H   4
Pickering WH   22
Robinson J   8
Roebuck N   13
Rogers A   21

Schofield E   7
Smith A   2
Smith RL   6
Swift HM   2
Thompson J   20
Walker CJ   2
Ward TA   2
Westlake FA   3
Wynn J★   2

Goals (55): Melling 12, Burgin 8, Thompson J 8, Robinson 7, Rogers 5, Drury 3, Howsam 3, Cockroft 2, Nelson 2, Driver 1, Lowes 1, Millership 1, Roebuck 1, Schofield 1.

1942–43

Ardron W★   2
Ashley JA   35
Burgin M★   5
Catlin AE   37
Cockroft J★   37
Driver A   1
Everitt RE   2

Froggatt R   1
Gadsby KJ★   1
Gill L   9
Hainsworth L★   1
Herbert F   16
Laking GE★   1
Lowes AR   1

Melling F   31
Millership W   38
Morton A   36
Reynolds W★   38
Robinson J   32
Rogers A   1
Russell DW   16

Smith J★   2
Swift HM   38
Thompson J   32
Thompson R   2
Ward TA   1
Westlake FA   2

Goals (104): Robinson 35, Melling 23, Thompson J 14, Burgin 8, Cockroft 6, Reynolds 6, Swift 5, Thompson R 2, Ardron 1, Everitt 1, Millership 1, own goals 2.

1943–44

Ashley JA 27	Everitt RE 2	Massarella L 7	Swift HM 17
Barton H* 4	Fox O 9	McCarter JJ 1	Thompson J 8
Beddows J 3	Froggatt R 23	Millership W 23	Thompson R 2
Briscoe J 1	Gadsby S 2	Morton A 9	Wakley IJ 2
Brown WJ 1	Goodson H 3	Napier CE 1	Ward TA 7
Burton S* 3	Hall A 1	Pickering WH 7	Westlake FA 13
Catlin AE 33	Herbert F 28	Poulston L 1	Wilkinson N* 7
Cockroft J* 33	Hinsley G* 1	Reynolds W* 19	Wiseman K 1
Curnow J* 6	Hunt DA 1	Robinson J 18	Woodhead D 1
Donaldson HA* 7	Ibbotson W 5	Rogers A 26	Wright H* 19
Driver A 4	Laking GE* 1	Russell DW 22	
Drury W 4	Lowes AR 3	Schofield E 2	

Goals (61): Robinson 12, Rogers 10, Wright 9, Ward 5, Massarella 4, Driver 3, Froggatt 3, Reynolds 3, Ashley 2, Cockroft 2, Thompson J 2, Barton 1, Beddows 1, Fox 1, Millership 1, Russell 1, Swift 1.

1944–45

Ashley JA 4	Froggatt R 23	Massarella L 14	Thompson J 12
Bannister K 2	Gadsby S 7	Medhurst HE* 2	Thompson R 2
Bates GR 9	Gale T 9	Millership W 20	Tomlinson CC 43
Beach D* 2	Goodson H 9	Parkin FW 10	Turton C 23
Calverley A* 1	Hanford H 1	Pickering WH 34	Wakley IJ 12
Catlin AE 9	Hawkeswell JC 9	Robinson J 16	Ward TA 17
Cockroft J* 43	Herbert F 12	Rogers A 22	Westlake FA 1
Donaldson HA 3	Ibbotson W 3	Schofield E 1	White F* 8
Driver A 5	Kippax DH 1	Smith J* 1	Wright F* 5
Fisher S* 1	Lindsay JM 15	Stewart R 1	
Fox O 23	Lowes AR 1	Swift HM 37	

Goals (87): Tomlinson 14, Lindsay 13, Robinson 12, Rogers 11, Massarella 7, Thompson J 6, Froggatt 5, Hawkeswell 5, Herbert 3, Ward 2, Bates 1, Catlin 1, Cockroft 1, Fox 1, Ibbotson 1, Lowes 1, Schofield 1, Thompson R 1, Turton 1.

1945–46

Aveyard W 1	Hunt DA 5	Pickering WH 30	Turton C 29
Cockroft J 36	Kippax DH 11	Robinson J 21	Wakley IJ 2
Driver A 10	Lindsay JM 32	Rogers A 14	Wands AMD 17
Fox O 6	Lowes AR 2	Smith RL 1	Ward TA 14
Froggatt R 33	MacKenzie ML 2	Swift HM 42	Westlake FA 12
Gale T 30	McCarter JJ 3	Thompson J 5	
Goodfellow DO 22	Morton A 17	Thompson R 12	
Goodson H 1	Packard E 10	Tomlinson CC 42	

Goals (67): Robinson 17, Lindsay 12, Froggatt 8, Tomlinson 7, Rogers 5, Thompson J 3, Thompson R 3, Ward 3, Cockroft 2, Driver 2, Hunt 2, Fox 1, Kippax 1, Wands 1.

FA Cup goals (16): Tomlinson 4, Driver 3, Froggatt 3, Thompson J 3, Aveyard 2, Ward 1.

Southampton

1939–40

Affleck DR 3
Allen JP★ 5
Barry P 2
Bates ET 30
Bernard J★ 2
Bevis WE 7
Bewley D★ 1
Bradley J 32
Briggs F 30
Brophy HF 1
Buckley J 7
Burgess H★ 1
Collett E★ 1
Compton LH★ 1
Creecy A★ 2
Dean CG★ 2

Dodgin W 10
Emanuel T 3
Gilmour GR 3
Hapgood EA★ 2
Harris J 33
Hassell TW 19
Hayhurst A★ 1
Higham N 2
Holt AG 31
Hopper L★ 2
Jones LJ★ 2
Joy B★ 1
Kelly G 1
Kiernan T★ 1
Laney LC 6
Logie JT★ 1

McGibbon D 16
Mordey HV 7
Noyce LA 1
Osman HJ★ 10
Parkin R 2
Perez R★ 3
Perfect FT 2
Perrett RF 16
Pitts H★ 1
Roles AG★ 8
Roper DG★ 1
Roy JR★ 2
Salter J★ 1
Sanders JA★ 1
Scott JR 1
Smith C★ 1

Smith G 22
Spence R★ 1
Stroud WJA 1
Sykes J★ 1
Targett AN★ 4
Tennant AE★ 1
Tomlinson RW 2
Vaux E★ 1
Walsh W★ 1
Warhurst SL 33
Weaver S★ 1
Webber EV 36
West HC 2
Wilkinson CE★ 4
Williams FA 1

Goals (74): Bradley 21, Bates 13, Briggs 11, McGibbon 7, Hassell 3, Holt 3, Perrett 3, Higham 2, Osman 2, Roy 2, Webber 2, Bevis 1, Dodgin 1, Gilmour 1, Logie 1, own goal 1.

War Cup goals (2): Bates 1, Osman 1.

1940–41

Angell R 4
Barry P 30
Bates ET 11
Brophy HF 1
Creecy A 28
Cummins A 2
Dean CG 1
Eckford J 3
Ellerington W 10

Fisher KW 9
Fox G 9
Harris J★ 31
Harris N 3
Hassell TW 32
Higham N 3
Hooper S★ 2
House AG 6
Laney L 19

Lanham H 5
Lewis J 1
McSweeney T 4
Mee B 16
Messom G 14
Noss R 3
Permain A 9
Perrett RF 2
Roles AG 19

Roper DG 28
Salter R 2
Smith C 9
Southern L 1
Stroud WJA 22
White CJ 23
White LA 1

Goals (57): Roper 12, Stroud 11, Hassell 10, Laney 6, Harris J 4, Bates 3, Dean 2, Mee 2, Smith C 2, Fox 1, Harris N 1, Messom 1, White L 1, own goal 1.

1941–42

Abbott D 1
Affleck DR 4
Barnes W★ 3
Bernard EG 9
Bidewell S★ 7
Bryant S★ 1
Creecy A 14
Ellerington W★ 21
Ellis EH 1

Fisher KW 8
Fox G 1
Hankey C★ 3
Harris J★ 21
Harris N 2
Hassell TW 15
Higham N 8
Houldsworth FC★ 9
House AG 1

Howard B 2
Laney L 21
Lanham H 2
McGibbon D 1
Messom G 6
Middleton AG 1
Perrett RF 2
Roles AG 19
Rolfe A★ 1

Roper DG 22
Smith FJ 1
Smith VJ 3
Stroud WJA 21
Tait T★ 10
Young RG★ 1

Goals (54): Roper 21, Tait 6, Higham 5, Howard 4, Laney 4, Harris J 3, Hassell 3, Ellerington 2, Stroud 2, Bidewell 1, Creecy 1, Fisher 1, own goal 1.

1942–43

Barnes W★ 28
Bates ET 30
Bevis W 1
Buchanan PS★ 10
Bushby TW★ 1
Creecy A 7
Cruickshank J 2
Davie J★ 2
Ferrier R★ 2

Finney T★ 1
Griffiths M★ 2
Harris J★ 34
Harris N 1
Hassell TW 10
Houldsworth FC★ 3
Jones JT★ 6
Laney L 8
Light WG 13

Messom G 4
Mitten C★ 21
Pond H★ 18
Rigg T★ 2
Roles AG 31
Roper DG 4
Rothery H★ 11
Rudkin TW★ 3
Stamps JD★ 14

Stroud WJA 31
Tann BJ★ 29
Tomlinson RW 2
Tweedy GJ★ 8
Wardle W★ 3
Whittingham A★ 29
Wright RCA★ 3

Goals (100): Whittingham 31, Barnes 14, Bates 14, Stamps 11, Harris J 10, Mitten 5, Stroud 3, Buchanan 2, Davie 2, Hassell 2, Griffiths 1, Harris N 1, Laney 1, Pond 1, Wardle 1, own goal 1.

1943–44

Affleck DR 1	Crossland B★ 1	Jones JT★ 20	Shimwell E★ 15
Allen JP★ 1	Davie J★ 7	Laney L★ 1	Smith JD★ 1
Almond K 2	Dodgin W 28	Lewis D 1	Sneddon T★ 3
Anderson JC★ 3	Drinkwater J★ 21	Miles AJB 1	Staton N 5
Arnold J★ 1	Eggleston T★ 2	Mitten C★ 1	Stroud WJA 28
Bates ET 35	Evans HA 17	Pond H★ 15	Tann BJ★ 5
Bonass AE★ 3	Fisher F★ 1	Ramsbottom E★ 1	Thomas RA★ 1
Carter VFT 1	Freeman A 1	Ramsey AE 5	Wardle W★ 13
Clements SFT 1	Grant W★ 7	Roles AG 36	Warhurst S 6
Corbett NG★ 4	Halton RL★ 6	Roper DG 36	Webber EV 2
Corbett WH★ 1	Hamilton DS★ 10	Seddon EA★ 3	Whittingham A★ 28
Coupland J★ 3	Houldsworth FC★ 9	Sheppard DF 2	Whitworth H★ 1

Goals (79): Whittingham 27, Roper 19, Bates 8, Davie 4, Stroud 4, Wardle 4, Grant 3, Evans 2, Dodgin 1, Roles 1, Seddon 1, Sheppard 1, Smith 1, Staton 1, own goals 2.

1944–45

Bates ET 36	Evans RG★ 11	Pond H★ 1	Stroud WJA 36
Bradley J 4	Grant W★ 10	Ramsey AE 11	Summerbee GC★ 1
Clements SFT 2	Hassell TW 24	Roberts E 6	Swindin GH★ 1
Corbett NG★ 1	Jones C★ 1	Roles AG 36	Tann BJ★ 2
Dempsey AJ 1	Lonnon C 1	Roper DG 33	Taylor RE★ 2
Dodgin W 30	McDonald JC★ 1	Rothery H★ 1	Walker S★ 13
Dorsett R★ 16	Miles AJB 1	Sheppard DF 1	Warhurst S 21
Eggleston T★ 9	Mills GR★ 7	Stansbridge LEC 14	Whittingham A★ 20
Evans HA 20	Moss F★ 15	Stear JA 7	

Goals (125): Whittingham 26, Dorsett 23, Roper 23, Bates 13, Hassell 8, Bradley 7, Walker 7, Grant 6, Mills 5, Ramsey 4, Stroud 2, Evans H 1.

1945–46

Bates ET 40	Eggleston T★ 5	Kingston A 1	Stansbridge LEC 4
Bevis W 7	Ellerington W 28	McDonald JC★ 1	Stear JA 3
Black J★ 5	Emanuel T 5	McGibbon D 30	Stout L 1
Bradley J 25	Ephgrave G 6	Mountford RC★ 1	Stroud WJA 36
Brooks W★ 1	Evans HA 34	Powell S 1	Veck R 28
Clements SFT 1	Gregory J 3	Ramsey AE 13	Warhurst S 19
Cruickshank J 4	Hancon W★ 1	Roles AG 40	Webber EV 14
Davies M 2	Hassell TW 12	Roper DG 42	Whittingham A★ 1
Day E 2	Heathcote W★ 1	Sibley ET★ 6	Wilkins L 3
Dodgin W 18	Jones JT★ 3	Smith G 15	

Goals (97): McGibbon 27, Bates 14, Bradley 14, Roper 11, Ramsey 7, Evans 6, Veck 5, Hassell 3, Smith 3, Bevis 1, Day 1, Heathcote 1, Stroud 1, own goals 3.

FA Cup goals (9): Bradley 2, McGibbon 2, Bates 1, Bevis 1, Ellerington 1, Roper 1, Veck 1.

Southend United

1939–40

Bell S 39	Holliday JW★ 1	McEwan W★ 1	Sherborne JL★ 1
Black T 3	Jefferson A★ 1	Milne JD 20	Sibley A 28
Blott C 1	Jones C 32	Morris R★ 1	Sidey NW★ 1
Bolan LA 22	Leighton W 24	Morris T★ 4	Singleton EA 1
Bower RWC★ 1	Levine –★ 1	Muttitt E★ 1	Smirk AH 31
Chalkley AG★ 11	Lewis HH★ 4	Ormandy J 36	Tucker C 1
Fairchild CC 4	Lovery JB★ 1	Paryote S★ 1	Walton FH 20
Fuller CE 5	Ludford GA★ 3	Reay EP★ 2	Welsh D★ 1
Hague JK 3	Mackenzie D★ 1	Reeve FW★ 20	Wright JD★ 2
Hankey AE 4	Mangnall D★ 1	Robinson D 30	
Harris A 14	Martin TJ 13	Scott L★ 1	
Hillam CE 35	McCormick J★ 1	Shallcross T 1	

Goals (74): Bell 13, Ormandy 10, Bolan 7, Smirk 7, Ludford 6, Sibley 6, Reeve 5, Martin 3, Robinson 3, Leighton 2, Lewis 2, McCormick 1, McEwan 1, Sherborne 1, Walton 1, own goals 6.

War Cup goals (8): Bell 2, Ormandy 2, Bolan 1, Ludford 1, Sibley 1, Walton 1.

1940–41

Baldry G★ 1	Fuller CE 24	McLuckie JS★ 13	Smirk AH 4
Bell R 1	Galley L 1	Millar NH★ 1	Tidman O 2
Bell S 19	Hillam CE 2	Parry W★ 32	Turton J 11
Bolan LA 2	Hollingsworth H★ 1	Phypers E★ 1	Walsh W★ 1
Burley B 32	Jones C 1	Pierson J★ 1	Walton FH 8
Calland R★ 22	Jones EN★ 6	Pyle L 2	Ward TA★ 1
Chadwick FW★ 2	Jones F★ 25	Rickett HK 31	Wright E 20
Edwards D★ 2	Jones L★ 24	Sibley A 1	
Fieldus S 15	Leighton W 23	Sliman A★ 31	

Goals (71): Jones F 18, Burley 16, Bell S 14, Wright 7, Jones L 5, Chadwick 2, Calland 1, Fieldus 1, Fuller 1, Leighton 1, McLuckie 1, Smirk 1, Walsh 1, Ward 1, own goal 1.

1941–42

Did not compete.

1942–43

Did not compete.

1943–44

Did not compete.

1944–45

Did not compete.

1945–46

Bell S   1
Bell SE   20
Bennett K★   11
Briscoe J★   3
Brown –   1
Burley B★   1
Calder JH   2
Chalkley AG★   2
Conway H   26
Dudley FE   23
Dutton LL★   1
Fairchild CC   1
Ferguson L   4
Gallimore F★   1

Gardiner J   10
Gibson R   20
Gilberg H★   9
Goodyear GW★   9
Harris A   3
Harvey J   12
Hemming JM   2
Hockey E   1
Humphreys RH   15
Jackson H★   9
Jackson RG   31
Jenkins BW   3
Jones C   12
Jones L★   4

Joslin PJ★   1
Lane H   1
Leighton W   8
Linton TNG   3
Macklin J   5
Marshall E★   6
Milne J   9
Montgomery SW★   14
O'Brien JH   1
Oldfield JB★   1
Ormandy J   3
Peters TJ   6
Pierson J   4
Reid C   9

Richards S   2
Robinson J★   1
Savage J   2
Singleton EA   2
Smirk AH   24
Smith EF★   1
Smith W★   5
Squires A★   1
Thompson CA   13
Tippett T   1
Walton FH   32
Whitchurch CH★   2
Wilson J★   1
Woodward H   1

Goals (55): Smirk 9, Thompson 9, Jackson H 7, Dudley 5, Gardiner 3, Gilberg 3, Jenkins 2, Macklin 2, Walton 2, Briscoe 1, Gibson 1, Harris 1, Hockey 1, Jackson R 1, Jones L 1, Marshall 1, Montgomery 1, Peters 1, Richards 1, Singleton 1, Tippett 1, Whitchurch 1.

FA Cup goals (1): Smirk 1.

Southport

1939-40

Colclough W★   1
Davies GMD★   1
Eastham H★   1
Grainger D   22
Grainger J   21
Hamer L   2
Hampson H★   3
Hardy R★   2
Harrison H   19
Hawkins H   4

Hewitt JJ   3
Hill D   1
Hodgkiss R   21
Howard D   3
Hullett W★   1
Hunt SW★   10
Johnson P★   1
Jones R   2
Jordan W   2
Kitchen N★   4

Lewis T   1
Little J★   12
Morris GE★   1
Newcomb LR   7
Patrick JC   6
Preece JC   9
Rawcliffe F★   2
Rothwell J   20
Scott A★   6
Scott RH   18

Sinclair W   3
Spivey R   3
Stapleton A   2
Stevenson H   23
Taylor E★   2
Tomkin AH★   9
Wardle W★   3
Watson JF★   15
Watt J★   6
Wilkie W★   3

Goals (38): Rothwell 10, Watson 6, Hunt 5, Hawkins 3, Patrick 3, Grainger D 2, Hodgkiss 2, Sinclair 2, Hewitt 1, Scott A 1, Spivey 1, Tomkin 1, Wilkie 1.

War Cup goals (4): Patrick 2, Grainger D 1, Rothwell 1.

1940-41

Bradford L★   24
Cropper R   4
Curran F   13
Deverall HR★   10
Dobson TW   4
Dutton T★   1
Eden –   1
Fairclough –   1
Finch R★   8
Grainger D   27
Grainger J   21

Groves K★   9
Hardy R   1
Harker J   16
Harrison H   26
Hodgkiss R   1
Howard D   27
Hullett W★   13
Hunter E   8
Jackson –   1
Johnson J   8
Jones R   17

Kitchen N★   6
Little J★   32
Lowe H   2
Lowe J   1
Meek J★   3
Newcomb LR   26
Norton L   2
Oldfield A★   1
Owens C   5
Peacock T   1
Rimmer R   11

Sanderson JR★   7
Scott A   1
Stevenson H   1
Taylor H★   8
Thompson J★   8
Watt J   14
Woods –★   1
Wright C★   1
Young LA★   2

Goals (76): Hullett 19, Harker 14, Curran 10, Deverall 4, Grainger D 4, Howard 4, Rimmer 4, Newcomb 3, Thompson 3, Finch 2, Owens 2, Sanderson 2, Taylor 2, Watt 1, own goal 1.

1941-42

Blair D★   34
Butler S★   27
Cropper R   1
Cross R★   4
Curran F   10
Davies GMD   3
Deverall HR★   30
Finan RJ★   15
Flack WLW★   12
Grainger D   29

Groves K★   5
Harker J   29
Harrison H   28
Hockaday LN   4
Hodgkiss R   1
Horton JC★   1
Hurman R   2
James W★   1
Johnson J   27
Jones D   1

Jones R   1
King FO   13
Kirby N★   32
Kitchen N★   2
Maudsley RC★   6
McManus J   6
Middleton J   1
Newcomb LR   12
Norton L   9
Owens C   1

Patrick JC   4
Ratcliffe B★   1
Ridyard J   1
Rothwell J   4
Strong GJ★   1
Swinburne TA★   3
Wright R   13

Goals (63): Harker 25, Deverall 16, Grainger D 5, Patrick 4, Rothwell 4, Butler 3, Kirby 2, Curran 1, Finnan 1, Middleton 1, Ridyard 1.

1942-43

Ainsley GE★   9
Ainsworth –   1
Angus A★   1
Aspinall J   2
Ball JA   16
Beardshaw EC★   3
Blair D★   18
Broadhurst I★   1
Butler S★   30
Coats A★   1
Delaney R   6
Deverall HR★   30
Ellis M   1
Evans HWR★   13

Flack WLW★   29
Francis ET★   2
Frost AD★   12
Gibson –   1
Graham DR★   11
Grundy JA★   4
Hargreaves WJ★   2
Harrison H   1
Hooton T   4
Horton JC★   2
Hutton –   1
James –   1
John WR★   12
Johnson J   20

Jones R   6
Jones WM   1
Kesley J   1
King FO   7
Kinsell TA★   2
Kirby N★   30
Kirkham R★   1
Lee JS★   1
Marshall JR★   1
McFarlane J★   1
Millington –★   1
Mitton –   1
Patrick JC   1
Rawcliffe F★   1

Rawlings JSD★   29
Readett H★   1
Rist FH★   17
Roche J★   1
Rothwell J   18
Simpkin J   7
Taylor L★   1
Tennant AW★   5
Tierney W   2
Watson –   1
Weaver –   2
Wildsmith T★   3
Wood R★   6
Wright R   14

Goals (102): Rothwell 24, Deverall 21, Ainsley 10, Rawlings 11, Butler 9, Frost 6, Ball 4, Rothwell 4, Flack 3, Simpkin 3, Coats 1, Kesley 1, Millington 1, Rist 1, Tierney 1, Wood 1, own goal 1.

1943–44

Aspinall J   9
Baker C   1
Banks K   7
Barton C   3
Batey R★   2
Blood JF★   32
Brown G   8
Butler S★   27
Coats A★   11
Conway H★   2
Crawshaw C★   1
Davidson AM★   1
Davidson W   4
Davies A   1

Davies P★   1
Delaney R   2
Dellow RW★   19
Dougal J★   2
Flack WLW★   19
Fraser J   2
Frost AD★   8
Gardner T★   2
Goodyear G★   3
Grainger J   2
Hardy RA   1
Harrison H   1
Hawkins H   16
Hesketh A   1

Hill M★   3
Holdcroft GH★   24
Horton JC★   5
Johnson J   22
Jones J   3
Jordan W   1
King F   3
Kirby N★   29
Marcia –   1
Martin T★   3
Morris C   1
Mutch G★   30
Patrick JC   1
Poole B   2

Pryde RI★   1
Rawcliffe F★   1
Rawlings JSD★   35
Salkie A   1
Savage RE★   2
Setchell AG★   1
Simpkin J   13
Smith M   5
Taylor JG★   5
Tennant JW★   25
Todd H   9
Williams N   1
Woodruff A★   2
Wright R   1

Goals (68): Mutch 14, Hawkins 10, Rawlings 8, Flack 7, Frost 6, Butler 5, Dellow 3, Smith 3, Aspinall 2, Coats 2, Johnson 2, Crawshaw 1, Davidson A 1, Kirby 1, Simpkin 1, Tennant 1, own goal 1.

1944–45

Banks K   7
Barton P★   1
Bentham SJ★   2
Birkett W★   21
Blood JF★   14
Brown G   6
Butler S★   30
Carey WJ★   6
Chiverton EJ★   7
Coats A★   35
Conway E   7
Cook W★   5
Costello –   1
Curwen G★   24
Dellow RW★   30

Gallagher J★   3
Grainger D   1
Gray J   2
Harrison H   1
Hawkins H   5
Hewson –   1
Hilliard WR★   10
Hobson A★   3
Hodgson R★   10
Howshall T★   1
Jones JE★   20
Kemp DJ★   4
Kirby N★   6
Kirkham R★   1
Linacre W★   1

Longdon CW★   1
Lunn G★   5
Makin G★   1
Malam A★   27
Marsh CW★   2
Massam DC   7
McDonnell M★   3
Miller AG★   5
Murray T   7
Mutch G★   4
Newman TF   1
Oakes G   5
Reid JM★   1
Richards D   1
Simms HA★   19

Simpkin J   30
Smith H★   1
Smith S★   1
Snowden R   10
Sperring G★   1
Taylor JG★   1
Thomas W   2
Thompson R   5
Thorpe W★   15
Todd H   4
Underhill C   7
Urmston T   9

Goals (65): Coats 15, Dellow 9, Malam 9, Butler 7, Urmston 7, Simms 5, Massam 3, Mutch 2, Oakes 2, Blood 1, Hawkins 1, Jones 1, Simpkin 1, Snowden 1, Thomas 1.

1945–46

Atherton J   3
Ball JA   2
Banks K   32
Birkett W★   3
Bond A   24
Brown G   8
Carr SR   11
Chiverton E★   1
Clough J   8
Coats A★   7
Gemmell J   34
Goodwin R★   1

Grainger J   11
Grant AF★   6
Green T   2
Grimsditch SW   24
Hanson AJ★   13
Hawkins H   25
Hodgkins R   6
Horsman W   3
Howarth H   25
Hulbert R   15
Johnson P   1
Jones J   6

Kelly L★   4
Linaker J★   2
McGough K   16
Neary J★   2
Oakes A   1
Oakes G   22
Pilling JJ   16
Preece JC   9
Rawcliffe L   4
Reid JM★   1
Robertson H★   1
Rothwell J   4

Shore A   1
Simpkin J   8
Sinclair W   6
Taylor R   4
Thorpe S★   8
Todd H   2
Underhill C   11
Warburton A   2
Wright R   1

Goals (53): Hawkins 17, Bond 10, Oakes G 8, Hanson 4, Underhill 3, Banks 2, Clough 2, Hulbert 2, Ball 1, Jones 1, Pilling 1, Robertson 1, Rothwell 1, Sinclair 1.

Includes one extra-time goal.

FA Cup goals (2): Oakes G 2.

Stockport County

1939–40

Ashley J 1	Gee CW★ 3	Morris J 1	Smith WH 2
Bagley TH 22	Gleave C 4	Neilson R★ 18	Sullivan LG 5
Bowles JC 2	Groves A 9	Oldham G★ 2	Sullivan W 2
Catterick H★ 17	Hall J★ 8	Owens P 17	Titterington W 20
Chappell S 9	Hartill C★ 1	Pollitt J★ 1	Topping HW 21
Clark GV★ 4	Hollis H★ 1	Reid JDJ 19	Toseland E★ 10
Crawshaw C★ 1	Howe F★ 18	Rich L 2	Williams TR 1
Dean R★ 1	Jones L 1	Sanders RM★ 1	Winstanley W★ 1
Essex JR 5	Lumby WCW 9	Seagrave JW 2	Woodcock A 6
Fielding W★ 2	McDonagh F 12	Sherwood GW 3	

Goals (45): Catterick 14, Reid 11, Howe 8, Bagley 4, Toseland 2, Woodcock 2, Lumby 1, Neilson 1, Sullivan L 1, Titterington 1.

War Cup goals (0).

1940–41

Bagley TH 28	Green J 1	Maudsley RC 8	Ridgway F 6
Bowles JC 3	Haslam H★ 1	Middleton J★ 3	Self ER★ 2
Burgess H★ 7	Howe F★ 27	Minshall O 3	Stevens J★ 1
Burrows A 18	Johnson J 8	Moore –★ 2	Taylor T 8
Butler P★ 21	Johnson T★ 1	Neilson R★ 6	Titterington W 17
Catterick H★ 17	Jones GT★ 5	Newton W★ 1	Topping HW 29
Chappell S 19	Kitching N★ 1	Noble J 1	Toseland E★ 16
Egerton J 1	Leighton L 2	Park JB★ 1	Watson F 7
Fielding W★ 28	Lumby WCW 1	Percival J★ 21	Williams TR 3
Gleave C 2	Lyons E 3	Reid JDJ 10	Woodcock A 2

Goals (57): Catterick 12, Watson 7, Burgess 6, Howe 6, Bagley 5, Reid 4, Burrows 3, Toseland 3, Middleton 2, Titterington 2, Butler 1, Leighton 1, Ridgway 1, Self 1, Taylor 1, Williams 1, Woodcock 1.

1941–42

Bagley TH 2	Forrester C 1	Percival J★ 20	Topping HW 12
Barber A 1	Garfoot A★ 1	Reid JDJ 2	Toseland E★ 19
Basford S 1	Howe F★ 12	Ridgway F 12	Vincent E★ 2
Burrows A 4	Laurence O 12	Rigby W★ 16	Watson F 13
Caldwell AJ 1	Leighton L 2	Scott A 12	Williams TR 1
Catlin AE★ 6	Lyons E 4	Shaw K 1	Wilson C★ 3
Catterick H★ 26	Maudsley RC 1	Shawcross K 2	Woodcock A 1
Chappell S 25	Middleton J 1	Steele EC 19	Woods H 2
Cutting SW★ 26	Minshall O 1	Tagg G★ 3	
Fallows L 1	Morris J 1	Titterington W 10	
Fielding W★ 11	Noble J 1	Topping H★ 17	

Goals (46): Catterick 21, Watson 9, Howe 4, Percival 4, Cutting 2, Burrows 1, Chappell 1, Middleton 1, Reid 1, Ridgway 1, Scott 1.

1942–43

Ashley J 8	Jones BW★ 1	Needham F 2	Stuart A★ 1
Barratt LJ 2	Kirkwood SJ★ 1	Ramscar F★ 1	Sweeney F★ 1
Birch N★ 6	Lancelotte EC★ 4	Redfern F 17	Swindells H 16
Brierley A★ 1	Laurence D 2	Reid JDJ 1	Titterington W 1
Burrows A 34	Laurence NJ 9	Richardson R 1	Topping HW 14
Catterick H★ 18	Lievesley L★ 15	Ridgway F 2	Vose G★ 7
Chapple S 1	Littlemore R 3	Rigby W★ 20	Whatley WJ★ 6
Colqhoun DM★ 2	Lyons E 26	Robinson W★ 2	Wilson CM 13
Cutting SW★ 5	Matthews R★ 1	Scales G★ 5	Woodcock A 3
Gilmour T 1	McKay W★ 8	Scott A 7	Worsley H★ 35
Grant JA★ 1	McKenna J 1	Seddon H 6	Wright F★ 6
Harrison J 4	McPhillips L★ 1	Shaw K 35	
Hyde E 19	Morris J 1	Spencer F 1	
James GC★ 7	Moseley NA★ 4	Steele EC 18	

Goals (71): Shaw 16, Worsley 15, Swindells 9, Catterick 8, Hyde 6, James 4, Lancelotte 2, McKay 2, Scott 2, Wright 2, Jones 1, Matthews 1, Reid 1, Ridgway 1, own goal 1.

1943–44

Beasley E 2	Harman C★ 1	Needham F 7	Stuart D★ 1
Burrows A 18	James GC 22	Paterson J 1	Swindells H 1
Butt L★ 2	Johnson J 9	Rawcliffe F★ 2	Tabram P★ 7
Catterick H★ 25	Johnstone J★ 1	Redfearn F 32	Talbot M★ 20
Charlesworth S★ 16	Leigh J★ 1	Reece TS★ 18	Thomson A★ 2
Colquhoun DM★ 2	Lewin DR★ 11	Scholes J 1	Titterington W 8
Curran F★ 1	Liddell J★ 6	Seddon H 6	Woodcock A 1
Fenner DW★ 1	Lievesley L★ 32	Shaw K 34	Worsley H★ 25
Gallon JW★ 1	Lyons E 21	Shepherd G 2	
Geddes A 13	Martin H 31	Simpson J★ 1	
Gee H★ 3	McCulloch WD 18	Stuart A★ 1	

Goals (68): Catterick 20, Shaw 10, James 8, Johnson 6, Talbot 6, McCulloch 2, Rawcliffe 2, Reece 2, Titterington 2, Worsley 2, Burrows 1, Butt 1, Curran 1, Seddon 1, Shepherd 1, Stuart D 1, Tabram 1, own goal 1.

1944–45

Bardsley L★ 1	Dimond S★ 2	Leicester E 2	Redfearn F 31
Barkas T★ 5	Ellis J 2	Lewin DR★ 27	Ridgway F 1
Barnes JW 1	Gage A★ 19	Lievesley L★ 16	Rigby W★ 8
Beasley T 1	Gee H★ 26	Lunn G★ 1	Shaw K 30
Bentham S★ 1	Gennoe R 2	Makin G★ 1	Shawcross K 6
Blyth LR 2	Gleave C 19	Martin H 1	Stevenson J 1
Booth A★ 1	Gorrie W★ 1	Mathieson H 1	Topping HW 1
Booth JM 1	Heyward D★ 1	McCulloch W 29	Waring J★ 1
Brown W 5	Hill M★ 21	McKay W★ 1	Watters J 13
Burrows A 14	Hyde E 2	Morris J 5	Wheatley J★ 1
Catterick H★ 17	Ireland H★ 1	Morrison A★ 4	Wilson C 12
Cochrane D★ 2	James GC 5	Murphy M 1	Woodcock A 7
Cope E★ 18	Johnson J 4	Owens E 11	Worsley H★ 5
Crawford J 3	Jones R 5	Park T 1	
Crompton J★ 4	Jones TG★ 2	Quirk AC 1	

Goals (64): Catterick 21, Gee 7, McCulloch 7, Barkas 5, Shaw 3, Woodcock 3, Dimond 2, Hill 2, Shawcross 2, Crawford 1, Gorre 1, Hyde 1, Ireland 1, Johnson 1, Leicester 1, Lievesley 1, Owens 1, Redfearn 1, Watters 1, Worsley 1, own goal 1.

1945–46

Bowles JC 27	Gee H★ 2	Lumby WCW 1	Steele EC 5
Brown W 35	Gleave C 30	Morris J 16	Stock H 9
Bryant W★ 1	Haslam C 2	Oldnall WJ 1	Topping HW 4
Buckley A 25	Herd A★ 1	Rawlings JSD★ 1	Trentham D★ 4
Burrows A 29	Hyde E 7	Redfearn F 23	Weaver S 23
Catterick H★ 2	Johnson J 10	Reid JDJ 5	Williams F 3
Clarke W 11	Jones R 3	Rickards CT★ 35	Woodcock A 17
Cocker L 6	Keenan WG★ 1	Rigby W 10	Worrall J 12
Coen L★ 3	Kinnear D★ 1	Shaw K 30	
Davison A 6	Laurence O 5	Sherwood GW 1	

Goals (81): Shaw 19, Rickards 16, Brown 7, Reid 6, Weaver 6, Woodcock 6, Burrows 3, Hyde 3, Johnson 3, Catterick 2, Gee 2, Worrall 2, Bryant 1, Clarke 1, Coen 1, Steele 1, Stock 1, Trentham 1.

Div 3N (0).

Match not included in final table.

FA Cup goals (2): Hyde 1, Shaw 1.

Stoke City

1939–40

Antonio GR   1
Baker F   7
Bowyer F   1
Bridges PS   1
Brigham H   25
Gallacher P   3
Griffiths J★   8
Hampson E   1

Jones D★   15
Kirton J   4
Liddle R   20
Massey AW   13
Matthews S   15
McCue JW   1
McMahon P   3
Mould W   24

Mountford F   1
Oakes John★   1
Oldham G   1
Ormston A   21
Peppitt S   20
Sale T   23
Scrimshaw C★   10
Smith C   10

Soo F   23
Steele FC   5
Tennant JW   3
Tutin A   8
Westland D   4
Westland J   1
Wilkinson N   2

Goals (64): Sale 20, Peppitt 14, Ormston 10, Smith 4, Soo 3, Steele 3, Liddle 2, Matthews 2, Baker 1, Bowyer 1, Gallacher 1, Mountford 1, own goals 2.

War Cup goals (14): Steele 7, Sale 4, Liddle 1, Ormston 1, Peppitt 1.

1940–41

Basnett A   5
Blunt E★   1
Bowyer F   19
Bridges PS   18
Brigham H   32
Challinor J   5
Curtis C   1
Dunkley R   3
Franklin N   33
Glover S   20
Griffiths HS★   1

Griffiths J★   3
Hampson E   21
Harrison S   9
Hayward LE★   1
Haywood L★   1
Herod DJ   13
Holden T   3
Howell L   1
Jackson J   2
Jones D★   1
Kinson W   2

Kirton J   4
Liddle R   31
Longland E★   7
Massey AW   2
Matthews S   12
McCue JW   14
Mitchell AJ   6
Mould W   3
Mountford F   29
Ormston A   3
Peppitt S   14

Sale T   36
Smith C   6
Soo F   20
Steele FC   16
Stevens GL★   1
Thompson M★   2
Turner A★   11
Ware H★   1
Westland J   1
Wilkinson N   2
Wordley EH   2

Goals (79): Mountford 23, Sale 17, Bowyer 10, Liddle 6, Steele 5, Soo 4, Brigham 3, Basnett 2, Longland 2, Ormston 2, Smith 2, Dunkley 1, Franklin 1, Mitchell 1.

1941–42

Basnett A   33
Blunt E★   20
Bowyer F   37
Brigham H   33
Brown R   2
Caton WC   11
Clewlow S   2
Franklin N   32

Glover S   34
Griffiths HS★   3
Hamlett TL★   35
Harrison S   3
Hayward LE★   3
Herod DJ   38
Kirton J   7
Liddle R   31

Longland E   1
McCue JW   3
Mitchell AJ   2
Mould W   10
Mountford F   9
Ormston A   2
Peppitt S   5
Sale T   36

Sellars J   1
Soo F   12
Steele FC   8
Westland J   2
Williams E★   3

Goals (116): Sale 56, Basnett 18, Bowyer 10, Liddle 10, Blunt 6, Mountford 4, Brigham 3, Soo 3, Hamlett 2, Clewlow 1, Mitchell 1, Peppitt 1, Steele 1.

1942–43

Baker F   4
Basnett A   22
Basnett AE   2
Bates P   17
Bilton DH★   7
Blunt E★   1
Bowyer F   37
Brigham H   32
Brown R   2
Caton WC   9

Clewlow S   2
Cowden S   1
Foster E   4
Franklin N   31
Glover S   1
Hamlett TL★   34
Herod DJ   6
Howell L   1
Jackson J   4
Kinson W   5

Kirton J   1
Liddle R   32
Massey AW   1
McCue JW   38
Micklewright R   1
Mitchell AJ   2
Mould W   2
Mountford F   36
Mountford GF   21
Ormston A   1

Peppitt S   2
Sale T   37
Sellars J   2
Sherratt F   4
Soo F   13
Tutin A   1
Vallance T   1
Ware H★   1

Goals (88): Bowyer 19, Mountford F 19, Basnett A 14, Sale 10, Mountford G 8, Liddle 7, Soo 4, Basnett AE 2, Caton 1, Hamlett 1, Peppitt 1, Vallance 1, own goal 1.

1943–44

Basnett A   17
Blunt E*   1
Bowyer F   37
Brigham H   16
Caton WC   2
Clewlow S   2
Cowden S   3
Crossley R   2
Dunn D   1
Edwards JAB   3
Foster E   17
Franklin N   34

Glover S   1
Griffiths J*   4
Hamlett TL*   10
Harrison S   2
Hayward LE*   6
Herod DJ   1
Jackson J   3
Kinson W   18
Kirton J   8
Liddle R   27
Massey AW   2
Matthews S   3

McCue JW   34
Mould W   20
Mountford F   29
Mountford GF   19
Ormston A   10
Peppitt S   11
Podmore EV   13
Pointon WJ*   2
Sale T   39
Sellars J   3
Shufflebotham R   1
Simpson J*   2

Soo F   2
Steele FC   9
Vallance T   1
Watkin C   1
West K   1
Wilkinson N   8
Windsor R   2
Wordley EH   1
Wright H*   1

Goals (106): Sale 30, Steele 20, Basnett 9, Bowyer 9, Peppitt 9, Mountford F 5, Mountford GF 5, Liddle 4, Ormston 3, Franklin 2, Clewlow 1, Jackson 1, Kirton 1, Pointon 1, Sellars 1, Watkin 1, own goals 4.

1944–45

Basnett A   17
Basnett AE   1
Bayford DSJ   2
Bowyer F   24
Brigham H   36
Brown R   2
Cowden S   15
Cunliffe AJ*   1
Foster E   6

Franklin N   32
Herod DJ   25
Howshall T   1
Jackson J   23
Kinson W   4
Kirton J   11
Leigh W*   2
Liddle R   11
Mannion J   5

Marks WG*   2
Matthews S   15
McCue JW   33
Mould W   2
Mountford F   40
Mountford GF   23
Ormston A   4
Pearson TU*   1
Peppitt S   2

Podmore EV   6
Poulton W   8
Sale T   40
Sellars J   18
Soo F   8
Steele FC   17
Watkin C   9
Williams S*   3
Windsor R   2

Goals (104): Sale 34, Mountford GF 15, Steele 10, Bowyer 8, Basnett 7, Jackson 6, Matthews 4, Sellars 5, Poulton 4, Soo 3, Bayford 1, Kirton 1, Liddle 1, Mannion 1, Mountford F 1, own goals 3.

1945–46

Antonio GR   16
Baker F   9
Basnett A   17
Boothway J*   1
Bowyer F   4
Brigham H   42
Brown R   8
Challinor J   5

Cowden S   21
Craddock H   2
Dodd JT   1
Franklin N   23
Hampson E   2
Harrison S   1
Herod DJ   42
Jackson J   2

Kinson W   6
Kirton J   25
Matthews S   20
McCue J   15
Meakin H   3
Mould W   4
Mountford F   40
Mountford GF   32

Ormston A   12
Peppitt S   13
Sale T   23
Sellars J   21
Steele FC   36
Topsham C   12
Vallance T   1
Windsor R   3

Goals (88): Steele 36, Basnett 8, Mountford GF 8, Sale 8, Antonio 7, Sellars 7, Peppitt 5, Ormston 3, Matthews 2, Boothway 1, Brigham 1, Dodd 1, Mountford F 1.

FA Cup goals (10): Steele 7, Antonio 2, Mountford GF 1.

Sunderland

1939–40

Burbanks WE 3	Gorman J 3	Housam A 3	Mapson J 3
Carter HS 3	Hall AW 3	Johnston R 1	Robinson W 3
Duns L 3	Hastings AC 3	Lockie AJ 2	Smeaton J 3

Goals (6): Carter 3, Hastings 2, Burbanks 1.

War Cup goals (7): Carter 5, Burbanks 1, Hastings 1.

1940–41

Did not compete.

1941–42

Allan TA 3	Gorman J 30	McCormack CJ★ 3	Spuhler JO 35
Borthwick M★ 1	Gurney R 8	McMahon H 28	Stubbins A★ 3
Bradwell S 8	Hastings AC 25	Milsom D 4	Thompson H 4
Burns OH★ 1	Hewison WJ 18	Ramsay RG 5	Walsh W 3
Carter HS 27	Heywood AE 39	Robinson GH★ 29	Wheatman L 7
Clark J 1	Housam A 38	Robinson W 12	Whitelum C 28
Curzon WA 1	Ireland E 6	Rodgerson R 10	Wright AWT 3
Duns L 3	Lloyd WS 2	Slack T 1	
Eves JR 28	Lockie AJ 25	Smallwood F★ 1	

Goals (103): Whitelum 26, Carter 23, Spuhler 14, Robinson G 9, McMahon 7, Wright 4, Allan 2, Gurney 2, Stubbins 2, Bradwell 1, Duns 1, Gorman 1, Hastings 1, Ireland 1, Lockie 1, Milsom 1, Ramsay 1, Slack 1, Thompson 1, own goals 4.

1942–43

Ainsley GE★ 1	Dryden JR★ 1	Laidman F 17	Spuhler JO 35
Anderson D★ 1	Duns L 1	Lloyd WS 7	Tapken N★ 2
Bircham B 20	Eves JR 27	Lockie AJ 19	Thompson H 1
Boyd J 1	Frazer N★ 1	Milsom D 2	Tuttle EH 5
Boyes W★ 3	Gorman J 36	Nicholson WE★ 7	Walsh W 1
Bradwell S 18	Green JH 1	Potts HJ★ 17	Wensley L 1
Breen C 1	Hastings AC 25	Ramsay RG 2	Wheatman L 4
Burbanks WE 1	Hewison WJ 21	Robinson GH★ 23	Whitelum C 33
Carter HS 24	Heywood AE 5	Robinson W 5	Wright AWT 1
Clark J 10	Housam A 4	Rodgerson R 1	
Coupland J 1	Johnston T★ 1	Short JD★ 1	
Davies T 1	Kearney SF★ 1	Smallwood F★ 17	

Goals (104): Whitelum 31, Spuhler 22, Carter 15, Potts 8, Smallwood 8, Hastings 5, Robinson G 4, Lloyd 3, Robinson W 2, Boyes 1, Bradwell 1, Lockie 1, Ramsay 1, Tuttle 1, Wright 1, own goal 1.

Includes Counties Cup final second leg goal.

1943–44

Bell HD 12	Farey JA 1	Lloyd WS 1	Stokoe D 1
Bell J 14	Freeman A★ 1	Lockie AJ 34	Thompson GH 1
Bircham B 13	Gorman J 27	Mather H★ 5	Tulip H 1
Boyd J 1	Gurney R 1	McMahon H 2	Walsh W 1
Bradwell S 16	Hall JL★ 1	Milsom D 3	Walshaw K 3
Carter HS 5	Harrison JY 2	Mortensen SH★ 1	Weightman – 1
Clark J 23	Hastings AC 27	Potts HJ★ 7	Wensley L 15
Collins GE★ 17	Hindmarsh E 18	Reay T 2	Wheatman L 4
Cunningham L 1	Hodges CL★ 6	Robb N 1	Whitelum C 27
Dawson T★ 1	Housam A 9	Robinson GH★ 1	Williams G★ 1
Duns L 3	Irwin J 1	Robinson JS 1	Wright AWT 2
Ellison SW 1	Jenkins TF 1	Robinson W 2	
Elms CF 1	Kilgallon J★ 1	Scotson R 5	
Eves JR 23	Laidman F 22	Spuhler JO 36	

Goals (90): Whitelum 26, Spuhler 23, Laidman 6, Wensley 6, Bell H 5, Collins 4, Hastings 3, Hodges 3, Potts 3, Carter 2, Irwin 2, Dawson 1, Duns 1, Milsom 1, Mortensen 1, Reay 1, Robb 1, Wright 1.

1944–45

Bell HD 16	Gorman J 28	Laidman F 28	Scott WR★ 1
Bell J 5	Hamill GC 1	Lilley J 6	Spuhler JO 36
Bircham B 26	Hastings AC 23	Lloyd WS 2	Stelling JGS 24
Brown C 9	Hetherington H 2	Lockie AJ 42	Taylor JWR 5
Burbanks WE 14	Heywood AE 17	Maguire JE★ 1	Tulip H 1
Carter HS 3	Horton L★ 2	Merry T 1	Wallbanks H★ 35
Dixon JT★ 1	Housam A 13	Milburn JET★ 2	Wallbanks J★ 4
Ellison SW 1	Ireland E 1	Milsom D 3	Walshaw K 26
Eves JR 34	Jameson JW 1	Potts HJ★ 1	White T 9
Fleck JSS 9	Jones S 1	Reay T 3	Whitelum C 36

Goals (105): Whitelum 41, Spuhler 19, Walshaw 11, Laidman 10, Brown 5, Bell H 4, Carter 3, Horton 2, Wallbanks H 2, Burbanks 1, Hetherington 1, Housam 1, Lockie 1, Merry 1, Milsom 1, Reay 1, White 1.

1945–46

Anderson J 1	Ellison SW 8	Johnston R 2	Thompson R 4
Bett F 4	Eves JR 10	Jones JE 23	Wallbanks H★ 3
Bircham B 3	Fleck JSS 13	Laurie J★ 1	Waller H★ 3
Boyd J 2	Forde S★ 2	Lockie AJ 35	Walshaw K 8
Brown C 24	Gorman J 1	Mapson J 31	Watson W 2
Burbanks WE 35	Gray AE 2	Purvis B★ 1	Wharton G★ 1
Cairns WH★ 1	Hastings AC 6	Robinson W 3	White T 20
Carter HS 7	Hetherington H 4	Scotson R 2	Whitelum C 39
Davie J★ 8	Heywood AE 8	Spuhler JO 6	Willingham CK 16
Dunn E 13	Housam A 41	Stelling JGS 40	Wright AWT 7
Duns L 18	Humble D 3	Thompson H 1	

Goals (55): Whitelum 10, White 9, Burbanks 6, Davie 5, Brown 4, Carter 4, Ellison 4, Dunn 3, Duns 2, Humble 2, Cairns 1, Hetherington 1, Housam 1, Robinson W 1, Spuhler 1, Walshaw 1.

FA Cup goals (14): Brown 5, Duns 2, Hastings 2, Whitelum 2, Burbanks 1, Housam 1, Walshaw 1.

Swansea Town

1939–40

Allen BW 17	Edwards G 23	Harris TJG★ 16	Payne EGH 24
Bamford T 13	Emmanuel DL 25	James D★ 7	Peters S★ 4
Briddon S 23	Evans HWR 1	John WR★ 4	Richards LA 7
Brown G★ 1	Fisher CK 24	Jones D★ 1	Roberts A 6
Burrows J★ 1	Fold – 1	Maggs P★ 1	Rogers E 3
Comley LG 4	Francis K 3	Mears E 6	Sneddon WC 11
Coulter J 3	Gallon JW 3	Meek J 3	Squires F 26
Cumner RH★ 1	Haines JTW 5	Mercer D★ 1	Stuttard JE★ 1
Davies D 5	Hanford H★ 5	Moore S 3	Tabram P 6
Davies WG 25	Hangwell L★ 1	Paul R 24	Thomas DSL 3

Goals (59): Squires 11, Bamford 10, Allen 7, Edwards 7, Briddon 6, Payne 6, James 4, Emmanuel 2, Comley 1, Davies D 1, Davies W 1, Haines 1, Meek 1, Richards 1.

War Cup goals (6): Davies D 2, Paul 2, Bamford 1, Payne 1.

1940–41

Allen BW 10	Emmanuel DL 9	Graham G★ 1	Payne EGH 12
Comley LG 6	Evans HWR 12	Houston WF 1	Squires F 12
Davies G 11	Fisher CK 12	John WR★ 1	Thomas DSL 1
Eastman J 3	Francis K 1	Mears E 12	Williams R★ 2
Edwards G 11	Fursland S★ 3	Paul R 12	

Goals (16): Fisher 3, Squires 4, Allen 2, Comley 2, Edwards 2, Eastman 1, Payne 1, Williams 1.

1941–42

Allen BW 8	Edwards G 3	Granville A★ 1	Rees JL 1
Briddon S 2	Edwards R 4	Hanford H★ 6	Rogers E 3
Carney S 2	Emmanuel DL 6	Holland C 1	Sellars D 1
Collins J★ 1	Evans GA 3	Hollis H★ 4	Sneddon WC 1
Comley LG 9	Evans HWR 20	Houston WF 8	Squires F 17
Davies AB★ 2	Fisher CK 19	Lowry S 5	Thomas DSL 2
Davies G 16	France J★ 6	Mears E 3	Thomas HR 2
Davies WG 4	Francis K 2	Millership A 5	Thomas WJ 7
Davis JE 1	Frimston RD 1	Morgan G 3	Tomkin AH★ 1
Davis L★ 2	Fursland S★ 1	Paul R 20	Witcomb DF★ 5
Deere DJ 1	Giles G 3	Payne EGH 8	

Goals (29): Houston 8, Squires 5, Payne 3, Collins 2, Paul 2, Comley 1, Edwards G 1, Emmanuel 1, Holland 1, Lowry 1, Millership 1, Rogers 1, Thomas H 1, own goal 1.

1942–43

Allen BW 1	Evans L 9	Jones TG★ 3	Rogers E 23
Anthony EA 1	Evans ST 1	Jones TR 1	Shadrach T 1
Briddon S 1	Ferguson W 1	Lewis B 6	Shreeve JT★ 3
Brooks C 1	Fisher CK 32	Lewis DG 16	Smith JH 1
Browen D★ 1	Ford T 4	Lewis LC 4	Sneddon WC 1
Carney S 4	Fox D 3	Lowry S 8	Squires F 1
Clayton JG★ 1	Giles G 3	Metcalfe L 10	Symons RR★ 17
Comley LG 34	Hall AE★ 2	Millichip A 16	Thomas DSL 12
Curtis GF★ 4	Hanford H★ 1	Morgan G 1	Thomas HR 2
Daniel RNV★ 1	Herdman C 28	Mortensen SH★ 1	Thomas M 7
Davies G 8	Hope G★ 1	Owen JH 1	Thomas V 1
Davies WG 1	Hughes WM★ 1	Paul R 5	Thomas W 1
Eastman J 3	James WG 6	Payne EGH 7	Turner H★ 2
Edwards ET★ 1	Jones E★ 1	Powell R 3	Watson WT★ 1
Edwards G 5	Jones JL 13	Readshaw – 6	Wheatman JR 9
Emmanuel DL 11	Jones M★ 1	Rees JL 6	Williams R★ 11
Evans GA 4	Jones RD 2	Richards DT 3	Woolacott H 1
Evans HWR 8	Jones S★ 1	Richards L 2	Wright JD★ 3

Goals (62): Thomas D 9, Lowry 7, Rogers 6, Comley 5, Emmanuel 4, Jones TG 4, Readshaw 4, Curtis 3, Ford 3, James 3, Williams 3, Richards D 2, Carney 1, Clayton 1, Evans H 1, Hall 1, Lewis D 1, Sneddon 1, Squires 1, Symons 1, Wheatman 1.

1943–44

Allen BW 1	Ferguson W 3	Lewis DG 2	Richards DT 1
Barber L 2	Fisher CK 25	Lewis LC 15	Roberts JH★ 3
Chew J★ 1	Ford T 4	Maule JF★ 1	Rogers E 23
Clark GA 1	Gow WH 6	McCulloch D★ 2	Scrine FH 27
Clayfield R 2	Griffiths D 2	Millichip A 2	Stevenson A 7
Comley LG 25	Griffiths G 4	Morgan G 1	Symons RR★ 24
Corbett W★ 22	Harris R 1	Owen JH 4	Tabram P 3
Crisp GH★ 2	Hellier WJ★ 1	Parris JE★ 1	Taylor GC 17
Davies AR 6	Herdman C 2	Parry J 24	Thomas DSL 2
Davies G 4	Howe LF★ 2	Parry WAM 3	Walker JT 1
Davies WG 3	Hutchinson W★ 1	Passmore E 12	Watson JL 1
Edwards EJ 1	Jones E★ 1	Paul R 5	Watson WT★ 1
Edwards G 1	Jones JL★ 27	Payne EGH 5	Westacott J 1
Emmanuel DL 4	Jones T★ 2	Porch TR 1	White RN 2
Evans HWR 2	Jones WEA 24	Powell R 1	Whittaker RW 2
Evans ST 1	Knoyle TI 3	Prescott JR★ 4	Williams R★ 3
Evans T★ 1	Lewis B 2	Rees M 28	

Goals (67): Rogers 11, Passmore 10, Comley 6, Scrine 6, Jones W 4, Rees 4, Ford 3, Roberts 3, McCulloch 2, Paul 2, Taylor 2, Williams 2, Corbett 1, Davies A 1, Edwards G 1, Emmanuel 1, Ferguson 1, Jones E 1, Jones T 1, Knoyle 1, Morgan 1, Payne 1, Prescott 1, Thomas 1.

1944–45

Ainge RP 1	Dimond S★ 1	Lewis DG 1	Scrine FH 5
Allen BW 33	Duffy R★ 3	Lewis LC 25	Steele EC★ 1
Anderson R 2	Eastman J 1	Lewis N 1	Stimpson HA 2
Briddon S 8	Evans E 5	Longdon CW★ 1	Tadman GH 1
Browne RJ★ 1	Fisher CK 30	McNally WF 3	Thomas DSL 2
Burns F 32	Ford T 5	Medley TD★ 1	Thomas RG 2
Clarke F★ 1	Gilchrist TJ 21	Noonan MD 8	Townsend LF★ 2
Coleman D 2	Goodwin J 1	O'Reilly J★ 1	Wardle W★ 2
Comley LG 18	Gow WH 4	Owen JH 2	Weir R★ 1
Corbett W^ 29	Grogan J★ 2	Parry WAM 3	Weston R 7
Dalton J 3	Hanford H★ 1	Paul R 9	Whittaker RW 2
Daniel R 18	Ireland HW★ 1	Phillips PH 32	Wilkes GA 1
Davies AR 6	Jepson A★ 1	Rees M 11	Williams B 1
Davies C 3	John WR★ 1	Richards J 1	Williams D 2
Davies G 1	Jones EM 1	Richards LA 8	
Davies WG 4	Jones LJ★ 1	Roberts JH★ 1	
Davies WR 1	Jones WEA 34	Rogers E 3	

Goals (74): Burns 20, Allen 7, Comley 6, Fisher 6, Jones W 6, Ford 5, Evans 3, Scrine 3, Thomas D 2, Townsend 2, Anderson 1, Clarke 1, Coleman 1, Corbett 1, Davies A 1, Eastman 1, McNally 1, Owen 1, Paul 1, Phillips 1, Stimpson 1, Wardle 1, Wilkes 1, own goal 1.

1945–46

Allen BW 18	Davies G 32	Jones WEA 39	Scrine FH 19
Batty S★ 1	Davies T 3	Millichip A 1	Smeaton J★ 1
Blair J★ 2	Davies WG 6	Parry WAM 1	Sneddon WC 18
Boulton FP★ 3	Emmanuel DL 4	Paul R 9	Squires F 4
Briddon S 14	Fisher CK 33	Payne EGH 24	Stansbridge LEC★ 5
Burns F 37	Ford T 41	Phillips PH 1	Tabram P 7
Coleman D 4	Gallon JW 10	Prescott JR★ 2	Twigg W★ 2
Comley LG 16	Gilchrist TJ 4	Roberts D★ 1	Weston R 37
Corbett J 4	Goffin WC★ 1	Roberts JH★ 11	Wheatman JR 2
Corbett NG★ 1	Haines JWT 5	Roberts OJ 18	
Daniel R 1	Hodgson S★ 6	Rogers E 1	

Goals (90): Ford 41, Scrine 8, Comley 7, Jones 6, Payne 6, Burns 5, Roberts JH 4, Coleman 3, Allen 2, Squires 2, Briddon 1, Corbett J 1, Haines 1, Paul 1, Sneddon 1, own goal 1.

FA Cup goals (3): Ford 3.

Swindon Town

1939–40

Bailey H★　4	Emmanuel DL★　5	Imrie WN　2	Morton BW　2
Bowl A★　19	Emmanuel T★　7	Jones DG　2	Olney JH　3
Butcher WF　1	Fowler A　29	Jones EM　29	Painter EG　6
Carr LL★　1	Francis CT　6	Kelso J★　1	Parkhouse RR　27
Catterall G★　1	Geldard A★　1	Lawrence RS★　11	Ryan T　2
Collins JH★　2	Hampson H★　2	Lawrence SW　10	Thompson JV★　3
Cousins H　29	Hanford H★　4	Lloyd WL　1	Webb JH★　1
Cox FJA★　1	Harris N Jr　1	Lowe H　3	Wildman FR　29
Curran F★　1	Harris N Sr　1	Lucas WH　14	Williams CE★　1
Day A　28	Hedley F　26	Maggs P★　1	Winter D★　1
Egan H★　2	Howe D★　4	Martin H★　1	
Emery DKJ　13	Hurst J★　2	McKenzie JA　1	

Goals (68): Fowler 22, Bowl 9, Hedley 7, Jones E 5, Lucas 5, Howe 4, Painter 3, Emery 2, Emmanuel D 2, Francis 2, Harris N Jr 2, Cox 1, Day 1, Lawrence S 1, Williams 1, own goal 1.

War Cup goals (1): Fowler 1.

1940–41

Did not compete.

1941–42

Did not compete.

1942–43

Did not compete.

1943–44

Did not compete.

1944–45

Did not compete.

1945–46

Barlow RJ★　1	Hall FW★　4	Mather J★　6	Saunders R　1
Bicknell R★　1	Harris N Sr★　1	McDonald M★　22	Skinner G★　1
Bingham WP　1	Hedley F　1	McGibbon D★　5	Sturgess M　1
Blanchflower RD★　1	Hinton E★　1	Morgan SW★　2	Thomas DSL★　6
Brinton JV★　1	Holland EJ★　5	Morton BN★　1	Tovey S★　2
Burton S　13	Jakeman H★　11	Onslow LG　8	Tudor W★　7
Cousins H　34	Jones EM　21	Painter EG　14	Wildman FR　21
Denyer AFT　9	Kelso J　17	Parkhouse RR　1	Williams GG　28
Derrick AE★　17	Lloyd WL　23	Preece JC★　4	Woodman D　21
Emery DKJ　7	Lovesey WS　21	Pritchard RT★　1	Woodward T★　1
Forde S★　1	Low NH★　1	Reilly LH★　1	Young AE★　1
Francis CE　7	Lucas WH　22	Rosenthal A★　12	
Godwin RG　6	Manning G　1	Ryan T　1	

Goals (56): Williams 11, Derrick 6, Jones 6, Rosenthal 5, Emery 4, Lucas 4, Godwin 3, Jakeman 3, McGibbon 3, Painter 3, Thomas 3, Barlow 2, Denyer 1, Holland 1, Morgan 1.

FA Cup goals (2): Emery 1, Francis 1.

Torquay United

1939–40

Bennett L★ 4
Brown A   5
Brown F★   16
Calland R   1
Cann ST★   1
Clarke A★   23
Clarke RL★   20
Coley WE★   26
Conley JJ   3
Cothliff HT   4

Craig A★   6
Davies TJ★   1
Day AE   3
Ebdon R★   28
Fursdon RH   1
Green R★   1
Head BJ   25
Hellier WJ   27
Honeywill L★   1
Hutchinson A   29

Johnson R★   6
Jones J   2
Joslin PJ   25
Keeton A   2
Kernick DHG   7
Knapman AC   19
Laing D★   1
Mahon J   1
Markham C   21
Mercer AD★   5

Mitcheson F   1
Naylor JW   1
Preskett C   3
Pugsley T★   2
Reed AG★   3
Stabb GH★   1
Sutherley C★   5
Tait T   3
Wilson A   6
Wright TB★   2

Goals (77): Clarke A 23, Ebdon 21, Brown F 11, Hutchinson 3, Knapman 3, Bennett 2, Conley 2, Kernick 2, Mercer 2, Clarke R 1, Coley 1, Mahon 1, Markham 1, Mitcheson 1, Preskett 1, own goals 2.

War Cup goals (8): Mitcheson 3, Ebdon 2, Cothliff 1, Kernick 1, Knapman 1.

1940–41

Did not compete.

1941–42

Did not compete.

1942–43

Did not compete.

1943–44

Did not compete.

1944–45

Did not compete.

1945–46

Bennett R   1
Birkett RJE★   1
Brown A   4
Bull C   1
Calland R   10
Cole J   6
Coleman R   1
Coley WE   20
Conley JJ   2
Cooper S   1
Cothliff HT   16
Court JH★   4
Davies TJ★   1

Dyer H   7
Fowler H   1
Franklin N★   1
Glanville B   3
Griffiths KJ★   14
Harris JR★   2
Haycox J★   1
Head BJ   22
Hellier WJ   10
Henry R   1
Hodge J★   1
Joslin PJ   29
Keeton A   31

Kernick DHG   17
Knapman AC   7
Lavers G   2
Lewis D   6
Markham C   36
McDonough FR   2
McLaughlin RJ★   1
Mercer AD   19
Phillips RGT   28
Pugh JHB★   1
Randall A   1
Raybould E★   1
Rich L★   5

Sheppard HH★   1
Smale DM★   1
Smith C★   19
Smith W★   8
Spencer H★   16
Strange R   8
Tait T★   1
Tanner T   5
Tivendale J★   4
Vallance T   6
Vidgen J   5
Williams F   4
Wilson A   1

Goals (41): Phillips 7, Griffiths 5, Kernick 5, Conley 4, Dyer 4, Court 3, Brown 2, Cothliff 2, Smith C 2, Smith W 2, Williams 2, Glanville 1, Knapman 1, Mercer 1.

FA Cup goals (1): Coley 1.

Tottenham Hotspur

1939–40

Bennett LD 10	Duncan A 16	Lyman CC 7	Sargent FA 19
Buckingham VF 16	Evans N 1	McCormick J 6	Spelman I 11
Burchell GS★ 1	Hall AE 3	McEwan FF 2	Stephens – 1
Burgess R 17	Hall GW 30	Medley LD 24	Tomkin AH 3
Cox FJA 10	Hitchins AW 34	Morrison JA 30	Ward RA 24
Ditchburn EG 2	Hooper PG 36	Nicholson WG 3	Whatley WJ 33
Dix RW 18	Howe LF 31	Ottewell S★ 1	Wilbert G 1
Dorling GJ 11	Hunt DA★ 2	Page AE 9	Woodley VR★ 1
Dowers JA 1	Ludford GA 14	Piper GH 1	

Goals (86): Morrison 28, Medley 12, Dix 8, Ludford 8, Bennett 5, Howe 5, Duncan 4, Hall G 4, Sargent 4, Burgess 3, Cox 1, Hall AE 1, Hunt 1, Lyman 1, Stephens 1.

War Cup goals (3): Cox 1, Dix 1, Howe 1.

1940–41

Arnold W★ 1	Gibbons AH 14	McCormick J 2	Skinner G 3
Bennett K 5	Goodman A 1	Medley LD 6	Sperrin JR 8
Broadis IA 12	Hall GW 23	Newman A 1	Sperrin W 10
Browne J 1	Henley L★ 1	O'Callaghan E★ 8	Wallace J 1
Buckingham VF 15	Hitchins AW 30	Paton TG★ 4	Wallis J 2
Burditt J★ 1	Hooper PG 22	Piper GH 3	Ward RA 30
Burgess R 14	Howe LF 6	Sainsbury R 1	Whatley WJ 28
Duncan A 21	Ludford G 31	Sargent FA 6	White R 21
Flack DW★ 5	McCarthy SJ 1	Saunders W★ 3	

Goals (78): Ludford 16, Gibbons 13, Broadis 10, Burgess 8, Duncan 8, Sperrin W 4, Hall 3, Howe 3, Sperrin J 3, Ward 3, Medley 2, Buckingham 1, Sargent 1, Skinner 1, White 1, own goal 1.

London Cup

Bennett K 1, Bennett L 1, Broadis 8, Buckingham 3, Duncan 10, Gibbons 11, Hall 11, Hitchins 10, Hooper 11, Howe 1, Ludford 11, O'Callaghan 1, Skinner 1, Sperrin JR 5, Sperrin W 5, Wallace 1, Wallis 1, Ward 11, Whatley 8, White 10.

Goals: Gibbons 11, Broadis 5, Duncan 5, Ludford 5, Hall 2, Ward 2, Bennett K 1, Wallace 1.

1941–42

Bennett K 3	Fitzgerald AM★ 1	Mannion W★ 4	Sperrin W 9
Bennett LD 1	Gibbons AH 28	McCormick J 2	Stevens L 1
Broadis IA 35	Gilberg H 2	McFarland –★ 1	Tickridge S 36
Buckingham VF 3	Hall GW 34	Noble AWT 6	Trailor C 1
Burgess R 6	Hitchins AW 31	Pearson TU★ 2	Ward RA 36
Cox FJA 2	Hooper PG 18	Revell C★ 1	Whatley WJ 5
Ditchburn EG 15	Howe LF 10	Sainsbury R 1	White R 28
Duncan A 28	Jolliffe – 1	Sainsbury WH 2	Williams CE★ 3
Edwards R 2	Kiernan T★ 2	Sibley A★ 3	Woodward H 1
Finch LC★ 1	Ludford G 29	Sperrin JR 2	

Goals (70): Gibbons 19, Ludford 18, Broadis 12, Duncan 4, Howe 3, Noble 3, Burgess 2, Stevens 2, White 2, Bennett L 1, Hall 1, Revell 1, Sibley 1, Ward 1.

1942–43

Barron G 1	Ditchburn EG 9	Howe LF 22	Rowley JF★ 2
Beasley A★ 27	Dix RW 1	Jackson H★ 2	Sainsbury WH 1
Bennett LD 1	Duncan A 1	Ludford G 29	Sargent FA 1
Briggs CE★ 2	Eastham S★ 1	Marshall E★ 1	Sperrin W 3
Broadis IA 13	Edwards R 4	Martin JR★ 22	Staley R★ 1
Browne RJ★ 3	Finlay D 3	McCormick J 2	Ward RA 32
Buckingham VF 1	Gibbons AH 23	Muir A★ 1	Whatley WJ 17
Burgess R 4	Gurr HD 1	Nelson D★ 1	White R 27
Chapman E★ 1	Hall GW 31	Nicholson WE 1	
Chisholm J 34	Hares W★ 1	O'Callaghan E★ 9	
Cox FJA 3	Hooper PG 22	Pattison JM★ 13	

Goals (80): Ludford 20, Gibbons 17, Beasley 12, Martin 9, Broadis 4, O'Callaghan 3, Pattison 3, Cox 2, Hall 2, Sperrin W 2, Edwards 1, Nelson 1, Sargent 1, Ward 1, own goals 2.

1943–44

Adams W 5	Dix RW 2	Manley T★ 1	Smith T★ 2
Beasley A★ 35	Edwards R★ 1	Martin JR★ 15	Sperrin W 1
Bennett LD 1	Evans JL★ 1	Mogford R★ 5	Walters WG 12
Briggs CE★ 1	Flack WLW★ 2	Moseley WA 3	Ward RA 37
Browne J 3	Gibbins E 2	Nelson D★ 1	Whatley WJ 28
Bryant B★ 7	Gilberg H 2	O'Callaghan E★ 2	Whent JR 2
Buckingham VF 6	Hall GW 6	O'Donnell F★ 11	White R 25
Burgess R 25	Harris A★ 3	Page AG 2	Willis A 9
Chisholm J 30	Hooper PG 10	Parker C★ 1	Wilson J★ 1
Clayton S★ 2	Howe LF 7	Rowley JF★ 20	Young AE★ 2
Cox FJA 15	Hunt DA★ 1	Sainsbury WH 1	
Davie J★ 1	Jones EN★ 16	Sargent FA 1	
Ditchburn EG 26	Ludford G 14	Smith JCR★ 1	

Goals (79): Rowley 22, Beasley 10, Burgess 10, Jones 7, O'Donnell 7, Martin 4, Walters 4, Bryant 2, Cox 2, Bennett 1, Clayton 1, Howe 1, Ludford 1, Moseley 1, Smith T 1, Ward 1, Whent 1, White 1, own goals 2.

1944–45

Adams W 4	Dunn R★ 1	Jackson J★ 2	Rowley JF★ 3
Anderson A★ 1	Flavell R★ 14	Ludford G 14	Smith R★ 1
Beasley A★ 27	Foreman GA★ 5	Lyman CC 1	Stevens L 12
Boulton FP★ 1	Gibbons AH 16	Martin JR★ 5	Swift WN 1
Broadis IA 6	Gilberg H 8	Medley LD 11	Tunney E★ 1
Brown HT★ 3	Goodman A 1	Mogford R★ 3	Wallis J 4
Burgess R 29	Hall AE 5	Moodie J★ 1	Walters WE 36
Burke C★ 12	Hall FA★ 17	Muir WR★ 1	Ward RA 36
Burnett T★ 1	Henley L★ 1	O'Donnell F★ 2	Whatley WJ 1
Chisholm J 8	Hooper PG 1	Oakes John★ 1	White R 28
Dix RW 1	Howe LF 6	Page AG 3	Whittingham A★ 1
Duke HP★ 3	Hughes WA★ 24	Pryde RI★ 1	Willis A 32

Goals (94): Gibbons 16, Burgess 12, Walters 10, Beasley 9, Foreman 8, Gilberg 6, Ludford 5, Stevens 5, Ward 5, Broadis 2, Burnett 2, Hall AE 2, Medley 2, Rowley 2, Flavell 1, Henley 1, Howe 1, Martin 1, O'Donnell 1, Whittingham 1, own goals 2.

1945–46

Acquroff J★ 2	Dix RW 26	Howe LF 1	Rundle CR 3
Adams WH 1	Duquemin L 1	Howshall T★ 1	Sargent FA 2
Baily EF 1	Ferrier II★ 1	Hughes WA 27	Skinner G 11
Beasley A★ 2	Fletcher H 1	Jinks JT★ 1	Smith GC★ 4
Bennett LD 11	Ford FGL★ 3	Joslin PJ★ 4	Stevens L 14
Blair J★ 2	Foreman GA 10	Ludford G 30	Walters WE 2
Broadis IA 9	Garwood L 1	Lyman CC 21	Ward RA 26
Buckingham VF 19	Gibbons AH 21	McCormick J 3	Whitchurch CH 17
Burgess R 37	Gilberg H 1	Medley LD 17	White R 25
Chisholm J 1	Hall AE 24	Morrison JA 1	Willis A 32
Cox FJA 1	Hall FW★ 6	Nicholson WE 11	Young AE★ 1
Ditchburn EG 2	Hall J 9	Page AG 16	

Goals (78): Gibbons 14, Foreman 13, Burgess 7, Lyman 7, Broadis 5, Hall AE 5, Dix 4, Ward 4, Whitchurch 4, Ludford 3, Medley 3, Acquroff 2, Jinks 2, Skinner 2, Blair 1, McCormick 1, Stevens 1.

FA Cup goals (2): Burgess 1, Hall AE 1.

Tranmere Rovers

1939–40

Alldis GJ 6	Cox AW 4	Jones C★ 2	Rosenthal A 6
Anderson EW 14	Daniels JF 21	Jones J★ 9	Sloan JW 13
Ashcroft LL 12	Davies E 23	Kirkham J★ 1	Smith WL 1
Bell RC★ 7	Dellow RW★ 1	Malam A★ 1	Staniford H 3
Bellis G★ 7	Evans W 3	Martin A 5	Teasdale WR★ 2
Bridges H 21	Griffiths JE 13	Mitten C★ 5	Walkden EV 6
Buckley EC 3	Hassall JK★ 1	Needham FR★ 1	Walters TB★ 1
Byrom T 14	Hawthorn W★ 1	Obrey A 8	Yates R★ 2
Caffrey J★ 2	Hodgson R 11	Owen AA 24	
Cartwright WJ 9	Howarth H★ 2	Price WB 10	

Goals (47): Bridges 10, Sloan 6, Griffiths 5, Bell 4, Davies 3, Ashcroft 2, Mitten 2, Rosenthal 2, Yates 2, Buckley 1, Byrom 1, Cartwright 1, Cox 1, Hodgson 1, Jones C 1, Malam 1, Martin 1, own goals 3.

1940–41

Alldis GJ 1	Cox AW 18	Jones TG★ 1	Simpson BT 3
Anderson AJ 4	Davies E 23	Kieran G 1	Sloan JW 5
Anderson EW 19	Gerrard EG 1	King RAG 3	Spencer RBA 2
Ashcroft LL 29	Gibbons W 16	Martin A 2	Stanley P 3
Atkinson RF 3	Greenhalgh N★ 1	Mitten C★ 6	Stevenson AE★ 1
Bell H 5	Griffiths H 1	Moore NW★ 1	Teasdale WR★ 17
Bentham SJ★ 1	Griffiths JE 2	Noble P 1	Thomson J★ 1
Breeze JL★ 11	Gunn GD★ 8	Owen AA 26	Whitfield T 2
Bridges H 2	Hodgson R 25	Paterson J 6	Wishart A 25
Byrom T 1	Jeffes FS 1	Price JT 6	Wood JG 4
Caffrey J 2	Jones BW★ 2	Price WB 25	Wyles TC★ 1
Cartwright WJ 6	Jones CF 1	Rosenthal A 5	
Coley WE★ 2	Jones TB★ 8	Rosenthal G 1	

Goals (82): Davies 10, Mitten 10, Ashcroft 8, Cox 7, Jones TB 7, Hodgson 6, Sloan 6, Bell 5, Atkinson 2, Bridges 2, Griffiths H 2, Paterson 2, Rosenthal A 2, Wishart 2, Alldis 1, Anderson E 1, Griffiths J 1, Jones BW 1, King 1, Rosenthal G 1, Stanley 1, Wood 1, Wyles 1, own goals 2.

1941–42

Alldis GJ 8	Eaton D 1	Hullett W★ 2	Mitten C★ 1
Anderson EW 6	Ferguson AP 3	Jones JE 2	Newton C★ 1
Ashcroft LL 11	Foster R★ 1	Jones TB 13	Owen AA 32
Bell H 25	Gale R★ 3	Kieran G 2	Price JT 16
Breeze JT★ 3	Gibbons W 18	Lamb HE 4	Price WB 19
Bremner GH★ 1	Glidden GS★ 11	Lewis TH★ 11	Rosenthal A 15
Bridges H 10	Griffiths JE 1	Lovett PR★ 16	Rosenthal G 1
Caffrey J 4	Harlock DS 10	Malam A★ 1	Sloan JW 1
Cartwright WJ 15	Heydon C★ 5	McAdam DR 3	Spencer RBA 3
Climo NW 3	Higgins WC 1	McIntosh JM★ 1	Teasdale WR 8
Coats A★ 5	Hodgson R 21	McMahon JJ 1	Warrington E 1
Cooper J★ 5	Hornby EV 1	McPeake M 7	Wishart A 12
Cox AW 2	Hughes L 13	Miles LA 1	Yeardsley RW 2

Goals (59): Bell 14, Bridges 7, Jones TB 5, Lewis 5, Hodgson 4, Ashcroft 3, Cartwright 2, Hullett 2, Rosenthal A 2, Alldis 1, Climo 1, Cooper 1, Cox 1, Harlock 1, Heydon 1, Jones J 1, Lamb 1, Malam 1, McMahon 1, McPeake 1, Owen 1, Sloan 1, own goals 2.

1942–43

Alldis GJ   5
Anderson EW   9
Ashcroft LL   5
Bell H   25
Bridges H   11
Burnett GG*   1
Cartwright WJ   3
Chedgzoy S*   1
Coom C   2
Cox AW   1
Dunroe R   6
Evans WH   5
Foster R*   2
Frost AD*   5

Gibbons W   1
Glidden GS*   33
Hale D   1
Harlock DS   9
Haworth J   1
Heydon C*   1
Higgins WC   2
Hill M*   28
Hodgson R   30
Hornby EV   5
Hughes L   26
Hunter E   1
Jackson WP   33
Kieran G   1

Kieran LV   2
Lamb HE   34
Lewis TH*   1
Maddocks WE   1
Mangan W   1
Milburn James*   1
Newton C   2
Owen AA   36
Payne AC   5
Price JT   2
Ratcliffe B*   2
Reid J   1
Rosenthal A   12
Saint JHH   4

Saunders HS   3
Smith A*   1
Staniford H   1
Stuttart JE*   2
Threlfall T   11
Tickell E   1
Tunney E*   8
Urmston T*   5
Wheeler JW   4
Williamson J   1
Yeardsley RW   24

Goals (73): Jackson 15, Bridges 9, Bell 6, Frost 4, Lamb 4, Rosenthal 4, Coom 3, Glidden 3, Hill 3, Saint 3, Alldis 2, Ashcroft 2, Harlock 2, Higgins 2, Saunders 2, Urmston 2, Cox 1, Evans 1, Haworth 1, Lewis 1, Smith 1, own goals 2.

1943–44

Allder DA   1
Anderson EW   21
Ashcroft LL   6
Bell H   23
Bentham SJ*   1
Birkett W*   11
Bridges H   7
Campbell F   1
Coats A*   3
Cochrane –*   1
Curran F*   1
Davies E   4
Dennett JW   3
Drinkwater J*   4
Evans AH   2
Foster R   12
Gibbons W   4

Glidden GS*   31
Grundy JA*   3
Harlock DS   1
Harvey ER   1
Heydon C*   6
Higgins A*   1
Hill M*   13
Hodgson L   1
Hodgson R   8
Hornby EV   9
Horner L   1
Hughes S   18
Hyslop A*   9
Jackson WP   6
Jones A*   1
Jones J   2
Jones R   7

Kieran LV   37
Lamb HE   3
Lynch J   3
Makin G*   4
Martin A   1
Melaniphy EM*   1
Murphy E*   2
Nelson PC   3
Newton C   2
O'Donnell H*   1
Owen AA   12
Patterson GL*   17
Payne AC   2
Price JT   2
Rosenthal A   10
Saunders HS   1
Sloan JW   1

Spencer RBA   3
Staniford H   1
Steele PE   13
Thorpe S   4
Threlfall T   15
Walters T   6
Watts FJ   2
Wheeler JW   21
Wilder FM   1
Williamson J   1
Williamson SH   18
Williamson T*   1
Worthington LL   1
Wyles TC*   6

Goals (68): Glidden 28, Patterson 7, Ashcroft 3, Bridges 3, Walters 3, Wheeler 3, Bell 2, Jackson 2, Makin 2, Anderson 1, Bentham 1, Campbell 1, Coats 1, Curran 1, Heydon 1, Hill 1, Hodgson R 1, Jones R 1, Rosenthal 1, Sloan 1, Williamson J 1, Williamson S 1, Williamson T 1, Wyles 1.

1944–45

Allder DA   6
Anderson EW   27
Atkinson H   17
Barrett HA   12
Bell H   10
Bentham SJ*   3
Bridges H   4
Butler EAE*   39
Cartwright WJ   2
Davies E   2
Fisher J*   1
Forshaw JE   8
Gibbons W   5

Glidden GS*   32
Gould H   14
Hanson AJ*   27
Harlock DS   1
Heydon C*   1
Hodgson L   1
Hodgson R   3
Hornby EV   23
Jones R   3
Kane J   1
Kieran LV   11
Kinder J*   1
Lamb HE   1

Lee J*   15
MacIntosh H*   1
McCormick JM*   1
Morrey B   7
Newton C   3
Nightingale D*   1
O'Mahony M*   3
Owen AA   20
Philpotts J*   4
Purcell S   2
Ratcliffe B*   2
Richards E   9
Rosenthal A   12

Salmon L*   4
Smith J*   1
Southall W   9
Steele PE   20
Tunney E*   3
Webster W   3
Weir A*   1
Wheeler JW   10
Williamson J   8
Williamson SH   40
Wright S   2
Wyles TC*   14
Yeardsley RW   1

Goals (60): Glidden 15, Hanson 11, Wyles 8, Atkinson 6, Rosenthal 5, Williamson S 3, Gould 2, Heydon 2, Williamson J 2, Allder 1, Jones 1, Kinder 1, Lamb 1, Lee 1, Richards 1.

1945–46

Allder DA   6
Alldis GJ   1
Anderson EW   30
Archer JW★   2
Ashcroft LL   11
Atkinson H   14
Barrett AH   1
Bell H   22
Bridges H   28
Butler EAE★   6
Cartwright WJ   1
Curnow J★   5

Forshaw JP   4
Frost AD★   3
Gibbons W   4
Gould H   10
Grant JA★   2
Griffiths JE   3
Harlock DS   23
Hodgson L   6
Hornby EV   33
Jones TB   25
Kieran G   2
Kieran LV   4

Lamb HE   7
Lapsley D   1
Lloyd H   16
Nightingale D   1
Payne AC   17
Philpotts J   1
Powell A   2
Price WB   9
Read D   8
Richards E   10
Rochford E★   1
Rosenthal A   15

Sloan JW   2
Southall W   1
Spencer RBA   3
Steele PE   6
Webster W   1
Wheeler JW   2
Whitehead W★   7
Williams J   3
Williamson J   5
Williamson SH   31
Woodvine A★   1

Goals (66): Bridges 17, Jones 8, Gould 7, Atkinson 6, Harlock 5, Ashcroft 4, Rosenthal 4, Allder 3, Price 2, Williamson J 2, Bell 1, Frost 1, Griffiths 1, Lamb 1, Philpotts 1, Sloan 1, Whitehead 1, own goal 1.

FA Cup goals (10): Rosenthal 4, Ashcroft 2, Atkinson 2, Bell 1, Williamson S 1.

Walsall

1939–40

Adams R   1
Alsop G   31
Beattie JM★   8
Beesley JH   1
Beeson G   2
Biddlestone TF★   7
Brown WS★   22
Bulger CG   29

Buttery A★   1
Clarke I★   1
Dryden J★   1
Edwards GR★   4
Fisher FT★   1
Godfrey C   30
Grosvenor AT★   2
Hancocks J   21

Harper K   2
Hickman JA★   4
Male NA   28
Morgan LD   22
Richards D   22
Shelton JBT   18
Starling RW★   5
Strong GJ   3

Talbot FL   3
Taylor T   9
Thayne W   17
Walton G   3
Williams BF   21
Wood T★   22

Goals (54): Alsop 24, Brown 10, Bulger 6, Wood 6, Hancocks 2, Taylor 2, Edwards 1, Male 1, Starling 1, own goal 1.

War Cup goals (10): Alsop 4, Dryden 2, Brown 1, Hancocks 1, Hickman 1, Wood 1.

1940–41

Alsop G   2
Beesley JH   13
Biddlestone TF★   32
Brown WS   28
Bulger CG   1
Dryden J★   7

Godfrey C   32
Hancocks J   27
Jones GT   1
Male NA   31
Morgan LD   27
Richards D   19

Rowley JF★   14
Shelton JBT   32
Starling RW★   33
Thayne W   8
Vinall EJ★   29
Walton G   5

Williams BF   1
Wood T★   31
Wrigglesworth W★   1

Goals (104): Vinall 27, Rowley 24, Hancocks 15, Brown 13, Starling 8, Beesley 5, Dryden 3, Walton 2, Wood 2, Alsop 1, Richards 1, Thayne 1, Wrigglesworth 1, own goal 1.

1941–42

Alsop G   2
Arnold J   1
Ashley H★   12
Auckland DW★   2
Ball G   4
Batty SG★   12
Beesley JH   26
Biddlestone TF★   29
Brown WS   11
Bulger CG   9

Coles V★   1
Dudley G★   5
Duffy C★   3
Dyall SE   4
Embleton E★   1
Evans CJ★   1
Godfrey C   19
Hancocks J   6
Holland R   4
Jarvis L   9

Lane H★   1
Lewis J★   5
Lord I★   1
Male NA   18
Morgan LD   26
Newsome R★   5
Richardson WG★   1
Roberts F★   1
Shell FH★   6
Shelton JBT   31

Smith AJ★   1
Starling RW★   20
Thayne W   5
Tranter AR★   3
Vinall EJ★   25
Wilkie CH★   2
Williams BF   2
Wood T★   27

Goals (63): Vinall 18, Beesley 9, Brown 7, Wood 5, Ashley 4, Batty 3, Hancocks 3, Newsome 3, Starling 3, Shell 2, Alsop 1, Dudley 1, Embleton 1, Shelton 1, Wilkie 1, own goal 1.

1942–43

Alsop G   1
Arnold J   1
Ashley H★   16
Ball G   1
Batty SG★   15
Beesley JH   6
Bilton DH★   7
Brown WS   15
Bullock AE★   1
Clarke I★   2
Collins GE★   1
Colquhoun DM★   1
Dickie MM   2
Dickie P★   3

Doherty PD★   2
Dudley G★   14
Dunkley M★   4
Emmanuel DL★   6
Featherstone J   3
Grainger D★   1
Halliday G   1
Hancocks J   3
Hann I★   3
Harper K★   3
Haycock F   1
Hickman A★   2
Hird E★   1
Ireland HW★   2

Jarvis L   8
Lewis J★   24
Lindley WM★   2
Male NA   25
Martin E   3
Mason DW★   1
Mason WS★   1
Mitchell TG   3
Morgan LD   24
Newsome R★   21
Nicholls H★   14
Powell IV★   3
Reid M   1
Reid WM   2

Rist FH★   1
Russell DW★   1
Shelton JBT   30
Streten BR   2
Symons R   1
Timms C   2
Tranter AR   17
Vause PG★   6
Vinall EJ★   16
Watts J★   4
Wilkinson H★   2
Williams BF   25
Wood T★   17

Goals (55): Nicholls 11, Brown 9, Newsome 6, Wood 6, Tranter 4, Vinall 4, Ashley 3, Doherty 2, Dudley 2, Martin 2, Alsop 1, Arnold 1, Ireland 1, Lewis 1, Mason D 1, Streten 1.

1943–44

Alsop G   9
Batty SG★   30
Brown WS   27
Bulger CG   1
Childs F   1
Cooper T   3
Dougall C★   7
Dudley G★   16
Emmanuel DL★   23
Featherstone J   2
Griffiths EO   3
Hancocks J   3

Hardy R★   1
Harper K★   1
Hayward LE★   1
Hinsley G★   21
Jackson GA   1
Jarvis L   3
Jones B★   1
Lewis J★   32
Lowery H★   8
Male NA   30
Maund J★   4
McCormick J★   3

Morgan LD   2
Mullen W★   6
Mulligan E   2
Newsome R★   1
Nicholls H★   4
Penrose N★   3
Reid WM   3
Richman FW   7
Rist FH★   25
Roberts NE★   9
Robinson G   1
Shelton JBT   35

Streten BR   4
Taylor J   1
Tranter AR   1
Tully J   1
Turley –   1
Vause PG★   3
Welsh A   3
Williams BF   35
Wood T★   6
Wright EV★   1

Goals (44): Hinsley 11, Brown 10, Dudley 5, Alsop 4, Batty 2, Bulger 1, Harper 1, Lewis 1, McCormick 1, Penrose 1, Reid 1, Richman 1, Roberts 1, Welsh 2, Wood 1, own goal 1.

1944–45

Allan –   1
Alsop G   21
Archibald C   3
Armstrong M★   10
Barker J★   1
Batty SG★   5
Beach G   7
Beck H★   1
Beesley JH   3
Billingsley G★   3
Bilton DH★   1
Boonham G   5
Brown J★   2
Buckingham G   1
Bulger CG   4
Clough J★   1
Cromwell T   1

Crutchley R   7
Flack WLW★   1
Forrester G   1
Gallon JW★   1
Goffin WC★   1
Gregory A★   1
Haigh W★   1
Hall A★   1
Harper J★   2
Hinsley G★   14
Hobbis HHF★   3
Houghton R★   7
Jarvis L   2
Jenkins RJ   6
Jessop W★   1
Johnson J★   1
Kelly FC   1

Kendrick K★   1
Kernick DHG★   1
Layton W★   1
Lewis J★   30
Little JJ★   2
Lowe G   1
Lowery H★   17
Lycett T★   4
Male G★   2
Male NA   32
McKenna M★   1
McKenzie J   1
Meath G   13
Morgan LD   4
Morris J★   1
Mullen W★   2
Mulligan E★   8

Peace HJ   17
Pearson TU★   2
Price S   1
Ratcliffe J   1
Redwood DJ★   3
Richman FW   3
Rist FH★   21
Russell DW★   2
Shelton JBT   30
Smith A★   2
Smythe G   1
Snape H   1
Stone C   4
Streten BR   5
Vinall EJ★   28
White FRH★   7
Williams BF   26

Goals (51): Alsop 11, Armstrong 6, Boonham 5, Peace 4, Hinsley 3, Pearson 3, Vinall 3, Beach 2, Mulligan 2, Russell 2, Archibald 1, Kernick 1, Lewis 1, Meath 1, Morris 1, Ratcliffe 1, Richman 1, Shelton 1, Snape 1, White 1.

1945–46

Acquroff J★   1
Alsop G   33
Barratt H★   1
Beach G   3
Bennett S   4
Brown WS   3
Bulger CG   5
Clark G★   3
Clarke J   1
Crutchley R   36
Darby D★   1
Evans A   5
Finch L   1
Forder JL★   1
Foulkes RE   25

Gedders E   1
Goffin WC★   1
Hamers L   1
Hancocks J   30
Harding EJ★   2
Harper K   1
Harvey E   1
Heaselgrave SE★   2
Hinks HJ   1
Hinsley G★   1
Jarvis J   1
Jenkins RJ   8
Kelly FC   17
Lewis J★   2
Lewis John   34

Lowery H★   4
Male NA   15
McNab A★   2
Methley I   17
Mullard AT   25
Newman AD   27
Paxton J★   1
Payne LT   3
Peace HJ   4
Peck WT   2
Pritchard RT★   1
Rowlinson H   1
Sankey J★   10
Screen J★   7
Shelley A   1

Shelton JBT   16
Skidmore W★   1
Smith E★   1
Stone C   4
Strong GJ   1
Talbot FL   25
Vinall EJ★   5
Walker R★   2
Walton G   2
White FRH★   1
Wilkie W   1
Williams BF   2
Wilshaw DJ★   10
Wood T★   1

Goals (68): Hancocks 14, Kelly 12, Alsop 11, Mullard 8, Talbot 6, Wilshaw 4, Bennett 3, Darby 3, Barratt 1, Bulger 1, Evans 1, Foulkes 1, Goffin 1, Jenkins 1, Vinall 1.

FA Cup goals (4): Alsop 1, Bennett 1, Mullard 1, Talbot 1.

Watford

1939–40

Armstrong JH 39	Findlay W 1	Lewis DJ 36	Reed AG 1
Barnett TA 37	Fitzgerald AM★ 5	Lewis TG 37	Walls D★ 1
Curran PJ 1	Foss SR★ 3	McHugh J 38	Walters TC★ 21
Dabbs BE 2	Harris WT 36	Miller HS★ 4	Williams RF 1
Davies W 39	Jones TJ 39	O'Brien RV 36	Woodward A 38
Duncombe AJ 2	Lager EW 3	Perry E★ 1	
Evans DR 4	Law WGM 2	Postlethwaite TW 2	

Goals (89): Lewis TG 22, Davies 20, Barnett 13, Walters 13, Jones 6, Lager 4, O'Brien 4, Woodward 2, Duncombe 1, Evans 1, Law 1, own goals 2.

War Cup goals (5): Davies 3, Lewis TG 2.

1940–41

Armstrong JH 2	Drinkwater CJ★ 4	Jones W 5	Robinson T 8
Barker J★ 1	Duncombe A 8	Lewis DJ 20	Saunders W★ 9
Barnett TA 38	Dunsmore TH★ 1	Lewis HH 28	Tidman DE★ 1
Boulton FP★ 5	Findlay W 2	Lewis TG 33	Walters TC★ 1
Brown J 12	Galley T★ 31	Lowe HP★ 1	Waymouth D 3
Cock DL★ 1	Giddings P 11	Lunn G★ 1	Williams RF 38
Crawford E★ 1	Gray H★ 1	McGivern A★ 1	Woodward A 37
Cringan JA★ 2	Harris W 6	McHugh J 28	Young L 3
Dabbs BE 1	Hunt GA★ 1	Miller HS★ 16	
Davidson DBL★ 12	Jones EN★ 6	Pease A 1	
Davies W 10	Jones TJ 38	Ramsbottom A★ 1	

Goals (101): Lewis TG 27, Lewis H 19, Barnett 8, Davies 7, Brown 6, Jones T 6, Galley 5, Miller 4, Williams 4, Robinson 3, Jones E 2, Pease 2, Saunders 2, Walters 2, Drinkwater 1, Woodward 1, own goals 2.

1941–42

Armstrong R★ 1	Davies W 2	Hughes S★ 2	Robinson T★ 2
Bacon CW★ 1	Delaney –★ 1	Hutton H★ 3	Robinson TW★ 18
Barnett TA 9	Dougall C★ 5	Jepson A★ 11	Salltall A★ 1
Barrs –★ 1	Drinkwater CJ★ 7	Jobling J★ 15	Sliman A★ 1
Bearryman HW★ 1	Dugnolle JH★ 6	Jones –★ 1	Smith GC★ 1
Biggs AG★ 3	Durman –★ 1	Jones EN★ 15	Sykes J★ 1
Blandford –★ 1	Egan GD★ 3	Jones TJ 35	Wainwright –★ 1
Bonass AE★ 2	Evans R 3	Jones W★ 4	Walker –★ 1
Boulton FP★ 12	Findlay W 2	Killourhy M★ 17	Waller H★ 2
Briggs F★ 8	Fitzsimmons P★ 4	Kurz FJ★ 11	Walters TC★ 4
Broome FH★ 1	Galley T★ 8	Lancelotte EC★ 1	Ward –★ 1
Brown –★ 1	Gregory FC★ 1	Lane W★ 1	Watson-Smith N★ 3
Brown J★ 9	Griffiths J★ 4	Learmouth –★ 2	Weightman E★ 3
Burley B★ 1	Halford D★ 4	Lewis HH 7	Westcott D★ 3
Cockburn –★ 1	Hall A★ 1	Lewis J 2	Whittaker W★ 1
Cooke G★ 1	Hamilton –★ 1	Lewis TG 4	Williams RF 20
Cowie A★ 4	Harris T 20	Mansell N★ 1	Wilson –★ 1
Cringan JA★ 15	Henson –★ 1	McIntosh A★ 7	Wipfler CP 2
Croom W★ 1	Hitchins AW★ 1	Miller HS★ 1	Woodgate JT★ 1
Davidson D★ 5	Hobbis HHF★ 1	Morris T★ 14	Woodward A 13
Davidson DBL★ 6	Holliday –★ 1	Reece TS★ 1	

Goals (57): Westcott 8, Killourhy 7, Kurz 6, Jones T 4, Hutton 3, Jones E 3, Lewis TG 3, Morris 3, Biggs 2, Brown 2, Galley 2, Barnett 1, Briggs 1, Broome 1, Dougall 1, Cringan 1, Egan 1, Griffiths 1, Halford 1, Lewis H 1, Lancelotte 1, Robinson 1, Waller 1, Wipfler 1, own goal 1.

1942–43

Aicken AV★ 1
Barrett J★ 1
Bates WH★ 1
Broadhurst R★ 3
Brook L★ 1
Brown G 4
Brown HS★ 12
Brown J★ 1
Brown JB 6
Brown WH 21
Butterworth FC★ 1
Cooke G 2
Davies W 1
Davies W★ 1
Dougal N★ 2
Dreyer G★ 3
Drinkwater CJ★ 1
Driver A★ 4
Edwards R★ 1
Embleton E★ 3

Farmer A★ 1
Farrant R 1
Ferrier H★ 2
Findlay W 1
Gray R 9
Harvey J★ 1
Haver J 3
Haysman W 2
Head BJ★ 9
Hogg J 2
Horwood JS 5
Jackson H★ 10
Jepson A★ 2
Jobling J★ 7
Jobson TH★ 1
Jones C★ 5
Jones EN★ 21
Jones F 7
Jones TJ 31
Kurz FJ★ 6

Lane W 2
Lewis TG 3
Loom BC 3
Lowe HP★ 2
March R★ 1
Martin DK★ 11
Mason WS★ 11
Matthewson G★ 1
Maudsley R★ 1
McLachlan P 1
Milburn James ★ 5
Millar W 4
Molloy P★ 1
Morris J★ 17
Morris R★ 2
Moss G★ 1
Perkins LA 1
Pugh SJ★ 2
Quinney J★ 1
Rickett H 12

Roberts F★ 3
Robinson TW★ 6
Saunders K 1
Saunders W 1
Shaw J★ 18
Smith C★ 2
Smith JCR★ 1
Smith N 2
Thompson A★ 2
Ware H★ 10
Weir A★ 3
Westcott D★ 1
White AS 5
White HG 1
Williams RF 25
Winter DT★ 9
Wipfler CP 4
Woodcock A★ 1
Young AE★ 1

Goals (60): Jones E 10, Martin 7, Jackson 6, Morris 6, Lewis TG 5, Loom 4, Jones T 3, Jones F 2, Kurz 2, Ware 2, Weir 2, Broadhurst 1, Brown H 1, Brown J 1, Driver 1, Lane 1, Pugh 1, Robinson 1, Westcott 1, White A 1, own goals 2.

1943–44

Anderson JC★ 3
Annis G 2
Baines SN★ 7
Biggerstaff FS 2
Brain J 13
Brown G 1
Brown HS★ 2
Brown WH★ 31
Cruickshank J★ 2
Davies W 21
Drinkwater CJ★ 2
Dugnolle JH★ 14
Forder FF 1
Fowler A 6
Glaister G★ 3
Guest G★ 9
Gunner R★ 1
Hipkin R★ 5

Howe F★ 2
Jackson H★ 18
Jeffries A★ 1
Jepson A★ 11
Jobling J★ 1
Johnson R★ 11
Jones TJ 30
Jones V 1
Lewis TG 1
Liddell J★ 1
Loughran J★ 8
Lowe HP★ 1
Lowes AR★ 1
Malpass ST★ 1
Mason WS★ 12
McLeod D★ 5
McTavish H 1
Milburn James ★ 14

Morris J★ 4
Murray T 7
Muttitt E★ 1
Naylor TW★ 1
Needham FR★ 1
Reed AG 1
Robinson TW★ 1
Ross R★ 25
Sands HA 1
Saunders K 6
Saunders W 2
Shaw J★ 28
Smeaton J★ 1
Smith JCR★ 1
Smith P★ 1
Smith T★ 1
Smith TW★ 1
Spencer TW 1

Stone J★ 3
Taylor E 2
Taylor J★ 1
Taylor L★ 4
Walker C★ 1
Walls R★ 3
Ware H★ 4
Warner LH★ 20
Westcott D★ 4
White A 1
Whittle J★ 3
Williams EE★ 7
Williams RF 12
Williamson J 1
Younger A★ 1

Goals (65): Brain 12, Davies 12, Jackson 11, Guest 4, Brown W 3, Jones T 3, Walls 3, Warner 2, Westcott 2, Williams R 2, Baines 1, Loughran 1, Lowes 1, Milburn 1, Ross 1, Shaw 1, Stone 1, Smith T 1, White 1, Younger 1, own goal 1.

1944–45

Allen M 1
Baines SN★ 12
Barnett TA 1
Barnham R★ 1
Bastin CS★ 1
Bennett SJ 1
Birkbeck T 1
Bowles JC★ 1
Brain J 6
Brand N★ 1
Bright PW★ 1
Brown HS★ 3
Brown JH★ 3
Brown WH★ 29
Browne RJ★ 22
Burnicle WF★ 2

Croucher RGG 1
Curran PJ 2
Davies W 18
Denby S★ 1
Drinkwater CJ 7
Dutton T★ 4
Dykes H★ 1
Findlay W 1
Franklin JL★ 1
Gallimore L 1
Groves HG 1
Hartshorne J★ 3
Haywood EJ★ 1
Hipkin R★ 3
Hooper S★ 1
Hughes S★ 2

Hunt GH★ 1
Jackson H★ 20
Jezzard BA 5
Jobling J★ 1
Jones F★ 1
Jones TJ 28
Lewis DJ 2
Lewis TG 20
Matthewson G★ 1
McCracken J 1
McLeod D★ 1
McNeil J★ 1
Milburn James★ 14
Moffat J 1
Moody KG★ 2
Nisbet KH 1

Paul R★ 4
Rothery H★ 1
Saunders K 22
Saunders W★ 31
Shaw J★ 20
Smith TW★ 5
Spencer TW 2
Stone J★ 8
Tadman MR★ 1
Taylor E★ 1
Tivendale J 12
Walker S★ 7
Wicks F★ 1
Williams RF 31
Woodward A 4
Wrigglesworth JL 12

Goals (72): Lewis TG 23, Jackson 11, Wrigglesworth 10, Williams 4, Brain 3, Dykes 3, Milburn 3, Baines 2, Stone 2, Walker 2, Bennett 1, Curran 1, Davies 1, Dutton 1, Hooper 1, Jezzard 1, Jones F 1, Smith 1, Tivendale 1.

1945–46

Anthony DWJ 1	Farnen L 1	Lewis TG 27	Saunders W* 8
Beck J 1	Feeney E 1	Linsley G 1	Shaw J* 30
Beckett W 18	Gallimore L 17	Martindale L* 2	Smith –* 1
Bland GP 1	Gillespie P 33	Mee G 26	Smith T 2
Brown R* 1	Goodman H 2	Merrett G 1	Stamford H 1
Brown W* 11	Gray R 35	Mortensen SH* 1	Stocker T* 2
Curran PJ 14	Harris WT 3	Moss F 1	Store J* 8
Davidson DBL* 1	Howshall T* 5	O'Brien RV 18	Surtees H 1
Davies W 22	Jezzard BA 13	Paterson J 2	Tivendale J 1
Drinkwater CJ 24	Jobling A* 1	Poole B* 5	Weir A 18
Dunderdale WL 8	Jones TJ 22	Ratcliffe B* 1	
Edelston M* 1	Kelly A* 1	Saunders K 2	

Goals (65): Lewis TG 21, Davies 8, Beckett 6, Dunderdale 5, Gray 5, Jezzard 5, Drinkwater 3, Weir 3, Curran 2, Jones T 2, Brown W 1, Edelston 1, Saunders W 1, own goals 2.

FA Cup goals (12): Gray 4, Lewis TG 3, Davies 1, Jezzard 1, own goals 3.

West Bromwich Albion

1939–40

Adams J 6
Banks GE 7
Bassett ICH 6
Bell T 15
Butler S 3
Clarke I 2
Connelly E 28
Davies C 3
Gripton WE 24
Heaselgrave SE 12
Johnson JA 28
Jones EN 5
Jones HJ 30
Kinsell TH 3
Lowery H 4
McNab A 28
Newsome R 25
Richardson WG 1
Sankey J 29
Saunders W 25
Shaw CE 31
White H 23
Witcomb DF 3

Goals (95): Jones H 38, Newsome 14, Johnson 9, Connelly 8, Bell 5, Sankey 5, Banks 4, Heaselgrave 4, Jones E 4, Witcomb 2, Butler 1, own goal 1.

War Cup goals (12): Jones H 4, Connelly 3, Heaselgrave 2, Richardson 1, Sankey 1, own goal 1.

1940–41

Adams J 30
Alderwick J 1
Bassett ICH 19
Chapman G 12
Clarke I 9
Connelly E 14
Davies C 1
Dudley G 6
Edwards CI 24
Elliott WB 19
Evans CJ 2
Goodall EI★ 1
Gripton WE 28
Heaselgrave SE 26
Hodgetts F 2
Johnson JA 24
Jones EN 2
Jones HJ 4
Kinsell TH 24
Lowery H 6
McNab A 5
Newsome R 9
Price AJW★ 1
Quinton W★ 1
Richardson WG 26
Sankey J 30
Shaw CE 20
Wilkes GA 3
Witcomb DF 3

Goals (92): Richardson 29, Elliott 15, Heaselgrave 13, Johnson 7, Sankey 7, Newsome 4, Wilkes 4, Chapman 2, Gripton 2, Jones H 2, Price 2, Clarke 1, Evans 1, Hodgetts 1, Shaw 1, own goal 1.

1941–42

Adams J 25
Ashley H★ 3
Banks GE 1
Bassett ICH 29
Bowen TH 1
Clarke I 4
Dearson DJ★ 1
Dudley G 6
Edwards CI 27
Elliott WB 31
Evans CJ 31
Gripton WE 26
Harris W 2
Heaselgrave SE 9
Johnson JA 20
Jones CW 1
Jones HJ 3
Kinsell TH 1
Lowery H 1
May GC 1
McKennan P★ 15
McNab A 15
Merrick GH★ 3
Quinton W★ 1
Richardson WG 24
Sankey J 25
Shaw CE 30
Wilkes GA 1
Willetts G 1
Witcomb DF 3

Goals (115): Elliott 31, Richardson 31, Evans 14, McKennan 13, Johnson 7, Sankey 5, Jones H 4, Edwards 2, Ashley 1, Bowen 1, Clarke 1, Dearson 1, Dudley 1, Gripton 1, Heaselgrave 1, Wilkes 1.

1942–43

Adams J 33
Ashley H★ 9
Bassett ICH 19
Billingsley G★ 1
Brown A★ 1
Burgin M 2
Butler H 1
Butler K 1
Butler S 2
Bye JH★ 1
Chapman G 1
Clarke I 5
Davenport A 1
Davies C 4
Dearson DJ★ 4
Doherty PD★ 2
Dudley G 6
Dunkley M★ 1
Edwards CI 3
Elliott WB 24
Evans AJ 6
Evans CE 36
Finch LC 19
Green T★ 3
Gripton WE 29
Hapgood EA★ 3
Harris W 1
Heaselgrave SE 12
Hodgetts F 13
Johnson JA 2
Jones EN 3
Jones HJ 2
Jones S★ 1
Kinsell TH 1
Lane H★ 2
Marks WG★ 1
McDonald JC★ 6
McNab A 17
Millard L 35
Newsome R 4
Parker A 2
Richardson WG 14
Robinson E 1
Sankey J 26
Scott L★ 2
Shaw CE 11
Shelton J★ 5
Simms H 1
Smalley T★ 1
Smith AJ★ 30
Smith J★ 2
Walsh W★ 1
Witcomb DF 4
Wood T★ 1

Goals (84): Elliott 17, Richardson 17, Millard 7, Evans C 6, Ashley 5, Heaselgrave 4, Sankey 4, Clarke 3, Shaw 3, Doherty 2, Dudley 2, Evans A 2, Finch 2, Green 2, Jones E 2, Dearson 1, Hodgetts 1, Jones H 1, Lane 1, Newsome 1, Witcomb 1.

1943–44

Acquroff J★   5
Adams J   10
Adderley JB   1
Armstrong M★   8
Ashley H★   1
Ball HG   10
Bassett ICH   14
Bradley DJ   1
Clarke I   4
Duns L★   13

Edwards CI   4
Elliott WB   26
Evans AJ   4
Evans CJ   33
Finch LC   5
Griffiths J★   1
Gripton WE   38
Guest WF★   4
Heaselgrave SE   11
Heath NH   29

Hodgetts F   24
Jones EN   7
McCormick J★   6
McNab A   27
Millard L   39
Pears WG   1
Pemberton JHA   1
Richardson WG   19
Rowley GA   1
Russell TJ   4

Sankey J   6
Smith AJ★   32
Southam JH   23
White H   2
Wilcoxson GH   1
Williams G   6
Witcomb DF   8

Goals (88): Elliott 28, Richardson 21, Ball 8, Acquroff 5, Duns 5, Hodgetts 5, Heaselgrave 4, Evans C 4, Clarke 2, Guest 2, Witcomb 2, Armstrong 1, Jones E 1, Pears 1, Russell 1.

Includes two extra-time goals.

1944–45

Adams J   5
Ball HG   6
Barlow RJ   1
Bowen TH   5
Clarke I   35
Dudley G   1
Elliott WB   13
Evans CJ   23
Finch R   6

Gripton WE   39
Hardwick GFM★   3
Heaselgrave SE   35
Heath NH   6
Hodgetts F   40
Johnson JA   9
Jones EN   4
Kinsell TH   7
Lewis E   28

Lowery H   15
Male N★   1
McNab A   37
Millard L   38
Parker A   3
Parkes H★   6
Richardson WG   4
Rowley GA   6
Sankey J   9

Saunders DG★   3
Saunders W   1
Shelton J★   1
Smith L★   3
Southam JH   9
Tranter GH   16
Vincent EA   1
Williams G   21

Goals (75): Clarke 29, Heaselgrave 13, Elliott 7, Evans 6, Hodgetts 6, Johnson 2, McNab 2, Rowley 2, Smith 2, Ball 1, Bowen 1, Parker 1, Richardson 1, Saunders D 1, own goal 1.

1945–46

Banks GE   8
Barlow RW   32
Bradly DJ   1
Butler S   25
Clarke I   35
Connelly E   10
Edwards CI   1
Elliott WB   34
Evans CJ   4

Gomm B   4
Gripton WE   6
Harris W   12
Heaselgrave SE   1
Hodgetts F   29
Hood OG   1
Jinks J★   1
Kinsell TH   31
Millard L   37

Newsome R   12
Pears W   3
Rowley GA   9
Ryan RA   17
Sanders JA   27
Saunders DG   2
Saunders W   2
Shaw CE   29
Southam JH   2

Tranter GH   34
Twigg WL   1
White H   13
Williams G   1
Williams N   1
Witcomb DF   37

Goals (104): Clarke 19, Elliott 19, Barlow 12, Newsome 10, Hodgetts 9, Rowley 8, Butler 7, Banks 4, Millard 4, Connelly 3, Saunders D 2, Gomm 1, Jinks 1, Pears 1, White 1, Witcomb 1, own goals 2.

FA Cup goals (6): Clarke 3, Newsome 2, Connelly 1.

West Ham United

1939–40

Attwell RF 1	Corbett NG 6	Griffiths R★ 1	Pearson HF★ 1
Barrett JW 30	Curtis GF★ 16	Hapgood EA★ 2	Richardson R★ 1
Bicknell C 38	Drake EJ★ 2	Harris JB 2	Robinson GH★ 1
Brown ARJ★ 1	Dunn R 2	Hobbis HHF★ 2	Roles A★ 1
Brown W★ 1	Fenton EBA 32	Howe L★ 1	Sidey W★ 1
Burke JJ★ 1	Flack DW★ 2	Hubbard C 3	Small SJ 22
Burton S 3	Forde S 2	Jinks JT★ 1	Smith EJ★ 1
Cann H★ 4	Foreman GA 34	Jones LJ★ 1	Smith JCR★ 1
Cater R 1	Foxall JS 34	Joy B★ 1	Taylor GE 1
Chalkley AG 7	Gore R 2	Macaulay AR 9	Walker CE 30
Chapman E 2	Goulden LA 26	Masson W★ 4	Walker RWE 30
Cockroft J 19	Green GH★ 2	McLeod J★ 1	Wilkins GE★ 2
Conway H 16	Gregory E 4	Medhurst HE 10	Wood EJ 11

Goals (115): Foreman 36, Fenton E 17, Small 16, Foxall 15, Barrett 7, Goulden 5, Wood 5, Macaulay 3, Curtis 2, Dunn 2, Hubbard 2, Walker R 2, Bicknell 1, Wilkins 1, own goal 1.

War Cup goals (24): Foreman 7, Foxall 4, Macaulay 4, Small 4, Gordon 2, Fenton E 1, own goals 2.

1940–41

Barrett JW 26	Foreman GA 29	Macaulay AR 10	Walker REW 9
Bicknell C 19	Foxall JS 31	Medhurst HE 3	Waller H★ 4
Chalkley AG 25	Goulden LA 27	Nieuwenhuys B★ 7	Whittaker W★ 1
Chapman E 10	Green GH★ 1	Osborne J★ 1	Wood EJ 1
Cockroft J 3	Gregory E 10	Penny HC★ 1	Woodgate JT 1
Conway H 13	Hobbins SG★ 5	Phypers E★ 1	Yorston BC★ 2
Corbett NG 12	Hobbis HHF★ 12	Savage RE★ 7	
Fenton EBA 17	Joy B★ 1	Small SJ 28	
Ferris R★ 1	Lewis WA 13	Walker CE 9	

Ten players only v Clapton Orient 28.9.40.

Goals (80): Foreman 27, Foxall 15, Goulden 8, Barrett 7, Fenton E 7, Small 7, Macaulay 2, Nieuwenhuys 2, Chapman 1, Corbett 1, Hobbis 1, Lewis 1, Osborne 1.

London Cup

Banner A 1, Barrett 6, Bicknell 10, Chalkley 7, Chapman 1, Collier – 1, Corbett 4, Fenton 5, Foreman 10, Foxall 10, Goulden 8, Green 3, Gregory 5, Hobbis 9, Lewis 3, Macaulay 4, Medhurst 5, Nieuwenhuys 1, Savage 2, Small 10, Walker R 2, Waller 2, Wood 1.

Goals: Foreman 7, Small 5, Foxall 2, Goulden 2, Hobbis 2, Bicknell 1, Chalkley 1, Corbett 1, Fenton 1, Wood 1.

1941–42

Attwell RF 11	Forde S 1	Macaulay AR 15	Tann BJ★ 1
Banner A 6	Foreman GA 36	Mahon J★ 4	Taylor GE 3
Barrett JW 11	Foxall JS 32	Medhurst HE 14	Walker CE 3
Bicknell C 32	Gore R 2	Nieuwenhuys B★ 10	Walker REW 16
Chalkley AG 22	Goulden LA 35	Pryde RI★ 1	Waller H★ 2
Chapman E 7	Gregory E 16	Quickenden – 1	Whatley WJ★ 1
Corbett NG 20	Jobling J★ 1	Ricketts HF★ 2	Wood EJ 6
Dunn R 3	Jones LJ★ 1	Sliman A★ 1	
Fenton EBA 34	Lewis WA 15	Small SJ 31	

Goals (99): Foreman 28, Foxall 14, Goulden 13, Small 12, Chapman 6, Fenton E 5, Wood 5, Macaulay 4, Bicknell 3, Mahon 3, Nieuwenhuys 3, Barrett 1, Corbett 1, Quickenden 1.

1942–43

Aicken AV★ 1	Corbett WR★ 9	Jones E 1	Taylor GE 4
Attwell RF 19	Davies C★ 1	Kippax FP★ 9	Trigg SA★ 1
Banner A 4	Dunkley M★ 1	Lewis WA 31	Walker REW 2
Barrett JW 6	Dunn R 14	Macaulay AR 9	Walker TJ★ 9
Bartram S★ 1	Fenton EBA 21	Mahon J★ 12	Waller H★ 1
Bicknell C 22	Foreman GA 34	Medhurst HE 15	Watson-Smith S 1
Brown AW★ 1	Foxall JS 18	Muttitt E★ 1	Wood EJ 16
Chalkley AG 6	Gladwin G 7	Page AE★ 3	Woodgate TJ 2
Chapman E 2	Goulden LA 30	Riordan J★ 1	Wright H★ 1
Corbett NG 16	Gregory E 13	Small SJ 29	

Goals (99): Foreman 30, Goulden 17, Dunn 14, Small 9, Foxall 8, Wood 4, Fenton E 3, Mahon 3, Kippax 2, Trigg 2, Barrett 1, Macaulay 1, Walker T 1, Woodgate 1, own goals 3.

1943–44

Aldridge RE 1	Dunn R 11	Jones DO★ 25	Smith JT★ 1
Armeson LR★ 4	Fenton EBA 23	Lewis WA 32	Taylor GE 1
Attwell RF 7	Foreman GA 35	Lowes AR★ 1	Walker TJ★ 6
Bicknell C 31	Foxall JS 13	Macaulay AR 5	Weaver S★ 1
Cardwell L★ 1	Gibbs A 1	Mahon J★ 2	Wilson RG 1
Chalkley AG 3	Gillespie IC★ 1	Medhurst HE 18	Wood EJ 17
Chapman E 2	Girling HM★ 1	Morris R★ 1	Woodgate TJ 1
Corbett NG 16	Goulden LA 34	Muttitt E★ 1	Wright H★ 1
Corbett WR★ 22	Gregory E 14	Parsons EG 2	
Deans T★ 4	Hobbis HHF★ 10	Sanders JA★ 1	
Dunkley M★ 10	Hughes WA★ 1	Small SJ 34	

Goals (89): Foreman 24, Goulden 13, Wood 12, Small 11, Dunn 7, Fenton E 5, Foxall 4, Macaulay 2, Bicknell 1, Deans 1, Dunkley 1, Hobbis 1, Lowes 1, Mahon 1, Parsons 1, Smith 1, Weaver 1, own goals 2.

1944–45

Attwell RF 4	Corbett WR★ 2	Henley L★ 1	Ridyard A★ 1
Bainbridge KV 3	Deans T★ 2	Hopkins I★ 1	Robinson J★ 1
Banner A 2	Dodds E★ 10	Hubbard C 1	Small SJ 9
Barrett JW 4	Dunn R 14	Hunt DA★ 1	Smith EJ★ 1
Bell R 1	Fenton BRV★ 1	Jones DO★ 17	Taylor GE 4
Bicknell C 31	Fenton EBA 31	Lewis WA 35	Thomas DWJ★ 1
Briddon S★ 1	Ferrier RJ★ 1	Ludford G★ 3	Thomas RA★ 1
Buchanan PS★ 1	Foreman GA 15	Macaulay AR 12	Townsend L★ 1
Burke C★ 1	Foxall JS 2	Mallett J★ 1	Whitchurch CH★ 15
Burnett T★ 1	Goulden LA 31	Medhurst HE 29	Wilson RG 24
Chapman E 1	Gregory E 4	Medley LD★ 1	Wood EJ 14
Cheetham TM★ 1	Hall AG★ 6	Parker D 1	Woodgate TJ 30
Corbett NG 30	Hall JL★ 1	Pritchard HJ★ 1	

Goals (111): Goulden 17, Foreman 15, Dodds 11, Whitchurch 9, Woodgate 9, Wood 8, Hall A 6, Small 6, Dunn 3, Fenton E 3, Ludford 3, Bainbridge 2, Cheetham 2, Corbett N 2, Macaulay 2, Wilson 2, Barrett 1, Chapman 1, Fenton B 1, Foxall 1, Lewis 1, Mallett 1, Medley 1, Thomas D 1, Townsend 1, own goals 2.

1945–46

Attwell RF 7	Forde S 1	Medhurst HE 42	Wilson RG 11
Bainbridge KV 9	Foreman GA 23	Powell-Bossans P 1	Wood EJ 29
Bicknell C 41	Gray G 1	Small SJ 25	Woodgate TJ 39
Cater R 21	Hall AG 34	Travis D 6	Wright K 5
Corbett NG 26	Harris JB 1	Walker CE 19	
Dunn R 1	Hopkins I★ 1	Walker REW 40	
Fenton EBA 37	Macaulay AR 23	Whitchurch CH 19	

Goals (94): Hall 16, Foreman 13, Woodgate 12, Small 10, Macaulay 9, Travis 7, Wood 7, Wright 5, Bicknell 4, Bainbridge 3, Fenton E 3, Whitchurch 3, Gray 1, own goal 1.

FA Cup goals (7): Hall 3, Wood 2, Bainbridge 1, Foreman 1.

Wolverhampton Wanderers

1939–40

Alderton JH 2	Finch LC★ 1	McMahon D 6	Smith AJ 2
Bainbridge A 1	Galley T 25	Morris WW 3	Somerfield A 1
Brown HS 1	Gardiner J 23	Mullen J 31	Springthorpe TA 9
Burden TD 3	Glasberg LH 1	Parker WD 5	Steen AW 19
Buttery L 1	Goddard R 25	Pedley FI 2	Taylor F 29
Clewlow SJ 2	King FAB 2	Plunkett SE 1	Thornhill D 20
Cullis S 8	Maguire JE 3	Scott RA 9	Westcott D 21
Dorsett R 15	McAloon G 1	Sidlow C 22	Wright H 1
Dowen JS★ 6	McIntosh A 21	Smalley T★ 3	Wright WA 16

Goals (79): Westcott 26, Dorsett 16, McMahon 9, Mullen 7, Taylor 5, Wright W 5, Galley 3, McIntosh 3, Gardiner 1, King 1, McAloon 1, Somerfield 1, own goal 1.

War Cup goals (6): Dorsett 3, Wright W 2, Westcott 1.

1940–41

Did not compete.

1941–42

Alderton JH 15	Davenport F 6	McDonald JC★ 1	Springthorpe TA 23
Asbridge T 1	Dorsett R 15	McIntosh A 4	Stevenson E 28
Ashton D 29	Dowen JS★ 21	McIntosh T 3	Taylor F 14
Aston WH 1	Dunningham JY 1	Morgan R★ 2	Taylor T★ 1
Barrett HJ 1	Galley T 10	Mullen J 27	Thornhill D 34
Broome FH★ 8	Gardiner J 8	O'Donnell F★ 4	Trigg C★ 1
Brown HS 2	Goddard R 8	Pritchard RT 1	Turner L 3
Brown WS★ 1	Goldthorpe A 1	Robinson E 5	Walker D 4
Burton CG 1	Hambly MLJ 1	Rowley JF★ 2	Wardle JH 1
Christopher RW 1	Johnstone D★ 1	Scott RA 9	Westcott D 19
Clarke GS 9	Kirkham R 1	Shorthouse WH 1	Wright H 1
Crook WC 1	Leitch J★ 1	Sidlow C 17	Wright WA 27
Cullis S 1	Marsh R★ 1	Singleton B 9	
Curtis GF★ 2	McCormick J★ 4	Smith AJ★ 3	

Goals (79): Westcott 28, Mullin 11, Rowley 7, Wright W 7, Stevenson 6, Broome 5, Dorsett 3, Robinson 3, Galley 2, McIntosh A 2, O'Donnell 2, Alderton 1, Ashton 1, Brown 1, Curtis 1, Gardiner 1.

Includes one extra-time goal. Additional scorer in Cup-Winners' Cup: Mullen.

1942–43

Alderton JH 18	Dorsett R 7	Michael R 1	Singleton B 1
Ashton D 30	Dowen JS★ 22	Morby J 1	Skidmore W 2
Attenborough G 1	Dunn J 24	Morgan WA 1	Somerfield A 1
Bailey A★ 1	Emanuel DL★ 1	Mullen J 4	Springthorpe TA 1
Ball SW 3	Ford J 2	Mulraney A★ 4	Steen AW 1
Barrass MW 3	Franklin N★ 1	Mynard LD 1	Stephens AE 2
Battiste C 1	Galley T 14	O'Neill J 1	Stevenson E 3
Bilton DH 3	Gardiner J 16	Pleasant J 1	Taylor F 2
Bowden HN★ 1	Greenaway J 1	Pringle J 1	Thornhill D 9
Buchanan CC 7	Hooks J★ 1	Pritchard RT 12	Walker D 1
Burden TD 2	Jackman JW 10	Reece TS★ 1	Walters H 4
Clark GS 5	Kelly L 7	Reeves G 2	Westcott D 13
Crook AR 4	King R 1	Roberts DG 9	Wright H 2
Crook WC 19	Kirkham R 2	Rowley GA★ 8	Wright WA 10
Crowe V 4	McIntosh A 4	Rowley JF★ 1	
Cullis S 5	McLean A 28	Shorthouse WH 1	
Darby D 3	Methley I★ 2	Sidlow C 31	

Goals (66): Westcott 18, Dorsett 8, Rowley J 8, Wright W 7, Pritchard 3, Rowley GA 3, Barrass 2, Dunn 2, Galley 2, Gardiner 2, Stevenson 2, Bailey 1, Ball 1, Clark 1, Crook W 1, Crowe 1, McIntosh 1, McLean 1, Walters 1, own goal 1.

1943–44

Aldecoa E 32	Crowe V 5	Lee K 9	Skidmore W 6
Alderton JH 11	Cullis S 2	Lovesey WS 1	Stephens AE 24
Ashton D 30	Davies K 10	Malcolm KC 1	Streten BR★ 4
Atkins A 1	Dorsett R 6	McLean A 37	Taylor F 3
Bicknell R 3	Dowen JS★ 4	Morgan WA 3	Thornhill D 2
Billingsley G★ 6	Dunn J 25	Mullen J 2	Wagg W 1
Bilton DH 3	Galley T 7	Mulvaney J★ 1	Wallis J 1
Black R★ 1	Gardiner J 2	Owen ILT 4	Walters H 10
Blunt E★ 1	Haycock F★ 7	Pickstock S 2	Westcott D 5
Brooks GJ 1	Hayward LC 2	Prince H 10	Wilshaw DJ 11
Buchanan CC 3	Hazelton D 1	Pritchard RT 8	Wood T★ 2
Buckby M 1	Houghton R★ 1	Roberts DG 1	Wright H 1
Clark GS 1	Isherwood D 2	Rowley JF★ 3	Wright WA 3
Crilly G 1	Jackman JW 2	Shelton JBT★ 1	
Crook AR 8	Kelly L 22	Shorthouse WH 1	
Crook WC 33	Kirkham R 13	Sidlow C 14	

Goals (58): Aldecoa 11, McLean 8, Westcott 5, Davies 4, Lee 4, Stephens 4, Wilshaw 4, Dunn 3, Buchanan 2, Crook W 2, Dowen 2, Isherwood 2, Mullen 2, Bicknell 1, Dorsett 1, Jackman 1, Rowley 1, Wright W 1.

1944–45

Acquroff J★ 24	Fenton M★ 2	Kirkham J★ 16	Scott L★ 2
Aldecoa E 16	Finch LC★ 31	Lee K 4	Scott RA 39
Alderton JH 35	Green WC 1	McAloon G 1	Sidlow C 2
Ashton D 33	Harris J 6	McIntosh A 1	Skidmore W 1
Ball SW 1	Harris R 1	McLean A 25	Smith AJ★ 8
Bennett R 1	Haycock F★ 1	Mitten C★ 1	Smith LJ 3
Bicknell R 2	Heathcote W★ 2	Morris WW 32	Somerfield A 5
Brown ARJ★ 1	Iddon H★ 1	Mullen J 6	Stephens AE 2
Buchanan CC 7	Jackman JW 1	Mynard LD 2	Westcott D 1
Crook WC 37	Jinks JT★ 1	Parsons DR 1	Wharton G★ 4
Crowe V 1	Johnson WH★ 2	Patterson G★ 1	Williams G 1
Davies K 19	Jones DO★ 1	Paxton JW 2	Wilshaw DJ 2
Dorsett R 6	Kelly L 2	Pritchard RT 1	Wright H 2
Dowen JS★ 4	Kelly M 1	Roberts DG 6	Wright WA 21
Dunn J 28	King FAB 1	Rowley JF★ 1	

Goals (76): Acquroff 18, Wright W 9, Dunn 7, Finch 5, Davies 4, Aldecoa 3, Fenton 3, Jinks 3, Mullen 3, Alderton 2, Dorsett 2, Kirkham 2, Buchanan 1, Crook W 1, Haycock 1, Heathcote 1, Johnson 1, King 1, Lee 1, Mitten 1, Morris 1, Rowley 1, Smith L 1, Wharton 1, Williams 1, Wilshaw 1, Wright H 1, own goal 1.

Includes one extra-time goal.

1945–46

Alderton JH 31	Dorsett R 7	Maguire JE 1	Rowley JF★ 1
Ashton D 23	Dunn J 23	McIntosh A 9	Sanderson JR 1
Bennett R 6	Galley T 15	McLean A 34	Scott RA 10
Bicknell R 2	Gibson CH★ 2	Methley I 1	Sidlow C 3
Buchanan CC 2	Goddard R 4	Miller D 11	Smith LJ 10
Chatham RH 29	Green WC 2	Morris WW 31	Steen AW 5
Crook WC 31	Harris J 1	Mullen J 12	Stephens AE 4
Cullis S 13	Jackman JW 1	Paxton JW 8	Westcott D 13
Darby D 6	King FAB 25	Pritchard RT 1	Williams BF 29
Davies K 11	Kirkham R 3	Ramscar FT 10	Wright WA 31

Goals (75): Chatham 14, Westcott 12, Wright W 9, Dorsett 8, King 5, Mullen 4, Buchanan 3, Darby 3, Dunn 3, Smith 3, Crook 2, Davies 2, Bennett 1, Galley 1, McIntosh 1, Miller 1, Ramscar 1, own goals 2.

FA Cup goals (15): Galley 4, Wright W 3, Chatham 2, Davies 2, Crook 1, Dunn 1, King 1, Mullen 1.

Wrexham

1939–40

Antonio GR★ 3	Coen L 9	Mathias JT 3	Smallwood F★ 2
Astbury TA★ 2	Cook W★ 11	McKennan P★ 1	Snow GEG 25
Baker F★ 1	Cooper T★ 3	McMahon P★ 1	Sproston B★ 1
Bamford T★ 2	Cullis S★ 4	Milburn James★ 5	Stubbs PEG★ 1
Bell RC★ 1	Edwards GR 1	Morris W★ 4	Taylor N★ 2
Bellis TG 5	Hough F★ 1	Moss F★ 1	Tennant JW★ 1
Bradbury T 5	Hughes JH★ 21	Nelson AO 2	Tudor W★ 14
Bridges H★ 1	Jones C 1	Redfern W★ 4	Tunney E 14
Briggs F 15	Jones JT★ 19	Roberts J★ 7	White F★ 2
Brown AR 12	Kelly G 2	Rogers E★ 21	Williams JJ 11
Brown VC★ 1	Kelsall C 3	Savage RE 3	Witcomb DF★ 2
Bryan W 3	Martin JR★ 5	Screen J 14	Woodman JA 3

Goals (48): Rogers 15, Roberts 7, Brown A 4, Coen 4, Cook 3, McKennan 2, Antonio 1, Bamford 1, Bell 1, Edwards 1, Hughes J 1, Kelly 1, Martin 1, Morris 1, Nelson 1, Redfern 1, Snow 1, Stubbs 1, Woodman 1.

War Cup goals (4): Bell 2, Coen 1, Cook 1.

1940–41

Anderson AJ★ 4	Dearson DJ★ 1	Lloyd JH 1	Smallwood F★ 3
Anderson EW★ 3	Devlin J 10	Major A★ 1	Smith C★ 1
Anderson JD★ 2	Dickenson A★ 10	Matthews S★ 1	Snow GEG 8
Astbury TA★ 1	Emmanuel T★ 12	McAvoy D 5	Springthorpe TA★ 2
Bamford T★ 12	Ferrier J 2	McGratton H 2	Steen AW★ 12
Bellamy W 19	Foulkes RE★ 1	Morris W★ 18	Timms BV★ 7
Bellis TG 1	Gladwin G★ 1	Owen AA★ 1	Trentham DH★ 3
Bidewell SH★ 1	Griffiths T 1	Park J 12	Waring T★ 2
Blunt E★ 19	Hampson – 1	Redfern W★ 31	Williams G 1
Briggs F 1	Hanson AJ★ 1	Reece T★ 1	Woodburn J★ 5
Brigham H★ 2	Hayward LE★ 17	Roberts WH★ 13	Wright H★ 2
Bryan W 21	Howarth H★ 3	Rogers E★ 20	Yates R★ 2
Butt L★ 2	Hughes JH★ 3	Rugman K 1	
Buxton A★ 4	Jones NG 3	Sale T★ 1	
Cope G★ 1	Kelsall C 19	Sidlow C★ 7	

Goals (84): Redfern 17, Bamford 8, Morris 6, Park 6, Rogers 6, Butt 5, Steen 5, Timms 5, Blunt 4, McAvoy 4, Smith 3, Snow 3, Devlin 2, Waring 2, Anderson A 1, Astbury 1, Ferrier 1, Kelsall 1, Roberts 1, Smallwood 1, Trentham 1, Yates 1.

1941–42

Antonio GR★ 2	Ellis J 9	Jones TG★ 5	Roberts LH 2
Armitage LG★ 2	Franklin N★ 1	Lloyd C 3	Roberts W 1
Atkinson WH 6	Frost AD★ 1	Lloyd JH 13	Rogers E 6
Barrett JW★ 1	Graham W★ 11	Lovett PR★ 1	Sidlow C★ 2
Bellamy WE 5	Griffiths H★ 7	McAvoy DH 8	Smallwood F★ 1
Bremner GH★ 25	Haines JTW★ 1	Milburn James★ 16	Steen AW★ 7
Briggs F 2	Herod DJ★ 1	Moore NW★ 13	Stevens GL★ 2
Burnett GG★ 3	Hewitt H 2	Morgan G 1	Swain GS★ 1
Carver – 1	Horsman W★ 4	Morris J★ 1	Swinnerton KS★ 1
Clark GV★ 1	Jones C 21	Park JB 5	Turner A 27
Cole C 3	Jones CW★ 2	Pritchard FJ★ 2	Tutin A★ 4
Cope G★ 2	Jones DD★ 1	Pritty G★ 2	Wallbanks J★ 24
Davies CT 3	Jones JE★ 13	Prydderch I 1	White FRH★ 6
Davies GR 5	Jones JT★ 1	Reader G 1	Williams JJ★ 1
Devlin J 4	Jones NG 5	Redfern WJ★ 27	Wright – 1

Goals (66): Redfern 15, Graham 9, Bremner 8, Atkinson 7, Horsman 3, Lloyd J 3, White 3, Jones C 2, Jones CW 2, Steen 2, Turner 2, Antonio 1, Devlin 1, Hewitt 1, McAvoy 1, Moore 1, Morris 1, Park 1, Rogers 1, Wallbanks 1, own goal 1.

1942–43

Anderson –★   1
Baines PC   3
Blunt E★   24
Bremner GH★   16
Burnett GG★   1
Caton WC★   6
Clegg D★   11
Cole C   2
Collins GE   24
Crossley G   1
Dean G   1
Dolby –   1
Driscoll –   1
Dugdale TC   1
Fellowes WJ★   1

Frost AD★   6
Gill H   1
Graham W★   4
Hewitt H   1
Hill AE   1
Hill FR★   31
Hinton EJA   1
Hughes A   2
Hughes WM   1
Jones C   35
Jones CW★   1
Jones David   11
Jones Doug   1
Jones JE★   7
Jones JT★   4

Jones NG   3
Jones TG★   2
Jones TN★   4
Kirton J★   1
Lea GI★   13
Lewis TH★   3
Livingstone A★   12
Lloyd C   20
Lovett PR★   2
McGovern –   1
McNee C★   12
Meade T★   2
Milburn James★   6
Moore NW★   25
Muir MR   6

Payne EGH★   2
Presdee HG★   2
Reader G   1
Roberts W   1
Rogers E   3
Simms HA★   19
Smith –   1
Smith BR   1
Stearn AD★   1
Stuttard JE★   22
Thomas DSL★   2
Turner A★   4
Waring T★   9
White FRH★   4

Goals (79): Moore 12, Blunt 11, Simms 9, Waring 8, Collins 6, Baines 3, Livingstone 3, McNee 3, Muir 3, Rogers 3, Bremner 2, Frost 2, Smith B 2, Thomas 2, White 2, Graham 1, Hewitt 1, Lewis 1, Milburn 1, Stearn 1, own goals 3.

1943–44

Adams EF★   1
Ashton R   4
Baines PC   5
Bamford T★   2
Bellamy WE   4
Birkett W★   1
Bremner GH★   35
Caton WC★   1
Clegg D★   1
Collins GE   1
Davies I   1
Dellow RW★   6

Fairhurst DL★   2
Foxall JS★   13
Griffiths GJ   1
Hill FR   33
Hilliard WR   11
Horsman L★   21
Hughes JH★   6
Hughes L   1
Jefferson A★   15
Jones C   36
Jones JT   1
Jones NG   2

Jones V★   2
Livingstone A★   31
Lloyd C   5
Lovett PR★   1
Malam A★   27
Milburn James★   8
Morgan G   1
Pilling JH   5
Reid C   1
Reid J★   1
Revell C★   8
Rogers E   11

Savage RE   13
Screen J   1
Simms HA   23
Smith A   4
Smith BR   6
Smith L★   4
Stuttard JE★   16
Thomas DSL★   3
Tracey C   2
Tudor W★   22
White FRH★   10
Whitelaw D   20

Goals (105): Bremner 19, Horsman 14, Livingstone 14, Malam 12, Foxall 9, Revell 9, Simms 8, Rogers 4, Hughes J 3, Smith L 3, Dellow 2, Milburn 2, Smith A 2, White 2, Baines 1, Reid J 1.

1944–45

Antonio GR★   1
Armstrong M★   2
Ashton R   3
Baines PC   35
Bamford T★   1
Bellis TG   28
Boyes W★   1
Bremner GH★   30
Briggs F   1
Case D   1
Collins G   6
Cooper J   4
Davies RG★   1
Derrick A★   1

Dix RW★   25
Douglas D★   2
Duns L★   12
Foxall JS★   1
Franklin ST★   4
Fuller C   10
Gavin C★   12
Griffiths D   1
Hancocks J★   19
Hewitt L   1
Hilliard WR   1
Hughes JT★   8
Hughes T   1
Isherwood D   8

Jefferson A★   19
Jones C   40
Jones J   1
Jones JT★   1
Jones R   1
Livingstone A★   13
Lloyd C   15
Lunn G★   1
Makin G★   1
Milburn James★   3
Moss A★   1
Mulligan E   1
Newsome R★   1
Parton B   2

Pilling JH   8
Raven J   3
Revell C★   4
Roberts E★   2
Rogers E★   2
Simmonds G   2
Simms HA   8
Smith A   2
Tudor W★   36
Watson W★   12
Wheatley J★   5
Whitelaw D   36

Goals (95): Baines 27, Dix 12, Hancocks 9, Bremner 7, Isherwood 5, Tudor 4, Livingstone 3, Revell 3, Simms 3, Watson 3, Armstrong 2, Collins 2, Duns 2, Hughes J 2, Bellis 1, Foxall 1, Gavin 1, Griffiths 1, Jones R 1, Newsome 1, Pilling 1, Roberts 1, Rogers 1, Simmonds 1, Smith 1.

1945–46

Archibald M   7
Armstrong M★   5
Arthur J★   1
Ashton RW   21
Baines PC   9
Bellis TG   35
Birkett W★   11
Briggs F   6
Brown AR   11
Burkenshaw GA★   4
Collins AJ   3
Cook W   11

Cooper J   1
Dix RW★   7
Duns L★   5
Eastwood E★   3
Gardner T   22
Gripton WE★   1
Hancocks J★   5
Haycock FJ   16
Hayward A   10
Hewitt L   6
Holliday F   2
Hughes JT★   1

Hughes T★   2
Isherwood D   9
Jackson R   28
Jones C   29
Jones R   2
Jones Ron★   1
Jones TG★   2
Leyland J   1
Lloyd C   8
Malam A★   6
McLarty JJ   8
Oakley M   1

Raven J   2
Roberts W   4
Rogers E   16
Shepherd AL★   2
Speed L   5
Thomas GL   1
Tudor W★   16
Tunney E   23
Watson W★   1
Weaver S★   10
Whitelaw D   3
Worsley H★   2

Goals (58): Haycock 6, Armstrong 4, Baines 4, Dix 4, Hewitt 4, Rogers 4, Hayward 3, Isherwood 3, McLarty 3, Roberts 3, Weaver 3, Archibald 2, Cook 2, Hancocks 2, Malam 2, Arthur 1, Brown 1, Duns 1, Gardner 1, Jackson 1, Jones C 1, Shepherd 1, Speed 1, own goal 1.

FA Cup goals (9): Hayward 2, Lloyd 2, Jones C 1, Haycock 1, Hewitt 1, McLarty 1, Wainwright G 1.

York City

1939–40

Allen W   6
Antonio GR★   1
Barkas T★   1
Boyle MJ   12
Brenen A   10
Collier A   20
Everest J★   8
Ferguson R   16
Gledhill S   18

Hathway EA   3
Hawkins J   19
Hodgson G★   5
Hogg F★   1
Hurst J★   2
Hydes A   5
Kelly JE   3
Lee GC   23
McMahon H★   2

Milner L   2
Milton S   7
Pinder JJ   13
Porritt W   11
Roberts SG   3
Scaife G★   7
Scott FH   3
Sherwood GW★   6
Stephens A★   1

Stockill RR★   16
Thompson JE   3
Tilson SF★   4
Wardle G   7
White N★   2
Woffinden RS★   13

Goals (39): Lee 12, Stockill 6, Hydes 5, Allen 4, Porritt 3, Brenen 2, Hodgson 2, Gledhill 1, Hawkins 1, Sherwood 1, Thompson 1, own goal 1.

War Cup goals (7): Hydes 3, Gallagher 1, Lee 1, Roberts 1, Ward 1.

1940–41

Bargh GW★   10
Beasley A★   1
Brenen A   26
Dawson T★   13
Eastham GR★   4
Everest J★   5
Fallon J   1
Ferguson R   23
Flinton W   2
Forrest –★   1

Gledhill S   31
Halton RL★   12
Hawkins J   10
Hodgson S★   22
Holley T★   1
Hydes A★   1
Jepson A★   8
Jones RG   26
Kelly JE   2
Lee GC   28

Lievesley L★   10
Little G★   22
McGowan J★   1
Mennie F★   4
Mortimer G   1
Patrick A   1
Patrick M   15
Pearson J   1
Pinder JJ   24
Porritt W   11

Rex –   1
Robinson E★   13
Scott FH   1
Stockill RR★   3
Surtees J★   2
Walsh W★   3
Woffinden RS★   1

Goals (66): Brenen 16, Lee 16, Dawson 7, Patrick M 7, Gledhill 4, Robinson 4, Little 3, Halton 2, Mennie 2, Porritt 2, Walsh 2, Flinton 1.

1941–42

Atkinson J★   6
Bentall CE   3
Bradley C   10
Brenen A   28
Brown ARJ★   20
Brown T★   3
Butt L★   1
Carter HS★   1
Collier A   3
Cooke WH★   18
Corbett NG★   1
Davis H★   1
Dawson T★   14

Dean WR   1
Dryden H★   1
Duggan EJ★   2
Fallon J   1
Ferguson R   16
Frankish AW   6
Gillamotte –   1
Gledhill S   31
Halton RL★   1
Hawkins J   5
Hindmarsh JW★   1
Hodgson JV★   31
Jones RG   28

Jones WH★   5
Joslin PJ★   11
Kemp DJ★   2
Lee GC   31
Livingstone A★   8
Lockwood –   1
Marshall CR   3
McGarry T★   4
McInnes JS★   2
Melaniphy EM★   5
O'Donnell F★   3
Patterson GL★   1
Pinder JJ   18

Porritt W   10
Ramsden B★   1
Reagan CM   3
Redfern R★   4
Rudd J★   1
Sargent FA★   7
Waddell W★   4
Waller H★   1
Wilson J★   13
Woodhead C★   13

Goals (80): Lee 26, Brenen 18, Dawson 6, Livingstone 4, Brown A 3, O'Donnell 3, Sargent 3, Bradley 2, Jones R 2, Marshall 2, Melaniphy 2, Bentall 1, Brown T 1, Dean 1, Dryden 1, Gledhill 1, Jones W 1, McGarry 1, Porritt 1, Rudd 1.

1942–43

Barnard R 1	Emmerson W★ 1	Livingstone A★ 1	Reagan CM 3
Bartram S★ 22	Farrington R★ 1	Marshall CR 3	Sanderson T★ 1
Bell R 1	Ferguson R 11	McCormack CJ★ 5	Scott AT 1
Black A★ 1	Forster LR★ 1	McPhie J★ 1	Scott FH 29
Bowden AJ 1	Gledhill S 32	Mills D★ 1	Shimwell E★ 1
Brenen A 21	Hawkins J 3	Milner L 1	Spelman I★ 1
Brown ARJ★ 28	Hodgson S★ 30	Mordey H★ 3	Stone J★ 1
Campbell R★ 13	Jones RG 28	O'Donnell F★ 10	Tutill NA 1
Compton LH★ 3	Knight J★ 20	Pearson W 1	Wilson J★ 34
Coultate C 1	Laing FJ★ 1	Pinder JJ 26	
Cullen J★ 1	Lee AH★ 2	Pollard H★ 5	
Dawson T★ 8	Lee GC 35	Powell A★ 1	

Goals (99): Lee G 26, Brenen 13, O'Donnell 11, Brown 10, Scott F 10, Knight 9, Campbell 4, Compton 2, Gledhill 2, Hodgson 2, McCormack 2, Dawson 1, Marshall 1, Scott A 1, Shimwell 1, Stone 1, Tutill 1, Wilson 1, own goal 1.

1943–44

Barnard R 6	Fenton EBA★ 8	Lawson JR 5	Rayner HJ 2
Bartram S★ 30	Ferguson R 6	Lee GC 31	Reynolds GAC★ 13
Bentall CB 2	Fitzsimons MJ★ 2	Litchfield EC★ 3	Savage RE★ 2
Billington HJR★ 17	Forde J★ 3	Lovell C 1	Scott FH 9
Bowden AJ 3	Gledhill S 34	Makinson J★ 2	Stone J★ 2
Brenen A 20	Harvey J★ 1	Martin J★ 3	Thompson H★ 1
Brown ARJ★ 6	Hastie A★ 1	Massey AW★ 4	Tindale JE 2
Brown T 1	Hawkins H★ 12	McDonald JC★ 2	Walker A 5
Campbell R★ 26	Hick DL 4	McMenemy H★ 1	Walker CH★ 7
Collier A 1	Hill DGD★ 1	Milligan GH★ 1	Wilson J★ 17
Davies CJ★ 1	Johnston A★ 1	O'Donnell F★ 1	Withington RH★ 1
Dawson T★ 33	Killourhy M★ 24	Pickering PB 1	Woodgate TJ★ 14
Dooley GW★ 1	Kirk J★ 1	Pinder JJ 33	
Dunn R★ 8	Knott H★ 1	Poole B★ 1	

Goals (72): Billington 17, Lee 9, Dawson 8, Killourhy 7, Hawkins 6, Walker A 3, Woodgate 3, Brown A 2, Brown T 2, Dunn 2, Fenton 2, Litchfield 2, McDonald 2, Scott F 2, Wilson 2, Brenen 1, O'Donnell 1, Stone 1.

1944–45

Bannister K★ 24	Ellis N★ 1	Makinson J★ 1	Stocker TM★ 1
Barclay R★ 7	Ferguson R 12	Milton S 1	Sutherland H★ 2
Barron J★ 1	Foxcroft G★ 1	Mulraney J★ 3	Taylor A★ 1
Bartram S★ 23	Gledhill S 40	Murphy G★ 1	Thompson H★ 15
Bates D 2	Haddington R★ 1	Nettleton E★ 12	Walshaw K★ 1
Bonass AE★ 1	Halton RL★ 1	Oakes L★ 1	Watmough D 2
Bowden AJ 3	Harvey J★ 1	Oliver J 1	Westlake FA★ 2
Brown T 1	Hatfield B★ 1	Pickering PB 2	Wilson J★ 40
Campbell R★ 4	Hawkins H★ 32	Pinder JJ 31	Wilson K★ 6
Cockcroft W 1	Hays CJ★ 1	Poole B 21	Woods P★ 1
Coyne C★ 1	Johnson JW★ 14	Rayner HJ 1	Woollett C★ 1
Cunningham L★ 2	Lawson JR 24	Riddle H★ 3	Wrigglesworth W★ 3
Dalby M 1	Lee GC 3	Robbins P★ 14	
Dawson T★ 27	Machin AH★ 1	Scott FH 19	
Dix RW★ 15	Maddison R 2	Smith CJ★ 6	

Goals (97): Dawson 21, Hawkins 21, Dix 8, Johnson 7, Thompson 7, Nettleton 5, Scott 5, Wilson J 5, Bartram 3, Bowden 3, Maddison 2, Riddle 2, Bates 1, Haddington 1, Sutherland 1, Taylor 1, Wilson K 1, Woollett 1, Wrigglesworth 1, own goal 1.

1945–46

Allen W   20
Armitage LG★   2
Bentall CE   13
Bilton DH★   1
Blair JJ★   5
Boothroyd S   1
Bowden AJ   3
Bratley G   6
Brenen A   21
Collier A   8
Cooke WH★   6

Daniels J★   2
Dawson T★   9
Dazzleby S★   1
Fensorne W   5
Ferguson R   22
Follon G★   1
Gledhill S   33
Green S   3
Hamer A   1
Iddon H★   11
Lawson JR   1

Lee GC   2
Maddison R   1
Mahon J   11
McMahon E   1
Nettleton E★   11
Oliver HS★   1
Payne EGH★   1
Pickering PB   10
Pinder JJ   28
Poole B   6
Porritt W   11

Reagan CM   1
Robbins P   26
Rodgers C   25
Routledge A   8
Scott FH   19
Thompson H   19
Turnbull R★   1
Walker F   1
Wilson J★   10
Winters IA   17
Young A   11

Goals (64): Winters 16, Allen 12, Dawson 5, Scott 5, Gledhill 3, Nettleton 3, Porritt 3, Thompson 3, Cooke 2, Iddon 2, Mahon 2, Robbins 2, Brenen 1, Maddison 1, Pinder 1, Routledge 1, own goals 2.

FA Cup goals (15): Winters 4, Scott 3, Allen 1, Brenen 1, Gledhill 1, Lee 1, Maddison 1, Mahon 1, Robbins 1, own goal 1.

Aberaman Athletic

1942–43

Goals (68): Carr 7, Crisp 7, Roy 6, Clayton 5, Tompkins 5, Cumner 4, Evans 3, Ford 3, McKenzie 3, McLaren 3, Chilcott 2, Smith 2, Airlie 1, Astley 1, Brinton 1, Chedzoy 1, Comley 1, Davis 1, Derrick 1, Hall 1, Hanford 1, Jones 1, Lewis 1, Lowry 1, Macaulay 1, Mahoney 1, Milsom 1, Rogers 1, Thomas 1, Williams 1.

1943–44

Goals (52): Hall 10, Carr 5, Tadman 4, Williams 4, Brown W 3, Brooks 2, Brown 2, Edwards 2, Pitt 2, Roy 2, Sharpe 2, Swinfen 2, Woodward 2, Armstrong 1, Cumner 1, Day 1, Evans 1, Hooper 1, Moses 1, Murphy 1, O'Mahoney 1, Prescott 1, Tucker 1.

1944–45

Goals (70): Williams 18, Brain 8, Comley 8, Griffiths 7, Brooks 5, Crisp 5, Woodward 5, Tennant 3, Hanford 2, Lewis 2, Brown 1, Burgess 1, Davies 1, Howarth 1, Jones 1, Roy 1, own goal 1.

Bath City

1942–43

Goals (115): Mortensen 13, Ball 12, Thompson 11, Rothwell 10, Smith J 10, Barley 5, Little 5, Machent 5, Hamilton 4, Stock 4, Hall 3, Knight 3, Brain 2, Carr 2, Davidson 2, Davies 2, Kirkham 2, Litchfield 2, Metcalfe 2, Millward 2, Passmore 2, Bailey 1, Barnes 1, Feltham 1, Johnson 1, Lay 1, McLachlan 1, Markham 1, Morris 1, Owen 1, Southam 1, own goals 2.

1943–44

Goals (119): McCulloch 24, Little 12, Parris 12, Turner 12, Howe 11, Tadman 9, Rosenthal 7, Hall A 5, Clarke 4, Liddle 4, Law 3, Thompson 3, Hull 2, Knight 2, Wigmore 2, Edwards 1, Gregory 1, Johnson 1, Mortensen 1, Owens 1, Sheen 1, Stock 1.

1944–45

Goals (92): Sloan 18, Sheen 10, Little 7, Murphy 7, Hall A 6, Tadman 6, Brown 4, Sibley 4, Urquhart 4, Butterworth 3, Pearson 3, Talbot 3, Markham 2, Barron 1, Barrow 1, Clarkson 1, Feltham 1, Harrison 1, Holland 1, Jones 1, Laing 1, McDonough 1, Sargent 1, Simmons 1, Warren 1, Wigmore 1, own goals 2.

Lovell's Athletic

1942–43

Goals (122): Owen WM 29, Shelley 24, Clarke 22, Crisp 12, Nieuwenhuys 12, Williams 6, Jones 5, Lucas 5, Tadman 4, Hobbis 1, Rogers 1, own goal 1.

1943–44

Goals (110): Owen WM 41, Lucas 13, Shelley 9, Crisp 7, Hardwick 7, Jones E 7, Wetter 6, Nieuwenhuys 5, Clarke 4, Watkins 2, Williams 2, Derrick 1, Lowe 1, Thompson 1, Witcomb 1, Wood 1, own goals 2.

1944–45

Goals (84): Clarke 13, Jones E 13, Lucas 13, Guest 10, Edwards 8, Hardwick 7, Holland 6, Ware 4, Murphy 3, Connor 2, Sheen 2, Duns 1, Wetter 1, Witcomb 1.

With the exception of Cardiff, all west clubs played League West Cup games against Plymouth on a home and away basis, though Bristol appeared to play once only at home. Scorers in these games were as follows: Aberaman Ath 2 (Brain 2); Bath C 8 (Urquhart 4, Sloan 3, Mortensen 1); Lovell's Ath 3 (Hardwick 1, Jones 1, Witcomb 1); Swansea T 4 (Burns 3, Jones 1); Bristol C 3 (Thomas 3).

Plymouth scored 19 goals in these games: Brown 6, Prescott 4, Loft 2, Adams 1, Court 1, Jewell 1, Thomas 1, Tugwell 1, Williamson 1, own goal 1.

The League Cup West Final was between Bath C and Bristol C. Bath won 5-3 on aggregate. The scorers were: Bath C 5 (Rosenthal 3, Turner 1, Urquhart 1), Bristol C 3 (Hargreaves 1, Thomas 1, Williams 1).

1939–40

DIVISION A 1939–40

	P	W	D	L	F	A	Pts
1 Rangers	5	4	1	0	14	3	9
2 Falkirk	5	4	0	1	20	10	8
3 Hearts	5	2	2	1	14	9	6
4 Aberdeen	5	3	0	2	9	9	6
5 Partick T	5	2	2	1	7	7	6
6 Celtic	5	3	0	2	7	8	6
7 Albion R	5	2	1	2	12	7	5
8 Motherwell	5	2	1	2	14	12	5
9 Third Lanark	5	2	1	2	9	8	5
10 Kilmarnock	5	2	1	2	10	9	5
11 Q of S	5	2	1	2	10	9	5
12 St Mirren	5	1	3	1	8	8	5
13 Hamilton A	5	2	1	2	7	11	5
14 Arbroath	5	2	0	3	9	9	4
15 St Johnstone	5	2	0	3	7	8	4
16 Hibernian	5	2	0	3	11	13	4
17 Alloa Ath	5	2	0	3	8	13	4
18 Ayr U	5	2	0	3	10	17	4
19 Clyde	5	1	0	4	10	14	2
20 Cowdenbeath	5	1	0	4	6	18	2

DIVISION B 1939–40

	P	W	D	L	F	A	Pts
1 Dundee	4	3	1	0	13	5	7
2 Dunfermline A	4	2	2	0	10	5	6
3 King's Park	4	2	2	0	11	7	6
4 East Fife	4	2	1	1	12	6	5
5 Queen's Park	4	1	3	0	7	5	5
6 Stenhousemuir	4	2	1	1	6	5	5
7 Dundee U	4	2	1	1	8	7	5
8 Dumbarton	4	2	1	1	9	9	5
9 East Stirling	4	1	2	1	7	7	4
10 St Bernard's	4	1	2	1	7	7	4
11 Airdrie	4	2	0	2	7	8	4
12 Edinburgh C	4	1	1	2	9	8	3
13 Montrose	4	1	1	2	7	8	3
14 Raith R	4	1	1	2	8	12	3
15 Morton	4	1	1	2	4	7	3
16 Leith Ath	4	1	0	3	4	7	2
17 Brechin C	4	0	2	2	3	8	2
18 Forfar Ath	4	0	0	4	7	18	0

WEST 1939–40

	P	W	D	L	F	A	Pts
1 Rangers	30	22	4	4	72	36	48
2 Q of S	30	17	6	7	77	55	40
3 Hamilton A	30	15	8	7	78	55	38
4 Motherwell	30	15	8	7	64	56	38
5 Morton	30	14	5	11	64	46	33
6 Albion R	30	15	2	13	62	60	32
7 Clyde	30	11	9	10	68	51	31
8 Kilmarnock	30	13	5	12	63	63	31
9 Airdrie	30	14	2	14	63	61	30
10 St Mirren	30	11	4	15	59	66	26
11 Partick T	30	10	6	14	57	74	26
12 Third Lanark	30	10	5	15	53	78	25
13 Celtic	30	9	6	15	55	61	24
14 Queen's Park	30	7	7	16	55	82	21
15 Ayr U	30	7	5	18	50	66	19
16 Dumbarton	30	7	4	19	48	78	18

EAST AND NORTH-EAST 1939–40

	P	W	D	L	F	A	Pts
1 Falkirk	28	19	5	4	97	47	43
2 Hearts	28	17	4	7	101	64	38
3 Dunfermline A	28	18	2	8	77	55	38
4 Aberdeen	28	15	4	9	78	49	34
5 St Johnstone	28	12	8	8	81	69	32
6 Dundee	28	11	7	10	69	61	29
7 Alloa Ath	28	12	4	12	54	59	28
8 Hibernian	28	11	5	12	78	65	27
9 Dundee U	28	12	2	14	66	73	26
10 East Fife	28	11	3	14	78	87	25
11 Raith R	28	10	3	15	66	80	23
12 King's Park	28	9	4	15	60	83	22
13 St Bernard's	28	8	5	15	44	73	21
14 Stenhousemuir	28	7	3	18	50	93	17
15 Arbroath	28	6	5	17	44	85	17

Cowdenbeath resigned after 15 matches. Rangers defeated Falkirk 2-1 in deciding match.

1940–41

SOUTHERN 1940–41

		P	W	D	L	F	A	Pts
1	Rangers	30	21	4	5	79	33	46
2	Clyde	30	18	7	5	99	61	43
3	Hibernian	30	14	7	9	74	61	35
4	Airdrie	30	13	8	9	75	62	34
5	Celtic	30	14	6	10	48	40	34
6	Falkirk	30	13	7	10	78	73	33
7	St Mirren	30	12	8	10	55	57	32
8	Motherwell	30	13	4	13	73	65	30
9	Morton	30	9	11	10	67	62	29
10	Hearts	30	12	5	13	64	71	29
11	Hamilton A	30	11	6	13	67	75	28
12	Partick T	30	9	8	13	55	62	26
13	Third Lanark	30	9	7	14	56	80	25
14	Dumbarton	30	10	4	16	58	78	24
15	Albion R	30	6	5	19	45	80	17
16	Queen's Park	30	6	3	21	46	79	15

1941–42

NORTH EASTERN 1941–42 1st Series

		P	W	D	L	F	A	Pts
1	Rangers	14	10	2	2	52	22	22
2	East Fife	14	8	5	1	34	16	21
3	Aberdeen	14	8	3	3	49	23	19
4	Dunfermline A	14	6	3	5	38	44	15
5	St Bernard's	14	5	3	6	36	48	13
6	Dundee U	14	3	4	7	32	45	10
7	Raith R	14	3	1	10	40	57	7
8	Leith Ath	14	2	1	11	31	57	5

NORTH EASTERN 1941–42 2nd Series

		P	W	D	L	F	A	Pts
1	Aberdeen	14	9	2	3	37	15	26
2	Rangers	14	10	1	3	49	33	26
3	East Fife	14	8	2	4	32	27	22
4	Dundee U	14	7	3	4	37	25	21
5	Raith R	14	6	2	6	38	38	17
6	Dunfermline A	14	4	2	8	30	42	12
7	Leith Ath	14	3	2	9	29	46	9
8	St Bernard's	14	1	2	11	19	45	4

In North Eastern League an extra point awarded for better goal aggregate over home and away matches.

SOUTHERN 1941–42

		P	W	D	L	F	A	Pts
1	Rangers	30	22	4	4	97	35	48
2	Hibernian	30	18	4	8	85	46	40
3	Celtic	30	15	9	6	69	50	39
4	Motherwell	30	16	3	11	76	62	35
5	Hearts	30	14	4	12	85	72	32
6	Clyde	30	13	6	11	79	75	32
7	Third Lanark	30	14	2	14	79	90	30
8	Falkirk	30	13	4	13	60	72	30
9	Morton	30	12	5	13	60	54	29
10	Queen's Park	30	11	5	14	55	56	27
11	St Mirren	30	10	7	13	60	82	27
12	Partick T	30	8	10	12	68	70	26
13	Dumbarton	30	11	4	15	73	90	26
14	Airdrie	30	10	4	16	57	76	24
15	Albion R	30	8	5	17	68	97	21
16	Hamilton A	30	5	4	21	\56	100	14

1942–43

NORTH EASTERN 1942–43
1st Series

		P	W	D	L	F	A	Pts
1	Aberdeen	14	11	1	2	51	16	23
2	Dunfermline A	14	10	0	4	28	23	20
3	East Fife	14	8	1	5	27	19	17
4	Rangers	14	6	0	8	30	31	12
5	Hearts	14	6	0	8	26	32	12
6	Dundee U	14	5	0	9	24	36	10
7	Hibernian	14	4	1	9	29	44	9
8	Raith R	14	4	1	9	23	37	9

NORTH EASTERN 1942–43
2nd Series

		P	W	D	L	F	A	Pts
1	Aberdeen	14	10	2	2	39	12	29
2	East Fife	14	9	2	3	38	23	25
3	Raith R	14	9	1	4	42	34	23
4	Dunfermline A	14	6	3	5	30	28	18
5	Rangers	14	5	2	7	32	23	16
6	Hearts	14	4	3	7	36	45	13
7	Dundee U	14	5	1	8	25	32	13
8	Hibernian	14	1	0	13	19	64	2

In North Eastern League an extra point awarded for better goal aggregate over home and away matches.

SOUTHERN 1942–43

		P	W	D	L	F	A	Pts
1	Rangers	30	22	6	2	89	23	50
2	Morton	30	20	5	5	81	48	45
3	Hibernian	30	19	6	5	86	40	44
4	Clyde	30	17	5	8	78	55	39
5	Motherwell	30	15	4	11	60	54	34
6	Hamilton A	30	14	5	11	61	67	33
7	Hearts	30	12	7	11	68	64	31
8	Falkirk	30	12	6	12	68	58	30
9	Dumbarton	30	11	6	13	76	76	28
10	Celtic	30	10	8	12	61	76	28
11	Partick T	30	9	8	13	63	67	26
12	St Mirren	30	8	5	17	49	78	21
13	Third Lanark	30	8	4	18	58	83	20
14	Queen's Park	30	7	4	19	55	76	18
15	Airdrie	30	7	3	20	55	97	17
16	Albion R	30	6	4	20	53	99	16

1943–44

NORTH EASTERN 1943–44
1st Series

		P	W	D	L	F	A	Pts
1	Raith R	14	11	0	3	42	24	22
2	Hearts	14	9	1	4	35	27	19
3	Aberdeen	14	7	3	4	36	22	17
4	Dunfermline A	14	8	1	5	35	22	17
5	Dundee U	14	7	0	7	36	43	14
6	Rangers	14	4	1	9	24	22	9
7	East Fife	14	4	1	9	22	31	9
8	Falkirk	14	2	1	11	15	54	5

NORTH EASTERN 1943–44
2nd Series

		P	W	D	L	F	A	Pts
1	Aberdeen	14	9	2	3	40	18	24
2	Rangers	14	9	2	3	42	25	24
3	East Fife	14	6	3	5	26	14	18
4	Dundee U	14	6	1	7	30	39	15
5	Hearts	14	5	2	7	28	33	14
6	Dunfermline A	14	5	1	8	27	33	13
7	Raith R	14	4	3	7	19	29	13
8	Falkirk	14	4	2	8	27	48	12

Home win 2 pts, home draw 1 pt, away win 3 pts, away draw 2pts.

SOUTHERN 1943–44

		P	W	D	L	F	A	Pts
1	Rangers	30	23	4	3	90	27	50
2	Celtic	30	18	7	5	71	43	43
3	Hibernian	30	17	4	9	72	54	38
4	Hearts	30	14	7	9	67	50	35
5	Motherwell	30	12	8	10	69	53	32
6	Dumbarton	30	13	6	11	54	58	32
7	Clyde	30	13	5	12	62	58	31
8	Morton	30	12	6	12	63	61	30
9	Hamilton A	30	13	3	14	80	88	29
10	Partick T	30	11	5	14	62	66	27
11	Queen's Park	30	10	6	14	64	75	26
12	Falkirk	30	10	5	15	79	80	25
13	St Mirren	30	9	7	14	58	78	25
14	Airdrie	30	9	5	16	54	72	23
15	Third Lanark	30	7	3	20	60	100	17
16	Albion R	30	7	3	20	43	85	17

1944–45

NORTH EASTERN 1944–45
1st Series

	P	W	D	L	F	A	Pts
1 Dundee	18	13	2	3	53	30	28
2 Aberdeen	18	13	1	4	65	21	27
3 Raith R	18	10	2	6	42	32	22
4 Dunfermline A	18	8	5	5	49	36	21
5 Rangers	18	7	2	9	32	32	16
6 East Fife	18	6	4	8	31	44	16
7 Arbroath	18	6	4	8	30	43	16
8 Dundee U	18	5	3	10	34	49	13
9 Hearts	18	5	2	11	31	49	12
10 Falkirk	18	3	3	12	16	47	9

NORTH EASTERN 1944–45
2nd Series

	P	W	D	L	F	A	Pts
1 Aberdeen	18	11	3	4	61	19	31
2 Rangers	18	10	3	5	41	25	29
3 East Fife	18	10	3	5	39	29	28
4 Dundee	18	10	0	8	49	36	24
5 Dunfermline A	18	8	4	6	37	35	24
6 Dundee U	18	7	2	9	31	54	19
7 Arbroath	18	5	4	9	28	43	18
8 Raith R	18	7	1	10	39	47	18
9 Hearts	18	5	5	8	27	39	18
10 Falkirk	18	4	1	13	32	57	11

Home win 2 pts, home draw 1 pt, away win 3 pts, away draw 2pts.

SOUTHERN 1944–45

	P	W	D	L	F	A	Pts
1 Rangers	30	23	3	4	88	27	49
2 Celtic	30	20	2	8	70	42	42
3 Motherwell	30	18	5	7	83	54	41
4 Clyde	30	18	0	12	80	61	36
5 Hibernian	30	15	5	10	69	51	35
6 Hearts	30	14	7	9	75	60	35
7 Morton	30	16	1	13	71	60	33
8 Falkirk	30	14	3	13	67	57	31
9 Hamilton A	30	12	5	13	77	86	29
10 Queen's Park	30	12	4	14	60	62	28
11 Third Lanark	30	11	3	16	55	65	25
12 Partick T	30	12	1	17	55	74	25
13 Dumbarton	30	9	3	18	51	84	21
14 St Mirren	30	7	6	17	45	71	20
15 Albion R	30	7	2	21	42	104	16
16 Airdrie	30	4	6	20	43	73	14

1945–46

SOUTHERN DIV A 1945–46

	P	W	D	L	F	A	Pts
1 Rangers	30	22	4	4	85	41	48
2 Hibernian	30	17	6	7	67	37	40
3 Aberdeen	30	16	6	8	73	41	38
4 Celtic	30	12	11	7	55	44	35
5 Motherwell	30	11	9	10	54	55	31
6 Clyde	30	11	9	10	64	54	31
7 Hearts	30	11	8	11	63	57	30
8 Queen's Park	30	11	8	11	60	60	30
9 Third Lanark	30	14	2	14	63	68	30
10 Morton	30	9	11	10	72	69	29
11 Falkirk	30	11	5	14	62	70	27
12 Partick T	30	11	4	15	54	65	26
13 Q of S	30	9	6	15	62	82	24
14 St Mirren	30	9	5	16	54	70	23
15 Kilmarnock	30	7	8	15	56	87	22
16 Hamilton A	30	5	6	19	44	88	16

SOUTHERN DIV B 1945–46

	P	W	D	L	F	A	Pts
1 Dundee	26	21	2	3	92	28	44
2 East Fife	26	15	4	7	64	34	34
3 Ayr U	26	15	4	7	69	43	34
4 Airdrie	26	14	5	7	69	50	33
5 St Johnstone	26	12	6	8	66	60	30
6 Albion R	26	14	2	10	45	41	30
7 Alloa Ath	26	12	4	10	59	53	28
8 Dumbarton	26	11	4	11	59	54	26
9 Dunfermline A	26	10	4	12	63	47	24
10 Cowdenbeath	26	8	5	13	43	62	21
11 Stenhousemuir	26	6	5	15	36	89	17
12 Dundee U	26	6	3	17	46	70	15
13 Raith R	26	6	2	18	48	80	14
14 Arbroath	26	6	2	18	40	88	14

LEADING GOALSCORERS OF SCOTTISH LEAGUE CLUBS 1939–46

1939–40

SOUTH AND WEST

Airdrie	15 – Mooney
Albion	20 – Burke
Ayr	28 – Clark
Celtic	12 – Divers
Clyde	14 – Taylor & Wallace
Dumbarton	7 – Stewart
Hamilton	13 – Wilson
Kilmarnock	20 – Collins
Morton	26 – Calder
Motherwell	15 – Wood
Partick	9 – Picken
Q of S	30 – Connor
Queen's Park	23 – Kyle
Rangers	13 – Smith & Venters
St Mirren	20 – Linwood
Third Lanark	11 – Dewar

NORTH AND EAST

Aberdeen	23 – Williams
Alloa	21 – Rice
Arbroath	8 – Miller
Cowdenbeath	15 – Walls
Dundee	25 – Coats
Dundee U	20 – Milne
Dunfermline	16 – Black
East Fife	21 – Adams
Falkirk	31 – Dawson
Hearts	24 – Walker
Hibernian	21 – Cuthbertson
King's Park	19 – McDowall
Raith	10 – Kinnear

1940–41

SOUTHERN LEAGUE

Airdrie	30 – Flavell	Hibernian	27 – Cuthbertson
Albion	8 – Burke	Morton	18 – Calder
Celtic	12 – Crum & Murphy	Motherwell	22 – Bremner H
Clyde	28 – Wallace	Partick	13 – Sharp
Dumbarton	12 – Williams	Queen's Park	11 – Browning
Falkirk	23 – Dawson	Rangers	24 – Smith
Hamilton	23 – Wilson	St Mirren	19 – Linwood
Hearts	12 – Walker	Third Lanark	13 – Jones

1941–42

SOUTHERN LEAGUE

Airdrie	14 – Flavell	Hibernian	23 – Combe
Albion	23 – Calder	Morton	14 – McGillivray
Celtic	22 – Delaney	Motherwell	17 – Mathie
Clyde	26 – Wallace	Partick	29 – Newall
Dumbarton	13 – McGrogan	Queen's Park	13 – Dixon & Wilkie
Falkirk	10 – Dawson	Rangers	20 – Gillick
Hamilton	10 – Wilson D	St Mirren	21 – Linwood
Hearts	20 – Walker	Third Lanark	27 – Connor

1942–43

SOUTHERN LEAGUE

Airdrie	18 – Flavell	Hibernian	26 – Smith G
Albion	11 – Louden	Motherwell	16 – Reid
Celtic	19 – Delaney	Morton	20 – Crum
Clyde	40 – Wallace	Partick	13 – Newall
Dumbarton	17 – Gould	Queen's Park	15 – Kyle
Falkirk	17 – Campbell	Rangers	20 – Gillick
Hamilton	17 – Wilson	St Mirren	14 – Linwood
Hearts	16 – Walker	Third Lanark	21 – Connor

1943–44

SOUTHERN LEAGUE

Airdrie	22 – Aitken	Hibernian	14 – Smith & Bogan
Albion	8 – McIlhatton & Mooney	Morton	11 – Kelly
Celtic	19 – Gallacher	Motherwell	21 – Mathie
Clyde	23 – Wallace	Partick	21 – Newall
Dumbarton	20 – Brooks	Queen's Park	14 – Dixon
Falkirk	18 – Fitzsimmons	Rangers	27 – McIntosh
Hamilton	27 – Herd	St Mirren	17 – Linwood
Hearts	15 – Kelly	Third Lanark	24 – Henderson

1944–45

SOUTHERN LEAGUE

Airdrie	11 – Aitken	Hibernian	17 – Smith
Albion	11 – McIlhatton	Morton	15 – Crum
Celtic	22 – McLaughlin	Motherwell	27 – Mathie
Clyde	22 – Johnstone L	Partick	8 – Sharp & Doonan
Dumbarton	14 – Reid	Qeen's Park	17 – Harris J
Falkirk	20 – Fitzsimmons	Rangers	16 – Waddell
Hamilton	20 – Herd	St Mirren	21 – Linwood
Hearts	33 – Kelly	Third Lanark	14 – Dawson

1945–46

DIVISION A

Aberdeen	16 – Pattillo
Celtic	19 – Gallacher J
Clyde	19 – Mathie
Falkirk	25 – Brooks
Hamilton	11 – Jones
Hearts	15 – Kelly
Hibernian	15 – Smith G
Kilmarnock	20 – Walsh
Morton	26 – Garth
Motherwell	13 – Brown
Partick	16 – Sharp
Queen's Park	12 – Harris J & Aitkenhead J
Q of S	13 – Connor
Rangers	18 – Waddell
St Mirren	19 – Linwood
Third Lanark	13 – Dawson

DIVISION B

Airdrie	34 – Aitken
Albion	9 – Hannah
Alloa	20 – Stephenson
Arbroath	9 – Lamb
Ayr	29 – Morrison
Cowdenbeath	9 – Browning W
Dumbarton	13 – McGowan
Dundee	30 – Juliussen
Dundee U	6 – Pacione
Dunfermline	11 – Forbes
East Fife	12 – Adamson
Raith	8 – Penman
St Johnstone	27 – McIntosh
Stenhousemuir	9 – Buchan

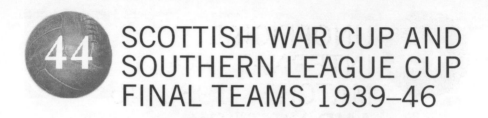

SCOTTISH WAR CUP AND SOUTHERN LEAGUE CUP FINAL TEAMS 1939–46

WAR EMERGENCY CUP FINAL
Hampden Park, 4 May 1940   71,000

Rangers 1 *(Smith)*
Dundee U 0

Rangers: Dawson; Gray, Shaw, Bolt, Woodburn, McKillop, Waddell, Thornton, Smith, Venters, Little.
Dundee U: Thomson; Miller, Dunsmore, Baxter, Littlejohn, Robertson, Glen, Gardiner, Milne, Adamson, Frazer.

SOUTHERN LEAGUE CUP FINAL
Hampden Park, 10 May 1941   75,000

Rangers 1 *(Marshall)*
Hearts 1 *(Woodburn (og))*

Rangers: Dawson; Gray, Shaw, Bolt, Woodburn, Symon, Gillick, Thornton, Smith, Marshall, Johnstone.
Hearts: Waugh; McClure, Miller, Philp, Dykes, Brown, Dougan, Walker, Hamilton, Massie, Christie.

SOUTHERN LEAGUE CUP FINAL REPLAY
Hampden Park, 17 May 1941   60,000

Rangers 4 *(Venters, Smith, Thornton, Johnstone)*
Hearts 2 *(Hamilton 2)*

Rangers: Dawson; Gray, Shaw, Bolt, Woodburn, Symon, Gillick, Thornton, Smith, Venters, Johnstone.
Hearts: Waugh; McClure, Miller, Philp, Dykes, Brown, Dugan, Walker, Hamilton, Massie, Christie.

SOUTHERN LEAGUE CUP FINAL
Hampden Park, 9 May 1942   45,000

Rangers 1 *(Gillick)*
Morton 0

Rangers: Dawson; Gray, Shaw, Little, Young, Thomson, Waddell, Gillick, McIntosh, Venters, Johnstone.
Morton: McFeat; Maley, Fyfe, Campbell, Aird, Whyte, Cumner, Orr, Hunter, Steele, Kelly.

SOUTHERN LEAGUE CUP FINAL
Hampden Park, 8 May 1943   20,000

Rangers 1 *(Gillick)*
Falkirk 1 *(Campbell)*

Rangers: Dawson; Gray, Shaw, Little, Young, Symon, Waddell, Duncanson, Gillick, Venters, Johnstone.
Falkirk: Matthews; White, Peat, Pinkerton, Shankly, Busby, Ogilvie, Campbell, Inglis, Fitzsimmons, Dawson.
Rangers won 11-3 on corner kicks.

SOUTHERN LEAGUE CUP FINAL
Hampden Park, 20 May 1944   50,000

Hibernian 0
Rangers 0

Hibernian: Downie; Fraser, Hall, Finnigan, Baxter, Kean, Smith G, Bogan, Nelson, Woodburn, Caskie.
Rangers: Dawson; Gray, Shaw, Little, Young, Symon, Waddell, Gillick, Smith, Duncanson, Johnstone.
Hibernian won 6-5 on corner kicks.

SOUTHERN LEAGUE CUP FINAL
Hampden Park, 12 May 1945   70,000

Rangers 2 *(Gillick, Venters)*
Motherwell 1 *(Watson)*

Rangers: Jenkins; Young, Shaw, Little, Woodburn, Symon, Waddell, Gillick, Smith, Venters, Johnstone.
Motherwell: Johnstone; Kilmarnock, Shaw, Ross, Paton, Miller, Gibson, Watson, Mathie, Gillan, McCulloch.

SOUTHERN LEAGUE CUP FINAL
Hampden Park, 11 May 1946   121,000

Aberdeen 3 *(Baird, Williams, Taylor)*
Rangers 2 *(Duncanson, Thornton)*

Aberdeen: Johnstone; Cooper, McKenna, Cowie, Dunlop, Taylor, Kiddie, Hamilton, Williams, Baird, McCall.
Rangers: John Shaw; Gray, Jock Shaw, Watkins, Young, Symon, Waddell, Thornton, Arnison, Duncanson, Caskie.

UNOFFICIAL INTERNATIONAL MATCHES 1939–45 AND VICTORY INTERNATIONALS 1945–46

11 NOVEMBER 1939

Ninian Park, Cardiff 28,000

Wales (1) 1 *(Glover)*
England (0) 1 *(Goulden)*

Wales: John (Swansea T); Turner (Charlton Ath), Whatley (Tottenham H), Burgess (Tottenham H), Jones TG (Everton), Dearson (Birmingham), Hopkins (Brentford), Astley (Blackpool), Glover (Plymouth Arg), Jones B (Arsenal), Cumner (Arsenal).
England: Woodley (Chelsea); Bacuzzi (Fulham) [sub: J Lewis (Walthamstow Ave)], Hapgood (Arsenal), Crayston (Arsenal), Oakes (Charlton Ath), Fenton (West Ham U), Smith L (Brentford), Hall W (Tottenham H), Compton L (Arsenal), Goulden (West Ham U), Smith JCR (Millwall).

18 NOVEMBER 1939

Racecourse Ground, Wrexham 17,000

Wales (0) 2 *(Astley 2)*
England (0) 3 *(Martin, Balmer, own goal)*

Wales: Sidlow (Wolverhampton W); Hughes (Birmingham), Smith AJ (Chelsea), Burgess (Tottenham H), Jones TG (Everton), Witcomb (WBA), Hopkins (Brentford), Redfern (Derby Co), Astley (Blackpool), Jones B (Arsenal), Cumner (Arsenal).
England: Swift (Manchester C); Sproston (Manchester C), Crook (Blackburn R), Willingham (Huddersfield T), Cullis (Wolverhampton W), Mercer (Everton), Matthews (Stoke C), Martin (Aston Villa), Lawton (Everton), Balmer (Liverpool), Brook (Manchester C).

2 DECEMBER 1939

St James' Park, Newcastle 15,000

England (1) 2 *(Clifton, Lawton)*
Scotland (1) 1 *(Dodds)*

England: Swinburne (Newcastle U); Richardson (Newcastle U), Greenhalgh (Everton), Goslin (Bolton W), Harper (Barnsley), Mercer (Everton), Matthews (Stoke C), Carter (Sunderland), Lawton (Everton), Clifton (Newcastle U), Pearson (Newcastle U).
Scotland: Dawson (Rangers); Carabine (Third Lanark), Ancell (Newcastle U), Pinkerton (Falkirk), Baxter (Middlesbrough), Brown T (Hearts), Finan (Blackpool), Walker (Hearts), Dodds (Blackpool), Napier (Sheffield W), Caskie (Everton).

13 APRIL 1940

Wembley 40,000

England (0) 0
Wales (1) 1 *(Jones B)*

England: Bartram (Charlton Ath); Bacuzzi (Fulham), Hapgood (Arsenal), Willingham (Huddersfield T), Cullis (Wolverhampton W), Copping (Leeds U), Matthews (Stoke C), Hall W (Tottenham H), Westcott (Wolverhampton W), Goulden (West Ham U), Compton D (Arsenal).
Wales: Sidlow (Wolverhampton W); Turner (Charlton Ath), Williams (Millwall), Green (Charlton Ath), Davies R (Nottingham F), Witcomb (WBA), Hopkins (Brentford), Dearson (Birmingham), Astley (Blackpool), Jones B (Arsenal), Jones L (Arsenal)

*Initials preceding surname indicate amateur player.

11 MAY 1940

Hampden Park, Glasgow   75,000
Scotland (0) 1 *(Dougal)*
England (0) 1 *(Welsh)*

Scotland: Dawson (Rangers); Carabine (Third Lanark), McClure (Hearts), Shankly (Preston NE), Baxter (Hearts), Brown T (Hearts), Caskie (Everton), Walker (Hearts), McCulloch (Derby Co), Venters (Rangers), Dougal (Preston NE).
England: Woodley (Chelsea); Sproston (Manchester C), Hapgood (Arsenal), Willingham (Huddersfield T), Cullis (Wolverhampton W), Mercer (Everton), Matthews (Stoke C), Martin (Aston Villa), Broome (Aston Villa), Welsh (Charlton Ath), Smith JCR (Millwall).

8 FEBRUARY 1941

St James' Park, Newcastle   25,000
England (2) 2 *(Birkett, Lawton)*
Scotland (2) 3 *(Wallace 2, own goal)*

England: Bartram (Charlton Ath); Bacuzzi (Fulham), Mountford (Huddersfield T), Willingham (Huddersfield T), Cullis (Wolverhampton W), Mercer (Everton), Birkett (Newcastle U), Mannion (Middlesbrough), Lawton (Everton), Goulden (West Ham U), Hanson (Chelsea).
Scotland: Dawson (Rangers); Hogg (Celtic), Beattie A (Preston NE), McDonald (Celtic), Dykes (Hearts), Brown G (Rangers), Milne (Middlesbrough), Walker (Hearts), Smith J (Rangers), Wallace (Clyde), Caskie (Everton).

16 APRIL 1941

City Ground, Nottingham   13,016
England (2) 4 *(Welsh 4)*
Wales (0) 1 *(Witcomb)*

England: Mapson (Sunderland); Bacuzzi (Fulham), Hardwick (Middlesbrough), Britton (Everton), Cullis (Wolverhampton W), Buckingham (Tottenham H), Fisher (Millwall), M Edelston (Reading), Welsh (Charlton Ath), Hagan (Sheffield U), Smith JCR (Millwall).
Wales: Sidlow (Wolverhampton W); Hughes (Birmingham), Williams (Millwall), Burgess (Tottenham H), Turner (Charlton Ath), Witcomb (WBA), Hopkins (Brentford), Astley (Derby Co), Perry (Fulham), Jones B (Arsenal), Dearson (Birmingham).

3 MAY 1941

Hampden Park, Glasgow   78,000
Scotland (1) 1 *(Venters)*
England (1) 3 *(Welsh 2, Goulden)*

Scotland: Dawson (Rangers); Carabine (Third Lanark), Shaw J (Rangers), Shankly (Preston NE), Dykes (Hearts), Brown T (Hearts), Gillick (Everton), Walker (Hearts), Smith J (Rangers), Venters (Rangers), Caskie (Everton).
England: Swift (Manchester C); Bacuzzi (Fulham), Hapgood (Arsenal), Goslin (Bolton W), Cullis (Wolverhampton W), Mercer (Everton), Matthews (Stoke C), Mannion (Middlesbrough), Welsh (Charlton Ath), Goulden (West Ham U), Compton D (Arsenal).

7 JUNE 1941

Ninian Park, Cardiff   20,000
Wales (1) 2 *(Woodward, James)*
England (2) 3 *(Hagan 2, Welsh)*

Wales: Sidlow (Wolverhampton W); Hughes (Birmingham), Turner (Charlton Ath), Dearson (Birmingham C), Jones TG (Everton), Witcomb (WBA), Rogers (Swansea T), Woodward (Fulham), James (Cardiff C), Jones B (Arsenal), Jones L (Arsenal).
England: Bartram (Charlton Ath); Bacuzzi (Fulham), Hapgood (Arsenal), Britton (Everton), Cullis (Wolverhampton W), Buckingham (Tottenham H), Kirchen (Arsenal), Hagan (Sheffield U), Welsh (Charlton Ath), Goulden (West Ham U), L Finch (Barnet).

4 OCTOBER 1941

Wembley   65,000
England (2) 2 *(Hagan, Welsh)*
Scotland (0) 0

England: Marks (Arsenal); Bacuzzi (Fulham), Hapgood (Arsenal), Goslin (Bolton W), Cullis (Wolverhampton W), Mercer (Everton), Matthews (Stoke C), Mannion (Middlesbrough), Welsh (Charlton Ath), Hagan (Sheffield U), Compton D (Arsenal).
Scotland: Dawson (Rangers); Carabine (Third Lanark), Beattie A (Preston NE), Shankly (Preston NE), Dykes (Hearts), McDonald (Celtic), Caskie (Everton), Walker (Hearts), Smith J (Rangers), Wallace (Clyde), Williams (Clyde).

25 OCTOBER 1941

St Andrews, Birmingham   25,000

England (2) 2 *(Hagan, Edelston)*
Wales (0) 1 *(Hopkins)*

England: Marks (Arsenal); Bacuzzi (Fulham), Hapgood (Arsenal), Goslin (Bolton W), Cullis (Wolverhampton W), Mercer (Everton), Matthews (Stoke C), M Edelston (Reading), Welsh (Charlton Ath), Hagan (Sheffield U), Compton D (Arsenal).
Wales: Poland (Liverpool); Turner (Charlton Ath), Hughes (Birmingham), Green (Charlton Ath), Jones TG (Everton), Witcomb (WBA), Hopkins (Brentford), James (Cardiff C), Dearson (Birmingham), Jones L (Arsenal), Cumner (Arsenal).

17 JANUARY 1942

Wembley   64,000

England (1) 3 *(Hagan, Lawton 2)*
Scotland (0) 0

England: Marks (Arsenal); Bacuzzi (Fulham), Hapgood (Arsenal), Willingham (Huddersfield T), Cullis (Wolverhampton W), Welsh (Charlton Ath), Matthews (Stoke C), Mannion (Middlesbrough), Lawton (Everton), Hagan (Sheffield U), Compton D (Arsenal).
Scotland: Dawson (Rangers); Carabine (Third Lanark), Beattie A (Preston NE), Shankly (Preston NE), Dykes (Hearts), Busby (Liverpool), Caskie (Everton), Walker (Hearts), Gillick (Everton), Black (Hearts), Johnson (Rangers).

18 APRIL 1942

Hampden Park, Glasgow   91,000

Scotland (2) 5 *(Dodds 3, Liddell, Shankly)*
England (1) 4 *(Lawton 3, Hagan)*

Scotland: Dawson (Rangers); Carabine (Third Lanark), Beattie A (Preston NE), Shankly (Preston NE), Smith T (Preston NE), Busby (Liverpool), Waddell (Rangers), Herd (Manchester C), Dodds (Blackpool), Bremner G (Arsenal), Liddell (Liverpool).
England: Marks (Arsenal); Bacuzzi (Fulham), Hapgood (Arsenal), Willingham (Huddersfield T), Mason (Coventry C), Mercer (Everton), Matthews (Stoke C), M Edelston (Reading), Lawton (Everton), Hagan (Sheffield U), Kirchen (Arsenal).

9 MAY 1942

Ninian Park, Cardiff   30,000

Wales (1) 1 *(Lucas)*
England (0) 0

Wales: Poland (Liverpool); Turner (Charlton Ath), Hughes (Birmingham), Dearson (Birmingham), Jones TG (Everton), Witcomb (WBA), Hopkins (Brentford), Squires (Swansea T), Lowrie (Coventry C), Lucas (Swindon T), Jones L (Arsenal).
England: Marks (Arsenal); Scott (Arsenal), Hapgood (Arsenal), Britton (Everton), Mason (Coventry C), Soo (Stoke C), Kirchen (Arsenal), Hall W (Tottenham H), Lawton (Everton), M Edelston (Reading), Smith L (Brentford).

10 OCTOBER 1942

Wembley   75,000

England (0) 0
Scotland (0) 0

England: Marks (Arsenal); Bacuzzi (Fulham), Hapgood (Arsenal), Britton (Everton), Cullis (Wolverhampton W), Mercer (Everton), Matthews (Stoke C), M Edelston (Reading), Lawton (Everton), Hagan (Sheffield U), Compton D (Arsenal).
Scotland: Dawson (Rangers); Carabine (Third Lanark), Beattie A (Preston NE), Shankly (Preston NE), Corbett (Celtic), Busby (Liverpool), Waddell (Rangers), Walker (Hearts), Dodds (Blackpool), Bremner G (Arsenal), Liddell (Liverpool).

24 OCTOBER 1942

Molineux, Wolverhampton   25,000

England (1) 1 *(Lawton)*
Wales (1) 2 *(Cumner 2)*

England: Marks (Arsenal); Hardwick (Middlesbrough), Hapgood (Arsenal), Britton (Everton), Cullis (Wolverhampton W), Mercer (Everton), Matthews (Stoke C), Rooke (Fulham), Lawton (Everton), AH Gibbons (Tottenham H), Mullen (Wolverhampton W)
Wales: Poland (Liverpool); Turner (Charlton Ath), Hughes (Birmingham), Dearson (Birmingham), Jones TG (Everton), Powell I (QPR), Hopkins (Brentford), Lucas (Swindon T), Lowrie (Coventry C), Jones B (Arsenal), Cumner (Arsenal).

27 FEBRUARY 1943

Wembley   75,000

England (3) 5 *(Westcott 3, Carter 2)*
Wales (2) 3 *(Lowrie 3)*

England: Marks (Arsenal); Bacuzzi (Fulham), Hapgood (Arsenal), Britton (Everton), Cullis (Wolverhampton W), Mercer (Everton), Matthews (Stoke C), Carter (Sunderland), Westcott (Wolverhampton W), Hagan (Sheffield U), Compton D (Arsenal).
Wales: Poland (Liverpool); Turner (Charlton Ath), Hughes (Birmingham), Dearson (Birmingham), Jones TG (Everton), Powell I (QPR), Hopkins (Brentford), Lucas (Swindon T), Lowrie (Coventry C), Jones B (Arsenal), Cumner (Arsenal).

17 APRIL 1943

Hampden Park, Glasgow   105,000

Scotland (0) 0
England (2) 4 *(Carter 2, Westcott, Compton D)*

Scotland: Dawson (Rangers); Carabine (Third Lanark), Shaw (Rangers), Shankly (Preston NE), Young (Rangers), Kean (Hibernian), Waddell (Rangers), Buchan (Blackpool), Wallace (Clyde), Venters (Rangers), Liddell (Liverpool).
England: Swift (Manchester C); Hardwick (Middlesbrough), Compton L (Arsenal), Britton (Everton), Cullis (Wolverhampton W), Mercer (Everton), Matthews (Stoke C), Carter (Sunderland), Westcott (Wolverhampton W), Hagan (Sheffield U), Compton D (Arsenal).

8 MAY 1943

Ninian Park, Cardiff   25,000

Wales (1) 1 *(Lowrie)*
England (0) 1 *(Westcott)*

Wales: Sidlow (Wolverhampton W); Lambert (Liverpool), Hughes (Birmingham), Dearson (Birmingham), Jones TG (Everton), Powell I (QPR), Powell A (Leeds U), Murphy (Bradford C), Lowrie (Coventry C), Jones B (Arsenal), Cumner (Arsenal).
England: Swift (Manchester C); Hardwick (Middlesbrough), Compton L (Arsenal), Britton (Everton), Cullis (Wolverhampton W), Mercer (Everton), Matthews (Stoke C), Carter (Sunderland), Westcott (Wolverhampton W), Hagan (Sheffield U), Compton D (Arsenal).

25 SEPTEMBER 1943

Wembley   80,000

England (4) 8 *(Welsh 2, Carter 2, Hagan 2, Compton D 2)*
Wales (1) 3 *(Lowrie 2, Powell A)*

England: Roxburgh (Blackpool); Scott (Arsenal), Hardwick (Middlesbrough), Britton (Everton), Cullis (Wolverhampton W), Soo (Stoke C), Matthews (Stoke C), Carter (Sunderland), Welsh (Charlton Ath), Hagan (Sheffield U), Compton D (Arsenal).
Wales: Sidlow (Wolverhampton W); Lambert (Liverpool), Hughes (Birmingham), Dearson (Birmingham), Jones TG (Everton), Powell I (QPR) [sub: Mortensen (Blackpool)], Powell A (Leeds U), Murphy (Bradford C), Lowrie (Coventry C), Burgess (Tottenham H), Cumner (Arsenal).

16 OCTOBER 1943

Maine Road, Manchester   60,000

England (5) 8 *(Lawton 4, Hagan 2, Carter, Matthews)*
Scotland (0) 0

England: Swift (Manchester C); Scott (Arsenal), Hardwick (Middlesbrough), Britton (Everton), Cullis (Wolverhampton W), Mercer (Everton), Matthews (Stoke C), Carter (Sunderland), Lawton (Everton), Hagan (Sheffield U), Compton D (Arsenal).
Scotland: Crozier (Brentford); Carabine (Third Lanark), Miller (Hearts), Little (Rangers), Young (Rangers), Campbell (Morton), Waddell (Rangers), Gillick (Everton), Linwood (St Mirren), Walker (Hearts), Deakin (St Mirren).

19 FEBRUARY 1944

Wembley   80,000

England (1) 6 *(Hagan 2, Carter, Lawton, Mercer, own goal)*
Scotland (1) 2 *(Dodds 2)*

England: Ditchburn (Tottenham H); Scott (Arsenal), Hardwick (Middlesbrough), Britton (Everton), Cullis (Wolverhampton W), Mercer (Everton), Matthews (Stoke C), Carter (Sunderland), Lawton (Everton), Hagan (Sheffield U), Smith L (Brentford).

Scotland: Crozier (Brentford); Kilmarnock (Motherwell), Stephen (Bradford PA), Macaulay (West Ham U), Kirton (Stoke C), Busby (Liverpool), Flavell (Airdrie), Stenhouse (St Mirren), Dodds (Blackpool), Duncanson (Rangers), Caskie (Everton).

22 APRIL 1944

Hampden Park, Glasgow 133,000

Scotland (1) 2 *(Dodds, Caskie)*
England (3) 3 *(Lawton 2, Carter)*

Scotland: Crozier (Brentford); McDonald (Celtic), Stephen (Bradford PA), Macaulay (West Ham U), Baxter (Middlesbrough), Busby (Liverpool), Delaney (Celtic), Walker (Hearts), Dodds (Blackpool), Duncanson (Rangers), Caskie (Everton).
England: Swift (Manchester C); Compton L (Arsenal), Taylor F (Wolverhampton W), Soo (Stoke C), Cullis (Wolverhampton W), Mercer (Everton), Matthews (Stoke C), Carter (Sunderland), Lawton (Everton), Hagan (Sheffield U), Smith L (Brentford).

6 MAY 1944

Ninian Park, Cardiff 50,000

Wales (0) 0
England (1) 2 *(Lawton, Smith L)*

Wales: Sidlow (Wolverhampton W); Barnes (Arsenal), Lambert (Liverpool), Dearson (Birmingham), Davies R (Nottingham F), Burgess (Tottenham H), Hopkins (Brentford), Lucas (Swindon T), Lowrie (Coventry C), Davies W (Watford), Morris S (Birmingham).
England: Ditchburn (Tottenham H); Scott (Arsenal), Compton L (Arsenal), Britton (Everton), Cullis (Wolverhampton W), Mercer (Everton), Elliott (WBA), Carter (Sunderland), Lawton (Everton), Rowley J (Manchester U), Smith L (Brentford).

16 SEPTEMBER 1944

Anfield, Liverpool 38,483

England (2) 2 *(Carter, Lawton)*
Wales (2) 2 *(Dearson, Lucas)*

England: Swift (Manchester C); Scott (Arsenal), Hardwick (Middlesbrough), Mercer (Everton), Flewin (Portsmouth), Welsh (Charlton Ath), Matthews (Stoke C), Carter (Sunderland), Lawton (Everton), Mortensen (Blackpool), Mullen (Wolverhampton W).

Wales: Sidlow (Wolverhampton W); Barnes (Arsenal), Lambert (Liverpool), Dearson (Birmingham), Hughes (Birmingham), Burgess (Tottenham H), Rogers (Swansea T), Jones L (Arsenal), Lowrie (Coventry C), Lucas (Swindon T), Cumner (Arsenal).

14 OCTOBER 1944

Wembley 90,000

England (0) 6 *(Lawton 3, Carter, Goulden, Smith L)*
Scotland (1) 2 *(Walker, Milne)*

England: Swift (Manchester C); Scott (Arsenal), Hardwick (Middlesbrough), Soo (Stoke C), B Joy (Arsenal), Mercer (Everton), Matthews (Stoke C), Carter (Sunderland), Lawton (Everton), Goulden (West Ham U), Smith L (Brentford).
Scotland: Cumming (Middlesbrough); Stephen (Bradford PA), Cummings (Aston Villa), Thyne (Darlington), Baxter (Middlesbrough), Macaulay (West Ham U), Smith G (Hibernian), Walker (Hearts), Milne (Hibernian), Black (Hearts), Caskie (Everton).

3 FEBRUARY 1945

Villa Park, Birmingham 66,000

England (1) 3 *(Mortensen 2, Brown A)*
Scotland (1) 2 *(Delaney, Dodds)*

England: Swift (Manchester C); Scott (Arsenal), Hardwick (Middlesbrough), Soo (Stoke C), Franklin (Stoke C), Mercer (Everton), Matthews (Stoke C), Brown A (Charlton Ath), Lawton (Everton), Mortensen (Blackpool), Smith L (Brentford).
Scotland: R Brown (Queen's Park); Harley (Liverpool), Stephen (Bradford PA), Busby (Liverpool), Thyne (Darlington), Macaulay (West Ham U), Delaney (Celtic), Fagan (Liverpool), Dodds (Blackpool), Black (Hearts), Liddell (Liverpool).

14 APRIL 1945

Hampden Park, Glasgow 133,000

Scotland (1) 1 *(Johnstone)*
England (1) 6 *(Lawton 2, Brown A, Carter, Matthews, Smith L)*

Scotland: R Brown (Queen's Park), Harley (Liverpool), Stephen (Bradford PA), Busby (Liverpool), Harris J (Wolverhampton W), Macaulay (West Ham U), Waddell (Rangers), Bogan (Hibernian) [sub: Johnstone (Clyde)], JR Harris (Queen's Park), Black (Hearts), Kelly (Morton).

England: Swift (Manchester C); Scott (Arsenal), Hardwick (Middlesbrough), Soo (Stoke C), Franklin (Stoke C), Mercer (Everton), Matthews (Stoke C), Carter (Sunderland), Lawton (Everton), Brown A (Charlton Ath), Smith L (Brentford).

5 MAY 1945

Ninian Park, Cardiff   25,000

Wales (1) 2 *(Cumner, Edwards)*
England (1) 3 *(Carter 3)*

Wales: Sidlow (Wolverhampton W); Winter (Bolton W), Hughes (Birmingham C), Dearson (Birmingham C), Davies R (Nottingham F), Burgess (Tottenham H), Astbury (Chester), Lucas (Swindon T), Rees (Cardiff C), Cumner (Arsenal), Edwards G (Coventry C).
England: Williams (Walsall); Scott (Arsenal), Hardwick (Middlesbrough), Smith G (Charlton Ath), Franklin (Stoke C), Mercer (Everton), Matthews (Stoke C), Carter (Sunderland), Lawton (Everton), Brown A (Charlton Ath), Smith L (Brentford).

26 MAY 1945

Wembley   60,000

England (1) 2 *(Carter, Lawton)*
France (1) 2 *(Vaast, Heisserer)*

England: Williams (Walsall); Scott (Arsenal), Hardwick (Middlesbrough), Soo (Stoke C), Franklin (Stoke C), Mercer (Everton), Matthews (Stoke C), Carter (Sunderland), Lawton (Everton), Brown A (Charlton Ath), Smith L (Brentford).
France: Darui; Dupuis, Swiatek, Jasseron, Jordan, Samuel, Aston, Heisserer, Bihel, Siklo, Vaast.

15 SEPTEMBER 1945

Windsor Park, Belfast   45,061

Northern Ireland (0) 0
England (0) 1 *(Mortensen)*

Northern Ireland: Breen (Linfield); McMillan (Belfast C), Feeney (Linfield), Todd (Blackpool), Vernon (Belfast C), Jones S (Blackpool), McKenna (Linfield), Sloan (Tranmere R), McCarthy (Belfast C), Doherty (Manchester C), Bonnar (Belfast C).

England: Swift (Manchester C); Scott (Arsenal), Kinsell (WBA), Soo (Stoke C), Franklin (Stoke C), Mercer (Everton), Matthews (Stoke C), Carter (Sunderland), Lawton (Everton), Mortensen (Blackpool), Smith L (Brentford).

20 OCTOBER 1945

The Hawthorns, West Bromwich   54,611

England (0) 0
Wales (1) 1 *(Powell A)*

England: Williams (Wolverhampton W); Scott (Arsenal), Kinsell (WBA), Soo (Leicester C), Franklin (Stoke C), Mercer (Everton), Matthews (Stoke C), Fenton (Middlesbrough), Stubbins (Newcastle U), Barrass (Bolton W), Watson (Huddersfield T).
Wales: Sidlow (Wolverhampton W); Winter (Bolton W), Hughes (Birmingham C), Dearson (Birmingham C), Davies R (Nottingham F), Burgess (Tottenham H), Powell A (Leeds U), Astbury (Chester), Lowrie (Coventry C), Lucas (Swindon T), Edwards G (Birmingham C).

10 NOVEMBER 1945

Hampden Park, Glasgow   97,000

Scotland (1) 2 *(Waddell, Dodds)*
Wales (0) 0

Scotland: R Brown (Queen's Park); McPhie (Falkirk), Shaw (Rangers), Campbell (Morton), Paton (Motherwell), Paterson (Celtic), Waddell (Rangers), Smith G (Hibernian), Dodds (Blackpool), Deakin (St Mirren), Liddell (Liverpool).
Wales: Sidlow (Wolverhampton W); Dearson (Birmingham C), Hughes (Birmingham C), Witcomb (WBA), Davies R (Nottingham F), Burgess (Tottenham H), Jones J (Swansea T), Squires (Swansea T), Lowrie (Coventry C), Cumner (Arsenal), Edwards G (Birmingham C).

19 JANUARY 1946

Wembley   85,000

England (2) 2 *(Brown A, Pye)*
Belgium (0) 0

England: Swift (Manchester C); Scott (Arsenal), Hardwick (Middlesbrough), Wright (Wolverhampton W), Franklin (Stoke C), Mercer (Everton), Matthews (Stoke C), Pye (Notts Co), Lawton (Chelsea), Brown A (Charlton Ath), Mullen (Wolverhampton W).

Belgium: Daenen; Paverick, Pannaye, Puttaert, Vercammen, Devos, Lembrechts, Coppens, Declyn, Mermans, Sermon.

23 JANUARY 1946

Hampden Park, Glasgow   49,000

Scotland (0) 2 *(Delaney 2)*
Belgium (0) 2 *(Lembrechts, D'Aguilar)*

Scotland: R Brown (Queen's Park); McGowan (Partick T), Shaw (Rangers), Campbell (Morton), Paton (Motherwell), Paterson (Celtic), Smith G (Hibernian), Baird (Aberdeen), Delaney (Celtic), Deakin (St Mirren), Walker (Hearts).
Belgium: Daenen; Paverick, Pannaye, Puttaert, Vercammen, Devos, Lembrechts, Coppens, Declyn, D'Aguilar, Sermon.

2 FEBRUARY 1946

Windsor Park, Belfast   53,000

Northern Ireland (2) 2 *(Walsh 2)*
Scotland (1) 3 *(Liddell 2, Hamilton)*

Northern Ireland: Breen (Linfield); McMillan (Belfast C), Feeney (Linfield), Todd (Blackpool), Vernon (Belfast C), Aherne (Belfast C), Dr K O'Flanagan (Arsenal), Stevenson (Everton), Walsh (Linfield), Carey (Manchester U), Bonnar (Belfast C).
Scotland: R Brown (Queen's Park); McGowan (Partick T), Shaw (Rangers), Campbell (Morton), Paton (Motherwell), Paterson (Celtic), Waddell (Rangers), Hamilton (Aberdeen), Dodds (Blackpool), K Chisholm (Queen's Park), Liddell (Liverpool).

13 APRIL 1946

Hampden Park, Glasgow   139,468

Scotland (0) 1 *(Delaney)*
England (0) 0

Scotland: R Brown (Queen's Park); Shaw D (Hibernian), Shaw J (Rangers), Campbell (Morton), Brennan (Airdrie), Husband (Partick T), Waddell (Rangers), Dougall (Birmingham C), Delaney (Manchester U), Hamilton (Aberdeen), Liddell (Liverpool).
England: Swift (Manchester C); Scott (Arsenal), Hardwick (Middlesbrough), Wright (Wolverhampton W), Franklin (Stoke C), Mercer (Everton), Elliott

(WBA), Shackleton (Bradford PA), Lawton (Chelsea), Hagan (Sheffield U), Compton D (Arsenal).

4 MAY 1946

Ninian Park, Cardiff   45,000

Wales (0) 0
Northern Ireland (0) 1 *(Sloan)*

Wales: Shortt (Plymouth Arg); Sherwood (Cardiff C), Hughes (Birmingham C), Warner (Manchester U), Jones TG (Everton), Burgess (Tottenham H), Powell A (Leeds U), Morris W (Burnley), Ford (Swansea T), Lucas (Swindon T), Clarke (Cardiff C).
Northern Ireland: Breen (Linfield); McMillan (Belfast C), Aherne (Belfast C), Carey (Manchester U), Vernon (Belfast C), Waters (Glentoran), Dr K O'Flanagan (Arsenal), Sloan (Tranmere R), Walsh (Linfield), Doherty (Derby Co), McKenna (Linfield).

11 MAY 1946

Stamford Bridge, Chelsea   75,000

England (0) 4 *(Carter 2, Brown, Lawton)*
Switzerland (0) 1 *(Friedlaender)*

England: Swift (Manchester C); Scott (Arsenal), Hardwick (Middlesbrough), Wright (Wolverhampton W), Franklin (Stoke C), Johnson (Charlton Ath), Matthews (Stoke C), Carter (Derby Co), Lawton (Chelsea), Brown (Nottingham F), Smith L (Aston Villa).
Switzerland: Ballabio; Gyger, Steffen, Springer, Andreoli, Courtat, Bickel, Fink, Amado, Friedlaender, Fatton.

15 MAY 1946

Hampden Park, Glasgow   113,000

Scotland (3) 3 *(Liddell 2, Delaney)*
Switzerland (1) 1 *(Aeby)*

Scotland: Brown (Rangers); Shaw D (Hibernian), Shaw J (Rangers), Campbell (Morton), Brennan (Airdrie), Husband (Partick T), Waddell (Rangers), Thornton (Rangers), Delaney (Manchester U), Walker (Hearts), Liddell (Liverpool).
Switzerland: Ballabio; Gyger, Steffen, Rickenback, Andreoli, Bouquet, Amado, Fink, Friedlaender, Maillard, Aeby.

19 MAY 1946

Colombes Stadium, Paris   58,481

France (0) 2 *(Prouff, Vaast)*
England (0) 1 *(Hagan)*

France: Darui; Grillon, Salva, Prouff, Cuissard, Leduc, Aston, Heisserer, Sinibaldi, Ben Barek, Vaast.
England: Williams (Wolverhampton W); Bacuzzi (Fulham), Hardwick (Middlesbrough), Wright (Wolverhampton W), Franklin (Stoke C), Johnson (Charlton Ath), Matthews (Stoke C), Carter (Derby Co), Lawton (Chelsea), Hagan (Sheffield U), Smith L (Aston Villa).

UNOFFICIAL HOME INERNATIONAL CHAMPIONSHIP 1945–46

	P	W	D	L	F	A	Pts
Scotland	3	3	0	0	6	2	6
Northern Ireland	3	1	0	2	3	4	2
England	3	1	0	2	1	2	2
Wales	3	1	0	2	1	3	2

46 MOSCOW DYNAMO TOUR OF BRITAIN, NOVEMBER 1945

13 NOVEMBER 1945

Stamford Bridge, Chelsea est. 85,000

Chelsea (2) 3 *(Goulden, Williams, Lawton)*
Moscow Dynamo (0) 3 *(Kartsev, Archangelski, Bobrov)*

Chelsea: Woodley; Tennant, Bacuzzi (Fulham), Russell, Harris, Taylor (Fulham), Buchanan, Williams, Lawton, Goulden, Bain.
Moscow Dynamo: Khomich; Radikorsky, Stankevitch, Blinkov, Semichastny, Soloviev L, Archangelski, Kartsev, Beskov, Bobrov, Soloviev S.

17 NOVEMBER 1945

Ninian Park, Cardiff 40,000

Cardiff C (0) 1 *(Moore)*
Moscow Dynamo (3) 10 *(Bobrov 3, Beskov 4, Archangelski 3)*

Cardiff C: McLoughlin; Lever, Raybould, Hollyman, Stansfield, Lester, Moore, Carless, Gibson, Wood, Clarke.
Moscow Dynamo: Khomich; Radikorsky, Stankevitch, Blinkov, Semichastny, Soloviev L, Archangelski, Kartsev, Beskov, Bobrov, Soloviev S.

21 NOVEMBER 1945

White Hart Lane, Tottenham 54,620

Arsenal XI (3) 3 (Rooke, Mortensen 2)
Moscow Dynamo (2) 4 (Bobrov 2, Beskov, Kartsev)

Arsenal XI: Griffiths (Cardiff C) [sub: Brown (QPR)]; Scott, Bacuzzi (Fulham), Bastin, Joy, Halton (Bury), Matthews (Stoke C), Drury, Rooke (Fulham), Mortensen (Blackpool), Cumner.
Moscow Dynamo: Khomich; Radikorsky, Stankevitch, Blinkov, Semichastny, Soloviev L [sub: Oreshkin], Trofimov [sub: Archangelski], Kartsev, Beskov, Bobrov, Soloviev S.

28 NOVEMBER 1945

Ibrox Park, Glasgow 90,000

Rangers (2) 2 (Young, Smith)
Moscow Dynamo (2) 2 (Kartsev 2)

Rangers: Dawson; Gray, Shaw, Watkins, Young, Symon, Waddell, Gillick, Smith [sub: Duncanson], Williamson, Johnstone.
Moscow Dynamo: Khomich; Radikorsky, Stankevitch, Blinkov, Semichastny, Oreshkin, Archangelski, Kartsev, Beskov, Bobrov [sub Demetriev], Soloviev S.

# ROLL OF HONOUR

Gordon Addy (Norwich C)
Brian P. Atkins (Everton)
Arthur G. Baxter (Barnsley)
Albert Bonass (York C)
George F. Bullock (Barnsley)
Joseph Carr (Sheffield U)
Charlie Clark (Luton T)
Albert Clarke (Blackburn R)
Frank C. Chivers (Blackburn R)
Henry B. Cook (Arsenal)
Tom Cooper (Liverpool)
Joseph L. Coen (Luton T)
Joe Croft (Nottingham F)
Bobby N. V. Daniel (Arsenal)
William A. Darby (WBA)
Ernest Davies (Tranmere R)
William B. Dean (Arsenal)
Stanley H. Docking (Tranmere R)
George H. Fairbairn (Fulham)
Tom O. Farrage (Birmingham C)
Fred W. Fisher (Millwall)
Alan Fowler (Swindon T)
James Gillespie (Luton T)
Hugh Glass (Arsenal)
Harry Goslin (Bolton W)
Keith Haines (Tranmere R)
Harold Hampson (Sheffield U)
Ray G. Harris (Birmingham C)
Dennis Higgins (Fulham)
Frank Ibbotson (Reading)
William A. Imrie (Swindon T)
William Isaac (Brighton & HA)
Alex Johnson (Norwich C)
Frank Johnson (Nottingham F)
Glynn Jones (Doncaster R)
Alfred J. Keeling (Manchester C)
Leslie M. Lack (Arsenal)
Charles J. Ladd (Luton T)
Donald A. Marriott (Derby Co)

Leonard Milner (York C)
Peter Monaghan (Bournemouth)
Robert Montgomery (Leeds U)
Alfred H. Moult (Nottingham F)
James H. Olney (Swindon T)
Jack Owen (Preston NE)
William W. Parr (Arsenal)
Colin Perry (Nottingham F)
Frank Pollard (Bury)
William G. Poole (Bury)
Sidney Pugh (Arsenal)
Frederick J. Pritchard (Cardiff C)
G. A. C. Reynolds (York C)
Grenville Roberts (Nottingham F)
Herbie Roberts (Arsenal)
Hubert Redwood (Manchester U)
Eric Robinson (Wolverhampton W)
Joseph Rooney (Wolverhampton W)
Gordon Rosenthal (Tranmere R)
George B. Salvidge (Hull C)
Percy Saunders (Brentford)
Colin Seymour (Newcastle U)
Wilfred Shaw (Doncaster R)
Walter Sidebottom (Bolton W)
Charles Sillett (Southampton)
Colin Smith (Northampton T)
Albert Stanton (Sheffield W)
J. Eric Stephenson (Leeds U)
Harry Strike (Halifax T)
William Summer (Everton)
P. Tommy Taylor (Preston NE)
William Taylor (Birmingham C)
Allan Thornley (Crystal Palace)
John Tompkin (Fulham)
Cyril E. Tooze (Arsenal)
Jack Wilkinson (Sheffield W)

and many others.